THE INDIGNANT GENERATION

THE INDIGNANT GENERATION

A Narrative History of African American Writers and Critics, 1934–1960

4/8/11

Lawrence P. Jackson

For Dr. Badia Ahad

Congratulations on your tenure!

Lawrence Jackson

PRINCETON UNIVERSITY PRESS PRINCETON AND OXFORD

Copyright © 2011 by Princeton University Press
Published by Princeton University Press, 41 William Street, Princeton, New Jersey 08540
In the United Kingdom: Princeton University Press, 6 Oxford Street, Woodstock,
Oxfordshire OX20 1TW

Library of Congress Cataloging-in-Publication Data
Jackson, Lawrence Patrick.
The indignant generation : a narrative history of African American writers and critics,
1934–1960 / Lawrence P. Jackson.
p.   cm.
ISBN 978-0-691-14135-0 (cloth : alk. paper)   1. American literature—African American
authors—History and criticism.   2. African Americans—Intellectual life—20th century.
3. African American critics.   4. African Americans—Race identity.   5. African American
arts—20th century.   I. Title.
PS153.N5J37 2010
810.9'896073—dc22   2009049322
Includes bibliographical references and index.

The following publications and publishers have given permission to reproduce portions of
previously published materials: "A History of African American Literary Critics from
1900–1960," *Cambridge Companion to African American Literature*, ed. Jerry Ward and
Maryemma Graham (New York: Cambridge University Press, forthcoming); "The Irredeemable
Promise: J. Saunders Redding and Negro New Liberalism," *American Literary History* (Fall 2007),
712–44; "Bucklin Moon and Thomas Sancton: Crusaders for the Liberal Left," *Southern Literary
Journal* (Fall 2007), 76–97; "The Aftermath: The Harlem Renaissance Twenty Years Later,"
Cambridge Companion to the Harlem Renaissance, ed. George Hutchinson (New York: Cambridge
University Press, 2007), 239–53; "Ralph Ellison's Integrationist Politics," *Oxford Historical Guide to
Ralph Ellison*, ed. Steve Tracy (New York: Oxford University Press, 2004), 171–205. "The Bean
Eaters" by Gwendolyn Brooks is reprinted courtesy of Brooks Permissions.

British Library Cataloging-in-Publication Data is available

Publication of this book has been aided by Furthermore: a program of the J. M. Kaplan Fund.
This book has been composed in Minion Pro text with Bodoni Std Poster display
Printed on acid-free paper. ∞
press.princeton.edu
Printed in the United States of America
10 9 8 7 6 5 4 3 2

For My Parents
Verna Mitchell Jackson
and
Nathaniel Jackson Jr. (1932–1990)
And the long black and tan line

Charles Dugger	Emmanuel Blow
Harold Macklin	Webster Claiborne
Wilbur Macklin	Milton Allen
Danbridge Macklin	Stuart Simms
Roland Dougherty, Sr.	Edward Rosemond
Raymond Mitchell	Bruce Hodge
Roy Borom	Franklin Beard
Donald Rigby	John Murphy
Victor Dates	Ralph Doram
John James	Prentiss Nolan
Ernest Colvin	Bruce Edemy
Edward Anderson	Dr. Eugene Ford
Otis Washington	George Barrett
Walter Gray II	Harcourt Brace
Donald Smith	Arthur Harris
Peter Miller, Sr.	Chester Lovett
Raymond Harcum	Cyrus Marshall
Percy Johnson	Howard Rawlings

and
Nathaniel Henry Jackson
Vernon Mitchell

CONTENTS

ILLUSTRATIONS

ACKNOWLEDGMENTS

I would like to thank Frank Moorer and the late Lorenzo Thomas, who wrote the earliest serious reviews of my first book. On my dedication page I have tried to recognize the black men who as role models were very important in shaping my early life; professors Moorer and Thomas were two black men who did not know me personally but extended themselves in a public intellectual capacity that was invaluable to me personally and professionally. They encouraged me to go on, and they are an example of scholarly practice. Also, professors Michael Eric Dyson and Cornel West deserve specific thanks for their affirmation of my writing.

Dolan Hubbard was always excited about this project and believed that it needed to be done. It is, as he called it in 2003, a "College Language Association story." To that end it is important to thank the people who are the direct, immediate descendents of many of those who are discussed at length in this work. These people were generous and unselfish enough to think that their time was well spent in discussion with a young African American man living in Columbus, Ohio, and working on a master's thesis on Sterling Brown: Dolan Hubbard, Maryemma Graham, Jerry Ward, Joanne Gabbin, Lee Green, Richard Yarborough, Arnold Rampersad, Sandra Drake, and Sandra Adell. I also thank James A. Miller for guiding me into this discussion with his class Black Writers of the 1930s. I also thank Horace Porter for his longstanding support of this work and his belief in my ability as a writer.

For room and board, use of an automobile, and sundry pleasantries, I especially thank my cousins Saundra and Roland Dougherty, Camille and C. Andrew McGadney, Diane and Edward McClure, Caitlin Nass and Tom Adams, Doris and Luis A. Despaigne, Shirley Ostine, Alan L. Smith, Greg Carr, Damian Rouson, Marie and Claude Ostine, Dana Williams, and my mother Verna Jackson. I thank Christian B. Allen for filming interviews in Atlanta during the summers of 2008 and 2010. I also thank Baba Nati Nataki and the family at Everyone's Place bookstore on North Avenue in Baltimore for providing knowledge to the community for more than twenty years.

My agent Regina Brooks tried to sell this project for many years, but American publishers preferred books with "hip hop" or "nigger" in the title. I appreciate the work of my editor Hanne Winarsky, her assistant Adithi Kasturirangan, production editor Ellen Foos, the three anonymous readers for my project, and Princeton University Press.

I have been the generous recipient of grants and fellowships made possible by United States tax dollars and privately endowed institutions. I thank, in order of receipt, the National Endowment for the Humanities Extending the Reach Grant, which I hope will be granted to more professors from historically black colleges and universities; the National Humanities Center in Research Triangle Park, North Carolina; the Emory University Transforming Community Project; Emory's Department of English; Emory's Department of African American Studies; Emory University College's Major Project Completion Grant; and Emory University College's Subvention Fund. I also thank Pennsylvania State University Distinguished Professor Keith Gilyard, Emory's Dean of the College Robert A. Paul, Emory's English Department Administrator Gerri Moreland, and the staff of the National Humanities Center, especially Geoffrey Harpham and Kent Mulliken.

The following librarians and libraries deserve my sincere thanks: Naomi Nelson, Susan McDonald, and Teresa Burke of the Emory University Manuscripts Archives and Rare Books Library; Marie Hansen of the Emory University Woodruff Library Interlibrary Loan; Jenn Hoberer of the Boston University Howard Gottlieb Archival Research Center; Ms. Cook of the Vivian Harsh Collection, Carter G. Woodson Branch, Chicago Public Library; the Newberry Library; Regenstein Library Special Collections, University of Chicago; Beth Howse of the Franklin Library, Fisk University; Rollins College Special Collections; Beinecke Library, Yale University; Diana Lachatnere of the Schomburg Center for Research in Black Culture; Andrea Jackson, curator of Special Collections, Woodruff Library, Atlanta University; Schlesinger Library, Harvard University; Lee Hampton, Brenda Square, and Christopher Harter of the Amistad Research Center, Tulane University; Rare Books and Special Collections, Library of South Carolina; the Lilly Library, Indiana University; Special Collections and Research, Syracuse University Library; the John Hay Library, Brown University; and Joellen El Bashir, Dr. Ida Jones, and Donna Wells of the Howard University Moorland-Spingarn Research Center; and the Library of Congress. Carmelita Pickett, the African American Studies librarian at Emory, was wise and diligent in obtaining materials. Emory University's Manuscripts Archives and Rare Books Library staff member Randall Burkett's talents extend beyond those of curator of African American special collections.

I thank Bruce Kellner and the Carl Van Vechten Trust, Mrs. Lesley Himes, the late Mrs. Grace Killens, Nancy Smith Fichter, and Elisabeth Petry.

For recommending books to read and taking valuable time to discuss, read, and comment upon elements of the project and black intellectual history generally, I thank Farrah Griffin, John Bracey, Jerry Watts, Corey Walker, Mark Sanders, Greg Adams, Horace Porter, Akinyele Umoja, William Chace, Shelly Eversley, Harvey Klehr, Ani Mukharji, Robin Kelley, William Darrity, George Hutchinson, Peniel Joseph, Barbara Ladd, William Maxwell, James A. Miller,

Robert O'Meally, Cynthia Willett, Eddie Glaude, Ben Reiss, Carol Anderson, Joanna Levin, Rudolph Byrd, John Stuhr, Leroy Davis, Shelly Fisher Fishkin, and Preston King and my intellectual mentor for many years, Greg Carr. A great deal of the scope and breadth of this project, especially its postwar segments, grew from over ten years of probing, heuristic, extended colloquy with Professor Michael Hill.

I am indebted to David C. Miller, Eron Miller, and Nathan McCall for giving a damn about my peace of mind.

Mark Sanders, Frances Smith Foster, Cris Levenduski, Horace Porter, Brenda Green, Regina Brooks, E. Ethelbert Miller, Darryl Scott, William Donaldson, Corey Olds, Keith Gilyard, Bernard Bell, Thabiti Lewis, Corey Walker, George Hutchinson, Susan Ashmore, Maryemma Graham, Carol Marsh-Lockett, and Frank Moorer invited me to lecture and participate in conferences connected to this work. I thank the Association for the Study of African American Life and History, the College Language Association, the American Studies Association, the American Literature Association, and the Midwestern Modern Language Association.

I thank Gerald Horne, Werner Sollors, Alan Wald, Jerry Watts, and Keith Gilyard for sharing their feedback with me regarding the manuscript. I am deeply pleased to have received generous scrutiny from such honest and committed intellectuals. I am excited to enjoy the life of the mind with such people.

The anonymous readers from Oxford University Press, *African American Review*, *American Literary History*, and *American Quarterly* and the editorial staffs of these journals helped contribute to this work. The editors and anonymous reviewers at University of Virginia, Grove Atlantic, and Oxford University all provided extensive criticism of this work as a proposal, as a writing sample, and as completed manuscript. For taking the care to use encouraging language in his correspondence with me, I especially thank Gordon Hutner of *American Literary History.*

The following persons were exceedingly gracious with their time: T. J. Arnold, Mary Sewell Smith, Louise and Charles Stone, Richard Gibson, Ruth Sheffey, Amiri Baraka, the late John Hope Franklin, Sonia Sanchez, Edward Bland, Jr., Albert Murray, Margaret Burroughs, Philip Bonosky, Thomas Sancton, Preston King, and Richard Long.

For research assistance, I thank my new colleagues Drs. Folashade Alao and Brittney Cooper. I am grateful to the resourceful and wonderful Roopika Risam and to the impressive scholar and excellent translator Guirdex Masse. I also thank Levin Arnsperger, Asha French, Keisha "Fort" Green, and the next generation Sachelle Ford.

My affectionate love goes to my mother, to my wife Regine Jackson, whose labors allowed me to devote time to this project, to my daughter Katani, and to the little men who arrived while the book was being written, Nathaniel and C. Mitchell, who are joyful additions to the planet. Bumby and Usabu-Sabija, the two of you running to greet me when I come in the door is the best happiness I have known.

THE INDIGNANT GENERATION

Irredeemable Promise: The Bittersweet Career of J. Saunders Redding

On the downward slope of a thirty-year publishing career, the fifty-two-year-old writer, professor, and literary critic J. Saunders Redding (1906–1988) brimmed with a final project. He wanted to work with the best fiction editors around to publish his second and as yet unwritten novel, a book that would redeem his career and confirm as worthwhile his efforts as a writer and teacher of literature. That early winter of 1959 Redding was going into his fifteenth year of teaching English at a small college in coastal Virginia and wondering about posterity's opinion of him.

A lean man with a confident air, who dressed in the Ivy League style, Redding was from an elite Delaware family and a devotee of the Protestant work ethic. Daily he labored over his books and articles in an upstairs room that his wife and sons were forbidden to enter during specific hours—the edict countermanded rarely, such as when Franklin Roosevelt died. In this upper room Redding had stacks of books, an unframed picture of his father, yellow pads and pencils, and cigarette smoke curling up the walls. It had been a place of productivity, but even his proven sanctuary rebuffed him as the year 1959 unwound.

The fretting that Redding showed that year was what he had displayed his whole writing life, and it was curious because he had already experienced unequivocal success as a writer. He had published long essays in *Harper's Magazine* and *Atlantic Monthly*. *Time Magazine* had reviewed his books and carried his photograph, along with *Saturday Review of Literature*. Redding had cornered literary prizes, like North Carolina's Mayflower Cup, awards noticeable enough that Dean Acheson's Department of State asked him to represent the United States on an extended tour of India as the country emerged from British satrapy to world power. Redding's second book, *No Day of Triumph* (1942), had been published by Harper and reviewed all over the nation. His first novel, *Stranger and Alone* (1950), had also been widely reviewed and deemed significant. He was personally gracious to the literary movers and shakers who supported him. When his sixth book, *An American in India* (1954), came out, he dedicated it to his editor Hiram Haydn. But when he put out feelers to publish a second novel, he did not generate the excitement of a well-known writer, prize winner, and potential best seller.

Gloomy and filled with a sense of foreboding, Redding reacted like any well-connected writer in a similar situation. He wrote his most powerful friends to steady him. On New Year's Day 1959, Redding sent a note to Henry Allen Moe, the head of the Guggenheim Foundation for more than twenty years. In the letter he chronicled his interminable delays before coming to terms with Bennett Cerf of Random House, a prize among New York literary publishers. Moe, who had authorized a fellowship for Redding in 1944, was in a position to offer another grant so that Redding could finish his project. The professor was disappointed that it had taken a year and a half to relieve himself from a contract clause with the earnest but not profoundly distinguished Indianapolis publishing outfit Bobbs-Merrill, where Hiram Haydn had worked.

In the new year, magic began. In March another Guggenheim went to Saunders Redding, and Bobbs-Merrill released him so that he could follow Haydn to Random House. He would call the new book *Cross and Crown*. To friends like Moe, he described a straightforward program for the novel: it would be a sequel. "My plan can be stated simply: it is to write a novel in which the protagonist of *Stranger and Alone* is again the protagonist and in which he brings about his redemption."[1] The redemption of his identity as an American figured highly in the mind of J. Saunders Redding.

The task of narrative rescue went unfinished. Even with a Random House book contract to match his prestigious Guggenheim, Redding neglected the project and spent the year at conferences and in turning himself into a better spokesman. For the liberal arts colleges he prepared a lecture series on international affairs called "People, Policy, and Propaganda." Redding traveled the country and fielded more lucrative job offers than the one he had at Hampton Institute. The five chapters he had written of *Cross and Crown* remained in the desk of the upper room.

Considering what he was up against, perhaps Redding's inability to complete the novel makes sense. "I want to get on to other things. The obligations imposed by race on the average or talented Negro are vast and become at last onerous," Redding had written in a moment of self-reflective torment. Perhaps to a proportion greater than any single one of his contemporaries, J. Saunders Redding resented his situation as a black American who came of age in the late 1930s, wrote successfully in the 1940s and 1950s, and finished a career in publishing by the early 1960s. For Redding, the entire era was characterized by grand opportunity diminished by his own immobilizing feelings of guilt toward his ethnic inheritance, self-loathing, distorted patriotism, and rage. In his book *On Being Negro in America* (1951), he revealed a cry of anguish that resonated deeply for the African American writers of his time. "I am tired of giving up my initiative to these demands. I hope this piece will stand as the epilogue to whatever contribution I have made to the 'literature of the race.'"[2]

J. Saunders Redding never shook the suspicion that his duty toward the "literature of the race" had ruined his abilities as a writer. He sensed that his creative talents had curdled because he had to work so diligently to integrate American society; and none of the trinkets he earned lastingly satisfied him. Why did he feel so strongly at the very end of the 1950s that an optimistic, redemptive statement in fiction was necessary to give his career lasting merit? Why was Redding ignored by the next generation, and his work forgotten? What struggles did he have with his fellow black writers that have made it impossible for his contribution to be recognized? How did the African American intellectual's attitude toward accepting the values of liberal American critics and intellectuals dramatically shift? The intellectual and artistic struggles during the twenty-five-year arc of Redding's career from the mid-1930s throughout the 1950s is emblematic of an indignant generation of black writers.

In 1940 Ralph Ellison applauded the "indignant consciousness" of Richard Wright's character Bigger Thomas. He praised the black character by writing, "He, Bigger, has what Hegel called the 'indignant consciousness' and because of this he is more human than those who sent him to his death; for it was they, not he, who fostered the dehumanizing conditions which shaped his personality. When the 'indignant consciousness' becomes the 'theoretical consciousness' indignant man is aware of his historical destiny and fights to achieve it. Would that *all* Negroes were psychologically as free as Bigger and as capable of positive action!"[3] Twenty-seven-year-old Ellison understood well the impact of *Native Son* and its electricity for black writers and intellectuals, a group who theoretically transformed their indignation at Jim Crow to manufacture a strata of artworks that secured and pronounced a new era of psychological freedom for African Americans. But the black artists' startling aesthetic, institutional, and commercial successes have overshadowed history's awareness of their "positive action" or contribution to a group "historical destiny." Individual black writers did so well, especially between 1940 and 1953, that the idea of the artists operating as a cohort has been obscured.

Redding started his career during the Great Depression, a time when writers like Sinclair Lewis, John Dos Passos, Ernest Hemingway, and James Farrell portrayed human life with naturalist or social realist techniques. The portrait of ordinary American life was often undergirded by a positive belief in the perfection of human society, generally compatible with Marxism, and in favor of eradicating gross material disparities in America. The focus on problems of masses of working-class Americans and their day-to-day lives positively signaled a new willingness to extend justice to African Americans. But during Redding's middle writing years, "modern" writing methods arrived, or rather embedded themselves at elite academic institutions and the intellectual journals. These were elaborate and often difficult literary techniques that made a case for individual, not societal, transformation. The modernist literary tradition insinuated that the writer's prime obligation to improve society was fulfilled by creating literature that shaped the moral, ethical, and psychological structure of the individual. Yet to Redding's mind, neither the slogan of the social realist nor the individual preoccupation of the modernist was fully satisfying.

If economic disaster in American society in the 1930s had a hand in making a physical place for Redding, the theoretical mechanics for this had existed earlier. A generation before Redding's debut, the American liberal intellectuals on the edge of World War I had encouraged a kind of cultural pluralism, enabling the participation in American life of non-Nordic ethnic stock. And it was not the economic radicals in the vanguard. Horace Kallen had prepared Americans to capitalize on the specific attributes of an integrated ethnic American experience in the 1915 essay "Democracy versus the Melting Pot." Kallen thought of America as capable of profitably bringing together diverse composites that retained their distinctions. "As in an orchestra," he concluded, "every type of instrument has its specific timbre and tonality, founded in its substance and form; as every type has its appropriate theme and melody in the whole symphony, so in society each ethnic group is the natural instrument, its spirit and culture are its theme and melody, and the harmony and dissonances and discords of them all make the symphony of civilization."[4] Kallen found reason to celebrate ethnic particularity, but he had not dealt with the relationship between producing fine cultural artifacts and having access to society's resources.[5] How would black artists learn to play their tunes without teachers, instruments, and freedom from everyday labor in order to practice? A young black writer of a certain privilege, Redding had an additional struggle. His first angst—widely shared by his peers—was finding and feeling comfortable with the idea of his own ethnic melody. Then, by the time that he did that, the wind had shifted and subordinated culture to economics.

Following the stock market crash of 1929, the wide-scale intervention by the federal government into the American economy and the increasing prominence of communists and left-wing political groups signaled a passionate, rambling renewal of the liberal pledge to individual rights and social welfare, and one that increasingly saw culture as utterly subordinate to economics and politics. In a 1935 lecture at the University of Virginia, John Dewey redefined the crisis in American liberalism and in the process secured culture to economics and considerably reduced the power of ethnic distinctiveness. The marriage between culture and economics prepared the way for a new term: social liberalism. Dewey reminded the listeners of the classic liberal tradition that descended from John Locke through Thomas Jefferson and grew up in the nineteenth century with John Stuart Mill. Dewey hoped to convince his audience that it had become necessary for classic liberals to become social liberals. He argued for the poverty of the classic position, which took the term in practice to mean nothing more than a laissez-faire government approach to business regulation, relying on the theory that the only condition necessary for free action was the absence of constraint.

The dire poverty of the Depression immensely helped Dewey's arguments in favor of refining classic liberalism, as did increasingly relational and contingent global political affairs. Dewey proposed that the majority of America's liberals "are committed to the principle that organized society must use its powers to establish conditions under which the mass of individuals can possess actual as distinct from merely legal liberty."[6] Distinguishing between freedom from constraint and freedom to act, Dewey defined the contemporary liberal mission in terms that must have cheered a then twenty-nine-year-old Saunders Redding for what it said about a fundamental recognition of disparity in American life. Social liberalism "signifies liberation from material insecurity and from the coercions and repressions that prevent multitudes from participation in the vast cultural resources that are at hand," Dewey told his listeners.[7]

Dewey primed an audience including publishers, philanthropists, and educators that would transform the scope of American culture and greatly ease the obstacles to at least partial participation for blacks like Redding. From the time of Dewey's pronouncement through the end of the 1940s, a windfall of resources did open up and national public attitudes changed. But an assumption underlying the discussion about democratizing resources was that blacks would achieve full success when they had assimilated to white American values and cultural models.

The touchstone for the liberal repudiation of Kallen's orchestra of ethnic distinctiveness and Dewey's "freedom from material insecurity" was Gunnar Myrdal's 1944 *American Dilemma*. Approaching the situation of racial segregation directly, Myrdal defined the country's racial dilemma as a moral problem, a failure to live up to a creed of belief. The Swedish economist affirmed that Americans' idea of themselves was properly grounded in liberal traditions in private property and Western individual rights philosophy; the problem was only that blacks were excluded. Myrdal did not make an argument for black misery on account of poverty of resources; nor did he believe that there was anything culturally specific or historically important about African American life. The only question revolved around whether or not whites would permit complete assimilation.

Even with those caveats, the window for the country's liberal soul searching was narrow. By the later 1940s, American liberalism made what Irving Howe would call "the turn in politics toward an increasingly conservative kind of liberalism."[8] Ex-communists and ex-leftists redeemed their radical pasts by making what historian Michael Kimmage calls the "conservative turn"—overtures to American patriotism, traditional religion, and the voicing of some cynicism about the potential for human change.[9] Their revisionist work began to obscure the idea that racial prejudice had ever been a dominant layer of American thought or that resources had been monopolized and blacks excluded.

By 1950 the highly regarded Columbia University English professor Lionel Trilling could comfortably announce in a collection of essays called *The Liberal Imagination* that a broad public sensibility of fairness and ethical judgment abounded all over the nation and that liberalism was the only source and viable flower of the American intellectual tradition. Trilling proposed that only a robust criticism and complex literature—as in one that borrowed from works that both sustained and critiqued the status quo—could safeguard individual choice and political and religious freedom, guarantee lack of interference, and, of course, deal with racial prejudice. Turning himself into a kind of Whittaker Chambers of literary criticism, Trilling implied that instead of radical politics, smart and dissenting liberals would account for themselves in literature, the "human activity that takes the fullest and most precise account of variousness, possibility, complexity and difficulty."[10] Trilling's reliability as a judge of American tradition was strongly reinforced by his own Jewishness; it was understood that he could be relied upon to record candidly the existence of prejudice in America.

But Trilling's willingness to erect a myth of liberal America and to embrace writers and ideas that had been hostile or indifferent to a concept like a racially pluralist American society was always a difficult maneuver for black writers. In the dozen years before *The Liberal Imagination*, African American writers had emphasized the crisis in resources and the cruelty of whites. Their characterizations had been studies of human ugliness, frustration, and bitterness. They had hoped to demonstrate the deep humanity within the individual African American life that was curbed by punishing social and economic injustice.[11] Redress of inequality had seemed a prerequisite to entering the mainstream of American culture. But in the wake of Myrdal and Trilling, the cultural field-generals who Ralph Ellison had in mind when he once described the unwitting treachery of "neutrals," "sympathizers," and "disinterested military advisors,"[12] black writers were told to shift their focus to things like "possibility," or optimism in the American scene, and "difficulty," which also meant courting the elites. These were among the terms of the new definition of American liberalism by the end of the 1940s. As the longed for era of liberalized racial relations began, it brought with it the aesthetic practices of high modernism and cast out those of literary realism that had described social and racial catastrophe.

The dust had not settled by 1956 when *Phylon*, the flagship literary journal for black academics during the era of segregation, published one of Redding's most alert peers, the literary critic Arthur P. Davis. A Howard University professor and Columbia University Ph.D., Davis wrote in bittersweet tones of the impact the disruption of the old racial order was having on black writers. "I think we can safely say that the leaven of integration is very much at work," Davis announced.[13] He was torn because the victory after nearly one hundred years of postbellum struggle carried a sharp and unintended consequence for black creative artists. "It has forced the Negro creative artist to play down his most cherished tradition." The "cherished tradition" that black writers had to shuck in the face of the "new climate" was the style of writing, elegant or vitriolic, that wailed against racial conditions. While protest fiction's effectiveness in the giant political goal of ridding the country of racial persecution and discrimination was debatable, it had, as a force distinct from the Harlem Renaissance and for more than twenty years by 1959, reopened the publishing industry to black writers.

The shift in publishing taste to protest writing and back again, and the relationship between the emerging black writer, aesthetics, and politics in the United States, were markedly different from the black writing boom of the 1920s. Around the time of the Supreme Court's 1954 *Brown v. Board of Education of Topeka* decision, most of the major publishing houses enlisted the work of at least one black novelist, dealers in words who lifted their pens in the struggle of art and life, but who also served notice to the new American racial liberalism. Harper touted Richard Wright, who in two works sold nearly one million hardcover copies; Random House claimed the erudite Ralph Ellison but shored itself up commercially with the blockbuster sensation Willard Motley; Farrar, Straus published all four of William Gardner Smith's books; Houghton Mifflin supported Ann Petry; James Baldwin started out with Knopf and then settled in at Dial; and even the poet Gwendolyn Brooks tested the waters of seminarrative fiction at Harper.

Some of the better established journals carried a regular Negro writer to report on the episodes of racial realignment in the country: *Commentary, Nation, New Republic, American Scholar, Partisan Review, New Leader, Reporter, Saturday Review of Literature*, and *Survey Graphic* would all have at least semiregular Negro contributors before the end of the 1940s. Obviously the inclusion of black writers, which began in earnest during the Second World War, was prima facie evidence of a new world: the very presence of the writers symbolized the end of the conditions that they described. Less a report from the frontiers of apartheid, the black writers and their protest books had the effect of depicting a door closing on an era.[14] But had racial oppression, and the imperative requiring artists to contribute to its demise, really dissolved? The liberalism that amassed itself in American centers of learning and in dense urban areas tended to say that it had.

The new assumptions were not easy for everyone capable of taking advantage of them. "Play[ing] down his most cherished tradition" damaged a man like

Saunders Redding, who had been talked of, between 1942 and 1952, as the most promising black prose writer in the country. But during the lift-off years of his career, a feeling of self-described "morbidity" weakened him. Redding worried that he was misperforming his role as a black American, and he maintained a brittle exterior to impress the public. In his novel *Stranger and Alone* he had described the condition that affected him and his generation, especially men like Chester Himes: "it was the horrible thing the retreat from their ambition had done to them. It had made them very hard and brittle outside, and very soft inside, like two-minute eggs. If you crack the shell, she said, everything runs out."[15]

Redding's yolk ran at least in part because he witnessed himself losing his audience. *No Day of Triumph* was among the most important narratives published by an African American in the 1940s, a book that belonged in the company of Wright's *Native Son* and *Black Boy* and Petry's *The Street*. *No Day of Triumph*'s disappearance in favor of the novels of Redding's much better known contemporaries Ellison, Petry, and James Baldwin emphasizes the neglected historical moment of influential writers and critics in the 1940s and 1950s.

Once the movement abandoning protest writing was under way in earnest, as early as Baldwin's biting 1947 reviews in the pages of *New Leader* and culminating in 1949 with his frontal assault on social realism, "Everybody's Protest Novel," critics were quick to chide anything smacking of too much bitterness. It seemed to be a sign of victimhood. In a span of five years, Americans went from shock at the moral ugliness Myrdal had exposed to a feeling that the protest fiction genre was overworked exaggeration. Black writers were reminded that Richard Wright had exhausted the genre's possibilities with *Native Son* in 1940.

The speedy transformation of American society from racial indifference to racial liberalism rode on the back of a paradox. Negro writers were encouraged to find a new home in the "mainstream," and their mortgage was loyalty to it. At the same time that justice impartial to race in American courtrooms became at least not impossible, American civil liberties faced increasing jeopardy in congressional hearing rooms. Americans seemed to be on a very different path than white South Africans were to addressing racial division following the Second World War. But the outward face of increasing tolerance concealed the political economy of a dangerous interior. When it was happening, Bob Bone, an important white critic of African American literature, found the country's accelerated efforts at racial integration necessary to feed the growing needs of the military industry. America's "unconscious drive for national unity" served to strengthen the "permanent war economy."[16]

Redding's public brittleness and emotional runniness reflect the precariousness of an entire movement of black writers, critics, and poets from the second half of the 1930s through the end of the 1950s. They were sometimes called the

"Richard Wright School" or were pulled together even more vaguely as an "Integrationist" literary movement. In a sense they were both and neither. Richard Wright was the dominant figure of African American literature, from the time he started publishing in 1935 to his death in 1960. His concerns—to develop a literary style that competed on the stage of world opinion and a literature of ideas—were ambitions widely shared by his fellow black writers. Wright's life-long relationships with writers in Chicago and New York touch on the prime geographies and include very many of the personalities that wrote the books that proved the downfall of racial segregation in American public life and the maturity of African American literature. Furthermore, never before had so many liberal integrated institutions been available to more than a handful of black writers and thinkers. The Federal Writers' Project, the Communist Party and its umbrella groups like the National Negro Congress and the Committee for the Negro in the Arts, the Julius Rosenwald Foundation, the Artists' Colony at Yaddo—all these famously welcomed and cultivated African American artists at one point or another during the 1930s, 1940s, and 1950s.

But to name the period after its star is yet a misnomer. Wright, whose influence, reputation, and intellectual energy may have dominated the movement briefly during the early 1940s, largely disappeared after he left for France and the widespread overturning of social realist literature took place. Nor were all the writers, like the famous iconoclast Zora Neale Hurston, or the members of the two Harlem Writers' collectives of the late 1940s and 1950s, committed integrationists. Certainly black writers wished to see the prohibitions of segregation struck down, but integration into the "mainstream" was hardly uncritically endorsed. In his early years a man like J. Saunders Redding had never even liked the stance; he was uneasy with and had accepted the standpoint of integration as a drowning man gasping for air. "It was rather like the action of one who kicks and splashes frantically to save himself from drowning and suddenly finds that he has reached a shelf on which he can stand in the river bed. His objective was not the shelf, but just to be saved. I kicked and splashed in all directions, and suddenly there I was."[17]

Swimming in the direction of integration had one greatly tangible benefit, which was to increase the number of educational facilities for black America. Perhaps the principal component of the sweeping historical change was the bona fide generation of African Americans with access to colleges, graduate schools, and liberal institutions, who made up a reading public and comprised the group of artists that came of age during the World War II and cold war eras. Redding's life, frustration, and aspiration touched on similar yearnings experienced by a large and historic cadre that included Alger Adams (who published under the name Philip B. Kaye), William Attaway, James Baldwin, Alden Bland, Edward Bland, Arna Bontemps, Gwendolyn Brooks, Lloyd Brown, Sterling

Brown, Alice Browning, Anatole Broyard, Horace Cayton, John Henrik Clarke, Harold Cruse, Arthur P. Davis, Charles T. Davis, William Demby, Owen Dodson, Ralph Ellison, Nick Aaron Ford, Fern Gayden, Eugene Gordon, Richard Gibson, Hugh Gloster, Rosa Guy, Lorraine Hansberry, Robert Hayden, Chester Himes, George Wylie Henderson, Carl Moses Holman, Eugene Holmes, Langston Hughes, Zora Neale Hurston, Blyden Jackson, LeRoi Jones (who later became Amiri Baraka), Ernest Kaiser, John O. Killens, Curtis Lucas, Paule Marshall, Julian Mayfield, Claude McKay, Marian Minus, Albert Murray, Ann Petry, Dorothy Porter, Willard Savoy, William Chancellor Smith, William Gardner Smith, Will Thomas, Melvin B. Tolson, Waters Turpin, Margaret Walker, Theodore Ward, Dorothy West, Richard Wright, and Frank Yerby.

Not all whites pivoted toward the center as sharply as Lionel Trilling. Writers and critics like Bucklin Moon, Lillian Smith, and Thomas Sancton made it possible for politically radical black writers like Ralph Ellison, Ann Petry, and Chester Himes to get book contracts, to meet publishers and agents, and to place their work in magazines. Edwin Embree of the Julius Rosenwald Fund administered a large philanthropic grant to black artists from the 1920s through the 1940s, which the lion's share of black creative writers during this era received. Fascinatingly and in an era of overt, palpable bigotry, the spearhead of the integration movement included the best of white America's liberal intelligentsia. This was the cohort who yanked the country into a new era; *The Indignant Generation* is their story.

The Indignant Generation is a synthetic social movement history that charts the overlooked achievement of J. Saunders Redding's generation in mostly three-year chunks. The book follows the writers as they circulate in and through the intellectual hubs: Washington, D.C., New York, and Chicago. It begins by looking at the genesis of the politically committed writers' movement during the 1930s and then follows it through its most spectacular success in the first half of the 1940s. The signal origin year of 1934 sees Richard Wright gaining national notice, the beginning of the Communist Party's Popular Front strategy, and the death of New Negro movement icons Wallace Thurman and Rudolph Fisher. But crucially, for a twentieth-century literary movement, 1934 is the year of the publication of a rare black "little" magazine, *Challenge*, edited by Dorothy West.

The middle portion of the book looks at the great climb to literary modernism and liberalism in the 1940s and early 1950s. During this period black writers found the elusive quality of artistic success and intellectual respect. The transformative "long decade" introduced to the national scene a group of amazingly mature and brilliant black writers. The fifteen-year period began with Wright's *Uncle Tom's Children* and ended with a blockbuster 1953 that witnessed James Baldwin's first novel, Gwendolyn Brooks's only fiction, and Ann

Petry's finest high modernist tour de force. In this important epoch, black American writers became best sellers and prize winners, and their much celebrated individual accolades seemed to outstrip the very notion of a cohort. Richard Wright became the first writer of African descent to sell copies of his books in the hundreds of thousands; and added to that was the fact that he was a major intellectual force in his era. J. Saunders Redding won a southern literary prize in 1943; Willard Motley's 1947 novel *Knock on Any Door* did so well that Humphrey Bogart starred in the film version; Gwendolyn Brooks's *Annie Allen* of 1949 was the first work by a black American to win the Pulitzer Prize; and Ralph Ellison's *Invisible Man* of 1952 claimed the National Book Award. Indeed, in 1953 it could seem as if racial discrimination against black writers was a thing of the past.

The final period of *The Indignant Generation* examines the artists who repudiated mainstream aesthetics and political compromise and prepared the ground for the militant writers of the 1960s and the aggressive rejection of American liberal ideals. The modernists of the 1940s and early 1950s had redeemed a historical past that enabled black writers to challenge more fully the prominence of the Western artistic tradition itself, a move that began to question the value of integration and cut against the assimilation politics that was at the core of the 1940s black liberal stand. But as they ran counter to the public mood, writers faced deadly isolation and difficulty in articulating their ideas and asserting themselves in opposition to those who had supported them. The "new" liberalism of Lionel Trilling went hand-in-glove with the conservative backlash that followed the Second World War and created conditions ripe for McCarthyism as well as a more general quieting of dissent. The struggle of the later 1950s revealed the key tensions that determined the artistic and aesthetic approach of black writers during the 1960s. Surprisingly, the writers of the integration era paved the way for the black aesthetic movement of the 1960s through a variety of responses to the "new" freedom available in the "liberal" age: among them, anger, expatriation, disillusionment, and artistic silence.

By posing a new period—1934 to 1960—and suggesting that there is a confluence in the career arc between ghostlike J. Saunders Redding and the much better known Richard Wright, we can gain important insights into the anguished artistic and political choices facing African American writers who embraced artistic naturalism in the 1930s and modernism after the second half of the 1940s. The period approach helps us to understand the deep suspicion toward Western society that encouraged the younger generation of black artists to advocate a radical departure from Western models particularly by the mid-1950s and flowering in the 1960s. By focusing on the quarter century between the Great Depression and the Bay of Pigs as a social movement, we regain access to a vital time during which key formal barriers fell that had prohibited

African Americans from full participation in the cultural and literary life of American society.

What happens when we examine the twentieth-century breakthroughs for African American writing within the context of a group, such as the commercial breakthroughs of Richard Wright, Frank Yerby, and Willard Motley, and the artistic breakthroughs of Gwendolyn Brooks and Ralph Ellison? To take one example, Frank Yerby examined in isolation seems merely the creation of a Madison Avenue advertisement and publicity machine. But in closer relation to his network at *Challenge* magazine and the Chicago Federal Writers' Project, Yerby's fuller, more complex, and radical literary achievement emerges. By concerning ourselves with milieu, we can better approach the resounding authority of the individual achievement, especially since all the benchmark achievements of Wright, Yerby, Motley, Brooks, and Ellison occurred within twelve years. Additionally, two of the people, Wright and Ellison, were collaborators, and four of them—Wright, Yerby, Motley, and Brooks—were Chicago-bred intellectuals and social realists.

Only recently have we begun to reckon fully with the import and prominence of the American Communist Party as an engine of intellectual and artistic development for black Americans who were committed to issues of social and economic justice. But how much more can we learn if we look over time at the multiple organizations and ideological tendencies that came out of the American Communist movement in conjunction with the other significant institutions shaping African American writers at the time, such as the Federal Writers' Project and the Julius Rosenwald Fund? When we do this, we see the political limitations of the mainstream organizations, as well as the ambiguity that many of the writers regularly exhibited toward demanding ideological movements. Perhaps most important, a study of a twenty-five-year movement and historic group presents for the record the challenges and contributions made by black Americans to a more broadly conceived liberalism in American public life before and after the Second World War.

As consequential as the black writers' relationship to liberal, communist, and anticommunist politics is the work and point of view of the significant African American intellectual class teaching at black colleges—people like J. Saunders Redding, whose contribution too often has been ignored. When we attach less well-known artists and critics to the mid-twentieth-century literary bloc, our orientation shifts. For example, when African American critical voices are added to the famous debate between Zora Neale Hurston and Richard Wright over the uses of folk realism and political naturalism, we find less evidence of a squabble with roots in misogyny than we do of a rather strong clash in the sphere of cultural politics, particularly the ideological challenges put to traditional philanthropic organs by Communist-backed institutions during the

Popular Front era. By including black critics from historically black colleges, writers with only coterie followings, and fledgling black journals, we enhance the possibilities for generating new definitions for black literary politics in the 1930s, 1940s, and 1950s.

By examining a temporal chunk and sifting through the literature, newspapers, journals, literary archives, and institutional records for their ample conjunctions, we can also reconstruct the valuable relationships between visionary white liberals—the professional critics as well as those in the publishing industry—and black writers. Carl Van Vechten is well regarded as an important custodian of black letters during the 1920s and 1930s, but who replaced this white broker in the 1940s and 1950s? How was the message of emerging black writers shaped and contained during the period? How much of mid-twentieth-century liberalism and cold war anticommunism was foisted upon black writers as a requirement for their acceptance in circles of influence and prestige?

Disillusioned and unable to finish his novel, J. Saunders Redding certainly paid the price of black liberals dissatisfied with liberalism and with even fewer places of relevance to go by the end of the 1950s. However, he was not alone in his dimming. Several of the bright lights that had shone so fiercely in the 1940s and early 1950s had burned to dull embers before the end of the decade. There were several examples of the flicker and snuff of talents that were the equal to Redding. Globally, Richard Wright would be dead by 1960, and even his legacy as an internationalist dismissed. Chester Himes had taken to writing detective fiction to support himself in Europe, since it had become impossible to earn a living as the writer of serious fiction in the United States. By 1960 Gwendolyn Brooks would write poems for Emmett Till and Little Rock, evidence of an emotional fire that would lead her to reclaim the black audience and reject white publishers entirely. Ralph Ellison, a fellow at the American Academy in Rome between 1955 and 1957 and already renowned as a slow writer, had in effect finished the chief creative output of his years. Ann Petry, one of the most gifted and successful of the black writers, ended her career as a writer of adult fiction in 1953. William Gardner Smith, the precocious and phenomenal talent who published a well-received novel at the age of twenty-two and who went on to write three more, neither gathered a collective of interest around his work nor developed his talent. He remained an expatriate. And James Baldwin, who would become the most famous of them all, distanced himself from his early liberal backers and embraced black suffering.

The next generation of writers born in the 1930s and 1940s would answer central questions about racial and cultural politics differently from their older predecessors. They soon challenged the idea that America had much to offer in the way of culture or civilization. Julian Mayfield captured much of this new discontent of a postintegration generation in his poignantly titled 1959 speech, "Out of the Mainstream and into Oblivion." By the end of the decade America was poised to explode, and even had he finished it, it is doubtful that Redding's novel of redemption would have prepared them.

CHAPTER ONE

Three Swinging Sisters: Harlem, Howard, and the South Side (1934–1936)

A t the tail end of May 1934, thirty-five-year-old Malcolm Cowley, the young man-on-the-scene of the American literary radicals, published his first and best-known book, *Exiles Return*. In it, Cowley characterized the American writers who had left America for Europe as the "Lost Generation." He described the Gertrude Stein–named "Lost Generation" as having absconded from itself.

> It was lost, first of all, because it was uprooted, schooled away, almost wrenched away, from its attachment to any region or tradition. It was lost because its training had prepared it for another world than existed after the war (and the war prepared it for nothing). It was lost because it chose to live in exile. It was lost because it had no trustworthy guides, and had formed for itself only the vaguest picture of society and the writer's place in it. The generation belonged to a period of confused transition from values already fixed to values that had to be created.[1]

Cowley and his better-known peers like Edmund Wilson, Allen Tate, John Dos Passos, Ernest Hemingway, Robert Penn Warren, and F. Scott Fitzgerald had ventured out to clutch the fragments of European culture after the disaster of World War I. Perhaps some of these young Americans wanted to follow the paths of Henry James, Ezra Pound, and T.S. Eliot and preserve what war and greed and time had threatened.

But writers like Hemingway, Warren, and Cowley, whose talent equaled their drive, wanted to develop into skilled modern artists—equipped with both a vast technical facility and a real appreciation for the richness of ordinary life—a task for which they believed American institutions and customs had left them ill prepared. In the end, venerating tradition and hallowing Europe failed to open their eyes to the American scene. And, since so much of the war's senseless carnage could be traced to the interest of international financial empires and the cruelty of the moneyed class, the ideal of the free market got a shaking as well. American elites like Wilson, Dos Passos, and Hemingway had veered to the left by the mid-1930s; but none took to the path with the commitment of Malcolm Cowley. "They were taken in by 'the religion of art' and now they are taken in by the religion of Leninism," a reviewer snapped. "When will they grow up?"[2] Cowley believed that maturity lay beyond the narrow grooves of privilege. He felt that the artists of the 1930s needed to choose the side of the "worker" in the class struggle and range over ethnic and racial bonds too. The writers who had left for Europe before the United States declared war to drive in the Norton-Harjes ambulance corps must now suture themselves to "people without manners or distinction, Negroes, hill billies, poor whites, Jews, Wops and Hunkies."[3]

Cowley hoped that his generation would connect with the unmannered and the disesteemed to recover the balance lost in the war, the expatriation, and the Depression. However, in his own work the liberal writer completely ignored the works and attitudes of another group of bold young Americans, which might have added genuine depth to his comment. This native group had achieved their everlasting notoriety a bit closer than Europe was to Cowley's offices at the *New Republic* on West 21st Street in Manhattan. These writers had made a stand for the "religion of art" at the northern end of New York City, at 125th Street and Lenox Avenue. As the college professor J. Saunders Redding said in 1939, "Negro mothers, too, bore children into the 'lost generation.'"[4]

But what Redding meant by native belonging and what Cowley gestured toward were different. Redding's Lost Generation assertion fell on deaf ears for two reasons. By the end of the 1920s, major American liberal intellectuals like Dewey, Kallen, and Chicago sociologist Robert Park were playing down the struggle against racial discrimination: the crisis of social class ruled the day. Cowley had perceptively called forth the unranked Americans and acknowledged the power of ethnicity, but he also proposed an equivocacy of ethnic heritages that ignored reality. Second, Cowley shared a view with other liberal whites that doubted from the start that blacks—or other ethnics—could have much of a literary tradition. A fine example of the view appeared in 1939 in *Partisan Review*. Harold Rosenberg believed that "lowercase Americans have been and remain 'aliens'" and held that for this group "culture exists in the future not in the past."[5]

Cowley's inability to see the black artists, combined with his hope that his peers would see the American value in "Negroes," touched on the major problem of American cultural identity and the most glaring contradiction of a society grounded on the principles of democratic government and universal suffrage. Even if their flight to Europe had not taken place under precisely the same conditions, even if the Sacco–Vanzetti case had not been the brook of fire for their political radicalism, it made sense for African American intellectuals to inhabit the same world of ideas and experience as their white peers.

Besides, black writers had experienced exile—in their own native land. They had been estranged from the rural past and moved into the swift urban and black international current that was Harlem. Several of them had traveled to

Europe, but they had also traveled back to the rural South, to the Caribbean, and, for that matter, to Chicago. They traced their political radicalism not just to personal slights but also to nationwide racial clashes during the "Red Summer" of 1919 that left twenty-three blacks dead in Chicago alone. They had wrestled with and been a bit disfigured by expectations from culture brokers and backers that they drip with "primitive" vitality. Their position as modern artists against the Victorian moralists and utilitarians in the art-for-art's sake struggle was compounded by their political liability: they were a visible ethnic minority in a vigorously white nationalist country. The overriding pressures of duty to the race often tempered their artistic creativity. And Redding accurately joined Cowley's generational estimate to them. By 1930, the best known of the black scribblers had become expatriates of sorts, and their exile would send them not just out from the physical neighborhood of Harlem, but away from the very idea of a Harlem Renaissance itself.

Understood by the people who participated in it as the "New Negro Renaissance," the Harlem Renaissance, almost "so-called" from the time it began, necessarily flourished with the support of institutional sponsors like the Urban League and the commercial New York publishing industry. It had gotten under way in 1924, and the trend of black writing connected to it collapsed as the economy ground to halt in the early 1930s and unemployment and breadlines became common American realities. The end of the cash patronage and the flamboyant interracial cabaret lifestyle that had characterized the 1920s exposed the special vulnerability of black writers who depicted the American scene. They lived in a still proudly racist country that had not yet established a traditional role for artists and intellectuals. Which was not to say that icons from the academy and literary salons had no standing criticism of black writers. Try as it might, the Harlem Renaissance had thus far not shown the Yankee puritan industry that had produced a Hawthorne, a Melville, or a Henry James. And, the door shut quickly on the Renaissance. As early as 1934, key writers like Wallace Thurman and Rudolph Fisher, upon whose future work the Harlem Renaissance had been predicated, had died.

The assailing of black literary talent from the 1920s came internally from Thurman, the man reported to be the group's indisputable genius, the editor of the Renaissance journals *Fire* and *Harlem*. According to Thurman, the energetic but dilettante novelist Walter White (the most regularly published black writer by large New York houses during the 1920s), the prim sonneteer Countee Cullen, and the reliably genteel Jessie Fauset represented the narrow literary abilities, and Zora Neale Hurston and Richard Bruce Nugent the outrageous personalities, that Thurman had in mind when he wrote that white critics thought of black writers in the 1920s as "a highly trained trick dog doing dances in the public square."[6] Five years later Thurman went further with his critique of the movement in his engaging roman à clef, *Infants of the Spring*. In the book Thurman complained of the multiple paradoxes that haunted the new generation of black writers: blacks who excelled at proving white stereotypes of blacks; prejudiced whites leading the liberal vanguard for racial justice; untalented blacks promoted as virtuosos; black artists personally disdainful of folk culture; make-believe black artists scaling the dramatic heights of bohemian burlesque to escape the label of race; and perhaps most critically, the inability of the black writer to find an audience.

Despite the slight orbit of Thurman's own career, his objections were received as more than petty caviling. Two of his contemporaries both called into question the organic connection to black folk and the aesthetic value of the writing after 1925. One of them was Howard University philosophy professor Alain Locke. In yearly book reviews for the Urban League's *Opportunity* journal, beginning in 1929 and ending in 1942 (and excepting 1930), the godfather of the Renaissance fired on the group of writers whom he had first helped to launch, many of whom he now thought petulant, irresponsible, and ungrateful. As black writers began to shift away from sentimentalized "beauty" into the field of realistic "truth," Locke admitted that the group had been guilty of "spiritual bondage"—to primitivism—and that "much exploitation has had to be admitted."[7] That was in 1929. Two years later Locke decided that the entire movement had suffered from "inflation and overproduction."[8] Langston Hughes, no special admirer of Locke's, concurred in some respects with the estimate, if for different reasons. When in 1940 he published his memoir *The Big Sea*, he contributed the most frequently cited passages that proposed a truncated chronology for the artistic movement as well as the chief source of its demise. At the end of "the generous 1920s," black artists were "no longer in vogue," at least in the minds of white consumers of black culture.[9]

However, three of the gold standards of 1920s black writing were flourishing in the Depression, notably enough the strong prose stylists: Langston Hughes, Claude McKay, and Zora Neale Hurston. All three were widely traveled investigators of the African diasporic condition (in fact, the Jamaican-born McKay would not return to the United States until 1934). But yet, at the formal end of the Harlem Renaissance they verged on their greatest artistic and commercial successes, a compelling rejoinder to the notion of their degraded vitality by 1934. Hughes and Hurston both would wield a qualified degree of artistic and public influence in the latter 1930s and 1940s; Hughes would carry on through the 1950s. The energetic acrimony with which McKay and Hurston fought the Communist Party, and certain leftists and civil rights leaders more generally, combined with their fairly early deaths (McKay in 1948; Hurston in 1960 after being off the scene for ten years), distorted and foreshortened the reach of their influence. They did not live long enough to see their views substantiated and their reputations redeemed.

By the later 1930s, Langston Hughes had left behind his image as the "boy wonder" of the group. Unlike his two black peers, but like Malcolm Cowley, he traveled with the country's cultural and political left wing during its best years, the 1930s.[10] Like Cowley, Hughes had enrolled as an undergraduate at an Ivy League university. But it took his attending all-black Lincoln College for him to receive a degree. He was vulnerable in the mainstream and on the Left in ways that Cowley could not imagine. In payment for his commitment to social justice, Hughes spent much of the 1940s and 1950s having to extricate himself from his most radical works and looking for succor from welcoming black audiences. Despite this sometimes-exhausting trek, Hughes possessed a genuine courage and intellectual flexibility. These qualities enabled him to cultivate the next cadre of artists whose work would project them successfully beyond the confines of racial segregation in the arts. A viable network of writers in Harlem remained, and Hughes, whose regular address shifted only once, from 634 St. Nicholas Avenue to a house at 20 West 127th Street in 1948, often stood at the center. But by the time of Cowley's defining of the Lost Generation, a geographic metaphor like "Harlem Renaissance" could no longer connote the brilliance and vitality of African American writing.

On the other side of the Mason-Dixon line from New York stood the "capstone" of Negro higher education, Howard University. Named after Oliver Otis Howard, Union Civil War general and Freedmen's Bureau commissioner, Howard in the 1930s was flypaper for a new phenomenon in the United States: the modern black intellectual. The famously regarded social scientist and organization man W.E.B. Du Bois, the more conciliatory but formidably influential sociologist Charles Johnson, the esteemed and cultivated philosopher Alain Locke, and the "father" of African American history Carter G. Woodson had opened the door for black intellectuals to become professionally trained and internationally traveled, and to use their scholarship and public positions to improve the status of American blacks. It had been Du Bois, Locke, Woodson, and poet James Weldon Johnson who had nearly single-handedly uplifted the very idea of an African-rooted culture and people.

By the mid-1930s a generation of equally ambitious young scholars stood poised to take advantage of the groundbreaking work and to leap forward. Howard collected black professors, the youngest of whom were two generations removed from chattel slavery. Trained at the most distinguished of the American liberal arts colleges and graduate schools, they flat-out rejected the modes and attitudes of racial accommodation, especially in their scholarship. Greatly influenced by Marixism, they tended to understand politics globally and to see the racial problem in economic terms. While the older group continued to build their reputations, the younger academics—poet and critic Sterling Brown, political scientist Ralph Bunche (who had field research in Africa under his belt), plucky and already prolific sociologist and historian E. Franklin Frazier, commissioned officer and historian Rayford Logan, economist Abram Harris, philosopher Eugene Holmes, education professor Doxey Wilkerson, the Harvard B.A. and inspector general of Africans in the ancient world William Leo Hansberry, and the archive-minded librarian Dorothy Porter—courageously expanded the publicly accepted models for activism and scholarship. Sterling Brown, who had been born walking distance to the campus and had earned degrees at Williams and Harvard, called the young crowd "faculty insurgents determined to develop Howard into a first-class college."[11]

The younger Howard cadre, turned out mainly by the Ivy League, also spoke for and with colleagues at the other black colleges. The combined group formed the intellectual groundswell of the literary critics who taught in America's segregated southern college system and started a major publishing enterprise in the 1930s and 1940s. There were several good college departments: Howard, Hampton Institute on Virginia's eastern tidewater coast, and Fisk College in Nashville, Tennessee. The important critics would grow to include the unfailingly genteel Arthur P. Davis, who started teaching at Virginia State, then moved to Hampton Institute before coming to Howard; Nick Aaron Ford, who after World War II and many years in the field finally settled into a job as an English professor at Morgan College in Baltimore; Blyden Jackson, educated at the University of Michigan and the most opinionated of the group; and Hugh Gloster, literary historian and Morehouse Man. The best known and most successful among them, but who went on to share their anonymous fate, was J. Saunders Redding, a Hampton Institute professor from 1943 to 1964. From their institutional platforms, the black college group broadcast and transformed the two most exciting ideas of their day: cultural and racial liberalism, and an economy planned by the government and not the business market.

But a home for the critic was not necessarily a home for the writer. In the mid-1930s African American schools south of the Mason–Dixon line very much retained their traditional impediment: racial subjugation. Thus, west of the Appalachian Mountain range and at the junction of the vital American Mississippi waterway lay the future of black writing. With the grand World's Fair of 1893 and a well-funded, cutting-edge university, Chicago, Illinois, had transformed itself from a gargantuan slaughterhouse to a place of literary consequence. By the 1930s the city had even put behind it the Riot of 1919. The midwestern metropolis remained a prime destination for southern blacks seeking refuge, work, and possibility. More than a quarter million had relocated to Chicago by the 1930s, and the human flood from Mississippi, Arkansas, Tennessee,

Louisiana, and Alabama continued, adding another one hundred thousand African Americans to the total by the mid-1940s.[12]

The scope of transformation available to formerly rural and small-town sharecroppers and their families was enchanting. In 1934 Richard Wright, an occasional mail sorter at the U.S. Post Office and recipient of public relief but also a member of the Communist Party's organization for young writers, the John Reed Club, traveled to New York and became recognized in the pages of the Communist daily newspaper, the *Daily Worker*, as a fellow writer alongside the likes of Langston Hughes, Sterling Brown, and Eugene Gordon. Easy to get along with and mild and joking in his manner, Wright did not seem obviously scarred by poverty or racism. His tenacity, quickness, and aplomb confused people who underestimated him. In Chicago Wright found other black writers restlessly leaping from the feudal South to the supersonic age. A man who had only graduated from junior high school in the state of Mississippi was destined to become the 1930s representative of the black artistic avant-garde. His intellectual work, tireless energy, and pending celebrity galvanized the historical ferment of Harlem, the college elites, and the Chicago Hotspurs. Relative to what this large group of black writers and intellectuals would accomplish, Wright was the modern man who had canned the dynamo of historical forces. The shift they were engaged in was a dramatic one that swiftly flowed beyond a basic premise of racial acceptance to a principal demanding that American readers acknowledge the richness of native black American culture.

The creative vitality of the Harlem Renaissance had been nurtured and developed in the house journals of the two leading reformist civil rights organizations of the early twentieth century: the National Association for Colored People's (NAACP) *Crisis* and the National Urban League's (NUL) *Opportunity*. Soon after its inception in 1909, when it was the platform for W.E.B. Du Bois, the NAACP had spread its views with a house journal. Rooted in the academic discipline of sociology and social work, the National Urban League was more interested in the amelioration of urban social conditions than in fighting racist American laws. Its members realized the importance of the arts in their fight. Founded in 1921, the league journal *Opportunity* had published the leading artists of the Harlem Renaissance to help spread the good news of social reform. During the 1930s the magazine sharpened its focus on the urban conditions of African Americans, journalistically recording the migration from the rural South to urban centers. Edited by Elmer Carter, *Opportunity* far outstripped its rival *Crisis* in ushering in the new, politically determined literary sensibility.

The civil rights organizations headed by black Americans had a long and distinguished interracial character. But they could not attract the attention of elite American cultural opinion; obviously they did not cater to or have at their disposal a broad-based literate African American audience. A not insignificant swathe of American philanthropy funded and supported the civil rights organizations, which, in turn, hesitated before endangering their public reputations with controversial causes, like criminal cases involving destitute blacks. Then the tightened belts of the Depression began to exhaust even those sources of financial support. The journals were reluctant to showcase images of black working-class life, and, except for the fact that they published black writers, they were reluctant participants in the literary experimentation that was becoming the modernist movement in the arts. By and large, the same sources backing the major civil rights organizations funded the black colleges and universities. In the case of the NAACP and the Urban League, the necessity of a pristine public image compromised their ability to cultivate the more radical, innovative, and intelligent of the next wave of artists. In the main, the protocols of *Crisis* and *Opportunity*, with their combined circulation of perhaps twenty-five thousand, eliminated writers without academic credentials, lacking upper-crust pedigrees, or failing to amass credible records of publication. By the same token, the didactic uplift publications were not the choice destination for writers with skills and contacts to do better.

The mounting difficulty of finding employment by 1934 strengthened the argument for radical and dramatic changes to the American economy. Americans, even the comfortably educated, were looking for answers and were prepared to venture into nontraditional avenues to achieve them. The beginning of an exodus of black Americans away from the rural South in the direction of significantly better resourced northern cities and states during the rough era of the First World War also had a hand in producing, between 1936 and 1942, nearly twenty-four thousand black college graduates.[13] This figure represented more black Americans with a college education than had ever previously graduated from college in the United States. By 1942, 46,000 blacks would be enrolled in college, and 2,500 black teachers were their instructors; among them, 381 were holders of a doctoral degree.[14]

The making of a credentialed intelligentsia was under way, an intelligentsia dramatically different from its seminary-educated predecessors, such as Howard University's first black president Mordecai Johnson who had done his post-baccalaureate work at Gammon Theological Institute in Atlanta. But already vulnerable and without sure-fire opportunities for professional work even when the economy hummed, black college graduates in the Depression made careers from such lines of work as "indoor aviation"—elevator operation—and red-capping at the train station. The unemployed black writers, artists, and activists were making a beeline for the political parties and artistic clusters on the left wing.

All kinds of black intellectuals had cut their teeth during the 1910s on the giant issue of the delegation of the resources of society, the kind of leadership group needed to begin the redistribution of power and the involvement of the rank-and-file. Sorting all of this out was among the many rich debates between socialism and communism. The most important early radical group was black socialists, mainly West Indians, who met in New York before 1920. There was George Schuyler, a World War I veteran originally from Syracuse, New York; the Jamaican Claude McKay, who had studied at Tuskegee and Kansas State; another Jamaica native, the schoolteacher Grace Campbell, who had helped to found the communist-skeptical Friends of Negro Freedom;[15] Hubert Harrison, an immigrant from the Virgin Islands whose legendary feats of erudition earned him the name "black Socrates" and who served as political theorist for the famed back-to-Africa nationalist Marcus Garvey; Richard B. Moore, from Barbados, who became a Harlem institution as a bookshop owner; Andy Razaf, a popular Virginia-born songwriter; the Texas bohemian and Tuskegee graduate Lovett Fort-Whiteman, who was the first African American to join the Communist Party; and the theoreticians of the African Blood Brotherhood (soon to be disbanded by the Communist International and transformed into the American Negro Labor Congress headed by Fort-Whiteman),[16] *Crusader* newspaper editor Cyril Briggs of Nevis and Otto Huiswoud of Surinam.

Though one fabled afternoon in 1921 or 1922 they apparently all (except Fort-Whiteman) came together at Claude McKay's offices at the *Liberator* magazine, this was a fractious group. McKay himself left his editorial post at the magazine for the Soviet Union to address the Fourth World Congress of the Third International and do extensive global travel. Moore, Campbell, Briggs, and Huiswoud would officially join the Communist Party. Other radical black intellectuals like *Emancipator* editor W. A. Domingo, along with the black American socialists Chandler Owen and A. Philip Randolph, believed that American blacks were reactionary—capitalist pawns—and only a hindrance to the international socialist movement.[17] Others were more reluctant to button the whole cloth of a foreign movement's philosophy. Briggs and Moore, for example, believed that a black nationalist left-wing movement was best suited to the conditions of the United States' domestically colonized black population. This intelligentsia still percolated through Harlem's libraries, street corner rallies, and intellectual events, but the American-born blacks in the group, led by A. Philip Randolph and George Schuyler, eschewed outright defiance by the 1930s. They had both decided to work within the system: Randolph in organizing a black union of railroad porters called the Brotherhood of Sleeping Car Porters, and Schuyler in journalism.

The mixed destinies of the socialists vividly illustrate the Communist Party's success in either corralling the talented black radicals or, as in the case of Schuyler and McKay, making permanent foes. Part of the difficulty owed to the growing pains of a new movement trying to span the distance between the New

World and the Old World. Founded in 1919 in Chicago, the American Communist Party (CPUSA) went through periods of tight and loose affiliation with the Communist International or Comintern. The American Communist leadership was not spectacular, bold, or especially creative. It faithfully sent envoys to the Comintern meetings where Communist policies were developed, changed, and transmitted. Compared to the Communist parties working toward socialist governments in England, France, Spain, and Germany in the 1920s and 1930s, the U.S. party did not succeed in recruiting a mass movement. If communist labor organizers and pamphleteers jeopardized life and limb when they went to Gastonia, North Carolina, Scottsboro, Alabama, and Atlanta, Georgia, the movement also "bored from within" and spent its energies working within the readily available avenues in a democratic republic. The CPUSA attempted to develop labor unions, organize public opinion, and field candidates for political office. Americans seemed more naturally "menshevik," prone to majority politics, than "bolshevik," inclined to form Lenin's revolutionary vanguard.

Anti-imperialist activist and trade-union organizer Earl Browder took over the post of general secretary of the CPUSA in 1932 from William Z. Foster. Headquartered in New York, the CPUSA could claim about ten thousand members. According to Waldo Frank, the Yale-educated liberal novelist and former associate editor of *The Seven Arts*, Browder was "dry, pleasant, reliable" and "had read books," qualities that attracted intellectuals when compared to the manner of the man he replaced. Foster made "no pretence to culture" and was devoted, Frank thought, "as a machine might be called devoted, to its single task."[18] A tough man, Foster had left school at the age of ten and spent most of his life working in plants and mills and heading strikes. But the party's years under Browder between 1932 and 1945 were those of its greatest popularity, influence, and mainstream legitimacy. Browder embraced Roosevelt's New Deal social reforms and included two African Americans in the upper ranks of party leadership, the charismatic Alabama native, college graduate, and front man James Ford, and Harry Haywood, the plebian theoretician handpicked by Joseph Stalin. Ford regularly ran for vice president on the Communist ticket.

When Browder took over, the Communists' directives to attract black membership helped to clarify a central black American political tension between belonging and independent freedom. Haywood had returned from the Sixth Communist International in 1928 with new a race-relations doctrine for the United States. Principally, the new platform called for dramatic efforts to eradicate racial discrimination, such as the decision to integrate workers' unions.[19]

Controversially, and not in complete sympathy with the principal goal of ending racial discrimination, the party also had adopted the "Black Belt Nation" thesis toward African Americans in the United States. Haywood, a World

War I veteran who had grown up in Nebraska and whose parents had been slaves, wrote the thesis. But its adaptation by the Communist International had as much to do with the schism between Joseph Stalin, William Foster, and the extensively Russian schooled Haywood himself, on one hand, and Nicolai Bukharin, Jay Lovestone, and Lovett Fort-Whiteman, on the other, as it did with the internal merits of Haywood's ideas about self-determination for the Black Belt. The real area of dispute was around the timing of the collapse of American capitalism, and whether or not blacks would move north en masse and become industrial workers.[20]

Haywood and Stalin believed they would not. The Black Belt thesis held that Negro Americans were an oppressed nation, sharing a common land, heritage, and culture, and that American blacks deserved the right to self-determination and their own national territory. In the portions of the American South where blacks were in the majority, they were imagined to constitute a "national" group whose right to self-determination was thought important enough for preservation, similar to the Ukraine in the Soviet Union.[21] The geographic zone would take the form of a belt of land stretching across the American South, coterminous with the old "Black Belt" where cotton had been extensively grown. The Black Belt would be the black homeland after the proletarian revolution had been successfully carried out. By 1935 Jewish communist James Allen brought out a pamphlet with a diagram showing the contours of the proposed state. It stretched from Washington, D.C., to encompass coastal Virginia, South Carolina, and Georgia and then veered west toward Texas. The Black Belt resembled an enormous Italy with its foot arching across the southeastern U.S. coastline and then forming a huge booted leg that lumbered diagonally across the continent and ended in New Orleans.

But the "scientific" and sometimes geographically distant communist theorists were challenged by the steady migratory pattern of blacks leaving the rural South. Objections to the Black Belt thesis persisted. A "highly intelligent Negro professor" in Moscow surprised writer Edmund Wilson during his extended visit in 1935. The black man had traveled to gain a hearing before the Comintern in hope of getting them "to change its line" on the Black Belt. "Negro culture" was simply "a part of the general American culture," the black professor insisted to Wilson and two American communists.[22] Some black Americans wanted not self-determination, but "their rights as Americans," and some wanted both.

The separate nation ideal had a long past. Enslaved Africans and American blacks and had pursued elements of a national project since perhaps the time of the 1739 Stono River Rebellion in South Carolina, in which the rebels deliberately sought to reach Florida. The Seminole "Indians" of Florida were actually territorially sovereign Africans who had escaped their Spanish captors.

Throughout the eighteenth and nineteenth centuries "New Negroes" from Africa and from the Caribbean brought traditions of both total freedom and the circumspect freedom of outlying, sometimes warlike, sometimes friendly, maroon communities. Merchant seaman Paul Cuffee clarified the determined goal for a black free nation in the early nineteenth century and began taking American freedpeople to West Africa. The expatriate plans and schemes continued in the middle of the century with explorers and ministers of black consciousness like Martin Delany and Henry Wilmot Blyden. After the Civil War, droves of Exodusters fled the cotton-belt South for Kansas and Oklahoma, and when that dream was sullied after the century's turn, Chief Alfred Sam of the Akim nation organized dozens of black westerners to go to Africa. Black nationalism culminated after World War I with the United Negro Improvement Association of Marcus Mosiah Garvey, which proposed the operation of commercial shipping lines to return the descendents of slaves to Africa. The communist-led version of black separatism, which gathered its steam during the African American Great Migration to urban centers, especially to New York and Chicago, would ultimately prove fantastic.

But sensational claims about black rights and racial justice and banners slung with them helped to build an audience. And the Communists were more than just their talking points. They continued to raise a profile with most black Americans, even those put off by their lofty theoretical projections. Their legal defense in two sensational trials of the early 1930s—the 1931 Scottsboro rape trial and the 1932 Atlanta case of labor organizer Angelo Herndon, charged, literally, with inciting slave rebellion—enabled the CPUSA to popularize nationwide their credo of economic transformation and racial equality. Middle-class organizations like the NAACP thought the nine poor and uneducated young men condemned at Scottsboro, or Herndon, a self-professed communist agitator, nearly impossible cases to win.

The Communist Party, however, used both opportunities to subject the U.S. legal system to international scrutiny. By providing free legal counsel through the International Labor Defense and publicizing the facts of the trial in their newspapers and media outlets, the CPUSA became a ranking defender of black American rights. In both cases, they helped the defendants avoid the death penalty, and, with the help of the NAACP, Herndon was freed outright. In the Herndon case, the Communist Party also recruited one of the premier African American talents of the 1930s and 1940s, the Harvard-trained lawyer and trophy of Atlanta's Negro middle class, Benjamin Davis, Jr. Nearly a communist celebrity, Davis was a crucial figure in the 1930s and 1940s who represented the natural attraction between the black radical intelligentsia and the Communist Party. Davis worked as director of the Harlem branch of the Communist paper *Daily Worker* and was on the CPUSA's decision-making Central

Committee. With his work and credentials, he ultimately developed enough of a leadership base to replace Adam Clayton Powell, Jr., on the New York City Council in 1943.

Beyond popular figures like Davis or James Ford, the magazine *New Masses* enabled American communism to present a coherent, reasonable anticapitalist point of view on topics of racial exploitation, politics, and culture. Founded in 1926 with the help of a grant from the antiwar Garland Fund, the magazine owed its approach and style to the tradition of its predecessors *Masses* and *Liberator*. *New Masses* provided a good home for vigorous criticisms of American culture and civilization. The editorial line regularly exposed the sham of Victorian era propriety and the hollow money-grubbing mores of the American middle class. By the mid-1930s, under the Communist "Popular Front" strategy, the journal would take on much greater significance for a large American public by publishing commercially famous writers, even to the point of what some called "a new literary snobbism of the left."[23] Comfortably placed on a coffee table alongside the *New Yorker*, the magazine gave its writers a "burgeoning, avid audience of awakened American readers," with articles about the complex nature of African American life and the fight for racial equality in the United States. It published articles by the Los Angeles lawyer Loren Miller, Langston Hughes, philosopher Eugene Clay, and a young Richard Wright. By the end of the decade and into the 1940s, the magazine's best and most distinguished black writer, Ralph Ellison, would hold down a post as contributing editor. Over the course of its twenty-two year history, *New Masses* would provide a cutting edge of African American journalism and cultural thought in the United States, written by blacks and whites.

New Masses was an excellent example of the sort of radical democratic possibility available to black writers in the 1930s. But early on in the decade, the Communists offered something vital to the young writer. In 1934, the hardest year of the Depression, the CPUSA was operating perhaps the only incubator for unpublished, uncredentialed literary talent, the John Reed Club. The club was named for the Harvard-educated American journalist John Reed, who had devoted himself to the emerging Soviet nation; Reed had even talked with Lenin about the problem of Jim Crow.[24] The membership typically combined young idealists and budding artists with dues-paying members of the CPUSA, who were sometimes both. The club had started in New York in 1929, and spread rapidly to support over thirty branches with twelve hundred members by 1934.[25] The largest groups were in New York and Chicago—unsurprisingly, as these were the strongholds of Communist Party cultural life. Cities with an identifiable "proletarian" industrial working population, New York and Chicago were home to large numbers of first- and second-generation European immigrants who identified closely with Marxism's demand for industrial workers to

control factory production and to participate actively in the basic political mechanics of urban life.

Black members were still not prominent—in New York especially so—but
their very presence was an index to the party's ideological commitment to dismantle white chauvinism. While these John Reed Clubs never had sizable black
participation, they did manage to promote a spirit of interracial camaraderie
and championed the art of debunking social-class privilege that was modern
yeast for expanding the opportunities and the sphere of interest of black writers. And in spite of these low numbers, some of the clubs managed to introduce
black writers to the public. A novelist of proletarian realism from the Midwest
named Jack Conroy devoted his August 1932 issue of the journal *Rebel Poet*,
organ of the Missouri John Reed Club, to African American writing.

In an early example of the collation of two distinct communities, *Rebel Poet*
carried a review by one Philip Rahv of Langston Hughes's illustrated folio of
poems and play *Scottsboro Limited*. A twenty-four-year-old Ukrainian-born
Marxist critic who had named himself after the Hebrew word for teacher, Rahv
waved the red flag in his favorable portrait of Hughes. "Nothing is more symp-
tomatic of the vitality and integrity of the revolutionary movement than the
fact that of late, due to the efforts of the Communists, Negro workers and intellectuals are being increasingly drawn into the class-conscious sector of the proletariat," he wrote.[26] As the editorial force behind the magazine *Partisan Review*,
which began as the New York City John Reed Club's journal, Rahv would sit out
the second half of the 1930s and the first half of the 1940s without ushering into
print much relative to racial issues. However, it is worth noting that he did not
begin his career that way.

More significant in their efforts at racial integration than the New York or
Missouri clubs was the Chicago arm of the John Reed Club—mainly because it
could claim Richard Nathaniel Wright. In a remarkably short period of time,
Wright irrevocably shaped the course of the river of the black writers' movement that emerged by using modernist techniques in the promotion of liberal
racial attitudes and political justice. He was very nearly the eponymous figure
of his age, who represented a particular American zeitgeist. Wright's achievement within his own generation ranks him alongside other key American writers who strongly influenced their peers, like Mark Twain, Ernest Hemingway,
and William Faulkner.

A twenty-five-year-old Wright joined the Chicago John Reed Club in 1933
and published his first poem, "Rest for the Weary," in *Left Front*, the Chicago
club's journal. He accepted a position on the editorial staff of *Left Front* and
then joined the Communist Party itself to improve his ability to protect the
technically unaffiliated club from Communist bureaucrats. A refugee from
Mississippi and Tennessee, Wright called the club, "my first contact with the

modern world."[27] And an unusually modern world it was for him. On his first evening, stumbling into a meeting, he found a hive of active writers about to make it big. First was twenty-four-year-old social realist writer Nelson Algren, on the verge of publishing his novel *Somebody in Boots*, a book that originally had centered on an interracial love affair.[28] Besides Algren, there were the writers Abraham Chapman (whom Wright became closest to personally) and Laurence Lipton, and poet and future *Direction* magazine editor Howard Nutt. At least for one black writer, the club's utility would be difficult to overstate. Talented and well read, but black, poor, and with limited formal education, Wright had the opportunity to enter into a companionable relationship with aggressive young writers and artists serious about their work. Wright's artistic journey was, from its inception, one of interracial association. He never cultivated "Negro" standards of success.

Wright's flourishing signaled the value of the institutional framework within the CPUSA, but communism was not democracy. At the 1934 Midwest Writers' Congress in Chicago, Wright's magazine *Left Front* was dissolved, a move that prepared the way for *Partisan Review* briefly to become the major literary organ for the American Communists. Faced with the Nazi parliamentary victory in Germany and the subsequent communist purge there, the Comintern decided to move aggressively to make alliances with former ideological foes. One part of the strategy was to dissolve clubs aimed at developing "proletarian" talent in favor of a broader coalition that could accommodate already established artists; this new coalition became known as the "Popular Front." The swift dispatch of Wright's journal forewarned of the upcoming dissolution of the John Reed Clubs themselves in September 1934 at the annual congress of John Reed Clubs and served to the wary as a cutting example of the strength of the foreign influence on the leadership of the American Communist Party. Wright, himself president of a club, thought, "This thing is cold!"[29]

The most famous black writer with Communist ties in the year 1935 was Langston Hughes, who had journeyed to Soviet Russia in 1932 and stayed for nearly a year, traveling the newly formed Soviet Union and Asia. From his briar patch on St. Nicholas Avenue in Harlem, he traveled abroad as well as toured the American South to read his works to black American audiences. The year before his sojourn to the Soviet Union, the genial Hughes, a famous recipient of fêtes by wealthy whites in the 1920s, began making a series of fervid proclamations. He decried the immorality of the moneyed class with works such as "To Certain Negro Leaders," "Advertisement for the Waldorf-Astoria," and, after his return, "Good Morning Revolution," "Revolution," and "White Man." These incendiary poems appeared in *New Masses*.

Also evocative of his strong bond with the militant left, Hughes had become, by 1934, the president of the League of Struggle for Negro Rights. The league became the Communist Party's frontline organization for black Americans, and it had actually evolved from Lovett Fort-Whiteman's American Negro Labor Congress.[30] In 1934 Hughes published his short stories, *The Ways of White Folks*, a narrative collection that reverberated with white brutality and black defiance, if it lacked the fresh execution for which his best poetry was known. To communist-minded friends like Evelyn and Matt Crawford, Hughes inscribed the book "Black and White until the Red book comes."[31] Around the same time, he said to his wealthy San Francisco patron Noel Sullivan that he was "string[ing] along with the Left," in order to last out the Depression.[32] Hughes easily called to mind the classic tug-of-war for the artist's loyalty between rich benefactors and radical social movements. This struggle fatigued Hughes, but not until well after his 1937 sojourn to Republican Spain to serve as a war correspondent for the African American press. Until the mid 1940s, Hughes would conspicuously ply his art for human rights and social justice.

The energy of the early 1930s reached other colleagues of Langston Hughes, though they did not all team up with the radicals. The writer Dorothy West had been an avid teenage participant in the vanguard group of black artists at the outset of the Harlem Renaissance. Born in 1907 into a cushy Boston family, the precocious graduate of Boston Latin had shared second prize with Zora Neale Hurston in a 1926 *Opportunity* journal contest for her short story "The Typewriter." They became friends, and in 1927 Hurston sublet to West her apartment at 43 West 66th Street.[33] West had spent the 1920s in close camaraderie with a talented group: her friend and roommate Helene Johnson, Hurston, Phi Beta Kappa poet Countee Cullen, model and artist Bruce Nugent, and Guyanese short story writer Eric Walrond.

At the prodding of Meharry Medical College graduate and socialite Mollie Lewis, West took a boat in 1932 to Russia with Langston Hughes and a crew of other impressive young black college graduates. They had their in-country expenses paid by the Soviet government in order to make a film that could not be made in Hollywood: they would present the cruelty of racial terror in the American South. The cast included the teacher and activist Louise Thompson, journalists Henry Lee Moon and Ted Poston, and Los Angeles attorney Loren Miller. But West did not give her heart to Marx, perhaps because the movie project never came off. The Soviets stalled on the filming, partially at least on account of the energetic maneuvering of an American engineer at the Dniepostroi dam project named Colonel Hugh Cooper. Cooper was already "agitated over the reception and kindly treatment which American negroes have had in Russia," and upon learning of the film he demanded meetings with Soviet officials, including Molotov, until he received assurance that the project would be abandoned.[34] When the well-connected West returned to New York, she used her native resolve to conceive, edit, and publish *Challenge*, a periodical designed, at first, to carry over the Harlem Renaissance into the mid-1930s. She published the magazine from 1934 until 1937, and she promoted the black writers of the 1920s with enthusiasm. Besides Hughes, Hurston, and Cullen, she counted among her personal friends the irascible Claude McKay and Renaissance editorial flame Wallace Thurman, as well as benefactors like Alain Locke and James Weldon Johnson.

West designed *Challenge* as a literary monthly that would showcase the talent of recognized and well-mannered younger black writers. She was trying to bring off what the Harlem Renaissance crew had tried with *Fire!!!* in 1926: to produce a regular journal taking advantage of black thematic material and smart enough to be cognizant of the modernist innovations that the prominent race journals—*Crisis* and *Opportunity*—were reluctant to publish. The only problem revolved around the fact that West seemed mainly interested in cuddling a kind of polite aestheticism. Protests against racial conditions, investigations of the economic crisis, and sometimes even the development of black themes seemed to her a bit turgid and artificial. In fact, she hoped to see black writers addressing something other than racial persecution.

Her preoccupations blunted the early dynamism of the magazine. She had been mentored in the craft of writing by Columbia professor Blanche Colton Williams, a Mississippian who had served as a judge for the *Opportunity* contests. Colton seems to have encouraged West to imitate the O'Henry Memorial Award short stories, which Colton edited, and which were known at the time for their contrived plots and sentimentality.[35] The journal's first two issues were built up with the old cadre: Langston Hughes, Claude McKay, Zora Neale Hurston, Arna Bontemps, Helene Johnson, and Countee Cullen. It was an inauguration of the sort to make the old guard smile. The elder Negro literary statesman James Weldon Johnson responded with pride to the March 1934 first issue of the journal. "I heartily congratulate you on *Challenge*," he wrote to West, "[i]t is away and beyond superior to any Little Magazine that we have yet launched. I hope it is going to be a success. It deserves to be. It is certainly a necessity."[36] Johnson inferred an unhappy estimate of the past. In spite of the impressive array of talent from the Harlem Renaissance, the group of writers and poets had been a bit too bohemian, eclectic, and erratic to organize a successful, long-lived literary journal.

Johnson famously endorsed the belief that the best way to end race prejudice was through a movement in the cultural arts. "[T]hrough artistic achievement the Negro has found a means of getting at the very core of the prejudice against him," he had written in *Harper's* magazine in 1928.[37] But the talented covey of writers had not flown as highly as their counterparts in music and dance. A year after the *Harper's* essay, Johnson had reprimanded black prose writers hunched together like "numerous small coteries of unsuccessful writers," making a "fetish of failure," and consoling their inability to publish with the canard that their books "portray Negro life on too high a level."[38] A Fisk professor, public relations expert, and Taft-era politician, Johnson encouraged the creation of the black front parlor. He feared that the popular explorations of black crime and vice, with their "accessible" and appealing "dramatic values," would overshadow works that painted the lives of the "respectable [middle-class element." Where was a resource that might codify the values of the black writers and bring into conversation those devoted to the life of the front parlor with those more attracted to the back alley?

Johnson thought that in West, a product of the black New England middle class, he had found a personality steady and attractive enough to organize a new showing of literary talent. And he was not alone in these hopes; other writers from the vainglorious days of the Renaissance wanted to rescue black talent and black themes from the "small coteries" of failure. The remarkable poet Countee Cullen, upon whose professional and academic achievement a good deal of the Renaissance claims for reputation and aesthetic fitness had been made, and who after several soul-searchingly infertile years was on the verge of making a full turn in favor of communism, responded to West's invitation for poetry with alacrity and favor. But he also signaled a recurring note: everyone who had participated in it considered the Harlem Renaissance a tragic failure. "Lord knows I wish we could recapture the spirit of '26," wrote Cullen. "I hope the bird hasn't flown forever. And there must be new recruits who would flock to the sort of banner you are raising! I rather look to them instead of to us who have grown old before our time."[39] Cullen implored Dorothy West to venture out and remain steadfast.

West's journal *Challenge* appeared six times, becoming a quarterly by its second issue of September 1934, and appearing only once in 1935, in May. West ran two issues of the journal in 1936, with a new associate editor, another veteran from the 1920s, Harold Jackman. It took a couple of issues, but eventually she did make contact with a new crowd. Among them was the seventeen-year-old Georgia writer Frank Yerby, trying to place his first national work and landing in *Challenge* with his imagistic poems. Yerby's verse, "To a Seagull" and "Drought," published in May 1935, emphasized the raceless themes that were important to West in the earliest issues. By the mid-1940s Yerby would abandon the notion of trying to win American audiences by exploring black frustration and start writing the historical romances that made him famous. But in 1935 he did not imagine that he was escaping race or that *Challenge* was a journal too staid and smug to deal with the realities of inequality and the necessity of group action for a remedy. He proudly wrote to West that "[t]he idea of a Renaissance in Negro letters appeals to me very strongly; I hope to be in the vanguard of those who will foster such a rebirth. If your magazine is successful, which I believe it will be, it will be the very hub of such a movement."[40]

Less cheery than the youngster Yerby was Wallace Thurman, dying of syphilis on a hospital bed on City Island. When Dorothy West sent him an issue, he disparaged the effort: "Frankly I was not impressed by its contents," Thurman told her, confirming West's suspicion that *Challenge* might not fare well against the literary rivals. "[Y]ou've expressed only the dead spirit of seven or eight years ago, ignored? the pulsations of a new day." He added, "the magazine lacks significance."[41] Thurman died within weeks of writing to West, but his stinging rebuke hung on. As a matter of fact, he was right.

West wanted to turn to new sources of talent, but she was not particularly in sync with them. The black colleges regularly frustrated West because of what she thought was the poor caliber of their literary submissions. In reality, it was hard to distinguish her journal's work from the 1934 collection of poetry published out of Memphis and with Fisk and LeMoyne colleges backing it, *Brown Thrush*. And then there was a choice distinction. Edited by the up and coming literary critic Hugh Gloster, *Brown Thrush* included poetry that had begun to state more plainly than ever the condition of psychological tension and angst that West wanted to approach more distantly. In Tennessee, black students were writing poems like "Jungle Revenge," and "Once I Was Black," descriptions of lynched lovers, and showing pride in African origins. But the Renaissance talents of the 1920s gave up Harlem as home base and broke themselves up over whether or not to write celebrations of the folk, racial persecution, or social-class critique. To remedy the absence of spirit, in 1937 Dorothy West's *Challenge* would find itself in an odd, short-lived, but crucial collaboration with Richard Wright.

One Harlem Renaissance anchor who did contribute to *Challenge* and who bristled with significant literary energy in 1934 and 1935 was Zora Neale Hurston. Acknowledging that industrial growth and migration to the city would radically affect the traditional lives of rural Negro Americans, Hurston spent the first half of the 1930s scouring the South and the Caribbean for folklore, tales, songs, rituals, and ceremonies. An intellectual as well as a commercial writer, she published her researches in, among other places, the *Journal of Negro History* and the *Journal of American Folklore*. Her work pored over black life and exclaimed its native, unadorned beauty and linguistic complexity. A mature woman in her forties, Hurston had scuffled around enough to know that if she would ever be more than precocious, and having to hide her age to do it, the 1930s would have to be her time.

One way that she made the 1930s the era of her prime output was by cultivating, nonstop, white allies. Arguably part of the way Hurston did this was by resisting the temptation to appeal to their guilt. Hurston did not put racial discrimination at the center of her work, and she refused the goal of "uplifting" blacks from unpolished modes of behavior and conduct. She had an ultramodern education, particularly from such groundbreaking cultural relativists as Alain Locke and anthropologist Franz Boas, but she seemed to believe in elemental characteristics belonging to black "folks," particularly the "[un]tampered" cultures that had evolved in places like Florida, Georgia, Alabama, and Mississippi. Conscious of the squabbles that she would incite, she suggested that black speech was an example of willful choice and not lack of education or exposure. "[T]he stark, trimmed phrases of the Occident seem too bare for the voluptuous child of the Sun," Hurston wrote.[42] She complicated her sense of language by agreeing with books like agrarian critic Cleanth Brooks's *The Relation of the Alabama-Georgia Dialect to the Provincial Dialects of Great Britain*, which tried to prove southern speech a pure form of Elizabethan English without any influence from West Africa. To Hurston, experience and belonging were more important than scientific method or objectivity. In the words of Hurston's protagonist at the end of the magnificent *Their Eyes Were Watching God*: "you got to *go* there tuh *know* there."[43] Hurston seemed to regularly if playfully trod against Boas's idea of the staying power of culture and environment over biology.

Around the time *Challenge* began, Hurston hit her stride. In 1934 Philadelphia bookmaker J. B. Lippincott published her tale of a heroic but tragic preacher, *Jonah's Gourd Vine*. Hurston had written the story in her hometown of Eatonville, Florida, where she had been guest of Robert Wunsch, who taught at nearby white Rollins College. In an act of interracial collaboration quite typical in the career of a successful black writer, Wunsch had read Hurston's 1933 short story "The Gilded Six-Bits" and sent it to *Story* magazine, which published it that August.[44] Lippincott, who had undertaken the series "The Peoples of America" and set as its director Hungarian expatriate writer Louis Adamic, was impressed enough by the short story to ask Hurston if she had any more material. She responded with the plot for her first novel. Written in only eight weeks, the narrative evoked the metaphorically rich language and imagery of the black church and the complex dynamics of Hurston's family near the time of her birth in 1891. It probably did not seem at all odd to Hurston to avoid completely the cruel poverty of the Depression, kicked off by real estate speculation in Florida. The next year, Hurston published *Mules and Men*, her justly famous study of black southern folklore.

Mules and Men fairly began the controversy that muted Hurston's impact among writers and intellectuals in her own time. The white reviewers at the mass media organs like the *New York Times* and *Saturday Review* welcomed the book and its "natural" earthy portraits of the black working people in dusty camps spinning yarns around the fire. The stories Hurston included were teeming with characters using the comic mask, misdirection, and cunning. But, significantly, her portraits of tale-telling, courtship protocols, and knife fights at juke joints made it possible to forget the existence of racial bigotry and structurally organized racial inequality. Hurston was hardheaded about the distinction between artistic purity, especially folk art, and political pamphleteering, an obdurate stand that would sour some blacks and liberal whites to Hurston for the rest of her career. For her part, Hurston believed that the "sobbing school of Negrohood" overplayed the race issue and produced distorted images of black Americans. "We talk about the race problem a great deal," she admitted, "but go on living and laughing and striving like everybody else."[45] But in her work, black characters did not talk about the race problem a great deal.

To a degree, Hurston believed that her real battle was outwitting the racially mixed elites (of whom she was a part) who she believed had strangled the appearance of undiluted black music, lyric, dance, and folk narrative. She steadily expressed frustration and outrage with philosophy professor Alain Locke, W.E.B. Du Bois, and NAACP secretary Walter White, a well-known dandified trio who seemed to connote physically the ideal of racial caste. And she often railed about these blacks to whites. A letter that Hurston wrote in 1934 to Fisk's white president Thomas E. Jones illustrates what people regarded as Hurston's brashness and indiscretion. In it she described her bilious reaction to the handling of her own music by the renowned arranger and choirmaster Hall Johnson. She charged the dilution of Negro spirituals at the hands of black performers and arrangers. "[I]t was thought that no Negro vocalist was an artist unless he or she could take good negro music and turn it into mediocre white sounds," she exploded. If Hall Johnson believed that "the world was not ready" for the "barbaric melodies and harmonies" of "Negro music unless it were highly arranged," then he was a fool. "I knew better," Hurston wrote to Jones.[46] To Hurston, the battlefield of cultural purity mattered, perhaps even more than the fight against white racism. Neither the race of her opponent nor her correspondent softened her candor.

From the perspective of those involved with and training people for the nascent civil rights movement, Hurston's black folk characterizations carried a noxious aroma. Sterling Brown, the only writer who approached Hurston's devotion to the classic black southern idiom, thought that Hurston's folk characters "should be more bitter; it would be nearer the total truth."[47] White reviewer Harold Preece called Hurston a "literary climber" because she described black characters similar to those of southern white sentimentalist novelists like Julia Peterkin and Roark Bradford. Thus, for Preece, her "resentment in some Negro circles" was "easily explained." Preece also believed that blacks owed one another loyalty. "Angelo Herndon was condemned to break rocks in Georgia; but a member of his own race, Miss Zora Neale Hurston, was devoting her literary abilities to recording the legendary amours of terrapins."[48]

In her mid-forties, the prime of her writing life, the effervescent Hurston, torpedo of New York salons, ignored the crisis and the critics. She was in the midst of a creative jag that would net her no less than seven full-length works. But the friend to influential and acclaimed whites, like nationally recognized figures novelist Fanny Kemble, mentor and salonnard Carl Van Vechten, millionaire Charlotte O. Mason, Guggenheim Foundation head Henry Allen Moe, and anthropologist Franz Boas, was wandering into the rearguard.

The poet and critic Sterling Brown preferred to fulfill his obligations to his race in *Opportunity* and his obligations to his understanding of social change in *New Republic* rather than in *Challenge*. A dynamic poet in a generation filled with dynamic poets, Brown spanned the distance between the Harlem Renaissance of the 1920s and the integrationist avant-garde of the late 1930s. He had been brought up in the bosom of the elite. Born in Washington, D.C., in a house at Sixth and Fairmount in 1901, close to the campus of Howard University, Brown graduated from Dunbar High School (renamed from the "M Street School" to honor the famous black poet in 1916), the stomping ground for the country's black giants.[49] He went through mythical Dunbar crossing paths with the likes of lyrical writer Jean Toomer and historian Rayford Logan, Dunbar upperclassmen in the year Brown began high school. Other classmates included future French scholar Mercer Cook and future inventor of blood plasma and blood banks Charles Drew. Negroes all, none of the men had even faintly brown skin. At Dunbar, the black Washington upper crust learned from a group of well-trained and worldly professionals, like future *Crisis* editor and Cornell University Ph.D. Jessie Fauset, poet and Wellesley graduate Angelina Grimké, Sorbonne Ph.D. Mary Church Terrell, and Harvard Ph.D. Carter G. Woodson. Brown went on from this rock-solid foundation in black achievement and excellence to Williams College and then to graduate work at Harvard in English.

After securing his academic credentials, he began making valuable contributions to the field of literary aesthetics with criticism that began appearing in *Opportunity* in 1926. He won even more acclaim in 1932 with a sheaf of poems published by Harcourt Brace called *Southern Road*. Brown's verse—rich, sensual, ironic, epic, and refusing any other but the idiom of the African American southern vernacular—laid claim to the highest honors among Renaissance poetry, with the possible exception of Langston Hughes's *The Weary Blues*. But perhaps the chief distinction derived from Brown's solidly urban upbringing and the New Negro spirit he accepted as a matter of course. His work emphasized racial tension, black pride, black resentment, and black resilience.

Tall, with very light colored skin and straight hair, Brown's unflagging allegiance and perpetual voicing of the aspirations of the harshly stereotyped black poor caused concern. It was rumored that his commitment to the poor blacks of the rural South was merely an aspect of his devotion to communism. But Brown's remarkable determination to provide a voice for the downtrodden and his pride in his heritage appropriately claimed simpler, more basic sources. Brown's father, the reverend Sterling Nelson Brown, had been born a slave in Tennessee in 1858. The Dunbar school's second principal, Mary J. Patterson, had been the first African American woman to graduate from college, and her father had been a fugitive slave. Publisher and historian Carter G. Woodson's parents had both been slaves. The direct living memory of bondage was no abstraction for Brown.

The rarest of his gifts, though, was the gift of perception. Brown rejected the slave legacy as a source of shame that lay at one end of the "southern road." Rather, he identified that heritage as an energetic base of mythic creation. And he allowed it to orchestrate his poetry. In his blues stanza poem "Southern Road," a brew of equal parts paean and elegy, the complex wisdom of African American vernacular culture sings through.

> White man tells me—hunh—
> Damn yo soul.
> Got no need bebby
> To be tole.[50]

Like literary man J. Saunders Redding, Brown could be counted among Harlem Renaissance literary figures. After all, he was older than Langston Hughes. His poetic saga "Odyssey of Big Boy" had appeared in Countee Cullen's anthology *Caroling Dusk* of 1927. But Brown's early success as a poet seemed nearly secondary to his career as a professional advocate of black arts. He labored four decades in the classrooms of Howard University, an effort that culminated with his personal instruction of the next generation of writers like John Killens, John Hicks, and Ossie Davis, and after them, LeRoi Jones (Amiri Baraka) and Chloe Wofford (Toni Morrison). In the 1930s he headed the Division of Negro Affairs for the Federal Writers' Project, and he authored two important installments of the *Bronze Booklet* series edited by Alain Locke. In *Opportunity* and various other magazines he was the ombudsman black critic during the 1930s and early 1940s, who decried sloppy representations of black characters by whites and championed social realism by blacks. Brown's peak years of influence and shaping the arts ran from about 1933 through the late 1940s. Shuttling back and forth from Washington, D.C., to New York, talking to editors and publishers, Brown added an impressive organizational talent that stamped together a literary movement in Chicago, New York, and Washington. A committed aficionado of blues and jazz music, Brown had a swagger that did not alienate, but inspired.

After getting as much as he ever would out of Harvard, a master's degree in English in 1923, Brown began a peripatetic odyssey along the black college circuit. He taught at Virginia Seminary in Lynchburg, Lincoln in Jefferson City, Missouri, Fisk in Nashville, until he landed the plum post at Howard's English department in 1929. There he began a career as a regular reviewer for the Urban League's *Opportunity* magazine. Brown observed white writers getting into print and some of them making reputations out of Negro subject matter. This fundamental dynamic of American cultural production—black creativity and white commercial success—infuriated him. It had played out ten years earlier on Broadway and ten years before that with ragtime and Dixieland jazz music. Over and again, throughout his career, such as in the introduction to the collection *Negro Caravan*, Brown stated, "Negro authors . . . must be allowed the privilege and the responsibility of being the ultimate portrayers of their own."[51] The question was whether or not the privilege was given by courtesy or taken by force.

His work as an informed and courageous literary selector became pacesetting around 1933. That year Brown published his most influential essay in Howard's *Journal of Negro Education,* "The Negro Character as Seen by White Authors." His report captured not just the new defiance of black intellectuals and their rejection of patronage. It also reflected the immense libraries now open to a small but growing group of black Americans educated at exclusive American colleges and universities in the North and West. Brown took seriously journalist Walter Lippmann's warning in *Public Opinion* that "stereotypes," a printing term referring to metal plates made from type, would create permanent and narrow portraits of human beings. "There is neither time nor opportunity for intimate acquaintance," Lippmann noted of Americans in the 1920s. "Instead we notice a trait which marks a well known type, and fill in the rest of the picture by means of the stereotype we carry about in our heads." He added that the stereotypes, "preconceptions" really, "govern deeply the whole process of perception."[52]

In the essay Brown rejected an entire stratum of American literature as being completely false to black life. He dismissed as especially harmful the Roark Bradfords of the world—a popular novelist who qualified the accuracy of his assertions regarding black Americans on the basis of his birth on plantations worked by slaves and his having been nursed by a black woman. "All this, he believes, gives him license to step forth as their interpreter and to repeat stereotypes in the time-hallowed South," began Brown. "It doesn't." Instead, the Howard professor identified seven recurring stereotypes: contented slave, wretched freeman, comedian or buffoon, brute, tragic mulatto, "local color" negro, and "exotic primitive."[53] His catalog would be revisited, revised, and enumerated by most of the major critics of African American literature in the twentieth century. But it was never surpassed. Unafraid to offend whites or burn bridges,

Brown also swung a bit of the sword of historian Vernon Parrington's economic determinism: American culture was driven by economics. Slavery expanded in the nineteenth century due to the cotton gin and the profit margin, and the result, insofar as the development of American fiction, was a stereotype of black contentedness under bondage.

American culture needed protection from the false black images. Brown showed genuine frustration toward the conclusion of his essay, as well as a final example of a stereotype, the "exotic primitive." He pointed to Carl Van Vechten, the best-known white enthusiast of African American writing and culture, especially during the 1920s, as among the culprits. Instead of an original exploration of the vitality of modern black life, Brown saw "cabarets supplanting cabins, and Harlemized 'blues,' instead of the spirituals and slave reels." Van Vechten benefited from the steady devotion of Langston Hughes, Zora Neale Hurston, and James Weldon Johnson, but this sort of time-tested liberalism had become inadequate. Brown readily rejected Van Vechten in the 1930s and in the subsequent decades provided additional epithets like "rascal" and "voyeur" and a judgment: "[Van Vechten] corrupted the Harlem Renaissance and was a terrible influence."[54] Brown's shot over-the-bow at whites of "good will" who produced the lion's share of America's black literary images staked a claim of independence and fitness that pinched the liberals who thought they had been doing blacks a favor. He strove to put images of that creature of myth, "the Negro," to rest. Brown chalked a line between art and prostitution in the pages of *Opportunity*, with reviews that crackled with energy and insight.

The standout example of *Opportunity*'s creative artists yoking together the crisis of race, class, white liberals, and urban America was Renaissance era prose-stylist Marita Bonner Occomy. Her 1934 story "Tin Can" eulogized the desperate young men growing up black in America's cities ("they only rattle, rattle, with a hollow sound") and squandering their lives in dance-halls. She slyly indicted the liberal whites who "felt responsible since Ma was in [their] cellar cleaning, instead of being at her own home to talk to Jimmie Joe."[55]

What Occomy presented in fiction, Sterling Brown devoted himself to in criticism. Among his most memorable battles to humanize black life and chastise profligate liberals, in March 1935 he severely admonished the immensely popular film *Imitation of Life*, based on Fannie Hurst's novel. Brown knew he was bucking the trend. Both actresses Louise Beavers, in the role of Delilah, and Fredi Washington, as Peola, had executed their roles with dignity. Delilah's bandana had been replaced by a white chef's cap, grinding poverty did not surface in the movie, and words like "darkey" had not appeared. "All of these things are undoubtedly gladdening to our bourgeois hearts," he noted in a tone that dripped with sarcasm, holding up the mirror to his bourgeois colleagues suspicious of politics. But in the images so gladdening to the new middle class, Brown saw the old meanness. "It requires no searching analysis to see in *Imitation of Life* the old stereotype of the contented Mammy, and the tragic mulatto; and the ancient ideas about the mixture of the races."[56]

In response to Brown's thoroughgoing catalog of the film's infidelities to real life, an irate Fannie Hurst dispatched an admonishment of her own. *Opportunity* printed Hurst's letter in April, accompanied by a vintage Brown reply. Hurst believed that Brown had remembered only the bones after a fish supper straight from Galilee. Throttling him for his "ungrateful" and "unintelligent" attitude, the famous writer, public liberal, and patron of Zora Neale Hurston claimed that the film based on her novel "inaugurates into the important medium of the motion picture, a consideration of the Negro as part of the social pattern of American life."[57] Brown rejected the heroic stature of a film that caused the black audience to laugh at its moments of tragedy and to weep at its scenes of purported triumph. To the mind of Sterling Brown, *Imitation*, with its mammy and tragic mulatto stereotype played to a "T," never left the realm of "pity" or "sentimentality." "This picture breaks no new ground," he reminded readers. Brown ended his reprisal on a personal note; he was too "unintelligent" to understand what in the world he had to be grateful for to Hurst.[58] The Dozens, a signifying ritual, had been brought into the sphere of American social and cultural criticism, and Brown, who later visited as a professor at several white colleges, never won a major prize or fellowship.

Brown's reputable criticism defended the value of a folk idiom, a grammar of blackness, but without the residue of cultural essentialism. During his last full year as a regular critic for *Opportunity*, 1935, he examined the same signs of progress and prostitution. The novels *Come in at the Door* by William March and *Unfinished Cathedral* by T. S. Stribling featured the "new style" of Alabama and Mississippi life, with their Negro characters "well understood and portrayed." On the other hand, Roark Bradford had resumed his collected doggerel with a group of short stories, "affectionate" but "unreliable," as did the southern apologist Richard Coleman in the novel *Don't Weep, Don't Moan*. Especially piquant to Brown, Bradford's book had been set off again with a seal of authority from the publisher, Harper, at the book's beginning: "By birth, environment and education, Roark Bradford is perhaps better fitted to write of the Southern Negro than anyone in the United States." Macmillan went even further on the dust jacket when it endorsed *Don't Weep*: "The true southern Negro . . . all the superstition, the primitive fanaticism, the sensuality, lightheartedness, easy humor, and violence of the black man." The jacket copy revealed the queer combination of politeness and bigotry that passed for Madison Avenue liberalism in the era before World War II.

Brown noticed a liberal trend. Toward the end of the year, Erskine Caldwell's *Kneel to the Rising Sun* and Robert Rylee's *Deep Dark River* somewhat made up for the endurance of caricatures. Their work remained grounded in "frank honesty" and delivered "the bitter ring of truth." Berry Fleming's novel *Siesta* portrayed black characters "hard and unflattering, but always convincing."[59] Brown gave to *Opportunity*'s readers a new kind of criticism. It wasn't the stodgy genteel biography that people typically associated with literary analysis; nor did it amount to cheering praise songs of black poets. Brown stressed over and again fidelity to realistic portraits of life as an antidote to the corrosive influence of racist stereotypes. His standard of excellence was realism.

The appearance of books with racial themes showed the new elasticity in American publishing. New institutions got set, like Yale professor Henry Seidel Canby's weekly *Saturday Review of Literature* and his Book-of-the-Month Club, both of them designed to raise the standards of taste of all Americans. In 1934 Book-of-the-Month-Club selected George Washington Lee's sociable folk history *Beale Street: Where the Blues Began* as the eight-year-old club's first selection by an African American. Lee's book worked in dollops of black history and local color to present the music and mayhem of black America's original Tenderloin district, the hallowed Beale Street in Memphis. Among the glowing reviews was Tennessee's *Sewanee*, which judged the book, the first it had ever reviewed by a black author, and its author quite talented. (*Sewanee* would review only two other black writers for another twenty years: Gwendolyn Brooks and Ralph Ellison.) A forty-year-old World War I veteran and officer, the Atlanta Life and Insurance district manager Lee had depicted Memphis's famous street of ill repute; he touted the blues as Americans' key to surviving five years of economic catastrophe. Lee's folksy style enabled whites to champion the book without necessarily having to promote racial equality.

By the middle of the decade, new American magazines were aiming for wide circulation and, without the moralizing mission of the Book-of-the-Month-Club, took on black writers and their sometimes distinctly modern concerns. George Wylie Henderson broke into the pages of *Redbook*. The new periodical for men, *Esquire*, carried a short story by Langston Hughes and two stories by newcomer to fiction and guest of the Ohio State Penitentiary, Chester Himes. One of the Himes stories, "To What Red Hell," offered a rambling, deadpan treatment of the horrific fire at the penitentiary the day after Easter in 1930. Himes's emergence in 1934 foreshadowed the trends to come for new black writers, whose works were gritty, urgent, and in the social realist mode. Black newspapers and civil rights journals, mass-market periodicals addressing shifts in tastes of the postflapper generation, the interracial philanthropic organizations, and black colleges were shaping and allowing to flourish the most audacious generation of black writers the world had seen.

CHAPTER TWO

The Black Avant-Garde between Left and Right (1935–1939)

A wave of young black writers and activists broke into the modern present by way of the American Communist Party's broadly inclusive "Popular Front," or "People's Front," strategy of the mid-1930s. The Popular Front stood for a coalition of writers and artists, regardless of social class background and erudition, enlisted against the forces of fascism. For a time the party supported liberal capitalist policies, although the Popular Front never allowed vigorous questioning of the Stalinist regime. The party proposed to replace the John Reed Clubs with the League of American Writers, a loose-knit organization of writers and artists who had committed themselves to oppose fascism. Their publication efforts shifted from a training ground for the proletariat to a show-case for the best and brightest.

Despite the trepidation of young poet-critics like Richard Wright, whose journals and clubs were threatened, by October 1934 the American Communist Party, in the words of its general secretary Earl Browder, was asking for a "united front" "[t]o fight off the imminent danger of fascism and war."[1] A few months later, in the January 22, 1935, issue of *New Masses*, critic Granville Hicks had put together the call for a congress "to accelerate the destruction of capitalism," defend the USSR, strengthen labor, and end white chauvinism.[2] Hicks proposed a merger of the prevalent radical magazines published by regional John Reed Clubs. Missouri's *Anvil*, Chicago's *Left Front*, and New York's *Partisan Review* were the most consequential club journals. By April 1935 the ground was ready for the first American Writers Congress to take place in New York at the Mecca Temple on West 51st Street.

For American writers, the congress represented the dedication of the new Communist Party "line." From the founding of the party's literary magazine *New Masses* in 1926 through the early 1930s, the line had found most succinct expression in a 1928 Mike Gold editorial. A disputant of Claude McKay's from the *Liberator* days, Gold had become the best-known Communist proponent of proletarian literary aesthetics. He asked for a literature comprised of "[l]etters from hoboes," "[r]evelations by chambermaids and night club waiters," and "[t]he poetry of steel workers."[3] Now the CPUSA was making an about-face, and one that seemed promising. For a year in 1936, the New York and Missouri club magazines would be published jointly as *Partisan Review/Anvil*; in 1937 *Anvil* would be completely subsumed by *Partisan Review*. These radical journals piloted by political dissidents, self-trained literati, and some Ivy Leaguers welcomed and sometimes solicited the art, poetry, and criticism of black writers. Both Richard Wright and Sterling Brown would see their work published in *Partisan Review* during the years of the Popular Front. The coalition officially held, with many bumps and shocks, until the Hitler–Stalin pact of 1939 when the Soviet Union privately readied for war but publicly suggested that the Nazis were no worse than any other imperial power. After the German attack on the Soviet Union in the summer of 1941, the CPUSA revived the Popular Front amid controversy and bitter skepticism.

But when it was strong, the Popular Front brought a fair number of blacks in New York and Chicago into the orbit of the Communist Party and their cultural affairs. At the start of the decade, Earl Browder admitted that less than one thousand blacks all over the United States were active members: five hundred in Chicago; one hundred in both Pittsburgh and Philadelphia; several hundred in Alabama; and only seventy-four on the rolls in New York City.[4] In 1934 New York counted about 240 black members, mainly on the basis of the organizing around the Scottsboro campaign. But the racial calculus in the North would change in a stroke, shortly before the first Writers Congress.

On the afternoon of March 19, 1935, a bantam Puerto Rican teenager named Lino Rivera was arrested for shoplifting at the Kress Store on 125th Street. What happened next is unclear. New York police claimed that several white men, thought to be Communists, organized a milling black crowd to swing into violence. The police assaulted and held incommunicado Harry Gordon, a white City College student, on the charge of standing atop a 125th Street mailbox and shouting to the black crowd that Rivera had been murdered. Whatever the case, a violent fury was unleashed in the streets of Harlem. To preserve their property, black storeowners painted their windows to say "Negro owned," and white shop-owners adorned similar prophylactics: "We employ Negro workers."

A day and a half later, the remains of twenty-five thousand square feet of plate glass pebbled the sidewalks and streets of Harlem's business district. Four men were dead and more than a score injured. The police had arrested over one hundred people, and Harlem's central business corridor had sustained two million dollars in damage. The finger pointing took different directions. After the riot, the City of New York offered eighteen-year-old Margaret Mitchell a choice between a ten-dollar fine or three days in the workhouse for screaming uncontrollably when Rivera was brought out by police and thus, apparently, driving black passersby into uncontrollable outrage.[5] Mayor Fiorello LaGuardia appointed an investigative subcommittee headed by civil liberties lawyer Arthur Garfield Hays, and including on its staff poet and schoolteacher Countee Cullen, sociologist E. Franklin Frazier, and social worker and civil rights activist Louise Thompson. The furthest to the left, Thompson had organized the African American actors and writers who had journeyed to the Soviet Union in 1932 to make the antilynching film *Black and White*, and in 1940 she would marry the important black Chicago Communist lawyer William Patterson. The subcommittee's report vindicated Harlemites of charges of savagery and exonerated Communists for inciting mayhem. The Communist leaflets, it turned out, had tried to stave off the bloodshed, the destruction of property, and looting. On the other hand, it was learned that the police force had killed a Negro high school boy without provocation. In fact, the unrest in Harlem was linked to the partial blinding by police of a man whose only crime was to stand in a relief line on March 13, six days before the riot.[6] One of the final reports, issued by the New York County Lawyers Association, admitted that a riot in a community of three hundred thousand that had gone twenty years without a new school or facilities for juvenile recreation "surprised no one."[7]

A year after the riot, CPUSA vice presidential candidate James Ford could happily put the number of black Communists in Harlem at eighteen hundred.[8] By the end of the 1930s, black Communist attorney Ben Davis, Jr., would lead membership drives and claim to have swollen the numbers of black Communists in Harlem to twenty-eight hundred, with seven blacks guiding policy on the Central Committee.[9] An admonishing Claude McKay was only exaggerating slightly when, speaking of New York, he averred that "[m]ost of the negro intellectuals . . . were directly or indirectly hypnotized by the Popular Front."[10] More than any other single event, the Harlem Riot of 1935 united the issues of racial persecution and economic exploitation for blacks in the North. The Carnegie Fund manager initiated a study of black life in America. New York and the nation went on notice, and artists in particular.

A month after the glass had been swept up, black intellectuals and artists listened keenly to Secretary Earl Browder's League of American Writers address at Mecca Temple. He declared the new direction for the party's revolutionary art. "[W]e think an organization of writers should be concerned, first of all, with the establishment of certain standards . . . with winning new collaborators, broadening and deepening the movement by drawing in more established writers and training new ones."[11] The main tropes of Browder's inaugural were a comfort to the non-Bolsheviks in the audience: "standards," "collaborator," and "established." The Communist Party was no longer insisting that only the working class or the anointed revolutionary cadre could write honestly.

Several black writers figured prominently in the 1935 American Writers Congress. The league considered thirty-three-year-old Langston Hughes important enough to put him on the advertising marquee alongside the novelist Waldo Frank and Malcolm Cowley. Although Hughes's address had been announced in the newspaper, when the 1935 American Writers Congress met in New York from April 26 to April 28, Hughes stayed in Mexico and mailed in to congress chairman Frank his manifesto "To Negro Writers."

In his role as titular head of the Communist-backed League of Struggle for Negro Rights, Hughes scoffed at the puffery of Negro patriots, "talking about the privilege of dying for the noble Red, White and Blue, when they aren't even permitted the privilege of living for it."[12] In 1926 Hughes had reacted against the "racial mountain"[13]—the aesthetic presumptions of white supremacy—but his 1935 speech lashed out at the tangible agents that made racism operational: crude religion; stereotypes promoted by press, book publishers, and Hollywood; the powerful philanthropy that eased Jim Crow conditions enough to make racism palatable; and "the false leadership . . . owned by capital, afraid to open its mouth except in the old conciliatory way so advantageous to the exploiters." This would become a vintage black leftist intellectual's exercise: a critique of the ideological superstructure.

Two men, Eugene Gordon and Eugene Clay (Holmes), introduced the concerns of the academic black critics. A contributing editor at *New Masses*, former student of Alain Locke, and mentor to Dorothy West, forty-four-year-old Eugene Gordon had been editor of Boston's annual *Saturday Evening Quill* from 1928 through 1930. He had served on the National Executive Committee of the John Reed Clubs since 1932.[14] In 1934 Gordon had published a snippet of harrowing memoir, "Southern Boyhood Nightmares," in the Moscow journal *International Literature*. The Communist publication afforded him a forum where he could emphasize the racial violence he had witnessed firsthand; Gordon had lived through the notorious Robert Charles affair in New Orleans, where a black man had shot twenty-seven whites before being killed, and white mobs roamed the city killing blacks in the aftermath. An older Gordon had endured an even more intimate horror: he had seen a black man lynched in Hawkinsville, Georgia.

But after the Renaissance among black middle-class writers slowed to a crawl, Gordon got his fulfillment by addressing social crises far from the genteel *Quill*. *Opportunity* had published his 1933 short story "Agenda," a study of a Communist organizer in Georgia. At *New Masses* and later on the staff of the *Daily Worker*, Gordon created pamphlets like "The Position of Negro Women" (1935), cowritten with black nationalist Cyril Briggs; "You're Not Alone" (1940), produced for laborers and brought out by the International Workers Order; and "Equal Justice under the Law" (1944), a broadside written with journalist Earl Conrad to protest the rape of a married black Alabama woman named Recy Taylor. In the later 1930s he worked for a year in Moscow, writing for the Moscow *Daily News*.

Gordon aimed for an uncompromising analysis of black writing with social action as its chief criterion. He called his theoretical paper "Social and Political

Problems of the Negro Writer." In the essay he strove to point out the ideological limits peculiar to the situation of the black writer—an artist with a crucial racial theme, but without a natural audience. Gordon insisted that the black writer was "chief propagandist" for his people, and that the writer served to "interpret[s] and plead[s] for them to the white ruling class." And despite the fact that black writers did not produce for the proletariat, their approach to the elites was ineffective. There were three problems: inept craftsmanship "owing to the sharpness and bitterness of the struggle to exist"; writing material that offended the publishers and "block[ed] up all avenues of expression"; and finally, if the works were published, the writers' "fear of retaliation from the ruling class."[15]

Gordon explored the underside of the Black Belt self-determination thesis and determined little salvation emerging from the folk. He argued that "the Negro people of the Black Belt were nevertheless a suppressed nation; they were a slave nation," and that the condition of national oppression had produced a folk culture of song and tale that had at its formation "national psychosis." Gordon suggested that black America had evolved a reactionary culture in response to white supremacy. The future Gordon hoped to project needed to come from a new class: younger black writers and whites friendly to the cause. Hope for the future, Gordon thought, lay in the work of Richard Wright, who would publish his poem "Between the World and Me" in the July–August issue of the journal *Partisan Review*, the "revolutionary literary magazine edited by a group of young Communist writers."[16]

Gordon's fellow Communist Eugene Clay Holmes, who published in the Communist press under the name "Eugene Clay," concentrated on the work of the contemporary black writer. Holmes worked with Alain Locke in the department of philosophy at Howard University, and he shielded the school from anticommunist scrutiny with his pseudonym. Howard, beholden to congressional appropriation for 65 percent of its annual budget, protected its faculty in the same manner that the faculty protected it. The university's first black president, Mordecai Johnson, had on more than one occasion offered praise of the Soviet Union. Johnson testified before the House Un-American Activities Committee in the late 1930s: "I am not in accord with those who believe that the best way to deal with communism is to persecute those who believe in it."[17]

Born in New Jersey, Holmes had earned his undergraduate degree at New York University. He would finish his doctorate in 1942 at Columbia and remain at Howard for the entirety of his career. Clay's work on black writers praised them for protest. Clay felt that the writers had misunderstood their proper response to the Great War and instead relied upon figures like Booker T. Washington and Du Bois, who, according to his calculations, misled the black masses. He continued with dismissals of the writers. In an analysis that would eventually become orthodoxy, Clay thought the inevitable result of poor cultural stewardship was the "Harlem tradition" of "amusements and new thrills" for the white American bourgeoisie. The Harlem Renaissance writers' movement earned its most baneful epithets from the black Left.

To Holmes, Langston Hughes was the only valuable writer to emerge from the 1920s black Renaissance. He properly congratulated Hughes's recent collection of short stories, *The Ways of White Folks*, because it devastated the stereotype of the happy servant and Negro American satisfied with race relations. Hughes had delivered a "bludgeon" against "the pseudo-rapprochement of Negro and white in their artistic relations."[18] Holmes's other champion was his Howard colleague Sterling Brown, whose poem "Slim Hears the Call" was read to the audience in full. Holmes liked the spleeny anguish of *The Ways of White Folks* and Brown's working-class folk poetics, but his breakfast of social realism tasted best when he approached the work of a bona fide Communist. That man was Richard Wright, whose poetry drew significant praise because it did not rely on the color of its writer for its effectiveness. "Is this desirable?" Clay asked his audience before replying, "Of course it is." To prove the interracial point and tip his hat in the direction of Sterling Brown, he closed the essay by praising contemporary whites who had written their black characters well. Like Brown, Holmes found competent representations in William March's *Come in at the Door* and T. S. Stribling's *Unfinished Cathedral*.

Both Gordon and Holmes promoted black writers who emphasized the condition of the working class and the "next step" toward integration, when the race of the writer and the subject matter bore no necessary relation. This perspective countered Soviet critic Lydia Filatova, who in 1933 had asked Hughes to "draw closer to the Negro masses and talk their language."[19] The African American Communists were confident and provocative and effectively combined arguments against segregation with the Black Belt self-determination thesis during the Popular Front years.

New friendships and creative exchanges at the league produced an environment allowing for flexible approaches to communist doctrine. The new hero, Richard Wright, making his largest address before an audience, presented a paper called "The Isolation of the Negro Writer." At the congress, Wright met Chicago novelist James Farrell, who was completing the final volume in the valuable social realist trilogy *Studs Lonigan*. A maverick on the Left, Farrell registered an early and not completely popular criticism of Communists in the arts. He felt betrayed by their rump-style politics and the elevation of writers on the basis of their "proletarian" credentials at the expense of literary craft.

In his 1936 book *A Note on Literary Criticism*, Farrell would have had the previous year's American Writers Congress in mind when he condemned the flaws of two prominent Communist men-of-letters: Michael Gold fetishized proletarian realism and encouraged "a literature of simplicity to the point of

obviousness, and even of downright banality." The other bricklayer was Granville Hicks, a Marxist of mechanical determinist orientation, who "usually as-
sumes implicitly, if not explicitly, that literature follows economics obediently
and directly."[20] Sometimes Farrell sensed insincerity at the center of the new
aesthetic direction of the party, but he noticed nothing of the untalented minion in the rising star Richard Wright. The two men became friends. After hearing Farrell read a paper on the short story, Wright went back and revised his
own short story "Big Boy Leaves Home." He also began working on the important story of the avenging mother called "Down By the Riverside." Farrell would
soon advise Wright to send his manuscript *Cesspool* to Vanguard Press.[21]

The young critics from New York's John Reed Club like Philip Rahv and William Phillips thought well of Farrell, and he published regularly in their journal
Partisan Review. Around the time of the 1935 American Writers Congress,
Wright got to know these critics. *Partisan Review* stood behind the call for a
League of American Writers, with its platform "against all forms of Negro dis-
crimination and persecution."[22] As a result of his exposure at the conference, in
1936 Wright accepted a position alongside Rahv and Phillips (then using the
name Wallace Phelps) as contributing editor to the fourth and fifth numbers of
Partisan Review/Anvil. He published a review of Arna Bontemps's novel *Black
Thunder* in April, and in June he wrote a short letter to the editor defending the
Chicago cultural scene and the novelist Meyer Levin. In November his short
story "Big Boy Leaves Home" appeared in a massive anthology called *The New
Caravan*. Wright was recognized immediately for having "unusual dramatic
talent."[23]

Sterling Brown seems not to have attended the 1935 Writers Congress, but if
not, it was not because he thought it unimportant. He served his own stew of
political ideology and craft in 1936 in his *Opportunity* reviews. For the entire
year he analyzed only Arna Bontemps's important historical novel of slave revolt, *Black Thunder*, and Frank Marshall Davis's protorevolutionary *Black Man's
Verse*. Despite a handful of minor flaws, such as Bontemps trying to digest "a bit
too-much of post-Marx revolutionaries" and the book's lean size, Brown applauded the "elegiac music" of the charming prose. Most important, Bontemps
had captured "the winning humanity of these early slaves who went down fighting."[24] Brown showed his sympathy toward black social realists in a review
of Davis's exceedingly direct *Black Man's Verse*, which he called a "valuable
contribution."

That October, Brown published in *Partisan Review* two singular pieces of
southern protest poetry. They were twin testimonials against the violence and
brutality of everyday black life. In both poems, Brown was able to sublimate his
bitterness into finely honed descriptive understatements, rife with irony and
steadied by vernacular idiom. The poem "Transfer" recorded the brutality of

the streetcar, then enlarged the metaphor of riding a one-line car and receiving Jim Crow justice until the narrative voice achieved a sermonic timbre:

> These cars doan git us where we got to go
> Got to git transferred to a new direction.
> We can stand so much, then doan stand no mo.'[25]

The other poem, "Southern Cop," was a kind of anti-elegy to a homicidal police officer named Ty Kendricks, patrolling "darktown" and shooting down whatever runs. Brown began each of the four stanzas with a plea for compassion toward the errant policeman: "Let us forgive," "understand," "condone," and finally "pity" the poem's antihero, officer Kendricks. The poem was a successful protest against racial injustice because it was impossible to misconstrue the bite of Brown's irony.

About a year after Brown published with *Partisan Review*, in the fall of 1937, the magazine's staff left their old John Reed Club offices at 430 Sixth Avenue for a rebirth at 22 East 17th Street. Conducting their discussions at Stewart's cafeteria in Sheridan Square, the editorial staff and its friends repudiated the cruel Soviet dictator Joseph Stalin in favor of the oppositional position of the exiled Marxist Leon Trotsky. Phillips corresponded with Trotsky to get straight the views of Marx and Engels on the cultural superstructure and then published the article "Art and Politics" by Trotsky in the August–September issue of the journal in 1938.[26] *Partisan Review* saw itself shorn free from the ideological commitments obvious at *New Republic*, *Nation*, and *New Masses*, which continued to publish articles that favored Stalin's policies and rationalized the purges of Soviet leadership during the famous Moscow Trials. "[W]e think the cause of revolutionary literature is best served by a policy of no commitments to any political party," announced the editors when the new edition of the journal came out that fall.[27] The group of intellectual sharpshooters headed by Rahv, Phillips, and Dwight McDonald decided that "literature in our period should be free of all factional dependence." Artistically, writers were growing "less responsible" under the hegemony of the Communist Party, and now the editors were convinced that "the totalitarian trend is inherent in that movement."

The 1937 issue opened to the pages of Delmore Schwartz's "In Dreams Begin Responsibilities," a short story that became one of the premier brief examples of American literary modernism. Curiously enough, the growing influence of the Trotskyite group would have a boomerang effect for black writers. In its new form shorn of Stalinist politics, *Partisan Review's* editorial staff included graduates of Yale and Vassar, like Dwight McDonald and Mary McCarthy (Rahv, who introduced Kafka to American audiences and whose intellect was revered, had never attended college; Phillips had finished City College and done Ph.D. work in literature), and the theoretical pretensions of the journal soared. The journal shifted its aesthetic preoccupation from the social to the individual; the radical critique of domestic racial equality was silenced. This change would basically preclude the further participation of black writers in the magazine for almost fifteen years.

Even Trotsky himself was concerned by these changes, worried that the magazine might become a "small cultural monastery, guarding itself from the outside world by skepticism, agnosticism, and respectability."[28] While Trotsky's *Partisan Review* article did not mention the crisis of America's largest racial minority, in April 1939 he entertained the Trinidadian Marxist C.L.R. James for a week in Coyoacan, Mexico. Their discussions were primarily about the role of African descended workers in the United States and the Western Hemisphere, and the black masses' potential as a revolutionary vanguard. At the end of the week, Trotsky sent James on to the United States specifically to begin organizing African Americans and promoting the value of black Americans to the committed socialist workers' party revolution. James, whose master work *Black Jacobins* had been published a year before his 1939 arrival in the United States, worked in America for the next fifteen years and was keenly interested in American literature and mass culture. But the *Partisan Review* never published him.

Perhaps the situation was not explicitly racist. When Philip Rahv was still getting the magazine together out of Beekman Place in Greenwich Village, Richard Wright tried to publish an article on "working-class Negro literature." Rahv liked the essay but thought it carried "too many overtones of the type of criticism we read in *International Literature* and in the *New Masses*." Combining the salt of sharp criticism with the pepper of snobbishness, Rahv dismissed Wright's work for its "generalities, pious appeals, half-truths, and, above all, a certain remoteness from the actual literary process."[29] Rahv thought Wright an apprentice writer and thinker in the 1930s and did not take him very seriously. He did not have to—for the simple reason that Wright was without venues to publish a Marxist essay critical of race in America but not a Communist tract. This is the situation that poet Melvin B. Tolson, a graduate student at Columbia in the early 1930s, recounted to black composer T. J. Arnold. "Outside of the Communist Party, we had nowhere to go."[30]

All things considered, the Communist Party in the United States during the Popular Front was not especially radical for black Americans, despite the party's connection to Hughes, Brown, Gordon, Clay (Holmes), and Wright. In fact, in the 1930s the CPUSA moved decidedly toward the center. During his 1936 campaign as the CPUSA candidate for the presidency of the United States, Earl Browder fondly told his audiences that "Communism is 20th Century Americanism" and that his party stood for the "democratic features of our Constitution, for the defense of the flag and the revival of its glorious revolutionary traditions."[31] If one circumstance in particular grounded Browder's statement, it was the remarkable existence of the federally funded programs of the Works

Progress Administration (WPA) to relieve the unemployment of America's fifteen million job seekers.

Begun in 1933 and directed by Harry Hopkins, the WPA included the Civilian Conservation Corps, the Public Works Administration, and the National Youth Administration. Beyond providing jobs for three and a half million people, the New Deal policies also included Federal Emergency Relief money for the needy, a Social Security Act for the retired, unemployed, and destitute, and a federal government guarantee for bank savings. In reality the programs did little for African Americans. Southern domestic and agricultural laborers, the overwhelming majority of the black workforce, were excluded from unemployment insurance, and statistically Africans Americans were unlikely to live long enough to receive old-age insurance.[32] But the federal government did intercede against poverty in a way that had direct ramifications for writers. After half of a year of public pickets by members of the Newspaper Guild, the Writers Union, and the Unemployed Writers Association—organizations believed to be Communist "front" groups—in July 1935 the Federal Writers' Project (FWP) was created.[33] Although the FWP would last for roughly only four years, in its brief run, and combined with its programs in the fine arts and theater, it would dramatically influence the growth of serious professional black writing.

New Yorker Henry Alsberg headed the Federal Writers' Project.[34] A Columbia- and Harvard-trained journalist who had covered the Russian Revolution in the 1920s, Alsberg was better known for his literary taste than for his administrative skill. He appointed such national associate directors as Waldo Browne, former editor-in-chief of *Dial* and one-time editor of *Nation*; the thickly accented Russian Jew Joseph Gaer, who could not be sent to the South or Midwest; and Lawrence Morris, a former assistant editor of *New Republic*. The proven achievement of the deputies indicated the literary merit that Alsberg hoped to achieve and also the governing political liberalism that would be seen as a sign of weakness and used to destroy the project.

Originally, the project aimed to get writers off the public relief rolls by putting them to work on "Baedekers," introductory travel-style guides to America's cities and states. Before it returned to state control in 1939, the Federal Writers' Project employed, at its peak, 6,686 writers and staff. The project was limited, in the main, to persons who could qualify as paupers, and it also maintained a quota for the numbers of the employed. It ultimately functioned like a combination of a large newspaper and a publishing house. The FWP worked with publishers to get contracts for its state guide projects and then tried to discipline its staff to submit the work on time. The editors culled the material from the researchers and reporters and then often tried to bring together a team of trained professionals, like the talented young short-story writer John Cheever, to tighten the prose.

Alsberg and his associates dodged controversy, congressional committees, and ridicule for the four years that the federal government sponsored the arts project. When Houghton Mifflin brought out the guidebook *Massachusetts: A Guide to Its Places and Peoples* in 1937 and it contained more extensive entries about the doomed anarchists Sacco and Vanzetti than about the Boston Tea Party, newspapers and critics were quick to cry "Communist subversion." Early on, there was considerable skepticism about hiring writers, especially since effective and aggressive protest by the unions was thought to be evidence of Communist influence. The historian Bernard DeVoto, then editing the *Saturday Review of Literature,* was probably in the center of public opinion when he wagged his finger at the very possibility that something like an "unemployed writer" could even exist. "[N]o one becomes a writer merely by calling himself one, and as further projects are prepared for unemployed writers, it would be well for someone to determine what an unemployed writer is," challenged DeVoto.[35]

DeVoto's fear that people were being paid for merely calling themselves writers could afford to ignore completely the problem of black writers hoping to become poets, novelists, and journalists. And even on the project, blacks faced something fairly close to systematic barring from professional and supervisory positions. But the various state writing projects and the guidebooks that were generally brought out by commercial presses forged a timely sense of national identity. Even skeptics like DeVoto acknowledged the value when the first guidebook from Idaho appeared.

The writers too had some grounds for complaint. They felt that the issue of ownership and the manner in which they had to account for their time were unfair. Painters and muralists on the arts project were free to develop their own themes without supervision and sign their names to their own work. Writers were obliged to perform "hack work": they had to fulfill a daily word count on subjects that they did not choose, and when their work appeared it was published anonymously. *Amsterdam News* sports columnist Roi Ottley, who directed the project devoted to black life in New York, took extreme advantage of the powerlessness and anonymity of the writers. When the project finally closed, he spirited away all the files on New York blacks and Harlem, then published the book *New World A Comin',* the collected work of his unit, under his own name.

The assignments could be as tedious as the job itself was in jeopardy. Every election season the vulnerable projects in arts, theater, and writing came before Congress for their appropriation and were easy targets for reduction. Writers on the project scouted their mailboxes for the inevitable "pink slips," signaling an end to their tenure. Layoffs and cutbacks and union-led protests for larger staffs were a stubborn part of FWP life. In New York, for example, where, according to Writers' Union figures, 3,500 people were registered as destitute writers, the employment quota was 447.[36] After Roosevelt's reelection in November 1936, the WPA was forced to cut 40 percent of its positions, resulting in walkouts and sit-down strikes.

Even with the influence of Roosevelt's "Black Cabinet" of African American public policy experts—Mary McLeod Bethune, Robert Weaver, William Hastie, Alfred Smith, and William J. Trent—the numbers of black writers on the project nationwide ranged from a low of about 85 to a high of no more than 150. In southern states like South Carolina, Alabama, and Mississippi, the offices refused outright to hire blacks unless the Federal Writers Project provided money for dual facilities. In Missouri, director Geraldine Parker would not hire more than a single Negro American.[37] Northern states claimed it was difficult to produce numbers of people who could qualify as skilled writers.

Virginia, New York, and Illinois were the notable exceptions, though even these states never had more than token black representation. In late 1937, as Richard Wright eased onto the New York branch of the FWP, there were about 106 blacks working on the project that supported about 4,500 writers nationally.[38] The next year all of those numbers would be trimmed dramatically. A writer and paramour of John Dewey, Anzia Yezierska dramatized the fatal tension at the end of federal patronage of the writers' projects in her lightly fictionalized memoir *Red Ribbon on a White Horse*. In the novel, an old man on the project literally dies on the floor of the New York Port Authority office building after receiving his pink slip.[39] By 1939, the last year of federal government involvement, the Writers' Project had been reduced to roughly 3,500 participants.[40]

Sterling Brown was a major success story in terms of the history of blacks on the FWP. The Washington, D.C., black professoriate that reported to Roosevelt's secretary of interior Harold Ickes successfully lobbied for a division of "Negro Affairs"; Brown was the division's captain. Just prior to Brown's appointment, Alsberg and his assistant George Cronyn met with Alain Locke and James Weldon Johnson.[41] After the consultation, Alsberg decided that each of the state guidebooks would feature a section dealing with black life, history, and folklore. Newly minted as a division chief, Brown hired as research assistants Ulysses Lee, a Howard University undergraduate, and the philosophy professor Eugene Clay Holmes. Brown prided himself on his unstinting admiration of black folk life and chiseling of a line of prideful racial justice in prose and verse. When the fourteen-hundred-page *Washington: City and Capital* appeared in 1937, printed by the U.S. Government Printing Office, Brown's "The Negro in Washington" was immediately among the most arresting analyses of an African American urban community, from privies to lace curtains, ever written. Brown did not pull punches, writing that American blacks experienced "a denial of democracy, at times hypocritical, at times flagrant."[42]

Brown's project tasks culminated with the 1940 publication of *The Negro in Virginia*, edited and supervised by Hampton Institute chemistry professor Roscoe E. Lewis. Under the leadership of Lewis, sixteen blacks collected interviews from roughly three hundred ex-slaves for the guidebook. The book gained the highest praise that American whites knew how to give to a work during that time. Jonathan Daniels, writing for *Saturday Review*, lauded the book as "free from both bitterness and prejudice and equally free of sentimentality and pretentiousness."[43] It was an ironic tribute to Brown, who had exercised a deadly wit toward white writers in his review column for *Opportunity*.

But probably the greatest single contribution he made to American culture came from his work and leadership dealing with the collection of more than two thousand interviews with and several hundred photographs of former American slaves, totaling seventeen volumes. Brown especially helped to shape and refine the protocols used when transcribing black speech. The ex-slave interviews were arguably the most important research undertaken by the entire Federal Writers' Project and produced books like *Drums and Shadows: Survival Studies among the Georgia Coastal Negroes*. When historians began to examine them exhaustively in the 1970s, these interviews transformed the understanding of slavery in North America.[44]

Although the project owned the prose and directed the efforts of its writers during the workday, the necessity of a nationally sponsored creative writing outlet became impossible to ignore. At the outset, a mimeographed broadsheet journal called "Material Gathered" came out, hoping to attract the favorable impression of the national director. In the spring of 1937 Alsberg put out a call for manuscripts that resulted in the anthology *American Stuff*, issued by Viking that same year. The anthology was one of the earliest examples of a modern, impartial selection process in the history of American letters. The book included poems by Sterling Brown and the young Detroit project writer Robert Hayden, but its standout piece was Richard Wright's uncompromising essay "The Ethics of Living Jim Crow."

Sensing the value of project creative work as a tool to defend the programs from critics, Alsberg proposed the creation of a regular magazine that would go under the name *Direction*. The magazine went through a brief run, but its editorial mission was clear. "In the fight for democracy the American people are slowly forging a cultural front. Here is its vanguard," wrote the editors in February 1938.[45] "*Direction* is the lively, entertaining and crusading magazine of the People's Front in the arts."[46] It began as a monthly in December 1937 and ran through the summer of 1941, when it came out as a bimonthly through 1942. In its final three years, it appeared as a quarterly. But Alsberg ran into difficulty when the Communist-backed Writer's Union vigorously objected to the appointment of editor Harold Rosenberg, whom it had labeled a Trotskyite. The

Writer's Union proceeded to scuttle the distribution strategies of *Direction* when it came out in New York.

New Republic, Poetry, and *New Masses* brought out special issues featuring the works of the project's writers. *New Masses* used Wright's short story of interracial alliances, "Bright and Morning Star." *Poetry* featured "The Young Ones" by Sterling Brown and introduced a superb and defiant talent, twenty-year-old Margaret Walker, who contributed "The Struggle Staggers Us" and "We Have Been Believers." Black writers were achieving recognition in the plebian democracy of the Depression. And they tended to owe something of themselves to lands west of the Mississippi.

In 1935 the United States was home to two metropoles with populations in excess of three million: New York and Chicago. The movement of black social realist writers that evolved into modernism proper was pioneered almost completely by the cadres of black writers who worked on the Federal Writers' Project in Chicago and New York. Sheer numbers boded well for the large population centers. In both New York and Illinois, a sizable group of African Americans earned a living as writers. Most of them already had college training, and they could profitably interact with whites without embarrassment about their ancestry or the fear of losing their own personalities. The "modern world" of literature and criticism that Wright had first found in the John Reed Club abounded at the project, in the shape of politically engaged social realism, the new (and often still banned) and difficult modernism, Marxist theory, and formalist literary criticism. The American Communist Party in Chicago had afforded Wright an outlet for his talent, but the FWP allowed him to make a living writing a novel. Wright joined the Illinois Writers' Project sometime in the fall of 1935, as a field reporter for the state guidebook.

Housed in a loft at 443 Eerie Street on Chicago's North Side, the Illinois Writers' Project had an unparalleled rate of accomplishment. Directed by Northwestern University English professor John T. Frederick, the Illinois project included veteran writers like the forty-seven-year-old black poet Fenton Johnson (who had published with editors Alfred Kreymborg and Harriet Monroe at *Poetry* since the 1930s), and novelists Nelson Algren, Arna Bontemps, and Jack Conroy. Young black writers like Wright found a decent welcome, but this is not really surprising. Simply put, they were the elite. Their numbers included the recent Northwestern University graduate Margaret Walker; the young Georgia prodigy and then University of Chicago graduate student in English Frank Yerby; Willard Motley, who had been raised in a family of distinguished artists like his uncle, the painter Archibald Motley, and who wrote a *Defender* column; and Katherine Dunham, professional dancer, University of Chicago anthropologist, and already writing about her expedition to a village of Jamaican Maroons in *Journey to Accompong*. In 1937 Richard Wright made a name for himself

both on Eerie Street and at the national office in Washington by drafting a proposal for a book project on Negro American life that Sterling Brown adopted
for the federal project.[47] Not only the black writers had a share of the exceptional talent. Counted among the other neophytes on the Illinois project were
Saul Bellow, Lionel Abel, Isaac Rosenfeld, and Studs Terkel, who would all go on
to make sterling reputations for themselves as writers and critics.

Only a couple of months after the FWP had begun, the key Popular Front
organization for African Americans, the National Negro Congress (NNC), held
its inaugural convention in Chicago. The NNC hoped to bring together black
Americans from all over the United States in a body that would emphasize the
joint problems of class and race.[48] Its roots stretched out to black academic
Marxists. It had been founded at Howard University's May 1935 National Conference on the Economic Crisis and the Negro. The organizers of the initial affair had been Howard political science department chairman Ralph Bunche
and Harvard Law School graduate and executive secretary of the Joint Committee on National Recovery John P. Davis. Although the 1935 conference had
chiefly featured labor and civil rights organizations, by the time of the Chicago
inaugural in February 1936, African American cultural elements had risen in
significance. The Chicago congress drew its five thousand participants chiefly
from three areas—labor, political, and religious organizations—but the special
emphasis on its cultural divisions sharply focused the extraordinary possibilities to young black writers.

Richard Wright published an article about the congress called "2,000,000
Black Voices" in *New Masses* that February, but the black artsy crowd noticed
the NNC too. An alert Dorothy West printed a *Challenge* report of the auspicious meeting, held at Chicago's Eighth Regiment Armory. *Challenge's* reporter
Louis Martin noticed a theme tying together the many sessions: "an Olympian
protest against racial injustice and an excoriating attack upon its infinite manifestations."[49] Here was the indignant calling card of the new generation. While
one example of the radicalism of the National Negro Congress was its steady
support from the Communist Party, the decision to hold the meeting in Chicago indicated the pivotal importance of that city in the new direction of black
thinking and writing. "There was plenty of evidence that the congress was seeking new race leadership. The old ballyhoo artists along with the gentlemen of
the cloth were snubbed," Martin submitted. "Du Bois, Woodson, Kelly Miller,
James Weldon Johnson, R[obert].R[ussa]. Moton and Charles Johnson, all
stayed at home while the 'younger prigs went to market.'"

Instead of the leaders from churches and white-moneyed institutions, the
NNC relied on the fiercely independent convener Davis, black American YMCA
official Max Yergan (just returned from South Africa), Lij Tasfaye Zaphiro of
Ethiopia, Communist official James Ford, and former socialist and Brotherhood

of Sleeping Car Porters chairman A. Philip Randolph. Langston Hughes addressed the congress's general session before a throng estimated at more than four thousand. Spitting fire in the 1930s, Hughes closed his remarks by reading a poem—perhaps "Goodbye Christ"—that sent running the bishops from the Colored Methodist Episcopal and African Methodist Episcopal Zion churches.

A Chicago journalist observed that the congress seemed a model of the "earnest effort of young people who are seeking by intelligent methods to break out of the prison house of oppression and restriction."[50] The new leadership that the journalists noted was setting a brisk agenda for Negro America found its epicenter in the person of twenty-seven-year-old Richard Wright. NNC convener Davis had selected the Chicagoan Wright to bring the new spirit of literature in a session on Sunday, February 16, called "The Role of the Negro Artist and Writers in the Changing Social Order." "We want you to play a significant part in this great congress," Davis had written to the up-and-coming poet and critic Wright that winter.[51]

Wright, who had already run into trouble with censorship from James Ford, was far from the only black Communist in the organization. Benjamin Davis, Jr., Ford, journalist Abner Berry, and 1920s radical Richard B. Moore were all on the NNC executive council. In the beginning, the presence of so many Communists and outspoken leftists did not stir up distrust. *Chicago Defender* columnist A. N. Fields admitted candidly, "The black man in this country is not in position in the present American scheme of things to turn aside help from any source when the ultimate aim and object is aid to him in reaching his proper destiny in his own country."[52] Plainly put, by 1936 communism was helping blacks to become twentieth-century Americans.

The Communist Party's participation in the National Negro Congress coincided with its greatest numbers of black members. By 1936 there were some 3,895 blacks making up nearly 10 percent of the total Communist membership; in 1938 black membership reached a peak of 6,900.[53] But the NNC also included people like the NAACP's Roy Wilkins, Lester Granger from the Urban League, and the Baptist minister Adam Clayton Powell, Jr., unlikely to have allied in public with a "front" organization. More to the point would be the remarkable sympathy in programs and outlooks between political liberals and reformists and the publicly articulated agenda of the CPUSA. NNC founding organizer John P. Davis himself would recall that between 1935 and 1942 he was "agreeable to carry out a Communist program."[54] Davis was not, initially, alone. At the end of the Chicago meeting, A. Philip Randolph was elected head of the organization.

At the Sunday afternoon meeting, Langston Hughes took the opportunity to introduce Wright to New Orleans poet Margaret Walker. Wright then welcomed Walker to a conversation with Arna Bontemps and Sterling Brown.[55]

There was talk of developing a club for unpublished black writers. Walker, herself an unemployed young writer trying to get on the Illinois project, asked Hughes to take her unpublished manuscript. Before leaving the talk, Hughes said to the Chicago men, "If you people really get a group together, don't forget to include this girl."[56] Six weeks later Wright mailed Walker a postcard inviting her to a club meeting; not too long after, she and her sister Mercedes joined the Communist Party.[57]

Richard Wright, in turn, organized what became known as the South Side Writers' Club and started its meetings near the end of April 1936.[58] The actor Robert Davis held the first workshop at his South Parkway home; from then on, the group met weekly at the Abraham Lincoln Center on Oakwood Boulevard. The members included Wright; Margaret Walker; the two-book poet and Association of Negro Press correspondent Frank Marshall Davis; William Attaway, the up-and-coming novelist; Louisiana native and playwright Theodore Ward, whose grandmother had had her hand cut off during slavery; Russell Marshall, a member of the exclusive social club the "400" who worked at the George Cleveland Hall Branch of the library and at Friendship House; Fern Gayden, who would become the founding editor of *Negro Story* magazine and who had served as the Wright family's relief case-worker; Arna Bontemps, finishing his Ph.D. coursework in English at the University of Chicago; anthropology Ph.D. student and Fisk College graduate Marian Minus; and the critic Edward Bland, a dialectical materialist working for the U.S. Post Office.

The group's concern with connecting Marxist ideology and the recovery of Negro folk heritage were well represented by Ward's play *Big White Fog*. Ward read the play to the group as he developed the script during 1936 and 1937, prior to the play's successful two-month run at the Great Northern Theater in the Loop beginning in April 1938.[59] In Ward's play, an educated farmer named Vic turns to Marcus Garvey for his salvation, only to be disillusioned. His son moves toward the Communist-led Popular Front. After the sheriff kills the hero Vic during the play's climactic eviction scene, a broad, interracial coalition emerges at the finale. It was clear that Ward's new work profited from the group's active critical engagement, their emphasis on art from the perspective of the working class, and the philosophies of literary Marxism and black political self-determination.

For Frank Marshall Davis, a midwesterner who had worked as a newspaperman in rigidly segregated Atlanta and virtually segregated Chicago, the South Side Writers' Club afforded him an opportunity to grow in a new direction: toward the League of American Writers. Here, Davis found something extraordinary that he had been looking for: "[t]he league partially emancipated me from the ghetto."[60] Davis became personal friends with novelists like Meyer Levin, who went on to discover Anne Frank's diary, and Stuart Engstrand, who published books in the 1930s and 1940s, and the best of the lot, Nelson Algren.

Algren and Engstrand also worked on the Illinois Writers' Project. A working writer, ten years beyond his university days at Kansas State, Davis was unconcerned about the league's political origin out of the John Reed Clubs. Instead, he was interested in the league's goal to resist fascism and in working alongside "a Who's Who among U.S. writers." Nearly everyone connected with the South Side Writers' Club itself went on to establish national reputations. It was a luxurious collection of talent.

Wright galvanized the Oakwood Avenue critics, especially through his example of national leadership. He was publishing his reviews in nationally distributed journals, writing on issues of literature and culture not confined to the race question, and working in diverse genres: poetry, short story, and literary criticism. The main activity of the group seems to have been the afternoons spent in workshops on the short stories "Big Boy Leaves Home" and "Bright and Morning Star" and the critical essay "Blueprint for Negro Writing." Fern Gayden could not forget her pleasure at hearing the moving revenge drama "Bright and Morning Star," or Wright's large ego when he read it.[61] The short story combined the Marxist and Garveyite passions that regularly flared up, especially among Wright and two young black intellectuals, John Gray and George McCray, the other dominant personalities at the meetings.

That year Attaway invited Wright to read at the Urbana-Champaign campus of the flagship state university. Attaway had a reputation as a popular campus playwright, at least among the black students; his play *Carnival* had been performed during the academic year. But when Richard Wright finished reading "Big Boy Leaves Home," Attaway was the only person left in the room. The audience had no stomach for the realistically detailed story of southern violence and lynching. Realism was provocative, but its sharply drawn dramatic windows exposing southern racial tension could also be embarrassing and even humiliating. In 1936 and in 1937 eight black Americans had lost their lives to lynch mob violence; in 1935 the number had been eighteen.[62] When blacks became successful and confident enough to mix on white campuses, they liked to keep the raw evidence of their oppression hidden.

On the Illinois campuses Wright was something of a lightning rod on the battlefield of race and politics and the lines of commitment to both. In October 1936 Dorothy West received a letter from her girlfriend Marian Minus, taking classes at the University of Chicago, describing the youthful political strife. Minus recognized shock waves among her Communist peers after they had absorbed some of the black Marxist theorizing from the young, articulate, but uncredentialed man off of Indiana Avenue. She also admired Wright's work.

Someone just rushed to me to tell me that Dick Wright is a Trotskyite. If only you could have seen the horror in her face! I must talk to Dick because I think he's going through the same thing which I am just recovering from. The Party is, of course, embittered because Dick was the [C]ommunist front in literature, so far as Negroes are concerned. Now, he will always have a message because he has always been proletarian. But thank heaven he won't be forced to type out shibboleths just because he is a Communist. They should have seen long ago that he was beyond that stage and was crying to be allowed to let his mature work be born.[63]

Minus provides one of the earliest pieces of evidence that gets at the literary and ideological struggle for young black artists in 1936. Wright had uncontested proletarian credentials, and the Communist networks and friendships decidedly benefited his work. But Wright tired early from the expectations of the disciplined members, a tension he recalled in the second half of his memoir *American Hunger*. No matter that he carried the burden of representing the proletariat, Wright would conduct his art with characteristic independence.

Richard Wright charged young blacks to think of themselves seriously as writers; he did little ushering to Communist Party cell meetings and picket lines. Margaret Walker was one of the most gifted that he met, and she and Wright went on to have an intense friendship. After Walker finished Northwestern and got on the Illinois Writers' Project, Wright would accompany her on the train back to the South Side where they lived, or to the Newberry Library, where they researched their assignments. Some of Walker's colleagues on the Illinois project, like poet Frank Marshall Davis and Jack Scher, warned her that Wright belonged to the radical political outfit. "I hope you will get to know all these people on the Project without getting to be a part of them and all they represent . . . observe them but don't join them," was the advice she heard.[64]

Wright, by then an Illinois project supervisor, was not clumsily ideological or professing revolution by rote. He presented himself as a politically committed artist in pursuit of a nuanced understanding of the cultural, social, and psychological conditions that shaped the ground of radical political action. And to get there, Wright read. He shared books with Walker, discussing Marx, Nietzsche, Gorky, Dostoyevsky, Joyce, Stein, Hemingway, and Faulkner. The controversial modern writers had not been part of her English bachelor's degree coursework at Northwestern. In turn, Walker typed the manuscript of Wright's first novel *Cesspool* (published in 1963 as *Lawd Today*), which he modeled after Joyce's *Ulysses*.

Wright's climb from poverty and segregation to rising Communist star compelled and inspired his peers. But the South Side Writers' Club was unable to sustain its energy beyond the late 1930s, and in fact, Margaret Walker believed that its vitality was compromised by the end of May 1937, when Wright departed for New York.[65] In any event, Ted Ward left for New York in 1938, and Walker herself finished a master's degree at the University of Iowa and then went to teach at Livingstone College in North Carolina. In a letter to Alain Locke, Frank Marshall Davis too regretted the passing of the group, a fate of "disintegration" that he connected to the near-pathology of middle-class blacks, the "morbid, almost psychopathic effect of prejudice; this suspicion, jealousy, and libidinous envy."[66] Davis offered multiple penetrating insights about black artists, middle-class identity, and the disguise black writers wore when encountering whites and each other. "I know the mask of the happy carefree Negro conceals deep hatred, cynical nihilism, etc." Within ten years, Davis himself would join the Communist Party and then leave the U.S. mainland for the comparatively colored island of Hawaii. (Almost forty years later, he would take under his wing a boy of mixed raced named Barack Obama.)

When Richard Wright put together his memoir, he deliberately slighted the experience in Chicago in the 1930s. Instead of getting the group off the ground, he recalled, "I met a Negro literary group on Chicago's South Side." The other writers were bourgeoisie parrots, "more formal in manner than their white counterparts" and "preoccupied with twisted sex problems." "I could not understand why they were so all-absorbed with sexual passion," he said to his audience. His answer was an archetype. "I was encountering for the first time the full-fledged Negro Puritan invert—the emotionally sick—and I discovered that their ideas were but excuses for sex, leads to sex, hints at sex, substitutes for sex. In speech and action they strove to act as un-Negro as possible, denying the racial and material foundation of their lives, accepting their class and racial status in ways so oblique that one had the impression that no difficulties existed for them."[67] Wright's dismay at black middle class sexual restraint and the subsequent channeling of libidinal energy into literary activity was insincere. In his *American Hunger* drafts, called at first "Black Confessions," he included a terrifying account of his own sexual initiation at the age of four.[68]

Wright shuffles the order of the chronology, placing his participation with the writing group anterior to his joining the John Reed Club, when the writing group clearly grew out of the National Negro Congress. He also has his revenge on his slighted romantic target Marian Minus, who was gay, or an "invert" in the parlance of the 1940s, as well as Margaret Walker, who had a sloppy schoolgirl's crush on Wright, which, apparently, she had not triumphed over when she wrote her own memoirs in her seventies. Fern Gayden remembered Walker telling the crowd that she was "going with" Richard Wright.[69]

But even without Wright's misrepresentation of the facts, the collective was difficult to hold together. During the club's year of vitality, Walker did become passionately committed to the transformative potential of Marxism in the United States. While everyone was affected, the Marxist mood did not carry the day. The South Side club's preoccupation with individual relationships seemed a failing to Walker. She rendered a caustic estimate of the group in a letter to

Wright after he had moved to New York. The group members had talent but "do not want to take it seriously enough to create a Craft group where we can work out individual and national problems of contemporary literature and writers." A Communist by then, Walker also agreed with Wright's social-class criticism of the group: "most of them look upon the group as a social outlet, a sort of bourgeois fad, and they do not see writing nor the group as a social and individual necessity."[70] Her view suggests that the Chicagoans who were publishing had a sharp-edged perception and valued a commitment to critique. To the politically committed few, literature written by black Americans was a "social and individual necessity."

But not everyone thought Chicago capable of creating a mecca for the new consciousness. Black Federal Theater Project unit director Shirley Graham held a more broadly disparaging point of view regarding the Chicago scene. An Oberlin-trained musicologist who would become the last wife of W.E.B. Du Bois in 1951, Graham produced Ted Ward's play in 1937. She found the Chicago scene artistically depressing, a cross between Joe Louis and Al Capone. "Frankly, the Negroes here care for only one thing—money. The city as a whole is utterly devoid of cultural interest."[71] Graham missed the forest because of the trees. A core nucleus of writers and critics would remain in place and advance a second and related group in the 1940s.

Wright's departure to New York at the end of May 1937 and his enthusiastic involvement in the writers' circles there shifted the center of gravity back to the East. In New York as in Chicago, the intellectual and artistic lines between the Communist Party and the Federal Writers' Project were blurred. Though the Communist Party facilitated his move by way of a job heading the *Daily Worker*'s Harlem Bureau, Wright would regain his position on the Federal Writers' Project before the end of 1937. Few places in the country took government support of writers more seriously than New York City. The New York branch of the project fully earned its title as a place of "quixotic good intentions, hysterical folly, pitiful bungling and general bedlam."[72] Much of the bedlam stemmed from the conflicts between the Communist writers' groups and basically everyone else.

The efficient Communist minority in the New York branch of the Federal Writers' Project operated as a syndicate. They worked as a machine to keep their members on the rolls of active writers. They voted in blocks and fielded candidates for positions of influence and clashed openly with the noncommunist Federal Writers' Association. Most characteristically, they created front organizations both to provide the illusion of numbers and to spread their influence without the stigma attached to the word "communist." These front groups included the Writers' Union, the Workers' Alliance, the City Projects Council, the Unemployment Council, and the Newspaper Guild. They took seriously the job of shaping and molding the opinions of their fellows, and they aggressively published and sold a variety of literature from the *Daily Worker* and *New Masses* to the *Red Pen* mimeograph sheet. They collected donations for the Abraham Lincoln Brigade, then fighting fascist armies in Spain, and recruited young fans to join the fight overseas. It was their hour. Recently moved to New York from Chicago, poet, translator, and critic Lionel Abel found the Red-tinged ambience impossible to ignore. Describing Manhattan in the mid-1930s, Abel said, "[T]he whole of New York City had gone to Russia."[73]

But to some of the black writers on the project, like the very light skinned journalist Ellen Tarry, the Communist activity seemed vague and distant from conditions of quite tangible racial oppression and injustice in the United States.[74] Besides Richard Wright, it is difficult to identify other blacks who were active Communists and employees for the New York Writers' Project. In fact, several of the most promising blacks were pulled into putative sympathy with the Trotskyites because of the blunt maneuvering of the Communist groups. In response to a set of charges around 1936, Lionel Abel, Philip Rahv, and writer Harry Roskolenko circulated a leaflet that claimed the Communists were out to punish and eliminate from the project all of their "political opponents whom they label Trotskyites, whether they be Socialists, Syndicalists, former members who dared leave the Communist Party, or liberals."[75] African American journalists Henry Lee Moon and Ted Poston included their names in the denunciation of the Communist tactics, apparently in an unsuccessful try for supervisory positions on the Writers' Project.[76]

With the exception of Claude McKay, Moon and Poston, both former reporters for Harlem's *Amsterdam-Star News*, were the best-known blacks on the New York Writers' Project. A product of Cleveland, Moon had graduated from Howard and journalism school at Ohio State. He had reviewed for the *New Republic*, wrote regularly for the *New York Times*, and in 1938 started working for black New Deal administrator Robert Weaver as a race-relations press associate. He went on to write the important study of the black voter called *Balance of Power*. Ted Poston is typically credited with breaking the color barrier at large-circulation white daily newspapers. In 1936 he accepted a job at the New York *Daily News*. Both Poston and Moon traced their distrust toward Communists from their botched film trip to the Soviet Union with Louise Thompson, Langston Hughes, and Dorothy West in 1932. The two journalists became leaders of the malcontents, loudly insisting that the Soviets had decided to avail themselves of improved political relationships with the U.S. State Department in exchange for abandoning a film that would show the truth about lynching.

The famous film episode inevitably contributed to the ambivalence and suspicion that talented black writers held toward the Communist Party. Black members and Communist sympathizers called "fellow travelers" neatly symbolized the social radicalism of the party, but when choosing among a pool of blacks for favorites, or when the issue of race relations had to be temporarily subordinated to other political imperatives, the Communists came off like sleazy opportunists. For African Americans who had never known anything like decent social intercourse from whites, the CPUSA's bold public policies and stentorian advocacy of racial equality were showily attractive. Blacks looking to answer questions about the failing economy with a new religion, and one that had proved capable of accepting them on the basis of merit, found soothing the tones of the arm-banded writers plotting sit-down strikes and singing the "International." But small numbers and a peremptory attitude of smug confidence alerted other black writers to the flaws of such an ideologically charged movement.

For young writers and those hit hard by the Depression, the directives and activism conducted out of Communist Party headquarters at 35 East 12th Street set the tone for a decade of fierce political and cultural struggle. The New York Writers' Project was a perfect example, as it tried to balance the Communist presence with the necessity of justifying itself to a U.S. Congress often hostile to its basic premise. For the first year of the New York project, there was total gridlock regarding the production of the state guide. After administrators Walter Van Olinda and Samuel McCoy were reassigned, a former Communist and editor of *New Masses,* the alcoholic, one-legged poet Orrick Johns, took over control of the unit in the early winter of 1936. Under his leadership the project offices became a hub of hunger strikes, protests, manuscript theft, character assassination, petitions, accusatory mimeographed broadsheets, and libel by agents provocateurs. According to Anzia Yezierska, the habitually drunken Johns (called "Barnes" in her novel) grew to despise the writers and their strikes for more jobs and better pay. Increasingly the sympathetic leftist sounded as skeptical as Bernard Devoto. "You know what you can do with your demands! . . . More pay? For what? Misfits, bitches, bums calling themselves writers, just because the government is giving them a handout."[77] Johns held the post for a year before resigning in scandal.

When the employees themselves weren't targeting the Writers' Project, the government sought to shut it down. By December 3, 1936, the New York project was forced to drop 1,936 people from its rolls.[78] The Writers' Union protested the size of the cut in the New York quota by flooding the new project offices on the seventh floor of 10 East 39th Street with 150 writers. Supervisors refused to submit the lists of terminated employees. By the middle of 1937 the writers had moved their offices to 235 East 42nd Street and the second floor of the cavernous Port Authority building. More space only indicated the severity of the general crisis. In May 1937 the City Projects Council successfully got 525 writers either to walk out or to join pickets in opposition to the shortfall in congressional appropriations.

Around 1939 Alfred Kazin, verging on the publication of his history of

Around 1939 Alfred Kazin, verging on the publication of his history of American literature, *On Native Grounds*, visited the Port Authority building to interview for a position as a supervisor. Faced with hallways "crowded with men and women lying face down on the floor, screaming that they were on strike," Kazin decided to reject the job and the environment of supreme chaos.[79] Kazin also noted that by 1939 the Communists and their arch-enemies the Trotskyites had joined ranks, an ironic signal that the resistance from conservative opponents was preparing to close down federal support of the writers' project. At least three times between 1936 and 1939, the mayhem of the New York project wound up on the front page of the *New York Times*, solid evidence for those bent on dissolving the government's wing of the literary arts.

In spite of the environment of contention, the New York City branch of the Writers' Project produced an early model of a moderately racially integrated workspace, and one that was unique for the city. The rest of the commercial world kept its doors shut tight. Henry Lee Moon sent his clippings to the *New York Times* in search of a job in 1936, reminding the newspaper that its faithful Harlem readers were ignored in the paper and completely unrepresented on its staff. Publisher Arthur Sulzberger wrote him back and admitted, "The point that you make merits consideration. On the other hand, it entails difficulties which cannot be overlooked."[80] Proving Moon's point, the paper was content to print half a dozen articles by him on issues of Harlem and black voters over the next several years, but full-time employment remained elusive.

But on the project, a different kind of interracial democracy emerged. The writers showed up in the morning at the Port Authority, rode the service elevators to the project floors, and then went out again, often to the main library on Fifth Avenue for research. On Fridays many hundreds of them waited in the same line for their checks. These were opportunities to share their views on the art they believed significant, to discuss their own writing, and to talk about the technical achievement of it. Benefiting from an esprit de corps that grew out of people from diverse backgrounds setting oars together to outlast a national tragedy, and in an informal setting that enhanced intimacy, the writers engaged in rich discussion of the political implications of art and artistic form, and they tried to differentiate their efforts from those of earlier generations. Their sense of shared effort and the possibility of transforming the American scene stemmed also from the regularity of contact, the self-esteem possible from employment, and the inevitable romances that broke out. Of course, memorable gatherings of import to literary history occurred. Trotskyite poet Harry Roskolenko fondly recalled a cafeteria bull session around July 1937 that included Claude McKay, Richard Wright, John Cheever, Lionel Abel, and Philip Rahv.[81]

Young Ralph Ellison joined the FWP division led by New York University English professor Harry L. Shaw in the early spring of 1938. He could easily qualify as a pauper, but he probably needed Communist support to "verify" that he had lived in New York for two years, which he had not; Ellison had just returned there after living six months in Ohio. The other black writers in New York had reputations for talent. Richard Wright wrote the section on blacks that appeared in the guidebook *New York Panorama* and was one of about thirty editors and supervisors. Roi Ottley served as editor of research on blacks for the project, and he saw that the materials, some forty boxes worth of government property, ultimately made their way to the Schomburg Library. Carl Ruthven Offord, perhaps the most disciplined of the committed leftists, was intensely interested in the attraction blacks felt toward fascism. Ellen Tarry, a competent journalist originally from Louisiana, wrote of her experiences in *The Third Door: The Autobiography of an American Negro Woman*. The group of blacks on the New York Writers' Project also included the outrageous gay writer and artist of the memorable 1920s Harlem salons Richard Bruce Nugent, his fellow Harlem Renaissance poet and Washington, D.C., native Waring Cuney, and the great champion of black antiquity and detective of racial miscegenation, the West Indian historian J. A. Rogers. Other writers who gathered information on Harlem included Lawrence Gellert, Bella Gross, Ted Yates, Everett Beane, Harry Robinson, Floyd Snelson, Abraham Hill, and Simon Williamson. New York had more than twenty African American writers on the project.

The infighting over the nature of art and politics was a fertile proving ground for the young talent, especially since the publishing industry itself was hard hit by the Depression. And yet, the relatively slow pace of work on the New York guidebook made the project an easy mark for congressional hawks. In the summer of 1938 Texas Congressman Martin Dies launched an investigation into the New York project for subversion. Here was a case when success turned into failure. The project's brief triumph in cracking the marble plate of U.S. racism was ignored for the dust it had stirred. Dies accused the theater and writers' projects of being "a hotbed of Communists." When the hearings were fully under way, the committee chose as evidence of the immorality and wastefulness of the project Wright's "Ethics of Living Jim Crow," frequently talked of in the national media as the best work in the entire volume of *American Stuff*.

If the consequences had not been so serious for the nation, the antics of the tin pot guardians of American political and cultural life would have made fine comedy. When the Dies Committee compelled the testimony of the assistant director of the WPA, Ellen S. Woodward, she defended the FWP by saying that the writers produced books like *American Stuff* outside of their project-related duties. She reminded the bureaucrats that creative work rehabilitated people who had been brought low by years of unemployment. The venom and fatuousness of the committee rose to the surface in discussion of the theater project. Congressman Joe Starnes from Alabama achieved a dubious fame when he uttered his famous demand to Ms. Woodward: "[T]ell us who this Marlowe is!" Woodward had clarified earlier that she was talking about Christopher Marlowe, but the southern congressman was a stranger to Elizabethan drama. Tough-talking Starnes did, however, recognize a cussing, and he made great use of the profanity in Wright's "Ethics" to whiten his own gown. "That is the most filthy thing I have seen," he claimed, making sure the court stenographer entered the words into the record without him having to sully himself by reading them. He challenged Woodward with a rhetorical question: "Do you find anything rehabilitating in that, I ask you?"[82] The assistant director agreed with the Dies Committee that she could not.

CHAPTER THREE

A New Kind of *Challenge* (1936–1939)

In 1934 the forty-four-year-old Jamaican-born poet and novelist Claude McKay returned to Harlem after an absence of more than ten years, planning to win final literary success. McKay's career was and continued to be rife with intellectual and artistic significance, but only slight commercial fortune. He had spearheaded black militancy in verse with his 1919 sonnet "If We Must Die." Committed to radical social change and socialist principles, he had served as an editor at *Liberator* alongside such pacesetting voices from the 1910s and 1920s as Max Eastman and Mike Gold. He had been venerated in Soviet Russia and had helped formulate global Communist policy towards blacks and he had published novels and books of poetry. His reward for all of this was to live hand-to-mouth for his entire adult life.

By the time he settled permanently in the United States, McKay was ambivalent about many of his black peers, fashioning for themselves a Harlem aristocracy that skirted the Polo Grounds on Edgecombe Avenue in Harlem. Like his colleague Zora Neale Hurston, McKay was wary of and prone to resent the pink-skinned black petit-aristocracy, with the notable exception of his lifelong friend James Weldon Johnson. Also like Hurston, McKay was more comfortable in traditional relationships with white patrons like NAACP funder Joel Spingarn and Eastman, relationships similar to those in which he had distinguished himself in Jamaica as a youth. The Communist radicals had become anathema to him.

His return to the United States and inevitably Harlem was not especially glorious, though he had recently published a distinguished novel, *Banana Bottom*. Soon enough he was borrowing from friends and trying to find rent-free accommodation. The process could not but have infuriated the sensibilities of a man who had lived as the guest of the Soviet government, and then in Morocco, Tangiers, Paris, and Germany. But in Manhattan he was limited to Harlem. Soon enough, McKay had two goals, besides making enough of a living to support himself. First, he hoped to generate a new journal, tentatively titled *Bambara*, after the language popular in Mali and Guinea, and touching the lands watered by the Senegal and Gambia rivers. Second, he wanted the journal to begin what he thought of as the intellectual contribution of his mature age: the separation of black American intellectuals from coziness with the Communist Party. Already at work on a memoir, he managed to get a room at Augusta Savage's house on West 136th Street.

Of his literary contemporaries, McKay had gone furthest with the left-wing politics, and because of his subsequent disillusion, he directed considerable disappointment toward the Comintern. (McKay heard from Max Eastman, whom he had traveled with in Russia in the 1920s, that Lenin, on his deathbed, had endorsed Trotsky and not Stalin.[1]) More important, McKay's years abroad had shown him ethnic minorities living comfortably in societies that did not fully embrace them, because they had embraced their common roots and pulled together economically. He had recovered from his experiences abroad the primacy not of social class, but of "group consciousness," a spirit that, often in spite of material circumstance, enabled "an unusual quality of dignity and assurance of living."[2] McKay established himself in 1934 with a Julius Rosenwald Fund grant and went to work on the autobiographical memoir and travelog *A Long Way from Home*. In late 1935 he began petitioning the New York Writers' Project for a position, and he was hired near the middle of the spring of 1936. He was one of the first blacks, if not the first, to join the New York project.

For a time McKay furnished material on contemporary black life for the New York City guidebook. Then New York director Orrick Johns granted him the distinction of working at home under his own supervision and on whichever topic suited him. By September 1936 McKay had completed his autobiographical manuscript. On the project, McKay gravitated toward the left-wing anti-Stalinists and toward cultivating his own brand of black nationalism. After having served on the project about a year, he helped to found the Negro Authors Guild in the spring of 1937, a unit similar to the Writers' Union. McKay apparently lent the small group's support to the organized strike against the May 1937 congressional appropriation bill, but when, over the summer, the question of white Communist participation loomed, McKay reached a boiling point. He tried to rally the black writers away from the popular Communist talking point of interracialism in favor of ethnic self-determination. But it was difficult to win young blacks over to the austerity of self-determinationist ethnic cultural politics amid the interracial pleasures available during the Popular Front years. Waldo Frank recalled the young white women, some from southern families, who "proved their freedom from 'race chauvinism' by going to bed with black comrades."[3] For the remainder of his career, McKay publicly preached the gospel of black unity that resisted the panacea of interracial communism. In private, he consoled himself with pious Catholicism.

During that summer, when Communists tried to nominate white Helen Boardman as a member of the Negro Authors Guild, he sharply resisted the efforts to integrate his small group. Arguably he failed to disentangle both issues— the control of a dominant ideology from the participation of a member of the dominant race. But McKay kept working, this time with an all-black unit, to create a "democratic association of Negro writers" that operated in the fall of

1937. On his new roster he counted James Weldon Johnson, novelist and Ph.D. Jesse Fauset, Countee Cullen, Henry Lee Moon, bibliophile Arthur Schomburg, artist Gwendolyn Bennett, and Ellen Tarry. McKay's hope that this group would prosper and function as a unit suffered from the same weakness as the Communists' Popular Front strategy. He pursued well-established writers, who would offer only sporadic token participation and whose security and conservative outlook would make the group unattractive to the young artists bursting with creative energy and striving to make themselves known. The irregular collection of NAACPers and journalists ceased meeting by the spring of 1938.[4]

McKay's years on the Writers' Project and living on the edge of poverty had entitled him to more than a small measure of perception concerning the feelings of his fellow artist. His attempt to form a movement and journal resonated with a growing number of writers who shared his basic premises: they lacked complete sympathy with Communists, were impatient with the philanthropic and civil rights organizations, and sought to raise the artistic standards of black writing. The irascible McKay strutted conspicuously, but on the sidelines. When he published his autobiography in 1937, he claimed that he had come to believe that Negroes were "haunted by the fear of segregation," a phobia that caused them to make inappropriate alliances and to compromise their "group spirit." The intrusion by white liberals had to be resisted for sake of high literary ideals. "As a member of a weak minority," he began with deliberate obscurity, "you are not supposed to criticize your friends of the strong majority." The strong majority included Popular Front liberals, wealthy philanthropists, and hard-line Communists. "You will be damned mean and ungrateful," McKay said, raising the volume, "and your group must be content with lower critical standards."[5]

McKay's effort to promote the critical standards that might have brought the Communists and liberals into range was about ten years ahead of its time; his younger colleagues were impressed by the League of American Writers and were not yet prepared to reject the Communists and their sponsored organizations. And not everybody had given up on the question of high critical standards. A rebirth was under way, but neither the middle class nor the established writers would lead it. McKay's impatient young peers at *Challenge* would light the path.

The fifth number of *Challenge*, in June 1936, showed the combination of greater editorial fire and vastly different materials by contributors. If the Renaissance holdovers had congratulated themselves on producing a "little" magazine in the modernist tradition in 1934, they had been a bit overly optimistic in the first two years. But by 1936 the encomiums were much better placed. The lead story, "Tale of the Blackamoor," was by the young social realist William Attaway. In three years Attaway would write a critically acclaimed novel, *Let Me Breathe Thunder*, that had no central black characters. His "achievement" was not to become a trend until after the second half of the 1940s. Eslanda Robeson, wife of the left-wing gallant Paul Robeson, contributed an article on black life in Paris, and Dorothy Peterson reviewed Arna Bontemps's novel of slave rebellion, *Black Thunder*. Bontemps's novel used the story of slave revolt to drive home the principle of interracial alliances and the spirit of socialism. West herself offered an article under the pseudonym Mary Christopher. And Louis Martin gave a hearty endorsement to the National Negro Congress in Chicago.

Challenge's salute to the NNC prepared the way for the Chicagoans. When the journal appeared again in the spring of 1937, it included the work of a new contributor, Marian Minus from the South Side Writers' Club. Minus wrote the article "Present Trends of Negro Literature," an essay about the state of contemporary minority fiction that pushed against the old boundaries. Minus forecast the development of an aesthetic bedrock for Negro writers: "the many sided[ness]" "racial idiom," folk prose and poetry, refinements in dialectical thinking, and an explicitly "Negro ideology."[6] She applied Marxist criticism to deal with the cultural economy of a racial formation. Despite her bracing language and somber tone, *Challenge* did present an alternative. The new radicalism that had been in the foreground at the Chicago conference and the emerging Chicago style of criticism rolled from her pen. "The time is past," she reminded the audience, "when the patterns of veneer of a class which is foreign to the great bulk of Negro life shall guide creative work." Chicago writers, responding to the incredible poverty of the South Side slums—and noting, through their close contact with sociologists, the roots of some of the poverty—promoted the Marxist cultural politics that encouraged social realism. They championed literature that reflected the lives of the masses of workers and featured the environmental conditions that so narrowly channeled their hard fate.

At the conclusion of *Challenge* that April, Dorothy West confessed her embarrassing struggle to round up subscriptions and copy for the magazine. Her results were unimpressive for a progressive magazine aimed at stimulating and exposing young Negro talent. Where might the talented readers and writers be found? Competent at training students for the middle class, Negro colleges—despite their surging enrollments—were less successful shepherds of intellectual and artistic pioneers. "We contacted Negro schools with unbelievably poor results," Dorothy West confessed to the editorial page.[7] So instead of schools, West was ready to tap into the increasingly vital literary band in Chicago. "We have become greatly interested in a young Chicago group," she said in an editorial. Referring to the "lively and well attended" South Side Writers' Club without revealing its name, West admitted the "considerable dispraise" her magazine had received from them. She playfully shrugged off Marian Minus and Richard Wright by offering them "a special section in a forthcoming issue, that they may show us what we have not done by showing us what they can do." Thus the single issue of *New Challenge* was born.

West was sly regarding her own feelings about left-wing radicalism, but the result of the literary riposte from the Chicago South Side Writers' Club was a metamorphosis. In the fall of 1937 *Challenge* changed its name to *New Challenge*, and in the months leading up to the historic publication it boasted new associate editors: Minus and Wright. For its single issue, *New Challenge* would exude "social necessity," even if some of its radical leftists were more blasé than ardent. Before the end of the summer, West had stationery bearing the new name of her journal, run out of her apartment on West 66th Street.

But the announcement was not just a change in the header. During the second week of June, within days of arriving in New York, Wright had written a column for the *Daily Worker*, where he was now editor of the Harlem Bureau, celebrating the revitalized journal and the creation of a new avant-garde with centers in Chicago and New York. A dash Panglossian, Wright identified a new audience of "thousands of Negro workers, students and intellectuals" turned radical by the Depression.[8] He continued the analysis of Eugene Gordon, which sharply criticized black writing of earlier eras because it pleaded to the "ruling class" and had no native audience. And Wright cast out the immodest patrons and professional friends of the Negro. "In contradistinction to the Harlem School of expression," he railed, "in part exploited by publishers for the jaded appetites of New York Bohemians, the new movement among Negro writers is receiving its stimulus from below rather than from above." Wright insisted that artists' work and the artists themselves needed to be organically generated from the black masses. By targeting a new audience, he could well argue for a dramatic departure from the traditional literary formula.

Wright's widening influence in New York was odd. Officially a Communist, and with his southern origins on his tongue and in his manner, he struck people with a useful combination of sincerity and intelligence. Certainly, he did not leave anyone, black or white, man or woman, feeling threatened or intimidated. The greatest boost to his stature was through his very public position as a delegate to the League of American Writers' second conference, held in New York in June 1937, where Dorothy West may have met him for the first time.

This second meeting of the league was a public event of the first order. Not even conservative analysts, writing during the cold war, could fail to note that for the New York literary community, the league's second congress was "probably the most massive social event in the community's history."[9] Future librarian of Congress and legendary poet Archibald MacLeish opened the conference, and Ernest Hemingway addressed the writers after showing a film on the Spanish Civil War that he had helped to produce. Black writers, including Wright, Claude McKay, Ralph Ellison, Margaret Walker, and Langston Hughes, were conspicuous participants at the conference; at one session Wright was asked to introduce the Federal Writers' Project director Harry Alsberg. It was probably the first time in American history that a congress of artists and intellectuals without a special mandate to address racial injustice had tolerated such a degree of black and white intercourse.

It did not take long before the fireworks started. Claude McKay had been seated with other guests on the stage during CPUSA secretary Earl Browder's evening address. The text of Browder's speech refuted the theologian Reinhold Niebuhr and Waldo Frank, who had both complained that communism was as rigid as orthodox Catholicism. Not even needing to point out Stalin's showy persecution trials in Moscow, Niebuhr and Frank criticized the handling of charges against Leon Trotsky. Browder shifted attention away from the Communists and turned to throttle the traditional scapegoats—the socialists—during the era when the CPUSA courted the bourgeoisie. "Is it possible for us to adopt an attitude of broad toleration of those who preach and practice such treason," he asked of his audience, referring to anarchists, followers of Trotsky, and socialists.[10] As his dramatic climax became obvious to the well-stocked auditorium, Claude McKay got up and walked off the platform in protest. McKay would spend the next two years trying to produce a position on race and progressive economics, without the influence of those he snarlingly called "dirty communists."[11]

McKay was not alone with his dramatic gesture of disapproval. The young socialist critics expressed their bitterness and signaled preparations to foil the coalition. Writers' Project workers like Philip Rahv, Harry Roskolenko, William Phillips, and Mary McCarthy disrupted some sessions with loud calls for Trotsky's rights. They went on to condemn the entire league as a "pure Stalinist Front."[12] Although League of American Writers secretary Franklin Folsom argued that his organization was fully impartial, the league did share a suite of offices at 381 Fourth Avenue with International Publishers, the press run by Communist cultural secretary Alexander Trachtenberg.[13] Over the next several months, Rahv, Phillips, McDonald, and McCarthy would be hard at work on *Partisan Review*, now shorn completely from the aegis of the Communist Party. The magazine would no longer be solicitous of Richard Wright and Sterling Brown. Few American blacks on the Left could afford to make the nimble jump into the Trotskyite unknown.

Around June 10, a couple of days after the congress, Wright, who had been in Manhattan less than two weeks, went down to the Port Authority building at 42nd Street and Eighth Avenue, obviously seeking a Federal Writers' Project position. Claude McKay spotted him. Curious about Wright's politics, McKay wanted to challenge the young black Communist from Chicago. McKay reported his sighting to Dorothy West, who was in the process of holding informational meetings with people like Wright and Henry Lee Moon to help transform her journal. McKay felt that West, still only in her late twenties, was turning her allegiance toward the younger writers and Chicago migrants. "I also saw your friend, Mr. Wright, down on the job," McKay wrote, "but he 'evaded' me (to use his word)." The evasion had not ennobled Wright to McKay. "Personally I think he has an extremely weak face, the type you see in a person who can be easily influenced and become fanatical about causes."[14] Intelligent, energetic, gregarious, and articulate about his convictions, Wright had a buzz around him. When Nancy Cunard approached Langston Hughes for an anthology of radical verse that spring, Hughes recommended Richard Wright. McKay claimed to fear that Wright was becoming a Communist pawn, but he also had ego enough to espy another younger writer gaining stature among the leftist literati, the same group that had at one time supported McKay.

The rub between McKay and Wright had inevitably to do with their centers of support. McKay was confirmed in his view that West's journal not only needed to be run by blacks but also needed a base of black subscribers for an anchor. This was the mercurial group that the writers needed to thrive but could never identify with complete certainty. Wright might have dreamed of "thousands of Negro workers" as an audience, but *New Challenge* pursued white liberals to prop up its endeavor, people like the twenty-seven-year-old future historian of the Underground Railroad Henrietta Buckmaster, and New York University professor and folklorist Mary Elizabeth Barnicle. Ralph Ellison successfully lured a contingent of Swarthmore professors into purchasing a subscription. *New Challenge* featured left-leaning Negro talent, but it could identify tangible support from the officially liberal white intelligentsia.

Salt in the wound between McKay and Wright during the summer of 1937 had another obvious source: Wright's attempts to publish his manuscripts were foundering, and all published writers inevitably seemed a part of the conspiracy to keep him out of print. The New York houses responded unenthusiastically to Wright's bleak realist manuscripts treating African American life. The most prestigious of the risk-takers turned him down. Rejection came in a warm note from editor Saxe Commins of Random House, the four-year-old publishing house that had taken on an obscenity lawsuit in 1934 to bring out James Joyce's *Ulysses* to American audiences. The seasoned Commins appreciated Wright's manuscript "Tarbaby's Dawn," from which the short story "Big Boy Leaves Home" was drawn. And the internal reviewers at Random House had the sense to realize that Wright presented an entirely new quantity in black writing. However, they feared that a public did not exist that was capable of accepting such raw violence (especially between the races), bitterness, and despair. Commins and all his readers agreed that the novel had been written with "skill," but he rejected the manuscript on a business principle: "such a book would have to overcome almost insurmountable commercial hazards."[15] The verdict against a literary confrontation with the race problem was a business decision.

On those occasions when he did not evade Claude McKay in public, Wright played up to the older man's reputation and celebrity. But he was disingenuous. Wright hoped to see McKay's body of work overturned. He desired a complete repudiation of the Harlem Renaissance. Privately, to help bring this about, he had already called upon Alain Locke to review McKay's new autobiography *A Long Way from Home*. He hoped to see *New Challenge* publish an essay "that would sum up the work of McKay and the whole period he represents."[16]

There was little love lost for McKay, who was by the summer fighting Wright and the new magazine "for all he is worth." Frank about his opponents and the places he expected to find encouragement, Wright prepared to jettison a tradition grounded in race-based alliances. He anticipated a genuine watershed shift in literary affairs and personnel, so calumny from McKay's breed mattered little. "[W]e are depending [more] upon support from west of the Hudson River than upon these boys and girls in Harlem," Wright wrote to Alain Locke.[17] He identified his literary peers as "moving in a Left direction," but not yet "out and out Communist." "We want to build," Wright admitted, "a Negro peoples movement in writing." A card-carrying Communist since 1933, Wright seemed reluctant toward orthodox membership by 1937. Congruent with the Popular Front tactics but preserving the strategy of self-determination from the Black Belt nation thesis, Wright hoped for a third term, a "Negro people's movement."

In the move to generate a new direction in writing for Negro people, Wright figured that Locke, the disgruntled "godfather" of Renaissance writers, would be the ideal person to signal the shift. For one thing, Locke's yearly retrospective columns on black literature in *Opportunity* journal had always reserved judgment for the appearance of strong black literary efforts. And Locke had grown increasingly disaffected with the artists he had helped to cultivate, like Langston Hughes, Zora Neale Hurston, and Claude McKay. In September Dorothy West wrote to Locke, thanking him for adding to the journal's critical edge. Speaking of his review of McKay's book, "Spiritual Truancy," West thought that "Its strength is objective, we feel, and therefore makes your analysis so much more effective. So far as we are concerned, it is not tainted with any personal grudge."[18]

But Locke's essay was a grudge-filled rebuke. He criticized McKay's flighty writerly trajectory, from Jamaican folklorist, to radical protestor, Communist, and black exotic, and finally returning to Harlem once again, and this time filled with color consciousness. Locke summed up the writers of the 1920s with his dismissal of McKay's latest effort: "[I]n some vital sense these aberrations of spirit, this lack of purposeful and steady loyalty of which McKay is the supreme example have to a lesser extent vitiated much of the talent of the first generation of 'New Negro' writers and artists."[19] In step with the general reassessment bubbling, Locke believed that the New Negroes of the 1920s had shown "spiritual truancy and social irresponsibility."[20] The black writers of the 1920s had failed to deliver relevant artistic products because of their alienation from black audiences. They had been "exhibitionists" posing for the "gallery of faddist Negrophiles." Operating in the final third of his career, Locke comfortably maneuvered himself into the camp of social realism and its concern with the black working class.

With Locke's review in hand, Wright's job of dramatically breaking from the black writers of the 1920s was neatly authorized, and he did it in *New Challenge* with the manifesto "Blueprint for Negro Writing." The essay had taken early shape as a collaborative effort during meetings of the South Side Writers' Club, though Wright assembled the draft in his rooms on 67th Street in New York during the summer of 1937.[21] In "Blueprint," Wright made a formal demand for black writers to reject the ethic of racial celebration for which the Harlem Renaissance group had been known. "Blueprint" brutally faulted the New Negro artists "curtsying to show that the Negro was not inferior, that he was human."[22] Wright emphasized a remarkable failure in black writing and offered as culprits the neglect of nationalism and the fawning obsequiousness toward white backers. These missed steps were compounded by the Renaissance writers' utter inability to erect a commanding literature off of what already had been recognized as a superior folklore tradition. Instead of celebrating the beauty of the race as a kind of primping necessary to enter the white mainstream, Wright suggested embracing black nationalism: the obvious model at hand was the National Negro Congress. "Negro writers must accept the nationalist implications of their lives, not in order to encourage them, but in order to change and transcend them. They must accept the concept of nationalism in order to transcend it. They must *possess* and *understand* it."[23] In "Blueprint," Wright returned to and enlarged the aesthetic scaffolding that Minus had developed in the final issue of *Challenge*.

In February 1937 the good news of the National Negro Congress had gone to Richmond, Virginia, under the front name Southern Negro Youth Congress. To a degree, the fortress of southern prejudice was under direct assault. Wright thought that the reluctance of the black middle class to use poems and novels to hammer the shape of an aggrieved political situation reflected a poor understanding of international events. He seems to have found the status quo of black artists ignorant of Gorky, Kafka, and Malraux, and for that matter of James Farrell. In his eyes their education, their fluency in foreign languages, their knowledge of Western culture amounted to nothing. They seemed blithely uninterested in the exciting new literary techniques exploring the unconscious and fearful of Marxism. Nor were they adept at digging out the basement of Negro life: its folklore and its church. Richard Wright hoped both to take black writers abroad and to bring them down-home. They needed to think of themselves as coworkers with writers all over the globe, and they needed a more rigorous understanding of what it meant to "be" black.

Marian Minus put "Blueprint" principles into action with her review of Zora Neale Hurston's September book *Their Eyes Were Watching God*. The novel was Hurston's second effort in narrative fiction, and a monument to the tradition of folk realism. Minus first called attention to the artistry and beauty of the book and its rejection of the "veneer" of a "foreign class" by concentrating on dry-longso blacks. But then she rapped Hurston hard over the knuckles for her slight treatment of racism and social-class strife. In stiff prose that seemed uncomfortable with its task, she reproached the Florida Writers' Project star for hiding the anger of a character named Tea Cake.

In her novel about a café-au-lait Cinderella searching for love and self-identity, Hurston had offered as the paladin Tea Cake, a lady's man, gambler, day laborer, rogue, troubadour, knife-fighter, and crack shot. In a couple of passages centering on Tea Cake, Hurston had broached the racial situation, but she had not deeply engaged it. In a scene of some length, Tea Cake is pressed (and called "suh") onto a work gang to bury the dead. He offers an estimate of segregation and unequal burial practices: "Look lak dey think God don't know nothin' 'bout de Jim Crow Law." Then he escapes and returns to his wife Janie and confides, "It's bad bein' strange niggers wid white folks."[24] Minus approved of the "bitterness in his reaction to his compulsory activity," but she also thought the response was inadequate. "[O]ne wonders that there is no elaboration of thought or act to involve change which would vitiate the habit of employment without consent," Minus commented obliquely. Hurston had clearly not written a book that would dwell upon racial conflict. Finally, the young critic said almost straightforwardly: "Here one wishes that Miss Hurston had allowed Janie and Tea Cake to be less in love for enough paragraphs to show the depths of this bitter reaction."[25]

The criticisms showed the determination of the young cadre to obliterate the genres of entertainment and romance, because Hurston, arguably without peer as a developer of black folklore into a refined artistic statement, was a natural one for the group to claim. Hurston always earned points for conveying the importance of black folk art, but she was steadily upbraided for failing to capture the sound of the modern era, the treble of social-class distinctions and the bass of racial oppression. Hurston had erred by using "understatement" and "avoidance" when showing her characters' "relations to the whole of southern practices." Racism and class strife were issues that should be confronted directly and explicitly, unless the writer had some aversion "to being called 'social conscious.'" Among the black intellectuals and writers in New York, in Chicago, and on Howard's campus in 1937, to aver being called "socially conscious" was tantamount to being a reactionary, or being a person who was an Uncle Tom. Of course this was an especially bitter pill to Hurston personally because she was something of a backer of Dorothy West.

Hurston's pursuit of white readers, and her assessment of the kind of fare that would sit well with American whites, informed the choices she made during her great run in the 1930s. After two novels and a collection of folktales, she brought out an anthropology, *Tell My Horse*, in 1938, a novel, *Moses, Man of the Mountain*, in 1939, and an autobiography, *Dust Tracks on the Road*, in 1942. Publishers asked her to remove portions from her books that would seem to aggrieve her niche audience, and she followed the advice. Her personal ethics were grounded in her own self-preservation and her sense that she was defending and speaking for blacks who could not do it on their own. She was known for playing fast and loose with other kinds of truths when it suited her. The famous example of her freewheeling ethical sense is her 1927 *Journal of Negro History* interview called "Cudjo's Own Story of the Last African Slaver." Hurston claimed to have talked to the last surviving African brought to the United States in chains. Instead, she had mightily plagiarized from Emma Langdon Roche's *Historic Sketches of the Old South*.[26] By the second half of the 1930s, Hurston felt like she was developing an audience, and she saw no reason to irritate them.

Sterling Brown's social conscience moved him out of himself, though it did not help his career as a writer. As director of Negro affairs, Brown had the prerogative of shooting out the memorandums of advice to the regional directors like Benjamin Botkin and Alan Lomax, who put into the field hundreds of writers who gathered more than three thousand narratives of ex-slaves. This devotion to the living memory of slavery was extraordinarily important for Brown and formed the basis of his October 1937 review of *Their Eyes Were Watching God*, published in *Nation*, a new perch for the Howard professor.

Their devoted work capturing the lives and folkways of African Americans in the deep South seemed so similar as to make Brown and Hurston nearly literary twins. But politics busted them up. Although Brown did not grow up in luxury or ease, his urban college upbringing among light-skin-colored elites and the social connections he took for granted were leagues different from Hurston's rural, nomadic, and uphill hike through early life. Privilege made Brown more sympathetic to the overarching economic plight of common folk, while indigence helped commit Hurston more fully to individual excellence. So, the WPA, the League of American Writers, and the Communist-influenced periodicals turned to Brown as their darling. During roughly the same period, Hurston published chiefly with *American Mercury* and *Saturday Review*, magazines that, like most of American popular culture, tended toward "sentimental" portraits of black life. Like Hurston, in 1937 Brown won a Guggenheim fellowship, and in 1938 and 1939 he would lecture at New York University as a visiting professor. Brown's combination of politics and folk dynamism was legendary. He gave one vantage on his position about fifteen years later, in a government interview. When an FBI agent attempted the interrogation, generally begun with the remark, "Are you now, or have you ever been, a member of the Communist Party?," Brown had a ready answer.

"Listen son, any Negro who has been to the seventh grade and is against lynching is a Communist. I have been to the eighth grade and am against a hell of a lot more than lynching."[27]

But fellow traveler or not, when Brown looked at Hurston's book, he seemed to grasp the nettle as reluctantly as Marian Minus. He celebrated Hurston's attention to black peasant workers and her formidable ability to invent and reproduce the southern vernacular idiom. "'Their Eyes Were Watching God' is chockfull of earthy and touching poetry," he readily admitted.[28] But the praise was only prelude to a genuine disappointment regarding the most important scenes in the book to Brown. Nannie's recitation of her past as a concubine, itinerant farmers and their children eking out a living in a swamp, and the segregated treatment of black and white corpses after the hurricane, these moments had no thunder in them, no extended narrative treatment of roiling discontent. He stretched to find evidence of the new black spirit in the book, and when he did, he sounded awkward: "there is bitterness, sometimes oblique, in the enforced manner, and sometimes forthright."[29]

Further left than Brown, Richard Wright told the *New Masses* crowd that Hurston worked "in that safe and narrow orbit in which white America likes to see the Negro live; between laughter and tears."[30] The most unmasked disappointment appeared in the pages of Howard's *Journal of Negro Education*. Hurston had done most of her undergraduate work there. Like the other reviewers, English professor Alphaeus Hunton liked the folk idiom but was embarrassed by the absence of the problems of race and social class. "It is too late in the day for such myopia."[31] It would take better than forty years and a different political climate before the book became a classic.

Nick Aaron Ford, an English teacher in Texas who had a master's degree in political science from the University of Iowa, talked to Hurston at her Florida home about her politics-of-the-novel shortly after the publication of *Jonah's Gourd Vine* in 1934. Though a respectfully polite academic, in his self-published 1936 study *The Contemporary Negro Novel*, the third academic study of black writers, Ford thought that there was no way for the black writer to choose "art for art's sake" in the 1930s. "[S]ince the Negro novelist has not produced even a first rate novel, is he not justified in laying aside the pretensions of pure artistry

and boldly taking up the cudgel of propaganda?"[32] Ford argued that the historical stage determined the role that black writers had to play; they were public
reformers and literary social workers.

In his study, Ford reported Hurston's awareness that she was already a controversial figure three years before *Their Eyes Were Watching God*. Referring to
Jonah's Gourd Vine, Hurston told him that "[m]any Negroes criticize my book
because I did not make it a lecture on the race problem." Hurston said then that
she was writing novels and not sociology. "I have ceased to think in terms of
race; I think only in terms of individuals."[33] A dark-brown-skinned man himself, Ford's reply to all of this was to look closely at Hurston and see if she could
possibly pass for white. In his experience, skin color might have explained Hurston's ability to distance herself from the problems of race in America during an
era especially thick with deadly tension and demanding political responsibilities. When he decided that the freckled Hurston, though light tone for a black
person in Florida, could not possibly pass as white, Ford was dumbfounded and
bitter. Nearly forty years later, when Ford prepared the anthology of black writing *Black Insights*, he still made a point of excluding her.

There was a book that had slipped the problem of representing black workers
without becoming a treatise on racism. Published two years earlier than *Their
Eyes*, George Wylie Henderson's *Ollie Miss* combined a masterfully drawn and
authentic female heroine with an attentive regard to the African American
rural peasantry, and without the heavy language of ideology. It also disregarded
whites entirely and, as Hurston had done, welcomed the white reader. A lyrical
tale of the summer and fall seasons and farm planting told with sympathetic
grace and unpretentiousness, *Ollie Miss* offered as protagonist a sensual ama-
zon who drifts onto a farm in Alabama. With one notable exception all the
characters were black, and the emphasis was on the tight space of Uncle Alex's
farm and the wandering laborers like Ollie and her various lovers whom she is
drawn to and alienated from, Slaughter, Lil Willie, and Jule, the father of her
baby. The fact that sex appeared naturally and without sensation seemed to assure Henderson's modernist pretensions, and that intercourse between woman
and man ultimately resulted in children made him certainly something of a
naturalist. But the key triumph was his protagonist's choice to assert her independence after a nearly fatal fight with Jule's other woman Lena, and to live
alone with her child.

The book focused on peasant laborers working for a landowning black, and
the heroine, at the conclusion of the tale, herself becomes a member of the yeo-
manry. It was a remarkable exposition concerning the transference from psychological independence, to reproducing the next generation, to gaining economic independence, and checking patriarchy along the way. Labor itself was
portrayed with dignity, and the critics loved the book. "Mr. Henderson works

with material that is almost entirely absent from the body of serious fiction by or about the American Negro."[34] Henderson was "what critics of Negro literature have long been waiting for," said an Urban League reviewer in *Survey Graphic*.[35] Hurston's classic fancy-girl protagonist, with her bank account, house, sweet man, and dreams of telling tales, seemed by comparison carried on palanquin.

With a new editorial board representing Howard (Sterling Brown and Eugene Holmes), Chicago (Margaret Walker), and Detroit (Robert Hayden), *New Challenge* began accepting work for another issue. The name change and invigorated direction indeed spurred submissions: there was, in fact, a new movement afoot. Wright, who was performing a great deal of the editorial work, solicited a short story from his twenty-four-year-old friend Ralph Ellison, called "Hymie's Bull." It was the first attempt at fiction by the trumpeter from Tuskegee's music department. Marian Minus reviewed Malcolm Cowley's book *After the Genteel Tradition*. Margaret Walker entered a folksy short story called "Yalluh Hammuh," and the Detroit City College graduate Robert Hayden sent in the antilynching poem "Diana." The work collected for the never published second number of the journal was more auspicious than the first issue, and it must be noted that all the young contributors were so heavily involved in the Communist Party that it is difficult to consider them other than Communist Party members.[36] *New Challenge* was tapping the strength of the emerging black college crowd and the urban literary radicals.

Minus's "Retrospect and Analysis" of Cowley's latest book signaled something central to the group: the necessity of expanding the range of interests beyond a racial outlook. The journal's young staff had the synthesis of avant-garde literary techniques and political struggle as its chief concern. "Our greatest interest lies," she began, "in those essays wherein not only the mechanics of the writer's craft as such are discussed, but also the mechanics of his thinking, and the correlation of this with the form of expression which it takes." In essence, Minus advanced the importance of theory, the "mechanics of [his] thinking." This sort of girding would again enable a move beyond the 1920s: "the young writer . . . resolves to shun the shell of imitation and borrowed cultural appendages."[37]

The new work that they hoped to publish accomplished it all. To boot, the roster of unknown writers—Walker, Ellison, and Hayden—would rapidly move to the head of their class. Margaret Walker used the general template of the black hero to elaborate a long folktale in dialect about the fun-loving bad man, "mah cousin, Yalluh Hammuh." Ralph Ellison's short story of hoboes on railroad cars centered on a violent episode and echoed Hemingway with a clipped narrative style. Nor did he put blacks completely at the center; instead, he had the narrator describe a Jewish hobo named Hymie. "Diana," the work-in-progress of young Robert Hayden, shrilly exposed the myth and the ritual behind lynching, the "obscene, black satyr," and the ironic "venereal virginity" of the harlot that gave lynching its justification.[38]

In the end, a poor subscription base ruined the journal's ability to reappear, especially since Ellison, the most diligent of those attracting subscribers, so-journed for several months to Ohio to bury his mother. Fractiousness ensued in the relationships between West and the recent Chicago arrivals, especially as romance between West and Minus deepened. But the prime culprit derailing the organizational energy of black America's short-lived modernist journal was a December message from *Story Magazine*'s Whit Burnet to Richard Wright: "It is a great pleasure for STORY Magazine to announce that the judges of the WPA contest have voted the $500 first prize award to you as author of *Uncle Tom's Children*, a book of novellas." The John Reed Club, the Communist Party, the Federal Writer's Project, the League of American Writers, and the National Negro Congress had launched the ambitious and prolific Richard Wright.

3.1. Langston Hughes, 1939   Photograph by Carl Van Vechten, James Weldon Johnson Collection in the Yale Collection of American Literature, Beinecke Rare Book and Manuscript Library, Yale University

3.2. Zora Neal Hurston, 1935   Photograph by Carl Van Vechten, James Weldon Johnson Collection in the Yale Collection of American Literature, Beinecke Rare Book and Manuscript Library, Yale University

3.3. Claude McKay, ca. 1933   Countee Cullen- Harold Jackman Memorial Collection,
Robert W. Woodruff Library of the Atlanta University Center

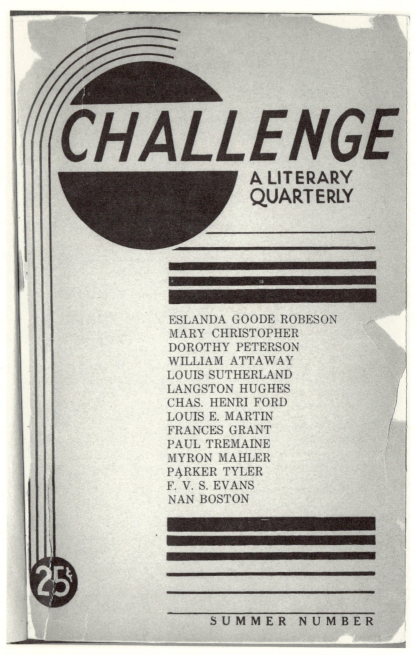

3.4. *Challenge*, June 1936   Manuscripts, Archives, and Rare Book Library, Emory University. Courtesy of the Estate of Dorothy West.

CHALLENGE

A Literary Quarterly

DOROTHY WEST, Editor

HAROLD JACKMAN, Associate Editor

VOLUME I   JUNE 1936   NUMBER 5

CONTENTS

Published quarterly by Boston Chronicle, 794 Tremont St., Boston, Mass. Make checks or money order payable to Dorothy West, c|o Challenge, 442 Manhattan Avenue New ork City, N. Y.

3.5. *Challenge,* June 1936, table of contents   Manuscripts, Archives, and Rare Book Library, Emory University. Courtesy of the Estate of Dorothy West

3.6. Dorothy West, 1948 Photograph by Carl Van Vechten, Carl Van Vechten Photographs, Countee Cullen-Harold Jackman Memorial Collection, Robert W. Woodruff Library of the Atlanta University Center

3.7. Sterling Brown and Abram Harris, Howard University, 1938   Cedric Dover
Collection, Manuscripts, Archives, and Rare Book Library, Emory University

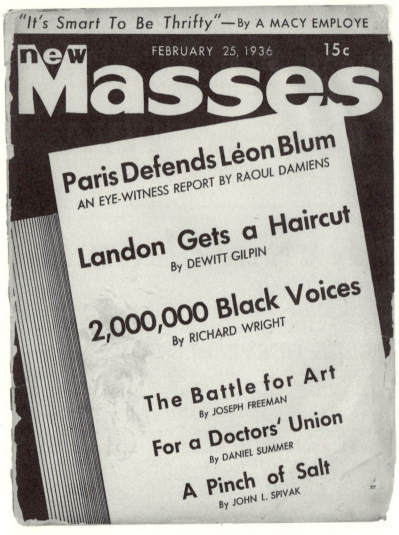

3.8. "2,000,000 Black Voices" by Richard Wright, *New Masses*, February 25, 1936   Billops-Hatch Collection, Manuscripts, Archives, and Rare Book Library, Emory University

3.9. C.L.R. James, 1944   Photograph by Carl Van Vechten, Carl Van Vechten Photographs, Countee Cullen-Harold Jackman Memorial Collection, Robert W. Woodruff Library of the Atlanta University Center

STILL TIME TO UNITE by A. B. MAGIL

NEW MASSES

MAY 10, 1938   FIFTEEN CENTS A COPY

VOL. XXVII, NO. 7, NEW YORK, N. Y., IN TWO SECTIONS OF WHICH THIS IS SECTION ONE

MONTHLY LITERARY SECTION INCLUDED WITH THIS ISSUE

FEDERAL WRITERS' NUMBER

Edited by S. Funaroff and Willard Maas

Bright and Morning Star

A COMPLETE NOVELETTE

By Richard Wright

The Brown Coat	by Alexander Godin
Medicine	A "Living Newspaper" Script
A Tall, Dark Man	by Saul Levitt
My Grandfather	by Arnold Manoff
Home	by Sam Ross
Street Songs of Children	Compiled by Fred Rolland
She Snaps Back Into Harness	by Ruth Widen

Verse by Raymond E. F. Larsson, Kenneth Rexroth, William Pillin, H. R. Hays, Lola Pergament, Kenneth Fearing, Alfred Hayes, Opal Shannon, Weldon Kees, Maxwell Bodenheim, Charles Hudeberg, Willard Maas, Dorothy Van Ghent, Eli Siegel, and A. T. Rosen

Inside France by Theodore Draper

What Lenin Thought of Trotsky and Bukharin A Review by Joshua Kunitz

3.10. "Bright and Morning Star" by Richard Wright, *New Masses*, May 10, 1938 Billops-Hatch Collection, Manuscripts, Archives, and Rare Book Library, Emory University

CHAPTER FOUR

The Triumph of Chicago Realism (1938–1940)

Black America had trudged seventy-five years from chattel slavery in 1940. An ex-slave had raised roughly eight of every nine black adults over fifty. The respected leaders of Afro-America had grown to adulthood enmeshed in a folkways and philosophy of life that grew directly from an epoch of bondage. But the radio, rocket, airplane, and atom of the modern era put up eons between modern Negroes and the slave auction block. The city of Chicago, a place that had no native tradition of bondage but owed plenty of its character to modern industry, was the apt locale to measure the distance between the whips and shackles of the cotton field and jive-talking Cab Calloway blaring from a jukebox on a street filled with skyscrapers.

Spurred by black real estate mogul James Washington, Chicago played host to the festive Negro Exposition in the summer of 1940. The Negro Exposition was a grand pageant commemorating the seventy-five years of freedom from slavery for African Americans. The location of the celebration also made fitting poetic justice, since the city itself had been founded by a Haitian Negro trader named Du Sable in the second half of the eighteenth century. The fair took place through July and August and emphasized the spectacular riches and steady advance of millions of Americans whose ancestors had once been chattels personal. In two weeks more than fifteen thousand tourists, black and white, visited the showcases at the Chicago Coliseum.[1] The glitter and gleam of the Negro Exposition promised that the age of fulfillment was at hand. The decade of the 1940s held true to the expectation, and it was especially writers from Chicago who shared in that fulfillment.

The energy to honor the American Negro found a natural source among the more than 370,000 African Americans living in Chicago in 1940. Chicago had become a comfortable upriver destination for Mississippi, Alabama, and Arkansas blacks seeking economic opportunity in stockyards and steel mills. The majority of Chicago's black Americans lived in a segregated corral on the city's South Side between 31st and 61st Streets north to south, and jammed together along the major corridors: Cottage Grove Avenue, South Parkway, Michigan Boulevard, and State Street.[2] The Depression hit them hard. Unemployment rates hovered at 30 percent for black workers of all classes except the professions.

White street gangs and racially exclusive residential "covenants" kept blacks from escaping the South Side and finding homes for the best value. Instead, the two room, roach-infested "kitchenette" family apartment served as the standard.

But activism against racial ceilings and codes persisted. Tenement dwellers ingeniously fenced the teeny squares of littered mud in front of their apartments and grew buoyant gardens. Black Americans renamed their community "Bronzeville" for the sake of self-worth and supported five newspapers to convince themselves of a more flattering reality. The biggest weekly newspaper, the *Chicago Defender*, sold forty thousand copies and circulated among more than twice that many citizens. Black Chicagoans also had more tangible, concrete sources of pride that more than matched that of black Americans from other parts of the country, even New York. Within walking distance from the black crossroads of the world—47th Street and South Parkway—stood Provident Hospital, the country's only private hospital staffed by black doctors, the George Cleveland Hall public library, the Hotel Grand, the luxuriously impressive Michigan Boulevard Garden Apartments, and five black churches that could seat two thousand and claim ten thousand members apiece.

The Negro Exposition gala owed its execution, thoroughness, and heft to the important batch of African American social realists. The novelist and Federal Writers' Project Researcher Arna Bontemps was director of research; poet and newspaperman Frank Marshall Davis held the title director of publicity; and sociologist and head of the Good Sheppard Community Center Horace Cayton served as assistant to the director. But the recognition of the value of emancipation did not come merely from established members of the black community. President Franklin D. Roosevelt opened the fair, and his vice president, Henry A. Wallace, closed it. Large corporations, as well as a special endowment from the Illinois State Legislature, supported the festival. The black colleges trucked in elaborate exhibits, reassembled at the state fairground. Every kind of musical performer, including concert artists, jazz bands, and choirs, and displays and floats glorifying black contributions to the nation, bunched on the promenade at 47th Street. Howard University librarian Dorothy Porter selected the books for the literature exhibit, and Horace Cayton arranged the showcase. After more than forty years of economically, socially, and psychologically devastating racial apartheid, black American institutions, coupled with some philanthropic giants, had rallied. This was a new development, and the writers, protesting and imagining a new world, took the first steps.

The brilliant perpetual student Horace Cayton bridged the divide between University of Chicago academics and the South Side artists. Cayton brought the races together, brokered power, and provided the crucial organizational energy that helped anchor "social" to "realism" during the World War II years. He had arrived in Chicago in 1931 from Seattle, Washington, and possessed a famous pedigree. He was the grandson of Hiram Revels, a Mississippi Negro who in 1870 had taken Jefferson Davis's old seat in the U.S. Senate. Cayton's father, Horace, Sr., had risen up from slavery to become a newspaper publisher. Cayton himself had seen something of life by the time he got to Chicago. He had been to reform school for robbery; worked across the Bering Sea as a ship's mess man; and served as a police officer while finishing college at the University of Washington. He capped what was for many Americans the Roaring Twenties of inebriation and libidinal release by marriage to a white woman. Then he went to the University of Chicago to work with the famed American sociologist and race relations expert Robert Park.

In the sociology department at Chicago, Cayton had taken classes with Park and Louis Wirth, the well-known pioneer of the study of ethnic immigrants adjusting to American cities. Cayton learned the mantra of the Chicago School analysis of race relations: contact, competition, conflict, accommodation, and, assimilation. In Park's theory, the hope for African Americans lay in the future assimilative stage; Park suggested that such vicissitudes as enslavement, subordination, and exploitation were part and parcel of the accommodative phase, but that the final result was ineluctable. Park had written that "racial barriers may slacken the tempo of the movement; may perhaps halt it altogether for a time," but the artificial dams against racial assimilation "cannot change its direction; cannot, at any rate reverse it."[3] At the outset of perhaps the bleakest era of American history, an economic depression lasting more than ten years and one that spelled devastation especially for vulnerable black workers, Cayton staked himself to the optimistic philosophy of progressivist social science. Park believed that conflict would occur during the different stages, but that the ethnic progression from one stage to another, and geographically in the city from one zone to the next, was inevitable.[4] The optimistic theory predicted upward social-class mobility.

With relationships to Park, Wirth, and another Chicago graduate and pioneer black statesman, Charles Johnson, Cayton landed a job as researcher for Secretary of Interior Harold Ickes and academic posts at Tuskegee and Fisk. Cayton successfully applied for a Julius Rosenwald Fellowship, the primary body of private funds enabling blacks to complete degrees in higher education or creative projects. In 1939 he and George S. Mitchell published *Black Workers*, while he served for three years as the only Negro director of a Works Progress Administration research project, housed in the basement of the Good Sheppard Community Church on the South Side of Chicago. As supervisor of District Three of the WPA, he enabled more than twenty monographs studying black Chicago in fine detail and published essays sifting through the problems of urban adjustment among black Chicagoans.

Energetic, witty, and a nonstop race man, Cayton had more in common with fact-finding realist fiction writers than with the bureaucratic-minded professors. He stepped away from the road open to him as either an academic or public policy consultant in favor of another calling: social work. In early 1940 Cayton accepted an appointment as executive director of the Good Sheppard Community Center at 5120 South Parkway, renamed the Parkway Community House, and the major outreach center devoted to improving the social, educational, and recreational lives of Chicago's South Side blacks. A massive Greek revival mansion that overlooked Washington Park and which Cayton bragged required a ton of coal to heat every winter day, the Parkway Community House was unmatched by any other black-run institution in North America for size and comprehensiveness.[5] Cayton told the *Chicago Defender* his reasons for leaving academe. "Instead of sitting in an ivory tower and making my investigations, I am trying to do three things in a practical way," he began. "First, I am applying sociological principles to a particular place; second, I am working toward the greater participation of the Negro in American culture; and third, I can best be served by institutional, recreational, and welfare agencies, both white and black."[6] Although Cayton had to abandon a second Julius Rosenwald Fellowship and the remainder of his University of Chicago doctoral studies to take over the Parkway Community House, he continued to draw on and make available the resources of the sociology and anthropology departments to the South Side community. Within roughly a year of Cayton's directorship, the community center included a clinic for mothers, a birth certificate office, a relief bureau, a selective service office, an auxiliary serviceman's center, and the Henry George School of Social Service. Cayton put social service principles into action.

He also recognized the power of the arts in building and sustaining community life. Under his leadership, the Parkway became an artistic center of consequence on the South Side and in national black life by hosting readings and dance and theatric performances, and offering gallery space. Olive Blackwell began a Negro playwriting guild at the Parkway. Cayton attracted the young brilliant radicals to him. Bryn Mawr graduate Grace Lee, a Chinese American passionately committed to the cause of racial and economic injustice and bemoaning the June 1940 fall of France (and with it, to her, Western civilization), fled New York for Chicago that summer and sought out Cayton. "It was the turning point of my life," she recalled, thinking about the moment when she read a speech written by Cayton at a rally protesting the death of black GIs.[7] Prowling the hallways of his center in an ascot on festive occasions, Cayton regularly entertained Langston Hughes (who during the 1940s sometimes stayed at the center for several weeks at a time), Arna Bontemps, Paul Robeson, and Katherine Dunham. Politically progressive, black-managed, community-based social welfare agencies like the Parkway, which combined educational, vocational, and recreational features for twelve hours per day, were precisely the kinds of brakes on social unrest that prevented a major race riot from taking place in Chicago in 1943, as occurred in Detroit and Harlem and a dozen other places.

Cayton tied together the worlds of liberal philanthropy and black intellectual life, closing the distance between African American 47th Street and the nearby Julius Rosenwald Fund, the most important grant-giving body to African American intellectuals in the 1930s and 1940s. Directed by Edwin Embree, the Rosenwald Fund operated out of the Hyde Park Rosenwald Mansion, donated to the fund after Rosenwald's death in 1932 and about five blocks north of the University of Chicago campus. Born during the American Civil War to German Jewish immigrants in Springfield, Illinois, and one of the original managers of the Sears and Roebuck mail-order company, Julius Rosenwald took over the presidency of the company in 1909. He retired in 1924 and endowed philanthropic gifts of more than twenty million. An intimate of Booker T. Washington and a man concerned with racial justice in the United States and abroad, Rosenwald earmarked four million dollars for "Negro education and welfare," then constructed rural schools in the South under the general administration of Tuskegee during his early years of extensive private giving.[8]

Initially the Rosenwald trustees sought to develop primary schools and four university centers in the South as a means of improving the quality of black life. When the poor caliber of teaching in the schools became evident, the fund began to support both public libraries and fellowships that trained Negro educators. However, in 1928 the endowment was reorganized into a corporation and Edwin R. Embree, then general secretary to the Rockefeller Fund, became director of the Julius Rosenwald Fund at 4901 Ellis Avenue in Chicago.

What Joel Spingarn, the Jewish cofounder of publishing company Harcourt Brace, had meant to the early years of the NAACP and to the careers of W.E.B. Du Bois and James Weldon Johnson, Edwin Embree became to the black writers and intellectuals who began their careers in the 1930s and 1940s. Embree had graduated from Yale in 1906 and was the grandson of southern abolitionist John G. Fee, founder of Kentucky's Berea College, where Embree spent part of his childhood. Like Spingarn, he was an effective front-man working for African American interests in a hostile or indifferent public climate, with publishers and magazines, but he had the power of a large endowment at his fingertips.

Embree approached the issue of race and rights from the perspective of the South's best interests, and he defused antagonisms. He presented the cause of the Rosenwald Fund and interracial relations to the readers of *Atlantic Monthly* and *American Scholar,* and he tried even more thoroughly to present the work in several books: *Brown America* (1931), *Thirteen Against the Odds* (1944), and *Investment in People* (1949). Of his accomplishments, Embree was perhaps most fond of his leadership integrating American university faculties. He mailed personal entreaties to nearly one hundred college presidents asking them point-blank if they would, in hypothetical principle, hire a qualified Negro applicant. The letter's next page supplied the names of dozens of eligible professors. Beginning with Allison Davis's appointment at the University of Chicago in 1942, by 1947, forty-three white universities had appointed seventy-seven blacks to teaching posts.[9] When he had finished his career with the Rosenwald Fund, Embree published an analysis of American philanthropy called "Timid Billions" in *Harper's Magazine*. In the article, Embree criticized the major endowments for their extensive bureaucracies and general lack of vitality. He hoped to awaken slumbering charitable titans. "The real criticism is not that foundations are vicious, but that they are inert," he insisted.[11] Two years after the fund closed, Embree died of a heart attack at sixty-six.

The Rosenwald Fund had one unique feature that chiefly accounts for its anonymity in the twenty-first century. Unlike other large philanthropic endowments set up by Rockefeller, Mellon, Ford, Guggenheim, and Carnegie, which invested their principal and spent the profit of their interest on programs, Rosenwald required his agents to spend both principal and interest. The fund was designed to have an explosive impact for a brief run.

It did. For twenty years, from 1928 until the gift was exhausted and Edwin Embree shut the doors in 1948, the Rosenwald Fund contoured dramatic change in the literature produced on the American race problem. For much of the time the leadership core consisted of Embree, the renowned southern race-relations expert Dr. Will W. Alexander (1930–1948), and Dr. Charles S. Johnson (1934–1948). These three provided the direct administration over the distribution of fellowships to some 798 individual black Americans (excluding multiple awardees), a genuine intellectual and artistic elite in the United States. Additionally, Rosenwald was the first and, for a generation, the only major fund to include blacks on the board of directors.[10]

The Rosenwald Fund had not originally sought leadership in the development of black writers and artists. Its leaders set out to erect an educational infrastructure in the South within the confines of the segregated society. However, following the considerable diminution in value of Sears stock during the Depression years, a shrewd narrowing of the fund occurred. According to Embree, the board of trustees saw the transformation of U.S. society as requiring a shift in values and custom, as much an event of shifting attitudes as of changing material conditions.[12] So in addition to supporting fellowships that enabled black academics to finish their advanced degrees in the northern and western United States, the trustees decided to stake creative projects in the arts and literature.

At the beginning of the 1930s and the fellowship fund's first active years of service, most of the recipients, even in the creative field, were prominent black

educators and statesmen. The elder statesmen among black academics—
W.E.B. Du Bois, William Stanley Braithwaite, Kelly Miller, and James Weldon
Johnson—accounted for eight of the ten fellowships granted creative writers
between 1928 and 1934. Fund managers liked the recognition that achievement
in the arts provided. By the time of the 1934 annual meeting, the Rosenwald
Fund hoped to concentrate its resources "on a relatively small number of persons of distinctive or unusual promise who may be able to exert leadership in
Negro life."[13] By 1937 Embree formally organized the Division of Fellowships,
and immediately he and George M. Reynolds, director of fellowships until
1941, started to reward the younger talent who had proven their ability to gar-
ner public recognition. Until 1941 the division solicited the help of Guggenheim Fund secretary Henry Allen Moe to identify talented writers and artists.

In the 1940s the division entered its most radical phase and granted creative
writing fellowships to authors without published books. During this period,
William "Billy" Converse Haygood and his wife Vandi V. Haygood, who served
as acting director while her husband was in the U.S. Army in Europe, conducted much of the administrative work. In his early thirties when he took over
the administration of the fellowship program, Haygood, like administrators
R. R. Paty and Reynolds before him, had attested to his personal fitness for the
post of directing grants and fellowships for black educators and artists by working in the South. He had been librarian of South Georgia Teachers College, had
literary ambitions of his own, and went on to receive a fellowship himself before the fund closed. (White southern writers and academics seeking to relieve
racial injustice accounted for 538 of the Rosenwald awardees.)[14] Vandi Haygood was a habitué of the intercontinental interracial social milieu, which took
place at Mollie Moon's famous soirées at 940 St. Nicholas Avenue in New York,
and at Horace Cayton's community center in Chicago. Vandi Haygood's distribution of fellowships to Chester Himes and Ralph Ellison in the 1940s introduced a new scale of intimate social interaction between artists and administrators, blacks and whites. Charles Johnson believed in the new direction so much
that he called these artists of the 1940s, "a new group of superior mentalities."[15]
The awardees included the prominent Chicago social realists Frank Marshall
Davis, William Attaway, Arna Bontemps, and Margaret Walker. The Rosenwald
Fund's support of the "superior mentalities" contributed to an atmosphere on
the South Side that bubbled with artistic vitality.

Margaret Walker used the term "renaissance" to describe the beer- and
salami-fueled studio parties "held in smoke-filled rooms, with much intellectual or political conversation" that ended the 1930s in Chicago.[16] A couple of
years later, in the 1940s, Gwendolyn Brooks could also embrace a "party era,"
where she and her husband Henry Blakely "knew writers, knew painters, knew
pianists and dancers and actresses, knew photographers galore."[17] Neither poet

exaggerated. Brooks was of course thinking of writers like trailblazing dialect expert Fenton Johnson, Frank Davis, professional librarian Charlemae Hill Rollins, radio personality Richard Durham, *Negro Story* editor Alice Browning, award-winning journalist Era Thompson, the famed Chicago realist painters Eldzier Cortor, Charles White, Charles Sebree, Rex Goreleigh, and Margaret Burroughs, pianists like Earl Hines, Thomas Dorsey, and Margaret Allison Bonds, and dancers like Katherine Dunham.

The ferment in the arts had help from local institutions within the narrow geography of the South Side. The George Cleveland Hall branch of the public library, opened in 1932 and directed by Vivian G. Harsh, contained nearly forty thousand volumes that emphasized elements of black life. Harsh organized weekly discussions of books, published reviews, and established a great-books course, all designed to create, in the words of a Marxist-leaning librarian, "a newer approach to the scientific knowledge and intelligent appreciation of the Negro race today."[18] Harsh ushered neophyte but serious writers, like Gwendolyn Brooks and Margaret Burroughs, into her own office where she kept the most important volumes of black literature and history under lock and key.[19] The University of Chicago campus, with a library open to nonstudents, sprawled between 55th and 59th streets and enrolled energetic African American leaders in its graduate departments. In the late 1930s and early 1940s, the English department was home to graduate students Arna Bontemps and Frank Yerby; critic Ulysses Lee was in history. Katherine Dunham, Marian Minus, and St. Clair Drake were all pursuing advanced degrees in anthropology.

Less than a year after the emancipation celebration, a converted three-story mansion at 3831 South Michigan Avenue was transformed into the South Side Community Art Center and opened with a combination of municipal and federal support to provide gallery space for black visual artists. Immediately an affluent North Side white socialite and writer named Inez Stark organized a regular poetry class, gave out *Poetry* magazine subscriptions to members, and even invited them to her swank apartment in the Loop, where the doorman had to be upbraided for sending the South Side writers to the service elevator. The star pupil of the South Side Community Art Center's creative writing forum was Gwendolyn Brooks, who had been publishing poetry in Chicago papers since the mid-1930s.

The Marxists had a place of their own too, the Abraham Lincoln School on Oakwood Boulevard in the Loop, with its writers' club, a critics' den for the Bland brothers, Edward and Alden (who published the novel *Behold a Cry* in 1947). The Allied Arts Guild held Sunday morning breakfast meetings and included musicians, visual artists, personnel from the *Chicago Defender*, and the poets. Horace Cayton's South Parkway Community Center at 47th and South Parkway added its new buildings and opened up a newly refurbished center by

1942. After 1946 the offices of *Negro Digest* and *Ebony*, the glossy but nonmili-
tant John Johnson and Ben Burns popular magazines, occupied the two-story
brick building at 5125 South Calumet Avenue, off the rear corner lot shared
with the South Parkway Community Center. And Embree's Rosenwald offices,
where he often entertained over cocktails local and out-of-town writers, grant
recipients, policy wonks, and celebrities, was a short walk away. Chicago built
and sustained institutions and associations that enabled the production of the
new kind of assertive, intellectual black literature.

The gusto and spirit of the midwesterners in the Chicago arts movement of
1930s and 1940s was captured well by the pugnacious journalist Frank Marshall
Davis. Born in Kansas, Davis had attended Kansas State and then determined
to wade into the teeth of discrimination and prejudice. In 1931, at age twenty-
six, Davis took a job at the *Atlanta World* newspaper and stayed in Georgia for
three years before returning to Chicago. Bitterly resenting racial segregation,
Davis did not share the temperament of the black southern middle class.

He announced his own personal revolt in 1935 when he published *Black
Man's Verse*, a jolting book of social realist poetry. Leading the collection was
"Chicago's Congo," a defiant poem revealing the battle of a black man against
the racist environment. "I'm a grown up man today Chicago / My bones are
thick and stout / (when I moved to new districts bombing couldn't break
them)."[20] The poem's aggressive spirit was sunk in the reality of black urban
politics. Three years after the book came out, defiant Chicago realtor Carl
Hansberry actively resisted the exclusive residential covenants and did not
waver when confronted by bombs. In 1940 before the U.S. Supreme Court,
Hansberry successfully won a legal decision called *Hansberry v. Lee* that tore
apart the legal basis for racist covenants.

Davis's muscular poetic energy was more in keeping with the shop of the
working man than the salon of the literary artist. Priapic and brash, he wrote
his words with the kind of modernist zest and confidence that seemed unafraid
of risk and confrontation—and some might have said disregarded the concept
of tradition. He gloried in repeating the word "spermatozoa," and he understood his own fertility as his chief force against the sterility of a bygone era that
Davis believed denied him manhood and citizenship. Editors uniformly saw
his poetry as unpolished, but they did not miss the sharp claw of truth at the
center of his work.

Davis derided the lives that black artists were forced to endure with poems
like "Roosevelt Smith," an elegy to a black bard whose greatness is destroyed by
"conscience and the critics."[21] In the poem, a young poet dies trying to appease
the learned assessment of the professional reviewers. The poet-tasters doom the
black artist on account of their inexhaustible fronts of attack. Variously they
employ condescending praise; hostility for insufficient black "uplift"; scorn at

pretentious language; cries of unoriginality at the sight of classic forms; and finally the condemnation of too much African influence. Davis was in open revolt against the double standards of black and white critics. Adding to the unadulterated quality of protest and impatience in the book was the fact that Davis did not publish—may not have even tried to publish—with the mainstream New York houses. He brought out his books with Norman Forgue's Chicago outfit Black Cat Press.

Two years after his first book, and while working full-time with the Associated Negro Press, the black counterpart to the segregated Associated Press, he won the first Julius Rosenwald Fellowship for poetry and published another uncompromising volume, *I Am the American Negro*. In an introductory poem he compared his book to a meal of "coarse victuals / A couch of rough boards," an exultation of the common man's prideful meal and encompassing a Whitmanesque touch.[22] Though Davis himself seems not to have signed on the dotted line with the Communist Party until 1945, his work was exuberantly proletarian. In the 1937 volume, Davis again wrote in a straightforward and epic style about life, love, confronting racism, and the artificial sexuality of the middle class. If the work was not widely reviewed, it did one thing well: it restored the confidence of young black poets. Chicago seemed to do that, and its magic worked for more than one writer.

Effervescent, smart, and filled with energy, a teenage Margaret Walker had left New Orleans with her fifteen-year-old sister Mercedes, a concert pianist, to work their way through Northwestern University. The sinew and fiber of the southern professoriate who worked a numbing seven-day-a week schedule at the small black colleges, Walker's Jamaican father and mother were both professors at Mobile's Central Alabama Institute. Walker had finished New Orleans University (now Dillard) at sixteen, but a white teacher and Langston Hughes convinced her parents that she might develop if she could leave the South. The sisters enrolled at Northwestern, where their father had spent six summers to graduate with a master's degree in biblical literature. Her mother believed in Margaret's talent so much that she had paid to have her early teenage poetry published. When Walker proudly told her Chicago classmates of her accomplishments, she was embarrassed to learn that publishers paid writers for their work, not the other way around.[23]

Northwestern challenged the devoutly religious, shy, and penurious young woman. Walker carried average marks throughout her undergraduate career, but two moments stood out for her. She published her first poem in the *Crisis* in 1935, and she took a senior-year class with American Renaissance scholar Edward Buell Hungerford. With Hungerford, Walker found an advocate, and she worked meticulously to master the ranges of verse rhythm schemes in English poetry. Hungerford rewarded her with an "A." Walker studied in an Anglo-Saxon department at an Anglo-Saxon time. A year behind her and a year older was a Jewish transfer student from University of Chicago named Solomon Bellow, who changed his name to Saul, and who had such difficulty fitting into the English department in the mid-1930s that he changed his major to anthropology. A person who struck everybody with her earnest sincerity, Walker stuck to Hungerford and the English major, while, ironically enough, Bellow devoted himself to Melville Herskovits, whose "Myth of the Negro Past" idea and explorations in African cultural survivals were shaking up long-held beliefs regarding the value and existence of black American culture. The two writers may even have overlapped in Hungerford's fiction writing class.

The African-descended Walker had a keener dilemma than the existence of African cultural holdovers, such as her own physical survival in Illinois. But after searching for a job for nearly a year in Chicago, she began work on the Illinois branch of the Federal Writers Project in March of 1936.[24] Walker accepted a job on the project with several hundred manuscript pages of a Civil War novel she had begun in Hungerford's class, as well as considerable work toward an epic poem. Northwestern had given her the opportunity to hear Harriet Monroe, the founding editor and spirit of the Chicago-based magazine *Poetry*, and also enabled Walker to learn about the Yale poetry competition and prize. She worked toward these twin goals, but nothing was as profound as her six-month-long relationship with colleague and friend Richard Wright. He made things fit together for her.

After Wright's departure for New York in June 1937 and the folding of the magazine *New Challenge* shortly thereafter, Walker began taking pointers from *Poetry* editor George Dillon, who urged her to read the French Symbolists. With her fluency in French and German, soon she was immersing herself in Rimbaud, Baudelaire, Valery, and Mallarmé and running into Muriel Rukeyser, winner of the Yale poetry prize for *Theory of Flight*, at cocktail parties at the *Poetry* editorial offices. While areas of Chicago maintained segregation, the opportunities within the cultural sphere were more plentiful and less pretentious than in New York.

Walker was able to thrive in the writing groups, and in July 1937 she began working at her typewriter, producing the poem "For My People." Her officemate Nelson Algren read the poem and advised her to build up the conclusion. The ten-stanza poem was a tour de force, an elegant kind of protest-and-praise-song combined. The epic concluded with a much-quoted line that seemed to clench the militant defiance that marked the indignation of a new black generation. "Let the martial songs be written, let the dirges disappear," counseled the young poetess. In 1938 Dillon published her poem "We Have Been Believers," which continued the prosodic storytelling style of "For My People" and offered a Marxist critique of religious belief and forecast, "the long-suffering [will] arise." The same year *Opportunity* brought out "The Spirituals," and "Ex-Slave." In 1939, in a special WPA commemorative, the poem "The Struggle Staggers Us" was published. After a year and a half in Chicago, not Evanston, Walker was coming into her own.

But the Depression lingered, and even with what was something of a salary for Walker, eighty-five dollars a month, she decided that her prospects would be improved with an advanced degree. She went to the Writer's Workshop at the University of Iowa in 1939 and finished the degree after a year. In her later memoirs, she claimed the experience nearly killed her, and she collapsed after returning to her parents' home in New Orleans. Her thesis included the poems that made up the book-length volume "For My People," which Walker submitted for the coveted Yale poetry prize. She had collected twenty-six poems, a few of them prosodic and incantatory like the title poem, but several others dug out from the vernacular tradition, like "John Henry," "Bad-Man Stagolee," "Kissie Lee," and "Yalluh Hammah." Walker, the product of the same ambitious southern black middle class that produced Chester Himes, William Attaway, and Sterling Brown, turned fully toward the working class for her material.

In 1941 she accepted a post at Livingstone College in Salisbury, North Carolina. But Walker claimed the attention of the nation in another year. "Negro Girl Wins Yale Poetry Prize," ran the November 1942 *New York Times* byline. At twenty-three she had become the first African American and the youngest poet to win the prize. Yale published her book in its poetry series, and Walker was celebrated by the League of American Writers at a party at 13 Astor Place hosted by the Broadway satirist Donald Ogden Stewart.[25] The next year she held a creative writing fellowship at the artists' colony at Yaddo in Saratoga Springs, New York. Her friendship with Richard Wright did not survive the 1930s, but Walker certainly did.

The most distinguished black Chicago writer was the most low-key. The writer of the acclaimed 1931 novel of a black jockey *God Sends Sunday,* Arna Bontemps moved to Chicago from Los Angeles in the late spring of 1935 and enrolled in the Ph.D. program in English at the University of Chicago that fall. He had made his way west from the Oakwood School in Huntsville, Alabama, where the white principal had threatened to burn his books. In January 1936 Macmillan published Bontemps's best-received novel, *Black Thunder*, one of the earliest examples of serious black historical fiction. Certainly the emphasis that Bontemps placed on the activities of the Jacobins in late-eighteenth-century Virginia was meant as an analogue to the vibrant Marxism used by radical blacks in his own time. But Bontemps, who supported a large family, never promoted his work full-bore. At the peak of his artistic powers, between 1935 and 1938, he served as an instructor and later principal at the emotionally and intellectually conservative Seventh Day Adventist Shiloh Academy in

Chicago. Then, after 1938, he accepted a job as a supervisor on the Illinois Writers' Project.[26]

While working in the offices on Eerie Street on *The Negro in Illinois*, Bontemps met the proletarian novelist Jack Conroy, editor of *Anvil*, and began a collaboration that continued into the 1940s when the men used their project materials that were not included in *Illinois State Guide Book* and published several joint projects, including a 1945 book of African American migration called *They Seek a City*. The joint project would be one of the first actually treating the migration of African Americans to the urban North, and the practice of genuine interracial authorial collaboration was, at the time, groundbreaking. Bontemps, who wrote and published three novels in eight years, contributed to the bristling energy in Chicago that forcefully reshaped literary traditions and changed cultural boundaries. The young writer Frank Yerby captured another side of the midwestern spirit as well, when he reputedly told Conroy after he moved from Missouri, "You intellectuals go ahead and write your highbrow stuff. . . . I am going to make a million."[27]

The Negro in Illinois project received grant money and office space from the Rosenwald Fund. Bontemps, who went on to serve on the board of the foundation, won a Rosenwald Fellowship himself in 1938 to complete his novel of the Haitian Revolution, *Drums at Dusk*, published by Macmillan. Bontemps's second historical romance concentrated on a young creole in pursuit of a mistress and was a giant step back from the militancy of *Black Thunder*. He showed a curiously tempered racial vision, and the chief point of view of the novel was not from the heroic Toussaint L'Ouverture, but from a young white *amis des noirs* named Diron. It was as if Bontemps was hoping to entice the new liberal constituency in New York and Chicago with a historical allegory showing the deep cords of friendship and sensibility between whites and blacks, even during periods of uprising and dramatic change that swept away the old racial order. Bontemps may never have known that C.L.R. James published *Black Jacobins*, the remarkable account of L'Ouverture drawn from French records, the same year.

Arguably the technique of writing with a white protagonist misfired. While critics were friendly, Bontemps's book did not obtain the politically and socially serious notice from the Left that he had earned before. *Nation* and *New Republic* did not review him. He was opening up a new path, though, with a historical novel and romance that featured white and black characters and edged around black themes but pursued no obvious political agenda. If, by setting his second novel in the nineteenth century, Bontemps had "vastly benefited his message," then the move to the earlier historical period enabled more freedom, or so was the logic of the *New York Times*. "Contemporary social prejudices will not interfere here."[28] Bontemps only bided his time in Chicago during the end of the Depression era. He changed his major at the University of Chicago to library science in 1941 and left with a master's degree to take over the Fisk College library in 1943.

The most meaningful novel in the 1930s set among blacks in the midwestern metropolis was not written by a permanent resident. Certainly as much as Bontemps, Zora Neale Hurston, and George Wylie Henderson, the Maryland native Waters Turpin seemed to hold considerable promise and have his finger on the pulse of black folklife in the 1930s. Ten years younger than Bontemps, and twenty years younger than Hurston and Henderson, Turpin was the comer. He called his Chicago novel *O Canaan!* but before that, in 1937, he had, at twenty-seven, published an important first novel titled *These Low Grounds*. Handsome and athletic, Turpin had grown up on Maryland's agricultural eastern shore, and he had spent his earliest years not far from the farms where Frederick Douglass and Harriet Tubman had labored in bondage—and then escaped.

Although Turpin had a college degree from Morgan in Baltimore and, by 1934, a master's degree in English from Columbia, he also had been encouraged in his career by Edna Ferber, the author of the novel *Show Boat*, which became a Broadway hit, and later the novel *Giant*, which became a Hollywood film. Ferber had employed Turpin's mother Rebecca Henry as a domestic during his boyhood and adolescence, and the wealthy author paid for Turpin's education.[29] Turpin accepted portions of segregated black American life, such as his jobs at Storer College in Harper's Ferry, Virginia, and then, in 1939, at Lincoln College outside Philadelphia. But when Ferber insisted that he serve as a butler at her home during the summer intercessions, he refused. Instead of working in service, he mailed off his manuscript to Doubleday editor-in-chief Malcolm Johnson. His patroness was nonplussed: "I am startled to learn that Waters Turpin's new manuscript was sent in to your office. I didn't know that he was going to send it to you."[30] Turpin intended to stretch the regular assumptions of American society in the field of creative writing as well.

His first novel covered the terrain he knew best. *These Low Grounds* called attention to African America family life in the mid-Atlantic region, mostly Maryland's eastern shore, augmented by characters' jaunts into the cities of Baltimore and Philadelphia. Turpin's novel had nearly a dozen major characters—one of his weaknesses as a novelist—but the fragmentary nature of his narrative also reflected his determination to rescue black folk voices from oblivion, a hallmark of his generation. And something else: as with Henderson and Hurston, the chief centers of consciousness in the novel are women—antebellum era Martha, her postbellum daughter Carrie, and Carrie's youngest daughter, the cakewalking Martha. The chief among them is Turpin's Carrie, the swashbuckling heroine of *These Low Grounds*, a hard-drinking, lusty, and engaging matriarch who lives in a bordello, sings the blues, leaves a husband, and is shot by a tormented lover.

Toward the end of the novel, Turpin brings himself into the book as the character Jimmy-Lew, the son of young Martha, and who finally achieves the education that his ancestors dreamed of. The young "New Negro" Jimmy-Lew wants to become a writer and " 'tap the untouched literary material offered by that little-known section of the American scene'" and write a "[s]aga of achievement" based on the life his own family. Jimmy-Lew settles for marriage and a career as a teacher, though he shows his manly courage by rushing from Baltimore back across the Chesapeake Bay to prevent, unsuccessfully, a lynching, as his grandfather Prince had many years before.[31]

The liberal press complimented him by saying, "Turpin is a Negro who is a credit to his race," by which they meant that he opposed the scourge of lynching but did not vilify all whites in the process. Since the book was unafraid to admit to out-of-wedlock birth, gambling and drinking, shiftlessness among Negroes, and a degree of magnanimity among whites, Turpin was thought to have written with "remarkable and just and fair balance."[32] The Negro left wing was more critical. Ralph Ellison reviewed the book in *New Challenge* and labeled it an achievement but yet naïve, filled with "undigested lumps" of characters who were driven by "superficial motivation." Ellison thought that "realism" required a high mark of political seriousness and that Turpin was a bit too satisfied to simply entertain his reader.[33]

Two years later and while working on a doctorate in education at Columbia, Turpin brought out *O Canaan!* with Doubleday, the first novel describing the "great migration" of rural blacks to the urban North during the first thirty years or so of the twentieth century. His speed as a writer and the breadth of his interest seemed just short of miraculous. This novel directly dealt with the World War I era migration of the Benson family from Mississippi to Chicago—the "Canaan" of the novel's title. The Benson family moves from the southern working class into the ranks of bourgeoisie by way of bootleg liquor, hard work, and education, but the race riots of 1919 and the Depression devastate the family and stretch its members to survive. Turpin showed the souring of the migrant dream, though in leading characters like Joe Benson, the humbled patriarch of indomitable spirit, and his daughter Essie, he also strived to point to definitive black heroism.

While he used many of the techniques of raw naturalism—urban and rural dialects, an unflinching examination of prostitution, abortion, murder, and razor-fighting, bleak portraits of the slums and speakeasies—Turpin's book was more comfortably a romance novel. The novel concludes with the melodramatic marriage of Essie to one of the characters from Turpin's first book, Paul Prince. The plot ends with the young couple triumphing over the pain of an unnecessary abortion and economic hardship to renew their vows. It was love conquerors all. "There is no color line in Mr. Turpin's middle-class world," wrote the young critic Alfred Kazin, who seemed only mildly capable of understanding the book. Instead of the strife and persecution he expected, Kazin noted African Americans "who felt themselves alien to nothing but their past." Kazin found a sensibility different from Wright's stories of violent revenge and Hurston's tale of unsatisfactory love. "And though it is not the whole truth, it is true of Mr. Turpin's people; and the joy he takes in them, the love with which he has described them, compose his achievement."[34] The young black critic Ulysses Lee, working toward his advanced degree at the University of Chicago, was a bit more critical when he declared that the weakness of the novel, "true" and "revealing" though it might be, was yet again in the characterization. "[T]here is little of the real substance of living beings in Mr. Turpin's people. . . . They are all allegorical shadows, playing parts which might as well be labeled x, y, z."[35]

Lee's assessment was perceptive and accurate; Turpin had in fact driven to Chicago over the summer of 1936, collected oral histories from migrants, visited churches, and read newspapers to construct the basis of his tale. He had become convinced of the acuity of Wright's "Blueprint for Negro Writing," and, after the novel's appearance, sketched out plans to write three more books that would follow an African American family from slavery to the modern age in rich detail. He began work on a novel called *The Rootless* and tried in 1939 and 1940 to win fellowship support. In 1941 he landed a Rosenwald Fund grant, and although he finished his novel, it took more than fifteen years to publish the book.

Turpin's novels passed from view not only because he sprinted through his descriptions of his characters, but because, a year after Turpin's second book was out, Richard Wright published a book that dramatically reshaped the twentieth-century American cultural sensibility. With the *Story* prize and *Uncle Tom's Children* breaking new ground, Wright had opportunities beyond the *Daily Worker* and putting together copy for the New York division of the Federal Writers' Project. In late spring 1938 WPA national director Alsberg approved Wright's transfer to the project's creative unit where writers worked under their own supervision. Wright began full-time work on a novel. In April and June 1938 he was interviewed on the radio, speaking about literature and his ideas. After several years of rejected manuscripts, publishers were now eager for his work, and he had a shocking premise he wanted to develop. Wright's colleague in Chicago, Margaret Walker, kept him abreast of the trial of Robert Nixon, an eighteen-year-old black youth charged with rape and murder. She began sending him clippings of the lurid newspaper accounts, which contained headlines like "Brick Slayer Is Likened to a Jungle Beast: Ferocity Is Reflected in Nixon's Features."[36] Wright had moved in with a young interracial Communist couple in Brooklyn and sat down to work at a pace of ten pages per day, hammering out a gripping narrative of murder and redemption with touches of Dostoyevskyan psychological penetration. Within a year of publishing *Uncle Tom's*

Children, Wright had completed the manuscript of the book he was unwillingly calling *Native Son,* in lieu of a better title.

When he began structuring the text, Wright showed a renewed authorial boldness merited by the broad support he received. In March 1938 Harper editor Eugene Saxton contacted Eleanor Roosevelt, the nationally recognized champion of liberal causes, to secure an endorsement for *Uncle Tom's Children.* The wife of the sitting U.S. president took seriously the racial crisis. To her mind, the tensions that Wright had shown operating in a story like "Big Boy Leaves Home" could have been resolved if the white woman had kept a cool head and had not shrieked at the sight of black male nudity. In his own emotional life, Wright was moving, rapidly, beyond the repair available to Roosevelt when she read "Big Boy Leaves Home." But he had survived the South by hiding much of his inner fire and taking advantage of the shape of opportunity, whether or not he believed in the ideals of his supporters. Months later, Wright pursued Roosevelt to provide a letter of recommendation for the Guggenheim. He described his new work: "this book will deal with the problems of youth among an unassimilated portion of our population from a Negro point of view."[37] Wright's concern to show "unassimilated" black life from the "Negro point of view" revealed the heart of his concerns. Roosevelt supported him, and he won a Guggenheim in early 1939. The book Wright was planning would not enable Roosevelt to believe, as she had written to Saxton in 1938, that "little things bring such tragic results" and that a simple act of lucidity would make everything "so easily understood."[38]

A measure of Wright's success with *Uncle Tom's Children* was the gratitude he received from the politically progressive and well-trained black critics like Sterling Brown at Howard University. *Uncle Tom's Children* was a giant hit and shot in the arm because it came through the WPA publishing machine and received high praise in the press. Wright managed to pull off, at twenty-nine years of age and the only time in his career, the combined praise of his black constituents, center-leaning white liberals, and the far Left. Wright broke new ground as the chronicler of black defiance and hostility toward malevolent white oppression. Sterling Brown reviewed him for *Nation,* and Brown's attitude favoring the social realism and vigorous protest against racial injustice flared from the page. Like Zora Neale Hurston, who disliked the book and said so in *Saturday Review,* Brown granted that Wright might have "too coincidentally contrived" the tragedies at the core of each short story, and he recognized that nearly the complete effort of the narrator had been bent to describe the victim's point of view. But Richard Wright's placement of violence at the heart of his stories resonated with Brown as the profoundly right message at the exactly right time. Mob rule, lynching, and casual brutality were "the way in which civilization keeps the Negro in his place," Brown wrote. The man from Chicago was no dramatizer of sensationalism: "[H]e knows what he is writing about." Brown approved of Wright's narrative voice and the new literary philosophy unafraid to shock with bitterness and violence. Here was a "wisdom brewed of suffering."[39]

Brown advocated for Wright's work at an especially intense moment in his own career. In 1939 the Folger Fund at Vassar College brought Brown to participate in a conference on the problems of the South, where he read his poetry. Naturally, he lectured at places like Fisk, when the college held a memorial farewell for the dean of African American letters, James Weldon Johnson, who died in 1938. But there were the additional pressures that made his artistic output difficult. In April 1939, when "The Negro in Washington" appeared in the D.C. guidebook, a Republican congressman from Wisconsin accused Brown of being a Communist. Representative Frank Keefe leveled the charge because Brown had dared to include factual data concerning George Washington's stepson's conjugal relationship with a black woman in the early 1800s. Beginning a line of reasoning that would grow as more uncompromising demands for civil rights were made, Keefe charged "insidious propaganda" from "communistically inspired agitators" and tried to have Brown fired from Howard.[40] Brown admitted that there was a price for his role and his intellectual integrity. "[T]hough I laughed at the affair, there was a little drain on my energies."[41] The drain inevitably widened into a sewer.

Brown's resentment at the difficulty of conducting a professional intellectual life of course endeared him to Wright. Wright's chiliastic visions of racial Armageddon were rooted in the sullen meanness that lay right on top of the easy surface of black life, a perceptible animus fortressed by generations of bitterness. Brown's poem "Bitter Fruit of the Tree," which appeared in the *Nation* in August 1939, emphatically pronounced his views on that question. The poem revealed the narrator's slave-born grandmother, who is asked, told, and then finally ordered by her persecutors to accept the final ignominious dose of racial subordination: "not to be bitter."[42] Meanwhile, her children die and are sold off, and her husband is brought to the dust. This was precisely the kind of sentiment pouring out from Richard Wright at the end of the decade when his relationship with Brown flourished.

Brown had gotten to know Wright as a member of the League of American Writers, sometime between 1935 and 1936, when, in New York and to interracial audiences, Brown regularly offered lectures like "The Negro Character in American Literature." The lectures and *Opportunity* column resulted in two 1938 monographs in Alain Locke's Bronze Booklet Series, "The Negro in American Drama" and "The Negro in American Fiction." The books became minor classics of literary history and the sociology of literature. With these short critical volumes, the easygoing and unflappable Brown collected a tool-kit to dissect black stereotype and caricature in American culture, a chief preoccupation of African American literary studies for the next fifty years. Among those in the know, his techniques were heralded as groundbreaking and provocative. But the books were explicitly designed as primers, with discussion questions at the conclusion of chapters and an emphasis on breadth rather than depth.

Brown garnered few converts among the literary tastemakers. He wrote to Wright in early 1939, hoping for something different from what was. "[T]hanks for what you've done for booklets. I suppose it would be asking too much for you to do a review of them somewhere—say the *New Republic*."[43] Black writers kept angling after serious and left-leaning audiences. If they reached them, they faced a problem similar to Italian Marxist Antonio Gramsci's, who sat out the 1920s in prison and had to write his masterpiece, *Prison Notebooks*, in a code that could outwit the censors. How could American audiences regard the mighty odds under which black intellectual labor was conducted and see value in the indirect and ornamented language that black college professors had to use in the South? Other than by folklorist B. A. Botkin, who published a review in *Opportunity*, Brown's intriguing and long-standing analysis fell "unnoticed."

By 1939 the committed folklorist Brown had found in social realism and literary protest a new doctrine capable of capturing not only the beauty of artistic expression, but also a quite reputable manner of advancing a black political agenda. In the essay "The American Race Problem as Reflected in American Literature," Brown singled out the "new literary force" of social realism, while lamenting that so far it had made only an "incomplete impression on Negro writers."[44] He felt that only George Lee, author of *River George*, Frank Marshall Davis, and Richard Wright had made use of the new approach. These artists were correcting the concentration on lynching, passing, and carefree romance that tended to characterize the middle-class novel. The recognition of the power of the new technique became apparent to Brown not only because of Mike Gold and James Farrell dealing with the Jews and the Irish, but principally after he had exhumed a fairly elaborate and dense literary history of black characterization in American letters, stemming from the antebellum era.

There were other concerns that forced him to look seriously at the prose-centered social realist style. Brown had another book of poetry ready for publishers, but the most receptive, Doubleday, Doran, asked him to set it aside. Instead of poetry, they gave him a contract for a novel. Brown tried to comply with the industry's narrative demands by working on a memoir, and he wrote several chapters of his journeys into the South during the 1940s, but he never published the book. It would not be until 1980 that his book of poems, *No Hiding Place*, was published. In 2006 two black college professors published Brown's memoir *A Negro Looks at the South*, almost twenty years after his death.

The black critic whose intellectual labors would increase in intensity during the 1940s and who did achieve critical notice in 1939 was the Delaware-reared,

Brown University graduate J. Saunders Redding. Redding claimed birth into the society of polite and educated black elites. His parents had met at Howard University's Normal School in Washington, D.C., and three of his four grandparents had known freedom prior to 1865. Born in 1905, he had started Lincoln College outside Philadelphia and finished his B.A. degree at Brown in 1928. At school Redding developed an aloof personality, perhaps a kind of constitutional requirement, considering his strong drive for success. He needed reserve and great drive to outlast the excruciating experience of being black and in the Ivy League during the mid-1920s, where he qualified for Phi Beta Kappa but did not receive the award during his undergraduate years. He recalled the immense paradox that often lay within the psyche of educated blacks. "I raged with secret hatred and fear. I hated and feared the whites. I hated and feared and was ashamed of the Negroes."[45] The social-psychologist and avid member of the 1940s literati Horace Cayton summed up this conundrum with his famous "Fear-Hate-Fear" syndrome, a condition in which blacks were victimized by overt white aggression as well as their own failure to respond aggressively to remedy injustice.[46] Redding fought himself emotionally to contain these feelings that moved from his anger at racial injustice to shame at black impotence and then wallowing in self-loathing.

He had done well as an undergraduate at Brown and published in the student papers, which led to better things. An anomaly for his era, Redding successfully nurtured his talent without the help of the Communist Party or the Negro social uplift magazines, like *Crisis* or *Opportunity*. Self-consciously jaunty and cultivating his membership in the avant-garde, Redding had titled his first short story "Delaware Coon" and appropriately published it in France in 1930 in the famed modernist journal *transition*, edited by Eugene Jolas. Appearing in the journal that published Gertrude Stein's "Four Saints in Three Acts" and James Joyce's early chapters of *Finnegan's Wake* entitled Redding to a bit of acclaim. He had become a modern writer by way of a defiantly social realist treatment of black squalor in his native Wilmington, Delaware. Putting black life of the ghetto onto the written page was a modernist act of creation. The story, without humor or irony, treated the depraved lives of the sporting men, gamblers, switch-blade-wielding "snow sniffers," and "yaller" women who tattoo their men's names across their bosoms. Redding narrated the tale of sex, drunkenness, brawling, and misery to a soundtrack of Bessie Smith and Ma Rainey, bellowing and moaning about the finer points of procreation.

When Redding showed the story to his father, son of an ex-slave woman, a college graduate, and branch chief of the Wilmington, Delaware, NAACP, the elder Redding expressed dismay. J. Saunders Redding showed up in Harlem the same year and, on the merit of the story, was counted by some as a member of the Renaissance, a putatively welcoming gesture that dispirited the tyro

Redding for what it seemed to indicate about the caliber of the other talents. For blacks like Redding, the result of the regular, nonstop rejection by white society was an unrelieved sense of slight worth. He seemed to believe that only a scrub group could want him.

Redding then rode out the Depression to conduct work on an advanced degree at Brown and at Columbia in the early 1930s. He did not linger long enough in graduate school to apply for a Julius Rosenwald Fellowship, and his dossier was too good for him to have to submit an application for public relief and subsequently gain employment with the Federal Writers Project. Instead, he accepted John Hope's offer of a position at Morehouse immediately after college, but he lasted only a year in Atlanta after a student died "at the hands of persons unknown." (Howard's prominent sociologist E. Franklin Frazier had also left Morehouse, under duress and in 1927, after he had published "The Pathology of Race Prejudice."[47]) Redding went on to teach at the Louisville Municipal College, the State Teacher's College in Elizabeth City, North Carolina, and Southern University in Louisiana, and there began his first book.

In 1939 Redding published his sweeping academic treatment of African American literature, *To Make a Poet Black*. The book held black writers to a litmus test of national fidelity and racial celebration, similar to the ideology Redding had known as a child. He shunned the idea of closing ranks with other blacks merely because they were black, but he also offered an assertive condemnation of black writers like Jupiter Hammon and Phillis Wheatley. "[N]ot once did she utter a straightforward word for the freedom of the Negro," amounted to his judgment against Wheatley and in favor of George Moses Horton.[48] He expressed a similar view of Countee Cullen, whose work suffered from "numerous disclaimers of an attitude narrowed by racial influence."[49] The cheeky estimates sometimes encouraged people to go after Redding. When Sterling Brown's student Ulysses Lee reviewed *To Make a Poet Black*, he revealed dissatisfaction with a book that was "neither so broad nor so penetrating as the earlier studies" and definitely "lacking the critical force" of the year-old pamphlet studies by Sterling Brown. Lee and Brown themselves, who were in the process of editing the mammoth anthology of black writing *Negro Caravan*, thought that the principal home for black writers was in American literature, something that Redding would eventually endorse, but not for many years.

Redding's rather hard-headed estimate announced the presence of a new and proud formation: African American literature. Redding divided the group into four parts—forerunners, abolitionists ("Let Freedom Ring" he entitled the chapter), adjusters, and New Negroes—fairly standard designations. But his sense that black writers belonged in the Lost Generation of expatriates hinted at a new assumptive possibility. Black critics had always made oblique reference to the main critical trends, but even though he was advancing the formation of a new body of work—African American literature—Redding made transparent the association between black and white like never before. There was a great deal to be gained from the move. If the 1920s expatriates had written chronicles of failure of the human spirit and ended destructively, then the resurrection of literary distinction in the 1940s was an exciting model for black literature. In the hands of Faulkner, Hemingway, Dos Passos, and Steinbeck, the 1930s had produced literature of considerable social significance. If the two traditions were indeed one and the same, as thought Sterling Brown and his coeditors of the *Negro Caravan*, then the 1930s boded well for black American writing.

If Redding had seemed deluded in drawing together a formally coherent black tradition, or by suggesting that little-known, less-bought black poets and novelists had something in common with Ernest Hemingway, the publication in a few months of Richard Wright's novel *Native Son* vindicated him. *Native Son* had the crowning virtue of being on an entirely different tack from the sort that black writers had commonly taken before. The book dared to suggest that an unemployed black slum-dweller was the suitable subject of a densely interior psychological portrait and could carry the tragic weight of the heroes in Shakespeare's *Hamlet* or Dreiser's *Sister Carrie*.

Wright gambled that it was possible to take the story of a black twenty-year-old reform school thug from Chicago's South Side, have him murder two women, and give him the standing of a tragic hero by the conclusion of the novel. Thomas Wolfe had shown the possibility of the stoic black hero of violence, the war veteran Dick Prosser, in the short story "Child By Tiger," published in 1939. Wolfe's neighborhood black handyman goes on a murderous rampage but draws the eerie admiration of his white pursuers for his resolve and dignity. But what Wolfe had left to the mist of conjecture, available only in the sparse details of the naturalist story, became another original point of departure for Wright. The narrator, from the opening pages of the book, presented a detailed psychological portrait of the protagonist's central tension as the racial struggle in the United States. Until Bigger Thomas, never had a black character, let alone the center of consciousness for a serious novel, been allowed to experience unfiltered disdain for and fear of whites, at least without the release of humor.

Wright basically prevented a white reader from an overt sympathetic identification with Bigger. Within hours of meeting a liberal heiress named Mary Dalton, Bigger thinks to himself, "he did not understand them; he distrusted them, really hated them."[50] Throughout the course of the novel Bigger grows in terms of his own perception of himself, but his awareness has nothing to do with adjustment to the middle-class norms that readers might have anticipated. At the conclusion of the novel, Bigger sits on the edge of violence with his own lawyer, after being asked if he had either erotic or platonic feelings for Mary Dalton. He shouts back to his attorney, "*Like* her? I *hated* her! So help me God,

I hated her!"[51] From start to finish, Wright pointed to the recognition of anger and its potential eruption in violence as primal antidote to racism.

This was revolutionary in a way that Wright apparently had not intended. None of the black writers who followed Wright's naturalist style over the next twenty-five years—Ann Petry, Willard Motley, Philip B. Kaye, Frank London Brown, and Claude Brown—dared to conclude their novels without adjusting their protagonist to some identifiable code of Western morality. The exception was Chester Himes.

Wright's revolt in *Native Son* did not stop with the idea that violence began liberation. He dirtied the work of mainstream philanthropy, embodied by the NAACP-supporting Dalton family, who dream of shaping Bigger into a new man by "inject[ing] him" into a "new environment," but who continue to profit from and sustain the slum conditions that dominate Bigger's possibilities.[52] The novel's melodramatic courtroom finale makes plain the malevolence of the thin liberal commitments of Mr. Dalton, the purported victim. Wright's liberal character Max, a communist-style lawyer, levies the social indictment in a series of sermons for the jury.

> The relationship between the Thomas family and the Dalton family was that of renter to landlord, customer to merchant, employee to employer. The Thomas family got poor and the Dalton family got rich. And Mr. Dalton, a decent man, tried to salve his feelings by giving money. But, my friend, gold was not enough! Corpses cannot be bribed! Say to yourself, Mr. Dalton, "I offered my daughter as a burnt sacrifice and it was not enough to push back into its grave this thing that haunts me."
>
> And to Mrs. Dalton, I say: "Your philanthropy was as tragically blind as your sightless eyes!"[53]

The boldest outright denunciation levied at white society from a black writer prior to Wright's books had been Langston Hughes's *The Ways of White Folks* (1934) and Du Bois's romantic epic *Dark Princess* (1928). Blacks had depicted individual whites as malevolent, but not since Charles Chesnutt's enormously unpopular *Marrow of Tradition* had something close to the entire loom and weave of American society been written of as a social fabric with an obvious and growing tear. Part of the strategic reason black writers had not spent much time traducing the American way lay in the fact that blacks were thought regularly oversensitive to prejudice. The topic of social equality for blacks itself was unpopular. As President Roosevelt had explained to NAACP head Walter White in 1935, to support vigorously a black cause like a federal antilynching bill was too risky.[54]

Wright's confidence in this area had a unique source. His agent, Paul Reynolds, Jr., asked him if he had ever read Booker T. Washington's famous bildungsroman of African American life, *Up From Slavery*. Wright replied with amusement, "I escaped being educated in Negro institutions and never quite got around to reading those books everyone is supposed to read."[55] Wright's "escape" fed the qualities of anger and resentment that black writers had not channeled previously for commercial success. Unlike Washington, who in the first three chapters of the 1901 autobiography repeatedly declares that he has purified himself from any residue of "bitterness" toward whites for his years of slavery, four decades later Wright would exalt in his own prideful spite. In *Native Son*, Wright was anti-Aristotelian, deliberately in opposition to art-as-catharsis. People had told him that *Uncle Tom's Cabin* made them weep. Now, he vowed, "no one would weep over it; it would be so hard and deep that they would have to face it without consolation of tears."[56]

He was on the mark. When his good friend Nelson Algren read the book, he confided to Wright that "I don't think any white person could read it without being frightened or angry at the end."[57] With Wright's popular and well-publicized works, a new form of racial and public intellectual consciousness emerged. Rebelliousness and outrage no longer were confined to the halls of the Oddfellows, Freemasons, or A.M.E. churches. White writer Bucklin Moon recorded the rapture of the book that opened wide his own opportunities as a writer when, in 1947, he made one of the colossal claims frequently connected to the book: "Anyone who has read Richard Wright's *Native Son*," said Moon, "has probably come as near to an approximation of what it is like to live in a racial ghetto as possible."[58] Wright was the first to present the American nation with this sort of experience. He learned that the nation was ready to hear him.

In spite of his message, Wright owed the book's commercial success to the orchestration of the inimitable American Fordist bourgeoisie, in the form of the Book-of-the-Month Club. Created by New York advertising executive Harry Scherman in 1926, the Book-of-the-Month Club recognized the profitability of direct subscription by mail over the anarchic democracy of the bookstore. By 1929 club membership stood at 110,588, and it was double that number by the time Wright published his novel.[59] The club legitimated its choices of the "best" available contemporary books by appointing a selection board, chaired by Henry Seidel Canby, founding editor of the *Saturday Review of Literature*. Canby, raised a Quaker and educated at Yale, believed that he was protecting Americans from the threat of modernist experimentation, technocracy, and commercialism; in their place he strove to enforce the purportedly timeless values of the liberal arts.

In the words of Farrar Strauss publisher John Farrar, the book club benefited the public by offering up books that were "daring," "unusual," or ones by new authors that "might entirely have escaped public attention."[60] With *Native Son*, they took on their second work by an African American writer. The other judges, including Heywood Broun (prominent defender of Sacco and Vanzetti) and Vermont's Dorothy Canfield Fisher, were excited by Wright's nonstereo-typical representation of the black poor, herded into ruin in the large urban America metropolis. While the club's board supported Wright, they asked him to remove anything that might be considered lewd, particularly a scene where Bigger masturbates to newsreel footage of the white heiress he will accidentally murder. This was all that Wright might have imagined, relative to good fortune, and probably the reason why he worked diligently to capture the support of the club and allowed them to shape his book to conform to their version of American tastes.

He revised to appease the sensibilities of mainly a single person. Dorothy Canfield Fisher had impeccable credentials as a racial liberal; nearly thirty years older than Wright, she had studied at the Sorbonne and written a novel in 1939 called *Seasoned Timber* that criticized prejudice against Jews. She endorsed *Native Son* by writing the book's introduction. However, in her introduction she directly compared Bigger to an animal, a move that must have made Wright queasy. "*Native Son* is the first report in fiction we have had from those who succumb to these distracting cross-currents of contradictory nerve-impulses, from those whose behavior-patterns give evidence of the same bewildered, senseless tangle of abnormal nerve-reaction studied in animals by psychologists in laboratory experiments."[61] Again, Wright was prepared to accept the support, whether misintended, naïve, or begrudged, and he calculatedly used a certain sensationalism so that even with concessions, his work struck with force.

Even so, the commercial success of *Native Son* during the season of Nazi military triumph was astounding. If *Uncle Tom's Children* had been a "critical success," enjoyed by fellow writers and Communists, reviewed respectably, but appealing to only a small fraction of the public, *Native Son*'s response was light-ning in a bottle. Wright had had his manuscript ready by the spring of 1939 and then worked it through editing and censoring to gain Book-of-the-Month Club approval. The result was that his publishers at Harper's were able to take full advantage of the critical networks and press prior to the publication. The re-views built up a great deal of momentum when the book was published on March 1, 1940. A week later, Harper's ran adds claiming, "Public stampedes bookstores for 'Native Son': Richard Wright's novel is a complete sell-out 3 hours after publication."[62]

For several weeks, *Native Son* was a blockbuster novel that set sales records at Harper's—200,000 copies in three weeks. The book company had preordered over 200,000 copies of the book to satisfy Book-of-the-Month Club demand, and one week after the book's release bookstores reordered 13,719 copies. After ten days the number had grown to 20,500. Two months after publication the book was still selling strongly in Chicago. By the second week in May, Wright had sold 250,000 total copies of his book. But a month later, by June 15, he was off of the best-seller lists, never to return, and he never closed on Richard Llewellyn, author of *How Green Was My Valley,* which sold at a clip from winter through summer of 1940 at about 2,000 copies per day. At the end of the year, booksellers would talk mainly of Hemingway's *For Whom the Bell Tolls* and Thomas Wolfe's *You Can't Go Home Again*; industry journal *Publisher's Weekly* did not feature Wright as a best-selling author of 1940.[63] Wright proved two things: black American themes could create a national buzz, meriting their adoption by the major presses; and Negro writers were still a world apart, too "special" in their direction to become blockbuster sellers.

The book did not make Wright rich, compared with his white peers. Although he earned $28,000 that year off book royalty income, he would have to continue writing for his living.[64] Wright was hit hard by federal income tax, and his agent Paul Reynolds went on to devise a new method of staggering royalties over time so that future writers would avoid being thrust into the highest income brackets for the relatively brief time of royalty payment for book sales.[65] Despite these caveats, the Mississippi-born and Chicago-bred writer had ranged far. The financial success meant that it was now possible to conceive of a black writer who spoke his own views, independent of foundations, educational and religious institutions, political causes, or races of people.

Native Son was a benchmark moment especially for two constituencies whose waning power can be traced to that moment: the traditional caste-derived black middle class and the Communists. The intellectuals, writing in *Crisis, Opportunity*, and Wright's hometown *Chicago Defender*, applauded the book's exposure of social conditions. James Ivy at the *Crisis* called it "the greatest novel written by an American Negro,"[66] and Sterling Brown at *Opportunity* believed that Wright's book would "silence many of the self-appointed 'white interpreters' of the Negro."[67] The *Defender* was unembarrassed to hope for a miracle. The book would "not only focus attention upon the evils," but "transform a rotten social, economic system into a living democracy for all."[68]

Arna Bontemps—the kind of black American who could move from Chicago to Nashville in 1943 for work and better quality of life—convinced himself that the "political" theme caused Wright to sacrifice an even greater level of popular success.[69] By 1940 Bontemps would be decidedly cautious. Reviewer Lillian Johnson of the *Baltimore Afro-American* newspaper showed the implicit threat of the novel with her title " 'Native Son' Is a Personal Triumph but of No Value to a Nation."[70] The leadership group had struggled to understand the importance of social movements among the overwhelming majority of unskilled African American laborers and semiskilled domestic workers. The key to Marcus Garvey's improbable success had eluded them, and into the 1940s the continued prominence of religious mystics like Father Divine and Daddy Grace shocked and mystified them. Partially because of their ties to wealthy philanthropists, a strident critique of social class typically was out of the question. Wright, son of a sharecropper and himself a junior high graduate, signaled the new wave of chaotic possibility that migration and Depression had made possible.

And then, even though the novel's most sympathetic character was a Communist, Wright's book represented an abrupt departure from the optimistic propaganda that the party wanted to see during the span of the Nazi–Soviet pact, the months of its renewed Black Belt thesis and nonintervention stratagems. Ben Davis, the intellectual and political leader of the Harlem branch of the Communist Party, wrote a long review that praised Wright for revealing the environmental conditions of the downtrodden black poor but harangued him for refusing to show more "progressive" black characters and more valiant Communists. Throughout the review, Davis thumped that "the Communist Party is the only organization profoundly interested in relieving the terrible plight of the Negro people."[71]

New Masses editor Samuel Sillen energetically endorsed the book on two occasions, once commenting on the reviews that the book received and a week later taking apart the symbol of Bigger Thomas. But he also showed the sizable difference in opinion between liberal whites and liberal blacks. For the Cleveland writer Chester Himes, Wright's characterization of Bigger Thomas was simply extraordinary. The key scene he identified took place when Bigger looked up to see a plane in the sky on a Chicago morning. The episode showed a human being seeing and feeling, "the beauty and importance of the vast, eternal, changing mystery of life." A convicted felon himself, Himes understood perfectly well what Wright was getting at in the book. The murder of Mary Dalton was accidental, but Bigger had to lay claim to the identity of murderer to transcend the guilt that society had ensnared him in since birth. And then in earnestness, Himes asked his reader, "But don't you feel the awful wrongness in a social system wherein any living human being has to believe that he has [to] commit a gruesome murder to ensure his identity as a human being?"[72]

The new breed of young blacks—exposed to college, seeking Marxism and relationships with Communists but not in awe of them, highly critical of white liberals and the traditional black middle class, and violently impatient with segregation—converted *Native Son* into a catalyst for political organization. At the spring 1940 National Negro Congress in Washington, D.C., and in spite of the national political scuffle that ended with A. Philip Randolph resigning from the organization, young African Americans used the novel to stimulate the buzz of political conversation—and conversion. Ralph Ellison, one of the delegates from New York, wrote to Wright to describe the thought-currents generated by the book, in spite of the attempts by some black Communists to finagle it into the current "line." In public forums on culture, black women and men were saying aloud that Wright had articulated their experience as Negroes. Sterling

Brown reported that the book was being debated in "grills and 'juke joints' as well as at 'literary' parties, in the deep South as well as in Chicago, among people who have not bothered much to read novels since *Ivanhoe* was assigned in high school English."[73] Ellison, a young Marxist radical, decided that Bigger's "indignation"—the violent eradication of the idea of moral and ethical justification in favor of Marxist "necessity"—was Wright's paramount achievement.[74]

By smashing the myth that all blacks needed to do to gain total freedom in the United States was move to the North, Wright naturally fell out with reigning liberal pieties. But his sod-busting went in another fertile direction. He proved himself unusually able at defending his work, and he renewed a tradition of defiant public black intellectual comportment that redounded to the nineteenth-century tailor and militant pamphleteer David Walker. And more so, Wright's voice appeared on newsstands all over the country. If his 1937 essay "The Ethics of Living Jim Crow" had been uncompromising enough to wind up on the desks of segregationist members of Congress, the essays he wrote in 1940 reached a broader audience and sounded just as loud. It was the first time in modern memory that a black writer had the advantage of shaping his audience's reception of a popular work.

At the Harlem branch of the New York Public Library (the modern-day Schomburg Library) in the spring of 1940, Wright gave a lecture explaining the genesis of Bigger Thomas, after an invitation by the library's curator Lawrence Dunbar Reddick. Reddick was an inspirational figure, a University of Chicago–trained historian who also broke segregation barriers by giving lecture courses in black history at City College. His pioneering work in Kentucky and Missouri in 1934 led to one of the early models for collecting the interviews of ex-slaves, picked up by the Federal Writers' Project. Wright turned in a performance so memorable that *Saturday Review of Literature* published a condensed version of his talk on June 7 under the title "How Bigger Was Born."

In July Wright published the full version of the piece in *Harper's*. Here was a Negro artist who had produced his own preface, a black writer who required no vouchsafing from a member of the white elite. Alain Locke, neither a prolific writer nor an inspirational leader, but who had a remarkable facility to gauge accurately the direction of literature and ideas, properly recognized in Wright a new threshold of integrity in the black writer, one that he thought both Langston Hughes and W.E.B. Du Bois had failed to show in their respective autobiographies, *The Big Sea* and *Dusk of Dawn*, also published that year. Locke had thought *Native Son* important as social realism and for putting up a portrait to compete with those done by Erskine Caldwell, T. S. Stribling, and William Faulkner. But he called the essay "How Bigger Was Born" "a great critical document."[75]

The most vicious scrap over the novel took place in the pages of the *Atlantic*, where Wright revealed his muscular wit. During the era of legal segregation, the American upper-class magazines tended toward three points of view. *Harper's* was the most liberal and proved it in 1938 by publishing the young writers Thomas Sancton and Bucklin Moon, who became the most vocal whites advancing liberal racial policies in the 1940s. *New Yorker* held the earthy middle ground of honesty, contempt, and pity and devoted a fair amount of ink to black Americans throughout the 1930s, including a three-part spread on Father Divine. But their attitude, which Horace Cayton went on to call "super-sophisticated" was typically best characterized as indifferent.[76] For example, in 1936 when writing about the Philadelphia-born contralto Marian Anderson, *New Yorker* used the insulting term "pickaninny."[77] Its profiles and short stories were indulgently sympathetic on the surface, but, until *Native Son*, with the smirk of caricature never far behind.

Atlantic was most solidly mired in nineteenth-century sentimentality and local color portraits of African Americans. It was in the rear guard of issues of racial justice, mainly because it retained the formula of appointing a white "southern liberal" to provide its racial commentary. The magazine steadily regarded the biracial character of the southern states through the eyes of David L. Cohn, a heavy-set journalist who spoke in preservation of the old magnolia traditions. Cohn obviously did not see himself with pitchfork and horns. The outspoken conservatives, like Mississippi senator Theodore Bilbo, who published that summer "An African Home for Our Negroes," called for the forcible removal of black Americans.[78] Alongside white liberals like Virginius Dabney, Mark Etheridge, and Hodding Carter, men who knew the depth of white supremacist attitudes, David Cohn believed that it would take better than fifty years before the legal enforcement of racial segregation could begin to relax and the U.S. Constitution could be enforced. But the canard of biological inferiority was the true source of his pessimism about change in the South. Cohn believed that the laboring class of blacks from the rural South were childlike and could advance only if they outgrew what he had determined was a system of comfortable patronage provided by southern landholders. "Delta Negroes are people without a culture," he had written in 1937. "They have not acquired the culture of whites, but merely ape their worst qualities. . . . if the rural Negro is ever to arrive at economic manhood, he must learn to forgo the soft pleasures of paternalism."[79]

For Cohn, Richard Wright was basically in masquerade, an ungrateful runaway metayer who had focused his preternatural barbaric inclinations on a novel that, in the words of the review's lead sentence was "a blinding and corrosive study in hate." Here was the argument, essentially, of reverse racism. Cohn thought that the course of contemporary history was exceedingly favorable for blacks, and that rebel attitudes like Wright's were simple folly. "Justice or no justice, the whites of America simply will not grant to Negroes at this time those things that Mr. Wright demands," the essay concluded.[80]

By June 1940 Wright, still calling himself "proletarian," had adopted the armor of sarcasm to deal with a caricature artist like Cohn. "I Bite the Hand That Feeds Me," Wright titled his essay. His problem as a realist writer interested in the flaws of society still lay in presenting raw experience about a psychologically charged public topic without having the evidence of the emotional tension surrounding the subject matter used as the chief argument to keep the taboos in place. He resented (and exposed) the fratricidal ethnic politics of suffering implicit in his being scolded by an American Jew. Wright called on the examples of Russia and Mexico to refute the conclusion that the race problem was impassable. He found himself needing to tell Americans how the book should be read. Bigger had been neither an endorsement of contemporary race relations nor an anarchist's cookbook. "In *Native Son* I tried to show that a man, bereft of a culture and unanchored by property can travel but one path . . . emotionally blind rebellion."[81]

To the whites who had reacted to claims that the book endorsed hatred, Wright showed the way to the dangerous frontline of the debate concerning the ongoing oppression of African Americans. Every generation of American blacks had worked to develop a cadre of intellectuals to explain the unique plight of the slaves and their descendents to the American ruling class and to fellow blacks. In 1940 Richard Wright strode to the rostrum. Finally—perhaps not since the 1845 appearance of Frederick Douglass's *Narrative*—a book had emerged that accomplished in the field of the public sphere the work that needed to be done. Wright's greatest asset lay in the fact that he did not subsist on an aesthetic diet of art alone, nor did he operate as only a skilled propagandist who titillated the middle class or the Left. He laid broad claim to the field of American public life. At bottom, *Native Son* introduced the spirit of transformation to American cultural politics.

CHAPTER FIVE

Bigger Thomas among the Liberals (1940–1943)

The productive national discussion of Richard Wright's work was only one example of the enriched liberal climate in 1940. In that year, the Common Council for American Unity founded the journal *Common Ground*, to "create among the American people unity and mutual understanding," to "overcome intolerance and discrimination," and to assist immigrants and their descendents with the "special problems of adjustment."[1] Around the same time as it brought Swedish social scientist Gunnar Myrdal to the United States, the Carnegie Corporation funded *Common Ground* and arranged for the journal's printing by Princeton University Press. Louis Adamic, a forty-one-year-old immigrant from what was then Yugoslavia, was council president and journal editor. Adamic had written so successfully and frequently of his ethnic experience and the composite ethnic character of the United States in books like *Native's Return*, *My America*, and *From Many Lands* that President Roosevelt invited him to dine with British Prime Minister Winston Churchill at the White House. *Common Ground* ran for nearly ten years and regularly carried the fiction and essays of black writers and reviewed their books, placing these works in a context of multiple ethnic narratives. Black critic J. Saunders Redding was pleased enough with magazine to say, "I am not sure that there is another magazine in America which has so uncompromising an editorial policy."[2]

Adamic picked from among the well-respected and least radical of the liberal intelligentsia to cement the idea of America as a functioning multiracial and multicultural affair. Zora Neale Hurston, George Schuyler, literary biographer Van Wyck Brooks, historian Arthur Schlesinger Jr., poet and dramatist Archibald MacLeish, and liberal journalist Carey McWilliams were among his best-known contributors. In terms of their fiction, the journal rarely devoted itself to attacks on the color line. Its most regular fiction artist was St. Louis author Fannie Cook, whose reputation relied on her touching portraits of black domestic servants in short stories like "A Killer's Knife Ain't Holy" (1942), "Seeds Without Soil" (1943), and "Mothers" (1946). Like a garrulous neighbor, Cooke retained an overly familiar "folksy" quality in her writing that would seem a rather unsophisticated residue of racism in the period that followed. For her era, her willingness as a white woman to go among the rough and tumble black working class was thought remarkable, if a touch unseemly.

If it drew from the most prominent of the anticommunists, *Common Ground* walked in step with Popular Front sentiment. But this carried burdens of responsibility. In the summer of 1941 Archibald MacLeish, librarian of Congress for two years, used his stature to emphasize the new liberal ideals. "There was a time—and it was not so long ago either—when people talked about something they called the Negro Problem in America or the Jewish Problem in America or the Japanese Problem in America," he intoned. "The idea apparently was that the Negro Problem was a problem for Negroes and the Jewish Problem a problem for Jews. . . . Good Americans regretted the existence of problems of this kind. They avoided talk about them whenever they could. But personally they weren't much bothered. It was none of their concern." He emphasized the point in a four-word paragraph, "That time is past."[3]

The shared agreement between a Social Register man like MacLeish and a journal headed by an immigrant funded by one of the country's richest private endowments and published at one of America's most prestigious private universities marked an obvious program for public racial tolerance. When war began MacLeish added to his responsibilities director of the Office of Facts and Figures, and he started shaping public consensus. Among his tasks was to rein in African American dissent. In March 1942 he called black newspaper editors together and chastised them as "defeatists," demanding that they lessen calls for racial equality during wartime.[4] Now that MacLeish had acknowledged the benign neglect, he wanted no further reports of discrimination or unrest. Thus, despite *Common Ground*'s rhetoric of good intentions, in 1940 the typical young black writer, like Marian Minus, Chester Himes, or John Henrik Clarke, was still faced with only Communist front groups or racial uplift magazines to publish their work.

The new journals that took a progressive and liberal view on race relations were not confined to the wealthy philanthropic trusts. Atlanta University produced a new magazine specifically designed to approach the new world of race relations in 1940. *Phylon,* edited and named by W.E.B. Du Bois, then seventy-three, and his coeditor and protégé Ira de A. Reid, paid homage to the school's famous studies from 1897 to 1914. "This quarterly review proposes to study and survey the field of race and culture, and of racial and cultural relations. It uses both designations more or less interchangeably; because it would emphasize that view of race which regards it as cultural and historical in essence, rather than primarily biological and psychological."[5] The journal pledged new views, especially in the social sciences, but quickly included criticism and belles-lettres in its purview. Bertram Woodruff published the journal's first literary criticism, "The Poetic Philosophy of Countee Cullen," in the third number of 1940. Fairly quickly the journal built a standout reputation. Nor did the editorial situation remain stable for long. Du Bois was dismissed from the university in 1944 and

Reid took over the journal, until he left Atlanta University, one of Embree's success stories, for predominantly white Hanover College in 1948.[6]

But the propaganda-like racial liberalism of *Common Ground* as well as the academic tabulations of *Phylon* were by-products of a far more radical reaction. The *Native Son* effect—really the Bigger Thomas effect—stimulated an enormous growth in consciousness in American audiences and publishers. The black critics could not help but want Bigger to smash the lurid stereotype of Uncle Tom and Aunt Dinah, which they found insulting. Bigger did replace the stereotype of Uncle Tom, and his brand of devil-may-care activism quickly made the techniques of patient black social uplift and the journals that carried the theme, like *Opportunity*, outdated.

What *Opportunity* had meant to the 1920s and 1930s it could not mean to the 1940s. To begin with, war rationing hurt the journal's ability to get paper. And the journal still hoped to put America first. Elmer Carter revealed the conservative sensibility in the early 1940s when he rejected the short story by the unpublished Harlem writer John Henrik Clarke. "I am sorry to have to return this story to you," Carter wrote back to Clarke. "I am distinctly in favor of having stories with good endings—not tragic frustration—for *Opportunity*."[7] Soon the longtime editor Carter resigned, and by 1943 the monthly magazine had become a quarterly. The journal closed its doors in 1949. New talent managed to get in the door during the first years of the war, continuing in the rich social realist tradition of Marita Bonner Occomy from the 1920s and 1930s. Marian Minus published two short stories, and John Henrik Clarke published four or five, with titles that revealed the Columbus, Georgia, native's evolving bitterness, like "Santa Claus Was a White Man." The heavyweight who went through *Opportunity* to better things was Chester Himes, perhaps the most devoted social realist of the 1940s. Himes, once described by his publisher as an author who "writes with his fist and in it a crowbar," bore the scars.[8]

If some traditional avenues for writing faltered, in Harlem flamboyant preacher Adam Clayton Powell, Jr., had founded his own newspaper. Called the *People's Voice*—"a new paper for a New Negro"—the paper was to keep track of the swiftly changing race relations and to serve as a platform for a Powell's political ambition. The dandyish minister had cornered the market on charisma and inspired talented people to gather round, like the pharmacist-turned-social-worker-turned-journalist Ann Petry, who worked as an editor for *PV* for eighteen months between 1942 and 1943.

In 1941 the most nationalist of the black press came out, this time directed at Harlem's young people. Called *Negro Youth*, this stridently Garveyite publication would, as a matter of course, have nothing to do with the light-skinned Powell. "Negro Youth is published in the interest of pure blooded black people throughout the Universe to bring about their complete freedom from domination by both white people and mongrel mulatto, mixed-blooded 'Negroes' and 'Colored' people."[9] *Negro Youth* examined blackness as a problem of pride and fought fire with fire, attempting to cultivate intolerant attitudes against the frequently color-prejudiced biracial aristocracy.

The most important early 1940s magazine of black American writing and critical thought was the short-lived journal *Negro Quarterly*, founded by Angelo Herndon in late 1941 and soon staffed by managing editor Ralph Ellison and fellow member of the Negro Publication Society Ernest Kaiser. Herndon, moving away from his long years in the bosom of the Communist Party, spent much of his time hunting donors, and for the most part the magazine seemed a kind of comfortable revival of Popular Front high-brow aesthetic policies, combined with a political point of view looking toward Africa and Asia. Unaffiliated with a paternalistic institution or editorial board like *Phylon* was, the journal showed political savvy, an international range, spunk, and an intensity that wouldn't be duplicated for another twenty years.

By the second issue, in early 1942, Herndon had secured as managing editor the most competent writer of the generation, Ralph Ellison. Herndon's move made the magazine a direct successor to *New Challenge*. Clever, humorous, intellectually dense, committed to combat against racism, and proud of his ancestry, Ralph Ellison served as managing editor of the *Negro Quarterly* for three numbers and the draft of a fourth.[10] Unlike the Ivy Leaguer J. Saunders Redding, Ellison had earned his literary reputation by working for the Communist magazine *New Masses*—the only publication in the 1930s with a national reach that was aggressively looking for black talent. Ellison studied his craft by joining the Federal Writers' Project in New York City and the League of American Writers. By the early 1940s he served on the league's executive board. His early fiction publications grew out of that milieu: the Writers' Project's club journal *Direction* and *Tomorrow*, and *Cross Section*, published by League of American Writers' secretary Edwin Seaver. The new spirit of what Wright had called the "Negro people's movement" could take a dropped-out music major from Tuskegee like Ellison and turn him into a recognized manager of literary affairs.

Ellison was an independent thinker, and that caulk held together the long and intense friendship he had with Richard Wright, from their days on *New Challenge* through Ellison's high-modernist breakthrough novel *Invisible Man* in 1952. And during that period, Ellison made the most of Wright's *Native Son*, which he saw as his generation's spur to a growth in consciousness. Ellison told the *New Masses* audience in August 1941 that he hoped to see "[t]he new Negro consciousness," of which Wright was a central engine, create a "new society."[11] Shortly after he took over the *Negro Quarterly*'s editorial duties, an unsigned editorial appeared criticizing black intellectuals and politicians for failing to solve "the riddle of the zoot suit," or, in other words, neglecting the political import of African American indigenous cultural forms of expression. Ultimately Ellison believed that the new consciousness of urbanized blacks might make a profound contribution to American life. His own work was at least partially designed to bring about such a transformation.

Negro Quarterly, "a review of Negro thought and opinion," relied heavily on the leftist New York intellectual network that was largely shaped by Communists. The network included people who regularly published in *New Masses*, like Alfred Kreymborg, Naomi Replansky, Herbert Aptheker, and Henrietta Buckmaster. But the journal's vocal repudiation of Jim Crow in the military sharply deviated from the Communist line of 1942 when the Germans were pressing the Soviet Army. *Negro Quarterly* claimed to present the "true experience" of the Negro people, to oppose "the old stereotypes" and correct "many of the falsehoods that have been spread."[12] Herndon and Ellison combined reprinted and original material, a strategy resumed by Fern Gayden and Alice Browning in 1944 with the Chicago-based magazine *Negro Story*. But the struggle to cultivate an audience and the wartime paper shortage tended to keep the entire operation on the precipice of ruin—that, and the sentiment expressed by Sterling Brown's essay in the first issue about the stubbornness of racism in the publishing industry. Brown thought that "[t]he market for Negro writers, then, is definitely limited as long as we write about ourselves. And the more truthfully we write about ourselves, the more limited our market becomes."[13]

Brown's conviction that the only success available to a black writer was to write dishonestly or about whites seemed partially proved and partially disputed by the arrival of William Attaway's second novel in 1941. Attaway throttled convention. The Mississippi-born son of a physician, young Bill Attaway ran away from home, hoboed on the railroad, and even within the college walls rebelled against the orthodoxy of the classroom. In Illinois Attaway briefly fluttered around Margaret Walker, Frank Marshall Davis, Frank Yerby, and Arna Bontemps at Erie Street Illinois Federal Writers' Project and then pursued his other talents. In 1939, in addition to his career working as an actor in New York on Hart and Kaufman's *You Can't Take It With You*, he published his first novel.

Attaway's 1939 novel *Let Me Breathe Thunder* struggled to step out of the dank puddle of assumption regarding black writers that Bontemps had struggled against and Sterling Brown thought whites wanted to read. The book did not have central black characters but explored Attaway's own experience gallivanting across the Southwest during the Depression. Reviewers rewarded him by saying, "[t]his first novel by a 25-year-old Negro quite definitely proves . . . that it is possible for a Negro to write about whites."[14] Attaway's novel looked back to Dunbar to exploit a genre that would gain in popularity in the 1940s, the so-called raceless novel. But even without black characters, Attaway's book reflected the serious political concerns of working-class Americans.

He triumphed enough with *Let Me Breathe Thunder* to convince Edwin Embree and the Rosenwald Fund of his worthiness for a fellowship in 1940. Attaway's new project was more ambitious and this time was solidly working out of black American thematic material. He conceived of a book about three brothers who migrate from the rural South to a steel-mill town. Like Waters Turpin's *These Low Grounds* and *O Canaan!*, Attaway's second book was a migration novel. But, importantly, Attaway was not writing out of his own personal experience. He pursued the work as an ethnographer trudging the field, and thematically the book was a companion to Horace Cayton's coauthored study of blacks in heavy industry. Two Rosenwald Fellowships, in 1939 and 1940, allowed him to travel around the Allegheny Valley and gather information about blacks who had migrated to the new steel-belt foundry towns.

Attaway called the novel *Blood on the Forge*, and it starred three brothers: Mat, Melody, and Chinatown. A compelling and tragic character like Wright's doomed paragon of masculinity, Big Mat leads his brothers away from sharecropping in Kentucky only to fall prey to the fascistic dream of becoming Riding Boss. For optimistic Marxist critics like Ralph Ellison, Attaway had represented the working class but failed to offer a vision of triumph. Attaway had teased out the differing ethnic relationships among Hungarians, Slavs, Irish, Mexicans, and blacks, striving to work their way from rural peonage to urban modern life. *Blood on the Forge* emphasized the destructive side of migration and values in flux.

In that respect, the novel was a great deal grimmer than *Native Son*, a book that insisted on naming its culprits and having Bigger transform his own conscience by the conclusion of the book. What discomfited Ralph Ellison about Attaway's realism was that it held out little hope for rural blacks to remake themselves or even to understand the process of their own dissolution. They were uneducated, disenfranchised, superstitious, and cruelly trapped by their own humble dreams of wish fulfillment. The novel's final scene showed the surviving two brothers in a car on their way to the slum section of a northern city, comparing wounds with a blind veteran returning home from the war.

More optimistic than Attaway about blacks in urban America and committed to the Communist Party was the college professor Melvin B. Tolson. *Atlantic Monthly* editor Mary Lou Chamberlain decided that she liked his poetry, and she published Tolson's "Dark Symphony" in September 1941. Tolson was a remarkable man, and he had known a kind of frugal thriving in the age of segregation. Born in 1898 in Missouri, he had tasted a bit of the eastern intellectual climate at all-male Lincoln College between 1918 and 1922. His classmate and friend was Horace Mann Bond, who later became the school's president. Located in rural Pennsylvania, not far from Wilmington, Delaware, Lincoln had as much of the prep-school fraternity feeling as any of the historically black colleges, and it also claimed people like Langston Hughes, Louis and J. Saunders Redding, and Thurgood Marshall. Like Tolson, several of the men were members of the Omega Psi Phi fraternity, equal parts Odin and Damballah; one of their mottoes was "Sons of Blood and Thunder."

Ten years later and teaching at small Wiley College in Texas, Tolson went back East, to Columbia, for master's work in comparative literature. He wrote a daring thesis on Harlem Renaissance novelists—the adventurousness being his assumption that a literary tradition of black Americans existed on its own native terms. Tolson made his real name during the period, though, by writing a newspaper column, *Caviar and Cabbage*, and directing a championship Wiley debate team that beat Oxford twice. In the 1930s and 1940s Tolson had matured politically and had become more than fond of the Communist Party. His friend and admirer, the *Modern Quarterly* editor V. F. Calverton, admitted, "I don't like your Stalinism, as I made abundantly plain, but other than that you are OK."[15] Tolson's political passions culminated with the determinedly socialist volume of poetry *Rendezvous with America* in 1944.

An accurate gauge of the difference between the pre– and post–*Native Son* world of African American writing was readily observable in the appearance of two memoirs, Zora Neale Hurston's 1942 *Dust Tracks on the Road* and Langston Hughes's 1940 *The Big Sea*. Hurston, who had written an allegory of African American life the year before with *Moses, Man of the Mountain*, was on the verge of turning herself into a cliché. Her ability to craft folksy types for Americans seemed painfully backward. Her kiss-and-tell memoir also rang false. Where were the great ideas? Where was the turmoil and strife? Young critic Hugh Gloster wrote in the *Journal of Negro History* that "*Dust Tracks on the Road* fails in at least two major ways: first, in self-portraiture, and, second, in re-creation of the times during which the author lived."[16] Arna Bontemps was more succinct: "Mrs. Hurston deals very simply with the more serious aspects of Negro life in America—she ignores them."[17] Hurston could fully expect to be taken to task; a reporter named Douglass Gilbert had quoted her as saying that the Jim Crow system worked in the South. The *Atlanta Daily World* printed a correction on March 3, 1943, where Hurston removed herself from the field of politics entirely. "I hate to talk about race problems. I am a writer, and leave sociological problems to sociologists, who know more about them than I do."[18] Once the public and the publishers allowed African American writers a smidgen of the national spotlight, they steadily voiced a desire to see the "Negro Problem" resolved. Unwillingness, indifference, and reluctance to do it signaled a black writer's doom.

Hurston and Hughes, who hadn't spoken in years, one turning fifty, the other turning forty, were remarkably similar. In terms of narrative writing, they were titans in the twilight, who would continue publishing but without the risk-taking and adventure that had characterized their early work. Hughes gummed up his memoir with the same problems of insignificance and navel-gazing that haunted Hurston. He had visited war-torn Spain and toured the South to benefit the Scottsboro trial victims, but his memoir was like a picaro of a prepubescent lad. "Too often it is undistinguished writing," sounded the *Phylon* review. The work did not earn distinction from its peers, though later generations would make great claims for its value, mainly because Hughes's memoir became the standard account of the Harlem Renaissance of the 1920s. Hurston had ignored the artistic movement of the 1920s and Hughes too was underwhelmed by what had taken place. "I had a swell time while it lasted. But I thought it wouldn't last long.... The ordinary Negroes hadn't heard of the Negro Renaissance. And if they had, it hadn't raised their wages any."[19]

The best example of a narrative writer in the early 1940s to build off the dense psychological realist exploration that Wright had begun came surprisingly from the young professional critic J. Saunders Redding. When *Native Son* appeared, the Phi Beta Kappa Redding sent to Wright an appeal for friendship such as he probably never had course to offer any other black man who had only finished junior high school. In fact, Redding heaped praise on the "great work" of *Native Son* for what the book had done to their field. "There is no doubt that *Native Son* did more to win Negro writers genuine respect (they had had that sort of patronizing respect since W[illiam].W[ells]. Brown[20]) than anything yet done. There is only one danger and that is that the deservedly great artistic and financial success of *Native Son* will cause a few plunging publishers to go all out for anything Negro and that we will be swamped in mediocrities, as we once were before. But no matter how many of the latter there are, so long as you are writing your great talent alone will keep the general level of Negro stuff high."[21]

Redding's adulation for Wright's work linked him to the critics who wished to battle racial injustice and also to champion African American literature as a body of study. Nearly as important, *Native Son*—a popular success—suggested the possibilities for a new relationship between black writers and white America that took advantage of the art of writing novels that described the American racial scene. Redding enjoyed greatly the articulation of his own frustration in Wright's work, but he also recognized the inner core of the book that sounded unpleasant to his ear. Black audiences could enjoy the presentation of their anger and frustration, but *Native Son* took away something from them too, their easy patriotism. He knew that black audiences, accustomed to romantic plots and "light" fiction, "did not want to believe what other Negro writers ... had been for years telling them in academic terms.... They did not want to believe that they were as helpless, as outraged, as despairing, as violent, and as hate-ridden as Wright depicted them. But they were. They did not want to believe that the America that they loved had bred these pollutions of oppression into their blood. But it had."[22] As his career developed, and in a more pronounced manner than any of his fellow writers, Redding would go on to reproduce this war: the hope for a relaxed, confident national identity steadily countered by the reality of his having to plot escape, actively, from pollution.

He did it in a magnificent memoir. In 1940 and with the assistance of a Rockefeller grant, Redding took a sabbatical from Elizabeth City State College and wandered the southern backcountry, talking to locals and keeping a writer's notebook. Two years later he found his greatest success as a writer with the wrenching travelog, *No Day of Triumph*. Richard Wright wrote the book's tart, single-page introduction. Noting Redding's attacks on black college administrators, Wright asserted that Redding was "the first middle-class Negro to break with the ideology of the 'Talented Tenth' in a complete and final manner."[23] His approach was curious and different from that of W.E.B. Du Bois, who had, in the 1903 *Souls of Black Folk*, written a book using fundamentally similar expository techniques and tackling similar questions. But Redding's book was no Wagnerian opera of mythic portent or pastoral refulgence. He revealed a miasma below the Mason-Dixon Line that the magnanimity of the New Deal had not begun to address. In realistic language and detail, the book steadily emphasized the damage wrought by generations of slavery and blistering racism. Here and there he found the earthy pride and resilience of the common man.

Redding introduced his sorrow song of black life in America with a chapter on his own family history. A childhood in Delaware had acquainted him with the absurdity of black life. Son of a light-complexioned mother and a dark-complexioned father, he had seen the prejudice among blacks that scorned excellence if it were dark skinned or came from the wrong side of the railroad track. One grandmother bitterly remembered slavery and never forgave whites or their version of American culture; another grandmother aggressively sought white favor and privilege. Redding portrayed his own adjustment as a largely uncomfortable one; by the time he had gotten to college, first at all-black Lincoln and then later at all-white Brown, his personality had fallen in on itself. He had become retrospective and prickly. When he recounted the extraordinarily privileged black collegians in New England's Ivy League system in the 1920s, he recalled chiefly their suicides and self-destructive behavior. Redding's account of his access to American upper-class life was written as if he were putting into words a companion piece to Harriet Wilson's forgotten 1859 novel *Our Nig, or, Sketches from the Life of a Free Black, in a Two-Story White House, North, Showing That Slavery's Shadow Falls Even There*. There was no marvelous democracy among talented and ambitious blacks in the urban North.

The heart of the book was the months spent meandering west from Virginia to Louisiana, and it continued the narrative tone of discomfort. Touring the South, noting the filthy conditions that the black traveler endured, the rank grub and seedy berths, Redding did not pretend to have any insider's knowledge that might elevate or ennoble the squalor. Even where he found pleasant entertainment, there was no getting around what segregation had done. Around October 1940 he stopped at a black college and interviewed the school's president. The resulting portrait revealed a fatuous Uncle Tom and proto-fascist, yet someone who believed himself to be a freedom fighter. In a controversial passage, Redding condemned the backbone of Negro elites: the educators. "Negro schoolmen are terrific snobs, the true bourgeoisie," he told his readers. "Grasping eagerly for the straws of recognition, a great many of them proclaim loudly their race-faith and avow social radicalism. Some let it be known discreetly that they are Communists. But theirs is a puerile profession of faith, a smart-alecky, show-off kind of radicalism." Redding allowed them nothing. "In reality they look to the upper-middle class whites for their social philosophy and actual practices ape that class's indifference to social and political matters and reforms. They are the bulwark against positive action, liberal or even independent thought, and spiritual and economic freedom."[24] Redding guarded himself by making the reference completely anonymous, a sensible precaution. The strongly unfavorable account revealed a pompous bureaucrat who had fired a teacher for voting, thought the WPA was breeding indolence among Negroes, and proudly snorting that he did not "educate" but "train" Negroes to fulfill their roles as second-class citizens. "I know what Negroes have to do, and I train 'em to do just that," the man told Redding.[25] Obviously, with such leaders, black America was walking out from slavery blindfolded.

The everyday black folks who talked to Redding were sincere and proud, but generally without the tools to navigate the modern world. In a small Tennessee town, an eighth-grade-educated teacher narrated the life of Alec Hill, a poor, befuddled farmer whose series of "wrong-turnings," mishaps, and bad luck culminate with what the teacher suspects is incest. And even when Redding's native sympathy was called upon, he found the dregs. In Kentucky, where he looked up friends of his family, he found a couple trying to pass for white, plainly angered by his having contacted them, and the gothic story of a young woman's spiral from small-town bourgeois propriety into alcoholism and what was then called sexual abnormality.

In contrast to the stories of woe, Redding offered up a passel of tragic heroes: Flap, a pistol-carrying pool-hall chief, the central opponent to segregation in his Tennessee hamlet; Coe Harvis, a drunken lawyer representing the black poor in a West Virginia coal-mining town; "Aunt Julie," a dignified woman who had in slavery endured beatings by her master and rape by the stud; and Redding himself, struggling with his own dignity in the face not just of poor, uneducated fellow blacks, but of white truculence. At a washed out bridge in southeastern Missouri, he faced down the bogey of the "typical southern white man," trying to jump his place in a line for a ferry over the river. In Memphis he withstood a policeman's bullying but then broke down tearfully along the banks of the Mississippi.[26]

Redding concluded the book with a rewrite of black nostalgia from the 1930s: Zora Neale Hurston's *Jonah's Gourd Vine* and *Their Eyes Were Watching God* and Waters Turpin's *These Low Grounds* had all romanticized the turn-of-the-century all-black town. Redding went to the Mississippi town River City, founded twenty years after the Civil War by ambitious black entrepreneurs who cleared raw land and built sawmills and opened banks. But the dream of economic success without political rights had sagged, become tattered, and was now broken. Some blamed an outsider for introducing skin-color hierarchy. But Redding's talks with the Yale-educated mayor, son of one of the founders, emphasized a broader climate of "[a]trophy and desuetude."[27]

Redding walked a tightrope between blaming whites for black degradation and putting on the hair shirt of black inferiority. He determined to accept responsibility not only for his condition, but also for his liberation. On occasion he described other blacks unflatteringly—"sullen animals guarding their lairs"—and, he left open the suggestion that Reconstruction was a "mess left by corrupted Negro political leaders."[28] Such rhetoric established direct points of sympathy with his editor W. T. Couch and other white liberals in the South.[29] Couch for one believed that segregation protected blacks while they underwent the process of civilization and acculturation to the white American way-of-life. Redding's manner of extricating himself from a tone that seemed to fault blacks for the realistic descriptions of southern poverty was to swing at the end. *No Day of Triumph* concluded in Louisiana at a Louis Armstrong concert with a girl named Mynola on Redding's arm. With a bit of effort, he was able to overcome shyness and, in the midst of the jumping crowd, breathe in the "air of freedom." "Only an utter fool would pretend enough discernment and insight and to a sympathy sufficiently broad to embrace the total meaning of all I had seen and heard and of all that there was to be felt," he decided in the roundabout logic that was his. Any attempt to grasp the totality of the experience was "an empty boast (it is also pure condescension), and it is based upon a fallacy. That fallacy is that the Negro is a problem both in vacuo and in toto, whereas in reality the Negro is only an equation in a problem of many equations, an equally important one of which is the white man. To know and understand and love the Negro is not enough. One must know and understand the white man as well." Although *No Day of Triumph* introduced no whites by name as speaking voices, the book gestured to them explicitly in its finale. The Negro problem was the American condition.

He had achieved nearly everything that was claimed black narrative writing had not then done. Redding was not a propagandist; his trademark was scrupulous, even self-deprecating honesty. He had not written a long rant wedged in an ideology, but his book was not glib, romantic, or lightweight. Nor could his work conveniently be used to endorse segregation. Redding showed rich psychological depth in his characters, and he filled the book with valuable, piquant descriptions of people and scenes. The accounts he provided would be reworked so steadily in the ensuing years that they became literary tropes. In ten years, Ralph Ellison would take the raw material of the corrupt college president, the incestuous farmer, the college-educated black Communist, artifacts connected to slavery, and the musical genius of Louis Armstrong to extraordinary dramatic heights in the novel *Invisible Man*. Redding's book also revealed a decided strength. *No Day of Triumph* avowed, in a voice far more reputable than the sensational Chicago Communist Richard Wright's, that blacks were no kin to Stowe's Uncle Tom, angelic martyrs patiently biding their time with love in their hearts. And they were not all Bigger Thomases. The book declared that though it was crucial to abolish racial segregation, access across the color-line alone would not resolve a heritage of black suffering. There would be no simple solution to racial crisis in the United States.

Redding had not ignored black destitution or racial tension, but he had not crusaded for the black man, and for that he felt guilty. He was overcome by the shame that in him whites had found a Negro to confirm their worst suspicions about the masses of American blacks. He had accepted a decree from the Rockefeller Foundation: "Go out into Negro life in the South. Go anywhere you like and see what you find."[30] Harper's emblazoned the words on the book jacket, unaware that, instead of freeing the book from the charge of white censorship and paternalism, they implied that Redding was not his own man.

Thus it did not help him so much that the book was a critical smash in the mainstream press. Despite their complex political differences, the white critics showed themselves to have a remarkably similar self-interest in promoting the book. The young California novelist Wallace Stegner, writing the review for the *Atlantic,* thought *No Day of Triumph* was "the sanest and most eloquent study of the Negro American that has appeared."[31] Malcolm Cowley supported the book in the pages of the *New Republic*: "[Redding] is surprisingly good-humored, objective and as willing to admit his own faults or those of his people as [he] is to describe their grievances."[32] In the *New York Times*, William Shands Meacham fully concurred with his peers: "[A] book by a Negro who is no apologist for his people, and one who can clearly see their faults."[33] Redding had been attractive to Aswell at Harper's because the editor found in him "the gift of true vision—the ability to look at life with a steady, level gaze and see it as it really is, and then put it down in words without distortion."[34] To top it off, in 1943 the state of North Carolina made Redding the first black recipient of the Mayflower Award for outstanding writing, and in the worst year of race-rioting since 1919 the national press gladly carried the news story of southern racial "good-will." White America may have liked his prose, but they loved that he did not seek, single-mindedly, to indict them for the existence of black serfdom and worse in the South.

Such well-placed applause turned chary black reviewers on the defensive. Redding was one of their own, but they could stand neither his scrutiny nor his acclaim. Redding's black constituents labeled him obsequious to white power and accused him of serving up reports of exaggerated black squalor to humiliate and weaken the fledgling black middle class. The reviewer for *Phylon* dismissed the "bizarre" examples of black life in the South that Redding had chosen and used the occasion of criticism to comment publicly on Redding as a man. "I do not feel that Redding has broken finally with his tradition," offered the reviewer. "The fact that he derides a college president and berates his colleagues does not bind him essentially to the mass of Negroes. Herein, perhaps, lies the difficulty he had in communing with his former associates. He may have been called snob, but seldom radical in his thinking; for he was then, as he is now, the victim of the stern discipline in cramped aloofness of his exclusive boyhood surroundings. And he has not yet attained a sympathetic understanding of Negro life."[35]

The brilliant young Howard English professor John Lovell, writing for the *Journal of Negro Education*, lamented Redding's overly personal approach to the topic. Lovell wanted to see a strategy that would "reindict and retry American civilization" in the manner of *Uncle Tom's Children* and *Native Son*. Instead, Redding's book had only produced one more "denial of the power of literature to trouble the water of muddy social forces."[36] But the reviewers who quibbled with Redding over personal and literary matters were mild in comparison with the more politically minded writers. When the *Journal of Negro History* reviewed the book in January 1943, they found Redding more than an obstacle in the path of racial uplift; he was a traitor, among the "miseducated colored Laval and Quisling writers for media publicity." By comparing Redding to famous Europeans who had easily switched allegiance to the Nazis, the *Journal's* verdict was clear: "Intentionally or unintentionally these writers are literary saboteurs betraying Negroes for the glee and satisfaction of their worst traducers."[37]

Redding had earned himself a sobriquet that would stick. He was now the infamous "traducer" of his race. Obviously the label did not matter to his white audience; but his being accused of racial disloyalty pained him. As a successful writer and a member of the black college professorate, he felt compelled to perform on the conspicuously different stages of black and white American life, and the gap between the assumptions, expectations, and resources of the two theaters was enormous. At the illustrious beginning of his career, Redding had to face the fact of losing the support of other blacks—certainly an important factor in *No Day of Triumph's* never appearing in paperback. Redding was also a bit ahead of his natural constituency: the American "new" liberals—political anti-communists and literary aestheticians interested in difficult recordings of the individual human experience—who claimed to champion racial justice would not comprise a group until after World War II. Redding's success d'estime could not get him lectures before audiences of white elites, job offers from their colleges, or even regular access to circles of other equally talented white writers.

For the most part, he rejected the whites who were keen to associate with him: the Communist Party and its journals and satellite groups, still key sources of interracial intellectual contact in 1942 and 1943. Redding claimed to have fallen out with the party personally in 1933, when, after attending several cell meetings, he decided, "I resented democracy for leaving me and itself so defenseless; but I hated Communism for putting me on the defensive."[38] Still, his point of view from the early 1940s coincided precisely with the Communists' putative principles of social justice. When *No Day of Triumph* came out, *New Masses* printed a chapter, and Redding's editor Aswell gave Ellison at *Negro Quarterly* a chunk to reprint for only a nominal fee. CPUSA members sent Redding fan mail.

But when he attended a party in his honor in New York, he felt manipulated by the Communist officers' exaggerated claims to make him a financial success. A black man seeking wide admiration as a writer might have extended them his consideration. In the early 1940s, Richard Wright, William Attaway, Theodore Ward, Ralph Ellison, Ernest Kaiser, Carl Ruthven Offord, Melvin B. Tolson, and others hovered in and around the orbit of the Communist Party in New York; certainly, at the time, Redding was their equal in talent. But Redding remained tied to the African American community's limited resources and approbation. From afar and to his white peers, Redding had a vigorous and enviable career. In reality, the elite sectors that congratulated his work remained rigidly closed off, and those that were open to him he did not particularly want. All told, *No Day of Triumph* launched Redding as the most visible African American humanist critic during the 1940s; and, unintentionally, it immediately set the terms for the counterreformation to Wright and the left-wing social realists.

One thing that Redding had left outside of his review of the racial situation was the case of black American young people, striving for change and new relationships. Although Redding understood Wright's work as definitive and powerful, he had not been personally interested in seeking out the Bigger Thomases, the lumpen proletariat considered to be a startlingly large proportion of black America. His contemporary Horace Cayton devoted his career to furthering Wright's ideas from *Native Son*. By way of his voluminous files, Horace Cayton had helped Wright to assemble the photographic essay *12 Million Black Voices*. (Wright returned the favor in 1943 by accompanying Cayton to the Harcourt, Brace offices and agreeing to write an introduction for the sociological treatise

Negro Metropolis.[39]) As World War II began and propagandists pitched the war to the American people as another bout to make the world free from dictatorship and free for democracy, Cayton found it impossible to countenance public U.S. discrimination, such as was practiced in the armed services. In the weeks before Pearl Harbor, Cayton published an essay in *Opportunity* magazine called "Negro Morale" that attested to seething discontent among U.S. blacks. The essay rang the bells of an interesting sort of project. Cayton's natural home was on the Left, but he did not see eye-to-eye with the Communists. He feuded with Chicago's prominent black Communists, like Fisk student Ishmael Flory and lawyer William Patterson.[40]

On the other hand, Cayton expressed the unapologetic opinion that the most important inspiration for blacks in the twentieth century had been the left-wing movement, and he provided historical evidence to add depth and detail to black discontent. His *Opportunity* essay contained the Bigger Thomas threat: "the next stage in the urban development of the dispossessed Negro will be, for many, the development of the hard, bitter, cynical personality types described by Richard Wright in *Native Son*."[41]

The younger radicals, like *Negro Quarterly*'s editor Ralph Ellison, thought well of Cayton's appreciation of Wright's fire and brimstone rhetoric. Ellison had an ecumenical vision that combined Cayton and J. Saunders Redding. Before the end of 1942, he reprinted the "Rosalie" chapter of Redding's book that confirmed the fetid mores of the black middle class. And Ellison hoped to print an article in *Negro Quarterly* by Horace Cayton, one that unsentimentally examined black life and leaders, and the techniques that might produce a consciousness of black historical destiny.[42] After having had discussions with Cayton and Wright and others, Ellison expected the men to move beyond the communists and the reformers. If they could successfully prove that blacks were an "oppressed" nation, Cayton was an excellent person to turn the findings into the concrete ground of a new struggle.[43] The American Communist Party might have formally shifted its emphasis away from Negro "self-determination" and the battle for immediate civic equality after the German invasion of the Soviet Union in the summer of 1941. But the genie was out of the bottle for black writers and intellectuals, increasingly groomed at black colleges and major research universities, who made and remade the elements of Communist positions and Garveyite doctrines to suit themselves.

Cayton moved the presentation of the "new struggle" argument from black audience to white. "Fighting for White Folks" appeared on September 26, 1942, in *Nation* and, as the title suggested, treated suspiciously the idea of Negro participation in the war effort to guarantee freedoms abroad that blacks did not share at home. Cayton targeted the dual system of race in America's twin regions: caste in the deep South and discrimination of a minority in the North.

And he hung a new sword of Damocles, not even that blacks would turn into Bigger Thomas, but that they would no longer confine themselves to picking their allies domestically. He confirmed for his audience in the liberal mainstream that the "growing identification of the American Negro with non-white people all over the world is no figment of Nazi propaganda."[44] He turned himself into the point man for black defiance in the 1940s that presented itself to the white public. The uncompromising, measured, and sociohistorically reflective attitude was new for his generation. His article did the trick of getting Cayton, already under active investigation by the Federal Bureau of Investigation, reclassified as 1-A by his Chicago draft board.[45]

For a brief period, the Negro journals kept pace with the far Left *New Republic*. *Opportunity* too hammered out the escalating anger of the black intellectuals, taking their cues from the masses. Chester Himes had exchanged Cleveland for Los Angeles, and was working on two novels, one about his prison experiences and the other about the struggle for racial equality and manhood in the wartime labor industry. Alert and gifted, Himes took advantage of connections he had forged with Sterling Brown and Langston Hughes at the League of American Writers. Hughes directed him to Knopf to get his books published. Only twenty-eight, Himes had served a doctorate's worth of time in the Ohio State penitentiary. A committed naturalist writer, concerned primarily with questions of race, communism, and masculinity, Himes's initiation into the life of semiprofessional crime afforded him a keener sense of the madness and surrealism sometimes at the core of black life.

Chester Himes was also a live wire, either a trait he carried that directed him to the penitentiary at nineteen or something that he had cultivated over seven years of imprisonment. Himes believed in violence and the macabre, elements from his earliest fiction depicting the Ohio penitentiary fire. By 1940 he had written about a marijuana-induced rampage in the pages of *Esquire* and the importance of Bigger Thomas in *New Masses*. He had chronicled his mother visiting him in prison with "The Things You Do" in May 1941, but by 1942 and the short story "In the Night," Himes had shifted to an interior psychological portrait and the crisis of social-class arrangements. Then the confluence of events around the Second World War transformed him.

Himes liked to pull the trigger, especially when it came to his political opinions. In September 1942 *Opportunity* somehow found the courage to publish his article "Now Is the Time! Here Is the Place," perhaps the most openly defiant article written by a black American that appeared in a mainstream publication during the Second World War. Himes encouraged martyrdom at racial incidents to foment more general rebellion against Jim Crow. "Now, in the year 1942, is the time; here in the United States of America, is the place for 13,000,000 Negro Americans to make their fight for freedom in the land in which they were born and where they will die. Now is the time and here is the place to engage and overcome our most persistent enemies: Our native American fascists."[46]

Horace Cayton had challenged the idea that blacks would continue to fight in support of whites; Himes believed that it was time for blacks to cultivate violent fervor against native American white supremacists. After the June 1943 riots in Los Angeles and Detroit, Himes would write for *Crisis* the primer "Zoot Suit Riots Are Race Riots." In August 1943 Harlem was ignited by several days of black rioting directed against police and businesses. Of all of these, probably pitched battles between armed black soldiers and white military police at Fort Dix, New Jersey, Fort Bragg, North Carolina, and Fort Huachuca, New Mexico, and the murder of a score of black soldiers in Alexandria, Louisiana, were the most suggestive of perdurable racial animosity that awaited proper circumstances to become open warfare.[47] Himes responded to hometown battles with the outright war cry "Negro Martyrs Are Needed," a call-to-arms to attack the American way of life, with a footnote to the correspondence between Karl Marx and Frederick Engels: "Martyrs are needed to create incidents. Incidents are needed to create revolutions. Revolutions are needed to create progress."[48] On June 12, 1944, a month after that article was published, the Federal Bureau of Investigation began regular and detailed scrutiny of the work and whereabouts of Chester Himes.[49]

The strident cries of the environmental determinists and protest realists were so strong that before the end of 1942, the respectable professor Alain Locke was revising his work of 1924 and joining the camp of sociologists and policy analysts. For the second time, Locke edited *Survey Graphic*, but his 1942 special issue "Color: Unfinished Business of Democracy" turned the presumption of his special 1924 *Survey Graphic* issue that had begun the Harlem Renaissance on its head. Locke no longer considered the cultural revolution capable of operating on its own. Sterling Brown was the only member of the literati to write a lengthy prose piece, and Brown showed his colors by merely transcribing and providing a context for the multiple and impatient black voices dotting the Mason–Dixon line. Locke was struggling to keep tabs on an increasingly independent and indefinable group.

Negro Quarterly, for instance, in the fall of 1943 was publishing full-out assaults on the tradition of erudite liberalism that Locke represented. The young Chicago Marxist named Edward Bland opposed the romantic tradition of the black middle class in the bracing essay "Social Forces Shaping the Negro Novel." A member of the South Side Writers' Club, Bland went after the 1920s black middle-class writer for the aesthetic sin of misidentification. He faulted black writers for nostalgia, inept technique, and poorly soldered connections to other American writers. The culprit was also new: the general Emancipation of 1865. The Union victory hobbled the black middle-class writers because as a social-class formation they had been created by fiat and their chief characteristic was passivity. Bland thought that the artists needed to work for a goal "to make other Americans see [our] suffering."

J. Saunders Redding also criticized the black middle class, and the suspicion other blacks had toward *No Day of Triumph* seems to have added a new boldness to his public journalism. "A Negro Speaks for His People" appeared in *Atlantic Monthly* in March 1943, just before the bloody riots between blacks and whites swept the entire nation. The article hit squarely on the racial crisis, serving notice that blacks understood the American war creed as a pledge to "wipe out racialism and the threat of racialism from the earth." Redding opposed well-liked "Southern liberals" like Richmond editor Virginius Dabney, who in a January issue of the magazine had blamed "Negro agitators" and "extremist Negro leaders" for stirring unrest.[50] However, writing from North Carolina, where whites had recently been ambushed, a race riot nearly touched off, and the state legislature was already threatening Elizabeth City State College with cuts as punishment for his *No Day of Triumph*, Redding badly did not want to be misconstrued or seen as a terrorist. With candor and stark facts, he chronicled the new spirit among blacks with clinical precision. At the essay's conclusion, he offered a succinct summary of the energies collecting among blacks that were leading them to overturn segregation. "The outstripping and supplanting of outworn Negro leaders, the effects of the growing class-consciousness on the race problem, the tremendous pressure of world forces generating the global war, the war itself for the equality of all peoples—all these taken together are a stupendous challenge to the South."[51] Increasingly, the new black critics of literature and culture seemed capable of cutting free from old ties.

A few months later Redding popped up in the two-year-old academic journal *Antioch Review*, a liberal and radically humanist magazine out of the college in Yellow Springs, Ohio. *Antioch*'s editors were outspoken proponents of the belief that "the social role of the intellectual in our time is to employ ideas to further democracy in the fullest sense."[52] The journal slashed into the field of race relations. In its second year Argentinean Luis Alberto Sanchez y Sanchez wrote "The North-American Negro" and set his exploration in Harlem to identify the deep psychological tensions between blacks and whites in democratic New York City.[53] One of the academic liberal quarterlies had begun to take seriously the work of democracy.

The first black to publish in *Antioch*, Redding appropriately called his essay "The Black Man's Burden." The early months of 1943 had soured black optimists. Redding now believed that, despite their outsized hopes, "nothing" that had taken place in the war served to "indicate a permanent dissolution of the old stereotypes that condition so much of our national thinking."[54] For *Antioch*'s audience he felt free enough to put into words the national disaster of race relations, a looming sense of ruin invoked by the term "social equality." "Social equality" was a lynching phrase when uttered by a black in the South and, as Redding spelled out, was always interpreted as an invitation for the rape of white women by black men. When he wasn't being provocative and deadpan in his delivery, such as comparing the state of blacks in America to "the lung in a tuberculous body," he ripped into controversy. "And what the Negro wants exactly is that the government recognize a sense of obligation to him and to extend its wardship to him on terms of equality with other people."[55] Counter to the NAACP's strong resistance to any policy that "set the Negro apart for special treatment," Redding supported Carey McWilliams's proposal to ease racism and its effects by creating an Office for Negro Affairs. Redding favored drastic liberal measures to replace the current black leadership and broadly alter the condition of Negroes in America.

This view was not necessarily popular among black Americans, who did not register with the Democratic Party by a large majority until 1948.[56] Even if a federal antilynching bill was perennially on the agenda, black Americans were also a religiously devout, socially conservative group that tended away from sweeping analyses of race prejudice that showed them unable to conquer injustice on their own. Chester Himes continued to support Redding's point about special requirements in his 1947 book *Lonely Crusade* by saying simply that "to a Negro equality meant special privilege."[57] And Himes's results were disastrous.

Chicago-based Horace Cayton, on the other side of the world from J. Saunders Redding's Hampton College roost, noticed the flinty position papers thinking through versions of racial equality from the purported white liberal crowd. *Nation* published James Boyd, a white southerner who predicted race riots and the extirpation of blacks if demands for wartime racial justice were not quickly put aside. Boyd's essay "Strategy for Negroes" reduced black struggle into a divided camp of either gradualism or "explosiveness"; citizens who accepted second-class status and rebels, basically. While the white liberals seemed to have common sense on their side—the white American majority showed repeatedly that it was resistant to treating blacks fully equally and that it was prepared to use violence to reject the implementation of the U.S. Constitution—their analyses typically returned to the turn-of-the-century standoff between manual education and liberal arts. Boyd, for instance, told his audience that "[Negro] efforts should be concentrated on the economic front."[58] Despite his opinion, he granted that Negro radicals had a tenable theoretical position; the question was whether or not their defiance would lead to race war.

Cayton thought blacks betrayed by Americans of the mainstream, and in his essay "The Negro's Challenge" in the *Nation* in May 1943 he articulated a position that strode against the mechanical solutions offered by the far Left and the paltry gradualism of the liberals. He continued to spur the liberals as he had in "Fighting for White Folks." In a sense, what he reported was the steady eclipsing of the domestic "Negro"—who had to understand himself partially by reference to white America—and the international "black"—who selected allies on the basis of mutual value. Cayton confidently described the new spirit seizing blacks throughout the country. "A change so profound that few persons realize its fateful meaning is taking place in the mentality of the American Negro," was how Cayton prepared his liberal audience, debating the implications of democracy to black Americans.[59] Cayton let everybody know that the modern African American no longer relied upon the United States for concepts of self-worth. "[H]e has broken out of his caste-bound mentality, transcended his purely racial point of view (which led him only to despair), and now sees his position in a society as identified with that of the darker races of the world."[60] In accord with the radical editorial board of *Negro Quarterly*, that summer Cayton thought he had identified a newly critical spirit within the growing urban masses of blacks, breaking from the analysis of what he called by 1943 not a complete but a "semi-caste" system of race relations.

Very much alone among politically connected blacks who had performed legitimate academic studies and who ran social programs, Cayton warned liberal whites that their notions of black progress were antique. "What many white liberals do not realize is that they are measuring the gains with an obsolete yardstick," he elbowed his reader. Instead of renewed black patience, as Detroit veered toward eruption, Cayton thought wiser the dogged pursuit of equal rights within a democratic nation trying to win a global war with the help of nonwhite allies. "Since America is just now deeply concerned not only with living up to democratic principles at home but, together with other United Nations, with guaranteeing democracy to all peoples everywhere, the present is a logical time for the Negro to seek to improve his position." Countering any sort of "close-rank" mentality and in opposition to the Communist line, Cayton took the occasion of public criticism to remind liberals that atomic-age blacks would battle back against their provocateurs and replace traditional friends.

The creative writers went alongside their fiery critics measure for measure. New York emboldened the radicalism of its recent arrivals too, even those who hailed from the African American upper middle class. A talented beauty with a strong sense of social consciousness, Ann Petry had unique credentials for a social realist writer. At fourteen she had graduated from high school in Old Saybrook, Connecticut, at fourteen, attended Hampton Institute, and gone on to earn a degree at twenty from the Connecticut College of Pharmacy in 1931. She came from a finely educated family; her aunt's husband had been secretary to Booker T. Washington. But in 1938 she abandoned her tame life at her uncle's small-town Connecticut pharmacy for the fashionable "progressive" social conscience of the age and started to work in Harlem for the *Amsterdam News*.

In February 1942 she joined Adam Clayton Powell's politically edgier newspaper *People's Voice*, which he was known to call "the Lenox Avenue edition of the *Daily Worker*."[61] A persistent social reformer, she had an early knack for revealing the environmentally grounded predicaments that addled black life in Harlem. Petry served as many organizations as seemed to improve the quality of life for Harlem's most vulnerable: its women and children.

Petry's career at Powell's *The People's Voice* was the high point of her radical career and seems to have directly shaped her early fiction, which might be to say it shaped all her fiction. *People's Voice* came out of the same radical genre, and was actually printed on the same press, as Marshall Field's *PM* newspaper, edited by the liberal journalist Max Lerner. Richard Wright and Horace Cayton had hoped to approach the Chicago millionaire Field with a proposal for a radical black magazine, but they had not moved beyond the planning phase of a simple anthology when, with Wright, Lawrence Reddick, Ralph Ellison, C.L.R. James, and Cayton, their colleague St. Clair Drake, had refused to accept that whites were responsible for black subordination.[62] Powell ran *People's Voice* out of a top-floor storefront on 125th Street overlooking the Savoy ballroom from 1942 through 1948, and for most of its existence the paper was ably led by Harlem's black Communist elite. Ben Davis, the head of the Harlem *Daily Worker* bureau and Central Committee member, posted a weekly column. Doxey Wilkerson, a fellow traveler who joined the Communist Party in 1944, served as the paper's executive editor between 1943 and 1947. Marvel Cooke wrote the articles and served as the de facto managing editor; Cooke had joined the CPUSA in 1936.[63] National Negro Congress head Max Yergan and Hollywood belle Fredi Washington were all connected to the paper and Communists.

The aims and directives of the far leftists coincided with Petry's direct participation in Harlem life. In the early 1940s she joined the Harlem Riverside Defense Council, the National Association of Colored Graduate Nurses, the American Negro Theater (where she played in *On Striver's Row*), and Negro Women Incorporated, which tied in to her duties on the newspaper. Negro Women Incorporated, for which Petry served as executive secretary, was a direct advocacy group that operated under the umbrella of the People's Committee, the street organization Adam Clayton Powell, Jr.[64] Wherever issues of labor, gender, and race seemed to cohere, Petry went to work. She paid her bills as a "recreational specialist" for the New York Educational Project, putting together programs for the children of laundry workers.

The weekly paper made exacting demands on a short staff, and few carried out tasks of greater breadth than Petry. Petry wrote a weekly gossip column called "The Lighter Side," edited the women's page, and reported on politics in Harlem and the nation. During her career as a journalist, she had found in Harlem extraordinary rates of domestic violence, alcoholism, rape, and murder.

She bent her fiction to explain the statistics that regularly confused people and seemed to support the hoary notions of biological inferiority. She tried to interest the big-time magazines in her stories but took only rejection slips from *Atlantic Monthly*, *New Yorker*, *Harper's Bazaar*, *American Mercury*, and *Story Magazine*. Finally, in December 1943 she broke into print in the pages of *Crisis* magazine with a short psychological thriller, "On Saturday the Siren Sounds at Noon." The gripping tale portrayed the eventual suicide of a war-industries worker after the death of his child.

Petry's early work showed the accumulated pain of racial suffering, and the terrible transference of violence from socially unacceptable to socially acceptable spheres, as in her short story connecting racial prejudice to domestic violence, "Like a Winding Sheet." Written in 1944 and sent to *Crisis*, the novella-length "In Darkness and Confusion" explained the mounting social frustration that led to the Harlem Riot of 1943. The riot was touched off by a mother whose son in the army has been shot by the military police. Despite the mounting casualties in her fiction, Petry's view of the environment in the early 1940s was basically optimistic. Behind her work lay the idea of extended governmental and philanthropic support; behind that, at least at first, was the suggestion of the assimilability of the segregated African American. The black magazines approved of her approach, and she saw her mission as a writer as alerting the black middle class and their supporters to crushing social despair.

While Petry believed in the mission of the civil rights organizations, she also showed a reluctance to connect herself to Communist-based organs or their satellites. The Communist Party, for example, funded American Negro Theater. But when National Negro Congress officer Ewart Guinier (future chairman of Harvard's Afro-American Studies Department and father of law professor Lani Guinier) appropriated her name for the letterhead of the Communist front organization Negro Labor Victory Committee, Petry reprimanded him for behavior she thought "highhanded." "I urge you to immediately remove my name from literature that is being put out by your Committee," she wrote to him.[65] Petry believed in many of the goals of the leftists, as much as they coincided with the New Deal social welfare agenda. But similar to J. Saunders Redding, her sense of American success precluded professions of socialism.

During the remaining years of World War II, Petry went on to publish in *Phylon*, *Negro Digest*, and twice again in *Crisis*. The relationship with black uplift magazines was not perfect, and the restrictions that editor James Ivy labored under at *Crisis* effectively prevented the magazine from serving as an important gateway for the creative writers of the 1940s. In 1944 when Petry sent to him the long riot story "In Darkness and Confusion," Ivy humbled himself before offering to return the story, which he privately considered "a little masterpiece." The editor didn't want to change the language, which he thought "would destroy the very pith and punch of the story." But it came down to his audience. "We, naturally, have no objection to appropriate use of profanity and verbal obscenity, but our readers do, and they object strenuously when they run across such words in the *Crisis* stories."

This was the frustrating condition for the writers who wanted to take the social world of black America seriously and were not satisfied by the Communist press. James Ivy and NAACP secretary Roy Wilkins advised her to send her story to *Harper's* or *Atlantic Monthly*, journals whose combined publications of black authors for the previous forty years had been only a single work each from Richard Wright, Rudolph Fisher, Langston Hughes, Horace Mann Bond, Frank Yerby, and Saunders Redding. Ivy's buoyant appraisal of the story was warranted, but the heavyweights among the slick magazines were not ready.

Mainstream America enjoyed from time to time a blast of black life, such as Wright had made available in *Native Son*. But the audience cared much less for black writers interpreting their own human experience, in either criticism or fiction. Dorothy West, trying in the early 1940s to crack the lucrative women's magazine market at *Collier's*, *Woman's Home Companion*, and *Ladies' Home Journal*, ran into a similar difficulty with publishers. If her stories weren't "too depressing," then they neglected the right kinds of blacks.[66] Elizabeth Boutelle at *Collier's* left no doubt as to the nature of the real double bind. "I notice that Miss West appears to be steering away from stories of colored people, and while that is easy to understand, I think it is rather regrettable. It does seem to me that there is a place for a warm human piece about Negroes, and, judging by what we have seen of Miss West's writing, she is a person who could turn one out . . . *all* Negro stories don't have to be problem ones."[67] In women's magazines Negro writers did not have to deal with the "problem," but that was also their chief distinctive attribute making them attractive to publishers in the first place.

The apparent contradiction about being black and publishing fiction, of interest especially to Langston Hughes and Sterling Brown in the early 1940s, was not all that the black writers faced. The convictions of the editors at the middle-brow American magazines like *Ladies' Home Companion* sometimes relied on a foundational and simple-minded racial cliché: blacks were carefree and happy. Hugh Kahler confided to West's agent George Bye, "I am afraid we'll never win the debate with this writer, but I cling to my conviction that most colored people manage to be a good deal happier than most white people."[68] West took off to her family home on Martha's Vineyard, where she remained for the rest of her life, writing two books, one of them the autobiographical novel *The Living Is Easy*, published in 1948. But if her set pieces about African American middle-class life, romance, and domestic relations had no market, it's unsurprising what happened to Petry's short fiction. Petry would not publish the hard-hitting "In Darkness and Confusion" until 1947.

Petry owed her introduction to the mainstream press to the same zones from which she had learned her writer's craft: white liberals. In winter 1942–1943, Petry had taken a Columbia University writing class under the direction of Professor Mabel Robinson. Robinson, who had something of a writers' colony in Maine at Bayberry Farm, maintained a long friendship with Petry. The connection led to Petry's first novel. After the 1943 short story "On Saturday the Siren Sounds," Houghton Mifflin editor Eleanor Daniels wrote to the young writer in February 1944, alerting her to the book company's generous literary fellowship and asking the magic words, "Are you by any chance working on a book?"[69] A year later Petry won a Houghton Mifflin literary fellowship for $2,400 to complete the novel. Doubleday editor Bucklin Moon had noticed the graceful and articulate woman and introduced her to Henry Volkening, one of the popular literary agents working in New York. Petry had not joined the League of American Writers, but interracial contact with liberal whites who believed it their responsibility to lead blacks to publishers was precisely the social intercourse necessary to pay tangible dividends.

Petry managed to launch herself in a sort of Harlem Renaissance kind of way: the uplift journal, black newspaper, and social organizations combined with a course or two in the Ivy League and then a fellowship and contract from a liberal New England publisher. But perhaps a more traditional story of a black writer being launched in the early 1940s happened in the case of the Trinidadian writer Carl Ruthven Offord. In June 1940 Offord had punched out a piece for the *Nation*, "Slave Markets in the Bronx," describing the street corners where black women gathered in hopes of a day of domestic work at the rate of fifteen cents an hour. Because he dared to mention the racial dynamic between blacks and Jews, he was accused of anti-Jewish bias. By 1943 Offord had joined the Communist Party and was a regular journalist for *New Masses*. Offord pulled together the punishing themes of race and class from the Stalinist point of view with his novel *The White Face*, published by Robert McBride in the last week of April 1943.

This novel about a Georgia sharecropper named Chris who flees peonage and falls into the trap of the anti-Jewish fascists in Harlem was probably the most vigorously environmental determinist novel of the 1940s. *The White Face* concludes with the narrator describing the man imprisoned by racial categorization, in a way that was artistically foreign to a writer as committed to realistic portrait as Richard Wright.

The white face had taken all that the black hand had produced, had made laws that governed the black hand, and withered it. His black life had been cut into a pattern by the white face to suit the purposes of the white face and he had no control whatever over it. The white face owned the land. The white face had stolen him from

Africa and brought him here to work the land and be governed by it. . . . That he should die within this pattern made for him by the white face! . . . His total nothingness in the world of the white face! The sneering whipping snarling lynching denial of the power of man in him![70]

Offord was as interested in showing the vestiges of still thriving racism in America as he was in sounding the alarm of the potential for a black fifth column, which would be disastrous for American war efforts and thus disastrous for the Soviet Union. He was not writing proletarian literature as much as he was writing literature of liberal coalitions between left-wing-minded middle-class Jews and blacks. Curiously enough, the leading black female Communist Claudia Jones panned the book in the *Daily Worker,* saying that Offord was dystopic: the writer "fails to give a clear-cut answer in his novel as to how these evils can be overcome."[71] Her criticism confirmed the steady position of highly placed Communist officials in the 1940s regarding novels tackling American race matters: the individual vision of the artist, especially a desperate or pessimistic one, should never conflict with the formulaic solutions provided by the party.

The mainstream press in this case had more to offer the novice talent. Henry Lee Moon, writing for *New Republic*, now edited by the young maverick Thomas Sancton, claimed correctly that Offord's "sordid story" was the first Negro novel to present an "American community differing from other American communities chiefly because of the restricted opportunities afforded its people for economic security, social welfare and cultural advancement."[72] Rose Feld at the *New York Times* called it "disturbing and provocative" and said it "makes a profound impression."[73] Diana Trilling, *Nation* book critic and wife of Lionel Trilling, thought that the book did not reach the mark as literature but offered "a chilling account of something that is much more than a footnote to the problems confronting us on the home front."[74] In Offord's case he followed a prescription—black nationalism led to fascism and interracial alliances led to liberal social democracy—but mysteriously there was no reward.

Horace Cayton believed that blacks should turn to friends abroad, but he did not take seriously the notion that these disgruntled Americans would become fascists. Unlike Offord, Cayton did not believe that the political IQ of black America was woeful or that black discontent was as simple as Nazi manipulation. His notoriety won Cayton few new friends, but the bloodshed in 1943 vindicated his commentary. Blacks had indeed lost patience, and whites were indeed resistant to accord them democracy, even outside of the traditional boundaries of the Deep South. Cayton's boldness began taking him out of the orbit of mainstream liberal circles, and he began to chafe under the powerbrokers who dominated the pace and emphasis of the national liberal racial agenda, like Rosenwald Fund director Edwin Embree.

Cayton had mailed Embree a copy of his *Nation* "Fighting for White Folks" article before it was printed. Offended, Embree replied to the implications regarding his own position of influence. "I do not quite understand your quarrel with the 'liberals'," he replied. "I do not know any considerable number of them who are urging the Negro to be patient. What they are asking is—what specific programs or what specific gains are proposed by impatient Negro leaders. Clearly the weakness of the 'The Negro Cause' at the moment is the lack of any clear-cut program, or even of any clear-cut statement of goals."[75]

Embree's response proved Cayton's point about measuring with obsolete tools. The famous philanthropic director promoted the concept of the "Brown American" (and title of his 1931 book). This American citizen was not "black," but fully indigenous to the American soil, disinclined to seek friends from other continents, and whose aims and destiny were inseparable from the majority white nation. Belief in the "Brown American" allowed Embree to ignore the radical programs of A. Philip Randolph, leader of the March on Washington Movement, John P. Davis, who had just left the National Negro Congress, as well as the program of "critical participation" in American national life espoused by the Negro Publication Society that put out *Negro Quarterly*.[76]

Embree could have had in mind the much applauded Durham Conference Manifesto of 1942, a document produced by a group of southern black ministers and educators articulating the goals of black Americans seeking to better their condition within the rough outlines of a segregated society. But even though the participants were well respected—James Shepard, president of Durham's North Carolina College for Negroes, was a Roosevelt advisor—they cared not to convey the irruptive and frustrated energy of black America. Cayton hoped to pierce the liberal's smug confidence that no new developments in black American life escaped them. Black writers and intellectuals, especially creative writers like Richard Wright, William Attaway, and unknown writers Ellison, Himes, Petry, Offord, and Curtis Lucas, were cutting a new path away from even their time-tested friends. Thus, when liberals such as Embree implored him to obtain a more fundamentally action-oriented program, a praxis in line with the instrumentality for which social science engineering is famous—and infamously flawed—Cayton bubbled over with frustration. By the fall of 1944 Cayton would write to Richard Wright that he had broken with the "corrupting influence" of Embree and the Rosenwald Fund.[77] Cayton felt deeply the limits of the social welfare model of ameliorative progress, one too inflexible in application and narrow in scope to satisfy the needs of black urban refugees, now flooding American cities.

CHAPTER SIX

Friends in Need of Negroes: Bucklin Moon and Thomas Sancton (1942–1945)

ugh Gloster, who would go on to serve as the president of Atlanta's More-house College from 1967 to 1987, had nearly completed his doctorate in English at New York University when he took a trip to visit his mother in Tennessee in August 1942. Thirty-four-year-old Gloster was a light-brown-skinned man of moderate stature, toward five-and-a-half feet tall, clean-shaven, his hair brushed back from the front, with an upright, almost military bearing. Like most professional black academics, he had not finished his terminal degree but, with a master's in English from Atlanta University, had been a college teacher for nearly ten years.

Although a Ph.D. degree was gaining in importance for college teaching, only a handful of blacks had the ability to win admission to an English literature Ph.D. program, spend several consecutive years in coursework and language training, sit for exams, and write a thesis. Harvard, which had admitted a handful of blacks to Ph.D. training, required proficiency in Old Icelandic, Old and Middle German, Old and Middle English, Latin, and modern languages. Limited to a handful of progressive northern universities, the black teacher then faced a narrow, segregated job market. Black professors needed to obtain and keep a teaching post as soon as one became available, immediately upon completion of a master's degree.

The capstone of an African American's career in 1942 was at Howard University, the highest plateau to which he or she might aspire.[1] The very best of the black humanists like Sterling Brown, J. Saunders Redding, or Melvin B. Tolson would parse together a summer here and a semester there at a good northern university, such as the University of Chicago or New York University, where it was possible to find decent quarters in nearby black neighborhoods and, over a considerable period of time, cobble together a degree. But none of these distinguished scholars ever finished a doctorate. Unlike most of his better-known peers, over time, Gloster eventually earned his Ph.D. degree. Most rare were the truly exceptional black literary scholars like Arthur P. Davis and John Lovell, who were able to earn scholarships outright and finish their graduate work at Columbia and Berkeley, respectively.

That August Gloster journeyed by train to Memphis from Atlanta, where he was teaching at Morehouse, the small and prestigious Baptist men's college.

He knew the country between the two places well since he had been traversing the ground with some regularity for many years. He had grown up and finished high school in Memphis at LeMoyne College, really a normal school, and then gone on to Atlanta for his young manhood, completing his B.A. degree at Morehouse in 1931 and taking his master's degree at Atlanta University in 1933 on the same historic campus. Gloster was a "race man," a member of a new breed of black educators, upstanding and forthright. He was not embarrassed about his racial ancestry, and he did not feel the need to apologize or compensate for it.

If anything, he wanted to know more about his heritage. He had founded, in 1938, an organization of black college-level English professors called the College Language Association, which remains in existence. The organization paralleled the Modern Language Association, which had admitted African Americans like William Scarborough in its earliest years but, after the 1896 *Plessy v. Ferguson* Supreme Court decision, had been unable to bring blacks in numbers into the annual conference hotels. The exception to this apparent rule was Howard University's English department chairman Charles Eaton Burch, a ranking scholar of the eighteenth century and British novelist Daniel Defoe. A native of Bermuda and an Ohio State University Ph.D., Burch had given a paper at the MLA conference in the 1920s. However, in Gloster's time, merely six blacks were members of the MLA.[2]

His academic work continued the fight for militant African American pride and recognition. In 1942 he was writing a dissertation that he would call "American Negro Fiction from Charles W. Chestnutt [*sic*] to Richard Wright," a direct assertion regarding the value of black literature, and an identification of interest with the two black novelists most explicitly engaging politics and social conditions. The Howard English professors Davis and Lovell, by contrast, had written dissertations on Isaac Watts's hymns and the Fourier movement of the 1840s, respectively. Gloster's investment was in black literature. He was steeped in black life, history, and culture and the struggle for black rights. He had made enough of a peace with the racist laws of the South to live there, but he was impatient and vocal.

Customarily the Atlanta-to-Memphis trains changed in Birmingham. Late on Saturday evening in the third week of August, Gloster boarded the Sunnyland, a passenger train that traveled up from Alabama and through Mississippi before stretching into Memphis. By the time the train reached Amory, Mississippi, about twenty miles over the state line, the single Jim Crow coach had become overcrowded, and a boisterous clot of late-night traveling black passengers stood in the aisle. Of all the Jim Crow indignities, educated and mannered blacks resented the segregated railroad cars in particular. In their memoirs they tended to single out the experiences that they suffered at the hands of the conductors who had police powers and enforced racial caste. Probably the black upwardly mobile class chafed because the situations on the cars so often defied logic. The railroad passenger coach behind Gloster, for example, had only two passengers in it. He asked the conductor if the white passengers behind him might be moved to the "white only" section to ease the overcrowding in the Jim Crow car. On more than one occasion that evening, Professor Gloster insisted on his request.

When the train reached Tupelo, Mississippi, the conductor appeared with three policemen who asked simply, "Where is the nigger?" After the conductor's positive identification, the four white men dragged Hugh Gloster from his seat and threw him bodily from the train onto the station platform. The policemen then beat the Morehouse professor on the head, face, and body for five minutes in front of the open door to the Jim Crow car, offering a sustained lesson in Jim Crow protocol to the black passengers. The Sunnyland pulled away, and Gloster was taken to the Tupelo police station, beaten again, and incarcerated for having "sassed" the conductor. After being searched and denied permission to contact his relatives, Gloster was nearly beaten a third time for having money in his pockets and hand-tooled luggage. The policemen threatened him with a stretch on the Tupelo chain gang.[3]

Toward evening on Sunday, almost twenty-four hours into his ordeal, the Frisco railroad agent appeared and, again threatening Gloster with a circuit on the chain gang for violating law, coerced him into signing documents relieving the Frisco railroad of culpability. The agent then transported the prisoner thirty miles back to Amory, Mississippi, where Gloster admitted to committing his offense of impudence and paid the local mayor a fine of ten dollars. The railroad agent, acting with police powers, then released Gloster to his brother-in-law W. C. McFarlin, who took him immediately to the Jane Terrell Memorial Hospital in Memphis. Having survived the police clubs and an evening in a putrid jail cell, Professor Gloster received treatment for his injuries. He was lucky. Black men were killed, even in the late 1940s and in the upper South, for violating segregation ordnances on train cars.

Gloster's inability to secure basic human rights in the U.S. South emphasizes the intellectual crisis for assertive black writers and critics of public culture. The ordinary, day-to-day style of living discouraged assertiveness but rather legally mandated diffidence and timidity. From what source would stir rigorous questioning, let alone defiance? How much literal independence of thought was possible on the college campuses? Obviously if minor breaches of unwritten protocols might result in near-death experiences, public commentary, even literary criticism, brought on potentially hazardous complications.

These crippling limitations were in place for whites as well as blacks. The outspoken Georgia writer Lillian Smith, a Julius Rosenwald Fellow, described in a letter to fund manager William Haygood the cascading punishment that thwarted white southern liberals from speaking out against injustice. Because of the antisegregation content in her journal *South Today*, in 1943 Smith was harassed by the Ku Klux Klan, white vigilantes, and the Georgia Bureau of Investigation. Eventually she requested a letter from the governor verifying that her journal was not being targeted for investigation. Then, Georgia postal inspectors refused her second-class postal privileges. Copies of the journal found their way to Atlanta police chief Marion Hornsby, who called it "subversive" and "indecent" and notified local officials and business leaders. When the mayor of Atlanta saw the magazine, he promptly pressured the owners of the property occupied by the local people who helped Smith publish the journal. Smith was forced to threaten the governor and the postal inspector with a publicity scandal (presumably in the North), and the pressure finally eased.[4] But what was a moment of courageous letter writing and holding her ground for Smith could easily have had more painfully immediate, if not deadly, consequences for Hugh Gloster.

For most of the 1940s, as a group, African American critics found it difficult to teach the exploding numbers of black students, overcome the entrenched conservative bureaucracies at the colleges, and establish standards for public consumption of African American images in literature. The problem of looming punishment for "radicalism"—which could range from the pursuit of simple dignity, to civil rights, to the expression of aesthetic form—captures the dilemma of an inchoate literary critical intelligentsia, still in need of help from the outside. White writers and critics who expressed sincerity to blacks, even of the more superficial sort, were in high demand.

For generations, white Americans had comfortably served as the literary amanuensis for the black character in fiction and the black point of view. During the 1940s a pattern complementing the 1920s emerged; the majority of the books written on "the Negro" were written by whites. But a new balance between civil rights crusader and local color portrait-maker emerged. The most ardent among the young gurus of racial liberalism in the 1940s was Bucklin Moon. And he had at least one unusual credential for a man whose most productive professional years were devoted to launching African American creative writers and demolishing the stereotypes that had accrued about blacks since the establishment of formal segregation in the United States: he was not a native southerner. Moon was born in 1911 in Eau Claire, Wisconsin, and had gone to prep schools in Minnesota and the Northeast. After a time, his family moved to Florida. By 1944 when he was applying for the Rosenwald creative writing fellowship, a grant made to blacks and southern whites, he would make a successful case for the award by telling fund director Edwin Embree, "I have spent most of my life in that region."[5]

Moon apparently gained deep personal feelings toward African Americans and an ability to depict the American South as a youth. His turning point came as a student at Rollins College in suburban Orlando, Florida, in 1930 when he watched a Ku Klux Klan parade being led by uniformed motorcyclists from the local police department. "I'd seen the Klan before, but never led by city officials," he told a black reporter in the ensuing years.[6] At Rollins, Moon learned from the writer-in-residence Zora Neale Hurston, becoming chummy enough with her to visit nearby Eatonville under her care. He also knew of Professor John Andrew Rice, who even then was something of a crusader for black rights. Rice was dismissed from Rollins in 1933 and founded Black Mountain College in Asheville, North Carolina, an experimental school with shockingly unorthodox racial policies.[7]

Moon graduated from Rollins at twenty-four, after taking time off to work on a stutter. He won some early recognition for a 1938 *Harper's* magazine short story called "Boats for Hire," a narrative set in coastal Florida or Louisiana that advanced Moon's concern about the tangled emotional connections of race that concluded with base acts of prejudice.[8] In August 1940 he started work at a Doubleday and Doran bookshop in New York, and within several months he had accepted a job as an editor at the firm, a post he held until 1951. During the rough era of Moon's tenure at Doubleday, America's largest book publisher in the 1940s, the firm became a national leader in publishing fiction and nonfiction that described African American life. Its books were written by black writers like NAACP secretary Walter White, Chester Himes, and Arna Bontemps and whites like Rackham Holt, Fannie Cook, and Moon himself. At Doubleday, under the name "George L. Hack," Moon anonymously submitted his first book for publication.

Doubleday brought out Moon's novel *The Darker Brother* in strife-filled 1943. The book established Moon's credentials as the most liberal white American novelist and, by extension, an expert in social and economic policy. Books dealing with African American life were understood broadly as "problem" books, not works of art, so their authors were considered more sociologists than literary stylists. Still, the scant years between Richard Wright's *Native Son* of 1940 and Moon's *Darker Brother* of 1943 represented a change of the epoch in terms of the imaginative depictions of blacks by white Americans. Moon edged the line of a new place.

Twenty-three-year-old Columbus, Georgia, native Carson McCullers had quickly arrived at the new outlook with her novel *The Heart Is a Lonely Hunter* in 1940. Her extraordinary portrait of the black doctor Benedict Copeland showed a heartfelt revolutionary wishing to lead a peace march on Washington, D.C., reading Spinoza in his spare time, and using his annual Christmas party to preach the gospel of Karl Marx. This was a departure not only from the abundant sentimental portraits of blacks but also more firmly from the oblique mysticism that enveloped the interracial portraits of the acknowledged literary pioneer

William Faulkner.[9] All of a sudden, white-drawn African American characters had gained depth and begun to articulate the contours of racial oppression.

Moon did not have McCullers's polish—or a sympathetic white narrator to hook into his liberal audience. In his first novel, Moon showed chiefly the trademark of a devoted social realist; he was a politically inspired novelist interested almost exclusively in a sympathetic portrait of black working-class life. His most interesting achievement was to offer one of the earliest portraits of the lingering poison of economic race prejudice in the urban North.

The Darker Brother is the narrative of a Florida immigrant family moving to Harlem. Widow Essie Mae takes her children Ben and Josie to live with her husband's brother Rafe. Soon enough, northern race prejudice begins to destroy them. Ben is beaten by whites at his interracial school and thus befriends neighborhood homeboy Slick, a youth whose ambition has already been crushed by poverty and discrimination. The conditions in Harlem are unjust and the family survives only due to the protection of Uncle Rafe, the numbers king of the ghetto. When white gangsters decide to take over Rafe's territory, he is betrayed and murdered. After the death of his uncle, seventeen-year-old Ben wanders the streets and tries to earn an honest living, but the tight job market is closed to him on account of his race. Responding to the religious escapism instilled in her as a child in the South, matriarch Essie Mae becomes a devout follower of Father Gabriel, an approximation of the historical figure Father Divine. She turns over the insurance money that Rafe leaves the family to Gabriel's Peace Movement, only to be crushed to death by fellow Peace followers in a boating accident.

The second half of the novel presents the relationship between Ben and his girlfriend Birdie, a domestic who dreams of becoming a nurse. Frustrated and unable to find work, and nearly participating with Slick in a deadly auto theft, Ben decides to join the army. In the military Ben finds himself at a southern training camp and his best friend, unable to cope with the racial pressure, commits suicide. In Harlem, Birdie is accused of theft at her job as an au pair and turns to prostitution to survive. Incredibly, the novel ends with the couple's reunion and Ben's determination to defend the country after Pearl Harbor has been attacked. At the novel's climax, Ben rallies with the Frederick Douglass–style credo of agitation and fidelity to the United States, a conclusion that connotes the winning spirit of a new generation of black Americans: "We got tuh fight for what we got comin to us over here. We been waitin uh long time. We liable tuh get knots beat all over top uh our heads. We goin to get shoved around. But we got tuh keep fightin."[10]

The heavy dialect prevented the novel from aging gracefully. But Moon had faithfully exposed the environmental severity of the urban ghetto and the triumphant spirit of those who could survive it. He reproduced the spectrum of black American emotional and psychological investment, from militancy to escapist religion, while emphasizing great optimism in the near future. The upbeat narrative that forecast the gradual assimilation of Bigger Thomases filling up American cities found immediate support among the liberal press. The *New York Times* noted that the book was "the first of its kind, combining a good story with authentic portraits of the Negro people." Moon gained critical advantage from the book's modulated tone—"not too strong and not too bitter"—as well as his unpretentious diction, "almost colloquial and always simple."[11] These were yet ideal qualities for Negro writing.

But a new kind of white critic noted something else in Moon's work, beyond what salved the conscience of white patrons or could work in the Communist membership drives. Thomas Sancton, managing editor of the *New Republic*, offered a cutting edge kind of literary criticism. He suggested a world uninflected by race bias, where whites might take cues from blacks. In Moon's book, Sancton saw the new terms for depictions across the color line. "[T]he Negro is going to take a new status in American fiction, as he has in life," the editor began. "Serious white writers in increasing numbers will enter Richard Wright's field of protest. The Negro's own fight for political and social equality is forcing this change in literature. In white men's books he is going to stop being a "nigger"— no matter how subtly this stereotype has been established heretofore—and become a person." Then Sancton presented an argument that most whites knew nothing about, and which had never been a part of the classic Harriet Beecher Stowe narrative of northern freedom and southern bondage. "What has happened to them is a vast cruel story. The South was built by their toil and suffering. So were Northern fortunes. So were English cotton-textile cities like Liverpool and Manchester. The Southerners must start to tell it right."[12] Only the Communists, whom Sancton had not joined, put the situation of black Americans so candidly, and even they, in 1943, were not arguing outspokenly for black equality. Sancton spoke out with fervor.

The precedent that Moon overturned as a northern-born white treating black characters sympathetically was considerable. Two years before, Elizabeth Lee Wheaton had won the *Virginia Quarterly's* Jefferson Award for her 1941 book *Mr. George's Joint*, an example of barely adequate vaudeville. The book's black protagonist, George, aspires to run a bawdy house and leaves small-town Texas for Houston so that he can manage his own beer-garden. Wheaton subscribed to the notion of the simon-pure racial type, and she offered her readers ample descriptions of black characters that were "simian" and "ape-like" in appearance. Typical of the level of motivation and rationale that she provided for her characters was the remark, "in common with his race, he had the happy faculty of reconciling himself to circumstances over which he had no control."[13] Wheaton was an excellent example of the nearly ugly ambivalence of the southern liberal. Her seriously treated work sustained deeply ingrained caricatures. And yet, despite the racism in her book, she sought the end of formal racial injustice. She dedicated herself to working tirelessly in engagements and public venues, particularly in the journal *Common Ground*. But when she looked for the humanity of American blacks, she saw an illusion, a fantastic bogey out of her own imagination.

Moon represented the dawn of another era of representation. A year after Moon had published his book, white writers no longer delved into extended caricature with the presumption that it might stand in for serious literature. In December 1943 Moon's Doubleday announced the George Washington Carver Award, "for any book dealing with American Negroes deemed worthy of [the] recognition."[14] Here was a structural support that pushed liberal racial attitudes into American homes. And a likelier figure could not have been chosen. The Carver cult generated biographies and encomiums about the meek ex-slave who had spent his life in loyal service and without any bitterness. But this model of a liberal attitude carried a painful contradiction: the celebration of black genius, but exclusively within the confines of humility, or even worse, obsequiousness.

Offering up an award in Carver's name was another achievement that can probably be attributed to Moon, who took on new responsibilities. Throughout the 1940s he worked as an editor at Doubleday and reviewed for *New Republic*, *Nation*, and the *New York Times*. From those posts he helped to deliver two of the decade's most important black writers: Ann Petry and Chester Himes. Moon believed that Himes had "power and rare insight" and that Petry was "exciting" and a "real writer."[15] He tried, but failed, to deliver Sterling Brown.

With the exception of Hurston, Moon knew very few blacks prior to the publication of his first novel. He gave a reading in fear and trembling at the 135th Street library shortly after the novel came out, avoiding the questioning face of a black teen who asked him how he dared to presume to write about black life.[16] An older member of the audience might have accused him of having the ethics of a poacher. After *Darker Brother* Moon's presumptions and his contacts with blacks would grow—even to the point of belittling his mentor Zora Neale Hurston. As a first move, he sent a copy of *Darker Brother* to NAACP head Walter White, who then invited him to lunch. A dilettante novelist and never one to miss out on a deal, White quickly hooked up a contract at Doubleday for his book about black troops in World War II, *A Rising Wind*.

Walter White and Bucklin Moon had one oasis for their camaraderie among other well-placed blacks and white liberals, and that was at the home of social worker, political activist, and Harlem belle Mollie Moon. Bucklin Moon became a habitué of Mollie and her husband Henry Lee Moon's parties, held variously at apartments on 66th Street and in Harlem's Sugar Hill on 157th Street and St. Nicholas Avenue. Mollie Moon was the glamorous hostess of Harlem's most celebrated interracial affairs in the 1940s, and she gained her post as a prominent organizer for Franklin D. Roosevelt's 1944 re-election committee. The years 1943 and 1944 hummed with spirited gatherings, in spite of the war. At these parties Bucklin Moon met chiefly dynamic black Americans. Henry Lee's first cousin Chester Himes made the parties during the fall of 1944, where Moon enjoyed the immense abilities of the raconteur Thurgood Marshall. Housing advisor Robert Weaver, Ted Poston, Charles Johnson, W.E.B. Du Bois, Shirley Graham, and other civil rights celebrities arriving to New York or preparing for battle in distant parts of the country unburdened themselves at the Moon's parties. During the era of tense interracial contact, guests must have deeply enjoyed the joke of black and white Moons.

Because of Moon's early years in Minnesota and Massachusetts and his having lived in New York for all of the 1940s, his foes could write him off as an unprincipled northerner meddling in southern affairs. And then Moon began his career, almost at the outset, as a novelist. Imaginative fiction seemed fluffy and not exactly a hard-hitting way to change American society. But the country evolved dramatically during the 1940s, when the now swinging bat of America's expanding racial liberalism hit the pages of the high-brow magazines and reshaped mainstream public discourse. Among the famous editors—Philip Rahv at *Partisan Review*, Allen Tate at *Sewanee*, Hiram Haydn at *American Scholar*, Bernard DeVoto at *Harper's*, Eliot Cohen at *Commentary*—none was more confrontational toward American racial prejudice wherever it might be found than Thomas Sancton, the man who had lavishly praised Bucklin Moon. The *New Republic's* managing editor in 1943, Sancton brought to these public debates over the "Negro problem" the impeccable credentials of a white man native to the deep South.

Intense and humorless, Sancton earned his reputation with most Americans at the flagship of the liberal magazines. The *New Republic*, a longstanding haven for the liberal intelligentsia, had hoped to keep its cutting edge sharp by appointing a scalawag, a southerner with attitudes liberal even in the North, to its helm in the early 1940s. Founded in 1914 by Herbert Croly, the stalwart *New Republic* had been designed "to start little insurrections in the realm of its [readers'] convictions."[17] The journal endorsed New Deal policies, among them the support of federal laws that banned any form of racial discrimination, and it advocated for labor—issues that were of keen interest to the new editor.

But it had not been that tradition that people remembered during the year that was the turning point of the Second World War. The journal in the early 1940s was reeling a bit in the murky political waters and attempting to recover from what was considered more than a Stalinist flirtation during the 1930s. Two years before Sancton became the day-to-day manager, Trotsky-leaning James Farrell had described portions of the journal as in full "renegade[s] from liberalism," and he also used the word "vulgarity" to describe its literary offerings.[18]

This was a jolt. During the 1930s the journal had been the billet of the prince of American letters Edmund Wilson. Wilson had graduated from Princeton, and he had used books like *Axel's Castle* and *To the Finland Station* to explain the challenging European modernism in the arts and Marxism in politics. But during the second half of the decade more radical voices than Wilson's grew in volume, especially the founding voice of the Lost Generation.

More or less, the literary editor Malcolm Cowley was thought to have besmirched the magazine's reputation by his procommunist views. In 1936, when the Popular Front was at its peak, Cowley said to Edmund Wilson, "It seems to me that the comrades are acting more sensibly these days." To which Wilson replied, "I liked them better when they were crazy."[19] As if to characterize the shift in American liberal thought away from radicalism, by the early 1940s Wilson had moved away from *New Republic*, was unhappily married to *Partisan Review* editor Mary McCarthy, and was publishing his regular work in the *New Yorker*. As late as 1946 George Orwell would include *New Republic* alongside *PM* and *Nation* as a "liberal Fifth Column" in the newly declared war against communism.[20] Cowley remained permanently humiliated about the period between 1935 and 1942, and when he wrote *The Dream of the Golden Mountains*, his memoir of the 1930s, he eliminated the Stalinist years.

A twenty-seven-year-old Sancton left the second half of a Harvard Nieman Fellowship and moved to New York to become *New Republic*'s managing editor in 1942. Louis Lyons, the curator of the Nieman Foundation for Journalism, and Professor Paul Buck of Harvard had given him high recommendations when Bruce Bliven, the magazine's president and editor, started looking for a new person to run the journal. Sancton provided *New Republic* with a new direction. When he arrived at the 49th Street offices, Sancton relentlessly presented to readers the grisly, unflattering pattern of American racial injustice and cruelty. A New Orleans native and 1935 Tulane graduate, Sancton emphasized his origins as a son-of-the-South and his experience living in New Orleans and Mississippi to rip the façade off of a congenial white southland, beneficent and united in its attitude toward "the Negro."

By the time he got to *New Republic*, Thomas Sancton had been a leader advancing liberal racial attitudes for five years. He had reached a national audience with short stories in *Harper's* that interceded against race prejudice. His 1938 short story "The Dirty Way" described the moral inadequacy of white police reporters and detectives in New Orleans, a failure that undergirded racist violence. In 1941 he published "The Parting," a stock piece of short fiction about a white boy's fond memory of a black servant dismissed from her job because of racial prejudice. By April 1943 Sancton believed he would write books on the race question constituting "a new approach to the South." His plans were elaborate. "I should hope [to be] one of the first of a new tradition of Southern treatment in fiction, based on real science, instead of murky mumbo-jumbo about Negroes, which passes for realism in the Southern realists."[21]

He worked from the sound presumption that much of the writing about black Americans was deeply flawed. Whether or not he had the capacity to write a different tradition would present the exhausting challenge of a lifetime, and it was a quest that did not always win him admiration. Tess Mayer Crager, a New Orleans bookshop owner and friends with Sancton's editor Lebaron Barker at Doubleday, described Sancton in a letter to Barker ten years after his *New Republic* stint. "I think he's crazy," she wrote Barker, doubting that Sancton would finish his proposed novel. "It is my belief that he will wind up in Jackson at the state asylum because they won't be able to afford DePaul's."[22]

There were other writers prepared to risk sanity and career in order to rewrite the cultural and political history of American race relations, like journalist Carey McWilliams, who published *Brothers under the Skin* in June 1943, a book with a chapter devoted to virtually every prominent American racial and ethnic minority. And here was the other tenet of Sancton's challenge to southern liberalism. During the fall of 1942, Sancton had wandered into Harvard's Widener Library and read his way through the historical literature on slavery. The experience deeply affected a sensibility already keen. Unlike the up-and-coming novelist Lillian Smith, Sancton believed in the radical historian's perspective, the code of Atlanta University sociologists W.E.B. Du Bois and Ira de A. Reid and the still brewing analysis of Trinidadian Eric Williams, whose book *Capitalism and Slavery* was still several years away. He believed this so sincerely that he secured a recommendation letter from Reid, a reversal of the usual pattern of white authority vetting black talent. Sancton held that the southern aristocracy of large-scale growers and industrialists was responsible for steadily fomenting and exploiting racial hatred to control whites, and in articles in 1943 he pointed his finger at Alabama's governor and Memphis's commissioner of public safety. Sancton's early ambition was rewarded by a Rosenwald Fellowship, the first of several.

Sancton's efforts at *New Republic* helped to make possible a significant transition in the United States by the second half of the 1940s, when even a moderately perceptive novelist like Fannie Cook understood that "Jim Crow is Public Enemy No. 1."[23] In the 1920s white writers had made careers writing about the Negro, but even the more generous of them, like Julia Peterkin and T. S. Stribling, had resorted to comic stereotypes and heavy regional folklore; making black uplift the center of a serious writer's career was unheard of. In the 1940s public tastes shifted, and the writers along with them. As Sancton had noted in his review of Bucklin Moon, Richard Wright's success showed for the first time the commercial viability of deeply penetrating psychological portraits that went beyond the old stereotypes and clichés about the "Negro problem."

New Republic presented a good bit of the information and analysis enabling Americans to grow beyond their racist heritage. In an effort to defeat Nazi racial propaganda, Columbia University anthropologists used U.S. Army intelligence tests to show that environment, not heredity, had the heaviest impact on the development of human intelligence. These would culminate with M. F. Ashley Montagu's 1945 article "Intelligence of Northern Negroes and Southern Whites in the First World War," published in the *American Journal of Psychology*.[24] Sancton wrote about the scholarship emphasizing that American Negroes scored higher than whites if the blacks were from the North and the whites from the South. And he revealed the wickedness of a certain Kentucky congressman who successfully stopped the report from being distributed to the army's officers.[25] In his chief dissident move, Sancton did not interpret black Americans' growing impatience with segregation as merely impudence leading inevitably to race war, like southern liberals Virginius Dabney and James Boyd, especially in his coverage of the widespread rioting in 1943.[26] Both dramatic moments—the downfall of biological inferiority arguments and the existence of undeniable black resentment and outrage—greatly complicated the fictional portraiture of black Americans. Sancton perceptively anticipated the new future where black aggressiveness would no longer be handled by lynch mobs but would be dealt with by the state.

Which all meant that Sancton became a specialist at telling people the things that they did not want to hear, and to hear them meant inevitably that the order of things would change. He showcased in his journalism the difficult stories of racial injustice with which whites were unfamiliar unless reading the Negro press. One of the early reports Sancton brought to the journal's readers presented the case of Odell Waller, a black farmer electrocuted for killing a white man in Virginia. Sancton showed a rural Bigger Thomas to the nation because, though Waller may have been technically guilty as charged, the overriding circumstances of the debt-peonage system in Pittsylvania County and the inability of black farmers to seek redress under law were among the "profound though subtle values" mitigating the case and requiring "no compromise and no apology in the conscience of a real liberal."[27]

Sancton used the term "real liberal" to distinguish the levels of commitment between himself and those he derogatorily labeled "southern liberals," who stood fast to racial segregation and insidiously aided the old planter regime. Sancton hoped to lead a crusade against the people he called the "arrogant malefactors," despots whom he believed had viciously corrupted the ignorant poor whites of the South. He argued regularly that it was far less the working-class white who would become violent at hearing the argument of racial equality, but rather the remnants of the Bourbon plantocracy clinging to power. In some distinction to his counterpart Bucklin Moon at Doubleday, Sancton concentrated on remonstrating whites for their failures to live up to the liberal creed of American democracy, rather than creating exemplary blacks worthy of integration.

Sancton hoped to expose the demagogues who stirred up racial hate and to use his personal experiences among southern whites to reverse the time-worn axiom that it was chiefly working-class southern whites who blocked integration and that southern elites protected Negroes out of genteel obligation. To effect this move, Sancton had freed himself from a tradition. Like many of his regional peers, his career as a thinker had begun with the manifesto *I'll Take My Stand*, the intellectual totem for young southern men of his generation. But when Sancton closed the book he repudiated it. "It is the kind of book to read once, understand for its unintended exposure of the weakness of regional culture, and then to dismiss, while passing on to books of genuine importance," he wrote to the Rosenwald committee.[28] The combined relinquishing of agrarianism and the Sambo historiography of U. B. Phillips set him apart. It made Sancton a one-man revolution prying off the mystique of whiteness and the romantic sentiment that lay within.

The 1930 book *I'll Take My Stand* had ascribed a racial policy to the Fugitive Agrarians, written by the group's youngest and probably most liberal member, Robert Penn Warren. In a cautious, unoriginal essay called "The Briar Patch," which praised Booker T. Washington and vocational education, Warren avowed that the "Southern negro has always been a creature of the small town and farm. That is where he still chiefly belongs, by temperament and capacity." Moreover, within that scheme of attentive "southern liberal" social concern, the Negro was to remain "beneath his own vine and fig tree," which was to say without any.[29]

But Warren's deep-seated paternalist racism was of the prep school sort next to the active passion of his older colleague, Vanderbilt English professor and poet Donald Davidson, who had thought Warren's "Briar Patch" essay too charitable in 1932.[30] (Warren would, in a sense, allow himself to be seen as charitable on racial issues in a 1946 *New Republic* review of Malcolm Cowley's *The Portable Faulkner* when he said, "The actual role of the Negro in Faulkner's fiction is consistently one of pathos or heroism."[31]) Unrelievingly galled by the national licking the South had taken by 1945 concerning its intention to continue segregating the races, Davidson produced a revitalized manifesto for apartheid called "Preface to Decision" in the pages of the *Sewanee* review in 1945. Unlike the New Deal–radical *New Republic,* which in 1946 turned over editorial control to Henry Wallace, Roosevelt's one-time vice president fired by Truman from the post of secretary of commerce, and basically ended their coverage of arts and literature, *Sewanee* was one of the most influential literary periodicals in the United States.[32] Davidson did not wish to forgo the label of cultured man of tolerance and one able to appreciate diversity, but he refused to acknowledge in the southern situation a case of cruelty and systematic injustice toward nonwhites.

Instead, he pelted the newly credentialed American intellectuals, the social scientists, whom Davidson claimed were the spawn of northern abolitionists. Behind an essay that indulged in the more vicious of racial stereotypes lurked a cry against the fact of gross regional underdevelopment and a prayer to retain the prominence of a humanist college faculty.

Davidson believed that the black American could not be incorporated into the southern way of life to begin with because he "cannot enjoy contemplating his own name in quite the same way the white man does, since there is hiatus or lurking humiliation where there ought to be history." Davidson went on to argue that segregation was begun to protect blacks and that citizenship and enfranchisement were not constitutional guarantees for African Americans living in the South. Reaching the crescendo of the essay, he surmised that the Fourteenth Amendment to the U.S. Constitution, guaranteeing citizenship to ex-slaves, created the modern-day totalitarian corporation. "The growth of industrial monopolies in the United States at large and 'colonization' of Southern resources by the financial-industrial East are a direct result of the Fourteenth Amendment," Davidson wrote. "In giving giant industry and speculative finance a free hand, the Amendment tore up the social and economic foundations of the older American life and substituted an abstract economic life."[33]

Davidson saw only continued abridgment of individual liberty under the "totalitarian" and "Leviathan state of the New Deal model," the same conditions that had produced the injustice blacks protested against in housing, public discrimination, and employment in the North.[34] He was uncontroversial when he observed that African Americans had gained only a "shadowy caricature of the democracy which the Constitution as a whole was intended to secure." The question of whether or not the Civil War had been fought as an inevitable action in keeping with the liberal rhetoric of the nation's founding documents or if blacks were inadvertently freed to join the ranks of common men who were subjugated totally by a victorious industrial behemoth remains hotly debated.

In any event, intellectual segregationists did not leave the field in the mid-1940s. There was a fairly clear line between Davidson and the political thinking of New Critical forebearers Ezra Pound and T. S. Eliot.[35] *Sewanee* editor Allen Tate, whose fellowships, international travels, and relationships with northern Ivy League writers made him a bit less comfortable with venting reactionary attitudes, feared that the case had been made too plainly. He wanted to avoid the appearance of proclaiming Nazi-like South African racial policies; America, after all, was not a white minority country. Tate's response to the essay proves the ubiquity of appearing the tolerant liberal by the mid-1940s.

In the next issue, Tate put the journal on record as advancing "simply the correction of extreme." He hoped to keep *Sewanee* safely tucked in the southern liberal intellectual center, but Tate could not help bogeying badly on the issue.

Where Davidson attacked the sociologists and their statistical tables, Tate could not resist a more underhanded call to white supremacy. He aimed his lance at what he thought a noble confrontation with "radical Negro leaders," encouraged by "certain anthropologists (we hesitate to say, of the white race)" who threatened Armageddon by proposing the slander that "the Negro is superior to the white."[36] Face-to-face with the works of Franz Boas, Melville Herskovits, and Margaret Meade, the proof positive of white supremacy would not survive the fall of Nazi Germany, and Tate was left with a sleazy appeal to white racial solidarity. White people like Thomas Sancton were traitors of the most despicable sort to Allen Tate.

Sancton considered himself leagues different from southerners who believed that segregation was wrong but that only prudence and forbearance could conquer it without another civil war. During the mid-1940s he tried to bend to the true path liberals who were actually productively working to improve the economic and social crisis but did not go far enough, like newspaper editor Hodding Carter of Greenville, Mississippi. When the swashbuckling Carter published the 1944 novel *The Winds of Fear*, Sancton let it be known that, despite the personal bravery of the author and the promise of the work, the characters and situations presented were adolescent, comforting perhaps, but inadequate guides for the future. Carter's book wanted mainly to show that racial violence originated with the rumor-mongering of the fearful. Essentially, the book details the white leadership in the town coming to grips with a few of the implications of modern-style race relations.

But in his novel Carter maintained the backbone of the contemporary system of race relations. In the book white violence reacts to black provocation. Carter refused outright the idea that innocent blacks felt the weight of white malice, and his black militants were impetuous scamps. When the only black doctor, a militant, leaves the ghetto Kirby's Quarters, only the doctor's discomforting attitudes receive comment, not the fact that the town's blacks no longer have access to medical services. From Carter's top-down perspective, white liberals lead the social transformation, in the person of a heroic newspaper editor and his son, who has been educated in the North and maimed in the Pacific. The wounded veteran represents the possibilities of a fructifying liberalism, though one that must always embrace loss.

For the black community, the accommodationist teacher Professor Monroe is the hero. Not even a third of the way through the book, he endorses the wise southern liberals. "We didn't stop them from lynching us," the professor thinks to himself after a black soldier has been killed by a cruel police officer. "They did themselves."[37] The implication was clear: the South could solve its own problems. Nor was Carter slipping in a point of view pulled from fantasy. The year before, Professor J. Saunders Redding had featured a long conversation in

No Day of Triumph with the principal of a Negro college who articulated exactly the same view.

Sancton did not let his partial admiration for the author (who, unlike Carson McCullers, still lived in the deep South) prevent him from exposing the dangerous myth of southern class relationships perpetuated by *The Winds of Fear*. He faulted Carter for upholding "the traditional view of Southern liberals that lynchers are to be found chiefly among a margin of malevolent poor whites, while many high-minded main-streeters and planters oppose mob action through an innate zeal for justice." Sancton dismissed the idea of the common rabble, like the feeble-minded Doc Hines and storm trooper Percy Grimm of Faulkner's dense treatment of lynching, *Light in August*, stirring up the town. "Southern life is not really like this . . . behind every lynch mob stalks the spirit of the Southern main streets and plantations, whose owners have the deepest investment in caste and economic serfdom."[38]

The culmination of his duties as manager of the liberal conscience appeared toward the end of 1943. Sancton dutifully brought to his *New Republic* audience his tart remedy with a special race issue for October 18. *New Masses*, of course, had led the progressive weeklies with a wartime race issue in October 1942 called "The Negro," followed by Locke's special *Survey Graphic* issue, "Color: Unfinished Business of Democracy," in November. *New Republic*'s contribution was a deluxe two-part special issue called "The Negro: His Future in America." Sancton tried to bring aboard a new audience, the "large, passive group of white Americans . . . uneasy about the mounting race conflict." But, as likely as not, he missed them. Because what he had in store for them was guilt, a heavy duty to change the country, and a condensed psychological rationale that had appeared before only in sketched-out form in the work of Faulkner. "The reason for the historic white faintheartedness grows out of the omni-present, insistent anti-Negro propaganda inherent in every facet of our culture," he entreated the audience, "it grew out of a deep psychological fear of a 'strange' race, a race with superficial markings dramatically differing from the white norm." He continued to investigate and detail the layers of the phobia: "The white soul is saturated with fear; white culture embedded within itself, and perpetuated at all cost, every educational device that was possible to teach this fear of the stranger and buttress it through customs, myths, and old wives' tales. And white America as well as black was victimized in the process."[39]

The connection between racism and fear, while obvious to modern readers, was new when still near the dawn of American psychoanalysis and around the time of the migration of the European expatriates trained in psychological theory. Rarely had white America looked at itself in the mirror with such courage and without sentiment. Sancton kept on and published a short essay, "The South Needs Help," in the Interracial Commission's journal *Common Ground*.

In it he stated plainly that the problem of the southern region was the moral problem of slavery. "Stealing these people from their own continent was a violation of a profound natural law and we are paying for it."[40] This was an apology to the enslaved, a rather spectacular admission from a southerner, when demagogues like Bilbo were calling for boats to return Negroes to Africa, in the same spirit as a doctor would rid a sick body of a disease.

The best evidence of a keel unable to keep a boat right, shortly after these articles Sancton officially left his duties as *New Republic*'s managing editor. He wanted to keep his options open until 1946 when his name was formally removed as contributing editor, the same year that *New Republic* went over to Henry Wallace's third party candidacy. Sancton returned to Mississippi in 1943 to repair his wife's health, no doubt made worse by her husband's Negro fixation. He took a high-paying job from *Life* magazine, which he clutched for a few months until he secured another Rosenwald Fellowship, this time to work on a novel about southern life.

Instead of southern elites transforming centuries of injustice, he proposed salvation by way of the celebration of the southern yeoman. During the same year as Carter's book, Sancton had fired off several chapters from his nonfiction study to Harper's editor Frederick Lewis Allen and, for three out of the first four months of 1944, *Harper's* published a near chapter-length excerpt. In January it ran "Race Clash," a short story of a young Sancton and his college pals, abusing their white privilege to instigate and then win a fight with Negro teens who are chaffing against the humiliating caste system. If he had been immoderate in his youth, he was now contrite and thoughtful. After the white men vanquish the black adolescents with the threat of ominous white violence, Sancton concludes that "the experience drove home to me the utter immorality of the Southern caste system."[41] "Silver Horn" in February was a reminiscing idyll of Boy Scout camp summers on the bayou for the sons of the upper working class. In his panorama of adolescence, Sancton included a memorable portrait of a Paul Bunyan–sized black man named Joe, who "got to be one of the people I liked best of all—not only in the camp but in my whole circumscribed world."[42] April's "The Tall Man" revealed a courageous but broken white laborer, relying upon his reserves of dignity to cheat death. This was the strength of the approach that Sancton brought to bear, insightful and deeply observant reportage, squeezing the lumps of quotidian coal to glean the sparkling gems inside. The literary sensibility that he had achieved as an advocate of racial equality now enabled him to perceive and grapple with the varieties of Americans. By 1945 Sancton had moved his project from Harper's to Doubleday and was calling the omnibus *The Southern People*. He never finished the book.

Sancton did not become giddy as America scored a few victories on the front of race relations, and there was good reason. If the publishing world had allowed him to flourish, other talented writers with similar stories, like African American Sterling Brown, who had been contracted at the end of the 1930s by Doubleday for a nonfiction prose book on the South, did not rate the prestigious magazines like *Harper's*. In *Phylon,* Brown did publish three short pieces in 1945—"Georgia Nymphs," "Georgia Sketches," and "The Muted South"—but they did not generate enthusiasm. As an editor, Thomas Sancton had perceptively counseled blacks to keep a healthy suspicion of the helping hands lent to them. "I believe that the Negro, in the long run, is the Negro's most trustworthy friend, and I believe he will never win any benefit he does not win by his own ability, independence, courage, and political organization."[43]

This was an unpleasant departure from the optimism and, at times, exceptionalism of the American liberal creed during the mid-1940s. And black writers, especially the committed social realists like Ann Petry, noted the problem of white literary allies. Petry wrote her aunt Helen Chisholm in 1943, rueful about white critics like Hurston's foe Harold Preece, who was "evidently making a career of writing about Negroes." "[A] good many people have found gold in them thar hills," she complained, "but too few of them were Negroes."[44] The liberal whites raising awareness would never be as good at helping blacks as they would be at helping themselves.

6.1. Paul Robeson, Sr. and Sterling Brown, ca. 1939   Courtesy of Moorland-Spingarn Research Center, Howard University

6.2. Horace Cayton, 1948   Photograph by Carl Van Vechten, James Weldon Johnson Collection in the Yale Collection of American Literature, Beinecke Rare Book and Manuscript Library, Yale University

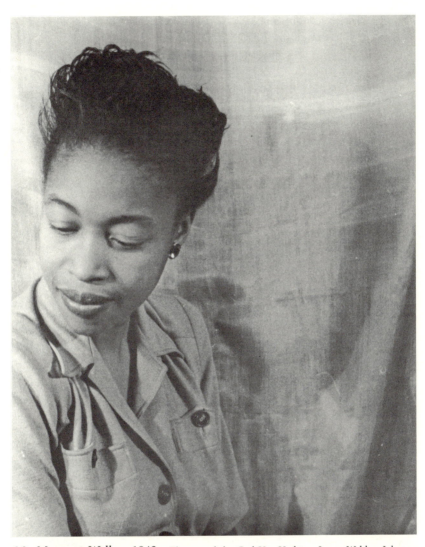

6.3. Margaret Walker, 1942   Photograph by Carl Van Vechten, James Weldon Johnson Collection in the Yale Collection of American Literature, Beinecke Rare Book and Manuscript Library, Yale University

NATIVE SON

BY

Richard Wright

Author of
UNCLE TOM'S CHILDREN

Even today is my complaint rebellious,
My stroke is heavier than my groaning.
—Job

HARPER *&* BROTHERS PUBLISHERS
New York and London
1940

6.4. *Native Son* by Richard Wright, 1940, title page   Copyright 1940 by Richard Wright. Copyright © renewed 1968 by Ellen Wright. Reprinted by permission of HarperCollins Publishers.

6.5. Richard Wright, 1946   Photograph by Carl Van Vechten, James Weldon Johnson Collection in the Yale Collection of American Literature, Beinecke Rare Book and Manuscript Library, Yale University

6.6. J. Saunders Redding, 1943   Photograph by Carl Van Vechten, James Weldon Johnson Collection in the Yale Collection of American Literature, Beinecke Rare Book and Manuscript Library, Yale University

6.7. William Attaway, 1941 Photograph by Carl Van Vechten, James Weldon Johnson Collection in the Yale Collection of American Literature, Beinecke Rare Book and Manuscript Library, Yale University

6.8. Chester Himes, ca. 1939   Julius Rosenwald Foundation Papers, Special Collections, John Hope and Aurelia Elizabeth Franklin Library, Fisk University

THE NEGRO QUARTERLY

A REVIEW OF NEGRO LIFE AND CULTURE

A SOUTHERN VIEW OF
THE RACE QUESTION
THOMAS SANCTON

ROSALIE
J. S. REDDING

AFRICA AGAINST THE AXIS
JOHN PITTMAN

IN THE FASCIST STYX
HARRY SLOCHOWER

3 FALL
1942
50 CENTS

6.9. *Negro Quarterly*, fall 1942, cover

6.10. Hugh Gloster, 1948, jacket photograph *Negro Voices in American Fiction*, 1948.
University of North Carolina Press. Courtesy of the private collection of Randall K. Burkett.

6.11. Bucklin Moon at his editorial desk at Doubleday, 1945 Ken McCormick/
Doubleday Papers, Library of Congress

CHAPTER SEVEN

"Beating That Boy": White Writers, Critics, Editors, and the Liberal Arts Coalition (1944–1949)

A literary crusader like Thomas Sancton was rare, but he was not without peer as American literary taste began to confront social fact. Edwin Seaver recomposed himself from his days as a League of American Writers executive secretary and as a staff writer for the *Daily Worker* by compiling the important anthology *Cross-Section* in 1944. Seaver had moved toward the political center with the rest at the end of 1930s. He had edited special issues of the Federal Writers' Project organ *Direction* in the early 1940s and then branched out to create his own volume *Cross-Section*, which regularly featured the latest literary innovators and stylists and included black writers. Seaver paid his bills with a regular job as publicity manager for the Book-of-the-Month Club, perfecting his instincts for popular trends. When he held the call for manuscripts for the legendary first volume of *Cross-Section*, the response stunned him. During the four years that the anthology came out, Seaver published 150 writers, plucked out from seven thousand submissions.[1]

Cross-Section showed a remarkable sense of literary taste and, significantly, a kind of ecumenicism several years ahead of its time. Seaver took no credit for it himself but rather thought the outpouring evidence of a fully shifting worldview in the United States. "An astonishing number of the manuscripts" addressed racial injustice, "what we call the 'Negro problem'," he told his audience in 1944. Black and white writers sent in these retributive manuscripts and confirmed for Seaver that the American author was preoccupied by "feelings of remorse."[2]

The inaugural volume proved extraordinary. Seaver published Wright's novella "The Man Who Lived Underground," which the editor himself called "one of the most notable short stories I have ever read"; "Flying Home," the short story that introduced Ralph Ellison's mature style; social realist Carl Ruthven Offord; and Langston Hughes.[3] The collection showcased new American writers displaying strong leftist leanings, like playwright Arthur Miller and Harvard graduate-turned-infantryman Norman Mailer. And in the third volume of 1947, Seaver published Ann Petry's novella "In Darkness and Confusion," her superb treatment of the Harlem riot.

Cross-Section was an obvious product linked to the 1930s, the League of American Writers, and the Communist Party. In a fashion, it remained true to the principles of radical social justice from the earlier period. Social realism, racial justice, working-class black American urban life, and popular culture featured prominently in Offord's Harlem-based "Low Sky" and Petry's riot narrative "In Darkness and Confusion." Ellison's short story splashed brushstrokes of deliberate modernist techniques to convince whites of their shared humanity with blacks: a psychologically revealing interior monologue; a highly educated, ambitious, and contemplative protagonist; and absurd symbols invoking tragedy and grotesque comedy. It concluded with the ironic hunger of blacks simultaneously seeking and fleeing their own people, and from themselves. Neither Petry, Offord, nor Ellison concluded their stories with interracial collaboration, a stock trope of Communist-backed fiction; instead they offered black racial collaboration. Wright's story of a wrongfully accused man toyed with the chief Western symbols for evil, time, and enlightenment, to suggest that only by accepting the imminence of violent death could the absurdity of morality and rationality be revealed and a new path generated. By 1944 the fiction writers were imagining black identity in the same terms that Horace Cayton had predicted—one that did not rely upon white liberals.

The role of even busy white liberals like Seaver and Bucklin Moon faded after the war. But the most successful writer in the 1940s who used the tropes that have become indelibly connected with African American writing—the lynching of the innocent, the prophylactic beating administered by parents, the lyrical catalog of the pastoral southern landscape, forbearance in the face of societal opposition, the tragic inertia of the light-skinned black—was neither African American nor a member of the political Left. Lillian Smith was a native Floridian, educated at Piedmont College, Peabody Conservatory, and Columbia University. From her quarters in Clayton, Georgia, the lesbian woman differed a great deal from her prominent southern peers who had tackled questions of racial oppression in serious fiction, such as Erskine Caldwell, Carson McCullers, and William Faulkner.

Dating at least as far back as Joel Chandler Harris's *Uncle Remus* tales, southern white writers and collectors had seen the value of black oral culture on the written page. In the twentieth century white writers like Frank W. Dixon and Thomas Nelson Page had used black characters in the emerging genre of popular fiction and propagandart as symbols of villainous evil. The venerable comic tradition in music, theater, and advertising thrived with the black characters of Octavus Roy Cohen, particularly his Florian Slappey detective fictions. But it fell to Erskine Caldwell to write popular exposés of the moral and constitutional bankruptcy of working-class southern whites. In famous works like *Tobacco Road*, he used Negroes as agents to further the ridicule of whites.

The same year as *Native Son*, Caldwell published a treatment of lynching called *Trouble in July*, and his book and Willa Cather's *Sapphira and the Slave Girl* were two notable efforts offering a newly serious treatment of black characters and themes from southern white writers. Cather's *Sapphira and the Slave Girl* telescoped the key dramatic tension of slavery into a mixed-race girl's struggle for virtue. Though Cather relied on fairly crude stereotypes—African blacks were cannibals; black "blood" was indolent and superstitious; the darker the bondsperson, the smaller their intelligence; blacks did not desire freedom; slavery was no worse than indenture—she suggested an intimacy and symbiosis between whites and blacks that had an excellent basis in historical reality and added dignity to the relationships. And her plot hinged on the pursuit of slave girl Nancy by the disreputable white nephew Martin Colbert, a pursuit condemned by the white community that engineers Nancy's escape.

Erskine Caldwell, after many years of writing scathingly of the South's white poor, constructed a book about lynching. As victim he included an extremely sympathetic black character named Sonny Clark, tracked by a mob of drunken, poor white farmers for the rape of a "cornfield slut" that he did not commit. After the innocent boy is hung, the accuser recants in front of the mob and is stoned to death, while the impotent sheriff watches from the bushes. The intense shaping of the plot around the drama and hysteria of lynching, and the satirizing of sheriff Jeff McCurtain's designs to escape what he calls a "political lynching" on the eve of an election, dramatized the local politics behind the reluctant federal efforts to pass an antilynching bill, as well as showing the impossibility of full citizenship rights for blacks. But while Caldwell's Hobbesian sort of satire judged most of the world as greatly flawed and unfit and effectively lumped the races together, Cather emphasized the distance yet to be traveled for the full humanity of black characters. Most of American liberals walked a middle ground between the two views.

Lillian Smith had several unpublished novels to her credit and had also edited one of the premier southern "little" magazines of modernism and liberalism, the journal begun as *Pseudopodia*, which became *North Georgia Review*, and by 1942 was called *South Today*. Smith had lived in China and worked with blacks in Baltimore, but she settled in a mountainous and rural Georgia town close to the border of South Carolina. After her book's publication she was regarded as one of the most outspoken southern liberals of the age. Smith developed contacts with and was much appreciated by African American writers and intellectuals working at Atlanta University, like Ira de A. Reid, Arthur Raper, and Owen Dodson, who all visited her retreat where she hosted a summer girls' camp.

She had a good relationship with Sterling Brown, whom she wrote in April 1943 to ask for a candid evaluation of the manuscript that would make her equally famous and infamous. "Sterling," she began, "I want most keenly for you to read my novel in manuscript. Your opinion would have great weight with me—indeed if you were to tell me I'd made a mess I would be utterly disconsolate."[4] Smith honed her credentials as a professional liberal in the pages of the journal *Common Ground*, where she published regularly her arguments for racial inequality and exposed racial injustice in Georgia politics and civil rights organizations.[5] The increasing literary, political, and public power of southern women assisted enormously in the evolution of U.S. literature in the 1940s and 1950s. Smith was joined by white women like Elizabeth Lee Wheaton, Fannie Cook, Carson McCullers, Elizabeth Hardwick, and Flannery O'Connor, whose collective works assisted in defusing the heavy southern taboos of friction and lust between the races and white women at the mercy of black men. But of them all, Smith was the most popular in the 1940s.

Smith had proposed the title for the novel *Strange Fruit* without any awareness of the famous Billie Holiday song, but she followed her agent Frank Taylor's advice and credited Lewis Allan, to whom the richly metaphorical line was popularly understood to belong. Smith had accommodated Taylor out of generosity, but she was a fierce woman who defied southern mores and never displayed typical liberal attitudes in the early 1940s. Smith went on to believe that the acknowledgment of the title credit was designed to "insinuate to the Commies of New York" that she was a "fellow traveler."[6] Smith's unique brand of southern liberalism that seemed to promote interracial sex between white men and black women did not brook association with the radical Left.

Her novel appeared the week of February 26, 1944, with an initial press run of twenty thousand, and because Smith had featured an interracial romance at the book's center, publisher Reynal and Hitchcock was bombarded with mail immediately.[7] The book featured several controversial topics, passingly mentioned but notorious nonetheless. The white central character Tracy Deen rapes his black concubine Nonnie, who has earlier in the novel proclaimed her willingness to bear a child out of wedlock and live in a shack near Deen and his betrothed, Dorothy. There was also some profanity, and Tracy's sister Laura becomes a lesbian.

Things came to a head regarding the book's controversial subject matter after about three weeks. On March 19 Boston booksellers voluntarily decided to pull the book rather than risk a ban. "The members of the Board of Retail Book Merchants, 'acting under a gentlemen's agreement of long standing,' withdrew 'Strange Fruit' from sale after a complaint against the language had been reported lodged with the Commissioner of Police of Boston," the Trade Board's statement read. Publisher Curtis Hitchcock fired back that this was the same as removing all the one-way street signs and then fining motorists for driving the wrong way.[8] Book sales peaked with the uproar.

By the first week of April, Reynal had run 67,000 copies; a week later they were up to 93,000.[9] *Strange Fruit* became a bona fide best seller on April 15, 1944, selling 19,000 copies per week, with 140,000 copies printed by April 22, roughly two months after the book was introduced.[10] These were blockbuster statistics. Reynal and Hitchcock quickly appropriated an $80,000 budget to advertise the controversial book and hitched its wagon to its new star. The advertising campaign, which the professionals labeled "a subtle use of sensationalism that is commendable," won them the *Publisher's Weekly* award for 1944.[11] The advertising was an example of what Ralph Ellison had begun to call "racial schizophrenia." In fifty-seven newspapers in forty-five cities and especially Georgia and Mississippi, the publisher's copy called the book "a dramatic love story of deep tenderness." The African American press carried this tale: "[t]the passionate story of what one town did to a white man's love for a Negro girl." Smith reached the number one spot in book sales in August and remained on the best-seller list through the year. Ten months after the book's release, Smith had sold just under half a million copies, more than Wright's *Native Son*.[12]

Literary merit or no, such a spectacle guaranteed attention. W.E.B. Du Bois's review of *Strange Fruit*, "Searing Novel of the South," appeared on the front page of the *New York Times Book Review* on March 5, 1944. Du Bois's review was appropriate since the structure of Smith's book followed so closely his "Of the Coming of John" short story collected in *The Souls of Black Folks*. Du Bois's review was appropriate since the structure of Smith's book followed so closely his "Of the Coming of John" short story collected in *The Souls of Black Folk*. However the doomed love story between two elite families of Maxwell, Georgia had reversed key elements from Du Bois's romantic tragedy. Black Nonnie Anderson, a Spelman College graduate, accepts a role as Tracy Deen's concubine. (Although he had earlier proposed marriage to her if they moved to France.) Tracy struggles to conform to the regimen of small-town propriety, signaled by his mother and the evangelical reverend, who seek to compel him to marry Dorothy, a safe and traditional mate. Since Nonnie is pregnant, Tracy determines to have her marry his black manservant Henry. Nonnie's college-educated brother Ed, visiting from Washington, D.C., and chafing against the primitive race relations of the South, kills Tracy Deen after he hears of the plan. Although Ed escapes Georgia with the help of the black educated class, in his place Henry is burned alive by the poor whites of the town.

Smith's narrative style was redolently modernist. Instead of hard-boiled naturalist description, she infused her terse lyrical accounts and sharp dialog with free-floating bits of unconscious interior monologue. She tried to show how a legitimate romance collapsed into ruin for the entire town on the basis of a psychological chimera for the lead character, prodigal Tracy Deen. Free-floating linguistic intruders into his consciousness staunch Tracy's most genuine romantic feelings. "*Colored girl. Negro.* Spoiling every moment, like a hair that's got into your food. Why under God's heaven did he keep thinking those damn words!"[13] This was a milder version of the technique that Faulkner had pioneered with *Light in August*, where character Joe Christmas is absorbed by "womanshenegro."

Despite the fact that Smith was labeled a radical for most of her life, she did not break much ground in her representations across the color line. Mainly her coquettish depiction of Nonnie, the unusually light-complexioned young woman who returns from college to become a domestic and live in a Georgia cabin, stretched the burden of credulity to its breaking point. Unsatisfactory are Nonnie's narrow range of motivation, her indifference to the customs and mores of her own black family and community, her willingness to embrace a demimonde tradition that was, perhaps, still popular among southern elites like South Carolinian Strom Thurmond but unlikely with Tracy Deen, a one-time promising young man who has squandered his potential. Nonnie's rationale for having a child in a situation that emphatically harkens back to slavery is, on the face of it, preposterous. "I want it. I'll have something they can't take away from me," Nonnie tells her lover at one of her moments of introspection.[14] These are the words of teenage victims of neglect, domestic abuse, and systematic undereducation. Even her lover Tracy cannot understand how Nonnie, smart enough to graduate from college, has allowed herself to become pregnant. The suggestion is either that Nonnie is an idiot or that she calculatedly chose to have a child with a white college dropout and soda jerk. African American reviewers were quick to challenge the character as a denigration of Negro womanhood, college graduates in particular, and an unfair silencing of the reality of the sexual abuse that black women, like Alabama gang rape victim Recy Taylor, were still suffering at the hands of white men.

If there was doubt about what the best-selling author was doing with Nonnie, less flattering depictions of African Americans in the novel fueled suspicion. Smith's characterizations of working-class blacks tended to fluctuate between martyrs and vaudeville performers. Most dangerously this happened in her depiction of Henry Macintosh, Tracy Deen's long-standing Negro companion, who is lynched for the crime of stumbling upon Tracy Deen's body. It is difficult to understand what makes the local blacks quite so obsequious. For example, Henry's father Ten McIntosh bitterly resents their living in the Deens' backyard and that his son is growing up in the old slave tradition. The father's feelings toward whites are noble. When Henry's mother violently punishes the little boy for sassing a white girl and forgetting his place, Ten cries out, "Gawd jesus, I hate the sight of one! Hate livin in Deen's back yard. Told you a hundard time it'd be better in the quarters where we'd be free to do as we like. I don want ma boy brung up wid no white boy—don want none of it!"[15]

Henry becomes his father's opposite. After Henry has attended school and lived in the Deens' backyard, he achieves what psychological historian Stanley Elkins went on to call at the end of the 1950s a "Sambo" personality, a permanent black, childlike dependency around whites. As the Deen family butler, yard-man, and confidant, Henry McIntosh is a prime caricature, a person who must play a clown's role as a survival skill. When Tracy returns from a long conversation with the Reverend Dunwoodie, who warns him to leave Nonnie and the terrible sin of "colored town" alone, Tracy asks his black comrade Henry for his views on God and the afterlife:

> Henry stared hard at the cup near Tracy's foot. His mouth worked around in circles, he licked his lips, frowned. Then he giggled, figuring now that Tracy had chosen a new way to be funny. "Whoopee, boy! Dat a good one!" He slapped his thigh. "Sho is," he opened his mouth to give a loud guffaw that would compensate for his slowness in catching on.[16]

Smith's portrait of the young black man showed the difficulty some writers had in moving into the modern era. In a scene shortly thereafter, Henry and the black cook prepare to take out razors against one another; readers learn that Henry sexually assaulted Nonnie as a teen; Henry accepts $100 to marry the pregnant Nonnie, and he announces this bargain to all and sundry at the neighborhood bar. Smith's readers can feel little remorse when he is burned alive.

The portrait was offensive enough that several readers doubted her actual attitude toward blacks, to the point that Smith went on to write an autobiographical polemic against racism called *Killers of the Dream* in 1950. When this book was reviewed in *Phylon*, the journal expressed relief at Smith's new clarity on the topic. "Anyone who, after reading the novel, had any doubts about Miss Smith's convictions along certain lines, will now find those doubts completely dispelled."[17] Smith's work epitomized the irony of white liberal participation. She merits her place of influence and leadership in shifting the course of southern race relations, but she chose a dubious path to achieve it. Nor did Sterling Brown find her especially disconsolate when he privately voiced his disproval of her portrait. Smith showed a kind of condescension that seemed to rise inevitably in the minds of southern whites toward what they believed was their own private preserve. "You seem puzzled by Henry," she wrote to him in 1945. "I know in a way Henry seems to you to be no more than a stereotype but there are some human beings whom stereotypes fit. Henry seemed more to me than the laughing, lascivious, stupid, backyard Negro. He was all of that, but his love for Tracy transcended any stereotype and his loneliness as a child, his experiences of always being left out are not stereotypes."[18] Smith was quite capable of missing the point, and to some degree the situation was remarkably similar to Brown's rift with Fannie Hurst in 1935.

But the ten years following *Imitation of Life* had stiffened the resolve of black critics and intellectual leaders. In the late fall of 1944, a group of broadly influential black American leaders showed their uniform impatience with segregation in Rayford Logan's edited volume *What the Negro Wants*. Logan's peers directly countered the sentiment that blacks were willing to work within the flawed segregationist system. But the book became legendary because in it an influential southern white liberal assailed the demand to end racial segregation. The condemnation emerged from the completely remarkable circumstances leading to the publication of the book.

University of North Carolina Press publisher W. T. Couch felt confident in his liberal credentials. He had arranged for J. Saunders Redding's *No Day of Triumph* and did not repress dissent. He had not expected in Logan's volume anything but trouble from the likes of anti-Jesus poet Langston Hughes, blackman-married-to-white woman George Schuyler, labor protestor A. Philip Randolph, or teetering-on-full-blown-communism Doxey Wilkerson. He had supported Logan's inclusion of the radicals, confident that their claims and rhetoric would expose them as fools. But he was dismayed at the change in tone of Logan's responsible black voices, like the college presidents Charles Wesley of Wilberforce, Lesley Hill of Cheyney Teachers College, Mary McCloud Bethune of Bethune-Cookman, and Frederick Patterson of Tuskegee. None of them seemed prepared to accept anymore the exclusive burden of lifting up their race. "I had been hoping that at least two or three of the fifteen authors would raise questions of how far the Negro is responsible for his condition, and deal with the problem of what Negroes themselves can do, regardless of what white people may do," Couch later wrote.[19] The publisher threatened to drop the contracted project altogether. But ultimately he decided that he would publish Logan's book only under one condition: if the editor conceded the publisher the unusual privilege of including a "publisher's introduction."

More to the point, Couch was profoundly disappointed by Logan's book. *What the Negro Wants* delivered the "old complaints against the white man" but failed to properly admit "that the Negro himself has some responsibilities." In the words of black critic Eugene Holmes, the introduction was "one of the strangest spectacles in American publishing history."[21] What the book and the introduction announced was a parting of the ways between a branch of white moderates and the black elites who had desperately relied upon them during the first four decades of the twentieth century. (Couch took his revenge in 1946 when he moved to the University of Chicago and brought out the project that many American presses were eager to see in print, Era Bell Thompson's *American Daughter*. Thompson, the daughter of a freedman and a talented journalist who became one of *Ebony*'s editors, had grown up in North Dakota.[22] Her black female coming-of-age story contained no bitterness on account of Jim Crow.) *What the Negro Wants* powerfully represented the unified disgust with segregationist practices and the resolve to transform the nation by the end of the war. Mary McCloud Bethune had gone as far as drawing an analogy between Harlem rioters—whom Kenneth Clark would psychopathologize in a *Journal of Abnormal Psychology* article in 1945[23]—and the bumptious colonials of Boston Tea Party fame.

The uproar was short-lived. Rayford Logan's edited volume was soon overshadowed by the Carnegie Corporation project of the same year, *An American Dilemma*, shepherded into creation by Swedish economist Gunnar Myrdal. Myrdal's book was a national sensation because of its scope and obvious thoroughness: one thousand pages devoted to a study of the American color line and the social and economic status of the Negro. And in spite of itself, Myrdal's book opened the door further for the creative writers and imaginative intellectuals by countering the economy-minded liberals and steering the conversation away from a disparity of material resources. Myrdal exceeded W. T. Couch by a long mile, but his carefully organized data got him not much further than the 1940 chirping of Archibald MacLeish in *Common Ground*. Instead the Swede pointed to the American Creed and said, "the status accorded the Negro in America represents nothing more and nothing less than a century long lag in public morals."[24] The "Negro Problem" then had nothing to do with the unequal distribution of resources. Black litigants, who strove to break the back of segregation by requiring equal facilities, were spun around. Instead of providing segregation deluxe—equal facilities—white Americans were importuned to discover their own guilt. The economy of racism and its network of social effects had become a problem in mind.

An American Dilemma accomplished one thing irrevocably. The book operated from a principle of racial tolerance that, with few exceptions after World War II, educated Americans would be unable to disavow and still lay claim to the inheritance of Amercan liberalism. The book appeared as the last of a six-volume series, guided at Harper by Ordway Tread. Fearing that a book about race relations would never appeal to the American public, Harper, well out in front on the issue of racial justice, had demanded that the Carnegie Fund underwrite the 2,500-copy print run, agreeing to buy at the end of two years, at full price, any of the unsold copies.[25] Although the double volume went on to exceed the sales expectations, it never would have been launched without the fund's commitment.

Still, with the focus turned to white morality, the Myrdal matrix of race relations left blacks with few options to change their own condition. In Myrdal's view, blacks reacted to a pattern of living laid out for them by the majority whites who Myrdal believed dominated all spheres of activity. Myrdal suggested that only "secondary reactions" were permitted to blacks, a social-psychological condition of subordination. But this, while squarely laying the moral problem of black discrimination at the doorsteps of whites, reduced black contributions to American society to nothing. Myrdal was dismissive of even the work that blacks had performed to expose racism. Black scholarship and writing amounted largely to "zealous dilettantism."[26] Writers and historians had transformed mediocrities into "great men"; "placed on a pinnacle" average cultural achievements; and "magnified into crises" "minor historical events." Despite the tendency for the claim to have the ring of truth, when it came time to support it with evidence, Myrdal and his aides had to resort to subterfuge, citing a pamphlet written by a barber and a book by Garveyite Joel A. Rogers that did not exist.

But weak evidence was no brake for Myrdal's sour estimate of the resources of black culture. "[I]t seems frankly incredible that the Negro people in America should feel inclined to develop any particular race pride at all or have any dislike for amalgamation, were it not for the common white opinion of the racial inferiority of the Negro people."[27] In his opinion blacks were human beings, but black culture was a purely defensive reaction to slavery and second-class citizenship. Chosen by Carnegie funders on the strength of his objectivity and distance from the racial crisis, Myrdal fired a scatter-shot against American racism that included half-truths diminishing black life in America. In an unpublished review, Ralph Ellison resisted Myrdal's tendency to reduce black life to either an assimilative move toward white society or a reactive gesture made to oppose it. "It is only partially true that Negroes turn away from white patterns because they are refused participation. There is nothing like distance to create objectivity, and exclusion gives rise to counter values," he wrote in 1944.[28] At his most suspicious, Ellison worried that the massive study might be used to exploit blacks in the South more effectively.

Myrdal's black researcher-writers like Sterling Brown and Horace Cayton were trapped between patience and confrontation. Toward the end of World War II, Cayton was voicing suspicions about liberals and their purported generosity and Myrdal in particular. He agreed that the question of moral fairness toward Negroes was important, and public events in Chicago easily showed the crass manipulations of racial morality. In one episode, Mayor Ed Kelly appointed an interracial commission to address a housing crisis that had its roots in economic racism. The public was satisfied by the mystical power of the newly appointed and glamorously interracial task force. But working alongside whites cut no ice for Cayton, who yearned now to expose public relations charades. Instead of pride at the committee's endorsement of publicly funded housing, he sensed another Frankenstein developing with the push for government-built residential projects, the original source of the racial tension in Detroit that led to the deadly riot in 1943.

To Cayton's mind, only Richard Wright, a creative writer whose thinking had been formed outside of academic channels, had the sensibility to perceive these flaws in American liberal logic. A catalyst in any circle, Wright was the appropriate source for confidence. "Ten housing projects, twenty housing projects for Negroes in Chicago would in my opinion intensify and make worse the race problem—I'm convinced of this. Now you can't say this, Dick, because people say 'What—you're against housing?'"[29] Due to these reservations, Cayton allowed his junior colleague Robert Taylor to accept the honor of having the major Chicago housing project on State Street bear his name. Chafing against normative modes of possibility, Cayton wanted both intellectual room and worthwhile intellectual comrades. "What we really need is a school of thought, a point of view, a philosophy," he wrote to Wright.

The appearance of token blacks and the addressing of sizable municipal problems like housing by liberal policy makers belied the stark reality of systemic inequality. But Cayton's perceptiveness and striving for new resources to confront the racial situation had dramatic consequences for him personally. As the decade wore on and Cayton's suspicion of traditional liberal allies continued, he admitted to harboring substantial psychological fears and paranoia. In 1943–1944 he began intensive psychoanalysis with Helen McLean, and for a number of years he submitted to as many as four sessions per week.[30] Cayton even became suspicious of his own work at the Parkway Community Center, coming to see his leadership and organization as "part of the machinery by which the subjugation of Negroes was perpetrated."[31] He responded to this sense of despair by raising his commitment to literature, where Cayton perceived intellectual freedom and integrity. He grasped that the raw emotional appeal of Lillian Smith and Richard Wright had done more to popularize awareness of racial injustice than the social sciences that studied the problem on committees and in colleges. If Myrdal was even partly right—that white Americans had to choose the correct response to a moral "dilemma"—then basic American mental habits would have to be rearranged. The new struggle took place on the terrain of human emotional organization, and because the terrain was fundamentally symbolic, the field of struggle was better suited to literature than to social science.

Ironically enough, Cayton's most genuine distress came at the moment of his keenest triumph and greatest power. He took the opportunity to respond to the liberals and to explore his own, more personal disagreements with Gunnar Myrdal in 1945. In 1945 Cayton's best-known achievement appeared, the book he coauthored with the anthropologist St. Claire Drake, *Black Metropolis*. Almost larger than *An American Dilemma*, *Black Metropolis* defined Chicago and drew from the research Cayton had conducted while he and W. Lloyd Warner ran a WPA research team there between 1936 and 1939. The enormous volume resisted offering any single methodology or theory to analyze the conditions affecting black Chicagoans but rather, in its more than eight hundred pages, combined an economic and sociological study with ethnographic vignettes and journalism. The authors offered a history of black migration to Chicago (called "Midwest Metropolis") up to the early 1940s, a detailed analysis of segregation and movement across the color line, especially as it affected employment, and a large socio-ethnography of the famous South Side "Bronzeville" upper and lower classes.

The book opened with a long introduction by Richard Wright, whom Cayton by then revered as the intellectual giant of the age. Challenging bromides about the triumphant progress of Western civilization, Wright connected the material destitution of the slums to the rise of the tyrannical, Hitler-style personality. The introduction reminded Americans of the depraved quality of American personal experience. Wright, who told his friend Ralph Ellison that in the introduction he had finally expressed himself without restraint, allowed that the black individual experiences described in *Black Metropolis* were of "so low a quality and nature as to preclude the deep organic satisfaction necessary for civilized, peaceful living."[32] But he made plain an important rider. The very existence of the shattered black lives revealed in the book condemned "the system that provides those experiences."[33] Twenty years later, Cayton remembered Wright's essay as the most important part of the book;[34] J. Saunders Redding thought it "discloses the *central stream*" of Wright's life work.[35]

And, in places, *Black Metropolis* itself condemned American society outright. The study did not praise America's growing liberalism for contributing to the reduction of race prejudice and racial inequality. "When major shifts in the Negro's status have occurred," the authors decided, "it has usually not been as the result of education and counterpropaganda or of engineered contacts operating in a vacuum; they have come in response to the demands of economic necessity and political expediency."[36] Not even migration out from the impermeable caste relations of the South altered the customary pattern. For Cayton, urban northern America was a society of active racial discrimination, where the boundaries between black and white were vigilantly patrolled. The book had its punch in the lines that northern industrial centers were forcing blacks to embrace "contradictory principles of social organization," "*free competition* and *fixed status*."[37] The contention broke ground by drawing attention to the hardening lines of economic racism in housing and employment in the North. But if the "major shifts" or catastrophes of war and depression caused elements of racial segregation to buckle and crack, blacks had profited by rebelliousness and alienation as much as they had a willingness to play by the rules. Essentially the force of Cayton's ideas and public commentary during the first half of the 1940s proved that blacks in America advanced along a new and undiscovered axis of possibility.

But what perhaps best indicated the uniting of sociology and fiction was the unusual opening of chapter 20, "Lower Class: Sex and Family," surely one of the most sensitive sections in the book. The chapter begins with a short fictional-ized narrative exploring the life and thought of a "dicty" black doctor treating a stabbing victim in a dilapidated tenement. Crafted from eyewitness events and interviews, the narrative had not been, as the footnote beginning the chapter testified, "subjected to imaginative recasting" by the authors.[38] Turning the raw data of black experience into a narrative was crucial. Cayton and Drake in-creasingly believed that the quest to reveal the "inner thoughts" of the objects of their study was of paramount importance.

Obviously the portrait excelled in its depiction of the internal torture the doctor undergoes, allying himself with his "race" and then feeling utterly alien-ated from fellow blacks whom he despises and who dislike him in return. The writers continued using the dramatic technique to render sympathetically the lower-class life patterns of real-life characters like "Baby Chile" and "Slick." Cayton seemed to believe that a prime attribute of liberal scholarship in a ra-cially segregated society was to recover the lost voice of the black poor. But his assumptions were falling out of fashion. By the middle of the decade, America's liberals were deeply questioning the leadership of the common man and the value of popular culture.[39]

Cayton's emphasis on the black voice of common America, the decision to combine anthropological depth with sociological breadth, reflected his pessi-mism regarding white America's commitment to racial justice. On the penulti-mate page of the book he wondered if "the Negro question—given the moral flabbiness of America—is incapable of solution," at least so long as Americans were not prepared to give up themselves to more conflict.[40] Four years earlier he had advised sociologists to move beyond looking at only the structural condi-tions of black life so that they might engage "the processes and the sentiments sanctioning the processes which allow the Negro to change his [social] posi-tion."[41] Cayton felt ever more acutely the need to uncover "sentiments sanction-ing the processes," and it was in the field of cultural artifacts—especially the novel—that he found the most alert material. However, a reliance on literature would also mean reliance on the critics, and they were in the process of chang-ing their minds.

For a generation of white critics, ethnicity outside of an "American" identity was something to resist. The leaders among the liberal writers in New York and Chicago were typically the college-trained children of eastern European Jews. Theirs was an assimilation pattern distinct from the Knopfs and Cerfs of pub-lishing fame, whose sometimes moneyed Jewish ancestors had migrated from western Europe during the antebellum era. The children of eastern European migrants of the industrial era saw their fortunes rise after the 1920s, and many of them had grown up confronting the woeful economy of the Great Depres-sion. They had started out at City College in Alcove Sixteen, radical Marxists,

Schachtmanites, socialists, Communists, or closely allied with the party. They had had profound Jewish teachers like Sydney Hook, Meyer Shapiro, and Elliot Cohen, so they had no particular burden to vindicate Jewishness—in a sense that had already been done. The end of the war was changing American society for this crowd that included Lionel Trilling, Philip Rahv, Stanley Edgar Hyman, William Phillips, and Isaac Rosenfeld and the younger men who shared their commitments, Alfred Kazin, Leslie Fiedler, Norman Podhoretz, and Irving Howe. The creative writers Delmore Schwartz, Saul Bellow, Bernard Malamud, and Norman Mailer filled out the ranks.

Men like Edwin Seaver of the League of American Writers or *New Masses* editor Samuel Sillen had flourished within the radical Left coincident with the intolerant anti-Jewish policies of the elite academy, the established publishers, and the elite magazines, especially in the South. After 1936 Lionel Trilling had won his tenure battle with the Columbia University English department, and by the time hostilities had begun in Western Europe, *Partisan Review* was an effective leader in the field of intellectual and cultural journals. Many of the thinkers responded graciously to the new inclusiveness and started looking abroad for their enemies. Certain accommodations were necessary for these victories, a kind of canny realpolitik in which emerging figures like the young public policy professor Henry Kissinger excelled. It could be safely assumed that African Americans would make the same adroit maneuvers for artistic and intellectual success.

From the mid-1940s through the mid-1950s, the most widely published critic of African American writing and of African American issues in the white American canon was neither a Negro himself nor a steward, per se, for new black writers. Charles I. Glicksberg, a native of Warsaw, Poland, taught English at Brooklyn College from 1946 until he retired in 1971, in addition to adjunct teaching at the New School for Social Research. While Glicksberg published two long essays on black American life in *Antioch Review,* he also published in *Forum,* in the *South Atlantic Quarterly*, and ten of them—more than any African American college professor during the era—in Du Bois's journal *Phylon.* Glicksberg was prolific, writing more than 250 academic essays in a long career. And his devotion to African American writing began as a tale of caution. He sensed at the beginning of the 1940s that African Americans had endangered themselves during the 1920s and needed to assimilate "white" American culture rapidly and perfectly. This was a commonsense observation. After all, educated black Americans, and virtually all the elites, with the possible exception of the ministers, spoke in a tone, style, and cadence that was completely indistinguishable from the flat-voweled, nasal twang of midwestern white America. The mastery of the accent was precisely what identified the smallish class of black Americans as educated.

In Glicksberg's first *Phylon* essay he approached the high bar of fitting in. "They [American blacks] must equal if not surpass the whites by incorporating American culture within their personality structure."[42] Glicksberg, who had only a passing academic interest in communism, wanted desperately, perhaps even stridently, to shape the field of African American literature into an outgrowth of American literature. His most formidable work, the bracing essay "The Negro Cult of the Primitive," appeared in 1944 in *Antioch Review*. Glicksberg the critic faulted the black writers of the 1920s because they had rejected American civilization with the rhetorical flourish of Negritude that he judged unsupportable and an intellectual dead-end. Instead, the road open was the universal, by way of the particular. "Negro-Americans must work in cooperation with the main trends of American culture," he wrote, "until such time when there will be no trace of differentiation between Negro culture and American culture."[43] Glicksberg responded sharply against the "the romantic glorification of the Negro as exotic, primitive, childlike," joining virtually all the 1940s black critical voices like Wright, Redding, Ellison, and Hugh Gloster.

The figure to be chastened here was Alain Locke, whose role in the Harlem Renaissance was now understood as irresponsibly romantic, almost intellectually shiftless. E. Franklin Frazier and others, like Ira de A. Reid, who had been influenced by the Chicago School of sociology, thought little of the Negro's purported African past. "Probably never before in history has a people been so nearly completely stripped of its social heritage as the Negroes who were brought here to America," wrote Frazier in his 1939 *The Negro Family in the United States*.[44] Even the researches of Melville Herskovits and Lorenzo Dow Turner failed to impress the group. Frazier in fact went on to take specific issue with Herskovits. In line now with the agrarians and the black sociologists, Glicksberg called Herskovits's work on African survivals "highly dangerous" because it pried open a closed door to those who believed in essential racial characteristics. For Glicksberg, assimilation was a more nourishing meal.

If Glicksberg was trying to shave black literature of its ethnic sentimentality, other critics were helping to shape the most inclusive kind of American liberalism and were prepared to embrace the strangest of bedfellows. No one was more earnest than Columbia professor Lionel Trilling, who tried to bridge the gap between the slowly evolving southern agrarian critics and the ex-Communists on the Left. Trilling's position on his own ethnicity signaled his capacity to overlook the sometimes formidable racial and ethnic prejudice of southerners and Ivy Leaguers. Trilling admitted to suffering "shame" at different points of his life at the outward "Jewishness" of others.[45] He had become a writer, while taking most of the 1920s and 1930s to finish a Ph.D. thesis, by enlisting with Eliot Cohen at *Menorah Journal*. But in 1945, when Cohen began the even more distinguished journal *Commentary* and asked Trilling, by then a figure of some import in New York, to participate, Trilling refused. "I had had my experience of the intellectual life lived in reference to what Cohen called the Jewish community, and I had no wish to renew it by associating myself with a Jewish magazine."[46] The letter he wrote to Cohen articulating the position caused furious, even violent responses from among Trilling's literary peers. Trilling determined that for him, the impulses of "intellectual life came from sources that were anything but Jewish." This was precisely the line of thought laid out by Glicksberg and others, and it was to be the ramrod for black assimilation.

Looking into the face of a world "dark and dubious," Trilling put his faith in the "critical intellect." The "critical intellect" was an organ "apt to study and praise elements that for the fullness of spiritual perfection are wanted, even though they belong to a power which in the practical sphere may be maleficent."[47] An intellectual, properly critical, could use important ingredients from flawed doctrines. Here Trilling offered an overture to pragmatism, or, rather, he put real teeth in the ideal of tolerance. If liberals were to appreciate diversity or progressive knowledge, they would necessarily borrow language and techniques from their conservative peers to help them resist intellectual sloppiness. Instead of the pat answers that Trilling observed in naturalist fiction, critics needed to embrace the "complication and possibility, surprise, intensification, variety, unfoldment, [and] worth" of the human experience. Trilling thought good criticism and critical literature could overcome the communist idea that mankind was only an "end," a destination point, with a negligible and better-off-if-left-forgotten journey. He thought lamentable the progressive insistence upon "the past as a failure, and of the present as nothing better than a willing tributary to the future." After Churchill's 1946 "Iron Curtain" speech, and Truman's subsequent Loyalty Act of 1947, communism itself was the obvious metaphor for intellectual sloppiness.

Trilling guardedly brought race into the discussion. In 1945 he published a short story called "The Other Margaret" in *Partisan Review,* where the revitalized creed of American liberalism cohered in the 1940s and 1950s. The short story articulated a key reorientation in liberal attitudes toward racial justice after the war. In his fiction, Trilling reinforced his prescription of fitness for the new liberal, especially as the intellectuals began to consider what American society owed black people. Trilling touched on one of the great urban legends from the 1940s expressed by whites, usually in the South, that described the vengeful conspiracies of black women on streetcars and in white women's kitchens. The phenomenon was known as the "Eleanor Club," after the liberal First Lady, and the disruptions were completely fictitious.[48]

"The Other Margaret" points out the weakness in understanding malevolent black behavior as mainly the product of white supremacy by reproducing the Elwin family's home life, particularly the relationship between the thirteen-year-old daughter Margaret and the family maid, who holds the same name.

Trilling paired the maid and young upper-middle-class girl to show the folly of blind liberal attitudes. Young, white Margaret strives for a grossly empathetic relationship with the servant in the face of her mother's empirical observations that "the other Margaret" is systematically destroying family heirlooms. The young teenager relies on her liberal and progressive education to explain to her father the reason for the servant's poor behavior: "'It's because—because society didn't give her a chance,' she said slowly. 'She has a handicap. Because she's colored. She has to struggle so hard—against prejudice. It's so *hard* for her.'"[49]

Young Margaret Elwin's education in the idea of social responsibility runs counter to the value of individual responsibility, a key ideal in the liberal Elwin home. Trilling's protagonist Stephen Elwin believes that everyone "bore their own blame. Exemption was not given by age or youth, or sex, or color, or condition of life." The child responds to her father's questions with the mantra of unspecific "liberal" clichés. When the Elwins compare the "other Margaret" to their loyal servant Millie, a black woman who returned to the South to nurse a sick relative, their daughter describes the former maid's loyalty to her employer as evidence of "slave-psychology." Her father's response indicates the shifting definition of liberalism in the 1940s and the growing impatience with the social critique that had its literary roots in naturalism. Stephen Elwin believes that the school's teachings have "corrupted" his daughter. The reader is to understand that Margaret Elwin has been misshapen by liberalism run amok.

Certainly W. T. Couch and Allen Tate were in sympathy with Trilling. It would have been difficult to find a noncommunist who did not share Trilling's judgment. But the question remained: did a conceptual space of freedom exist for blacks like the "other Margaret" to act? When *Negro Story* had the chance to tender a view even slightly touching on domestic work, such as in the short story "I Had a Colored Maid" by Margaret Rodriguez, it emphasized the adversarial behavior of some whites and the gutlessness of the so-called liberals.[50]

James Farrell, who had recently tried to revive his relationship with Richard Wright, published a brief commentary on the "The Other Margaret," faulting Trilling for his "reactionary moral view."[51] But his piece appeared in *New International*, a regular publication from the Worker's Party, still trying to find a place for socialism apart from the Stalinists. Farrell's counter was important, but his dissent was growing faint in the rousing chorus of postwar American liberals. Irving Howe, then a twenty-seven-year-old Schachtmanite socialist, placed his debut critical essay in *Partisan Review* by upbraiding Farrell for collapsing Trilling's imaginative short story with social reality.[52]

At the very end of 1949, Lionel Trilling would collect the influential essays he had been issuing for the second half of the 1940s and famously publish them under the title *The Liberal Imagination*. Trilling would make quite clear that he resisted the organizational orthodoxy of "liberalism"—such as it had been in the John Reed Clubs or American Writers Congresses—organizations for neo-phyte writers that he thought had greatly reduced the "variousness and possi-bility" of contemporary writing and thought.[53] Trilling hoped to reclaim and make liberalism "new"—ironically—by stripping it of its innocence and infus-ing it with the mature rigor. To do this Trilling diminished two authors, Vernon Parrington and Theodore Dreiser, and the creed of "social responsibility." "This is the liberal criticism, in the direct line of Parrington, which establishes the social responsibility of the writer and then goes on to say that, apart from his duty of resembling reality as much as possible, he is not really responsible for anything, not even his ideas."[54] Top American critics were finished with under-standing novels for the work that they conducted bending the American public toward the arc of racial justice by way of their resemblance to "reality." But the rectifying would have to wait until the end of the decade, after one black writer earned everlasting fame and another had been anointed to take his place.

CHAPTER EIGHT

Afroliberals and the End of World War II (1945–1946)

In both the year that *Native Son* was in production and the year it blazed up the charts, Richard Wright worked solidly on a new novel. A mild-mannered, almost boring man of dutiful and regular habit, Wright sat down and composed at his typewriter every day for six or seven hours, from morning until early afternoon. In the evening he read. Wright's amazing success had changed some elements of his life. With the money he earned from *Native Son*, including fifteen thousand dollars over a couple of months, he cultivated a kind of extravagance. He bought thick tweeds for his trousers and a Chicago tenement for his mother and aunt. But in his approach to the craft of writing he remained vigilant and hardworking, as if a typewriter were all that was between him and the poverty he had known when he cut out from Natchez to Memphis at seventeen, a daring move in a lifetime of daring moves. His literary labors were never frivolous nor capricious, but belabored, didactic, and filled with Wright's feverish imaginings, his slightly bizarre sense of drama.

The book he staked himself on in 1940 and 1941 was called *Black Hope*, and he submitted to his agent Paul Reynolds a draft of more than nine hundred pages by the end of 1940. If his first novel had addressed juvenile delinquency, the second project broached the other "big" issue making the papers and reaching the American consciousness: the struggle of black female domestic workers. The realist kernel for Wright's imagination this time was the newspaper report of a Brooklyn mansion that seemed expertly run by servants, but whose white owners never appeared. It turned out that the black "chauffeur" owned the immaculate home. Wright's book revealed the situation—philosophical, economic, and erotic—of Maud Hampton, a twenty-seven-year-old, light-skinned University of Chicago graduate who passes for white in order to land a respectable job cleaning houses. Having endured a failed marriage to a Russian ballerina, Wright's imagination seemed to have returned to Marian Minus.

Once again Wright wanted to force a stick into the wasp's nest—the bankruptcy of liberal approaches to the American racial dilemma. How did white America know black America, and how might that intimacy be increased, an intimacy that might disable racism? Perhaps this was also asking how the ranks of liberals might be swelled. In the early 1940s, the noncommunist white American liberal came from the ranks of the white-collar intelligentsia, which was middle, really upper-middle, class. It required a bit of education and exposure, book knowledge, to disengage from the racial stereotypes that crudely managed American race relations. Part of the problem had to do with the sheer demographic magnitude of slavery and the subsequent streaming migration of southern blacks into northern cities. It was quite possible for middle-class whites outside of the rural South and distant from the bleak areas of the cities, despite their intention, to disregard, ignore, or be absented from black life. There were few ritual places of interaction, even in places where racial segregation was outlawed.

There was a prime exception to the typical pattern of white upper-middle-class removal from the contour of black life: the maid. Like Lionel Trilling, most white Americans who could claim personal relationships with American blacks based their experience on interactions across racial barriers within the overall sphere of domestic labor. In 1939 in New York City, the stronghold of American liberalism outside of the academy and with the largest urban concentration of blacks, 80 percent of African American women in the labor force worked as domestics, and obviously they worked for white families.[1] The seen-but-not-heard dynamic of Pullman's porter "George" and the General Mills corporation's ubiquitous image of good service "Aunt Jemimah" permeated most elements of American life. In 1940 Hattie McDaniel won an Academy Award for taking the good-natured black servant role to dramatic height in the film "Gone With the Wind." It would be sixty-two years before another Academy Award went to a black woman.

Even in the highbrow fiction produced by the liberal intelligentsia, such as the comfortably Left-leaning Mary McCarthy, black Americans regularly cropped up as relics to verify the authenticity of the American scene. These characterizations were of humble and often comic people. In her masterpiece "The Man in the Brooks Brothers Shirt," McCarthy compared her heroine's acceptance of something vulgar but endearing from an avuncular and porcine paramour to "one of those home-made cakes with Paris-green icing that she used to receive on her birthday from her colored maid." When the heroine leaves a Pullman train, "the porter waited beside them with a large, Hollywood-darky smile on his face."[2] McCarthy was not racist and the depictions were at least benign and arguably rather complex. But she also captured perfectly the gap between what liberals thought they were doing and how blacks could feel that their lives were badly misrepresented and comically exploited.

This problem was compounded. The Negro maid of the middle twentieth century had an equally well-known and frequently described twin: the street-walker. If the stereotypical maid was imagined as distantly maternal, custodial, obedient, and clean, the prostitute invoked the opposite range of associations along America's submerged libidinal unconscious, starting with evil and ending with ruin. Sex-for-sale was as much a part of black American shame as out-of-wedlock birth, and both had grown pointedly acute during the drive toward urbanization. Fifty-four percent of women arrested for prostitution in New York in 1940 were black, and half of the arrests for the crime of "sexual immorality" took place in Harlem.[3] And like the customers of the better known Negro maid, most of the people who purchased the services of the black prostitute were white. This brew of race and sexuality, such as Wright had hoped to test with his novel, challenged the abilities of creative writers who were in the best position to help advance social mores. Everyone accused everyone else of sentimentality, often enough reflected in the portraits of ragged domestics and lipstick-and-nylon barflies.

The troubled circumstances were lost in the marvel of a commercial bonanza. The most concerted efforts of black writers to use literature in the fight for social justice took place in the mid-1940s, and there was a literal payoff from books like *Native Son*, *For My People*, and *No Day of Triumph*. The plums fell in 1945 and kept falling for a year and a half, during which time it became widely established in Washington, D.C., Chicago, and New York that black Americans were producing a second "Renaissance." It was true. In a sensational period of eighteen months, the black writers came out with grace and power and opened up new genres, set sales records, impressed the critics, and buried some traditions of cultural prejudice. They showed clearly the direction that the literature was moving in and also captured the peak of its historic style. Wright himself would contribute a key book that earmarked the period, but it was not *Black Hope*; instead it was Wright's enduring narrative about his childhood, *Black Boy*, that indelibly froze him and his career in 1945.

The sharpest criticism that Richard Wright faced after the success of *Native Son* was that he had limited the consciousness of the main character. After completing the manuscript, he wrote to his agent Paul Reynolds on March 7, 1939, and admitted that by relying on "the inarticulate Negro," he had made "some of the weaknesses almost inevitable."[4] Wright vowed to Reynolds then that his future fictional actors would "be more conscious, articulate, and will move in wider social areas."

Then, in April 1943, Horace Cayton convinced Wright to take a train ride with him to Nashville to Fisk and lecture on his life. Wright rode out to Chicago in Pullman-style comfort, and the two men began their trip down the length of Illinois, through Kentucky, and into Tennessee. The peculiar poignancy of those hours on board the train, where one morning Wright and Cayton were refused breakfast until after all the white passengers had eaten, was enough to prod Wright's imagination into arguably his most exceptional piece of work. He would offer his own life as stunning testimony. At one point on the return leg to Chicago, Wright told Cayton, who asked him why he lay in his berth fully dressed even though he prepared for sleep, "When I'm below the Mason–Dixon Line I want more between me and white people than a curtain. I want iron and steel."[5]

The iron and steel of Wright's views found their way into the world by way of steel type and ink on paper. About six months after his trip to Nashville, Wright had a roughly five-hundred-page manuscript detailing his life in Mississippi, Memphis, and Chicago. The narrative ended with Wright being bodily thrown out of the Communist May Day parade by former comrades and determinedly making his way to New York.

His book was initially held up because the legal counsel for Harper wanted to reduce the publisher's exposure to libel, so Wright censured his criticisms of black insurance companies, heads of the Chicago theater, and black Communists like Oliver Law and Harry Haywood. Then, *Atlantic Monthly* took two of the final chapters dealing with his breakaway from communism and planned to print them in July and August 1944. Wright's friend C.L.R. James took the second half of the autobiography, covering Wright's years in Chicago and with the Communist Party, and set it in a pamphlet to be published by his splinter socialist group, the Johnson-Forrest Tendency.[6] Toward the end of May 1944, Wright's editor Edward Aswell asked Book-of-the-Month-Club judge Dorothy Canfield Fisher for a blurb to promote the book. On June 6 she sent him a strong letter of approval. Aswell liked the endorsement so well that he wanted to turn it into a preface. Before the end of June, the Book-of-the-Month Club proper had extended its support to the book. For the second time, Wright's work found its way into hundreds of thousands of American homes by way of the imprimatur of the Book-of-the-Month Club.

Wright's second designation by the club belied the curious politics necessary to receive liberal support—one that guaranteed commercial success. Although he had established his craftsmanship, his intelligence, and his marketability, Wright still endured fairly tight supervision from his liberal patrons. Not even a month after she had mailed her letter of support, Fisher was sending Wright three-page-long, confidentially toned letters badgering him to remove the strongest doses of wrath and bile from the book. Fisher used every tool at her disposal: seniority, gentility, her recognized stature as public liberal champion, and Wright's debt to her, stewed together in a palaver of innocent request. But underneath it all was the simple fact that she had power over Wright's editor Aswell, and if Wright responded badly it would have ramifications not only for him but for the other black writers both men were trying to promote.

Fisher congratulated Wright's "intelligent reasonableness," which she had noted when she had required him to make changes to *Native Son*. But her request this time was in effect of a higher order. She wrote that she wanted only for Wright to provide the answer to a single question. What had made him "conscious of possibilities. From where had I caught my sense of freedom?" She gave him a possible answer. She wanted to "catch a passing glimpse of the fact" that Wright was "rooted in those 'American principles' so mocked and degraded" by racial discrimination.[7] And all that was only elegant prelude. What Fisher wanted Wright to do was not ornamental or even lyrical; it was didactic, specific, and ideological. "To receive, in the closing pages of your book, one word of recognition for this aspiration, if it were possible for you to give such recognition honestly, would hearten all who believe in American ideals." She asked Wright to cosign an increasingly popular trajectory of American liberalism.

Two weeks later, when writing to Aswell, Fisher was more succinct: "[I]t would add greatly to the maturity of his book if he puts in it only two or three words acknowledging the existence of Americans who have other ideas about racial discrimination than those of the South."[8] She wore Wright down. By the end of July he had rewritten the ending several times and finally come up with something that Fisher let stand. Instead of finding his salvation in Dostoyevsky and Marx, he made a half gesture in the direction of H. L. Mencken, Edgar Lee Masters, Sherwood Anderson, Theodore Dreiser, and Sinclair Lewis, white Americans who had enabled him to "overcome my chronic distrust" of the "straitened American environment."[9]

The book reached the American public the last week of February 1945, as the European war lurched to a close. That March, Saunders Redding described the tortuous landscape of the black writer in America, a person who typically had to publish himself in lieu of a publisher willing to create a market. He believed that there was only one solution available: the Negro writer must "make a common audience out of white and black America."[10] Wright seems to have accomplished the feat. One hundred years after Frederick Douglass's narrative, Wright's book helped to shape the conflicts and the sensibilities of young Americans only a few years from a crisis as dramatic and far ranging, if not as bloody, as the Civil War. The same week as its release, *Black Boy* became a "Candidate for the Best Seller List," and before the end of March, Wright and his publisher had a legitimate best seller. By April 28, 1945, Wright was beating out Ernie Pyle for the nation's leading nonfiction best seller.[11] Wright relinquished the lead to Pyle's *Brave Men* after a week, but *Black Boy* continued to sell vigorously, leading the *New York Herald Tribune* and *New York Times* best-seller lists. Four months after its release, at the end of June 1945, Wright had sold 450,000 copies of the book.[12] *Black Boy* remained a best seller throughout 1945 and finished the year with 195,000 copies sold at the bookstore and 351,000 sold through the Book-of-the-Month Club.[13] Of the books published that year, Wright's was the most popular nonfiction work that did not directly deal with the war. It would be thirty-seven years before another nonfiction book with an African American theme and written by an African American outstripped Wright's hard-cover sales. That book was *Roots* by Alex Haley.[14]

The public interest showed a sort of dawn in the sky because *Black Boy* was a tale of what Ralph Ellison would call in *Antioch Review* in 1945 "personal catastrophe expressed lyrically."[15] Wright's autobiography includes two father figures who are hunted by whites, one of whom is lynched, and the brother of a young friend who is also butchered by whites. Young Richard's earliest memory is a near-death beating that opens the text, followed by his father's abandonment of the family. Wright's early memories included experience as a first-grade drunk and time in an orphanage. These elements of destitution and the young boy's despondency are combined with a sense of defeat and dread overtly connected to the power of the white world. And once young Richard begins his ritualistic interactions with whites, he faces a long series of cuffings, humiliations, stinging insults, and episodes of being fit, procrustean style, onto the iron rack of racial subjugation. If anthropologists like John Dollard were working out theories of castelike relations between blacks and whites in the South in books such as *Caste and Class in a Southern Town*, Wright's narrative exploded the notion that all blacks easily accepted their subordinate role and embraced it as beneficial and mutually sustaining. In Wright's life, nothing compensated, not even remotely, for the cruelty of segregation and the cheap salve of American gimmickry.

Black Boy magnifies the fear and hatred of *Native Son* by duplicating the harsh social conditions that produced Bigger Thomas and then forcing a sentient protagonist, curious and alive to the world of ideas and values, through the painful straits endured by black Americans. The book's important contribution is its determination to show the significant role the black community plays in adjusting the young child to a life of injustice and deprivation. Two-thirds of the way through the narrative, Wright painfully realizes the contrived nature of racial roles. "I began to marvel at how smoothly the black boys acted out the roles that the white race had mapped out for them. Most of them were not conscious of living a special, separate, stunted way of life. Yet I knew that in some period of their growing up—a period that they had no doubt forgotten—there had been developed in them a delicate, sensitive controlling mechanism that shut off their minds and emotions from all that the white race had said was taboo."[16] Wright showed the manner in which the system of unequal and unjust social relations was inculcated and then independently reproduced by southern blacks as "natural." And once again, Wright pointed to struggle, subterfuge, and violence as among the tools necessary to escape the stupor of a racist conditioning process. These tools had been the necessary implements to enable him to reach writers like Mencken, Sinclair Lewis, and Dostoyevsky.

In *Black Boy* Wright showed the hallmark of his mature style: a series of enduring motifs of black American social interactions under the Jim Crow regime. They are elaborate dramatizations, and, as many critics reminded him then and into the present, examples not so much from historical fact as from a

nonfiction novel. But the book abounded in his construction of archetypal figures from black life in the South that maintain an enduring explanatory power:
blacks who caricature themselves before whites, especially a Chinese-looking
elevator operator named Shorty; the male victims who transgress the rigid economic or sexual boundaries and are lynched or assaulted; the black-on-black
pitted battle for white sport; black suspicion of reading and education; paternal
abandonment; starvation; blacks attempting to check and control ambition,
particularly school teachers; and perhaps the leitmotif under which all these
examples are gathered, feudal southern relations. Wright drummed this message into his readers from the second chapter: "Negroes had never been allowed to catch the full spirit of Western civilization, [that] they lived somehow
in it but not of it."[17] And, perhaps most glaringly of all, especially if his *Atlantic
Monthly* articles were considered, in the book Wright showed another new kind
of maturity: he had entered the realm beyond ideology. Neither Marxism, black
cultural nationalism, religious spiritualism, nor anything else propped him up.
He was staking himself on a realistic devotion to honestly revealing his life.

Wright's candor was sometimes reckless. His estimate of black folk life in
Jackson, Mississippi, ringingly indicted segregation but also grumbled about
the Negroes who submitted to it. His writing that blacks teetered on the edge of
barbarism in the semifeudal South had long-lasting implications, and few people liked what he had to say. In the most famous paragraph of the book, Wright
presented black America ignominiously: "I used to mull over the strange absence of real kindness in Negroes, how unstable our tenderness, how lacking in
genuine passion we were, how void of great hope, how timid our joy, how bare
our traditions, how hollow our memories, how lacking we were in those intan-
gible sentiments that bind man to man, and how shallow was even our despair."[18] Like Henry James, who in a piece of biographical criticism on Nathaniel Hawthorne had also cataloged "the items of high civilization . . . absent from
the texture of American life," Wright wanted to journey to the base of African
American life.[19] "I saw that what had been taken for our emotional strength was
our negative confusions, our flights, our fears, our frenzy under pressure. . . .
And when I brooded upon the cultural barrenness of black life, I wondered if
clean, positive tenderness, love, honor, loyalty, and the capacity to remember
were native to man."[20]

The passage fits logically within the text: Wright's father has just abandoned
responsibility for his children; Wright has become a six-year-old drunk shouting obscenities in the Memphis saloon where he spends his afternoons; and, for
his safe-keeping and moral betterment, his mother sends him to an orphanage.
And the passage was also one of the most worked over moments in the book.
In the earliest handwritten draft of the manuscript, instead of writing that
blacks exhibited an "absence of kindness," Wright had written, "To wide

stretches of Negro life, kindness is an alien thing."[21] When he had first typed up the manuscript he had reversed his emphasis and had written that he recalled an "abundance of naïve kindness,"[22] which became, in his next version, an "abundance of animal kindness."[23] On that round of revision in the manuscript, when he must have started to become pressed for space and the recipient of the importuning letters from Dorothy Canfield Fisher, he streamlined the entire paragraph for concision and coherence, deciding that "absence of kindness" would suffice.

But because of his final decision to propose a black community with no values, Wright was thought incorrigible, and had he not been embraced by the liberal mainstream, he would surely have been rejected by the black middle-class intelligentsia, literati, and the Communists. Offered a publishing contract by Harper partly on account of Richard Wright's recommendation, Gwendolyn Brooks admitted to her editor Elizabeth Lawrence, "Negroes here are very upset about two paragraphs on page 33."[24] Chicago blacks were confident that *they* had a culture. Despite the growing use of Wright's images of the "damaged" black personality by liberal sociologists, psychologists, and public policy analysts (sociologist Horace Cayton and psychiatrist Helen McLean were the most influenced by Wright) to demand changes in public policy, black and white liberals expressed frustration at the book's portrait of the educated classes.[25]

By May 1945 this topic had moved from the special journals to the editorial page of the *New York Times*. None other than W.E.B. Du Bois fired the big gun. "[W]here shall we look for 'the truth' about the Negro—in the violent pages of social protest and hot indignation, or in the routine account of Negro life as it is actually being lived by the Negro people?"[26] But Wright did not back down from his presentation; he ratcheted up his intensity. When a longtime friend and left-wing ally Jere Mangione heard Wright talking to an audience in Philadelphia, he noticed a change in Wright: "every word seemed charged with dynamite and disgust for his audience."[27] When Mangione described the talk twenty years later, he compared Wright in 1945 to the most vitriolic black speaker of the late 1960s, H. Rap Brown.

At the same time that the black middle class held up its traditional barrier against Wright, he found himself determined a pariah by others a bit closer to home. Wright had anticipated genuine rancor from the Communists. His former ally Samuel Sillen, who had praised *Native Son*, dunned him as soon as the *Atlantic Monthly* pieces appeared in 1944. Wright had forgotten himself by evincing a "curious remoteness from the democratic upsurge of both the Negro and white masses today."[28] Wright's sin was not only to have published the articles in *Atlantic Monthly*, but also to have delivered a quote to the *New York Herald Tribune* that impugned the Communists as "[n]arrow-minded, bigoted, intolerant and frightened of new ideas" on account of the Communist rejection of the African American public's "Double V" wartime slogan—victory against segregation at home and fascism abroad.[29]

It was Wright's book of "'truth' of the Negro people" that enabled an evolution in criticism. For the first time, an African American critic presented the finest interpretation of an African American creative work. *Antioch Review* brought out its second black writer, Ralph Ellison, in 1945. In the important piece of criticism, Ellison announced himself to a broad academic audience. "Richard Wright's Blues" also suggested that black American popular folk culture provided the appropriate vehicle to measure the value of narrative art. Black high art could be measured based on internal group standards and traditions. Ellison called his critical device "the blues." "The blues is an impulse to keep the painful details and episodes of a brutal experience alive in one's aching consciousness," he told his reader, "to finger its jagged grain, and to transcend it, not by the consolation of philosophy but by squeezing from it a near-tragic, near-comic lyricism."[30] Ellison focused on the utterances of "blues" implicit in Wright's tale as a source of value. He would go even further with the theory in his own fiction.

Horace Cayton was the other great advocate of *Black Boy*. That summer Cayton had defended Wright's autobiography in a series of articles that framed the debate as between the "hard-boiled realists" and the "sweetness and light crowd." Cayton thought, from a theoretical point of view, that blacks needed to overcome their fear of whites by making straightforward assaults against the mechanisms of oppression. For his money, Cayton thought of Ellison, Wright, and Chester Himes as members of the "blues school" of literature, a group committed to probing the "dark inner landscape of emotional conflict which is raging in the heart of all Americans."[31]

The summer of 1945 was the undeniable peak of the "blues school"; even the friendships upon which it was based would fray in another year and a half. Unlike the middle class or the Communists, Ralph Ellison privately struggled against *Black Boy* because of its stylistic pessimism and its reluctance to show an optimistic hero contending with postwar philosophical tools, such as Wright had displayed in "The Man Who Lives Underground." Ellison thought the book a step backward in terms of artistic form, "more basic" than Wright's previous work, and one that showed a bitter pessimism about the American scene.[32] Curiously enough, Ellison was holding Wright to the same standard set by Dorothy Canfield Fisher. And if an older white woman held the key to Wright's financial success, the same applied to Ellison, who around the time of his review started accepting loans from wealthy leftist Ida Guggenheimer.[33] Nor was the issue of whether or not the American scene merited optimism—Ellison's famous conclusion to the novel he had just broken ground for in 1945—simply theoretical. When Horace Cayton walked the streets of New York with his white girlfriend in August 1945 and heard that the atomic bomb had been used against the Japanese, Cayton, partly fearing a renewed white supremacist order, would suffer, in the middle of Times Square, a nervous breakdown.

The book that actually proved that the social realists had hit their stride was not by a member of the New York clique, or even written in prose narrative, but was rather the heralded collection of poetry *A Street in Bronzeville*, published on August 15 by the twenty-eight year-old Chicagoan Gwendolyn Brooks. Bronzeville was the regular synonym for the South Side of Chicago, and Brooks presented a series of poems that telescoped the landscape of urban black life, the blocks of shambling tenements and crowded apartment buildings, through the fresh eye of a young black woman from a humble but dignified family. The dignity of Brooks's characters enabled them to speak standard English and express familiarity with white middle-class customs and practices, from the lace-curtained parlors to visits to the doctor and multi-year mortgages. A native of a northern American city, Brooks called attention to structural racism and not necessarily the heritage of bondage or the humiliating slights of Jim Crow.

Brooks often represented herself to her literary friends and professional acquaintances as an ingénue. This was a classic American pose of dissembly; she was a long-schooled, consummately skilled poet. She had started writing in junior high and had become seasoned in the pages of the *Chicago Defender*, where she published more than seventy-five poems. Brooks was not merely the local favorite, pleasing the churchgoing crowd and elementary school principals. She worked to advance her art politically and intellectually. With her college friend Lula Battle, she joined the Chicago NAACP's Youth Council, along with other promising writers like Margaret Taylor (later Goss and then Burroughs) and John Johnson, future founding editor of *Ebony*, *Jet*, and a publishing empire. They created a club to pursue creative literature and attracted such people as William Couch, Jr., an aspiring critic who attended lectures at the University of Chicago. *Crisis* and *Opportunity* printed Brooks's work that came out of these immediate post-teen years: "Mrs. Corley's Maid," "Road," and a long poem about lynching. In 1943 Brooks won the Midwestern Poetry contest and journeyed to Harlem for the first time that year, where she tried to reach Langston Hughes and Ralph Ellison but missed them. In October 1944 she went up a notch and published "The Ballad of Pearl May Lee" in *Negro Quarterly*, just before the managing editor Ellison left for the merchant marine.

Brooks's intellect had been tamed by the Depression. She finished her education at Wilson Junior College, where the tuition was only six dollars a semester. But even though she was a legendary student at Wilson, her poetic sensibility had evolved from the delicate layers of her personality. Brooks was a child of racial integration, a caring family, and the North. Her native reserve and curiosity, and the fact that her parents were able to shelter her, had developed in her a highly sensitive perspective on the world around her. This predisposition was heightened by her educational experiences.

She had begun high school in mostly white Hyde Park where she had been ignored. Then, at black Wendell Phillips, she had not made the grade as "hip," which for girls usually meant "fast." She finished at Englewood High, where she was again in the racial minority. Also, there was, at least what seemed to her, a fearsome skin color hierarchy among blacks that systematically and hideously doffed its cap to those of lighter hue. She did not reach womanhood during an era that overtly praised beautiful skin darker than the proverbial butcher's brown paper bag. Undaunted, Brooks became precocious early on and sought out people to help her mature as an artist, like James Weldon Johnson, who actually return-mailed to her criticisms of her poetry, and Langston Hughes, who in the early 1930s offered her his trademark hearty encouragement. Still, the maturity that entered her work when she reached her mid-twenties had also something to do with the intellectual crowd that she now moved in and which included the survivors of the original South Side Writers' Club, like Theodore Ward, Fern Gayden, Frank Marshall Davis, and Edward Bland.

Ward, of "Big White Fog" fame, was a committed Communist when Brooks met him. For a time he lived next door to her apartment on East 63rd Street, where the elevated line thundered overhead on its way to Cottage Grove Avenue. The neighborhood was a gritty center of urban black life where, Brooks said, "if you wanted a poem, you had only to look out of a window."[34] Ward's vigorously advanced Marxist view in art and politics initially struck Brooks as overradical. She had a more important relationship with Edward Bland, a friend of William Couch's, the adored and suave intellectual of their group. Nine years older than Brooks, Bland hailed from New Orleans and worked at the post office. Self-taught and active in politics, Bland pursued a career as a disciplined adherent to the philosophy of dialectical materialism.

Bland's interactions with South Side artists took off when the South Side Chicago Community Art Center opened in 1941. The center, at South Michigan and 38th Street, occupied a three-story brick Georgian-Revival building, its interior remodeled the year before it opened in the unornamented Bauhaus style that harmonized function and form. Across the street in the Old Comiskey Mansion was the house the painter Margaret Taylor Goss Burroughs would eventually buy, which would later become the Du Sable Museum, the country's first museum of African American history. In the meantime, Burroughs lived in the rear carriage house, a barnlike building where red wine flowed and the house was opened up to writers, painters, and never-ending conversation. Margaret Burroughs "lived up from the root," Gwendolyn Brooks liked to say.[35]

The editor and activist Fern Gayden sat on the board of trustees at the art center and was coeditor of a literary journal that would appear in early 1944 called *Negro Story*; Brooks' vignette "Chicago Portraits" appeared in the inaugural issue. *Negro Story* featured black and white "blues writing" through 1946, specializing in "plotless realism"—short stories that, in the words of one journalist, took their greatest pleasure in "indicting a white supremacist society."[36] *Negro Story* included Ralph Ellison and Nick Aaron Ford on its advisory board. In 1944 and 1945 Ellison helped put flesh between the magazine's covers by reprinting his work that had appeared in the Communist and Federal Writers' Project publications, "Mister Toussan," "Afternoon," and "The Birthmark." Chester Himes published more short stories in the magazine than any other writer; his comic grotesques were popular with readers and especially with black soldiers in army camps.[37]

The founding editor of *Negro Story* was Alice Browning, a woman of dazzling good looks who had gotten the idea for the magazine while at work on her master's degree in English at Columbia under Vernon Loggins. Loggins encouraged her to submit a short story to *Esquire*. A prodigy, by age nine Browning had read all of Dickens, Thackeray, Eliot, Hawthorne, Cooper.[38] She had easily joined the New York writers' milieu and could be found bent over her work at the 135th Street library, and also at parties at Aaron Douglass's house at 409 Edgecombe. At one place she discussed literature; at the other, she flirted and skiffled with Ralph Ellison and Angelo Herndon.[39] When she returned to Chicago, she and Gayden went on to found the magazine and invigorate the literature scene she had participated in since the early 1930s when she was a student at the University of Chicago. The critics held their writing workshop on the second floor of the Community Art Center every week. Another writers' collective held a salon on the first floor of 3853 Calumet Street on Saturday and Sunday nights, which included painters Charles Sebree, Bernard Goss, and Margaret Goss Burroughs, sculptor Marion Perkins, and South Side Writers' Club members Margaret Walker, George McCray, Frank Marshall Davis, John Gray, and Bob Davis. The talented Chicago group continued to thrive.

With his criticism that was unafraid of smashing something and his steady mantra that reviled the "literary incompetence" of the 1920s, Edward Bland cut the edge for most of the Chicago writers. His essay "Social Forces Shaping the Negro Novel" seemed to devote an unsympathetic close reading, such as was the fashion in Cleanth Brooks and Robert Penn Warren's *Understanding Poetry*, to an entire social class. Similar to Horace Cayton, Bland recognized American blacks as uniquely positioned with their abundant international connections and not a few obligations. However, the epigonic black middle class, "reticent about the patterns and meaning of existence" and bereft of a consciousness of "the wider dimensions of life," was inadequate to produce a flourishing narrative tradition.[40] Bland described a classic breach of faith away from intellectual currents by the black middle class dependent upon the "social environment" for its consciousness, rather than the awe-inspiring power of Nature. The implications for the novel were great: "The creation of a sensibility whose contact with Man created only occasional and temporary feelings of inadequacy, this novel spurned the larger interests of the mind as seen through the major traditions of the West." To Bland, the novelistic tradition of Jessie Fauset and W.E.B. Du Bois unhappily emphasized "conformity to civilized practices" and missed the nineteenth-century revolt against the convention of sentimental melodrama by the romantic individual. African American intellectual leaders who were fully a generation behind had left poverty in place of tradition for the black novelist.

Bland added one coda to this thesis of general malaise in March 1944 when Harriet Monroe's Chicago-based *Poetry* magazine published his essay "Racial Bias and Negro Poetry." He found black poets, and black writers more generally, holders of "pre-individualistic values," a belief system nearly opposed to the Western enlightenment tradition of distinctive, individual humanistic examination. "Instead of seeing in terms of the individual, the Negro sees in terms of 'races,' masses of peoples separated from other masses according to color."[41] Bland decided that the "limitation" caused by this situation "detracts from whatever poetic skill may be otherwise present." Bland hoped that, in keeping with the American propaganda, the Second World War's successful conclusion would advance the humanistic elimination of white prejudice. And he also hoped that the "self-conscious 'race values'" that "impair and delimit the vision of the artist" would find their end.

Bland's articles and theories advancing the end of "self-conscious race values" were workshopped and argued in the poetry and critics' group meetings at the South Side Community Art Center. Gwendolyn Brooks's verse matured during these sessions, and, since *Poetry* and *Negro Quarterly* published the material, the Chicago style of militant social class observant expression probably also shaped the ripening literary aesthetic of Detroit poet Robert Hayden. After Bland died in the U.S. Army in Germany, Brooks appreciated him and his brother enough to say that Edward and Alden Bland "patiently taught me and Henry [Blakely, Brooks's husband] how to think."[42]

And think she did. *A Street in Bronzeville*, her book of forty-one tight, well-polished poems, reflected the internal lives of the African American working and lower middle classes. Brooks gave the public a dose of sweet verse that recorded a lurking unwholesomeness that insisted upon cure. She touched life in the kitchenettes, among the pimps, the youth on their way to the cemetery, the children aborted by poor mothers or burned to death by their siblings in the steady house fires that plagued the overcrowded tenements. The poems were grouped in segments that reflected prominent motifs: "A Street in Bronzeville" cut a swathe of black life at Cottage Grove and 47th Street; "The Sundays of Satin Legs Smith" reveled in the luxuriant hedonist satiety of a playboy; "Negro

Hero" memorialized the Pearl Harbor heroics of Dorie Miller; "Hattie Scott" recovered the life of the paragon of the black middle class, the female domestic; "Queen of the Blues" paid homage to the spirit of Ma Rainey and Bessie Smith; "Ballad of Pearl May Lee" presented a lynching through the eyes of a black girl scorned; and "Gay Chaps at the Bar" took the reader on an intellectual journey through the emotive life of black soldiers in the racially segregated U.S. Armed Forces. Her canvas took in Chicago, black war heroes, lynching, the lives of ordinary working black women, and color prejudice.

Brooks's best short poem, "kitchenette," presented the problem of the good life by juxtaposing the dream of the imagination with the "gray" environment of social reality—the shared bathroom, rent, and garbage in the hallway. Throughout her collection of poems she depicted the monotony and the dullness, the brutality and the amorality that characterized Bronzeville. She revealed black Chicago in nooks of wormy banality, accented by episodes of the dramatic violence so dear to Richard Wright. Richard Wright read the manuscript in September 1944 and made suggestions about increasing the content but noted the sharp grasp of life. What he liked most about the collection of poems was that a "quiet but hidden malice runs through most of them."[43] Wright then talked her up to Edwin Embree of the Rosenwald Fund and to editors Edwin Seaver of *Cross-Section* and Dorothy Norman at the magazine *Twice a Year.*

Brooks's signature poem might have been "a song in the front yard," where she described a proper young girl debating the virtues of the back alley with the implied reader and her own mother. She explored the same theme to more devastating and far less ambivalent effect in "Sadie and Maude," the tale of two sisters and their opposing stands on social propriety and human vitality. She proposed a cultural relativism in the life of Bronzeville. Black South Side might have produced unmarried mothers, or men with patent leather hair, teenagers dead before their time, maids at the hairdressers, and prosperous madams, but it was a culture of its own, with its own standards and access to humanity.

But where her point of view once corresponded closely with Wright's and Bland's was in the implicit criticism of the black middle class and its church-based social structure. Brooks pointed to them as the key upholders of Victorian mores that modern life was proving were blemished antiques. The marriages without vitality, the estimate of women based almost exclusively on their approximation to white standards of beauty, the hypocritical and immoral ministers, all this tendered a scorching critique. Brooks's views on racism and inequity in the military, the "Negro Hero" who has to "kick their law into their teeth" in order to fight fascism, were mild by comparison.

Brooks's gutsiness came through in her poem on abortion "the mother," an entire ballad devoted to "the children you got but did not get." Even her fans thought she was confessing unpleasant facts about her own gynecological past. She paid for this with the critique from the *Phylon* reviewer, who upheld propriety and criticized the inclusion of abortion and the very notion of skin color prejudice within the race, the subject of "the ballad of chocolate Mabbie."[44] But even *Phylon* had to admit that she presented "the Negro as he is." Howard University's *Journal of Negro Education* seconded the opinion that Brooks had slanted the book to explore the underbelly of black life. "[I]t includes no Negro homes with lovely lawns and awnings at the windows and all too few Brown Americans whose conduct is normal."[45] The national papers, *New York Times* and *Chicago Tribune*, applauded the arrival of a solid young poetic voice, and both papers were particularly impressed with Brooks's mastery of poetic form.

Brooks's chosen métier did not, however, thoroughly satisfy her publisher. As soon as the book was accepted, Harper went to work on Brooks for the prose material that they hoped would bring in a best seller. "[W]e feel that you will turn eventually to writing fiction. And fiction, of course, is far more profitable than poetry for both author and publisher."[46] Brooks was excited about winning the contract and working with Harper, which now wore the crown as the extraordinary liberal press of the mid-1940s. Harper's list included a poet, a fiction writer, and a nonfiction specialist, all Negroes, and all would win awards with their Harper books.

Brooks wanted to be a polished artist of Negro American life, but she did not seek recognition for pushing a radical political agenda. She wrote to her editor to defend her aesthetic. She wanted to offer proof "(by implication, not by shouting)" that black Americans were "merely human beings, not exotics."[47] She admitted disdain. "I resent pure propaganda," she wrote, and "I enjoy writing a thing that can't be considered propaganda in *any* form, pure or alloyed." When she met Elizabeth Lawrence face-to-face, Brooks was sure to remind her that she was a purist. She was afraid of portraying herself as overly concerned with poetic technique, and yet issues of formal competence and technique were typically of the first importance to her. She hoped to range beyond the humble office of cataloger of the ills of the race, not least because "the public won't accept, much longer, that pure propaganda dished out in broken-up lines and called 'poetry.'"[48]

It is unclear to whom she obliquely referred: Frank Marshall Davis, master of the direct, unpoetic line? Langston Hughes, the most widely published black American poet? It is a certainty that those like Edward Bland and Ralph Ellison, critics who had loudly rejected everything connected to black writing of the 1920s, shared her view. But if Brooks asserted her sense of difference from the "broken-up lines" of some of her peers, she did not feel ready to challenge the publisher. By February 1945 she told her editor Elizabeth Lawrence that she had stopped writing poetry, to develop the novel that Harper encouraged.[49]

As always, there was a subtext to the assertion of allegiance to artistic purity over propaganda-like necessity. Brooks had been contracted and given an advance, an unlikely circumstance for a poet whose work had not appeared in esteemed academic quarterlies or nationally circulated, paying magazines. Brooks needed to dramatize her ability to belong to a world quite different from the black Chicago Marxist bohemia, and devotion to technical excellence obviously was an avenue to do that. And then, Brooks may have needed to explain herself in the terms of antipropaganda. When Wright's *Black Boy* did come out, her editor Elizabeth Lawrence noted that the book both "disturbed and moved her." But then Lawrence thought this was wrong. "Frank books need to be written and published by and about Negroes in America, but I am a little afraid that too much emphasis will be given to the racial theme."[50] Lawrence went on to say that she subscribed to the "school" of thought that held that Wright had melodramatically inflated his own personal battles and anguish into an apocalypse for the race. Brooks liked to hold herself aloof from these quarrels as well as she could, and when she responded to Lawrence she dutifully replied that she had heard criticism and praise from a variety of schools and camps, but that her own view of the book remained balanced. But it was impossible to read *A Street in Bronzeville* and miss the "racial theme."

Another important poetic voice, from the Great Lakes region, also turned an artistic corner toward the end of 1945: Robert Hayden. An orphan adopted into a grim home in black Detroit, Hayden had prevailed over early obstacles to finish his baccalaureate at Detroit City College (later Wayne State University). He took a job with the Federal Writers' Project in Michigan and worked at his poetry. His feelings of racial loyalty were intense and balanced only by a deep sense of introspection; Hayden himself was a shy and reserved person with eyesight poor enough to exempt him from the draft. His poem "Diana," which he had sent to *New Challenge* for the second scotched edition, had finally been self-published in his 1940 collection *The Heart-Shape in the Dust*. While he lived in the North, Hayden tended to stress the pain of African American historical southern experience, especially lynching, in poems like "We Are the Hunted," "Coleman," "Religioso," and "The Negro to America." The Left also decidedly influenced him, and he sloganeered with poems like "Speech" and "These Are My People." He even had quaint dialect poems, but not with quite the humor of Langston Hughes. All in all, Hayden's first book sounded very much like a propaganda piece. He had diffused the elements more serenely than Frank Marshall Davis, but there was no getting around the emphasis of the finale poem, "These Are My People," an epic with the stridency of Margaret Walker, but without the rich images and poignant vernacular. It was good but apprentice work.

Hayden's gifts showed enough promise for him to enroll in the English department at the University of Michigan for master's degree work in 1941. That summer Hayden read about slavery at the Schomburg Collection in New York, and in the fall at Michigan he enrolled for a class with a new addition to the English department faculty, Professor W. H. Auden. In Auden's class on modern poetry, Hayden saw the magnificence of T. S. Eliot pinned to the board and unpacked by readings of Kierkegaard and Nietzsche. Students were encouraged to think more critically of Eliot's "The Waste Land" and the idea of the end of poetry. After finishing his degree and gaining Auden's backing, Hayden lectured to the undergraduate classes. He lived in Michigan during the moment of fiercely escalating racial tensions and then the dramatic Detroit riot of 1943. In the early 1940s Hayden gave in to his true passion, to "correct the misconceptions and to destroy some of the stereotypes and clichés which surrounded Negro history."[51] He was calling his new book *Black Spear*.

Phylon brought out the longest chunk of his latest work in the third quarter of 1945, and Hayden, then thirty-two, published what became his signature poem, "Middle Passage." In another year he would begin teaching at Fisk College, after having served a four-year apprenticeship at the University of Michigan, where he won the Hopwood Award for his poems. With "Middle Passage," Hayden had found his voice. He had always loved history, and now he epically dramatized a series of buried archival events that brought forth the best of his imagination. The leitmotif of the poem was the traumatic journey of African slaves across the Atlantic. But the modernist jam of the poem, the criticism of received tradition, the insistent, persuasive, and oddly complementary voices, turned the poem of a regrettable historical event into an evocative and compelling testament of human triumph.

"Middle Passage" offered a three-part lament, combining dirgelike, repetitious riffs of black plaintive cries, the biblically allusive names of slave ships, and long evidentiary notes from a slave ship's log and legal depositions, interlaced with the story of Joseph Cinque battling across the forecastle to freedom. Hayden hewed out a raw-edged irony between voices of the pious Christian enslavers and the devotedly rebellious slaves. The narrator guided the reader through the poem, emphasizing the sections that demanded a careful attention to social history with the refrain "to flower stubbornly."[52] Stubborn flowering was the new fate of the descendants of the stolen tribe, a new anchor for black identity. The result was a stunning masterpiece.

The poem's thematic heft seemed more than just a little germane to the contemporary problem of black artists and their establishing a foothold on the American scene. Hayden seemed to acknowledge the bane to black critical perception—the "gods false to us . . . kings betraying us"—of left and right on the political spectrum.[53] Black writers and thinkers also were trying "to flower stubbornly" in a place without mentoring or succor.

The increasingly sophisticated discussions of the "racial theme" rounded out the arrival of new talent in 1945, at least its arrival to the broad American public. Ralph Ellison, recently returned from the war zone, reviewed a new anthology published by Bucklin Moon, who had said for the dust jacket of Brooks's *A Street in Bronzeville*, "[s]he writes easily and with a deft touch that never strives for effect."[54] Moon's help was sought after. The 1945 article "Beating That Boy" in *New Republic* was Ellison's first crack at a nationally distributed magazine unconnected to the Federal Writers' Project or the Communists. The fact that New Dealer Earl Browder had formally dissolved the Communist Party in the United States and turned it into a political association in 1944 made the venues for Ellison's early career all but indistinguishable, and certainly *New Republic* continued to qualify as a "parlor pink" magazine. Moon's anthology had collected most of the widely distributed pieces on race published during the 1940s and also included some of the classics. Ellison took his theoretical discussion away from a vilification of the black middle class and started to look to the unconscious of white America, where he believed might be found the psychological confusion that embedded and perpetuated racism.

Ellison claimed that blacks were forced "down into the deeper levels of his consciousness, into the inner world," and that they stayed there because the "social sciences and serious literature have been conscripted . . . to drown out the persistent voice of outraged conscience." Arguing against Gunnar Myrdal, who pointed to moral cowardice in the perpetuation of racism, Ellison thought that racial oppression took place outside of normative conscious reality and inside a realm created by the "anesthesia of legend, myth, hypnotic ritual and narcotic modes of thinking." "[T]he 'Negro Problem' is actually a guilt problem charged with pain," he argued, redefining the common term.[55]

Ellison then set down a brief sketch of the nature of white American psychological life for which he won lasting notoriety. "For imprisoned in the deepest drives in human society, it is practically impossible for the white American to think of sex, economics, his children or womenfolk, or of sweeping sociopolitical changes, without summoning into consciousness fear-flecked images of black men."[56] The black artist's dilemma (and duty) was greatly magnified in such a cauldron of basic American social self-deception. As necessary an act as freeing the black was the responsible artists' coming to terms with the processes drowning the "outraged conscience" of white Americans. Instead of accurate perception, white writers tended to ignore powerful racial material, which consequently became distorted as it was forced down into the deep regions of the mind.

In the next issue of *New Republic*, the ex–managing editor Thomas Sancton publicly thanked Ellison and launched his work to a larger audience, an unheard of example of white editor claiming insight from a black literary critic. "In a single page he makes some essential observations about American writers and writing that one fails to find in most full-length critical books, which, whatever their other merits, lack an understanding of the withering influence of the race dilemma on so much American art and thinking," Sancton wrote.[57] And in one of the early important moments in the reversal of the intellectual ethnic ghettoes, Sancton observed that Ellison had shown him "why I dislike Hemingway."

Ellison's arrival on the national scene was an event because he had not been launched exclusively by either the black middle class and their colleges or the Communists, and really Richard Wright had been the only one to make it all the way from the far Left to legitimate literary success. But soon enough unaligned writers would hold the public attention, and writers like J. Saunders Redding, who had appeared widely in the early 1940s discourse of literature and cultural politics, would recede—at least in terms of their visibility to the white public. By fall of 1943 Redding had left North Carolina and begun teaching for Hampton Institute's English department, a job he held for nearly twenty-five years. Typical of the conservative black colleges, Hampton had never had an African American president and had appointed only one black department head by the early 1940s. Redding had chaired the English department at Elizabeth City State College, but he gained the new teaching position at Hampton on account of his recommendations from Harper and the University of North Carolina. Even if he could not seek a job at a white majority institution, he was not confined to the same narrow game of advancement as his colleagues who relied on the recommendation of fickle administrators for their livelihood. Redding seems to have imagined freedom entirely from the career of a lifelong academic. When he moved up to Hampton's campus, Redding determined to write a novel, and in 1944 he successfully applied for a Guggenheim to work on his book.

Criticism, however, if of a pedestrian variety, accounted for Redding's longstanding influence. Within a couple of years at Hampton he became the regular literary critic for the *Baltimore Afro-American* and quickly enough the most prominent black literary critic publishing in a newspaper in the United States. The paper circulated to 244,000 between Richmond, Virginia and Newark, New Jersey, and had its hub in Baltimore.[58] Redding shoved off with a weekly column called "A Second Look" on January 29, 1944, still fresh from the excitement of *No Day of Triumph*. More than his black academic colleagues, but in a fashion similar to both Horace Cayton and Langston Hughes, Redding tried to marry the worlds of black and white.

For nearly two years Redding made "A Second Look" a grab-bag general forum that discussed culture, race, and politics from a strongly centrist, integrationist, Christian American position. Anything that grew out of fundamental democratic principles and expressed liberal tolerance, Redding endorsed.

His liberalism suited the needs of his African American audience, which demanded a certain burden be placed upon white society. "[T]he bridge to the truly democratic future must be built by white people," he assured them in the opening weeks.[59]

Redding's implicit posture in his column was that of race protector, although he took his share of chiding for not being outspoken enough. He was interested in the psychological formation in the back of the American concept of race. He suggested that U.S. blacks existed on "two levels of reaction," an intense situation that required blacks "to do a lot of extra living."[60] This was not a wholesome condition, but rather one of doubling that precipitated psychic exhaustion, and Redding believed that in race-pride lay the core of the solution. "The only way a colored person can convey to others that he is human is by first insisting that he is colored," he lectured to readers.[61] Redding was an advocate of black pride insofar as it was an element of modernist psychological confidence, and he ground black humanity in uplifting racial narratives. Black Americans could only make a way into the universal modern world from the accurate cultivation of their specific historical experience. "Slavery, therefore, is not entirely a thing of odium, but, more important, a bit of the past that makes the present possible."

Such dramatic slogans of confidence signaled not only the departure from the embarrassment of slavery, but also the rejection of the African past as Hegelian prehistory, and here the new black writers were critical. At that moment, Redding saw in Wright's portrait of black depravity almost precisely the same gesture as being made by Lionel Trilling. "Richard Wright's is perhaps the first colored voice to cry 'Hear! Hear!' to universal values."[62] Redding led the 1940s trend to denounce the existence of double consciousness as weak-willed.

Among the other controversies, Redding dismissed the sexual taboo in the newspaper. He claimed that white southern resistance to black social equality lay in the distorted creation of the African male "[p]reternaturally endowed with sexual vitality and lust," which was undergirded by an unpleasantly malformed white femininity, "brutal, amoral and correspondingly lustful."[63] He commemorated the death of Thomas Dixon, of *The Clansman* and *Birth of a Nation* fame, with an anti-elegy. "Dixon died as he should have died—trailing the wilted plumes of his hate behind him."[64] He heaped manure upon the black status quo, saying that in the jet age, the black colleges were making do in a buggy driven by a "blind and spavine" horse.[65] He spread the blame around generously: the ideology of caste exploited by Booker T. Washington, "the stubborn idea that colored students in general should confine themselves to certain fields of endeavor"—meaning industrial education—and finally, "unimaginative and timid educational leaders." "The colored people in America, who above all people need a grounding in the humanities, in truly liberalizing knowledge, in sympathetic understanding of human society and its all too human foibles, have been taught only to make a living." He seemed to do more than just gesture at the culprits, "It is not mere coincidence that an inferior colored college should be rated Class A by the same rating board which rates the University of North Carolina, the University of Texas, and Duke University Class A." And he extended the critique to the students themselves. "[O]ne is hard put to distinguish the average colored college graduates from the unfortunate clodhoppers who have never seen a school," he noted.[66] Here was Redding's everlasting and painful fight against the administrators and sham bourgeoisie of the African American college system, and the reason why he valued so highly a social realism that hit at his enemies.

A modernist in his professional sensibility, Redding defended Lillian Smith's *Strange Fruit* from the obscenity charge that had caused it to be banned in Boston. But Redding was also precisely the kind of person who disapproved of Smith's curious fiction world, where a black woman graduate of Spelman College chooses to become a concubine. He tried to be statesmanlike with his review that caught anchor with environmental determinism. "There is no character in the book who is not to be pitied. All of them are caught, bound less by what they are (and this is the pity) than by what society has made them."[67] What he saw his way clear to stand by in Smith's work was her effective marshaling of a dark social realist vision of environment. Here lay her courage and power, he decided.

On May 28, 1945, Redding announced that "this column will concern itself with books for the next few weeks," identifying a regular commitment to book reviews that would hold him until 1966. About a year later, on June 29, 1946, the column changed its name from "A Second Look" to "Book Reviews." It was a good time to switch from public issues to books. That fall, the Eightieth U.S. Congress went Republican in both houses, and a historic bloc between southern "Dixiecrat" Democrats and right-wing Republicans rolled back the New Deal social welfare agenda.[68] The cold war abroad and conservative politics at home would introduce a new tendency among black critics at small southern schools or trucking along with the New York intellectual crowd: one of appeasement under the guise of "new" liberal politics.

Against snobbery, Redding accepted any book for review mailed to him by a publisher. He vowed to look at "all comers, good and bad," a practice that would gall him over the years, but to which he remained faithful.[69] Redding sought to build up black audiences, and he tried to erect a framework of concerns that would increase black participation. First, he thought cultural control was important and that black audiences failed to support their own. "It is strange, when you stop to consider it, how much more interested white people are in the literature and art of colored people than we are ourselves."[70] Redding presumed that greater freedom of self-expression would come only when black writers escaped the cultural assumptions and commercial directives of white America.

But Redding's desire for black audiences to pick writers with their pocket-books had its source in the conservative politics after World War II as much as it did in his mildly Garveyite sentiment. Contrary to the view of Langston Hughes and Sterling Brown, he believed that during the 1920s crude racism in American publishing had ended as a factor preventing the publication of books by black Americans about black topics.[71] Sterling Brown said flatly, "[o]pposition to honest treatment of Negro life in literature is certain and it is strong."[72] Redding took the other view. When he received letters from readers arguing that the publishing industry was racially prejudiced and decidedly reluctant to publish what one of his readers called the "real true facts about colored people," he responded without any ambiguity. "[T]he first-rate publishers are neither prejudiced nor averse to taking the necessary risk involved in issuing a new writer's work," he held forth.[73] The "day when good writing is ignored is largely past," Redding intoned, on the verge of overstating the case but striving to prevent self-created racial ceilings from setting up.

But the meager fraction of blacks on publishers' lists and on bookstore shelves suggested more active prohibition to his black readership. The reality of the situation was more racist influence than Redding cared to admit. Bobbs-Merrill publisher D.L. Chambers reprimanded Redding's editor Hiram Haydn for accepting Redding's project *On Being Negro in America*. When told by Chambers that his list for 1951 was unwisely filled with "Jews and Negroes," Haydn stood up and delivered a "philippic" exhorting antiracist modern liberal ideals and the obvious necessity of books about racial and religious minorities.[74] Redding was lucky that Hayden maintained his conviction; surely there were other editors unprepared to jeopardize their careers and fight so hard.[75]

Additionally, an oblique geometry shaped the production of black literary talent. Five years into his column, the goodly portion of the black authors Redding reviewed were paying to have their books published by two New York houses, Exposition and Pageant Press. These preachers, teachers, and social workers comprised the black "elite" "middle class" "intelligentsia" as it existed in the 1940s, and they dramatically outnumbered the tiny group of blacks published by the large commercial firms. Typically Redding railed against these "would be" writers, who threw "talent, truth, [and] profundity" to the wind, believing that "[i]f it's about colored people, it'll get published."[76] Probably what they believed was that their story was worth telling. In any event, the vanity press authors and their earnest and lightly edited books commented explicitly on educated blacks' estimate of the inexorable quality of racial prejudice. As a group, there was a strong belief that white racial prejudice would always close off access to commercial publishing.

A disciplined man who, after his success with *No Day of Triumph*, downplayed the forces of racism, Redding rarely accepted publishing company bias as the excuse for the slender work published by black Americans. But in terms of a network of effects shaping possibility, the assumptive basis that generated outcomes, it was there. In 1945 Redding published the only article that he ever wrote for *Publisher's Weekly*, "The Negro Author: His Publisher, His Public and His Purse." He supported the idea of widespread liberal attitudes in publishing, writing that "even now Doubleday, Doran is sponsoring a contest for the best book written by a Negro."[77] He had everything right but the preposition. The contest was for best book *about* Negroes. In the half-dozen or so years it was awarded, no Negro ever received the award for fiction. For blacks, the optimistic dream of new liberalism demanded keeping one eye always shut.

CHAPTER NINE

Black Futilitarianists and the Welcome Table (1945–1947)

J. Saunders Redding's twin was Horace Cayton, the frustrated artist who also published a weekly column in the African American press during the mid-1940s. Cayton was also alert enough to recognize the timely power of literature. After the 1945 publication of Wright's second blockbuster, *Black Boy*, Cayton turned his attention fully to the works of American novelists, and he even experimented with Socratic-style fictional dialogue in his *Pittsburgh Courier* column. He loved to use the imaginative space of fiction to explore difficult problems without the burden of providing programmatic solutions. Cayton's inspired commentaries on writing helped to make the concerns of black literary realists synonymous with the movement for racial justice. Fiction had the potential to popularize the environmental processes that contributed to the high levels of black degradation, as well as to show the faintheartedness of intervening white liberals. The success of the social realist writers exposed the twin canards of the "southern liberals," who continued to hint that blacks were biologically inferior and that white liberals already intervened too much. Cayton hoped to encourage other writers to become chroniclers of black tragedy, to fashion themselves into Horatios who would take Hamlet's plea to accept a life "in pain" and "tell my story."

In Cayton's view, two black writers took up Horatio's burden: a capital Richard Wright, and the bright and intrepid newcomer Chester Himes. During the peak years of Cayton's *Courier* column, Wright's *Black Boy* and Himes's 1945 novel *If He Hollers Let Him Go* were his touchstones. He regularly lauded the two stirring writers, whom he thought the captains of what he called by 1946 a "Negro Renaissance in Literature." The lesser known work was quite distinctive. Released in November 1945, Chester Himes's novel *If He Hollers Let Him Go* jolted and scraped bone. Himes published his book a couple of months after Wright's *Black Boy* had reinvigorated the terms of black anger. He completed the novel with the help of a 1944 Julius Rosenwald Fellowship. It was probably a good thing that the troops in the war zones did not get it in time. The novel showed that not only lower-class Bigger Thomases despised whites and resented their treatment—middle-class blacks harbored deep and potentially violent frustration as well.

Himes worked hard to develop a black audience. The year that followed his "Double V" polemics in *Opportunity* and *Crisis* brought him in close coordination with traditional middle-class aims, chiefly because he spent the time publishing in the *Crisis*—four short stories in 1943, then one each in 1944 and 1945. "Two Soldiers" and "All He Needs Is Feet" were set pieces exploring racist brutality. In "So Softly Smiling" Himes gave readers a love story occurring among the eighty thousand or so black college graduates. But in "Heaven Has Changed," Himes tried his hand at a mildly satiric political allegory. In the black heaven, Uncle Tom has just died and his son struggles to take over leadership from an overseer figure called Jim Crow. Not long before the publication of his novel, Himes offered a strongly autobiographical short story called "All of God's Chilluns Got Pride" that revealed his core concern: humiliating fear. The short story showed Himes at work on the Cleveland WPA, trying to keep a marriage going without income, and then in the army stockade at the end. At one moment in the story the protagonist Keith bluntly characterizes the pessimism of black Americans: "If I really loved you, baby, I would blow out your brains. Right now! Because all you can ever look forward to, baby, is never having nothing you ever dreamed about."[1] This was a bit acidic for the NAACP, but mellow in comparison with the novel Himes had gotten through his publisher at Doubleday.

If He Hollers Let Him Go supplied an adrenaline-filled four days in the life of protagonist Bob Jones, a charismatic young black man with two years of college and working as the lone black foreman at a California shipyard. A master of the "blues," Himes cued the novel's thematic arch to parallel the black pimp's wisdom, "Get a white woman and go from Cadillacs to cotton sacks."

The novel begins with Jones at the height of prosperity. He owns a car, is nearly engaged to the attractive daughter of a local physician, and holds a ranking position at a shipyard. By the end of the novel he has been arrested for the rape of a washed out, blowsy white biddy from Mississippi, mainly because, after a series psychologically intense dalliances, he refuses to have sex. All of Jones's tangible symbols of success are gone: job, fiancée, car, and draft deferment. The racial, environmental and biological tensions of the naturalist world prove steadily ruinous, but the psychology of internalized racial oppression is the novel's prime focus. Jones was a semi-intellectual who bridged the gaps between the slowly integrating black elites and the permanently segregated black working class. Himes continued the tradition of intellectual resistance common in Waters Turpin and Carson McCullers by including an African American college graduate named Ben who is both an intellectual and courageous. Unlike Bob, an uncomfortable intermediary, Ben offers uncompromising militancy. "You'll never get anything from these goddamn white people unless you fight them," Ben tells the black ship welders, "They don't know anything else."[2] But Bob Jones falls into a sexual tar baby and never approaches the principled fight against white power. The novel concluded with Jones physically broken and being mustered into the army, which for a black soldier meant at least a long drink of humiliation during basic training at a southern camp.

Of the three writers whom the *Chicago Defender* editor Earl Conrad called the leaders of the "Blues School" of literature in 1945, neither Richard Wright, Ralph Ellison, nor Himes wanted to abandon the option of violence as a proper remedy for racial injustice. In their own way, each of them saw it as an important component of masculinity. And of course, Himes had struggled for and with his masculinity in a different way from either Wright or Ellison. His mother had sheltered and favored him as the youngest and lightest in color of her three sons. Himes had rebelled in college and gone to prison at nineteen for seven years. In the Ohio Penitentiary he had a long-standing homosexual love affair, which he used to describe, with irony, as the greatest love of his life.[3] The protagonists he created in his 1940s novels were charismatic leaders and privileged men, sexually desirable across racial, class, and gender lines (though Himes did not publish on homosexuality in the 1940s), and men prone to respond to life's challenges with violence. They were also intellectuals, and Himes seemed to propose that masculine integrity saved them from either succumbing to liberal clichés or sacrificing the imperatives of black liberation.

The real target of *If He Hollers* was white liberal hypocrisy and black accommodation to the status quo. The book presents a series of flawed episodes of racial equality and the black pursuit of upward mobility. In the most detailed episode, Bob Jones's anger seems the only force capable of exposing the hypocritical and phony gradualism of white liberals who seduce educated blacks. Bob's socialite girlfriend Alice throws a hoity toity party hoping to impress a white liberal named Leighton. The casually lettered Bob easily shows the extraordinary distance between the problems of the liberals and their black lackeys and the majority of black people. The cultural flash point for issues of race and class was Bigger Thomas, but by 1945 Lillian Smith had arrived. Himes's hero takes a Neanderthal stand and defends Richard Wright.

> He waited for me, and when he saw I wasn't coming he said by way of appeasement, "Of course I think that Richard Wright makes the point better in *Native Son*."
>
> "Oh, but what Lillian Smith does is condemn the white Southerner," Arline said. "All Wright did was write a vicious crime story."
>
> "Personally, I think the white Southerner doesn't mind being just like Lillian Smith portrays him," I said.
>
> "I think Richard Wright is naïve," Polly said.
>
> "Aren't we all?" I said.

"*Native Son* turned my stomach," Arline said. "It just proved what the white Southerner has always said about us; that our men are rapists and murderers."

"Well, I will agree that the selection of Bigger Thomas to prove the point of Negro oppression was an unfortunate choice," Leighton said.

"What do you think, Mr. Jones?" Cleo asked.

I said, "Well, you couldn't pick a better person than Bigger Thomas to prove the point. But after you prove it, then what? Most white people I know are quite proud of having made Negroes into Bigger Thomases."

There was another silence and everybody looked at me. "Take me for instance," I went on. "I've got a job as leader man at a shipyard. I'm supposed to have a certain amount of authority over ordinary workers. But I'm scared to ask a white woman to do a job. All she's got to do is say I insulted her and I'm fired."

Leighton looked concerned. "Is that so?" he said. "I didn't realize relations between white and coloured were that strained in our industries."

"Of course Bob's problem is more or less individual," Alice apologized. "He's really temperamentally unsuited for industrial work. As soon as he enters into a profession, his own problem will be solved."[4]

Himes had needed a double intertextual reference to examine America at the end of 1945. Conversations across the color line were admirable, but not conversations that went to the nature of the problem. It was impolite and perhaps strategically unwise to suggest that large numbers of whites clung to public rituals that deliberately degraded blacks. Well-to-do and aspiring blacks were expected to rebuke Bigger Thomas, and to present Richard Wright, as Brooks's editor Elizabeth Lawrence had, as suffering from a painful individual experience. Bob Jones's girlfriend Alice Harrison, a svengali of accommodation, presented the intelligent view of the elites and their understudies. Advising Bob that conformity to segregation was necessary "to achieve any manner of financial success," Alice also heralds "spiritual values, intrinsic values, which are fundamental components of our lives." For well-to-do Alice, light colored enough to pass for white, racial barriers are finally inconsequential. "It depends darling," she tells Bob, "on our own sense of values."

Alice represents the viewpoint that had come out in Gunnar Myrdal's book, but in reverse. It was incumbent upon blacks to shift white attitudes by fighting to uphold their own values within a segregated society. But *If He Hollers* did not want to forget the disparity in material resources, or justified black resentment and bitterness at segregation. Instead of giving coy Alice the last word, Bob Jones is nearly beaten to death by a white mob, then forced to join the U.S. Army. The inevitability of martyrdom, pointless or ordained, seemed the only outcome for an honest black man. Himes would also end his next novel, *Lonely Crusade*, with his hero on the verge of being beaten to death.

Himes's unsettling quality to the American liberal milieu was proved by the reception of the book. In later years Himes described the novel's reception in legendary terms of sabotage. The situation was odd because racially bighearted Doubleday brought out the book. Himes's first cousin Henry Lee Moon read manuscripts for the press. Bucklin Moon, the most liberal white man in publishing, served as the editor. Moon recalled the experience as "memorable" and thought that he had stood up to help Himes remain uncompromising: "[T]here was no way out; to compromise further for either of us would have meant the emasculation of something which badly needed telling—the psychological lynchings which every Negro suffers almost daily and their impact on his psyche and personality." Moon led Himes to believe that if he softened the portrait, he would win the new $2,500 Doubleday "Carver Prize," named in honor of the black man of science.

But a few scant weeks before publication, Himes found Doubleday preparing to delete thirty pages of sexually explicit dialogue between Jones and his white antagonist Madge. Himes had to race by train to New York from California in June 1945 to argue his position and have the material restored. Then there was the question of publicity and the print run, which seemed to top off at seven thousand copies. Nor did Himes win the George Washington Carver Prize. The award went in early 1946 to Fannie Cook of St. Louis, the author of *Mrs. Palmer's Honey*, a novel about an unlettered and loyal domestic who joins the Congress of Industrial Organizations and votes the New Deal. Cook even had a character with the same job as Henry Lee Moon, an assistant to the director of the CIO's political action committee designed to help re-elect Roosevelt. When Doubleday ran its January advertisement in *Publisher's Weekly*, it used *If He Hollers* as an anonymous point of comparison by which to flatter Fannie Cook. "*Mrs. Palmer's Honey* is a book which you can sell to any reader. It is an honest, intelligent novel, devoid of lynchings, mixed love affairs, and profanity." Even the *New York Times* said, "it seems a little grotesque to honor as undistinguished a book as *Mrs. Palmer's Honey*." Himes felt betrayed by his publisher.

The reviews showed an awareness of the dilemma of race in America, and some analysts were happy about the vigor of Himes's discussion. Richard Wright reviewed him with praise, and *New Masses* picked the historian of Negro rebellions Herbert Aptheker to write up its favorable spread. *Saturday Review of Literature* called his book "the bitterest we have come across in a long time"—which meant ever—and while Isaac Rosenfeld in *New Republic* "liked particularly Mr. Himes' inclusion of sexual equality among the Negroes' demands for justice," he finally checked his enthusiasm for the book because of its "irresoluteness."[5]

Himes had had such success with *Crisis* in the early 1940s that he probably had come to believe that he was beloved by the black middle class. He never quite understood that his novel embarrassed them. *Opportunity* claimed that the protesting book reflected the deep feeling of Negro life but was trashy. "This story is too full of Negroes who seem mainly concerned with sex," wrote a prim Patsy Graves. "There is a maximum number of four-letter words, and an overflowing of four-letter implications," continued the review. "The characters are not well drawn. The unrelieved violence becomes tedious and unbelievable."[6] *Phylon* and the *Journal of Negro Education* thought Himes had written something that was significant but "harsh" and "sociological," or not exactly art.[7]

Himes received a wholly negative assessment from J. Saunders Redding at the *Afro-American*. Redding opposed the narrative choices of *If He Hollers Let Him Go*, which seemed to him utterly false: "There is nothing at all inescapable in what happens in it." Himes mainly offended Redding by using vulgarity in the book. Going a bit further than *Opportunity*, Redding even condemned "the extensive use of jive language," which he believed vitiated the novelist's ability to say something "important."[8] In his own work Redding had delivered up the dissipation and casual perversity of black life, but as he approached his forties, Redding was like a man getting religion. He believed that Himes had created a "stinker" for a protagonist. There was none of the powerful didacticism that had ruled Richard Wright. Redding did not anticipate the burgeoning French existentialist movement that many black writers felt was a native response of American Negroes to their circumstance. He rejected the meaningless suffering of a literary character. Instead, he thought that the writer should deliver materials that created sympathetic reactions within the audience. He faulted Himes for failing to show a belief in the strong moral principle necessary for the progressive betterment of society. Redding's religion would be one of the shallower branches of cold war liberalism.

The condemnation from the most powerful black critic of his time was evidence of the fracturing of any short-lived coalition among black writers between the camps of the Communists and the *Saturday Review*. Redding keenly yearned for stark realism and was prepared to encounter psychological depth, but, crucially, he resisted, to the point of resentment, anything that stung of obscurity or disdain for the audience. On the other hand, he accepted the existence of the forceful social realist movement in the black literature of restrained protest against the racial conditions, but he expressed sentiments that were almost entirely unsympathetic to the man-on-the-street views of his intellectual peers Sterling Brown and Horace Cayton. In one of the first examples of the criteria he put in place, he steadily rejected Himes, whose works in the 1940s best captured what came to be known as black protest fiction.

But what was poison in Hampton Roads, Virginia, was daily bread on 47th Street in Chicago. By 1946 Horace Cayton had identified twin tendencies in black writing. Appropriating Mathew Arnold's famous phrase, he had observed "a sweetness and light crowd who try to maintain the point of view that although Negroes have been mistreated in this country, they are not and should not be bitter."[9] Horace Cayton vigorously encouraged writers to become exponents of black tragedy, and he never ran out of encomiums for Richard Wright, the "genius, with gifts that have seldom been equaled," who had in "hard, tough, but beautiful writing" developed the indelible portrait of a Negro who had been brutalized. Cayton attributed to Wright a major psychological advance. Wright was the first Negro writer to say boldly and flatly that "Negroes hated and feared white men for what they had done to them and that hatred and fear warped the Negro's entire personality—conditioned all of his behavior."[10] Himes too was acknowledged for this clarity, the humorless recognition of painful feelings of inadequacy and rejection that shaped a generation of writers and thinkers. "Himes, writing out of a cold fury, lashed out at a world that had denied him his manhood," wrote Cayton.[11]

The voices that Cayton marshaled were so alarmist that *Pittsburgh Courier* editor P. L. Prattis had sarcastically termed them the "Scolding School" of black American writers. But Cayton was actually edging toward an analysis of fear among black Americans that looked similar to what would be called domestic colonialism. "This is not a neurotic fear based upon a vivid imagination," he began a column in the spring of 1946. "It is a real and constant fear of an enemy environment which attacks him psychologically and physically twenty-four hours of the day. This is true because the Negro is a suppressed and subordinated minority group."[12] This was as close as Cayton came to a colonial analysis of the black condition in America.

By looking closely at the works of the two writers, especially their presentation of the emasculation of black men in American society, Cayton produced one of the earliest racial syndromes, the famous "fear-hate-fear" syndrome of black racial pathology.

> Though some Negroes might deny it, none could live in the United States and not be afraid of white people when the means of keeping them down is terror. Wright goes a step further. He shows that, since Negroes are human beings, they resent this terrorizing. They hate white people, because white people have kept them down. This is the second phase of the complex.
>
> The last phase is that the Negro becomes afraid of his own hate, because it might bring on retaliation and further abuse.[13]

Imaginative fiction that registered protest promised a suitable metric to measure such statistically unquantifiable regions as black hostility and fear. It also gave vent to a new hostility: the cynicism behind liberal support of some black issues. Literary realists had the power to describe "the labyrinth of subterranean emotion which Negroes feel toward the injustice of the American system."

If they did not do it, Cayton figured, then the psychosis would go unchecked and continue to disable black attempts to fight Jim Crow.

His exploration culminated in the 1947 essay "The Psychological Approach to Race Relations." In it he talked about a deep-seated "oppression psychosis" among blacks. Based mainly on his readings of fiction, Cayton concluded that the "adult Negro is in all of his dealings with white men either consciously or unconsciously in a state of tension."[14] If white American liberals were demanding heavy doses of individual responsibility, Cayton was commandeering the black unconscious as a space of perpetual persecution. The fear-hate-fear syndrome resulted in "persistent and exaggerated mental states" in the subordinate group. "Fear leads to hate; but the personality recoils with an intensified and compound fear. This is his reaction to his own brutalization, subordination, and hurt. It is this vicious cycle in which the American Negro is caught and in which his personality is pulverized by an ever mounting, self-propelling rocket of emotional conflict." "Thus the Negro," he wrote, "is at war with his environment. There is a close analogy between a Negro living in America and a soldier under battle conditions." The notion of perpetual conflict had become excruciatingly dear. Cayton once remarked that he was "prouder of this little essay" than the entire book *Black Metropolis*.[15]

If He Hollers Let Him Go pivotally developed this controversial idea that blacks despised whites and resented their treatment. Cayton admitted that Americans were apt to find the book "over-drawn, hysterical, and too provoking." But the representation of sexual tension was new. "What Himes has done is to picture perhaps for the first time in American literature, the subtle horrible manner in which sex can be used to express racial hatred and racial revenge." Cayton responded favorably to a distinct Negro peevishness that had rarely before appeared in the public realm, the reason why Himes and Wright would mean so much twenty years later to black activists. To a critic like Cayton, this response was a defining moment of overcoming the abstract fear of white society. As the social realists matured and became more psychological in their explorations, their rhetoric of dissatisfaction with liberals and black leaders became more publicly painful. There was a cost. Twenty-six years later, when Himes published his memoir *The Quality of Hurt*, he insisted that the publishing industry in the United States repeatedly punished him for his indiscreet comments about American racism.

And so, for his part, Chester Himes continued to take to writing like a man battling for his life on the printed page, and he brought to the court of public opinion his resentment at the caviling directed at his book, the reluctance to point out his new perceptions and achievement, the tendency of the liberal press to react as if they had heard it all before. Himes genuinely believed that the book fell on deaf ears because Americans were in deep denial. In February

1946 he told them as much in a defiant blast in *Saturday Review of Literature.* Americans were afraid to "look upon the grim actualities of their own lives, the depths of their own depravities, the dangers of their own dissatisfactions, and the extent of their brutalities, accepting instead, with fulsome self-delusion, the utterly deliberate, premeditated falseness of their own picturization." To this breed, Himes would offer "the truth as I see it" and, as for solving the race problem, "I would not saddle an underprivileged, uneducated, poverty stricken, oppressed racial group with this responsibility."[16] This was an event. Regardless of the historical circumstance, American black writers had not been known to publish their resentments in reviews circulated into tens of thousands of American homes.

In effect, Himes declared war. When he wrote to Richard Wright expressing gratitude for his support, he also implied the existence of a new cadre and their distance from the old guard. "The manner in which Horace Cayton, you, [and] Ralph Ellison have come forward with such good will and interest and your realization and appreciation of the fact I have tried to be honest in the story, is indicative of a new day on the literary front," he warmed to Wright, whom he had met at Langston Hughes's house in the summer of 1945.[17] Himes thought Wright the leader of the "new school" of Negro writers. Although he had been in prison during the National Negro Congress's Chicago meeting of 1936, Himes was spiritually engaged by the mandates that extended from that congress, linked it to the South Side Writers' Club, and found expression in *New Challenge*: "I hope all this generation of writers will embrace this honesty of regard for one another's works—the pattern for which you have already established in many instances—no matter whether critical or to acclaim."

For Himes there would be much more "critical" and much less "to acclaim." He was on his way to becoming permanently enveloped in bitterness, and his dilemma was one of timing as much as anything. It was not a condition true for every black author. The most anticipated writer contracted in 1944 and who completed a manuscript in 1945 did not publish a book that year. Boston publisher Houghton Mifflin bet heavily on Ann Petry's stridently social realist document *The Street,* and it waited for an opportune time to release the book, after the exhilaration surrounding *Black Boy* and *If He Hollers* had subsided, in the late winter of 1946. Even better, the war had ended, and Petry's fiction writing instructor Mabel Robinson assured her, "Now that peace has come, people are going to listen to what you have to say."[18]

What Ann Petry had to say shocked everyone who would read it. Her book of social criticism and macabre tragedy detailed the odds against one black woman living on a destitute block in Harlem. The novel *The Street* was more barbed than what Petry had published in the previous two years, and Petry took advantage of the freedom the form gave her to peel back the rancid layers from urban African American life. The book appeared on February 7, 1946, to a substantial treatment by the black press, who had anticipated Petry not only because of her Houghton Mifflin literary award, but also because of her work that had appeared in the periodicals.

Houghton Mifflin splashed the face of lead character Lutie Johnson on the jacket's spine, a stock feature of its advertisement campaign that winter that included fetching young women on the covers of Anya Seton's best seller *The Turquoise* and Hester Chapman's *I Will Be Good*. The marketing division at Houghton Mifflin seems to have taken on faith that, unlike Wright's book, and most unlike Lillian Smith's *Strange Fruit*, the new benchmarks for fiction featuring black characters, Petry's novel would sell best among, if not exclusively to, blacks. About two weeks after the novel debuted, *Publishers' Weekly* printed Houghton Mifflin's lengthy marketing plan to reach the Negro market. Both publisher and publisher's journal showed the expansive consideration they were granting this unusual work, a cue they obviously wanted other publishers to know about.

> The book which deals with 116 Street in New York's Harlem is, of course, of great interest to the Negro press. And feature articles will be carried by a number of Negro periodicals including *Negro Digest, Ebony*, which covered the Houghton Mifflin party for Miss Petry on February 6, *Opportunity, Headlines, Phylon, Pulse* and *Journal of Negro Education*, which is published at Howard University. In addition a feature story with pictures will appear in the March issue of the *Crisis*, the magazine in which Miss Petry's work first appeared. The author's picture will appear on the front cover of the March issue of *Opportunity*.
>
> Sixty Negro newspapers were serviced with pre-release stories and pictures, mailed through Interstate United Newspapers, Incorporated. In addition, the United Negro College fund will send a story to 32 private Negro colleges and releases will go to some 70 other Negro schools.
>
> Copies of the book have also gone to the directors of several national organizations, including the Brotherhood of Railroad Trainmen, Ladies Auxiliary, the National Council of Negro Women, the Council Against Intolerance in America, and the National Association for the Advancement of Colored People.
>
> The Urban League is issuing a series of pamphlets on Miss Petry that will be included under "Thumbnail Sketches of Interesting People."
>
> Three of the Harlem bookstores, the National Memorial Bookstore, the Frederick Douglas Book Store and the Frances Reckling Book and Music Store, have given autographing parties, and featured the book in special display.
>
> Arrangements are now being completed for the presentation in early March of the Thalheimer Annual Award of the National Association of the Advancement of Colored People which is to be given to Miss Petry at Freedom House in New York by General Eisenhower.

In addition to all this, Miss Petry has appeared on several radio programs and she has been featured in stories and interviews in the *Pittsburgh Courier*, the *People's Voice*, the *Amsterdam News*, *PM*, the *New York Post*, and the *New York Age*. Miss Petry has also been interviewed by Carolyn Coggins of the *New York Herald Tribune*.

The *New York Times* is also doing a feature in pictures for the Sunday magazine section. Photographs for it will be taken in Harlem and posed by Canada Lee and Jane White who is now appearing in "Strange Fruit."[19]

The publisher had gone to a remarkable degree to identify and credential the Jim Crow reading networks in the American public, and to deliberately advance the manner in which the work might blossom without the assistance of the Left or, for that matter, the high-brow elites.

Although Petry did receive excellent notice in the *New York Times*, including reviews by Charles Poore and Alfred Butterfield during the week of publication, she did not wind up with a photographic spread in the magazine.[20] *Opportunity* showed her to fashionable and lovely advantage on the cover of its spring 1946 issue. Houghton Mifflin had available twenty thousand copies on publication day, but in its first six months of publication *The Street* was never a best seller or a candidate for the list, according to the statistics compiled by *Publishers' Weekly*, numbers based on a cross section of seventy to a hundred major bookstores in New York, Boston, and Chicago. Generally, a writer needed to have sales in excess of two hundred thousand a year after publication to make an annual best-seller list. Soon enough, the book seems to have been made available in paperback, and it is difficult to determine if the press printed again another hardcover run beyond its initial twenty thousand, or, if the book was issued quickly as a pocket paperback to achieve its broad distribution. However, *The Street* did not have to rely on book sales alone to reach American readers; in March *Omnibook* agreed to publish a condensed version of it, and Petry was paid two thousand dollars.[21] *Negro Digest* also serialized portions of the book. Not long after the book reached its audience, Petry and her husband George left New York for Connecticut, a certain sign of their new prosperity.

In her first novel, Petry's beguiling talent concentrated more on message than artistry. Petry accused from the perspective of a social worker, and what made her accusation unique was its precision: Lutie Johnson and her son Bub are defeated by their block of 116th Street between Seventh and Eighth Avenues. The book's dramatic action is condensed into a couple of hours during three or four days, and midway through the book two of the minor characters, Min and her common-law man Jones, take over the narrative and become more compelling than the heroine Lutie Johnson. The novel's conclusion is melodrama of a high order, rapidly escalated and forced, with the narrator supplying a formulaic rationale for the final action, the candlestick murder of the black bandleader Boots, the tangible substitute for the forces of oppression that have devastated the heroine. In his autobiography, Malcolm X described the same neighborhood, where he ventured to sell narcotics around 1944, as the "worst of the ghetto," where people bought street-corner drugs "to keep from having to face their miserable existence."[22]

Petry's narrator assumed the point of view of every character to drive home without any ambiguity the didactic orchestration under way. She needed the inside view of each character, even her villains, because she was determined to show that the observable deformity of Harlem life was due to poverty, squalor, and racism, and never any innate failing or human inadequacy. She did not let her audience choose if there was suffering and cruelty; the characters dripped with it. Her protagonist Lutie was a feminine version of the wooden code hero: classy, desirable, smart, talented, and, most important to the clubwoman that Petry was, morally irreproachable.

And this stroke contained genius. Petry successfully yoked two audiences— the black middle class and the white liberals—with a novel that made its working-class protagonist a paragon of moral virtue. A Harlem native, Lutie is a cut above the multitudes of laboring blacks she is related to by blood, works and walks the street alongside, and has married. But her distinction is unexplained. Her finale, where, instead of using her sexuality for commercial advantage, she accepts the complete ruin of her and her son's lives, showed the Victorian moral that shaped Petry's own sense of justice. Despite the influence of biology and environment in dominating human life—central to Petry's premise—Lutie is unlike all the other characters. She sublimates her sex drive completely, while the other characters—her father, her stepmother, the building superintendent, her husband Jim, and the bandleader Boots—are completely dominated by theirs.

In a manner that was impossible to misinterpret, Petry crafted the city into the vicious agent of black destruction. In her novel there would be no court-room melodrama to make plain the series of relations that brought urban blacks to the tipping point of despair; for Petry the city itself would take on anthropomorphic characteristics. One of the novel's most perceptive passages recorded the communal feelings of hopelessness and desperation abounding in Harlem. Lutie Johnson stumbles upon a cluster of people on the street staring at the corpse of a young man. Lutie notices the boy's waferlike shoe soles, detached from the uppers. The victim's sister appears and can only say about the young man's sudden death, "I always thought it'd happen." The woman can barely show remorse and certainly not pain. "It was as though for a fraction of a second something—hate or sorrow or surprise—had moved inside her and been reflected on her face. As quickly as it came, it was gone and it was replaced by a look of resignation."[23] The value of kin is reduced to an extraordinary thinness in the city that had begun the century as a refuge for blacks from the South. But Lutie is hardly surprised at the easy dispatch with which family bonds have etiolated; she reads a newspaper headline the following day that describes the justifiable killing of a "burly Negro."

> And she decided that it all depended on where you sat how these things looked. If you looked at them from inside the framework of a fat weekly salary, and you thought of colored people as naturally criminal, then you didn't really see what any Negro looked like. You couldn't, because the Negro was never an individual. He was a threat, or an animal, or a curse, or a blight, or a joke.[24]

Lutie has grown up in Harlem, rented a house in Jamaica, Queens, and worked as a live-in domestic for a white family in suburban Connecticut. Despite the complex variety shaping her perspective, 116th Street effectively destroys her Franklinian resolve for upward mobility halfway through the book. "For a brief moment she tried to look into the future. She still couldn't see anything—couldn't see anything at all but 116th Street and a job that paid barely enough for food and rent and a handful of clothes. Year after year like that."[25] With only a quarter of the book left, Lutie's feelings about her environment have become excruciating. "Even if she had the necessary funds, any apartment she moved into would be equally as undesirable as the one she moved out of. Except, of course, at a new address she wouldn't find Mrs. Hedges and the Super. No, but there would be other people who wouldn't differ too greatly from them."[26]

In another bounding leap of logic that placed her squarely in the camp of finger-pointers at society, Lutie decides that her block is an example of "the North's lynch mobs . . . the method the big cities used to keep Negroes in their place." And her geographical isolation is part of her racial punishment. "From the time she was born, she had been hemmed into an ever-narrowing space, until now she was very nearly walled in and the wall had been built up brick by brick by eager white hands."[27]

Petry's manipulation of Harlem into a horrific dungeon was not velvet-gloved. There were no churches or youth clubs, political movements or social reform drives in the world she created. Her nearest depictions that approximated a Negro professional class were the half-gangster, half-bandleader Boots and a fleecing lawyer whose deception fuels the final destructive action of the plot. After Lutie's young son has been arrested, the heroine engages in her most active analysis of the situation of black families. And in this, Petry molded the feminism available for her day, one that did not seek to blame black men for the poor standing of the group. Lutie angrily concludes that her family life has dissolved because of her husband's inability to find work. Instead of the comfortable patriarchy available to white women, black women produce the family's income. "The women work because the white folks give them jobs—washing dishes and clothes and floors and windows. The women work because for years now the white folks haven't liked to give black men jobs that paid enough for them to support their families."[28] Lutie concludes that whites have created "the Street" to addle black material advance and, even, their psychological well-being.

Petry hammered the head of the racial nail, expressing more direct bitterness than had been in the pages of *Native Son*, and from a character who was better educated and more moral than Bigger Thomas. Her protagonist is unwavering; every seventy-five pages offers a condemnation. "Damn white people, she thought. Damn them. And then—but it isn't that woman's fault. It's your fault. That's right, but the reason Pop came here to live was because he couldn't get a job and we had to have the State children because Jim couldn't get a job. Damn white people, she repeated."[29] Or in another place: "It all added up to the same thing, she decided—white people. She hated them. She would always hate them."[30] And then toward the book's conclusion, "In every direction, anywhere one turned, there was always the implacable figure of a white man blocking the way, so that it was impossible to escape."[31] Somehow white liberals managed to love the book.

The Street collected support in spite of its method and its message. It was curious. The black middle class liked the fact that her heroine did not give in to sexual indiscretion. *Phylon* noted that Lutie, unlike the black girl from *Strange Fruit*, was not "provoked by the desire for white men, for either pleasure or for profit."[32] White liberals enjoyed the reformist thrust of the book, the idea that a remedy was possible and plausible. The *New York Times* rewarded the "memorable simplicity and power" of the novel and then applauded Petry's sense of dramatic tension. "[S]he has created as vivid, as spiritually and emotionally effective a novel as that rich and important theme has yet produced."[33] There was also safety in a smug presumption: the character Lutie might have thought she hated whites, but her epic struggle was "against those of her own race and neighborhood," problems that seemed to be of her own creation.

Petry's most penetrating critic was Arthur P. Davis, now teaching at Howard (where Eva B. Dykes, one of the first African American Ph.Ds., would soon retire and where Sterling Brown was taking several visiting appointments during the 1940s). Davis recognized the formation of the "hard-boiled school" of writers, which included Ann Petry, Richard Wright, Carl Offord, and Chester Himes, and he ascribed a new method to them: futilitarianism. The writers specialized in "sordidness and [the] social degeneracy" to depict the helpless victim whose personality was distorted by the black ghetto.

> Primarily writers of social criticism and protest, these authors make frequent use of obscenity . . . not inserted for wholly sensational effect. Another weapon in the arsenal of protest, it is used to shock the American conscience into an awareness

of the inequalities and injustices in our system. . . . Though futilitarian in their own works and attitude, they, by the very intensity of their attacks, have done much to enlist the aid of liberal America to the cause of the Negro.

Enlisting liberals to the cause of the Negro did not, in Davis's estimate, produce a formula for high art: "a thesis is one thing, a good novel another."[34]

Good novel or not, the book received notice from among the liberal elite crowd. Diana Trilling, wife of Lionel Trilling, played a sharp note in a *Nation* review that twined *The Street* and Fannie Cook's *Mrs. Palmer's Honey*. Trilling called Cook's novel "cerebral" because, even though it used nearly black caricature, it argued in favor of the New Deal and labor unions. Unlike Cook's two-dimensional black characters, Petry's portraits had achieved "verisimilitude." But Trilling's conclusion emphasized a point of view that exposed the fragile coalition between black and white liberals. What was extraordinary to her about the book was the simple fact that Lutie wanted a better life, at all. "[C]lass feelings are as firmly ingrained in the colored population of this country as in the white," she warmed up. And from there, Trilling went on to lay the seedbed of an emerging consensus regarding race in liberal circles after the war: "there is nothing inherently virtuous, from a political point of view or any other point of view, about being a member of a mistreated minority."[35] Inadvertent perhaps, a new postwar challenge was on the table: blacks needed to prove inherent virtue to merit relief from injustice.

The novelist Frank Yerby faced the same problem of literary audience and the value of social realism, but he expressed his particular desolation and bitterness in another way. He was thirty-five in 1946, the year he became rich. Yerby had been a young crackerjack member of the black avant-garde, and he had plowed within the narrow furrows available to the elite of black writers. After *Challenge*, he had linked up to Jack Conroy's *New Anvil* in 1939. He wrote for *Phylon*, for *Common Ground* in 1945 and 1946, and for the WPA's *Tomorrow*. Everything he wrote revealed the plight of black America. The novel that he worked on and was unable to place was called *This Is My Own*, and it revealed the lives of highly educated black Americans. In 1944 Yerby got a big break with a short story he did not particularly like called "Health Card," published in *Harper's*.[36]

Even with the magazine taking his fiction, the novel still did not meet the approval of Harper editor Edward Aswell. Yerby believed the problem was that his novel featured a black Ph.D. as its protagonist. He described the book's hero as an "intelligent, educated—no 'Bigger Thomas' in any sense of the word. He is myself and thousands of my friends and maybe a little bit of all the persecuted minority peoples all over the world."[37] The dramatic limitations of such a character, let alone the theoretical limitations of the class as explained by Edward

Bland, did not matter for Yerby. He disliked the absence of "the educated Negro," whose resemblance to whites seemed to stir their unconscious resentment. "The point is that the reading public, in common with the public generally, likes to pretend that such Negroes do not exist."[38]

So to prove to himself that he did exist, for the seven active publishing years of his literary career he had kept his eye on the structure and thematic lilt among the leaders of the best-seller categories. It frustrated him to see black writers limited to the rather rarefied liberal journals and magazines, and not really the cream of them, their publications staggered in those, and grudgingly allotted opportunities from the mainstream commercial press. Yerby had eked out the same occasional honors as all his peers—Chester Himes, Ann Petry, Ralph Ellison, and Willard Motley—working on the WPA and publishing in low-circulation magazines and race journals. However, he had more literary training than any of them, an M.A. degree in English from Fisk and a year of course work toward a Ph.D. degree at the University of Chicago. But after teaching a year at Florida A&M and a year at Southern University, taking a job at a defense plant in Detroit because it paid better, and then living through the viciously racist Detroit riot of 1943, where white policemen refused to save blacks from being killed by mobs, the bad taste of misery began to offend Yerby. He held two points of view: the first, "to follow the route I had mapped out for myself[,] was roughly analogous to shouting one's head off in Mammoth Cave"; and the second, "nobody ever went broke underestimating the taste of the American public."[39]

He had the misfortune to produce a sentient protagonist in the wake of *Native Son*, when publishers had tangible proof that the black bad man could, at least partly, sell. Additionally, the dilemma of racial antagonism as a theme of interest to the commercial press dried up considerably after 1945. Publishers wanted to acquire trendy new books, but no publisher wanted the label of house to activist Negro writers, whether the protest was made by Bigger Thomas or Ralph Bunche. At Doubleday, the largest commercial house, editor-in-chief Ken McCormick could understate this broad response from American institutions by writing to a book dealer near the end of the decade, "[T]he fact that at last someone has written a novel about the Negro Problem which doesn't have a lynching nor develop romances under the magnolia blossoms is very refreshing."[40] Critics from the "mainstream"—the large northern universities and the elite colleges and the southern New Critics—had not been overly swift to chart the rise of black literature, but they were swift to tire of it once it reached the scene. By 1947 Columbia professor and Joyce scholar William Tindall identified certain writers—including Lillian Smith and Richard Wright—who had produced "the sociological best seller." Pointing to the beginning of the tradition with Stowe's *Uncle Tom's Cabin*, Tindall thought merrily, "it seems that if an author wants his novel to sell better than the better sellers, he has only to choose for his subject either the evils of drink or the prejudice against Jews, Negroes, or, sometimes, Chinese."[41] Tindall's colleague at Columbia, professor and short story writer Robert Gorham Davis, candidly noted the movement of his colleagues away from an appreciation of the naturalist style and the political assumptions that undergirded it. In the climate following the war, Davis found that "[l]iberalism, progressivism and naturalism are not only dismissed as false and superficial, but they are said to make impossible literary understanding."[42]

Yerby's solution to the dimming opportunity was to work through the tradition that was thematically close to his heart and empirically guaranteed to appeal to the American public: the southern plantation romance, taken to its popular melodramatic height by Margaret Mitchell's 1939 blockbuster *Gone With the Wind*, and to its tragic modernist peak by William Faulkner in *Absalom, Absalom*.

The Foxes of Harrow appeared February 5, 1946, during what might be called the "interbellum," the brief lull between the wars against fascism and the often hot war against communism. Dial Press expressed supreme confidence that the book would sell well and, including the advance orders from book clubs, had six hundred thousand copies of the book on hand. By February 23, 1946, Yerby's book had raised the possibility of becoming a best seller, and by the end of March the book entered the national list of best sellers.[43] It would remain on the list for the rest of the year, and Frank Garvin Yerby of Augusta, Georgia, became the best-selling Negro writer of all time up to that point. When the year's tabulations were all in, Yerby had sold a startling 1.2 million books nationwide, and nearly two hundred thousand of them at bookstores.[44] He claimed second place that year in overall book sales in the United States and made a prophet out of Sterling Brown, who believed that a white cast was the key to success.

Yerby wrote what he called "costume" novels, and he adopted a kind of sexy, Horatio Alger–style of formula with a code hero who goes from rags to riches, luxuriates in an opulent mansion, comports himself in accord with the chivalric code, and experiences idyllic romance. In the process Yerby disabled a ring of the firewalls that had been accepted in the mystical elements of southern lore and identity, and sustained even by writers like Lillian Smith. By the Second World War, roughly one in three Americans could be identified by the U.S. Census as having "foreign stock"; in other words, either they or their parents had been born abroad.[45] Not only did new Americans have little stake in the antebellum cultural myth, but all U.S. citizens were growing increasingly remote from the nineteenth century as a period of historical time. At the same time, the influence of the William A. Dunning School of Reconstruction era U.S. history began to waver. It was no longer axiomatic, after Du Bois's 1935 *Black Reconstruction in America* and the up-and-coming C. Vann Woodward, that southern history between 1865 and 1877 was filled with overreaching freed slaves, carpetbag-carrying northern confidence men, and scalawag white natives who had betrayed the Lost Cause.

Obliquely yes, but clearly enough, Yerby brought the popular public up-to-date with the new work from the 1930s: the Marxist interpretation of slavery, Du Bois's new view of the Reconstruction, Herbert Aptheker's work on slave revolts, and Melville Herskovits's emphasis on African retentions in American Negro culture. Almost an allegory for the choices available to contemporary Americans regarding their identity as the country tried on its new shoes as world superpower, *Foxes of Harrow* introduced to the popular imagination multiple competing notions regarding American race relations in the South during the antebellum era. The hero is fearless riverboat gambler Stephen Fox, an Irish immigrant, who works his way into the French Creole society of New Orleans, an ancien régime on the verge of ceding its power to the boisterous Anglo-Saxon pioneers pushing into the Mississippi region to develop cotton and sugar empires. Yerby sculpts Stephen Fox into the embodiment of the chivalric white American myth, an iconoclastic lover of hard work, liberty, reason, and democratic principle.

Fox, a regular opponent to the martial romantics who advocate southern secession, reaches his climactic moment in the narrative by delivering an extended peroration defining the import of freedom and the working class.

> "I don't believe any longer in aristocracy. . . . Ye can't have a land like America unless the people—all the people—have a hand in its shaping. And the South has never dealt fairly with its people. Why we've treated the Negroes better than our own. What of your landless white? Your mountaineers—your swampfolk. Must they go on eating the clay of the earth to keep from starving?"[46]

Instead of taking on the problem of race frontally, Yerby effectively reached his audience's self-interest, their position in the social-class hierarchy, after massaging their fable of the white-columned southern past. For an American audience, Yerby's rhetoric made an effective appeal that did not rely upon an exuberantly liberal intellect or a commitment to Marxism.

He treated the problem of race with unusual tenacity, but only as secondary subplot, perhaps a division of thematic emphasis that Yerby believed more closely reflected the reality of American life. The hero Stephen Fox marries his dream woman the same day that his loyal black foreman Achille weds an African princess, a woman who gloriously refuses her fetters. Sons are the result of both unions: white Etienne, a spoiled and cruel man, and Inch, a remarkable African American who gains literacy, studies law in France, escapes slavery, and meets Frederick Douglass. Although Inch, in a dramatization of the Dred Scott case, is returned to his master Etienne, at the conclusion of the novel Inch has risen to a fitting office in Reconstruction era New Orleans and is a much better example of rational discourse, the book's model for enlightenment and success, than Etienne, the biological heir to the plantation.

Yerby's protagonist Stephen Fox is a Daniel Webster–style orator who regularly argues against the sanctity of slavery. He patriotically stresses the importance of the United States as an Eden regardless of race or previous condition. "Never upon earth has the poor man, the commoner, had such freedom; never has there been so much respect for the essential dignity of mankind."[47] When asked by his second wife, Aurore, if "[e]ven the Negroes?" will share in such a bounty, Yerby's Fox is unequivocal. "Even the blacks. We shall find men with minds like Inch's among them, and in the end they will take their part in the nation." Keeping the talented blacks at arm's length can only adversely affect the noble experiment of American democracy. "If there is any one thing upon the face of the earth that is unconquerable 'tis human freedom. And if they try to take it away again from the blacks they will end by losing it themselves."[48] Yerby's apparently innocuous historical romance had the capacity to touch an audience that a "professionally liberal" book might never have reached. Yerby used the pulp narrative to present without special pleading the commonsense arguments in favor of ending racial segregation. When his book came out, several of Yerby's peers, Nick Aaron Ford especially, noted this fact.

Yerby quit the cause of socially valuable black literature just as numbers of African American social realist poured out into the field and reaped scorn. After *Native Son*, critic J. Saunders Redding had suspected that "mediocrities" might flood the literary marketplace, but this, insofar as black writers were concerned, was merely hyperbole. Despite the letters that he regularly received at the *Afro-American* fearfully lining out the racist conspiracy, there were not enough would-be black novelists for the New York publishers to flood the public with. Secondly, the standards and acquisition processes of the presses would finely limit the appearance of such works. A small-time writer like L.A.H. Caldwell was able to get his gritty story *The Policy King* between covers in 1946, but it was with New Vistas, a Chicago vanity outfit. Caldwell's tale hooked its audience by purporting to show the inside of the "rackets," and the disintegration of the black family as a result of them. It also showed the psychology of the black street, which had begun to assimilate antidiscrimination rhetoric. When a racketeer is indicted because of his sister's testimony, the hustler calls his sister a "victim of white psychology." "How much longer will the Negro suffer like this before he cracks?," he accuses her.[49]

George Wylie Henderson tried to follow up his 1935 underground favorite *Ollie Miss* with a sequel called *Jule*. Henderson disliked the black exodus to the urban North and now showily promoted a Booker T. Washington philosophy. An unskilled laborer and son of the protagonist of *Ollie Miss*, Jule migrates from the South to Harlem, leaving his fiancé. But in the North, Jule struggles to find honest work, and his college-educated northern girlfriend Lou is little better than a whore. She concludes the book in the clutches of Dr. Jackson, who lives to exploit his race, while Jule, with an eighth-grade education and an astounding ability to "figure" without formal training, becomes a printer's apprentice and marries his southern sweetheart. It was a triumph for nineteenth-century accommodationism: humility, powerful white friends, and suspicion of higher education.

The best regarded of the lot came from Curtis Lucas, a bit of civil rights crusader himself, whose second novel *Third Ward Newark* was brought out by Ziff Davis and made a selection of the month by the Negro Book Club in January 1947. He had begun his better than ten-year career with the rags-to-riches murder mystery *Flour Is Dusty* in 1943. Lucas was as indebted to mysteries and "who-done-its" as he was to promoting the cause of racial justice. *Third Ward* looked frankly at black poverty and the prostitution poverty engendered, enfolded within the plot of a mystery. Lucas seemed out to tell the story that Ann Petry had rejected. The book presented the lives of the cousins Hattie and Wonnie Brown and showed how easily young black women slipped into prostitution. In a climactic episode, two white johns murder Wonnie's friend Mildred. Wonnie Brown is sealed in a world of despair. "What could she do? They were white, all of them. Mildred was dead, and they would do nothing. Nothing!"[50] And when not individual malevolent whites, the environment was to blame.

> It was the Third Ward, where they lived. Where they ate. And slept. Laughed and cried. It was the broken-down houses, where they had to live; the white men's stores, where they were overcharged. It was colored girls, scrubbing white folks bathrooms and selling their bodies, while the white girls worked in the department stores and doctors' offices. It was the colored men, robbing, stealing, pimping, gambling, working at jobs that white men didn't want. It was hell![51]

The book concludes with Wonnie's death and her reformed cousin moving out West. Lucas was barely a novice at the craft but he had a story to tell. J. Saunders Redding liked the opening portions of Lucas's tale, but then the narrative got "all loused up with a sermon he doesn't quite know how to preach."[52] The irony behind Redding's remark, of course, was that by 1947 no one would know how to preach the sermon of black degradation on account of the environment.

All the same, Redding felt like he could afford to be callous to the least polished of the new writers because so many reputable blacks were at work on groundbreaking projects. The published fiction and its theme of protesting against racial discrimination contributed to the climate that enabled black writers to spend several weeks in overlapping residence at the artist's colony at Yaddo in Saratoga Springs, New York. The creative retreat had been set up by financier Spencer Trask and his wife Katrina. Executive Director Elizabeth

Ames had started bringing artists, composers, and writers to Trask Mansion and the surrounding cottages sitting on four hundred acres in 1926. The cohort that went that summer of 1947 were not the first blacks—that honor belonged to Langston Hughes, who went in 1942. The original Yaddo charter carried nothing about racial discrimination, and when the flood of European refugees, especially Jews, began to appear at Yaddo, Elizabeth Ames was able to overcome the prejudices of "one or two elderly directors who were awfully afraid about blood mixing."[53] Ames, a committed liberal, believed that Negroes "should have come before," and that 1947 was a catch-up year, during which "one or two weird things" took place, she wrote to admissions committee member Malcolm Cowley.[54] Horace R. Cayton, when he was not feuding in bars and spouting Kierkegaard, devoted himself to multiple projects, including a novel and a work of literary criticism. Arna Bontemps worked on a book along with another intelligent W. H. Auden–trained poet writing his first novel, Owen Dodson. They were also joined that summer by Bucklin Moon. Clearly, black writers and their fellow traveler Moon seemed to be in for their share of recognition.

The members of the Yaddo admissions committee—Cowley, Newton Arvin, and Granville Hicks—all imagined themselves advancing the cause of amicable race relations by bringing in blacks and black projects. They noticed other important writers, such as Ralph Ellison, whose publisher Frank Taylor at Random House had heard of the goings on. Ellison wrote to Elizabeth Ames in late spring, trying to flatter himself into the retreat by the end of the summer. After Granville Hicks visited Hampton in the winter of 1948, the next fall the doors serendipitously opened for J. Saunders Redding. The committee recalled the significance of No Day of Triumph. Hicks vouched for Redding, even though he had not read any of the forty-two-year-old professor's work, by saying that the man was "likable"—the central thrust of the evaluation.[55] For his part, Redding worked hard trying to lift up the race high at Yaddo, with its added uncomfortable "strain of living in a more or less unnatural family-like situation."[56] Nonetheless, Elizabeth Ames invited him even to extend his stay there in the late fall of 1948, and Redding found himself chummy with southern writers like Ed McGehee and Kentuckian Elizabeth Hardwick.

Redding would have admired several things about Hardwick, a critic and novelist of The Ghostly Lover, a nimble portrait of white and black life that shucked sentimentality and minstrelsy equally well. Her book included two well-crafted scenes of recognition between white and black characters that stressed black abject poverty but allowed blacks and whites equal portions of human vulnerability and dignity. Hardwick had produced a memorable black domestic, the opposite of Trilling's "other Margaret," named Hattie Sipe, who possesses "alert, trigger-set, dry and scorched eyes," mimics the family she serves, and sizes up the people of the world "perpetually in a state of indecent exposure."[57] And, perhaps what best signaled Hardwick's decorous intelligence, on the printed page black and white southerners spoke the same language, the same dialect.

Redding got along easily with Hardwick and departed before the firestorm of accusation and recrimination in February 1949, when General MacArthur denounced Yaddo secretary Agnes Smedley as a Soviet spy to the press. Robert Lowell and Hardwick, who had remained at Yaddo as winter guests, then organized an ad hoc trial and accused fellowship director Elizabeth Ames of being a Communist and potential spy. Led by the high-strung Lowell, the rump group contacted the FBI, who had already been receiving information regarding the "disloyal remarks" of Yaddo guests from secretary Mary Townsend, and they demanded the board of directors fire Ames and replace her with Lowell.[58] It took several months and the work of a committee that included writers John Cheever, Eleanor Clark, and Alfred Kazin before the dust settled, leaving Ames in place and Lowell in the sanitorium. Notable about the liberal open door at Yaddo (especially for Cayton, who went for two successive years and was even married there on his second visit) was the meager result. Some of the invitees, like Bontemps and Cayton, would not complete any work at all; others, like Dodson, Redding, and Chester Himes, would not produce work of lasting distinction. What is more, following Lowell's legendary accusations about Communist infiltration at Yaddo, few blacks outspoken on racial issues were invited as guests. The public climate was shifting against radicalism.

The most robust publishing industry in history helped create the opportunities for the Yaddo cohort, but mainly it contracted new legions of white writers anxious to record the liberal conscience Americans were adapting toward racial issues. The liberal whites wrote as optimistically as the black writers had written pessimistically. Millen Brand published *Albert Sears*, a novel of a white man who helps a black family move into a white neighborhood. Worth Tuttle Hedden wrote an interracial love story, *The Other Room*, the tale of a young Virginia blueblood who falls for a black professor while teaching at a black college in the South. Florence Carnell Means suggested that Communists were destroying a black teacher's best efforts in South Carolina in *Great Day in the Morning*. (George Schuyler assisted the effort by getting out a sixteen-page pamphlet called *The Communist Conspiracy Against the Negro* in the same year.) Cid Ricketts Sumner's novel *Quality* appeared in September 1946 and would be successful in selling the story to Hollywood and having the novel made into a film called *Pinky*, directed by Darryl Zanuck.

The heavily marketed stories were not deep, and they never implied anything like protracted cruelty lurking behind the system of American race relations. They were moral passion plays with heroes and villains, atonement and redemption. And perhaps because the books were so shallow and offered such easy solutions, the intelligent reading public, who had had only minor contact with any literature written by black writers, began to tire of them. Helen Parker, reviewing *Albert Sears* in the *Times*, anticipated the mounting fatigue: "The issue of racial discrimination should logically have been atomized by now, what with the sheer weight of literary tracts against it."[59]

Parker was exaggerating, but the contrast between America of the 1920s and the late 1940s, in terms of the literary politics toward black American life, was as startlingly sheer as atomic warfare. Two of the best-selling books of the first half of 1947 gave the average American reader of the best-seller list the idea that the race problem was well on its way to resolution, if resolution could be achieved by having everybody talking about it. Sinclair Lewis neared the million mark by publishing *Kingsblood Royal*, a novel depicting a comfortable young banker who discovers that his mother has a black ancestor. One of America's most famous interrogators of the middle class, Lewis would try to direct race relations with his final work. Written in a blast of high liberal fury in 1946 and shaped by Saxe Commins, the Random House editor who had just dislodged Ralph Ellison from a contract at Reynal and Hitchcock, *Kingsblood* attempted to pose a universal dilemma that virtually any white American might face. What was the moral thing to do if they found out that they were technically black?

Some 790,000 copies had been printed for the release of the book on May 23, 1947.[60] Random House printed another 125,000 to keep up with bookstore demand by that July. The publishers delighted in Lewis's Mennipean satire about race: "The Literary Guild tells us this is its most successful book and has won a greater percentage of acceptance from members in the South than in the North." The irony about the country's traditional regional divide was lost on *Publisher's Weekly*: Lewis's book was set in Minnesota and designed precisely to ridicule northerners' false moral uprightness regarding racial discrimination.

J. Saunders Redding gave the aged man great credit for making Americans a bit uncomfortable and adding racism to the pantheon of Lewis's famed attacks against foundations, the middle class, and the priesthood. For Redding, *Kingsblood* was a courageous and moving indictment of American racism, "the most complex theme of modern times."[61] But Redding's approach to black life put him on the same side as Diana Trilling, who had thought Ann Petry chiefly important for presenting the reality of black life. In a sharply uncritical manner, Redding maintained the standard that merely the race of the black novelist was a satisfactory measure of truth and that white writers like Lewis "know next to nothing about colored people."

The most affirmative point of view held by an African American critic came from Horace Cayton, who felt indebted to Lewis. Toward the end of the book, when Neil Kingsblood is clumsily learning about his African American neighbors, Lewis had written that the sale of books "by Myrdal and Cayton and Du Bois" was a solid step forward in civil rights activity.[62] When he journeyed to upstate New York in the summer of 1947, Cayton happily accepted Lewis's invitation to his Thorvale Farm estate, where a black trio of cook, butler, and handyman took care of him. During the time he spent with Lewis, Cayton sought a reaction to his essay on the fear-hate-fear complex. The windy essay suffered from a flat tone, long quotes from Wright, Himes, and the case studies of Cayton's psychiatrist Helen McLean, and offered little new to the understanding of the dynamics of American life that had not been said with more pith and searching inquiry by Ralph Ellison's 1945 article "Beating That Boy" in *New Republic*. Lewis told Cayton only, "I guess there's a lot in what you say." Cayton thought to himself that his essay "deserved more consideration than he was giving it."[63]

If Lewis managed to leave him unfulfilled, Cayton too had little to say when Lewis had an unusual request. Cayton spent several days at the farm, some of them quite tense, culminating the week after July 4 when, following a profoundly awkward picnic with his servants, Lewis confessed to Cayton, "But you see why I need a Negro mammy, don't you."[64] For Cayton, this was profound confirmation of the racialized psychic energy dwelling in the crevices of the American liberal unconscious. Convinced that literature was one vehicle that might capture the bevy of unconscious American psychological processes, Cayton told friends that he was hard at work on a novel called "From Which No Traveler Returns."

The combined popular success of books like Smith's *Strange Fruit* and Lewis's *Kingsblood Royal* indicated a discernible preference in average American readers: they were capable of dealing with the problem of racial discrimination and environmental degradation best when the protagonist and author were white. The African American writer Willard Motley gained the most from this perception. Motley's race was kept from his audience (his photograph was not included on the dust jacket), but it was well-known to his publisher. He had the same excellent credentials as any of the Chicago writers. Born in 1909 in Chicago and from an artistic family that included his uncle the painter Archibald Motley (whom he referred to as his brother to hide the fact of his unmarried mother's teenage pregnancy), Willard Motley strove to combine artistic elegance with hard-hitting social realism. Precocious, he started his writing career in 1922 with a column for the *Chicago Defender* under the alias Bud Billiken, the name of a popular parade on the South Side. A slight man, Motley had proved himself as a citywide football player, but he always struck people as modest, a little diffident, and kind. The future critic Fanny Butcher once described him for the *Chicago Tribune* as "sensitive-faced," but Motley was also intrepid.[65] After Motley graduated from Englewood High School, he rode his bicycle to New York to join his uncle Archibald on the older relative's trip to Paris.[66] His grandmother convinced him that he could gain more by staying at home. Motley then hoboed the country, looking for experience to turn into fiction. He believed he should make his name the same way that Mark Twain and Ernest Hemingway had, by living and writing.

In 1940 he gained a position on one of the surviving WPA projects. He made the interracial relationships with writers on the Illinois Federal Writers Project pay off, and probably his contact with Jack Conroy, whose friendship he kept through the 1950s, and Nelson Algren shaped his literary style more than anything else. Perhaps part of his success was his committed bohemianism. Motley successfully led the life of an artist in integrated artistic circles, while not necessarily having to submit to the discipline of the Communist Party. Motley was quite serious about demolishing artificial class barriers. He met with other artists and writers at Hull House, Jane Addams's radical settlement home for the poor on Chicago's near West Side, and he helped to found the *Hull-House Magazine*, which ran issues in 1939 and 1940. A man more interested in the buffeting that human beings experienced at the hands of the environment than was Richard Wright, who was always captivated by the mental adjustments people made to their condition, Motley picked up the challenge of writing about the urban slum.

In 1941 he chucked what little desire he had for respectability and moved into a converted sweatshop on Halstead Street near Maxwell, Chicago's downtown crossroads of poverty and crime. He walked West Madison Street, the epicenter of raucous vice, and filled up his notebooks with observations while taking six hundred photographs. The Rockefeller Foundation, out of the Newberry Library, granted him a fellowship in 1944 to write a novel. (The next year Era Bell Thompson won the prize to publish *American Daughter*.) In 1946 he won a Julius Rosenwald Fellowship. By that time Motley had over 2,100 manuscript pages. After six years of work, cutting the manuscript in half and leaving Macmillan in favor of Appleton Century, he published the novel in 1947.

Motley's *Knock on Any Door* was a 240,000-word tour de force describing life in Chicago's famed Near West red-light district, specifically West Madison Street. Motley created for a protagonist an Italian American named Nick Romano whose family has been reduced to poverty by the Great Depression. Nick leaves the wholesome environment of lower-middle-class Denver for reform school, Chicago, and, finally, the electric chair. Instead of exploring the inner lives of blacks, Motley exposed his audience to the world of juvenile gangsters and of the "phoneys"—cruising gay men—and traced Nick Romano's attitude of rage and resignation to sexual ambivalence. Heavily interested in the influence of environment on wounding the human personality, the book did not champion the cause of African Americans. And for the first weeks of its reviews and publicity, no one knew that Motley was black.

At the end of Ann Petry's *The Street*, Lutie Johnson rationalizes that, after she has murdered a man, her son is better off as an eight year-old in reform school. "That way he may have some kind of chance," she imagines as she climbs aboard a train for Chicago.[67] By the second chapter of *Knock on Any Door*, Nick Romano is on a clear trajectory away from the church altar and to the reform school doorstep. The fundamental premise throughout the huge novel is that reform school is a one-way ticket to the dregs of American society and sociopathology. And while he exposed the short-sightedness of liberalism, Motley did so to generate interest in its revitalization. He structured his narrative as a crime-to-courtroom potboiler like *Native Son*, but all the techniques of modernist experimental realism came readily to him—the splintered consciousness, the interest with forms of human sexuality and the readiness to describe it, the notions of a subconscious operating and dividing the human being's ability for knowledge and control.

Unlike Petry, who maintained her protagonists' strict moral code to the verge of improbability, Motley proposed nothing like purity for his protagonist Nick Romano. His foil, which freed him from the scorn of the NAACPs of the world, lay in the fact that all his major characters, with one single exception, were white. This had become something of a Chicago conceit by that point, done first by Arna Bontemps, then William Attaway, then Frank Yerby, and then in 1947 by Motley. But for the man whose books would best embody the concerns of African American naturalists, there was something quite obvious that happened with a white cast. Both Richard Wright and Ann Petry had had their protagonists carry out heavily symbolic acts of lethal violence against blacks who had to stand in for the white world that simply could not be effectively reached. Though equally doomed, Motley's Nick Romano achieves a moment of catharsis by destroying his enemy, the police officer Riley, who has symbolically stolen Nick's vitality.

Despite the decision to make the book's protagonist white, Motley carried out elements of the racial politics discussed in the South Side Writers' Club meetings. Nick Romano's associations and his decision to remain a criminal are, like Huck Finn's, partially based on his discomfort with racial hypocrisy. His earliest dream is to be a priest who will "convert the little Jewish boys and the little colored boys. Then some day he might be a saint."[68] But at reform school, the dream becomes less lofty, specifically because of the reality of choosing democratic associations. "[O]n the long bench against the wall he saw a colored kid—a new kid. . . . He watched Nick for a long moment. Then he twisted his lips in the faint beginning of a smile. Nick grinned at him . . . ."[69] The vision of interracial fraternity is short-lived. Minutes later the bully "Bricktop" begins to enforce compliance to reactionary American attitudes.

> "They brought a nigger in today . . . We don't talk to no niggers in here . . . You ain't going to talk to no niggers, are you?" Bricktop told Nick, loudly bossing him. Nick hung his head and said, softly, hoping the colored kid, who was all of a sudden different and a nigger, wouldn't hear, "No, I won't."

Nick's fateful turn toward a life against social norms begins when he admires the defiance of Tommy, a small boy who faces the punishing bully Bricktop for his right to have black friends. The reform school episode culminates with an epic battle between Nick and Bricktop, which Nick wins, and which impels him completely into a world of violence and rebellion. Nick continues to associate with blacks, regular evidence of his moral depravity.

Motley had several black tough guys wander in and out of Nick's gang life, and association with blacks in defiance of the racial taboos was one of Romano's, like Huck Finn's, principal sympathetic traits. On the surface, Motley's descriptions of black characters seemed indifferent, nearly racist. He named his central black character Sunshine and described him in keeping with the heavy racial stereotypes popular throughout the United States during the 1940s.

> His brown, almost black face was shiny, greasy-looking on his forehead, on his cheekbones and across his flat nose. His kinky hair stood up all over his head and was in a tall cockscomb just at the front. His lips were pushed out in a sad pout. . . . Only the eyes were alive in the sad brown-black face. They came around sideways, showing white. All the rest of him was in a dead, lazy droop. Sunshine got up slowly, slowly shuffled over to Nick.[70]

But in spite of the opening description that exhausts the comic Step-n-Fetchit and Buckwheat image, the relationship between Nick and Sunshine is one of shared generosity and is the one relationship initiated by Nick where he acts as a mature citizen capable of rational thought and sympathy. In return, Sunshine loyally attempts to defend Nick during the trial for the murder of police officer Riley. During his testimony, Sunshine reveals the political education he has received from Nick Romano. His own disputes with the police have become explicable: "'ah guess they didn't like my color—Nick said so anyway.'"[71] Motley took care to show his readers precisely how they should react to this information, and how their assumption should be revised. "That got to the jury. Their eyes all came over and rested on Sunshine's face sympathetically." Sunshine's testimony nearly succeeds in winning Nick an acquittal, until the black youth is exposed as a perjurer by the prejudiced district attorney Furman.

If he only edged around the racial issue, Motley gave the heart of the book to the thesis of environmental determinism. Nick's young wife Emma, the novel's martyr, speaks the creed that appears during the novel's climax. "It isn't your fault Nicky! . . . It's what reform school did to you, the way you grew up."[72] Grant, a liberal reformer and writer, tells the jury, "I have seen a boy who lived in squalor and misery sent to reform school for a crime he didn't commit . . . a boy who is—I believe—the victim of his environment."[73] Defense attorney Morton's closing statement echoes completely the voice of the book's other sympathetic white characters, but the mea culpa is more dramatic: "Nick Romano was murdered seven years ago! I so charge! I accuse—Society!—of the murder of Nick Romano!"[74]

Motley's white characters are advocates of job creation and employment training, better schools, slum eradication, police review boards, social security, recreation clubs, and social hygiene, topped by weighty draughts of racial and sexual tolerance. Richard Wright had written of Communists and liberals as inept or indifferent to the crisis in the ghetto, and for Ann Petry slums thrived because reformists, far left or just liberal, black or white, did not exist. Motley's white fiction world contained a constituency of advocates for widespread social reform, and one that required little assistance from left-wing radicals.

Motley's publisher Appleton-Century had fifty thousand copies printed when *Knock on Any Door* debuted on May 5, 1947, and the book sold briskly, averaging about two thousand copies per week by the end of that spring.[75] *Knock on any Door* never made its way into the top five of the weekly best-seller category, and finally sold about 350,000 copies. Motley's optimistic view of the possibility for enduring urban reform popped out when he rationalized his choice to hide his race from the public. He claimed in a letter to Horace Cayton that he had guarded his racial identity from the early publicity information because he hoped to see "the book go on its own legs."[76] Extraordinarily, Motley suggested that "if it was known that I was colored some people would have bought the book and praised it because I am a Negro." The note to Cayton seems false. Few publishers seek to turn down praise for a book or limit the size of its reading public. And of course, nearly the opposite was true: there was as good a chance that if Motley's racial identify had been known, he might have alienated his audience and signaled to his reviewers that he supported a clandestine radical agenda that might have some kind of indirect benefit for African Americans. Motley's willingness to take seriously the preference of his audience for white characters and without anything smacking of leftist ideology to reform American postwar cities shows that he was ahead of the curve to internalize the tenets of the new liberalism at the end of the 1940s. In the second half of the 1940s and into the 1950s, several prominent black writers would write books with white casts, but in them, most writers confined themselves to tidy moral and ethical problems. The books were content to ignore "the problem" of poverty and racial injustice in the United States. The writers' disavowal was crucial because as blacks flooded northern cities for the industrial jobs available during the war, the problems of the inner-city slum and the African American would become one.

A contest took place over Motley's status, which the black reviewers were not quite sure how to handle. Because of his extraordinary devotion to environmental determinism, Horace Cayton wrote that only Motley, not withstanding Theodore Dreiser, "has presented the wealth of material and the richness of data in such an abundance to describe the social fabric of an area and a people."[77] Alain Locke said that the book was a "net gain" that broadened "the Zolaesque indictment to a common denominator of class and environment rather than mere race and environment."[78] Thomas Jarrett of Atlanta University thought Motley technically excellent: "one of the reasons for its greatness is that it exhibits, among other qualities, a superb employment of imagery."[79]

Apparently, without race to bog him down, the reviewers took on his argument. With Richard Wright, Chester Himes, and Ann Petry, the discussion often had centered on the degree of accuracy with which they reproduced black life and attitudes. "No abler recruit has joined the extreme naturalist school of fiction in a long time than Mr. Motley," wrote Orville Prescott in the *New York Times*.[80] Even when Charles Lee said that Motley wrote like a "whole glee club of sobbing sisters," he at least compared Motley to Dreiser and not Richard Wright.[81] Motley had worked hard on his book and the polish showed, but it was difficult not to notice the putative relationship between abandoning the cause of justice for the black poor and attaining literary success. *Knock on Any Door* seemed to prove the principle that blacks could be accepted on the same terms as whites, if they abandoned racial themes.

BY THE AUTHOR OF "NATIVE SON"

BLACK BOY

RICHARD WRIGHT

This true story of life in America will open the
eyes of many readers to things they never knew
before about our country and its people. It is the
story Richard Wright knows best, for it is his own.

"Beautifully written," says Bennett Cerf, "with the
impact of a battleship."

With an Introductory Note by
DOROTHY CANFIELD FISHER

HARPER & BROTHERS · ESTABLISHED 1817

9.1. *Black Boy* by Richard Wright, 1945 edition, cover   Copyright 1937, 1942, 1944 by Richard Wright; renewed © 1973 by Ellen Wright. Reprinted by permission of HarperCollins Publishers.

9.2. *Black Boy* by Richard Wright, advertisement, *Publisher's Weekly*, October 13, 1945

9.3. Gwendolyn Brooks, ca. 1945   Library of Congress

9.4. *A Street in Bronzeville* by Gwendolyn Brooks, 1945 edition, cover   Copyright 1944, 1945 by Gwendolyn Brooks Blakely. Reprinted by permission of HarperCollins Publishers.

9.5. Sterling Brown, Bucklin Moon, Owen Dodson, Chester Himes, and John Bright, 1945   Courtesy Lesley Himes

9.6. Ann Petry, 1948   Photograph by Carl Van Vechten, James Weldon Johnson Collection in the Yale Collection of American Literature, Beinecke Rare Book and Manuscript Library, Yale University

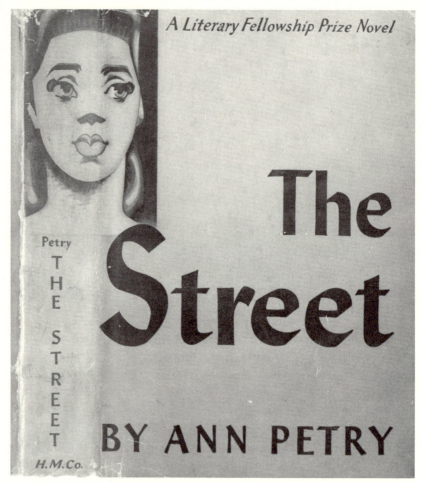

9.7. *The Street* by Ann Petry, 1946, dust jacket   From *The Street* by Ann Petry Copyright © 1946, and renewed 1974 by Ann Petry. Reprinted by permission of Houghton Mifflin Harcourt Publishing Company. All rights reserved.

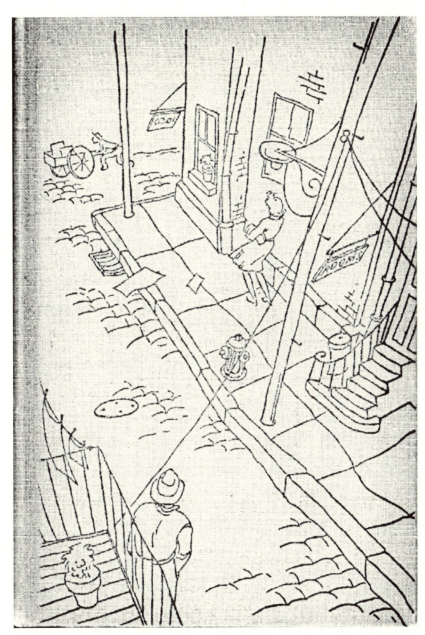

9.8. *The Street* by Ann Petry, 1946, cover illustration   From *The Street* by Ann Petry
Copyright © 1946, and renewed 1974 by Ann Petry. Reprinted by permission of Houghton Mifflin
Harcourt Publishing Company. All rights reserved.

9.9. Horace Cayton, 1947 Photograph by Carl Van Vechten, James Weldon Johnson Collection in the Yale Collection of American Literature, Beinecke Rare Book and Manuscript Library, Yale University

9.10. Willard Motley, 1947   Photograph by Carl Van Vechten, James Weldon Johnson Collection in the Yale Collection of American Literature, Beinecke Rare Book and Manuscript Library, Yale University

CHAPTER TEN

The Peril of Something New, or, the Decline of Social Realism (1947–1948)

In January 1947 Thomas Sancton carried out his final gesture of overt liberal race relations patronage. Sancton guest edited the journal *Survey Graphic*, the same journal that under the guidance of Alain Locke in 1924 had culled the Harlem Renaissance into being. The ranking force among southern radical liberals, Sancton called his special issue *Segregation: The Pattern of a Failure*. To drive home his point he collected the nation's heavy hitters, the sociologists, philanthropists, policy fund managers, and experts: Louis Wirth, E. Franklin Frazier, Will Alexander, Robert Weaver, Ira Reid, and even Alain Locke. But none of them broke new ground, and Sancton was probably aware of the fact. Bucklin Moon published a single journalist-style book that year called *The High Cost of Prejudice* that was more coherent and rhetorically effective than the one Sancton's interracial band of brothers proposed. To make his special issue memorably radical, Sancton needed to recognize not only the politics and sociology of race relations, but what Horace Cayton had already identified as the "sentiments sanctioning the processes." If Americans were unwilling to reveal honest sentiment or human feeling, how could their traditional biases be uncovered and effectively addressed?

By 1947 the country had reached the apex of its casual awareness of minority group rights, and it turned to the didactic and pithy solutions of popular culture to fix old problems. Americans looked to the work of Ann Petry, Chester Himes, and Gwendolyn Brooks, and papers that had never had much use for black writers before, like the *Washington Post*, announced "Another Renaissance Noted in Negro Arts."[1] The year before, Harry Overstreet, the famed adult educator and social psychologist, had reached a broad American audience in *Saturday Review of Literature* by giving a multi-point directive to black writers necessary to solve the "Negro problem."[2] Black writers had a duty to produce likeable heroes who might mend bridges to white America. In a nutshell, "The Negro Writer as Spokesperson," urged black writers to chuck bitterness, environmental horror, and ambiguity, and write optimistic books like the ones that white writers were turning out about the race issue.

Thomas Sancton was skeptical of simplification like this, but he was also becoming starkly aware of the government drive toward open hostility with the

Soviet Union and the obvious decline in value attributed to efforts that drama-tized stark racial tension in domestic American life. He also recognized that he was on the margin. People like Alfred Kazin remembered him during the war at the *New Republic* offices "weeping over attacks on Negro soldiers."[3] His sen-sitivity toward racial issues was being recognized now as a mark of intellectual sloppiness, an inability to face facts and advance the foremost liberal American agenda. Slowly enough, Sancton caught on. In two years, he would go on to cover the U.S. Congress for *Nation*, and he had wearied of black writers claim-ing the race problem unsolvable and too difficult to secure concrete solution. He returned to the Deep South and left off his racial crusading. He finished his custodianship in the tournament of black rights and arts in 1949 with two es-says in *Common Ground*: "Southern Train," which showed blacks on board a train in the South asserting themselves with a new confidence after fifty years of segregation, and "They Belonged," a description of the tempered pain of the black upper middle class integrating the Ivies.[4] After a ten-year run, *Common Ground* was shutting its doors. The work of overtly refashioning racial under-standing seemed to have run its course.

In the months following Churchill's appeal to Missourians that they must resist a Soviet-built "Iron Curtain" in Europe, Sancton's dull, manual-like ap-proach to curing American race relations lacked vision and vitality. When he was cobbling the *Survey Graphic* issue together in the late summer of 1946, Sancton wanted to bring aboard one of the important younger black writers. But the celebrity Richard Wright traveled to Paris that year as a guest of the French government. The reviews of Ralph Ellison now appeared in *New Repub-lic*; he was being considered for a job there. But after four long months working on an article, Ellison felt betrayed by Sancton and insulted by the journalist's attempts to put words in his mouth.[5]

Sancton should have turned from a writer in his thirties to one in his twen-ties. If *New Republic* lost its best black reviewer over the episode, another young black man, really a much younger man, barely old enough to have served in the military during the war, began publishing his reviews. The reviews, which started to appear that April, caused a sensation. The writer's name was James Baldwin. The eighteen months from 1947 through the end of 1948 would announce an almost completely new spirit of thought about what the liberal approach to black American life should be.

The publishing career of critic James Baldwin, the most consistent antinatu-ralist and antisocial protest critic of the 1940s and 1950s, began in the spring of 1947 and soared like a meteor for the next fifteen months, until it burst into long-lasting literary celebrity in the early 1950s. Baldwin's success continues to be a source of debate for the people who knew him, both casually and well, dur-ing the 1940s. After he was famous, he was adopted by the elites. In retrospect, colorful Mary McCarthy claimed him eagerly as the young black critic who possessed intuitive "taste." Her clever remarks tend to be supported by people who adored her at one time or other, like Philip Rahv, Alfred Kazin, and Norman Podhoretz.

Certainly some of the facts are indisputable. Basically three journals—*New Leader*, *Commentary*, and *Partisan Review*—provided Baldwin's education and turned him into a critical force. And of course this made Baldwin extraordinary. Black talent no longer collected on the left at *New Masses, Nation*, and *New Republic*; it was being raised by journals that had galloped from the left to the center, and which typically had been begun by American Jews, if *New Leader* and *Partisan Review* eschewed an outright ethnic focus. With the exception of Anatole Broyard and Richard Gibson, none of Baldwin's contemporaries could boast of that level of succor from something like a quarter of the makers of American literary taste.

In the 1960s Baldwin told his first biographer Fern Eckman that he was given reviews for the same reason that he was given fellowships: there were no other blacks on the scene, and white editors were oddly curious about a black boy who wanted to write.[6] But this is not really true. Plenty of blacks wanted to make it as writers, and Baldwin had known precisely the kind of poverty that would have kept him away from the literati who claimed to have eagerly embraced him in his youth.

Born in 1924 and bred in a New York tenement at 731 East 131st Street, about a block-and-a-half from the Harlem Hospital where he entered the world, James Baldwin grew into young manhood among black southern refugees trying to scrape by as janitors, laborers, laundresses, and servants in the most expensive city in America.[7] They had fled small towns in Virginia, South Carolina, and Georgia. His stepfather's mother Barbara, who lived on their floor, was ninety years old when Baldwin was born, and she had spent a significant portion of the nineteenth century enslaved in Louisiana. She gave birth to her son David when she was in her fifties. James Baldwin read his way out of the local library on 135th Street, but he was a shy youngster. He lived in a house dominated by his evangelical stepfather and including a mother who was pregnant nine of every eighteen months, a stepbrother nearly ten years his elder, and a grandmother who seemed from another era of time altogether.

Baldwin grasped the racial apartheid at work in his life and became adept at negotiating a different sort of path away from the career as a menial laborer that awaited most people he knew. He tried to please his father by joining the church in the Depression, but his ability and early recognition from white teachers freed him from the constraints at home. In junior high, the poet Countee Cullen taught him French. By high school he was writing stories and working on the school newspaper.

Baldwin used the war years well. He had attended League of American Writers lectures and workshops as a teenager and, like many of the young men from his school on their way to City College, gravitated toward the Socialist political party. He joined the Young People's Socialist League and later became a Trotskyite. He cultivated himself as he could, and the most self-conscious thing that he ever did was completely to affect his speech pattern, so that he sounded as if he had been raised in Greenwich, Connecticut, with the high lilt and bored tone of confident bluebloods. The young Baldwin shunned watermelon, fried chicken, Bessie Smith, and the idea of race pride.[8] But if he was consciously alienated from black people and black culture, he also had the black gamin's instinct for survival, and he was capable of turning white pity into something he could use. He was scrawny, a boyish brown-skinned man whose eyes seemed too big for his skull, and his skull too big for his body. He had little chance to play the role of Negro Casanova at which men like Ralph Ellison, Horace Cayton, Roi Ottley, William Attaway, Anatole Broyard, and Chester Himes excelled. Baldwin's initial turmoil was compounded by the fact that he went through his early years with strong homosexual desires, which he decided to embrace in his twenties. One important thing held him together; he believed in his natural gifts.

Baldwin wanted to be an artist, but it took him a while to narrow the field. He asked for jobs at newspapers in Harlem, probably in 1942 and probably at the *Amsterdam News* and the *People's Voice*. The editors "laughed [him]out of the office," disparaging his work history as a shoe-shine boy and his education that did not include even a semester at college.[9] He thought he might do better at acting or photography, and Max Lerner, the editor of the short-lived alternative newspaper *PM*, took on Baldwin as a messenger and printed a couple of his photographs. Baldwin was in step with the times and hoped to improve the plight of American blacks, or, as it was better known, of "race relations," and he proposed a book, "Unto the Dying Lamb," similar to Richard Wright's book of photo-journalism *12 Million Black Voices*. But it was depressing working at the liberal newspaper that imposed a caste system among its four black workers. Young Baldwin worked alongside a man his same skin color, while a very dark-skinned black man labored obscurely in the cellar. In front of the window facing the street, the position of esteem, sat a Negro of very light skin color.[10]

Inevitably, it seemed, Baldwin became known. An accomplished bohemian but also a young reader in the slush piles at Doubleday named Betty Arnoff met Baldwin in Greenwich Village and introduced his work to Doubleday's associate editor Bucklin Moon.[11] Always alert to new black talent, Moon befriended him and took him seriously. Moon thought Baldwin a talent-loaded urchin. Jimmy Baldwin was the kind of man "who comes in to mooch a cup of coffee . . . half an hour late because he didn't have subway fare and had to walk."[12] One thing stood out in the little friendship: despite Moon's connections in Harlem and his success publishing, he was not quite sure of himself around Baldwin; there was something that left him uneasy. "For all I know he may kill somebody with an ax tomorrow morning, but this kid has something," he wrote in a recommendation letter for Baldwin. The young black writer from Harlem possessed a murderous innocence. This quality, coupled with his improbably large talent, his determination to cultivate it, and his poverty, set people on edge.

Baldwin had the relative luxury to give himself over to his talent because he avoided the draft, the bane of most of the black artists. The writers and jazzmen did everything they could to slip Sam Brown. Dizzy Gillespie told the inducting examiner he might shoot a white man; on his way to prison and confrontation with the Nation of Islam, Malcolm Little did the same. Chester Himes was married and had medical troubles. Richard Wright was never called, but the service loomed over his head. Ralph Ellison dodged the army and eventually joined the merchant marine, an integrated unit. The U.S. Army, with its segregated outfits and basic training in the deep the South, could be torture. Vaudeville prodigy Sammy Davis Jr. worked in an integrated unit and was forced to drink his own urine. Perhaps the most famous disfigurement of a black artist occurred in the case of Lester Young, conscripted and then court-martialed for drug possession, but the army's destructive regimen was well-known and contributed mightily to the death of historian John Hope Franklin's college-educated brother.[13] There would be success stories in the case of some black men who traveled to Europe as GIs and returned only briefly to the United States, like William Gardner Smith and William Demby. William Attaway joined a special services unit, and Howard University professor John Lovell and critic Russell Marshall became army officers. But Baldwin was the oldest male in a household of nine. The government declared him "3-D" and did not call him up.[14]

In Greenwich Village, the traditional bohemian outpost in the United States, Baldwin was able to find a job at the Calypso, a Trinidadian restaurant filled with black jazz musicians, intellectuals, and artists, and a smidgen of cultural freedom. At the MacDougal Street restaurant he saw and heard and eventually talked to Richard Wright and the internationally famous Trotskyite C.L.R. James.[15] The Village was also a place of peril that he described as "an alabaster maze perched above a boiling sea," and to navigate the maze and avoid being scalded he would need help.[16] He formally introduced himself to two people and impressed them with his abundance of talent and artistic seriousness: Beauford Delany, the black impressionist painter whose works had been featured at the Downtown Gallery a couple of years before, and Wright, the most famous living black writer.

A twenty-one-year-old Baldwin walked up to 181 Green Street where Delany then lived and introduced himself. Delany was hip, urban and urbane, and homosexual, as were others in Harlem and the Village, like sculptor Richmond

Barthé, Richard Bruce Nugent, and Cullen, who died in 1946. A rather daring abstractionist painter, Delany fairly quickly initiated young James Baldwin into the world of the artist. Delany showed Baldwin how to see differently, to look at a puddle of water and, because of the motor oil, catch a reflection of the city's skyline. He introduced Baldwin to pot but kept him away from heroin. He bought tickets so that the two of them could attend Marian Anderson's Carnegie Hall concert. Delany played some of the great blues classics on the phonograph in his tiny apartment and made the place seem so rich with funky possibility that Baldwin imagined himself on a terrace when sitting on the fire escape.

Wright, on the other hand, was the most important black writer alive and, married to a white woman, father to a mixed-race child and living in a house at 13 St. Charles Place, must have seemed to Baldwin ensconced in a surreal inter-racial fantasy. After he bought the house in the spring of 1945, Wright received the twenty-one-year-old Baldwin by pouring out bourbon, combining elements of southern formality and southern clannishness, which Baldwin recognized from his own parents and relatives. Baldwin accepted Wright as an institution, somehow beyond friendship. Wright delivered for Baldwin a Saxton Fellowship in the winter of 1945, the first tangible proof of the young man's creative aptitude. "I wanted to thank you for your aid and your kindness to me. It's one of the most wonderful things that has ever happened to me," Baldwin wrote to his mentor in a rare moment of graceful satisfaction.[17]

Before the end of 1945 Baldwin felt like he had a workable draft of the novel "In My Father's House." Confident and always alert to the feelings of backers he was forever wounding, he wrote to Wright months after the award, after Wright and his family had moved to France, and requested an essay. He also reminded Wright that he respected him "and have for quite some time." By then he had taken liberty enough with Wright that it made sense, on occasion, to offer Wright praise. Baldwin was always polite, but he was never awed by Wright's stature.

The Saxton Fellowship gave Baldwin a sense of his ability, but his success as a published writer was owed to other courts. Through his Young People's Socialist League contacts, Baldwin became known to Sol Levitas, the editor of the socialist newspaper *New Leader*.[18] Housed on the fourth floor of the Rand School building at 15th Street and Fifth Avenue, *New Leader* had succeeded the American Socialist Party's paper *Leader* in 1924. When the Socialist Party headed by Norman Thomas split over its support of New Deal policies, the *New Leader* remained with Roosevelt and leftist politics and began a mounting campaign of anticommunism. With a bookstore at the offices and regular public lectures by the likes of Max Shachtman, the labor hero, the founder of analytic philosophy Bertrand Russell, and Professor Sidney Hook, there was an intellectual zing in the air at *New Leader*.

What *Partisan Review* meant to the anti-Stalinists on the cultural front, *New Leader* meant to them on the political front. The magazine exposed everything, from the Moscow Trials and Soviet massacres to the collusion over patents between German manufacturer I. G. Farben and Rockefeller's New Jersey–based Standard Oil. Young City College student Daniel Bell was one of its editors, and the newspaper operated with a sense of duty, daring, and antipropaganda zeal. There was also a more tangible feeling of excitement and consequence connected to the journal too. Popular Italian antifascist writer and lecturer Carlo Tresca had been assassinated on the street outside the office in 1943. The only African American to have published in the newspaper was Claude McKay, who had moved to Chicago, embraced Catholicism, and would die in 1948. But ten years earlier, McKay had used the paper as a forum to begin exploring the pernicious effects of communism among African American intellectuals.[19]

New Leader's literary editor was Isaac Rosenfeld, the man who had already put a torch to Chester Himes. Round-faced and heavyset, the University of Chicago graduate was frequently considered the bright star of his generation by people like Saul Bellow and Alfred Kazin. Rosenfeld was in the midst of accomplishing much of what Baldwin would increasingly see as important. He published a novel in 1946 called *Passage from Home* that had been rewardingly reviewed as developing away from a "Jewish genre novel" into a book of "profound universal meanings."[20] This seemed to be the triumph of universal humanism over sectarian ethnicity, which had been the traditional mark of acceptance for the Jewish writers, who still had not comfortably claimed the ethnic heritage of the ghetto neighborhoods of the American Northeast. Rosenfeld left the field of creative fiction and became known for his criticism. He came to know Baldwin well enough to write his recommendation letter for the Rosenwald Fellowship in 1948.

Rosenfeld's position on blacks was aggressively liberal but complicated. He could be understood as "pro-Negro," but Rosenfeld understood blackness in the classic sense of those around *Commentary* magazine. "Blackness" was a kind of stain of difference separating blacks from union with the majority of Americans. He had written in the novel *Passage from Home*, "Or, think for a moment, what was it like to be a Negro? I could only imagine myself to be obsessed if I were one: I should go about thinking, 'I am black, I am black.'"[21] For Rosenfeld, the central question for the Negro was the problem of overcoming physical difference, a difference premised on a white norm and an absolute blackness. Understandably Rosenfeld was attracted to Baldwin, who proved his liberal largesse and accepted the same viewpoint, that the physical manifestations of black speech and ethnic characteristics were to be transcended in the movement to universal humanity.

But even if he thought blackness a disability, Rosenfeld's opinion of Baldwin was tremendous. He believed the young man from Harlem noble. "His courage is two-fold—it consists in his honesty and in his desire (and great ability) to express the truth," he wrote to the Rosenwald judges.

> I value him as a man, a friend and a writer for his great personal dignity and understanding. . . . He has a sympathy, rare in the rarest of men, that can penetrate outward disorder to the inner meaning, where the fact that men suffer degradation, and the significance for human culture of that degradation, are one. This inner broader meaning, the "cultural sense" is not separated from him by any area of vagueness, rhetoric or morally self-conscious good will; it is an immediate, painful perception. It is this which gives him his right to say "we," "our," when he speaks both for Negroes and for America; he has instinctively. I know of no one with greater authority to speak both the part and the whole."[22]

In about fifteen years, the Nation of Islam national spokesperson Malcolm X would make the ideal of a black and white "we" the object of scorn in his most important speech, "A Message to the Grass Roots." But in the mid-1940s, for a black man to speak of "we," and include himself as an American and pretend to speak for whites, was nothing short of miraculous.

By the time Baldwin met *Partisan Review* editors Philip Rahv, William Phillips, and Mary McCarthy, he would remind McCarthy of Delmore Schwartz, the young prodigy of their set. McCarthy met him for lunch in the company of Phillips, probably in 1948, at the Blue Ribbon restaurant on the West Side. She was surprised by him and believed that the fact that his reading was not "colored by his color" was "an unusual trait."[23] McCarthy, who famously married Edmund Wilson while living with Philip Rahv, reflected the patronizing snobbery of her group. Her judgment that Baldwin was the first "black literary intellectual" she knew may indeed be true, but Baldwin was certainly not the first that she could have known. Her suggestion that Baldwin had some expert facility that enabled him to evaluate art without a flawed racial consciousness is also disingenuous. McCarthy did not read *Phylon* or know of other black critics. In 1947 and 1948 the best prose narrative stylists among African Americans—Ann Petry, Zora Neale Hurston, Frank Yerby, and Willard Motley—all published novels featuring white protagonists. The trend was thought to herald the dawn of mature race relations and black self-conscious identity. Since the *Partisan Review* crowd had, after their 1937 rebirth, ceased to interact with Sterling Brown, Richard Wright, Claude McKay, and then, as they came along, J. Saunders Redding, Ralph Ellison, C.L.R. James, Ann Petry, and Carl Offord, intensely intellectual New York black writers (with the exception of commuters Brown and Redding), they would now turn to precocious youngsters like Baldwin for what they needed.

James Baldwin's first *New Leader* review in May 1947 showed him quite different from what he would become. He scrutinized Irving Shulman's novel of Jewish gangs in Brooklyn, *The Amboy Dukes*, and thought the straightforward narrative had special meaning because, like *Native Son*, it made a broad and "pessimistic" social indictment. He was raw. "He does not say, but seems to know, that recreation halls and basketball games, the first resort of the civic minded, is a procedure about as effective as the application of Vaseline to a syphilitic lesion."[24]

A couple of weeks later and Baldwin popped up in *Nation*, where poet Randall Jarrell, a man of Vanderbilt agrarian aesthetics and slightly Marxist politics, was editor. The subject was more typical of what Baldwin's liberal friends had in mind for the young critic: African American literature. Baldwin reviewed the workaholic writer Shirley Graham's *There Was Once A Slave* and showed an impatient fury that probably hinted at his resentment for being pigeonholed: he was good enough to catch notice of the *Nation,* but not good enough to get a first-class book. On the other hand, it was appropriate to give the biography of Frederick Douglass to a fiction reviewer because the book was fiction. Baldwin called Graham's version of Douglass "unbelievable" and bereft of "dignity and humanity alike," chiefly because "she is obviously so determined to Uplift the Race."[25] In the treatment of Offord and Petry and Wright by the better class of intellectual reviewers, the "Uplift the Race" criteria had received some exploration, and now, in the hands of a young black reviewer and an unarguably second-rate book, a new bar had been set up. For ever more, race propaganda was ideology, plain and simple; the only valuable contribution lay in art and form. Baldwin would write again for *New Leader* in September, a review of the book *The Sling and the Arrow* by Frank Marshall Davis's friend Stuart Engstrand (whose plot anticipated a book Baldwin himself would publish in another nine years, *Giovanni's Room*). But his most important task in his debut year as critic was his fall review of the second novel of Chester Himes.

The world would always believe that Chester Himes had a rather unimaginative persecution complex. In September 1947, a short eighteen months after his novelistic debut, Chester Himes published the sophomore novel *Lonely Crusade*. The second book revealed the ugly joint between race, sex, and labor in wartime California aircraft plants. Himes created a protagonist named Lee Gordon, and he set the book within the range of American life in which he was expert. Gordon, a college-educated black, has firsthand experiences with communism, labor unions, corporate management, and interracial sex. The book epitomized the storm brewing over realistic representations of the interracial American landscape. For Himes, even the publicity received by the book bespoke the discomfort and jeopardy of the new climate to black writers. Himes thought that the new book would succeed and transform him into a major figure, like Petry, and bring middle-class acceptance, which he had still failed to win.

Instead, the September publication day of the book that should have put him into the league with Richard Wright turned into a nightmare. The ferry taking Himes from Brooklyn to Manhattan broke down and he was forty-five minutes late to Macy's flagship store in downtown Manhattan, where he had been scheduled to meet with the bookstore clerks before work began. At Bloomingdale's on East 59th Street, Himes did not even get to see the manager before he knew that no copies of the book were for sale. Then the Mary Margaret McBride radio program for the Central Broadcasting System (CBS) canceled his afternoon interview after a transcript that Himes had made for another program, *This Is New York*, was broadcast.[26] He had every expectation for success with the interview. A year earlier, in April 1946, Himes had shared the program with Ann Petry and Mark Harris, author of *Trumpet to the World*.[27] An ex-con who thought he might never get an even break, Himes took the experience to heart. "It was then that I decided to leave the United States forever if I got the chance."[28]

Lonely Crusade sold poorly, and in fact, the experience of publishing the work at all was excruciating for the author. Ralph Ellison, disappointed in his friend's book, thought that, among other things, Himes had misjudged the extent of the escalating "Red Scare," the euphemism used by the wary during the months between the Loyalty Oath and the indictment of CPUSA's leadership on charges of sedition.[29] Himes had concluded *Lonely Crusade* with a long, sympathetic conversation between protagonist Lee Gordon and a Communist, which influences Gordon's final pyrrhic gesture to unionism. Audiences would not gravitate to a book that showed Communists as wise liberators. *Opportunity* dismissed Himes's "paper-thin" characters and "unilluminated concern with violence."[30] The best that *New Republic* could do was to say that the overall achievement was "unsettling."[31] J. Saunders Redding condemned the same flawed, frightened men that he had disliked in *If He Hollers*. "In *Lonely Crusade*, the same error [as in *If He Hollers*] is made," Redding wrote in his weekly review. "[H]e deliberately creates heroes with a hundred petty flaws in order to show how weak and foolish and depthless even heroes are." The real theme Redding found was simply fear, "the fear that the author seems to believe is the only natural endowment of the colored man in the white world."[32]

There was one critic who unequivocally supported the value of the book. Horace Cayton fought with his black audiences to take to heart unflattering messages from black novelists. "It will offend a lot of people," Cayton admitted of *Lonely Crusade*, but "it's closer to the truth than most anything I've read recently." Cayton thought that the black audience was overly inclined to see the truth as relative only to their own personal experience. Cayton warned them away from judging literature by virtue of its ability to mirror their own lives. "You don't have to read the book and say 'I wouldn't have acted that way'," Cayton explained in a short course on literary criticism. "You don't have to make generalizations about all trade unions or about the Communist party or about the amount of anxiety you might have felt. But given the character Lee, given the situation, 'Lonely Crusade,' written by Chester Himes, is a great book."[33]

Himes was the first black novelist that James Baldwin reviewed, and though he would review more, it would never be that many. It seemed to Baldwin, immediately, that he was being pushed into the corner of "minority rights" book reviewer, and in his mind he saw thousands of tractlike, formulaic pamphlets emerging on racial and ethnic relations and goading Americans to "'do the right thing.'"[34] Nevertheless, the assignment for the October 1947 *New Leader* was difficult. Baldwin conceded, twice, that the prose of *Lonely Crusade* was "uninteresting and awkward," and "some of the worst writing on this side of the Atlantic," which was also a political jab aimed, it would seem, at Sartre. He claimed that Himes had tried to do too much, but that his integrity as a writer, the value he placed on honesty, commanded the recognition of some merits of the book. "The value of his book lies in its earnest effort to understand the psychology of the oppressed and oppressor and their relationship to each other." The book contained "an historical importance, not unlike that accorded *Uncle Tom's Cabin* or, more recently, *Native Son.*"

But the essence of what he had to say was directed against the unraveling of the plot and the creation of the lead character. Baldwin criticized Himes for leaving the protagonist no way out of his morass.

> Unlike Bigger Thomas, gone to his death cell, inarticulate and destroyed by his need for identification and revenge, and with only the faintest intimation in that twilight of what destroyed him and of what his life might have been, Mr. Himes' protagonist, Lee Gordon, sees what has happened and what is happening and watches helplessly the progress of his own disease. *And there is no path out.* In a group so pressed down, terrified and at bay and carrying generations of constricted, subterranean hostility, no real group identification is possible. Nor is there a Negro tradition to cling to in the sense that Jews may be said to have a tradition; this was left in Africa long ago and no-one remembers it now. Lee Gordon is forced back on himself, not even bitterness can serve him as a weapon anymore.[35]

About six months into his career, Baldwin had sketched out a critical paradigm that he adhered to throughout the 1950s. Looking to writers as cultural soothsayers, he believed that wallowing in bitterness and indignation was flawed because it led to violence and self-destruction, either of the black self, of the black people, or of the American nation. He also suggested that there was no cultural retreat for black Americans because they were a people without a tradition that might enable a conscious return. This was the price that came with the resurrection of Henry James, who thought American culture traditionless, a notion that appeared in the work of Lionel Trilling and Richard Wright. Baldwin seemed to suggest that to reach full maturity, black writers would necessarily be indistinguishable—thematically—from whites.

Baldwin's review for the anticommunist press differed in only one small way from *New Masses*. Himes had ridiculed the party's approach to African Americans by making the chief black leftist a kind of caricature. The black Communist Luther is described by the narrator as an "ape" on several occasions, and he participates in crude and degrading relationships with white women and men. Although Himes had written favorably of the other Communists, his work could be accused of endorsing black inferiority. Breaking into print with some of his earliest criticism, Lloyd Brown seemed like the CPUSA's biting black pit bull eliminating race chauvinism when he exaggerated, "I cannot recall ever having read a worse book on the Negro theme."[36] In the same character, Baldwin had found impeccable quality. "[T]he Uncle Tom named Luther, is handled and seen so accurately that no white man, ever again, should dare to turn his back on any Negro he feels he has bought and conquered."[37] The murderous potential of the harmless black toy fascinated Baldwin as well as Himes.

The problem was that racism in the form of assumptions, beliefs, and practices still functioned with power. Baldwin may have spotted the high ground, but it was far off. Milton Klonsky's review for *Commentary*, for example, compared the finesse of Himes's writing to lavatory graffiti. Klonsky even included a unique form of ethnic patronizing that was considered racist by radicals then and racist by everyone in the next generation. "Although the author is himself a Negro, his book is so deracinated, without any of the lively qualities of the imagination peculiar to his people, that it might easily have been composed by any clever college girl."[38] Klonsky was from Staten Island, and although he had studied with Allen Tate at the Cumberland School in Massachusetts, he was not revealing southern paternalism, he was revealing American liberal paternalism. His attitude represented the coziness that came about with integration and the cocksure sensibility concerning whites' obligations to amicable race relations at a journal like *Commentary*, home to a provocative cultural criticism. When he asked his black friend Anatole Broyard, a hip young critic, to collaborate on a jazz essay for *Partisan Review*, Klonsky conducted himself as he had in the *Lonely Crusade* review. "Milton suggested that I write the first draft and he would rewrite it," Broyard remembered. "What he meant was that I'd supply the facts and he'd turn them into prose."[39] In the 1940s this was a relationship—laborer to craftsman, raw material to finished product—that even blacks expected.

The record would eventually show that Broyard needed no protector, but the net gain for social realism had begun to fall into the debit column. Chester Himes was the classic case in the fall of 1947 of the decline, precipitous and ugly, of social realism in the hands of a black writer as a device for American racial justice. There was a gap of more than fifteen years. When Claude Brown and Alex Haley returned to the sex and violence of the urban streets in the mid-1960s, with the certainty that environment shaped the nature of individual choice, the genre would be starkly different in a key respect: it would be auto-biographical, like the slave narrative. It was as if a huge gate stood between black writers attempting to examine racism in American society and the bench-mark of fiction writing.

And there was also something about the social milieu that James Baldwin, Anatole Broyard, and, to an extent, Ralph Ellison began to be enmeshed in by the second half of the 1940s. William Phillips, the coeditor of *Partisan Review*, once described his circle of fellow editors and writers as adherents to "a super-rationalism, a competitiveness, an intellectual hardness, and an indifference to loyalty that was humanly destructive."[40] The reward for a selection of black writers was to jump into this world and not really, ever, to be able to return.

Not everyone was ready to reject the efficacy of realism. Since the art of pro-test had been demoted, apostles like Horace Cayton went to the intellectual barricades to try to show the redeeming value of these authors. The work of "subjective protest"—novels, short stories, autobiographies, poems, and plays—was for Cayton one of the chief forces capable of exploring and disseminating broadly the effects of the deep problem of racial inequality in America.

Cayton's exploration of black unconscious fear and his attachment to plain statements of black anger and fright lost ground in the second half of the 1940s, when he had fully worked up his fear-hate-fear syndrome in "The Psychological Approach to Race Relations." The terms of the battle for "freedom" and "equal-ity" shifted for liberals as America accepted a permanent military draft and entered the cold war with the Soviet Union and then rather quickly a hot war in Korea with China. "New" liberals, like Lionel Trilling, believed that "more than a document of misery and oppression" was necessary to prevent giving readers only temporary "escape" and providing a substitute for their "moral and politi-cal action."[41] This was something that everyone had become convinced of, and indeed Richard Wright had been convinced of since the publication of *Uncle Tom's Children*: the inadequacy of literary catharsis. No one wanted to write books that would expiate white guilt; the books, if they had value, were sup-posed to mobilize resistance to segregation.

By the second half of the 1940s, Lionel Trilling, who graduated years in ad-vance of James Baldwin from the same Bronx high school, had become the in-tellectual authority in the movement to reject issues-based social realism. He put himself in position to do part of this by drawing a line in the sand, with Richard Wright's *Black Boy* on one side and everybody else on the other. Trill-ing praised Wright for offering more than just an account of misery in *Black Boy*. But the putative adoption of Wright as an artist signaled a new wave of literary liberalism that had a different approach to race relations, one that, in the environment of the cold war, complemented the views held by southern liberals. Trilling claimed to appreciate the value and justification of black anger, but he also believed that it signaled a literal dead-end. If black writers revealed the condition of their lives honestly, "the full amount of anger that would be appropriate to the social situation alone would surely have the effect of destroying the person who felt it," he said.[42] This view indicated two things. In effect, ordinary "subjective protest" was only escape, and, worse, the evidence of anger revealed self-destruction more than it shone light on the objective world. In essence blacks were giving themselves catharsis by writing blunt books of degradation. What were the writers to do? Horace Cayton, who wanted badly to become a novelist, felt his subjective anger acutely. Indignant about the mistreatment of black people, he admitted to the readers of his column, "I want to get up on a housetop and scream."[43]

The social realists were also struck a blow when Richard Wright left the country and settled permanently in Paris in 1947. Wright had taken his family to France for seven months in 1946 and found that he acclimated well to the country. Moreover, he wished to raise his children beyond the taint of U.S. race relations. When the Baltimore *Afro Magazine* proudly ran a column describing Richard Wright's life in exile in France, Wright made the famous claim that, "There is more freedom in one block of Paris than there is in the whole United States."[44] The departure of Wright's manic and aggressive intelligence at the peak of his fame slowed the writing agenda of the social realists, and the book companies did not exactly look to replace him.

In February 1947 J. Saunders Redding wrote a short essay consolidating his views on the best-known black writer across the globe. The effect of the shock tactics of social realism had led Redding to determine Wright's key success to have been an entirely new victory for the black writer: the triumph over the problem of audience. To Redding's satisfaction, Wright had "extricated himself from the dilemma, the horns of which are, (1) to write exclusively for a colored audience and therebye limit oneself to a monotypical, glorified and race-proud picture of Afro-American life, and (2) to write exclusively for a white audience and therebye be trapped in the old stereotypes, the fixed opinions, the stock situations that are as bulwarks against honest fictional portrayal." Redding claimed that Wright's path breaking had cut a new way. "[C]olored writers are finding it easier to appeal to 'two' audiences without being either false to the one nor subservient to the other."[45]

Redding might have believed that Wright had shifted the terms of authorship, but the dilemma of audience remained inimical to black writers in the years after Wright's departure and never found satisfactory conclusion. After the burst of Himes's two books, which never sold well nor found support from their publishers, the later 1940s were fairly dominated by Frank Yerby and his style of success—a Jim Crow special that removed black protagonists. Writers were being warned off of social realism, and only the unusual or the young continued to appear with new books. Yerby, who was selling books by the hundreds of thousands, represented the most forceful trend by black writers at the end of the decade, the "raceless" novel. At the end of the 1950s, Yerby would dignify his turn away from the racially conscious social realist fiction he had published between 1938 and 1946 in *Common Ground, New Anvil, Phylon,* and *Tomorrow* by claiming that the "costume novel" of "light, pleasant fiction" actually lay at the heart of audience desires. He lied convincingly when he told readers "at bottom, the novelist's job is to entertain. If he aspires to instruct, or to preach, he has chosen his profession unwisely."[46]

Yerby refused to use black central characters, and his later novels, like 1947's *The Vixens,* even eliminated the black secondary characters that had been prominently featured in *The Foxes of Harrow.* Certainly Yerby's extraordinary success contributed to part of Ann Petry's experiment with *Country Place,* a slender, whites-only novel about gossiping, adulterous New England that Petry was able to get in print a mere year after her important debut. Others followed. In 1948 Zora Neale Hurston turned her eye to Florida's middling whites in *Seraph on the Sewanee,* which had echoes of *Their Eyes Were Watching God.* Young newcomer William Gardner Smith would play the literary game like Petry and devote his sophomore effort, *Anger at Innocence,* to white working-class Philadelphia. A young comer named William Demby tried a novel with three protagonists, one of them white. Chester Himes changed the color of the characters in his prison novel and published *Cast the First Stone* in 1952. James Baldwin did the same thing in 1956 with his second novel. Richard Wright joined the curiosity with his psychological case study *Savage Holiday* in 1954. And Willard Motley landed major book contracts by continuing to write books with a white character as the center of consciousness for his entire career.

None of the authors ever admitted that books with white characters seemed to be a kind of magic for black crossover appeal, and for most of them it was not. But they could not escape the publishing climate. The conservative wisdom held that black writers could not make a career of writing books with black characters and selling them to white audiences. If blacks wanted to have the high-flying careers of white writers and to prove their willingness to envision a world beyond Jim Crow, this was certain proof. But, with the notable exception of Hurston's final narrative effort *Seraph,* none of the writers seemed capable of imagining a world where the barriers of segregation did not exist or did not damage American lives.

At the end of the decade, Chester Himes had made the largest investment in showing the damage done to blacks. An emotionally sore Himes took time out from an eight-week visit to Yaddo in late spring of 1948 to give a talk to the

Creative Writing Forum at Chicago's Parkway Community Center on May 18, 1948.[47] Before the lecture he had written to *Commentary* in protest of the glib Milton Klonsky review. "Protest against racial injustice was not my principal objective," he explained. He had written *Lonely Crusade* rather to provide, "an inspirational value to all who are oppressed," the rejoinder began, mildly enough. But next, Himes claimed that, deep-down, Klonsky hated Negroes.[48] Himes had begun to bite the liberal hand that fed him.

Himes's response in *Commentary* was a model of restraint compared to what he had to say by the time he got to Chicago. Depressed by the criticisms aimed at his novel, Himes lashed out, quoting Cayton's essay and admitting the fury of "fear-hate-fear." "There can be no understanding of Negro life, of Negroes' compulsions, reactions and actions," he lectured the crowd, "there can be no understanding of his sexual impulses, of Negro crime, of Negro marital relations, of our spiritual entreaties, our ambitions and our defeats until this fear has been revealed." Not yet necessarily shameful, Himes continued and made the listeners uncomfortable. "If this plumbing for truth reveals within the Negro personality homicidal mania, lust for white women, a pathetic sense of inferiority, paradoxical anti-semitism, arrogance, Uncle Tomism, hate and fear of self-hate, this then is the effect of oppression on the human personality."[49]

The endorsement of "hate and fear" was the climactic moment of Himes's talk. He had outlined the conditions that caused talented and honest blacks to be thought psychotic by publishers. "For him to delineate the degrading effects of oppression will be like inflicting a wound upon himself. . . . And this must be the reward for his integrity; he will be reviled by the Negroes and the whites alike."[50] He was by that point in the lecture speaking candidly about his own problems. After he finished his delivery, and "not a single person, white or black, applauded," Himes returned to New York to Yaddo and went on a six-week bender.[51] It was a prologue. Himes foundered for the next five years, trying to publish books about homosexuality in prison and hatred inside of the black family. In the process, he lost his marriage and many of his friends. In 1953 he too would leave the United States for France.

Like Himes, Horace Cayton would find the price of honesty and being on the wrong side of the social realism literary debate a self-inflicted wound. To control his behavior and temper his emotions, throughout the 1940s he had become addicted to most of the powerful mind- and mood-altering substances then legally available: alcohol, nicotine, the sedative Seconal, and the stimulant Benzedrine. He conducted disastrous personal affairs. Nor did his overconsumption relieve his more general feelings of anxiety, helplessness, paranoia, and depression. Cayton's body shook when he got up in the morning. His psychoanalysis sessions drained him and never seemed to enable him to alter his self-destructive behavior. He would spend lengthy periods of his adult life in hospital care. The Parkway Community Center's board of directors saw Cayton drinking heavily and talking furiously of the import of literature and protest, and they placed him on furlough, which they politely labeled "sabbatical." When Arna Bontemps called the center that fall, the secretary told him that Cayton "is not at all well and will take a year off—at least."[52] Hoping to work into literary circles and escape embarrassment, Cayton, married for the third time, moved to New York for the next eleven years. It was fast becoming a time for black writers who knew the scene and who sensed the curve toward a new liberalism to take flight. The glamorous black retreat overseas, and even the outright casualties like Cayton, heralded the dawn of a new age.

CHAPTER ELEVEN

The Negro New Liberal Critic and the Big Little Magazine (1948–1949)

As a group, African American professional scholars—academics—never approached keeping pace with the critics in publishing or influence. J. Saunders Redding was the exception, though he never won the love of students or of his black peers. In 1948 Hampton Institute professor Hugh Gloster moved to the front rank of the academicians studying black literature with his book *Negro Voices in American Fiction*. Gloster treated black writers and black characters in American fiction from the Civil War through the Depression, building on the work already done by earlier critics, including Nick Aaron Ford, Sterling Brown, and J. Saunders Redding. He was good enough to become the second black academic to have his literary criticism published by a university press in the United States.

Gloster held out Richard Wright's *Native Son* as the benchmark of African American creative fiction, but he did a good job of bringing together a tradition that had grown remarkably from the time of the earlier studies. Gloster was encyclopedic in his identification of tradition, if he was not an unusually sophisticated analyst. He called books "significant" without justifying the decision, and he spent most of his own work discussing plot structure. Gloster used Columbia critic Carl Van Doren's *The American Novel* as a template for his study, but his training did not permit him to go beyond it. The research was drawn exclusively from Gloster's days as a student under Oscar Cargill at New York University. The work did not respond to the newly contrived liberalism of the mid-1940s; in fact, the book could have appeared in 1941, relative to the information that Gloster provided. He took his slight Marxism from *New Masses* or *Modern Quarterly* or not at all. However, in the précis that accompanied all five of the chapters of literary discussion, he produced a competent and optimistic literary history. And there would simply be a point of view, a standpoint from which Gloster would not move. The unadulterated opposition to racial persecution was the paramount credential for a narrative work of art. For him, the works of William Faulkner, T. S. Stribling, and Erskine Caldwell had turned the tide of southern romanticism in the treatment of blacks. Gloster described Caldwell's *Trouble in July*, widely considered a horrible novel, as "an outstanding attack upon racial persecution."[1] For Gloster, this was the prime criterion for excellence.

It must have been difficult for Gloster to take the full measure of the freshly liberated voices of white critics and "friends" of the fledging tradition of African American literature. Similar to his peers in background and training, he believed that amiable whites had, accidentally, torpedoed the Harlem "Renascence" of the 1920s. The mission for Gloster's generation was the correction of white influence that seemed to have tilted the Harlem Renaissance in the direction of the exotic. In 1945 Gloster's "The Van Vechten Vogue" sketched out the influence of the best-known white American—half architect, half voyeur—connected to the explosion of black writing in the 1920s.

A literary movement of blacks partly engineered by a bisexual playboy, one that left little evidence of confrontation or belligerent protest, seemed humiliating, perhaps especially so after the war. Gloster wrote that Van Vechten's 1926 book *Nigger Heaven* "dramatized the alleged animalism and exoticism of Harlem folk" and "influenced the writings of Negro Renascence authors."[2] Three years later in *Negro Voices* he said that *Nigger Heaven* "affected the work of Negro fictionist more than any other book in the history of American literature."[3] Thus the subsequent Van Vechten School of black novelists—which included Claude McKay, Wallace Thurman, and Arna Bontemps—stressed "jazz, sex, atavism and primitivism." Gloster, though not completely dismissive of Van Vechten's import as the first novelist to capture the Harlem scene of the 1920s and to develop an audience, articulated all the touchstones that would come to haunt the period. The Renaissance was "primarily a fad," and Van Vechten and his friends' "fatal mistake" was to "make a fetish of sex and the cabaret rather than to give a faithful, realistic presentation and interpretation of Harlem life." If the postwar American critical establishment wanted to call off literary protest, some of the young blacks were pushing back against the trend and beginning their skirmishing against long-standing friends.

Phylon's editor, the sharp-minded young sociologist Ira de A. Reid, had felt obliged to go to the still prominent and in some circles quite beloved Van Vechten for comment. Ever seeking the blessing of the young blacks, Van Vechten wrote back that Gloster was "eminently fair." The novelist, photographer, and spirited collector of African American letters could not avoid the fact that he was seeing something that he had predicted would end certain varieties of discrimination. "Negroes are kept down because they lack NERVE and initiative," Van Vechten had written to his friend Langston Hughes in 1942.[4] Gloster showed both qualities, hallmarks of a new generation of writers and critics, a cadre that would rely considerably less on the support of individual patrons like Van Vechten.

Gloster knew that in 1948 black writers faced a predicament to secure patronage and then sustain fidelity to an artistic vision. The Rosenwald Fund was in its final year and the Federal Writers' Project was a relic from the 1930s. And

now, with the critical rejection of social realism, writers faced an ongoing anxiety over which portions of tradition to claim. For J. Saunders Redding, too, the
Harlem Renaissance had been overvalued. "Almost every writer or would be
writer who so much as lived in or around New York in the middle or late Twenties" had claimed critical attention, he wrote in a column in the *Afro-American*.
"[S]ome of those who got attention simply were not worth it."[5] And some of
them were pointing to new culprits for the problem. Young critic Blyden Jackson exposed the flaws in Countee Cullen's work and then blamed scholars for
letting it happen. Jackson could not find the Negro literary historian to match
Alfred Kazin, a black biographer on par with Van Wyck Brooks, or a historian
of the cultural economy like Vernon Parrington. "The literature does not, and
should not come first, with the critics following in its wake. The critics, with
their revelations, their encouragement, their warnings, their guidance, should
come first, and the literature should develop behind them into a tradition which
not only the artists, but the critics have had a hand in defining and creating."[6]
There was some trepidation that perhaps Wright's work had not been enough to
sustain the movement.

A bit stodgier and less flexible than Jackson was Southern University's English department chairman, John S. Lash. He asked the question, "What Is Negro
Literature?" in October 1947 in the journal of the National Council of Teachers
of English, *College English*. The reply was essentially that Negro contributions
to American literature were slight and that as a genre the literature did not exist.
Lash stood on the broadly accepted principle that "[l]iterature must remain the
study of belles-lettres and must not be allowed to be prostituted to the cause of
social justice for any group."[7] The novelist Waters Turpin, teaching English at
Lincoln College for men in Pennsylvania, seconded the view that the humorless
black novelists, especially the tawdry Chester Himes, had pursued too narrow
a focus. Black prose writers were "too preoccupied with the racial theme to give
full rein to his powers."[8]

Blyden Jackson may have been closest to the truth of the matter: it took good
criticism to elevate the aesthetic standards sufficiently to produce enduring literary work. Richard Wright, J. Saunders Redding, and Ralph Ellison had all
gone through the rigors of criticism before struggling successfully with lengthier narratives. But the black American writer who came of age after the Second
World War, even if it was in September 1945, had a different consciousness
about the tradition, a keen sense of individuality, and a sense of loyalty to a
vastly different constituency than his forebearers.

After dismissing the protest tradition with Chester Himes, James Baldwin
moved from *New Leader* to *Commentary*, a destination among the New York
magazines in the 1940s and 1950s. Eliot Cohen had founded the journal in 1945
for the American Jewish Committee, who wanted to bring the Jewish intellectual

into the conversation about American life and identity. In spite of that mission of breadth and inclusion, the editor Cohen admitted that *Commentary* was "a Jewish magazine."[9] Cohen was also known for his fierce anticommunism.[10] A warren of rough cubicles in a loft in the garment district on 33rd Street, where large numbers of black men were seen moving racks of clothes through the street, *Commentary*'s offices were not as distinguished as the *New Leader*'s. But the magazine boasted young editorial talent in literature, criticism, and politics, people like Robert Warshow, abstract expressionist art critic Clement Greenberg, City College graduate Irving Kristol, and sociologist Nathan Glazer. The magazine's next editor, Norman Podhoretz, described Cohen's Moses-like leadership of Jewish intellectuals out from "the desert of alienation" to the "promised land of democratic, pluralistic, prosperous America," an identity as comfortable in "its Jewishness as in its Americaness."[11] The view that this group extended toward African Americans was not exactly charitable. In the 1940s it did not seem controversial for the editors to share Glazer's view that "the Negro is only an American and nothing else. He has no values and culture to guard and protect."[12]

Commentary wanted to do what the *Menorah Journal* had been doing but without purely ethnocentric inspection. The American climate changed rapidly during the 1940s: from an all-time high of anti-Jewish prejudice in the first half of the decade to the country's all-time low by the end of the decade.[13] In 1945 Jewish Bess Myerson took the crown of Miss America and successfully resisted the efforts to change her name for the competition. Four groundbreaking movies, *Crossfire, Gentlemen's Agreement, Prejudice*, and *Open Secret*, all released in 1947, presented the problem of prejudice against Jews. In 1949 *Pinky, Home of the Brave, Lost Boundaries*, and *Intruder in the Dust* would do something similar for black Americans.

At *Commentary*, under the tutelage of Robert Warshow, Baldwin wrote two pieces in 1948 that were not reviews: "The Harlem Ghetto," a social critique of a sacred black geography, and "Previous Condition," his first published short story. Baldwin linked the transformation in his perceptual abilities to Warshow's commissioning "The Harlem Ghetto" and then sweating it out with him. "He was the *greatest* editor I ever *had*," Baldwin emphasized to an interviewer in 1966.[14] Baldwin's contemporary Norman Podhoretz shared that complimentary view of Warshow. A plainspoken twenty-nine-year-old University of Michigan graduate, Warshow was antagonistic to the refinement and remove from the field of politics represented by a figure like Lionel Trilling.[15]

The result of the teamwork on "The Harlem Ghetto" was a new kind of essay for liberal American readers. First of all, it pointed to nothing practical and concrete for them to do to fix racial problems. It successfully adopted the point of view of a principled and trustworthy black critic, unprepared to compromise or "sell out" to ingratiate himself to whites, but who was also not unaware of larger problems of American reality. Baldwin described Harlem, black leaders, black newspapers, black churches, and, because it was *Commentary*, black and Jewish relations. He was not a social scientist or even a college graduate: his evidence was anecdotal and imaginative. He was a critic who had witnessed. He pointed to Richard Wright as the source for the observation that "the Negro is always acting," and he mocked Wright's black middle-class critics.[16]

Most singularly, Baldwin, who introduced the piece by acknowledging his position as a Negro native to Harlem, started to speak for his audience in the first person plural, "we," the affect he had developed that had caught the notice of Isaac Rosenfeld. In this early work, it was necessary to clarify his taking the first person plural, so that people would understand the bridge he was offering. "We (Americans in general, that is) like to point to Negroes and to most of their activities with a kind of tolerant scorn; but it is ourselves we are watching, ourselves we are damning, or—condescendingly—bending to save."[17] The confidence in his tone, and the assumption of a shared cultural life, was astonishing.

And yet Baldwin may have been more comfortable appropriating the voice of the white liberal than he was in accurately revealing the resentful attitudes of Harlem. The essay had been an aching tug-of-war between Baldwin and Warshow, who refused to accept the rather bland adage that Harlem had no calcified Jewish prejudice, and, furthermore, that Baldwin himself had no residue of it. Baldwin had not set out to reveal this kind of personal shame.

Over a period of six months, from the time that Warshow solicited the essay in the fall of 1947 until it was published in February 1948, the editor kept sending back the drafts until Baldwin admitted that bitter resentment against whites could take the form of anti-Jewish prejudice. "[T]hat was the first time I realized that writing was not simply the act of writing—that it was something *else*, something much *harder*. Which is to tell the truth," he told a biographer.[18] The discussion of difficulties between blacks and Jews was tricky because Baldwin expressed nothing like admiration for black liberals: "Concerning Negro leaders, the best that one can say is that they are in an impossible position and that the handful motivated by genuine concern maintain this position with heartbreaking dignity."[19] Harlem was not going to lead itself out from the ghetto.

The achieved candor of the essay, and its attitude that combines elements that are indifferent, sardonic, and deeply sympathetic, elicited waves of praise and excitement. Arna Bontemps called the piece "remarkable" in his regular correspondence with Langston Hughes. Having missed the early *New Leader* reviews, Bontemps was beholding a rare talent for the first time. "What a kid! He has zoomed high among our writers with his first effort."[20] Not long after the essay was written, Alain Locke, spending a semester as visiting professor at City College, would introduce himself to Baldwin. Locke was moved by the young writer and foresaw a considerable future. When Baldwin's short story "Previous Condition" was published by *Commentary* in October, Locke wrote to Eliot Cohen. "Artistically there has been nothing to equal it, in my judgment, since Jean Toomer's story, *Sketches in Cane*. . . . You have done a discerning service pioneering his work."[21] James Baldwin was officially launched and recognized.

Close on Baldwin's heels were two more articles written about Harlem by writers who had bigger profiles. But only one of them would be published. Ralph Ellison wrote "Harlem Is Nowhere" for *Magazine of the Year*, but, like his *Survey Graphic* essay and his Gunnar Myrdal review, the essay would sit in his desk for decades; *Magazine of the Year* folded before publishing the 1949 issue. In the important piece, Ellison described the Lafargue Clinic, a pauper's psychiatric center in Harlem that he and Richard Wright had been integral in founding. He pointed to psychiatry as a possible means of addressing "the Negro's perpetual alienation in the land of his birth."[22]

One evening William Phillips of *Partisan Review* encountered Ellison at the apartment of Catherine Carver, the *Review*'s managing editor. What Phillips recalled of the event was not Ellison's high seriousness toward the Lafargue Clinic or issues of craft, but his determination to stick to the idea that black Americans viewed life from a distinctive cultural perspective, such as the blues, as he had pioneered with his reading of Richard Wright's *Black Boy*. Phillips later claimed that Ellison "believed and kept insisting that black experience is always distinct from white experience, and always shapes black thinking."[23] The Jewish intellectuals that Ellison knew, like Phillips, who had started out like him, writing for the Communist press, were unreceptive to the idea of black Americans having any access to cultural repositories that might shape their outlook. The liberals would accept them as much as they renounced their own ethnicity, more or less. But African Americans were ten times the number of American Jews and had had a formative, if historically obscure, impact on the United States since colonial times. Sometimes a black writer could also get a glimpse of something, in the space between their assimilation and their bitterness, that felt like a dynamo.

Despite the possibility, it was a hard problem, unforgiving to more than one writer. Ann Petry published her article on Harlem in a place that decidedly brought more money than either Ellison or Baldwin would earn. When *The Street* was published, Petry had been dismayed by Bucklin Moon's criticism that she might turn to "slicks," the glossy, high-paying newsstand magazines. But her article "Harlem" in *Holiday* in April 1949 seemed to bear out the warning. By the time she wrote the piece she faced a personal irony, the fact that she had profited so handsomely from her representation of black despair, a condition that she had only ever known at second hand. In May the New American Library would bring out the twenty-five-cent pocket edition of *The Street*, 425,000 copies of them.[24] With financial security to match her Connecticut pedigree, Petry had become an unlikely muckraker.

In "Harlem," her exposé that reached a broad national audience, she admitted the horror of Harlem life—one black-and-white photograph featured a stabbing victim laying in the gutter. But she steadied the account by adoring the glamour of Sugar Hill. Another picture showed the beloved jazz torch singer Billie Holiday having dinner with Booker T. Washington's granddaughter at Frazier's Dining Room. Petry's profound social conscience would not ring out in the midst of such balanced platitudes of balefulness and benevolence. Toward the end of her bird's-eye view of black life for the advertisement-laden, large-circulation magazine, she turned from treble to bass. Harlem's "thousand faces" finally merged into "the face of a ghetto." Writhing with discomfort, Petry concluded, "Harlem is an anachronism—shameful and unjustifiable, set down in the heart of the biggest, richest city in the world."[25] And yet the plea only cast a weak light on the deficiency. Publishing in a glossy venue where she was shorn of her documentary evidence and her moralist naturalism, she could not make a compelling case. Like the black leaders described in "Harlem Ghetto," Petry was in an impossible bind.

For the season, James Baldwin seemed a better bet. And the young writer would not disappoint readers in search of new material. Baldwin debuted in fiction in 1948 with the short story "Previous Condition," and it signaled a relationship with *Commentary* that Baldwin would eventually outgrow at the end of the 1950s, but which dominated his early years as an American writer. The term that Hurston introduced, "Pet Negro," is impolite, but still probably appropriate. Between 1948 and 1949 Baldwin published five major works in the journal. He continued to fulfill obligations for the *New Leader*, reviewing books and sending them the important essay "Journey to Atlanta," which condemned the presidential campaign of New Dealer Henry Wallace, a nationally recognized antiracist and proponent of social welfare. The young black writer gravitated to the polish and sophistication of *Commentary*, which opened even more doors for him.

In the 1960s Baldwin described this same period shortly before he left the United States as "terrible years," during which time particular journal editors had helped to "save" him.[26] Baldwin's curious attitude toward his extraordinary early success caused some of his peers to think him disingenuous, shrill, and obsessively dramatic. He was fond of telling supporters and friends, typically after he had failed to fulfill some sort of obligation, that he was having a nervous breakdown. In fact, in the midst of his breakthrough, immediately after winning a Rosenwald Fellowship, he fled from the open doors in the United States. *Partisan Review* was now asking for his work. He explained himself to the journal's coeditor William Phillips after he hopped an expensive airplane to Paris. At home in New York his work as the black critic of wonder had been so demanding that "I didn't know where I was or where I was going or what I wanted."[27] Baldwin's willingness to voice indecision and ever-wavering loyalty contributed to the remark made by Richard Wright, that he sensed behind the sentences he read "echoes of a kind of unmanly weeping," and that throughout Baldwin's work there was "a certain burden of apology for being a Negro."[28]

Baldwin reproduced the genuine degree of conflict over this issue of allegiances in the short story "Previous Condition." In the story, the protagonist Peter has just finished performing in a theater where he plays "an intellectual Uncle Tom."[29] But Peter's role of a racial traitor is not merely the entertainer's mask. Peter realizes that he must continually re-examine all of the characters he has mastered in order to survive: in moments of police danger he plays Sambo; with liberal friends he manipulates their sense of guilty obligation and makes himself a nuisance or an exotic. "I knew these things long before I realized that I knew them and in the beginning I used them, not knowing what I was doing. Then when I began to see it, I felt betrayed. I felt beaten as a person. I had no honest place to stand."[30]

Baldwin explored the problem that still lingers after the more obvious steps of racial integration have begun. His narrator pals with the liberal cutting edge among whites. His friends are "diverse" by contemporary standards: Jules Weissman is Jewish; his matronly lover Ida is "shanty Irish" and married to a gay man. The peak of the action occurs when Peter, evicted from a cheap room on account of his race, is unable to emotionally unburden himself to Ida and screams at her in a crowded white restaurant. They part and Peter goes uptown to Harlem, where, to the casual white observer, he seems to be in his place, but where he actually feels an alienation similar to one he faced downtown. He admits to the reader, "I didn't seem to have a place."

The short story concludes with Peter buying beer for a leathery Harlem whore. When he approaches her, he goes through the same emotional convulsions that he had felt steeling himself for an inevitable eviction by a white landlord from a rented room downtown. The story concludes as the barfly asks him to reveal himself and Peter still is unsure that she has the equipment to grasp the truth of his life. Obviously he fails to understand at the end of the story that the local prostitutes would have catered to a white trade and would thus have access to precisely the same bank of problems that he too must confront. Here of course was Baldwin's own struggle to understand the value of the black experience. He did not know enough in the 1940s to tout the wisdom of the black working class as he would in the 1960s. Where did his own obligations lay? In a sense, the Village had extended the space for his arrival to adulthood, yet it was no real haven, with its "Goth" toughs and landlords refusing to rent to blacks. He felt sharply the crisis of trying to make a life between two worlds, *New Leader*'s office and 132nd Street, both on Fifth Avenue, downtown and uptown.

Baldwin made his mark the next year with an essay called "Everybody's Protest Novel," after he followed Richard Wright and Beauford Delany to Paris. And he did it with this single work that Philip Rahv and William Phillips seem to have gotten into the right hands, a heartbreaking essay that wound up standing for the eradication of naturalism such as Wright, Chester Himes, Willard Motley, and Ann Petry had been known for. Baldwin came on like a fine game cock, and everybody loved to see spurs and feathers and blood. But the enduring sense of the essay as a gem of American literary history was different from what it meant in 1949. The real adversary in Baldwin's "Everybody's Protest Novel" was Edmund Wilson.

In November 1948 Wilson, the eminent dean of American cultural criticism, published an essay in the *New Yorker* making the case for the literary value of *Uncle Tom's Cabin.* Wilson, who had divorced Mary McCarthy in 1946, had just finished covering postwar Europe for the *New Yorker* (to the mixed approval of *Partisan Review* associate editor William Barrett) and writing the steamy novel *Memoirs of Hecate County.* He was a corpulent lady's man who reminded everyone physically of Herbert Hoover. Toward the end of the 1940s he had begun to prepare lectures on the Civil War that would become his major work of the 1950s, *Patriotic Gore.* The book offered examinations of three principal Americans of the Civil War era: Abraham Lincoln, Ulysses Grant, and Harriet Beecher Stowe. Stowe's chapter would begin the book.

Stowe, the nineteenth-century queen of literary protest fiction, was being raised up in the world. To begin with, Wilson was greatly disappointed that no one knew the book anymore: "One might grow up in the United States and never see a copy of the novel," he lamented.[31] Wilson, who was then reading the novel aloud to his young son Reuel, which certainly got back to Mary McCarthy, believed that while the book had some qualities that were "undistinguished" and it was "carelessly written," there had been a synergetic phenomenon: "the characters spring to life with a vitality that is all the more striking for the dullness of the prose that presents them." He called the book "eruptive" and a "throbbing breathing creation suddenly turned loose on the world." Finally he announced that Stowe possessed a "first-rate modern social intelligence" and that *Uncle Tom* was "not unworthy to be compared" with what Lionel Trilling had convinced American critics was the high mark of literary realism: E. M. Forster's *A Passage to India.* Wilson, after having been pleasurably impressed by Roi Ottley in Rome during the final months of World War II, was on his way to a new relationship with people of African descent, one that continued with travels to Haiti in 1949. It is possible to imagine James Baldwin reading the essay on his way to Paris and considering it middlebrow puffery.

Wilson's *New Yorker* essay could not have found favor among the *Partisan Review* crowd. Delmore Schwartz had published a review obliquely sniping at

Wilson called "The Writing of Edmund Wilson" in *Accent* in 1942, pointing out a formalist error that meant something to the New Critics. Schwartz described Wilson's understanding of literary form as "the wrapping paper which covers the gift."[32] Stanley Edgar Hyman, an occasional editor for the *New Yorker* and disciple of the critic of symbolic grammar Kenneth Burke, tried, not with complete success, to win the esteem of the *Partisan* critics by opening his 1948 book *The Armed Vision* with a deeply critical chapter on Wilson. For Hyman, Wilson was "at his best as an 'introductory critic'," a "translator" and "popularizer," whose criticism amounted to little more than plot summary and overtures to the author's biography.[33] Perhaps most damnable was Wilson's central contention that great art went hand in hand with the artist's suffering or disability, the "wound-and-bow" condition of the hero Philoctetes of Greek mythology. Hyman insisted that it was a poor "cliché of critical thought" to make "a general statement that the artist will naturally express what chiefly concerns him, his own suffering, or that art is a product of suffering."[34] Nor did Hyman evade the criticism of the man. Wilson used words like "nigger" and "darky" in his books of social reportage. And he cribbed, using "other men's researches and insights, sometimes without credit."[35] Wilson became the epitome in the late 1940s of the patrician critic, whose interest in plot, theme, and author was uncomfortable. On top of all this was the fact that Wilson was thought to have made an anti-Semitic slur against William Phillips and Philip Rahv. At the offices and cocktail parties of *Partisan Review* editorial staff, Rahv called him a "schmuck."[36]

Mary McCarthy must have contributed to the attitude of frustration toward Edmund Wilson, his approach, and, inevitably, what he represented. McCarthy had sojourned from the New York clique of writers and intellectuals around *Partisan Review* and *Commentary* during her years married to Wilson, but during the second half of the 1940s she would be making her way back, most conspicuously through a friendship with expatriate existentialist philosopher Hannah Arendt. McCarthy's fierce description and piercing analysis was taken even more seriously because she reconciled by way of frontal assault: the 1948 roman à clef *The Oasis*. In her witty and biting satire of the New York intellectuals, she struck hardest at her former beau Philip Rahv. Attractive, devilish, and whip smart, McCarthy kept the attentions of Baldwin's mentors through equal doses of affection and bitters. In the eyes of William Barrett, "there was no real break in his [Philip Rahv's] friendship with Miss McCarthy."[37] And if, as she claimed, McCarthy met James Baldwin at the Blue Ribbon in 1948, it was almost certainly orchestrated by William Phillips and Philip Rahv.

Rahv had a high estimate of Jim Baldwin, as he called him, and the estimate paid Baldwin enormous dividends. By the summer of 1948 Rahv, the strong half of the *Partisan Review* editorial team, who was in the process of helping to make the reputations of writers like Saul Bellow and Elizabeth Hardwick, fully matched the enthusiasm for Baldwin shown by Isaac Rosenfeld. In the greatest gesture of patronage a writer can know from an editor, he took Baldwin's inchoate novel "Crying Holy" to Random House. Rahv told the publisher that Baldwin was a genius, the most promising Negro writer of the twentieth century. The house reviewer Belle Becker disagreed and called the draft juvenile, tedious, self-involved, and sophomoric. Undeterred, Rahv argued up the chain of command for Baldwin—whose fiction he had not yet published—until, by October, more than 150 pages of Baldwin's draft had been read by both Robert N. Linscott and Albert Erskine, Faulkner's editor.[38]

The results were the same. "I agree with you that Baldwin has real promise," wrote Linscott after a conference with Albert Erskine, "but I don't think—frankly—that he has matured enough yet to write a novel."[39] The Random House editorial staff was quite cognizant of the power of the *Review*'s senior editor toward the end of the 1940s. Linscott affected a placating tone to Rahv: "I know you won't agree with this decision, but I still think that on the evidence presented any publisher would feel the same way, i.e., that even a modest advance would be too chancy a gamble to take on this particular evidence."

The olive branch made sense, and Rahv was aware of his own widening influence. In 1947 a wealthy philanthropist named Alan Dowling deposited enough money for *Partisan Review* to appear on a monthly basis, and the circulation promptly jumped up to 14,000, about six times what competitors like *Kenyon* and *Sewanee* were posting.[40] When Harvard historian and public policy analyst Arthur Schlesinger Jr. remarked that one of the *Review* sketches was having a renaissance in Washington in U.S. State Department circles, Rahv glowed back that "the pieces in it do get read by the right people."[41] Disregarding Baldwin's powerful backer, Random House advised the young author to remove the autobiographical narrator Johnny from the story and to deepen Gabriel's character, to really make it a novel about the ruin and redemption of the father.

Receiving the final bad news in mid-October after a summer-long buildup expecting to win an excellent book contract left Baldwin unsettled and at odds. He had the full attention of several prominent and influential critics. With his novel on hold, he promised William Phillips a critical essay. Unlike Rahv, an autodidact who probably admired Baldwin's nervy acquisition of a proper literary education, Phillips had graduated from City College and begun graduate work at NYU and Columbia. William Barrett and Delmore Schwartz were both trained professors, and all three men had considerably milder dispositions toward Marxism than Rahv. The academic side of *Partisan Review* helped suture the left-of-center politics to a more centrist and slightly new critical textual approach. Baldwin always claimed that the two American writers whom he grew up reading were Henry James and Edmund Wilson; he had certainly impressed critics with his knowledge of Henry James. But knowledge was not enough to steady him in New York. He left the country for France in November.

His decision to leave the country was an astounding confluence of factors like race; his competing sexual drives that seemed to be more homosexual than heterosexual; Calvinist-anchored Christianity; his struggle, like Peter in "Previous Condition," to get an adequate apartment; and then a condition that Baldwin tended to guard more closely than all of the others. It was chaos, what he called "the kind of violent, anarchic, hostility-breeding pattern of all my life."[42] Baldwin recognized that he had already internalized this hostility—"uncontrollable" and "with a power to kill"—and accepting the job he was being groomed for— the arbiter of the liberal American conscience concerning racial issues in the United States—disoriented him. In the eighteen months he had spent reviewing American literature and African American history in *New Leader*, *Nation*, and *Commentary* before leaving the United States, Baldwin had excitedly expressed an ever-increasing impatience at the very idea of a black cultural tradition. He suffered a mild resentment that *Commentary* wanted him to keep pushing open the Harlem angle, and he could suppose that his friends at *Partisan Review* would be after the same thing. All this was lurking behind his May 1949 apology to William Phillips for leaving the United States: "I did not know who I was and could not even be resigned because I had nothing to be resigned to."

But he figured it out and anchored himself, for the few months left in the 1940s and all of the 1950s, with a single piece of work. In the spring of 1949 in France in an English magazine called *Zero*, edited by Themostocles Hoetis, Baldwin published the essay "Everybody's Protest Novel." In May William Phillips wrote to Baldwin telling him that he would take the unusual step of reprinting the essay in June for *Partisan Review*. Baldwin, who had apparently written on his passport application that he was working as "Foreign Correspondent *Partisan Review*," had some explaining to do to Phillips, who assumed proprietary rights to the material.[43] Baldwin made peace with Phillips by saying that he felt "wildly flattered" to be reprinted, and he lightly explained away his conduct by saying that "*Zero* was here and you were there."[44] Then he asked if Phillips might ignore protocol and immediately air-mail the honorarium.

At work on several projects in the spring of 1949, Baldwin judged "Everybody's Protest Novel" a very minor work. Obviously he did not think much of the essay as a condemnation of the career of Richard Wright. On page 53 of *Zero*, Wright's "The Man Who Killed a Shadow" ended; "Everybody's Protest Novel" began on page 54. Baldwin and Hoetis knew that a mild controversy would help to push the English-language journal. As it turned out and to the intellectual friends and colleagues Baldwin had made up to that point in his life, "Everybody's Protest Novel" was considered the finest thing that he wrote in a career of forty years, and everything else that he wrote only served as an extended base to increase the stature of this single work.

In the essay, Baldwin countered Edmund Wilson measure for measure, jumping in with both feet by calling Stowe's book "a very bad novel." His criticism was doubly improbable, considering the racial dimension of the poor boy from Harlem's slum, having grown up in a house with essentially two books, *Uncle Tom's Cabin* and the Bible, taking on the Princeton-educated bona fide from Cowley's Lost Generation. But Baldwin fixed the book as only a clichéd aphorism, such as were hung in the Bowery's furnished rooms.

Mary McCarthy and Philip Rahv loom as the logical people standing behind the Baldwin essay and throwing darts at Wilson—whom McCarthy accused of emotional and physical abuse until the end of her life, and whom Rahv was also critiquing for having abandoned political struggle.[45] Wilson, who had taken Marxism seriously in *To the Finland Station*, and who had by then made friends with Haitian writer Philippe Thoby-Marcelin, fits neatly as the target of Baldwin's essay, the "sentimentalist" with "arid heart" who harbors a "secret and violent inhumanity." But more curious to literary historians than the negation of what Wilson had had to say about Stowe was Baldwin's gratuitous castigation of his patron Richard Wright—the man whom Baldwin had sought out in Greenwich Village and who helped him win the Eugene Saxton Prize. It would be many years before Baldwin found other successful black writers to whom he would be loyal; perhaps his famous example of loyalty to Black Panther Eldridge Cleaver owes something to the tensions in his friendship with Wright.

But the essay was, at least for young black Americans at majority-white colleges like Kenyon undergraduate Richard Gibson, a liberatory statement, a kind of "Blueprint for Negro Writing" breaking the ground for the Eisenhower 1950s. "Everybody's Protest Novel" would enter the pantheon of twentieth-century critical watersheds for African American literature, revelations that freed black writers from the clichés of the previous generation. When the essay was reprinted a third time, in the Lionel Trilling–edited winter 1953 issue of *Perspectives USA*, a quarterly funded by the Ford Foundation for overseas distribution, it made renewed international rounds. Living in Puerto Rico in 1955, the actor and Harlem novelist Julian Mayfield was given a copy by his neighbor, an "ultra modern" painter. "He thought I would be especially interested in an article in one of the issues contained having to do with the Negro (that much talked about Negro) in American literature," Mayfield wrote his good friend and agent John Henrik Clarke. To Mayfield, the essay was quite alert and unusually stern in its tone. "Am I right in my impression that Baldwin is a Negro?," Mayfield asked.[46]

The uncertainty about racial origin undoubtedly grew out of the crisp unsentimentality of "Everybody's Protest Novel." Indeed, Baldwin seems to use the essay as a primer for new criticism. To that end, the essay survived the worst gaffe possible for a formalist-minded critic, the intentional fallacy that proposes to read a novel's characters as no more than an extension of the author's personally held views. Baldwin's first move reduces Stowe's characters to mouthpieces: "Miss Ophelia, as we may suppose, was speaking for the author."[47] After a couple of pages, though, he recovered to present the esteemed characteristics of modern personality: "resolutely indefinable, unpredictable . . . disquieting[ly] complex. . . within this web of ambiguity, paradox, this hunger, danger, darkness."[48] This was the same catalog for writing used by Lionel Trilling in *The Liberal Imagination* and also by Cleanth Brooks in *The Well Wrought Urn*. But the essay gained its significance over the years chiefly by caretaking the new liberal piety of the 1950s. Social protest written by African American "futilitarians" like Chester Himes, Ann Petry, Curtis Lucas, Carl Offord, William Attaway, and Richard Wright was condemned as "raging, near paranoiac postscript[s]" that "actually reinforce . . . principles which activate the oppression they decry." When he went into the formal flaws of expression that might never be rescued by the urgency of content, he wrote like a well-trained Yale critic. And then, famously, the essay concluded with a machine-gun burst in the direction of Wright's *Native Son*.

Wright did not take the criticism well, partly because Baldwin seemed to misread deliberately the dialectical pattern of the novel that stresses the importance of choice as a requirement to gain human potential. Wright deliberately has Bigger negate Marxist dogma to derive his own indignant meaning. Baldwin had also managed to find both Stowe's and Wright's books "wildly improbable," though one was based on a slave narrative and the other on newspaper accounts.[49] What perhaps made Wright believe that Baldwin participated in a conspiracy to ruin his reputation was the onslaught against him from *Partisan Review*. A month after the journal reprinted "Everybody's Protest Novel," philosopher Sidney Hook belittled Wright by name in *Partisan Review* as an ignorant stooge for Sartre. This rare and unusual punishment was amplified because Hook did not even bother to take him seriously. During the Paris Peace Conference of 1949, a giant international event designed to ease the accelerating cold war tensions, Wright had supported a general criticism of the Western powers, but he disagreed with Paul Robeson (waffling badly on the issue of Italy regaining its African colonies), who had proposed that American blacks would not fight against communist military forces. Hook wrote in *Partisan Review* that Wright had "broken with Stalinism more on personal than political grounds," and that Wright had "no understanding" of the French scene. He suggested that Sartre exploited Wright "as a kind of club against American culture," and that Wright was dumb enough to be tickled.[50] Behind Hook's rhetoric, though, was an old canard: Negroes were insufficiently cerebral.

Prominent white writers and intellectuals voiced steady displeasure that Wright had developed an audience with the French Left and was held in esteem. They were irked by the fact the Simone de Beauvoir praised him and told them so when she visited New York and Chicago in 1947. Neither American thinkers of Hooks's ilk, nor writers making their debut in places like *Partisan Review*, had achieved a similar acceptance in international circles. Wright's apparent success also tended to contrast with the French reluctance to adopt American "liberal" ideals, especially the attitude that equated communism with totalitarianism. But for Wright, soon his entire body of work would be in for a wholesale reevaluation.

On the other hand, Wright's entire pose, from his capitulation in *Black Boy*, where he had removed the second half of the book that called into question the possibility of freedom in the American North, to his decision to remove his immediate family from the United States, did not seem politically or artistically robust to the young generation of artists and activists. Initially it was difficult for him to understand precisely what Baldwin's essay would do to his reputation in the United States, though he flared into more open anger regarding the situation toward the end of his life. In the 1950s, a period during which he actively published, Wright was not so much eclipsed as erased. He kept up with U.S. news from occasional contact with the best among the black intellectual crowd, like Ralph Ellison and St. Claire Drake. And he too took his turn to publish with *Encounter* magazine, a publication funded secretly by the new American Central Intelligence Agency. In America it was the era of the "Vital Center," Arthur Schlesinger Jr.'s mildly Orwellian lingo to suggest a "moderate" mass in the middle of the political spectrum that successful candidates for public office would woo to win office and of necessity temper their platforms to appeal to.

The multiple accounts of Baldwin's feuding with Richard Wright in Paris suggest that Baldwin may very well have been inclined to see the battle in Oedipal terms. And perhaps this must be understood within the context of his relationship with his own stepfather, a violent and unrepentant man, who seems to have left Baldwin with a model of mean response to provocation. Baldwin touched Wright lightly in his review, but enough to have indeed expected a ferocity of newsprint, an essay that stated for once and all the highly serious dimension of the black political novel purporting to rearrange society. Certainly Wright's work, alongside that of Redding, Attaway, Petry, and Himes, was durable enough to sustain the argument. But nothing ever came. Instead, in 1953 Baldwin's essay received more widespread release in *Perspectives U.S.A.* Although Thomas Sancton was no Lionel Trilling. It is extraordinary to consider the shift in ground among liberals between 1943 and 1953, from Thomas Sancton brokering Ralph Ellison to Lionel Trilling distributing James Baldwin. The movement from Ellison, who had believed in Wright's *Black Boy* so much he had invented a new category of analysis, the blues, to Baldwin, who began his career by recognizing social realism's historical validity only to reject social realism as an endeavor, was profound.

When James Baldwin had published "Previous Condition," *Commentary* had started to build him up, calling him "an important new talent on the literary scene." In 1949 they were saying that "James Baldwin has been called the most promising young Negro writer since Richard Wright." But another young black writer, three years younger than Baldwin even and also from a major American city, reached not inconsiderable literary success in 1948. William Gardner Smith published his novel *Last of the Conquerors* with Farrar, Straus in August. A Philadelphian, twenty-one-year-old Smith had served with the occupation army in Germany and written a novel that combined elements of wartime Europe with vividly detailed interracial romance. After eight months overseas, Smith started writing the book on the troopship back to the United States.

Published in August 1948, the book delivered the biting social commentary of an American GI who finds considerably more democratic freedom in old Nazi Germany than in the postwar United States Army. Mainly the book was an update of *A Farewell to Arms*, with private Hayes Dawkins as Frederick Henry and a young fräulein named Ilsa as Catherine Barkley. The *New York Times* noted the well-paced book, decried segregation in the army, and pointed to its fantastic romanticism, its "revealing example of the tendency of minority groups . . . to project themselves into a fantasy world in which they enjoy rights that are inherently, if not actually, theirs."[51] But this was all right for a Temple University junior who had written up police reports for *Pittsburgh Courier* at sixteen and shipped out for garrison duty in Germany out of high school. Smith had never joined the Communist Party, but he had been a Philadelphia civil rights crusader, leading demonstrations against police brutality up and down South Street. Some of the critics thought he had grabbed a fundamental achievement, the synthesis between realism and the modernist touch, to have properly balanced the struggle of individual will in a formidable or hostile environment. Blyden Jackson credited him with style, an "elegiac tone that Smith gets immediately and sustains admirably."[52] This talent seamlessly combined "conception and the capacity" and gave "just the right pitch" to the fundamental irony of black American life: that more freedom was available abroad than at home.

Another writer publishing a first novel in 1948 was the erstwhile editor of the vanguard, Dorothy West, who completed *The Living Is Easy*. West had abandoned New York for a small cottage on Martha's Vineyard, in the historic African American section called Oak Bluff. If she had published the book, set in Boston in the early 1910s, in the late 1930s, she might have had some attention, and if it had appeared before the end of the Harlem Renaissance, it might have splashed. But the novel, dedicated to the deteriorating relationship and fortune between Judson the "Banana King" of Boston, an ex-slave who had become prosperous, and his light-complexioned wife Cleo, who is determined to ruin him, seemed in tune with neither stories of dramatic freedom nor high aesthetics. Even West's ailing buddy Alain Locke admitted, in a sugary review, that the book "glosses over too superficially the real pathetic import of these drives, for the conflict of value loyalties in the middle-class Negro are matters of real and pathetic significance."[53] The white hipster Seymour Krim wrote the review for the *New York Times*. A regular customer of black flesh for sale in Harlem's bars, Krim found unusual criteria for admiring the novel. He praised the book's "abundant and special women's energy and beat. The beat is a deep one, and it often makes a man's seem puny."[54]

West was undoubtedly shrewd to have stuck with a portrait of middle-class life, because while James Baldwin believed that the average liberal whites and wrong-headed blacks shielded themselves from the profoundly individual reality of racism and injustice with the weak literature of protest, his colleague Anatole Broyard believed that it was the "inauthentic" and illegitimate black performance of everyday life that drove racism along. Born in New Orleans in 1920 and educated at Brooklyn College and the New School of Social Research, Broyard was considered a talent of the first rank. For a time, between 1950 and 1953, he was thought to have the greatest promise among the prose writers of his generation. A tall, light-complexioned man with straightish hair, Broyard was a card-carrying member of bohemia and had run a Greenwich Village bookshop immediately after the war. He looked like a keener-nosed version of Harold Jackman, the famous Harlem Renaissance beau from the 1920s. In 1948 Broyard wrote an essay touching on African American life for *Partisan Review*: "A Portrait of the Hipster." After a couple of warm-up exercises, about eighteen months later, he would plant another strike in *Commentary* that signaled his métier. That essay was called "The Inauthentic Negro." His first works were dramatic, cerebrally exciting, and with a streak of cruelty. In Broyard's long career of writing essays and short stories and reviews, these two essays would be his best; after them, Broyard himself would cease to be known as a black American.

Broyard was praised because he seemed to have suppressed all evidence of racial sentiment, but he never peacefully resolved his own racial identity. He was a dancer, jazz aficionado, and sexual athlete, but Broyard worried that these aptitudes made him unfit him for the intellectual life. Probably he also supposed that they exposed him as a black man since they were a catalog of capacities to which blacks were widely thought to excel. In addition, Broyard's understanding tended toward material reality, not abstractions, and he feared being associated with so-called primitive qualities. "I've always been rather literal-minded and it's one of the things I'm ashamed of," he confessed.[55] When a friend reported to Anatole that he was dying of leukemia, Broyard admitted to the "homeliness" and "sloppiness" of his improper sentiment. "My feelings had no style. To Saul, my sympathy would have seemed almost bestial, the disorderly impulse of a more primitive civilization."[56]

Broyard left Brooklyn for Greenwich Village in 1946, where, according to friends of his like the writer Chandler Brossard, he started, selectively at first, passing for white. He never acknowledged his racial identity in print, but he did offer tantalizing metaphors for what was taking place. "I was like an immigrant who goes from a poor country to a rich one and can't quite believe the new prosperity" was how he described the multiple transformations.[57] Milton Klonsky's critique that Chester Himes was deracinated did not apply to Broyard as a person, but it certainly suited his own postwar literary character.

Published after his death in 1990, Broyard's memoir of the mid-1940s New York literary scene split his life into two sections. On the surface of the narrative, the first section culminates with his ex-girlfriend Sheri Martinelli (called "Donatti" in the book) seeking out his family in Brooklyn. But what the memoir actually describes is the moment when Martinelli learns that Broyard is undeniably African American. By the time that the young critic—guest of literary figure and sexual connoisseur Anais Nin and buddy to Delmore Schwartz—reaches his parents' living room, he finds the former girlfriend on his mother's lap thumbing through old family albums filled with his brown-skinned relatives, images which incontrovertibly prove Broyard to be an "authentic Negro." Speaking literally about sunlight and film exposure, Broyard describes a moment the full significance of which his reader cannot understand without appreciating the fact that a white woman is visiting an African American family and learning for the first time that her lover is not white, but black. "The light in our family album was like the glare of truth," Broyard wrote in his memoir with characteristic double entendre.[58] Even nearly fifty years after the event, Broyard could not quite bring himself to reveal what was at stake.

In his criticism he sought to resolve the tension of blackness that haunted him. "The Portrait of the Hipster" brought to the pages of the *Partisan Review* its first work by an African American—whether criticism, short story, poem, book review, or letter from abroad—since the publication of Sterling Brown in October 1936, twelve years before. Delmore Schwartz accepted "Portrait of the Hipster" for publication, and the work was obviously drawn from Broyard's own extensive prowling along the margins between Harlem and the Village, Negro and bohemia. The exposure of the theme caused its author some misgivings. "I didn't want to be typecast as an aficionado of the primitive. I wanted to be a literary man, like them. I felt too primitive myself to be comfortable talking about the primitive."[59] Broyard proved adept and graceful at psychologizing others but not himself. Simple and plain, his fear was the classic anxiety of racial exposure. William

Barrett admired Broyard's talents and thought it sad that *Partisan Review* ultimately did so little with him; but it might have been that for Broyard the task at hand and places that he had to go for revelation were too difficult to visit.[60]

His portrait of the "hipster"—a fairly direct racial synecdoche for black urban men of the street corner—asserted that the homegrown hipster was the illegitimate child of the Lost Generation and brought urban American street culture to the journal's readers. The essay conceded that hipsters, and black culture by extension, had been capable of providing valuable insight into the human condition, but by the later 1940s jive-talking hipsters had become "pretentious poet laureate[s]" of a "bureaucratize[d] jive."[61] Even their famous appendage, marijuana, fostered "sentimental values" and led the hipster to the shoals of philosophical ruin.[62]

The essay was so vigorously critical that it drew blood all over the place. But Broyard wanted to do two things that did not quite jibe. He wanted to say that originally, even in the late 1920s and early 1930s, the hip pose had been ridiculous and a retreat from the field of action; it was, like the Negro himself, he seemed to say, always supercilious and trifling. Too much was made of the hipster by his critical friends who had little contact with the real. But then, he also wanted to low-rate the latest evolution of black urban music, bebop. Like Ralph Ellison, Broyard found bebop annoying. "[T]here was too much cuteness in jazz. It stammered and strained. It took its sentimentality for wisdom."[63] Of Charlie Parker, who along with Dizzy Gillespie was generally accepted as the acme of "hipster" style, Broyard snapped that he "found in Parker's style a hint of the garrulousness that would soon come over black culture." Apparently this was a kind of indirect payback. One evening around the same time that the essay appeared, Charlie Parker is said to have spotted Broyard traipsing through Washington Square Park. Parker said, "he's one of us but he doesn't want to admit he's one of us."[64]

So, for a short while, Broyard served as the jazz man for the inner circle of New York's leading critics of art, literature, and politics. He took the livelier of the *Partisan Review* editors, Delmore Schwartz, Clement Greenberg, and Dwight McDonald, uptown to experience jazz in its native element. He told them about witnessing murders and showed them how to handle showgirls. There were intellectual dividends, of a sort. Hipster intellectual Milton Klonsky asked Broyard to supply facts about jazz for the journal's April 1949 article "Along the Midway of Mass Culture," which exposed the degeneracy of artificial jazz music. Klonsky, who had considered Himes not charming enough, advanced an especially unsentimental perspective on race. He jumped in and out of the Village, to Paris, to the West Coast, back to the Village, a kind of brave of the avant-garde.

Klonsky's investigations were, like his review of Chester Himes, designed to separate out the high culture from the low, a vocation that also carried elements of cold ethnic rivalry. In another article for *Commentary*, "Greenwich Village: Decline and Fall, Bohemia's Age of Lead," Klonsky coupled the decline of Greenwich Village with the hipster communities that frequented the blocks below 14th Street. In the finale to the essay, he showed a kind of intimate disdain that became the hallmark of other young Jewish writers, some of them beats, some of them flashing tendencies in the 1950s that would enable a turn toward neoconservatism in the 1960s and 1970s.[65] In the essay, Klonsky describes an encounter with a black man.

> I saw him then as he came loping toward me, his face so flat and black I could hardly separate his features. "Give me some skin, man," he said, "I want you to dig some of this charge."
>
> Ah well, ah well, it was my friend Saggy, an old viper out of Harlem, always frantic, always high, the kind of tea-pusher who'd pull a hype on his own mother if he knew who she was. Under his sleeve his wrist was pocked with a thousand bites of the needle. . . . Then he lit up with a deep sigh of smoke and, as the image of the burning match flared upon his eyes, I saw in that sudden flash of insight that they were pitch-black! they had no whites![66]

The vignette operated as key to Klonsky's extreme liberal democratic attitude: he recognized a black acquaintance, a heroin addict, that no American black could afford to admit to—not even, or perhaps especially not, as a relative. But Klonsky's playfully surreal description edged along the border of mean caricature. The threat of black eyes without the whites was a wonderful metaphor for what black writers feared they lacked in hip smart circles of the literary crowd. Could they ever be white enough? The two main black writers who walked this path had enormous areas to be whitened. If Baldwin swore off fried chicken, watermelon, and blues music, Broyard evaded his own sisters and the people who knew him from his days at Brooklyn College. Both men had exchanged one kind of sentimentality for another.

Broyard was certainly game enough to keep trying. By 1950 when he appeared in *Commentary* it was to issue forth an essay-length frustration about black American life, well beyond Klonsky's motherless black viper. Broyard dismantled the idea of any sort of wholesome African American identity, and he did it using Sartre's work on Jews. Sartre, seeing Jewish identity as a religious preference and nothing else, claimed that the Jew's supposed ethnic identity was merely a reaction to the articulate prejudice of the racist. Broyard suggested that blackness was only an optic phenomenon, and that its perception by whites had caused blacks to build, psychologically, "layers of unreality" around themselves, and to indulge themselves in a series of "inversions." As a result, "the Negro" personality, so to speak, had been "virtually usurped."[67]

For Broyard, these inversions and rejections of reality took multiple classic forms: the minstrel pose (which included a sadistic acceptance of racism), the romantic attitude of flight into the exotic and primitive, and the attitude of beastlike rejection—not quite indignant rebellion—which Broyard summed up in a paraphrase of Shakespeare's Sonnet 121, "You might as well play the game as bear the name." Broyard proposed that blacks deliberately spoke broken English and tried to appear simian, and in the final pose of "role-inversion," they affected ridiculously meek attitudes, including highly effeminate homosexuality. Handily, Broyard managed to forget the favorite stereotype from American films like *Imitation of Life*, *Pinky*, and *Lost Boundaries*: the "tragic" mulatto.

The nearly twenty years separating Broyard from Sterling Brown's 1933 essay "The Negro as Seen by White Authors" appeared to be years of the climbing popularity of American liberalism, but less tolerance. Now a black critic was speaking before a large white audience. But his analysis no longer dwelt upon the formation of caricature and prejudice from within American literary culture. By 1950 an embedded journalist widely read in psychoanalysis delivered another kind of verdict. Instead of a warped or malignant American culture, black people and blackness itself had now become psychopathological. Certainly this made sense if the argument held that blacks were without tradition. Broyard was the critic-as-clinician and claimed to have observed disturbingly odd forms of behavior among blacks, on the street, in the nightclubs, and during the war. Myrdal had pressed America's whites to live up to the rhetoric of the Constitution. Broyard wanted blacks to comport themselves to the most basic standards of mental hygiene.

His prescription for mental health fitness was complicated by the ambiguity over the race of the sharp-minded author. For Broyard this was much more important than for Willard Motley or James Baldwin. His earliest *Commentary* article's first page had carried a note describing him as a person who knew "at first hand" the "situation of the American Negro."[68] This description was fascinating doublespeak that did not ultimately define him as a black American; it did not necessarily verify to the reader what the magazine's editors and the inner circle knew to be true. The distance that Broyard set up between himself and the subject at hand, like the first-person "we" Baldwin used, was an important pose because of the great suspicion that blacks were unable to remove themselves sufficiently from their racial pain to write competently. However, the editorial description was imperative because it certified the liberality of the magazine, which would not seek to slander Negroes by presenting the views of a writer without credentialed expertise. It was also unusual. Not until his fifth *Commentary* publication, "The Death of the Prophet" in March 1950, was James Baldwin racially identified, as "the most promising young Negro writer since Richard Wright."[69]

Though Richard Wright, George Schuyler, E. Franklin Frazier, and Horace Cayton all believed that there was little culturally distinctive about African American life, the younger modernists among the black writers, influenced by Langston Hughes, Sterling Brown, and Zora Neale Hurston, would stake a claim to the unique cultural provenance of black America. Like Baldwin, Broyard discounted the possibility of a "cultural residue" to which an African American might "secretly return."[70] Broyard was a Pacific war veteran, the limit of his international travel, and fundamentally a kind of patriot, a modernist who loved being considered by American elites. This conservative apprehension always prevented him from deigning to debate the issue out with other black writers, who seem not to have existed for him. Necessarily then, instead of debating published experts of black culture, Broyard took the contest elsewhere, to a dissatisfaction with white liberals. "Those whites who have attempted to take ameliorative action have been, for the most part, 'liberals,' or 'progressive' persons who usually do as much or more harm than good," he chided. Broyard was repeating Virginius Dabney in public and Horace Cayton in private. He was cunning but not moderate, analytically complex, but also an artful concealer, and, finally, not controversial at all. "Until the Negro defines his self, then, he's not going to get very far in formulating a program for living."[71] The genuine question that remained to be answered was to identify the location where the self-definition might occur. For Broyard, it would never exist, and he would not tempt fate and try to find it.

CHAPTER TWELVE

The Communist Dream of African American Modernism (1947–1950)

In the company of Thomas Sancton, Ralph Ellison did not taste success or notoriety in 1947. But six months after the special segregation issue of *Survey Graphic* appeared, Ellison did have on his taste buds both qualities. His short story called "The Invisible Man" appeared in Cyril Connolly's English journal *Horizon* in October 1947. Connolly, a pudgy, round-faced friend of George Orwell's was London's version of Edmund Wilson, and he had created a special issue discovering America for Europe. The English editor had traveled to New York in the fall of 1946 and, in the company of W. H. Auden, wandered the literate portions of the great metropolis completely unscathed by the war and asking whether or not the Yanks were coming with intellectual and cultural leadership to match the military and economic assistance they had provided during and after the war.

His American audiences gave him mouthfuls of negative appraisals. One of his guides explained the problem of producing culture in a land dominated by The Man in the Brooks Brothers Shirt. Connolly cared to salvage English pride; in his estimate, dilettante Americans had ambition and a work ethic, but they were not worldly or exuding savoir faire. "Intellectuals thus have to join political movements or attach themselves to causes or become dons for they cannot otherwise survive," he told the British readers. "They become over-serious . . . [and] the intellectual becomes uncivilized, a pedantic variation of the business man."[1] Citing the problems of a massive consumer industry and best-seller lists, and making the point that "stimulating material perfection over-excites the mind," Connolly more than intimated that orthodox commercialism—the widespread machine-age technology, radios, railroads, automobiles, paved roads for them to ride on, and hot running water—doomed America to remain an intellectual and cultural backwater.

He did not achieve the judgment by himself. Connolly had invited several essays by the *Partisan Review* circle—editors William Phillips and William Barrett and art critic Clement Greenberg—and by the French-born and Columbia University–reared cultural historian Jacques Barzun. All the cultural commentators dutifully noted the various American problems, especially the relentless pursuit of the "middlebrow"—the populist ethos that scorned an elite and blurred the distinctions between high art and consumer culture. When Saul

Bellow, the young Chicago author of *The Dangling Man* and *The Victim* (published by Vanguard that November), read the special issue, he thought it a thinly disguised "louse-up of American life."[2] Bellow, who was bordering on literary stardom, decided that one work stood out in the special issue: a short story by Ralph Ellison.

Oklahoma native Ralph Ellison had begun writing a new kind of fiction between 1944 and 1945. Alongside a peripatetic Richard Wright, he had left the Stalinist crowd and, by himself, given up reportage-style, problem-based social realism. In the process Ellison glued himself more fully to the symbolist doyen Kenneth Burke, the man whom Stanley Edgar Hyman, another close friend of Ellison's, had posed as the antidote to Edmund Wilson in the book *The Armed Vision*. By 1947 Ellison had something new under way. His short story, which was also reprinted in the 1948 edition of *Magazine of the Year*, was chock-full of deliberate symbols, presented in a manner that took the quotidian struggle for African American rights into the land of universal human struggle. In a show of erudition and humor, Ellison mulled over age-old concerns of alienation and the search for identity in the wilderness. To do it, he brought into black fiction a new kind of literary character. The hero was a middle-class striver, anxious, self-reflective, more on edge than he was hip.

But the anchor of Ellison's short story borrowed little from experimental semiotics. The story hung on the unusual connection between the teenage narrator and his ex-slave grandfather. "I'm told I take after him," says the narrator.[3] The grandfather, who leaves his family with a deathbed riddle, was the embodiment of Ellison's black mythic archetype, one part tragic-hero and the other part Brer Rabbit. "I want you to keep up the good fight," declares the grandfather, singeing his family with his final words. "I never told you, but our life is a war and I have been a traitor all my born days, a spy in the enemy's country, ever since I give up my gun back in the Reconstruction."[4] It was a new way to grasp a downtrodden generation with a beaten down past.

The meek grandfather seems to his family the perfect Uncle Tom. Dying, he counsels his son to enjoy resistance, to live with "his head in the lion's mouth"; then the grandfather redefines himself as a life-long revolutionary, a spy for another nation, and traitor to America for another country. Ellison was cryptic, ambiguous, and "high" modern, but he moved with elegance when he embraced the tradition of chattel slavery. Richard Wright had also written of an ex-slave grandfather, a former Union soldier, in *Black Boy*. Wright depicted a man embittered and on the fringes of his own family. Zora Neale Hurston had written of an ex-plantation concubine in *Their Eyes Were Watching God*, and the achievement of the modernist heroine at the book's conclusion was to decide that she "hated" her slave-born relative.[5] Ellison's broad move to reconnect the contemporary black generation to its slave-born grandparents was a reclamation of the first order, a profound spiritual rescue. The riddle effectively immortalized the grandfather and celebrated generations of enslaved Africans and their descendants, the people whom poet and new critic Donald Davidson had libeled as having no name. Ellison turned a disgraced tradition into a source of pride. In the death-bed riddle story, Ellison had created a twentieth-century companion to the Uncle Remus "Tar Baby" story, where the mythical trickster rabbit escapes by cunning to his home, the briar patch.

This was an unusual note to play. The better-educated Negro Americans on the whole seemed quite happy at the possibility of joining white America and on precisely the terms laid out by the schools of ethnic assimilation. A black Chicago writer named Alyce McComb stated rather baldly the mentality coming out from the colleges as the 1940s ended. To her mind, the collegians were attempting the trick of assimilation, and the first thing they wanted to do was wash off the antebellum dust. "For the Negro" to make the first important step toward joining the mainstream, she began, "it would mean rousing himself from the stupor into which he sunk, when, reduced to slavery, he lost that thing to which every human has a right—dignity." Of course a giant question remained. "Could he do it?"[6]

The inevitable linking of human dignity to the assimilation to "white" standards in the arts seemed to point backward to the nineteenth century. Vigilant observers responded to the position. Kenneth Clark, one of a handful of trained black psychologists, replied strongly to the inference that a reality of black degradation lay at the center of segregationist practice. "The problem is fundamentally a problem of the lack of maturity, the lack of integrity, the absence of intelligence, the greed and frustrations of the perpetrators of prejudice," Clark seethed in response, also carried in the pages of the *Reporter*. "It is they who must become assimilated into forward-thinking currents of mankind."[7] The old war was between Robert Park's assimilationist theory and Gunnar Myrdal's demand for strengthened American fidelity to national ideals. Where Ellison's new brand of thinking—the implicit understanding that there were prideful moments within degradation—raised its head was in Clark's aside. He suggested that the "refined" author McComb was probably suffering from "not a little racial self-contempt."

There were signs hinting at the coming transformation of the broad understanding of the black historical past. Sixty-eight year-old Carter G. Woodson was an acknowledged leader in the fight, though certainly his older and more celebrated colleague W.E.B. Du Bois had the impressive intellectual range and scored the public attention. But Woodson's steady leadership of the *Journal of Negro History* from 1916 had provided a forum to produce the alternate view to the U. B. Phillips "plantation" school of history. It was Phillips who had emphasized the paternal care extended by whites to docile yet barbaric blacks.

Woodson did not use the journal merely to cultivate black voices, like stand-outs Luther P. Jackson, Alrutheus Taylor, Lorenzo Greene, and Charles Wesley; the white contributors were also noteworthy in the field. One of them was Frederic Bancroft, who in 1931 published *Slave-Trading in the Old South*, a book that emphasized the economic profit from slavery and struck out against the legend of the plantation as an idyll for master and bondman. Ten years later contributor Frank Klingberg wrote *An Appraisal of the Negro in Colonial South Carolina*, another formidable redress of racist historiography. Perhaps most confrontationally, if obtusely for the layman, historian Richard Hofstadter published a reassessment of U. B. Phillips's sampling techniques in the journal in 1944. And throughout much of the 1940s, Marxist Herbert Aptheker produced sensational historical narratives of black rebellion against slavery, notably his Columbia University Ph.D. dissertation, published in 1943 as *American Negro Slave Revolts*.

The same year as Ellison's short story, another Oklahoma native and Harvard Ph.D. named John Hope Franklin updated Woodson's twentieth-century history of black Americans, *The Negro in Our History*. Franklin's popular history book was called *From Slavery to Freedom: A History of American Negroes*, and it devoted four chapters to black Americans' African ancestry. Carefully pointing to African antiquity, Franklin began the book with the sentence, "Egypt was an especially attractive land."[8] And as if to emphasize dramatically the difference between groups of blacks and their supporters, the most damning review that Franklin received came from another black writer. Arguing that the book would have been more appropriately titled "From Freedom to Slavery," James Baldwin called the work "top-heavy," "very nearly fatuous and persistently shallow," and "pallid and platitudinous."[9] Studded to E. Franklin Frazier's theory, Baldwin considered it impossible for American blacks to have or recover an ethnic cultural tradition.

While mandatory ethnic assimilation to a comfortably white American norm held the field at the heavily Jewish journals like *Commentary* and *Partisan Review*, growing numbers of educated blacks hoped for something a bit more complex. For example, in 1948 when Frank Yerby consolidated his stardom with *The Vixens*, a continuation of *Foxes of Harrow* into the Reconstruction era, he secured the praise of black critics. Waters Turpin, now teaching at Morgan State College in Baltimore, and Blyden Jackson, a Fisk College English professor nearing the completion of a University of Michigan Ph.D. degree, understood Yerby's books as an advance in craft and spreading the new consciousness, the end of stereotypes for both author *and* representations of the black character. Although Jackson called Yerby's performance in *Foxes* one of "vintriloquism" [*sic*] and "acculturation," he approved of the newly available plateau that Yerby benefited from, the "heritage of assurance." For eighty-five years or more, southern whites had a developed a "Golden Legend" convention of wistful romanticism concerning the antebellum era, and blacks had taken the opposite side of the debate, recalling the period as "a dark and bloody ground." Yerby had played it safe with his white characters and had eliminated "the voice of any Negro speaking as Negroes have been wont to think of the principals in the tragedy of American slavery." But instead of masquerade, this might be viewed as another sort of liberation, this time by way of appropriating "whiteness" and southern myth, and eliminating stereotype.[10]

The cultural philosophy and the history reached a peak in 1956, when Kenneth Stampp could begin his book *The Peculiar Institution* by supposing that "innately Negroes are, after all, only white men with black skins, nothing more, nothing less."[11] Stampp described the slave regime as brutal, severe, and avaricious, and *The Peculiar Institution* would finally overturn the U. B. Phillips history of slavery that had celebrated the plantation regime. This was an extraordinary sort of revolution since 1935 when W.E.B. Du Bois's *Black Reconstruction* had attempted to overthrow the Dunning School version of the postbellum era, and Stampp's ideal of "white men with black skins" reflected the turnaround of a national mood. But somewhere between the late 1940s and 1953, the presumption that blacks were merely whites in black skins—George Schuyler had used the name "lampblacked Anglo-Saxons" in 1926 to mean the same thing— would become a source of discomfort for black writers. Their "heritage of assurance" seemed to give them more confidence to chance an affirmative reflection into the era of enslavement, a reflection that steadily shifted their perspective on their American identity. J. Saunders Redding's admonition, that slavery was "not entirely a thing of odium," had found support.

The shift to appreciate black culture and history, and the idea that there might be a culture to appreciate after all, were part of the staying power of the redrawn Communist Party of the USA after the Second World War. But in the period of formal cold war acrimony, especially between 1946 and the launching in 1953 of Senator Joseph McCarthy's Permanent Subcommittee on Investigations, the Stalinist Left continued to thrive. In the roman à clef *The Man Who Cried I Am*, the African American novelist John A. Williams, a navy veteran and Syracuse University graduate, described the years following the Second World War as a mission by the Communist Party to recapture its leadership of black artists from the liberals. "Communists were coming back big, riding the coattails of the liberal organizations that were being born with the speed of rabbits fornicating against a stop watch."[12] Williams, who broke into the segregated New York publishing circle as an editor and circulation manager in the 1950s, wrote about the lives of men like Richard Wright, Chester Himes, and Ralph Ellison. And, with the end of the Rosenwald Fund, the long-spent government aid to writers programs, and the "Red Scare" at places like Yaddo, young black writers had fewer sources of support by the end of the decade. Liberals might have claimed Baldwin and Broyard and even Ellison, and the mainstream or corporate publishers certainly held fast to Frank Yerby and Willard Motley, but for unknown black writers, the Communist Party still cultivated the lion's share of the black talent.

The Communists were successful in reconstituting something of a formal black intelligentsia after the departure of their higher-profile black writers from the early 1940s. They had transformed from a revolutionary "party" trying to overthrow the government by peaceful means into the Communist Political Association, which operated in polite accord with the New Deal. When the European war wound down in 1945, ranking French Communist Party official Jacques Duclos wrote a letter challenging Earl Browder's decision to dissolve the CPUSA and collaborate with New Deal policies. Duclos operated with the approval of the Comintern. The slogan "Communism is twentieth-century Americanism" was no longer true. William Z. Foster returned to leadership of the CPUSA, and the former secretary's name became a noun used to codify the errors of collaborating with capitalism: "Browderism." James Ford lost his position as second in command, new blacks began to filter in, and the CPUSA returned to a more vigorous discussion of black national development.

The most prominent sign was a 1946 discussion article by thirty-year-old Claudia Jones, the highest-ranking African American woman in the party. An editor at the *Daily Worker* and an activist since the mid-1930s, Jones presented a nuanced revival of the self-determination thesis. Most important, she made the "special" case for a combined movement to defeat the barriers of racial segregation and yet maintain a place for "self-determination," which she did not link exclusively to national territory. She insisted that "integration cannot be considered a substitute for the right of self-determination. National liberation is not synonymous with integration, neither are the two concepts mutually exclusive."[13] Additionally, Jones was intrigued by the question of black culture. "Negro culture is part of the general stream of American culture," she suggested, "but it is a distinct current in that stream; it arose out of the special historical development and unique status of the Negro people."[14] Jones analogized the relation between American blacks and whites to the testy relationship between eighteenth-century American colonists and the British, who despite similarities of language and culture eventually mutually agreed to part ways. From there she felt able to draw attention to the specific nature of black traditions, the spirituals, work songs, literature, art, and dance. "No other people in American could have developed this culture," she asserted. The new rubric gestured again to the black nationalists, the artists, and the radicals.

At first, Communist organizing in the South picked up with the Southern Negro Youth Congress, an affiliate of the Negro National Congress, and bright young black people like Eagle Scout James Jackson joined up. The outspoken war veteran Harold Cruse signed on in 1946. A semi-orphan without pedigree of any sort other than his intellect and a slightly combative personal style, Cruse combined working-class origins in Virginia together with the distinctive cultural stamp of Harlem and the Village. His company of friends included the abstract painter Norman Lewis.

Novice writers like Cruse were drawn to the tangible opportunities at New York community institutions like Harlem's George Washington Carver School at 57 West 125th Street. Lodged between Seventh and Eighth avenues, the adult education center had opened in October 1943 under the support of Paul Robeson and socially conscious actor Canada Lee. Directed by former New Negro poet and Howard University art professor Gwendolyn Bennett, the Carver School received additional staffing by new arrivals to Harlem, like the radical labor intellectuals Louis Burnham, Ewart Guinier, and Edward Strong. Cruse greatly admired the Texas-born and Columbia University–educated Bennett. When he wrote a roman à clef in the late 1950s called "The Education of a Rebel," he described the analogous character Grace B. as having revolutionary commitments without any ideological baggage. She was "an unusually unorthodox Communist," "completely non-sectarian in her outlook," and "neither bureaucratic nor dogmatic."[15] Fifteen years older than Cruse, Bennett had once run a salon out of her Washington, D.C., home when she taught at Howard University in the 1920s. She had moved to New York and operated the Harlem Art Center during the WPA years, until being suspended after a House Un-American Activities Committee (HUAC) probe in 1941.[16] She worked on her advanced degree at NYU, became the founding director of the Carver School, and married a white English teacher named Richard Crosscup, who also volunteered at the school. More magnetizing than her friend Claude McKay, Bennett emitted a personal charm and charisma that had a profound impact in making Communist Party life attractive to Cruse.

At the time that Cruse became a regular, the journalist and army air force veteran Lloyd L. Brown took over the battle stations of far left-wing literary and cultural judgment concerning the Negro. Brown was biracial, and he had grown up in Minnesota where whites had considered themselves tolerant. He always remembered his primary school teacher reassuring the class after a fight prompted by racial epithets, "in God's eyes *all* children are white."[17] But such lessons were balanced by other kinds of academic experiences, such as another school Brown attended that was organized by the Young Communist League to teach Marxism-Leninism. By the 1930s Brown had become involved in the radical movement and was writing and working as a labor organizer in Pittsburgh.

The young activist's Pittsburgh years were characterized by the execution of a black union organizer named Willie Jones in 1941 after a coerced police confession.[18] Immediately after his military service ended in 1946, Brown moved to *New Masses* as a managing editor, where he quickly devoted himself to litera-ture. Like Ralph Ellison and Paul Robeson, Brown apparently never formally joined the Communist Party, though he happily referred to himself as "only one of thousands of Negro Communists."[19] The effects of the federal government repression and internal shakeup at the Communist Party showed when the twenty-two-year-old, middlebrow *New Masses* was folded together with the one year-old, highbrow quarterly arts journal *Mainstream* in 1948 to become *Masses & Mainstream* in an attempt to compete for a liberal audience and remain unha-rassed by government agencies. From the end of 1949 through 1952, years of profound black literary expression, Brown held one of the editorial desks at *Masses & Mainstream*, alongside Samuel Sillen and Charles Humboldt.

By the time Lloyd Brown became the Communist press's leading black critic, he was working mostly as a sniper, fighting a guerilla-style war that rarely pointed out even the direction of the courageous battle. Brown described him-self as in the process of tying together those intangibles, "My People and My Party," race and ideology. In a call to arms to defend Communist leaders jailed under the Smith Act and lynched Negroes like Isaiah Nixon, Brown hung a shaky ladder from communism to black American folkways. He tried to con-vince anyone who would listen that "the defense of the Communist Party and the precious truth that it teaches—Marxism-Leninism—and the liberation movement of my people are one and inseparable."[20] When called for, Brown played the role of propagandist.

Communist hopes for black artists in the second half of the 1940s were stated clearly and woodenly by Theodore Ward in *Mainstream* in 1947. Ward carried on in flush circumstances, for the first time, after the war. Despite the success of his first play, *Big White Fog*, in Chicago and New York, he had had to shine shoes during the war years to make a living. He had written an unsuccessful play about longshoremen called *Deliver the Goods* but had managed to land on his feet and get into courses with the Theater Guild, where he wrote the script *Our Lan'*, a play about the anguish and triumph of recently freed slaves on the Georgia coastal islands. *Our Lan'* ran successfully at the Henry Street Playhouse in the spring of 1947 and made it to Broadway, however briefly, as a serious Negro drama. Ward then took a Guggenheim Fellowship to Dartmouth Col-lege in 1948 to work on a long play about John Brown.

Moving into middle age, Ward dug his thumb into the eyes of his own crowd of black realist writers, especially his ex-friend Richard Wright, with the essay "Five Negro Novelists." An impractical and inflexible kind of criticism, the report dismissed every well-known black prose expert. In the analysis, the artist had no right to any freedom of vision whatsoever, especially not one that viewed the race issue as beyond solving. Novels needed to depict the "well known" characteristics

of the "Negro people": "the greatest courage and stability and capacity for progress despite the most limited opportunity."[21] Ward commanded black writers to
produce heroes. He advanced fundamentally the same position as the restrained
centrist liberals and the middlebrow moralists scared of pushing artistic or political boundaries. Ward's communist literary agenda sounded like Henry Seidel
Canby's booklist for the Book-of-the-Month Club and Harry Overstreet's guide-
line for black writing in Canby's *Saturday Review of Literature*.

Nor should the heroic narrative be too difficult to perceive. The Communists
were reluctant to publish the high modernism of adventurous black writers, like
Melvin B. Tolson, who still thought that the radical Left had an important role
to play. Near the time that Tolson had begun to draft the poetic statements that
would lead him to his famous *Libretto for Liberia*, he tried to publish in *Mainstream*. Editor Samuel Sillen was polite—"I am very anxious for you to appear
in our magazine"—but he still brushed him off. "My opinion is that you have
attempted to cram too much within the framework of this poem. As a result,
much of the language has a telescoped and obscure quality."[22] *Mainstream* was
committed to publishing unknown talent—even black underknown talent—
but it also required transparency. Here was a key place where the needs of a
mass movement for drastic economic change and the desires of artists seeking
to overcome systematic undereducation did not always mesh. Perplexingly, the
professionally radical Sillen tendered almost precisely the same criticism as Tolson would earn from J. Saunders Redding and the African American press.

The rejection of the black Marxist high modernist belied the queer problem
of applying political standards to the arts. *Masses & Mainstream* editor Lloyd
Brown himself never criticized the social realist work published by writers on
the outskirts of fame or distant from the major publishing houses. In other
words, the radical press itself did not beat the bushes to alert its public to black
writers working outside the mainstream or to books like Alger Adams's *Taffy* of
1950, which kept up the tradition of a protesting urban naturalism. *Taffy*, the
story of a gang-banging, rampaging Harlem boy whose parents were solidly
middle class, revealed such a startlingly negative black world that its author, a
minister and Hamilton College Phi Beta Kappa member named Alger Adams,
had to use the pseudonym Phillip B. Kaye on the jacket cover. To that work, the
criticism of the solidly middle-class J. Saunders Redding displayed more inclusive social-class instincts, insofar as he insisted on reading books by black authors, mighty and meek alike. By 1949 Redding was trotting along predictable
critical paths and decided that "Phillip B. Kaye tried to reproduce the terrible
Wrightian world of the city jungle," which meant he found the book superflu-
ous.[23] But nothing before Petry's *The Street* had so thoroughly indicted both the
unforgiving urban environment and striving for middle-class success as *Taffy*—
thus the proper place to showcase a leftist critique.

A prime example of an intellectual who found the principle of communism important but tried to shape the orthodoxy of party belief to the reality of black life in Harlem was Doxey Wilkerson. Professionally dapper and evincing a mannered brilliance, Wilkerson joined the CPUSA officially in 1945 after many years of active struggle on behalf of the working class and democracy. A native of Excelsior Springs, Kansas, and a graduate of the University of Kansas, Wilkerson had attended graduate school at New York University. He had served as an advisor to Roosevelt and on the staff of the Office of Price Administration. His credentials and expertise took him to the capstone of Negro education in the 1930s, Howard University, where he served in the education department, and staunchly opposed some of the regimented maneuvers of President Mordecai Johnson. He divided his time in the 1930s and early 1940s between his position as professor of education at Howard and his contributions to New York's radical political environment.

Always he earned respect as a man of principle and hard work. When the Daughters of the American Revolution refused Marian Anderson the use of Constitution Hall in Washington, D.C., Wilkerson headed the protest committee that produced one of the twentieth century's greatest public relations coups for the cause of black rights: Anderson sang before thousands on the steps of the Lincoln Memorial. Wilkerson worked to bring the union movement to college teachers, and he eventually served as the vice president of the American Federation of Teachers. His central work in the Communist Party began in 1943, when Wilkerson became the editor of Adam Clayton Powell's vehicle of mild protest in Harlem, *People's Voice*. But Powell's paper did not enable Wilkerson enough leeway to get at class issues. In short order the *Daily Worker* began carrying his weekly column.

Wilkerson kept expanding his commitments, and in 1944 he joined the faculty of the Jefferson School of Social Sciences, the big brother to the Carver School in Harlem and a thirteen-year-long experiment in Marxist courses and a radical collegiate curriculum. Wilkerson headed up the faculty and curriculum at the building on 575 Sixth Avenue. The night school, an "evening adult center for popular education," sometimes enrolled more than five thousand students, 75 percent of them women, in semester-long courses on American history, literature, the arts, languages, science, economics, and postwar planning.[24] Gwendolyn Bennett taught Jefferson's courses in painting and drawing. Columbia University historian Philip Foner offered the course on Women in American History, alongside other teachers like Herbert Aptheker and Communist cultural leader Alexander Trachtenburg. In 1945, a few months after he started teaching at the Jefferson School, Wilkerson accepted a position on the Communist Party's National Committee, after the party's top-to-bottom reorganization and reassertion of its mission to battle capitalism to the end.

During the same year as the extraordinary outpouring of social realists books, 1946–1947, the Jefferson School's enrollment surged to fourteen thousand.[25] Former Schomburg head librarian Lawrence Dunbar Reddick and Anatole Broyard both remembered the mid-1940s as a time when "Kafka was the rage," but the art and high-society crowd's interest in alienation, the perdurability of despair, and the facelessness of oppression had its source in the hyper social conscience in New York, which the protest novel and radical schools had a hand in creating.[26] Some people were put off from going to the Jefferson School. The young black surrealist poet Ted Joans, who from a seat on the downtown bus used to spot W.E.B. Du Bois going into the buildings during the 1950s, was afraid to go near. "[T]here was a rumor" making its way through the college crowd, Joans recalled, "that anybody who went into the 'Communist School' as Jefferson was called, would be photographed from across the street in a vacant warehouse where the FBI had a huge, eternally moving camera."[27] Jefferson definitely suffered during the purge years, and in the meantime another black Communist, William L. Patterson, joined its board. After Attorney General Tom Clarke listed the school as subversive in 1947, the enrollments steadily declined until the school closed in 1956.

Resourcefully procommunist for many years, Doxey Wilkerson had spent most of his career as an academic measuring the performance of black children in segregated schools, but he also took his writing on race and socialism seriously. Wilkerson both supported the CPUSA vigorously and conducted an independent intellectual life, a move of necessity during the era of Browder's defeat and the renewal of interest in black self-determination. At the same time he believed in racial integration as a successful policy. When Wilkerson looked at the history of the country and black social participation, he concluded that only an interracial formula might relieve inequality. He believed that, "in unity with powerful allies and aided by progressive economic trends, the Negro people have moved forward to greater freedom." Without liberal white support and when "confronted with reactionary political trends," he surmised, "the Negro people have been defeated in their struggles."[28]

Wilkerson believed in the value of the tightly organized Marxist politics of the Communist Party, but he did not overvalue discipline. He was helping to bend the CPUSA toward a program better fitted to black needs, and he criticized American Communists in the Communist journal *Political Affairs*. Wilkerson wrote that the Communist Party was too greatly distanced from the ongoing civil rights struggle of American blacks.[29] His work in the 1940s and 1950s sought to bring the CPUSA in closer relation to black American struggles. He had the bravery to take the Communist theorists to task.

Most significantly for the artists, in the field of culture Wilkerson decided that African Americans had a foundation that might be a valuable and potentially revolutionary asset. This perspective had been either grounded in or profoundly shaped by his participation in a group called the Council on African Affairs. Paul Robeson and W.E.B. Du Bois had organized the council in 1937 as a public advocacy and lobbying group within the United States for African nations, whose goals of political independence had been consistently and deliberately thwarted by the British, French, and American powers in the Atlantic Charter.

Between 1947 and 1949 Wilkerson played a role in two dramas that sharply weakened black leftist organizations in the United States. In March 1947 the National Negro Congress, then headed by Max Yergan, sponsored a conference at New York's Murray Hill Hotel to attack discrimination and the derogatory representations of blacks in the arts, literature, and film. In the early 1940s Yergan seemed totally faithful to the Communist line. He took over the presidency of the National Negro Congress from a communist-skeptical A. Philip Randolph in 1940 and silenced black northern activism during the war years. At the end of hostilities, Yergan made the congress an interracial organization. At the 1947 Murray Hill conference, Alain Locke and Lawrence Reddick gave addresses and chaired panels, but Fannie Hurst, also scheduled to give an address, decided to stir up some publicity by a last-minute boycott of the meeting. She told the press that while she supported an end to derogatory caricatures, she did not care to associate with such groups as the Negro National Congress, an "organization with motives that are unknown."[30] The Marxist novelist Henrietta Buckmaster stood her ground and countered that Hurst seemed willing to entertain those "responsible for the plight of the Negro" in attempting to avoid the label of Communist sympathizer. In a sense, the conference, but no longer the organization, was important. To boot, the National Negro Congress and the Southern Negro Youth Congress were now included on the attorney general's "subversive" list and neither would survive the year. The demise of the two organizations signaled the funeral of that rare bird combining black militant activists, labor, and left-wing politics.[31]

The subversive list itself was a death sentence for the National Negro Congress, but the single-handed scuttling effort of the soul-searching commander Max Yergan cannot be overlooked. Apparently, after the replacement of Earl Browder in 1945, the Marxist-Leninist floor gave way in the mind of Max Yergan; then he entrapped himself in a blackmail scheme and became the patsy of the FBI.[32] By 1947 Yergan had managed to purchase controlling interest in the Harlem newspaper People's Voice and then fired all its Communist staff. Yergan released longtime editor Doxey Wilkerson, the reporter Marvel Cooke, and the famous Hollywood actress Fredi Washington.[33] The paper closed its doors in 1948. Wilkerson attacked Yergan in the Daily Worker in December 1947, calling the new People's Voice an "Uncle Tom" paper "trying to make its peace with the red-baiting enemies of the Negro people."[34] Their brouhaha, in the climate of public accusation and insult, silenced an institution that had been weekly urban black news and a proving ground for Ann Petry and political cartoonist Ollie Harrington.

Yergan's business did not end with *People's Voice*. Threatened with prosecution for the crime of extortion, and later for perjury, he became a professional instrument for the FBI. In 1947 Yergan would spend most his time working on the Council on African Affairs, where he had been organizational secretary for several years, driving home his now familiar "nonsectarian" theme. In April 1948 he accused the familiar black antiwar New Yorkers—Wilkerson, former Howard University English professor, Communist, and editor of the journal *New Africa* Alphaeus Hunton, and Paul Robeson—of "using the council as a feeder for communist activities."[35] Yergan caucused among the black ministers on the council to eliminate the influence of the leftists. Two months later, he had Doxey Wilkerson arrested for trespassing at the council's office on 26th Street. Even though Yergan eventually was forced out, the council, Robeson's brainchild and Du Bois's sinecure, would implode as a result, silencing a black progressive voice for the decolonization of Africa.

For his part, Yergan was just hitting stride busting up the work of black political progressives. After leaving in ruins the National Negro Congress, *People's Voice*, and the Council on African Affairs, he would pitch a tent with the CIA-sponsored Committee for Cultural Freedom, his home during a 1950s filled with legal testimony against his old friends and former associates. By the 1960s Yergan would become the most widely recognized African American supporter of white supremacist and politically reactionary regimes in Congo, Angola, Rhodesia, and South Africa.[36] Several American blacks moved from the Left to the Right during the twentieth century, but no one matched the propulsive intensity of Max Yergan.

Yergan's National Negro Congress closed its doors by folding into the political action group the Civil Rights Congress under the leadership of lawyer William Patterson, author of the daring "We Charge Genocide" petition to the United Nations. To resume cultural duties among writers and artists, the CPUSA created a new cultural organization, focusing mainly on the theater. The Committee for the Negro in the Arts (CNA) produced plays between 1949 and 1953 out of the Club Baron at 132nd Street and Lenox Avenue. The CNA grew considerably more important after 1949 in Harlem when the somewhat independent, somewhat prestigious American Negro Theater (ANT) ceased to operate.

Founded in 1940 by black actor Frederick O'Neal and with Abram Hill as its director, the American Negro Theater had given opportunities to untried thespians like Sidney Poitier, Ossie Davis, Ruby Dee, and Harry Belafonte. The black theater's high point came early in the life of the outfit in 1944, when the adapted play *Anna Lucasta*, written by Philip Yordan and telling the tale of a prostitute's reform, made the long march from the basement of the Harlem branch of the public library to Broadway. On account of the success of this play starring Hilda Simms, which was about "people rather than about a race," the mocking, super liberal *New York Times* quipped, "Negro actors will not be required to wear zoot suits this year."[37] The victory was only partial. After *Anna Lucasta*, all the ANT productions were based on scripts written by white playwrights.[38]

A few years later, the Committee for the Negro in the Arts struggled with elements of the same condition: it had an interracial board and a stated goal of "the integration of the Negro artist into all forms of American culture on a dignified basis," but it did not exactly encourage black playwrights and would not generate a writers' workshop until 1951.[39] The Communist organizations were the earliest laboratories for interracial equality among writers in the United States, but their practical problem was unavoidable: if whites had considerable social advantage in the society, how could the two races operate on equal footing within an organization without specifically elevating blacks? And would the CPUSA have to privilege blacks from the middle class, who already had achieved a measure of equality, contradicting the vaunted aim of empowering the proletariat or peasant?

The CNA, led by Harlem arts activists Walter Christmas, Ernest Crichlow, and Ruth Jett, had strong ties to the other Communist institutions like the Carver School and the Jefferson School, magazines like *Masses & Mainstream*, and Robeson's next venture after the collapse of the Council on African Affairs, the newspaper *Freedom*. Like the Anti-Defamation League, the committee functioned at first as the watchdog of Negro portraiture on radio and television, but soon creative writers asserted their needs over the critics, and writers like Lloyd Brown, Alice Childress, Shirley Graham, and Theodore Ward took part. Quickly enough, the early leaders were followed by young people attaching themselves to the new organization, war veterans and college students like Rosa Guy, John Henrik Clarke, Julian Mayfield, John Oliver Killens, Loften Mitchell, William Branch, Lonnie Elder III, Douglas Turner Ward, and Lorraine Hansberry. These writers, actors, and playwrights turned out to comprise the pediment of the next generation.

A dynamic intellectual leader like Wilkerson meant something to the younger artists reviving the radical cultural movement, no longer a priority of cold war white liberals who were rejecting racial protest and black claims of ethnic heritage. Wilkerson extended his greatest influence among the Harlem writers for the 1949 essay "Negro Culture: Heritage or Weapon." His meditation on the African American cultural legacy and political ethics perked up the ears of the literature-and-arts set who were nonplussed by the presence of large numbers of whites directing Harlem cultural organizations. The essay fought its battle within the disciplined rhetoric of the Communist Party. For example, it followed Theodore Ward's 1947 argument and continued to portray Richard Wright as persona non grata. Wilkerson found Wright "self destructive" because he chose to investigate "unfathomable psychological mysteries" rather than material reality.[40]

But if Wilkerson tore down the famous black writer, he sustained Wright's 1930s version of black cultural formation: black folk culture was a suitable base for high art, and black Americans possessed a distinct national cultural tradition. "The Negro arts defy adequate and fundamental understanding unless they are viewed as expression of a *distinct people*," he warned his audience, "within the general population of the United States, reflecting their *special* relations to the society as a whole, giving expression to their *special* memories, traditions and aspirations."[41] A term like "Negro culture" was meaningless for Wilkerson unless the "relation to the development of Negro Americans as an increasingly organized, self-conscious political entity within the American scene" could be preserved.

His final point in the article returned completely to "Blueprint for Negro Writing." He wrote that black artists trying to show how universal they had become by writing novels and plays about whites "would do well to understand that the high road to his goal lies, not in self-negation, but in the full and honest interpretation of his own consciousness—through the expression of those memories, ideas, sentiments and aspirations which constitute the special psychological make-up of the Negro people."[42] Here was an argument for cultural distinctiveness, the antithesis of what black commentators at American high-brow journals were turning out.

The article was a whetstone for young Harlem writers like Benjamin Brown and Harold Cruse, frustrated members of the CNA. Deeply agitated, both men went to Benjamin Davis's office, determined to address the problem of white powerbrokers directing the arts groups in Harlem and black leadership refusing to take black folk culture seriously. According to Cruse, a reluctant Davis capitulated to their demand for help with an independent vehicle to collect black thought. The younger group organized the Harlem Writers Club, and Davis agreed to help them launch a journal, *Harlem Quarterly*.[43]

The Harlem Writers Club began as a workshop that convened at 180 West 135th Street. They were a combination of the engaged "non-Communist Left" and younger Communists in Harlem. Under the leadership of Benjamin Brown, a Texan with a college education from Morehouse, the club tried to gather alms and succor from the better-known writers. The endeavor was only briefly successful: after sweating it out with *Harlem Quarterly*, Brown would move to Brooklyn and become the militant head of a Congress of Racial Equality branch. Stumbling and scraping was inevitable for a young project reaching out for professional help. Brown asked a politically pressed Langston Hughes to serve as an editorial supervisor. Then, in February 1949, they announced themselves with a Negro History Week program at the Harlem YMCA's Little Theater. The Harlem Y was the black version of City College's lunchroom alcoves, a place where impassioned discussions of politics and the arts took place. In the late 1940s and 1950s Cruse hung out in a vibrant and gutsy milieu where "anybody that couldn't argue Marx or Engels was considered a goddamn dummy."[44]

Harold Cruse's participation in the club showed the Communist Party's unique position as a springboard into the professional New York arts world. Cruse had received an education in politics and life as a supply clerk in the army. In North Africa the Algerian profiteers targeted black troopers like Cruse to fuel the underground market in prime commodities, a cycle of commerce with colonial and racial implications that Cruse did not understand until partisans explained it to him when his division landed in Italy.[45] By the time he was demobilized in 1945, he knew so much about the world that he sought out the Communist Party. After a while, he was hired to run errands at the *Daily Worker*.

Cruse believed that the *Daily Worker*, especially in cultural matters like theater, was powerfully influential in New York in the 1940s and early 1950s and read by everyone, especially the drama critics at the *New York Times*. The *Daily Worker* offices were on the second floor of the famed Communist headquarters on East 12th Street, a stone's throw from Union Square, and calling on the intellectual atmosphere of both New York University and the bohemia of Greenwich Village. Cruse started there as a copyboy who ran menial errands, even though he was almost thirty years old. But Cruse took advantage of the job and learned copy editing, layout, design, and rewriting. He started hanging around the better reporters, like the star African American John Pittman, who headed a bureau or a "desk" and had turned down an opportunity to integrate a white daily because he refused to compromise his progressive politics. Cruse admired other reporters like Milton Howard, Alton Max, Joseph Starobin, Joseph Clark, Louis Mitchell, and David Platt. He worked there, through a series of ups and downs, for five years and in the process, relying on his irascible nature, turned himself into a critic.

His natural area for analysis was the spate of plays generated to resolve the racial dilemma. He thought he deserved Barnard Rubin's job as theater reviewer for the *Daily Worker* ever since the spring of 1949 when he had struck so hard at Kenneth White's play *Freight* he left a tattoo. Mainly Cruse pointed to the limited horizon of the black characters: "none of these Negro youth have their roots anywhere, no direction, no vista." Worse, Cruse found at least one scene "insulting to Negroes." The play would have aroused a "heated controversy if people were politically mobilized and alert on the Negro Question."[46] By the end of the decade, the "Negro Problem" of racial oppression had become a "Negro Question" of black ethnic identity.

Energetic, Cruse went forward with the typewriter. He censured the MGM film *King Solomon's Mines*, which he called a "dangerous bit of film poison" designed to flatter imperialism on the eve of African independence.[47] He challenged the elimination of black roles when the Broadway musical *Call Me Mister* went to Hollywood, and he saluted Josephine Baker, who had performed before American soldiers in North Africa.[48] After the Baker review, which glowed with enthusiasm for black culture, Cruse felt the "mumble of disapproval" from Benjamin Davis Jr., on his way to prison following his July 1951 conviction for violating the Smith Act.[49] When a nostalgic Broadway revived Marc Connelly's 1930 success *Green Pastures*, Cruse rang out against theater's "steady descent into the lower regions of barrenness and uncreative sterility."[50] And here again, he felt throttled by an orthodox Communist view from James E. Jackson, who had studied with Arthur P. Davis at Virginia Union, and who informed Cruse that he needed only a brief statement to show why the play should be banned, not a bibliography of black folklore. Communist bureaucrats did not want to stress ethnic deep structures or racial difference.

Though Cruse lived and worked downtown, his significant social and political life took place in Harlem. He and several of the others on *Harlem Quarterly* were plotting a path to black cultural nationalism. Unsurprisingly, then, they also asked for backing from W.E.B. Du Bois, a Marxist and a lifelong black vindicationist, now shorn from the NAACP and living and working independently in New York. But it was not quite Garveyism. They sought support from Communist historian and favorite from *New Masses*, *Mainstream*, and *Masses & Mainstream*, Herbert Aptheker. Jewish and a Brooklyn native, Aptheker's work was so uncompromising that, like Bucklin Moon, people regularly presumed that he was an African American. In turn, Aptheker would receive extraordinary allegiance from black peers.[51] The critic Lloyd Brown, who worked in the office alongside Aptheker at *Masses & Mainstream*, "loved him" for his uncompromising militancy against capitalism and white supremacy.[52]

The spirit bubbling up from the ground among Harlem writers was naturally working class and shaped by a rancor directed against the crude racism in the United States during the 1940s and 1950s. Dark-complexioned and gently disposed, John Henrik Clarke, a Union Springs, Alabama, native and army veteran, had long desired mainstream success as a creative writer. To clarify his desires to himself, Clarke had taken his middle name from Ibsen. But he seemed unable to resist explorations into the history of racial prejudice and Africa. Clarke had moved North in the early 1930s, in part to study at the League of American Writers School, but he wound up spending more time in the history clubs of Dr. Willis Huggins in Harlem and devouring the ancient civilization lectures of William Leo Hansberry, the great black classicist who was unable to find an American university qualified to award him a Ph.D.[53] But Clarke's closest and most formidable relationship was with the Puerto Rican bibliophile Arturo Schomburg, who personally guided Clarke along the contours of African history through its many international permutations. After four years in the service, Clarke returned to Harlem in 1945 to work for the Board of Education and at LaGuardia Airport, determined to finish his formal education. He enrolled at New York University, but the treatment of African topics in the history classes infuriated him. He spoke up and was thrown out of the lectures. In 1949 he published a volume of poetry, *Rebellion in Rhyme*, but he had little talent for poetry. More to his own interest were Aptheker's essays on slave revolts, probably the reason why he and Aptheker began a close friendship that lasted twenty years.

Others who helped get the club and *Harlem Quarterly* under way were uncompromising analysts of American life and culture. Virginia-born Ernest Kaiser, member of the Negro Publication Society alongside Angelo Herndon and Ralph Ellison, had served as an aide to Lawrence Dunbar Reddick at the Schomburg Library after 1945. A veteran of the City College classrooms during the highly political 1930s, Kaiser had read his first black history in Herbert Aptheker's radical pamphlets—but this did not prevent him from critiquing Aptheker.

Kaiser proved himself by way of a finely written piece of intellectual history for *Phylon* in the fall of 1948 called "Racial Dialectics," which emphasized the relation between schools of thought like the bobbin-style black liberalism of Horace Cayton and more consistent black radicals. Noting the reluctance to discuss the durable race prejudice of poor whites, Kaiser pointed out the flaws of the Marxist doctrine when applied to conditions in the United States. Also he recognized an inability to admit that the ghetto had caused grievous injury to blacks. He lanced the ailment affecting white scholars and even acknowledged the harm of friends like Aptheker: "both an idealization of the common people and a condescension to them."[54] In addition, for Kaiser and others trying to work their way out of an artistic cul-de-sac, the far left of black critics—Du Bois, Wilkerson, and the young Lloyd Brown—all represented the same failure: what amounted to nearly a refusal "to deal with Negro psychology."[55] Kaiser chastised the writers for their inadequate psychological depth when analyzing masses of blacks as the fundamental challenge for the writer and intellectual. And this was also a routine failure of Marxism, a reluctance to integrate the dilemma of social psychology and material reality. Here was the genuine cradle for the creative writer to entwine a politically informed literary naturalism with all the discoveries in narrating language and describing individual consciousness—in other words, of modernism.

By May 1949 the group was prepared to launch a journal, which Benjamin Brown believed "will take root and grow in the hearts of the people of our community, and, who knows, maybe later branch out into a national magazine."[56]

Langston Hughes, working on Broadway shows and the book of poems *Montage of a Dream Deferred* and experiencing a fine degree of success transforming the *Defender* stories of Jesse B. Semple into book form, agreed to help Brown (but not as an editor) because "I have long felt that our community has needed a good literary journal."[57] In the process of becoming an older statesman of the literary world, Hughes retained his determined resolve. In 1941 he had been listed as having belonged to as many as forty-nine Communist front organizations, more than any other American, and he would be called to testify before the McCarthy committee in March 1953.[58] But he still committed himself to helping launch the next generation.

In the first issue of *Harlem Quarterly*, Kaiser wrote out the rationale for an ethnic-centered community journal of art and politics. Once again, African American writers were exceptionally cognizant of the strides made in recovering the historical narrative. Kaiser applauded "the great contributions to Negro history made by white Marxist historians like Herbert Aptheker, James S. Allen and Philip S. Foner," but he believed that "the main job of digging up and chronicling the Negro past has been done by the Negro historians—Carter G. Woodson, W.E.B. Du Bois, Luther P. Jackson, John Hope Franklin, and all the others."[59] Kaiser wanted both to preserve the space for blacks working on black subjects and to encourage blacks versatile enough to write about white subjects, the proverbial and still uneasy two-step.

Harlem Quarterly's inaugural issue showed spark. John Henrik Clarke wrote a short story about the enormously popular figure for educated American blacks during the 1940s, Haiti's Toussaint L'Ouverture. Louise Jenkins contributed the poem "To Bigger," which tried to reconcile religious morality and environmental determinism. A Nigerian Ph.D. candidate, Reuben Udokwu, wrote an introduction to the different ethnic groups on the African continent, and Langston Hughes contributed a poem, "Corner Bar Speaks of War," emphasizing dismay at the First World War.

The magazine worked through the same vein of culture, arts, politics, and history as *Negro Quarterly*, but minus three of that journal's main attractions: a major figure like Richard Wright; well-known Communist writers and supporters; and, for that matter, any prominent whites connected to the magazine at all. *Harlem Quarterly* proposed to succeed on the strength of blacks in New York, several hundred thousand of them to be sure, the same group Richard Wright had derided in 1937, but who had now sent Adam Clayton Powell Jr. to the U.S. Congress. The *Harlem Quarterly* slogged on through two more numbers, and if it did not quite become distinguished, it did at least simmer. "We feel that not enough portrayals of Negro life and interracial relations have been reaching the American people," the editors wrote. "[W]e are opposed to stereotypes of the Negro or any segment of the world's population . . . [and] we will not publish such distortions."[60] Their intent was noble, particularly at the moment that the television version of the popular radio program *Amos 'N Andy* was being readied for American audiences, but too narrowly special for a significant body of readers. Most of the group would fold itself into Paul Robeson's paper *Freedom* and the Committee for the Negro in the Arts writers' workshop the following year.

When Ralph Ellison ran into the editorial group that included Brown, Cruse, and Kaiser, he was convinced that, though he was not publishing much, his commitment to leftist publications like *New Republic* or black-focused journals like *Negro Story* had come to an end. Ellison thought by then that the combination of clear-cut politics and what seemed to him like the clumsy aesthetic posture of so many of the writers on the journal would curdle the overall content. He fancied himself artistically and intellectually bigger than the Harlem provincials. He let off some steam in a letter to Richard Wright and lamented the inevitable rift between amateur writers who sincerely wanted to learn craft and the wily politicians, some of them Communists, seeking manpower or publicity for a hidden agenda. And he knew Wright would recognize the eternal dynamics of Harlem or of South Side Chicago, "the same old mammy-made provincialism, envy, and ignorance."[61]

Ellison was unwilling to gather the forces of Harlem's literati, as Wright had tried ten years earlier. He was disillusioned and tired of having to keep battling so hard for his convictions. When Ellison participated in the bull sessions at William Attaway's, Attaway puffed him up as vastly intellectual, more than Wright even, who had made his reputation as a man of scholarly pretension. The most politically strident personality among the Communists, Shirley Graham, apparently took these opportunities to heartily disparage Wright. But although he did not publish in *Harlem Quarterly* or strenuously engage the members of the club, Ellison admitted the deep need for its existence.

He felt the need because in 1949 Ellison, a professional writer who enjoyed telling the unpublished Harlem writers "I know how to make a living"—a combination of his writing and making stereo amplifiers—had a single published work, in *Reporter*, and only then because they were running a special issue called "The Negro Citizen."[62] *Reporter* began its twenty-year run as a "fortnightly of facts and ideas" that could take to the barricades against communism, but with aplomb and a commitment to intellectual standards. Editor Max Ascoli, an Italian-born refugee and dean at the New School in New York, wanted to provide something of a cultural and political accompaniment to the Marshall Plan. He would include friends, like Arthur Schlesinger Jr., and bring in American writers like Edmund Wilson, Mary McCarthy, and Alfred Kazin. Himself a Jew, Ascoli had an active interest in black rights and hoped to pilot the magazine usefully between the "laissez-faire" domestic attitude of the political center and what was being derided as the "professionally liberal" position of those further left.[63]

Ascoli considered Ralph Bunche, a Harvard Ph.D. from Los Angeles and the newly appointed U.S. envoy to the United Nations, the shining example of America's commitment to becoming a society where race carried no special significance. After running the magazine a few months, Ascoli lured away from media mogul Henry Luce's *Time* magazine the editor Philip Horton. Horton had heard through the grapevine that Bunche wanted to do an exposé, no holds barred, and he proposed a serial. Ascoli and Horton decided that 1949 was a ripe moment for a Negro issue of the new magazine. Then Horton came through with real brainstorming: they would publish "a substantial piece on the current spate of Hollywood films on the Negro problem." Horton told Ascoli to "get some vigorous, even aggressive young Negro writer of talent to do the job from the Negro viewpoint and in a completely outspoken fashion," which would combine "social significance and great publicity value."[64]

Horton had noticed the stunning about-face in American film, prompted by the NAACP and the motion picture branch of the Office of War Information, whereby some of the more profound American racial prohibitions were lifted overnight, by fiat.[65] Ascoli himself minded less the outspokenness of the black writer than he did the idea that the writer needed to forecast important developments in American society. "The Negro issue," he replied, needed to verify "a change in the Negro's condition and the way he is thought of."[66] Ralph Bunche did not find time to write for the magazine, but his profile was handled by his friend from Howard, Sterling Brown. Ascoli dug up Ralph Ellison to write the piece on Hollywood cinema.

Horton knew that the appearance of an aggressive piece might not only sell magazines, but he also participated in the broader international tussle against communism led by the U.S. State Department. The editorial in the special issue even disclosed the stakes, the "military balance of power in the world for decades to come."[67] The American government had "the urgent problem of winning friendship and cooperation" from a billion people in Southeast Asia and India, who "like the U.S. Negro, are colored." "To them, far more than Europeans, the status of the U.S. Negro is the touchstone by which to test our integrity and our intentions." This was the same logic that prompted the State Department to make something of Bunche, to send the Illinois Cook County state's attorney Edith Sampson on the 1949 Round-the-World Town Meeting Tour and then make her an alternate U.S. delegate to the U.N., and to send J. Saunders Redding to India in 1952, which produced his book *An American in India*.

Precisely the bull that Horton was after, Ellison turned out the most formidable essay he had published since 1945, "The Shadow and the Act." The essay combined hope with hard-headed skepticism as Ellison rummaged for something useful among the spate of groundbreaking films that year: *Pinky, Lost Boundaries, Home of the Brave,* and *Intruder in the Dust.* While he thought that perhaps the film adaptation of Faulkner's *Intruder in the Dust* might signal a shift in American racial consciousness, certainly the other "black" movies that tended to star white actors did not. This gaggle of 1949 Hollywood race-dramas was the first serious dramatic effort to engage the problem of black prejudice in America, and, unlike 1935's *Imitation of Life,* the films brought two African American men onto the screen: Juano Hernandez and James Edwards. The next year would inaugurate the most formidable black leading man for the next twenty years, Committee for the Negro in the Arts product Sidney Poitier, in two films, *Red Ball Express* and *No Way Out.*

But Ellison's essay drove home his trademark idea that white representations of blacks in American culture offered mainly a window to overlook the chaos of white libidinal repression and ethical conflict. The white-drawn black character, as a realistic representation of black life, offered nothing. As a result, black audiences broke into laughter during the moments of piety and sentiment in these Hollywood river cries. When Ellison's essay came out, he wrote a note of thanks to Albert Murray for showing the report to his classes at Tuskegee. Ellison admitted that mainly whites read his work, and "I'm afraid that won't do much good in the long run."[68] He attempted to rouse his friend Murray, who had completed a master's degree in English at NYU in 1948, to take advantage of the expansive publishing climate and send something to *Reporter.* Not two years later and near the time that his own fiction was about to appear there, Ellison would encourage Murray to send his work to *Partisan Review.* The implication from Ellison, who had traveled easily in Stalinist circles through the early 1940s, was that the liberal center had changed and now welcomed blacks. He thought that Eliot Cohen at *Commentary* might take some criticism from Murray because the magazine was coming to see that "something is not quite right with Baldwin and Broyard."[69] With irony and suggesting the absurd madness of the circumstance, Ellison seems to have believed that neither Broyard nor Baldwin was close enough to black people—their idiom, culture, and political struggle—while at the same time he wanted to establish a barrier between himself and other writers who were too close.

But Ellison could not have been more wrong in his prediction of the New York intellectual taste in black writers. If anything, the magazines and New York scene could not get enough of the two black New Yorkers, Baldwin and Broyard. In fact Murray might have been better served by sending something to *Harlem Quarterly,* which obviously Ellison thought Murray too good for. Neither the Harlem Writers Club nor the *Harlem Quarterly* officially survived past 1951. (Harold Cruse thought that Communists working in the CNA, like Shirley Graham, had orders to clip an autonomous black arts group.[70]) *Reporter* was not necessarily an open door either. After Sterling Brown and Ellison, the only other black to write articles for *Reporter* was James Baldwin, who published the reportage piece "A Negro in Paris" six months after Ellison's work appeared.

Never distant from his own personal angst, Baldwin portrayed black life in Paris as a contest of willed alienation—from other blacks. "In general, only Negro entertainers are able to maintain a useful and unquestioning comradeship with other Negroes," he told his audience, reassuring them that black Americans retained no racial identification. Baldwin asked for recognition that the black American was a "hybrid," not unlike the American whites themselves. Homiletically he concluded that though African Americans looked black, they were really whites, "bone of their bone, flesh of their flesh . . . he cannot deny them, nor can they ever be divorced."[71] After a year and needing money, Baldwin appeared again with a review of Roi Ottley's travelog about Italy during the last months of the war, *No Greener Pastures*. Baldwin had grace as a writer, but the work of his earliest years as a critic tended to reinforce a politics that wanted blacks to live up to a whiteness that it was proposed they could never be without.

Bucklin Moon published too in *Reporter* in 1949, fatigued at the end of ten years as a lone white man on the parapet of the race conflict. Moon wrote a general literary roundup that would have been better left to Ellison, Baldwin, or Communist Lloyd Brown. Trying to shore up his reputation against charges that he was more than a fellow traveler, he had to hit out against social realism by name. It also did not hurt to downplay the originality of black writers. "[W]hat usually defeats the Negro writer, I think, is the fact that under the existing American mores he is always, in essence, telling the same story," Moon offered.[72] The worn tale over-repeated was the one of racial protest. Although racial conditions did not show signs of dramatic improvement, the tradition of protest needed an editor. "There will always be a place for the Negro protest novel, but until it becomes the exception, rather than the rule, American literature will suffer along with the Negro artist." Moon's line of reasoning indicated that black writers might be too "worn" and bitter a group to succeed on their own.

Moon would not leave the 1940s with his racial zeal in tact. His final novel, *Without Magnolias*, another foray onto "social message" terrain, appeared in 1949, the year of a spat with Lillian Smith. For the book he won Doubleday's George Washington Carver Award for excellence in the field of race relations, an award that could never quite go to an African American for fiction. *Without Magnolias* revealed the circumstances perpetuating racial segregation and identified possible solutions within higher education, labor unions, and the nuclear family. Set in Florida, the novel describes the interrelated circumstances necessary for an entire community to awaken its social conscience and to attack public racial discrimination.

Without Magnolia's main characters are industrial worker Luther Mathews, his sisters Bessie and Alberta, his wife Eulia, and his mother Esther. With a book that featured several college graduates, Moon believed that he was doing the heavy lifting for his adopted race. He prided himself on having the "other Negroes" in his books, the middle class, the people absent from the "novels of pure protest" written in the aftermath of the Harlem Renaissance. At Double-day he sent an intraoffice memo to his salesmen saying, "No novel in the past fifteen years has brought them to life. I think I have done so."[73] His novel had created a diverse group of blacks benefiting from wartime prosperity and the industrialization of the South. Luther joins the union and becomes a represen-tative for a war plant. Alberta has fled to the North, pursued an education, and fallen in love with a married white man. Bessie has taken a degree at the local Negro college and now works as the president's secretary. The college setting held a place of importance particularly because it allowed Moon to stratify blacks by social class, showing the bevy of recognition dramas they faced with whites and each other in their attempts at self-definition.

In his efforts to stress the resilience of black southern culture and its ability to nurture black people, Moon understood himself as writing deliberate antipropa-ganda. He refused to appoint the southern environment as merely a nest of so-cial backwardness and psychological malaise. Reviewers liked Moon's "effective sympathy" as well as his "unobtrusively smooth narrative style"; unlike the ma-jority of "problem" novels, Moon could tell a "good story."[74] Of course, Moon had neither set out to write nor achieved a "problem novel." Similar to *The Darker Brother*, Moon stressed the black romance theme and featured three marriages: Luther to Eulia, Luther's mother Esther to Eulia's father Jeff, and Luther's sister Bessie to black University of Chicago–trained sociologist Eric Gardner.

The main dramatic effort of the book was to show an increasingly bolder black American, chiefly through Luther and Eric, who reject the paths of grad-ual progress taken by their elders. At the conclusion of the novel, the college president is asked by his local white supporters—the newspaper editor and the wealthy philanthropist—to rein in Eric, with sensitivity like Horace Cayton's, who writes a national editorial citing the use of the Hiroshima atomic bomb as an explicit example of racial prejudice against Asian people. This climactic mo-ment enables Moon's ultimate revelation: the black college president Rogers, who symbolizes black success prior to Word War II, has fundamentally com-promised his integrity by submitting to powerful whites. During the gradua-tion ceremony the president recognizes his own complicity with the Jim Crow regime. He has made himself the tool of "that good and true white man whom he had always looked upon as even more of a father than the black man from whose loins he had really sprung." President Rogers realizes he has sold not just his body, but his "mind, his loyalty, but most of all his personal integrity, so that forever he could be nothing but his owner's creature."[75] Despite his being a near sentimental novelist, Moon was yet convinced of the improbability of the black leadership from the first half of the twentieth century exhibiting the vigor to destroy Jim Crow, root and branch.

The future of black generations lay decidedly with the middle-class characters, who took over the second half of *Without Magnolias*. The one-armed war veteran George Rogers, son of the college president, the professor Eric Gardner from Washington, D.C., too radical for the college, and Bessie, the one character who through marriage and talent shows the possibility of upward class mobility, represent the vibrant hope. But these characters leave the South to their working-class relatives and to the black compromisers with white racism. While Moon's book avoided dramatic violence between the races and coasted along with a surface optimism, its underlying plot structure could only underscore that the author did not completely believe the narrative of racial progress.

Despite Moon's devoted work, his black friends were alert to the distinctive light touch in the novel, which portrayed racial friction as a declining phenomenon. When Horace Cayton reviewed *Without Magnolia*'s at the end of the decade, he admitted his disappointment because the book lacked fury. He made his column an open letter to the black audience about his good white friend Moon specifically, and the value of white liberals more generally. "So when I first read 'Without Magnolias,' I said to myself, why is this guy who's supposed to be such a great white liberal pulling his punches?," Cayton asked rhetorically. Then Cayton decided that the book was not written for him. The value of *Without Magnolias* lay in the fact that a white man had written it. "White people should read your book because they can't laugh it off. They can't say, this is just some Negro-lover trying to make money out of these current fad of books about 'the brother.' "[76]

All the liberals were turning away from discussion of race discrimination in the field of the arts. Charles Glicksberg now tartly advised that "[t]oo much Negro fiction and poetry is of an aggressive racial cast, dealing obsessively and often monotonously with the theme of racial discrimination."[77] By 1953 *Commentary* could afford to issue "Black and White Unite," a near-satire of misguided liberal beliefs that simultaneously poked holes in communism and in obsessive racial equality. Marvin Elkoff had pitch-perfect tone in his short story showing the ruin of the idealist white collegian attempting to work on the Harlem branch of the CPUSA, where he feels "his whiteness as criminal an evidence of guilt as the striped clothes of a convict."[78] The Communists were not so much to be feared for their evil conference as to be driven from the field for the childishness of their convictions.

In reality it was the end to the era of social realism. Moon's book of romance-and-flight reflected the dwindling political will of the white and black critical realist avant-garde to battle for the significance of the social realist books. Peril awaited those who continued to try, even Whites like Moon. His marriage collapsed at the end of the decade and he lost his job at Doubleday in 1951. He took a desk at *Colliers* magazine in 1952, but he was dismissed in April 1953 after being publicly denounced for his participation in Communist front groups like the Independent Committee. Virtually all the work Moon had accomplished in the 1940s could be linked to radical groups. And though he recovered and became an editor at Bobbs-Merrill by 1955, in the first years of the 1950s he attempted suicide.[79]

Moon's reviewer and friend Horace Cayton, who desperately believed in the value of the novel as the most effective means of spotlighting the black plight in the United States and as a laboratory for solutions, hit the rocky bottom of alcoholism and drug addiction. Whether he abandoned his wife and friends or they abandoned him is unclear, but Cayton moved to a basement in an apartment on Virginia Place in Brooklyn, selling his blood so that he could buy cheap wine. Given over to fits of mania and depression, Cayton gave an occasional lecture and kept up his weekly *Pittsburgh Courier* assignment. Once he wrote to Max Ascoli asking him for help in getting a job at the New School. But Cayton burned at both ends and never recaptured his old prominence.

The published novelist Chester Himes was also in New York as the forties ground into the fifties, separated from his wife, working as a custodian, watching televised professional wrestling, and getting by in dingy flats. Himes was barely holding on to a career as a professional writer by sending a publication or two to *Crisis*. Insofar as what he thought of Bucklin Moon and the value of white liberals shaping the 1940s, when it came time to write his memoirs, he totally removed the experience of working with his editor at Doubleday.

CHAPTER THIRTEEN

The Insinuating Poetics of the Mainstream (1949–1950)

The struggle for the meaning of black literature, its sense of its own heritage, and its connection to politics collided with the publics looking at poetry. Poetry may provide the most precise insight into language, but in the era of the Second World War it had fallen nearly complete victim to the prose novel in terms of appealing to the cultivated tastes of the mass audience. Book publishers like Harper and Doubleday dangled fiction and nonfiction book contracts before poets Gwendolyn Brooks and Sterling Brown, and the writers spent years trying to fulfill prose obligations that were not at the center of their artistic cores. In his lifetime Brown never published the book he was under contract for at Doubleday, *A Negro Looks at the South*. Brooks's turn to prose after *A Street in Bronzeville* was also curious, debilitating, and wounding. The sum of her experiences made her an advocate of craft. Brooks would say in 1950, after winning a place in history, "The Negro poet's most urgent duty, at present, is to polish his technique, his way of presenting his truths and his beauties, that these may be more insinuating, and, therefore, more overwhelming."[1] She implied that black poets still needed hip boots to wade through sentimental sewage before reaching genuine artistic truth. But in back of this was also a plea for each artist to remain true to the hub of his or her own primary expression. For Brooks that meant poetry.

Certainly her experience trying to prepare a novel for Harper had shaken her own confidence in the polish of her work, stoking the ever-present suspicion that she was preparing a series of pamphlets about racial injustice. At the end of January 1946, Brooks mailed to her editor Elizabeth Lawrence ten chapters of her planned novel "The American Family Brown." Even though Brooks was positioned to have her work ready in the central year for black social realist fiction, her publisher was impatient with her work. Harper told her flatly that the draft had too much in common with an earlier era. "[T]he incident and situation [are] too patently devised to demonstrate the social and economic aspects of Negro life, inter-race attitudes and relationships, racial discrimination, etc.," Lawrence wrote back in polite displeasure.[2] The details of black life and their prideful resolution had become et cetera with amazing speed. In 1946, the year that African American citizens in urban Georgia began to be able to register to

vote, it is not completely clear which elements of the "social and economic aspects of Negro life" were "patently" a part of American thinking. But many
liberal Americans considered the artist's role in the struggle of American race
relations about over. Brooks speedily revised, thanking her editor for "sympathetic reactions," and mailed back new work.[3] This was the pattern for eighteen
more months, until the end of September 1947, when the staff decided that the
book did not constitute a unified, dramatic whole and would not be published
by their house.

A key problem mulled over by the editorial staff before rejecting Brooks's
narrative work was that she was a Negro and they might have been thought
guilty of prejudice. But they shrugged off the guilty feeling. "About Gwendolyn
Brooks' job. That is a harder decision to make, not because I feel less certain that
we are right, after reading it, but because, under the circumstances, there is inevitably a tendency to lean over backwards to be fair. Which is, I suppose, an
even more insidious form of discrimination. The fact remains that if she were
not a Negro and if the book had come in perfectly cold, I know I wouldn't hesitate a minute to decline it."[4] The Harper personnel surrounding Lawrence took
on the attitude of proven pioneers in racial equality. What Brooks received
from the experience was a steady attention to a couple of vignettes that she later
included in the novel *Maud Martha*, which was what became of "The American
Family Brown." One of her readers at Harper wrote in the memo that the
sketches were "(by a colored girl, I think)" and then pronounced "If you're light
and have long hair" the gem of the collection.[5] This short story was obviously
what Lawrence had in mind when she told Brooks that, to her credit, she had
provided an "almost shocking revelation of the negro psychology."[6]

"If you're light and have long hair" described the misery of a brown-skinned
girl married to a light-complexioned husband. When she published it in her
book *Maud Martha* years later, the anecdote revolved around a young couple
at an all-Negro private ball. After watching her husband dance with a voluptuous alabaster-colored redhead, "white as a white," the heroine consoles herself by psychoanalyzing her spouse. "[I]t's my color that makes him mad . . . he
keeps looking at my color, which is like a wall. He has to jump over it in order
to meet and touch what I've got for him. He has to jump away up high in order
to see it. He gets awful tired of all that jumping."[7] Publishers had grown tired of
the sociological protest, but their ears had become quite keen for evidence of
intraracial discontent. It seemed like blacks taking on responsibility for their
condition.

The year 1949 produced one of the most detailed versions of blacks taking
responsibility for their condition in the form of a novel called *Alien Land* by air
force public relations officer Willard Savoy. Savoy wrote as if he were a staffer at
meetings of the newly formed American Committee for Cultural Freedom, and

they had approved him for a book contract to assert that blacks were patriotic Americans. A heart-wrenching novelist, Savoy proposed "passing" and exogamous marriage, if it was possible, as solutions for the racial problem, and he drubbed professional black racial uplifters as obsessive compulsives. (Anatole Broyard had described the same group as classically "inauthentic.") The improbable narrative was a love story that took all its cues from James Weldon Johnson's *Autobiography of an Ex-Colored Man*. Protagonist Kern Roberts imitates his own father and achieves marriage to a white woman but struggles with his remote black past. Savoy proved he was not soft on crime, by orchestrating several of the key dramatic episodes around Negro brutality: a wild D.C. Negro rapes and kills the hero's mother; Kern comes of age by stabbing another feral and belligerent working-class black man. The other peaks involved the shame of Kern Roberts's exposure as a Negro by a southerner at a northern resort and then the lynching of his uncle (by marriage) in the feudal South.

Because Savoy was the right color, sensitive-faced, and a military officer, the black press loved him for what he had achieved. And ignored the rest. They treated his protagonist's marriage to a white woman as advance and not treason; his angst and shame they believed justifiable on the basis of the circumstance. The professional black reviewers were caught between deposing one of their own and disavowing the book's elitist and assimilationist politics. Arna Bontemps granted that Savoy did not "wince at delicate matters."[8] In her *Saturday Review* treatment of the book, Ann Petry called *Alien Land* an "unusual comment on the whole subject of race relations," then she praised all the sections where Savoy had written about the darker-colored black working class.[9]

The lucrative postwar prose market thrived on black internal criticism. But Gwendolyn Brooks's awkward turning toward prose must have been especially painful for her because during the same time she experienced phenomenal recognition for her poetry. *Mademoiselle* magazine invited her to New York for the award of Ten Notable American Women in 1945. Brooks met Richard Wright (whom she did not know) in the office at Harper.[10] Then in 1946 she started taking prizes. She won a Guggenheim Fellowship, followed by grants from both the American Academy of Arts and Letters and the National Institute of Arts and Letters, a sequence topped off by another Guggenheim in 1947. If her prose nibbled, her poetry still ravished. While things fell apart in 1947, to the point of her editor Lawrence recommending that she try to sell the book "The American Family Brown" to another house, and Brooks effectively separating from her husband Henry Blakely, she returned to her first love, verse. She wanted to grapple with new, weightier ideas and denser, more thematically elliptical poetic lines. Brooks had always been skeptical of racial propaganda, but the bona fide advent of the New Criticism timed well with her artistic evolution—her movement away from the brief, stanza-length themes of *A Street in Bronzeville*.

The new critical close reading methods had grown in seriousness since the late 1930s publication of Brooks and Warren's *Understanding Poetry*. In 1949 Rene Wellek and Austin Warren produced the book *Theory of Literary Criticism* and suggested nearly a scientific terminology to reveal poetic import. Most consequentially, the new theories completely separated the author's avowed meaning and the emotional affect from the overall value of the work of art. The true measure of value lay in the technical craftsmanship of the poem. The tension of a poetic line jammed with contrasting or only sketchily connected ideas appealed perfectly to Brooks, who learned through study and native ability to enjamb the epic of African American life onto the complex syntax of the poetic line. She had sent out portions of the new poems to the Chicago-based magazine *Poetry*, Edwin Seaver's *Cross-Section*, her friend Fern Gayden's magazine *Negro Story*, and *Common Ground*. But nothing that she sent out indicated the broad book she had in mind with its protagonist called Hester. In 1948 she sent her manuscript with the new poem "The Hesteriad" to Elizabeth Lawrence, who promptly mailed it to professor and Harper poet Genevieve Taggard. After receiving the reader's report, Lawrence offered Brooks a conditional contract, smaller than the one she had received for *A Street in Bronzeville*. Harper changed the title to *Annie Allen*, but, unlike her foray into prose, Brooks changed very little else.

Annie Allen was a daring artistic performance for the 1940s because Gwendolyn Brooks cut away completely from the base of her audience. Black readers who had Baudelaire, T. S. Eliot, and Wallace Stevens on their shelves would have a fine appetite for the book, but how many were they? And Brooks had some reason, other than book sales, to suppose that she had not necessarily connected all that well with her audience in *A Street in Bronzeville*. After the "Hester Brown" contract had been proffered, she wrote to Langston Hughes and hoped to correct the controversy over *Bronzeville*'s "Ballad of Pearl May Lee," in which the bluesy heroine "cut [her] lungs with laughter" at the fate of her man, lynched after having consensual sex with a white woman.[11] Readers had not been prepared for a black female version of *If He Hollers Let Him Go* anymore than they had been ready for the male version. With a stanza devoted to sex between the races in a Buick, some people thought Brooks was advocating miscegenation, but instead she had wanted to sink her teeth into her major theme between 1945 and 1953. The poem's heroine Pearl May Lee was not criticizing or promoting mixed-race couples, but rather her "guiding anger" was directed at her "boyfriend's preference for light-colored women, of the *negro* race."[12] "Yellow was for to look at/Black for the famished to eat," Pearl remembers about her lover Sammy.[13] The white woman was "merely an incidental, an instrument"[14] to punish Sammy, who in the poem's refrain "had it coming surely."[15] Brooks wanted the possibility of pure emotion, existing outside of the well-known conventions that installed standards of white beauty, but they were hard to supersede in the

1940s. To write and invoke complexion and preference was an invitation for confusion and worse. Brooks could be an assimilationist or a black chauvinist, but picking through the middle in a dense poetic idiom was a guarantee to cut the black audience.

To drive home the implied reader for her new material, she dedicated the book to and began it with a memorial poem to Chicago critic Edward Bland, killed in an assault on German positions in the spring of 1945. J. Saunders Redding raised the issue of audience in a deeply textured essay on the black literary tradition in the 1949 *American Scholar*, Redding's occasional bench as the best-known Negro Phi Beta Kappa. "Three times this century," Redding offered, black literature "has been done nearly to death: once by indifference, once by opposition, and once by the unbounded enthusiasm of its well-meaning friends." Redding proposed, however, that the challenges Brooks faced, the "cultivated fears, ignorance, race-and-caste consciousness," were nearing an end. Revisiting his exact words about Richard Wright from 1947, Redding decided that Brooks could appeal to "two audiences without being either false to one or subservient to the other."[16] Brooks did not dress up squalor or seek assimilation, the two problems that Redding foresaw. But the distance between her formal expression and the black audience would be a frustration that took Brooks many years to resolve.

Annie Allen was a suite of three units: "Notes from the Childhood and the Girlhood," "The Anniad," and "The Womanhood." The book canvassed the life of one woman to show a semivaliant contending against poverty, prejudice, and lovelessness in America. In the middle section Brooks mockingly compared her heroine Annie to Virgil's hero Anaeus to emphasize the epic weight placed on marriage in the life of an American woman. The middle section was a tour de force of forty-three rhymed, six- and seven-line Chaucerian stanzas of iambic pentameter. No rhyme scheme was repeated, a suggestion from the reviewers to eliminate monotony. In the middle poem, Brooks explored the issue that had been the thematic thrust of "An American Family Brown." Brooks took on the issue of marriage between a black girl and a "tan man" who lumbers off to war and returns from the ravages of the battlefield yearning for extramarital sensual excitement. Linked to the struggle of marital intimacy operative during wartime was the issue of aesthetic beauty, Brooks's overriding concern. Eventually, toward the end of the 1960s, this preoccupation would lead her to deep sympathies with black cultural nationalism. But it was in *Annie Allen* that Brooks claimed her identity as a "daughter of the dusk" and explored her repressed fury at a social order that belittled women generally and degraded specifically brown-colored skin and tightly curled hair.[17] In a fell swoop Brooks extended the front line of politics to the question of standards of taste and beauty. It was the issue of aesthetics chiefly that caused Brooks's protagonist to devote years to "taming all that anger down."

"The Anniad" dismembered the idyll of conventional marriage, and in that way it registered a much broader criticism of the nature of American life than merely the problem of social, economic, and hygienic discrimination against blacks. Whatever the gains accomplished in the civil rights arena, the problems of Western society would always interfere. But it would be a mistake to consider the document merely an obliging overture toward the doctrine of universality. And despite her dense, modernist delivery, the heroine expressed unmistakable bitterness throughout the poem, a feeling of bile that never hid, never found resolution or transcendence. The frustration and anger in the poem always seemed to mock the bunting and delft—the "bijouterie" in Brooks's lexicon—of middle-class American life. Additionally, the heroine's marriage seemed to have the same odds against it as the flawed nuptials of "If you're light and have long hair." Brooks chose the perspective of the vulnerable black everywoman, from the working class and dreaming of upward mobility, and, like Petry's Lutie Johnson, possessing considerable quantities of chaste dignity.

But unlike Petry's heroine, Annie is not a declared beauty. Annie knows the feelings of anxiety and timidity because of her life at home, a household with grudging reserves of warmth and kindness. The poem described what happened to an "unembroidered brown" girl, with her "harvest buttoned in," who is enchanted by a "paladin," the mythic chivalrous man. The poem was also on determinedly sure symbolic modernist footing, as multiple stanzas used metaphors from decoration and jewelry to parallel the consummation of the sexual act and to show the Edenic fall from purity of young Annie. The marriage of Annie to the "tan man" at first merely sours but becomes humiliating after the return of the husband from war, when he "[h]unts a further fervor." The poem's second half is devoted to the husband's pursuit of extramarital carnal fulfillment, until there is a reconciliation at the end. The poem concludes with Annie, in the kitchenette building that Brooks had immortalized in *A Street in Bronzeville*, hugging nostalgia, soul kissing the "minuets of memory."

Because it was poetry and because she was a woman and in Chicago, there was only a dull roar when the book first arced out. The mainstream press was a little disappointed that Brooks had not emphasized more typical racial portraits. "When Miss Brooks forgets her social conscience and her Guggenheim Scholarship and writes out of her heart, out of her rich and living background, out of her very real talent, then she induces almost unbearable excitement," said the *New York Times*.[18] Paul Engle of the *Chicago Tribune* was more supportive— he had even taught Brooks in a summer session at Northwestern—but not very deep. Brooks had authored a "warming, humanly rich book."[19] One thing was certain. The ornate technical execution of *Annie Allen* vaulted the pitfall of overt concern with protesting racial conditions, a preoccupation that would have caused Brooks to be seen as a poet imposter.

If she daringly combated the beauty standards, Brooks hesitated to directly confront politics and addressed the crisis of civil rights directly in only a single poem. "I love those little booths at Benvenuti's" portrayed a black couple integrating a white restaurant. But the couple faces more trouble from their own psychological anxiety than from outward prejudice. A slight poem, "old laughter," detailed Brooks's thoughts about elements of her African heritage.

Her restraint confronting racial issues and her "sophistication of thought" brought her a most unusual credit: a review in *Sewanee*. Brooks was the second African American author to receive consideration from the journal published at the University of the South, the elite liberal arts college outside of Nashville. Fearing that it might abandon its agrarian credentials, the journal tentatively called *Annie Allen* "a book of undeniable charm," though the poems were too "hastily" braided together. Interestingly enough, the rather reluctant *Sewanee* sensed what was at the heart of things for Brooks and the other black writers wanting to explore the world given to them without wearing the brand of pamphleteer. "The reader feels at times also the burden of the author's attempt to come to terms with, and yet avoid, racial bias."[20] Another southern journal, *Virginia Quarterly Review*, seemed transformed in the eight years since the time it had celebrated *Mr. George's Joint* in 1941. In a review of multiple books of poetry put out by the best of the American press, the *Quarterly* said that Brooks had written the collection that merited "the greatest amount of aesthetic excitement."[21] Part of what Brooks seemed to have proven was that by demonstrating glittering technical skills, black authors would make white America take notice. Margaret Walker frankly told an audience in *Phylon* that *Annie Allen* was a "racial vindication." "[T]he Negro has finally achieved full status in the literary world as a poet."[22] This was an ironic point—that the triumph of black poets was ever conferred by white society. It likened Brooks's accomplishment to Phillis Wheatley's similar feat some 186 years earlier.

Afro-America's gatekeeper J. Saunders Redding took the opposite point of view on the work, concluding that Brooks should have said less to titillate critics and tried better to hold on to the audience. He compared the fineness of her accomplishment to a burnished Cellini sculpture, but whose delicate inner working went unnoticed. After reading the third stanza of the poem "Intermission" that began with the line, "Stand off, daughter of the dusk" and then ventured into a discussion of "bronzy lads" hurrying to "cream-yellow," Redding cried foul. "Who but another Negro can get the intimate feeling, the racially particular acceptance and rejection and the oblique bitterness of this?," he complained.[23]

Here Brooks had also been responding to encouragement from the editorial staff and, of course, Redding may have been personally embarrassed. With only occasional exception, such as Chester Himes, the black male contemporaries of Brooks who were writers or intellectuals married either white women or very light-colored black women, the same women featured regularly on the covers of *Crisis* and *Opportunity*. Critic Blyden Jackson called it "the tendency among Negroes for black men to stampede into marriage almost whenever any yellow girl says yes."[24] Brooks had called into question certain mechanisms of racial oppression that would ever be unaffected by direct legislation. And Redding responded instinctively. "[I]s not this penchant for coterie stuff—the special allusions, the highly special feeling derived from an even more special experience—that has brought poetry from the most highly regarded communicative skill to the least regarded? No one wants to read a psychological treatise whatever for that matter, in order to get at the meaning of a poem."[25] A critic who could be as antimodernist as he could be anticommunist, Redding was not being exactly honest. The elements of caste society that were being critiqued by the poem were simply still in place. An increasingly jaundiced Redding missed an opportunity to celebrate an artist who had accomplished a portion of his standard; she had not been "false to one or subservient to another."

And then the seas parted. In May 1950 it was announced that Gwendolyn Brooks had won the Joseph A. Pulitzer Prize for poetry. She was the first African American to win a Pulitzer Prize award, in any category, and she had beaten out both Robert Frost and William Carlos Williams in poetry. When *Holiday* magazine ran a feature on Chicago and "Bronzeville," its photographer captured a smiling if shy Gwendolyn Brooks in a studio room with the painter Eldzier Cortor. And yet, the reality was such that Brooks felt so pressed between 1946 and 1950, supporting herself and her son Henry, that in December 1949 she had accepted a job as secretary at the South Side Community Art Center. Julian Mayfield, the young New York actor, playwright, and member of the Committee for the Negro in the Arts, recalled meeting the famous black Chicago poet at the receptionist's desk.[26]

The awarding of one of America's paramount literary prizes to a young Negro woman did not occur with complete serenity. After Brooks had been recognized, a mild controversy took place. On May 13, 1950, *Saturday Review of Literature* published a "feeler" poll that listed the personal choices of well-known editors for the prizes. Called only a "writer of promise," Brooks was not selected as the winner. In fact her book received only a single first-place vote. The next year, the National Book Committee would set up its own award, the National Book Award, to be given by the most prominent writers and critics to pathbreaking new work and distinct from the moral criteria connected to the Pulitzer. But offering the most conspicuous literary prize to a female African American poet was a public relations coup for the international prestige of American liberalism. The grand prize also served notice that African Americans had little to gain by endorsing social protest linked to unseemly radical leftist politics. The introspective, obtuse, ambiguous approach was properly endorsed as the gateway to a new freedom. The ethos of universalism by way of idiomatic difficulty and "shocking revelation of negro psychology" had a marquise.

To welcome these new writings, a colloquy was held in the pages of *Phylon* at the end of 1950, called "The Negro in Literature: The Current Scene." It was a kind of assembly of the black talent in the room—a corralling that became nearly an obsession with New York intellectuals like Mary McCarthy, Norman Mailer, Saul Bellow, Norman Podhoretz, and Alfred Kazin—but the *Phylon* group did it without overtly bitter testimonials. One circumstance aided to control the level of acerbity. With the notable exceptions of William Gardner Smith's and Margaret Walker's essays, politics were taboo. Neither Richard Wright nor any of the publishing black Communists participated: not Eugene Holmes, Eugene Gordon, Doxey Wilkerson, nor Lloyd Brown. Of course it was safer to respond to the aesthetic challenges and differences in a manner remote or isolated from the recently defeated Progressive Party candidate Henry Wallace, W.E.B. Du Bois's growing affinity with communism, the public attack against Paul Robeson, the death-penalty trials of six black men accused of rape in Trenton, New Jersey, or the trial of seven black men for the crime of rape in Martinsville, Virginia.

Politics and the crisis in American life had provided an ignition key for twentieth-century critical movements, but especially the Lost Generation symbolists, the agrarian formalists, and the New York intellectuals. The twenty-one *Phylon* critics agreed on the basic assessment: black creative writing had developed promisingly, but it had not reached full maturity and it painfully lacked a critical tradition. The old man of the group, Alain Locke, never one to miss the changing winds of fashion, declared the paradigm shift away from the 1940s to the 1950s, by now describing *Native Son* as an epic in lost virtue. "I think all would agree that the first two chapters of *Native Son* had such quality, not to mention how and why the book as a whole lost these virtues as it became more involved in propagandist formulae."[27] Locke was implying that Wright had become a propagandist by suggesting that government intervention on behalf of the nation's citizens, particularly a formerly enslaved racial minority, was an important component of a modern liberal society. Locke's inference was clear: there was another form of insidious propaganda to resist, the propaganda of racial protest. Propaganda for the race was as dangerous a sin as propagandizing for a political point of view, and Wright, living abroad, would serve for ten years as the convenient scapegoat.

The danger of propaganda also seemed apparent to the youngest contributor, William Gardner Smith, whose second novel, *Anger at Innocence*, had been published that year. Smith had shrugged off the label of propagandist in the best possible way: his novel set in Philadelphia had no black characters. By the logic of 1950 this was a fine, nearly imperative, artistic decision, and it found an

opposing voice mainly in the work of J. Saunders Redding. Inspired in his opposition to propaganda, and claiming the philosophy of relativity, slashing
away at the notion of absolutes in morality and art, Smith followed along the
line of ripping a soggy tradition. "I have not read one Negro novel which has
truthfully represented the many-sided character of the Negro in American society today."[28] If Smith seemed only repeating shibboleths from the work of
Eugene Gordon, Richard Wright, Ralph Ellison, and Edward Bland, it was the
first time this had appeared in a black college publication, and at time when the
"Negro novel" was a genre piece written by more whites than blacks. His verdict brought swift accord. Gwendolyn Brooks scolded black poets for throwing
out raw ingredients to audiences instead of finished material. Blyden Jackson
called African American writing "too often execrable," then noted that when it
was not, such as with Robert Hayden's excellent "Middle Passage," the professional critics ignored the work.[29] *Phylon* and its black critics set a high bar
against racial sentimentality.

Interviewed by *Phylon* editors Carl Holman, N. P. Tillman, and Thomas Jarrett, Langston Hughes applauded blacks for writing about "non-Negro" themes.
The position was seconded by Hugh Gloster, who hoped the writers would not
"suppress . . . ethnic individuality" but rather "shun the cultural insularity that
results from racial preoccupation and Jim-Crow esthetics."[30] Gloster beheld a
tragedy where the black writers were loyal to stereotypes, produced a shallow
perception of the human condition, rendered their work humorlessly, failed to
contribute to the world of ideas, and bricked themselves into a publishing ghetto.
Thomas Jarrett hoped to see the very notion of any racial grouping eased from
view. He noted with approval that "the expression 'Negro literature' finds less
acceptance among intellectual circles than ever before."[31]

Sterling Brown's student Ulysses Lee identified the problem as a moribund
critical tradition, which he believed had not had any legs since the 1930s works
of Benjamin Brawley, Alain Locke, and Sterling Brown. "No one in the Forties
emerged to challenge the critical standing which Brawley, Brown, and Locke
had achieved by the mid-Thirties." Lee hoped to claim the modern critical
problem-solving methods of the New Criticism as opposed to the catalogs of
achievement and loose biographical and bibliographical data that had characterized "criticism" of the turn of the century. He correctly noted that in the
more recent works of Nick Aaron Ford, J. Saunders Redding, and Hugh Gloster
there was not much more than plot summary and a sentence or two of critical
comment. But then the social condition yet intervened against "receiving and
transmitting ideas and standards," the basic activity of a critical tradition. The
black college professors were "too busy as teachers and missionaries," and having to judge art "less as literature than as new evidence of advance and achievement, to be shared and gloried in."[32]

And if Lee did make his reader aware of the psychologically bracing new critical work of Ralph Ellison in *Antioch Review* and *Reporter*, he neglected James Baldwin, Lloyd Brown, and Anatole Broyard, and white critics like Glicksberg and Sancton. Alain Locke commented on the intellectual development and saw more of a total problem. "The Negro intellectual is still largely in psychological bondage," he said, afraid of "breaking the taboos of Puritanism, Philistinism and falsely conceived conventions of 'race respectability'. Consciously and subconsciously, these conventions work great artistic harm, especially the fear of being accused of group disloyalty and 'misrepresentation' in portraying the full gamut of Negro type."[33] Clipping away ties to respectable group loyalty was precisely the forte of the blacks connected to *Partisan Review* and *Commentary*.

Margaret Walker, working at Jackson State Teacher's College in Mississippi, alerted the crowd to the reality behind the push for high modernism and New Criticism. She saw the gigantic turn toward the complex literary expression of Gwendolyn Brooks as an example of a "religious revival," the defense mechanism of Western society struggling against the threat of atomic annihilation. Noting the stampede of high modernist poets T. S. Eliot and Robert Lowell to orthodox Catholicism, and spiced by Lowell's psychopathic tirade to rid the artists' colony at Yaddo of Communists in 1949, Walker recognized a combination of "fear and hysteria" and the "desire for inner self-analysis, reflection and introspective knowledge that may lead, thereby, to a spiritual panacea."[34]

Sounding like no one other than her Mississippi beau Richard Wright, she wrote, "[w]hether to Catholicism, Existentialism, or Communism, modern man is turning to some definite belief around which to integrate his life and give it true wholeness and meaning." Walker called the emphasis on difficulty, ambiguity, and formal qualities a resurgence of the Augustan era's devotion to neo-classicism. She also prophesied a danger, a tendency "toward intellectual themes of psychological and philosophical implication which border on obscurantism."[35] Obscure reference and the slackening of racial prejudice had even more consequence. The impact of the special issues of *Survey, New Republic*, and *Reporter*, the desire for black writers to try their hand at depicting white American characters, all of this culminated in increasing reliance on the opinions of white critical venues, like *Sewanee*, to point out a standard of excellence. Obviously some writers would thrive under these conditions, but others, even some very dear to black audiences and black critics, would disappear.

Not all the critics agreed with Locke and believed that the work of propaganda had been completed. Nick Aaron Ford, Morgan State College English department chairman, acknowledged that at least there was a debate. For whatever vagary of circumstance, he continued to be concerned with addressing prejudice as it existed. In 1941 Ford had told a group of reluctant black educators that

Native Son had "done more to plead the cause of the underprivileged Negro than anything since Harriet Beecher Stowe's *Uncle Tom's Cabin*." Ford believed all that was necessary to "revolutionize America's treatment of the Negro within a decade" was "two or three more novels with the power and significance of *Native Son*."[36] By 1950 Ford was still awaiting *Native Son*'s worthy companions.

Ford's talent and hard work should have enabled him to produce a first-class work of criticism, but his own career points out that even as the barriers to racial segregation fell, the black intelligentsia struggled to hurdle the legacy of racial discrimination. A rare figure in 1940s literary circles, dark hued and manly featured, Ford could credit his appearance and his own unwillingness to amuse whites or genuflect at the shrine of Western culture for some of his slight success. He had spent his early years in rural South Carolina, and his parents had been slaves. Ford was prideful of his ancestry and diligent. His family had managed well during the Reconstruction era, though after the death of his father Ford had put himself through school unaided. In 1936 he paid the Boston vanity press Meador several hundred dollars to have his master's thesis, *The Negro Novel*, printed, bound, and made available in its catalog. Ford saw the book and its self-publication as a sacrifice, a component of his own personal mission. He dedicated his life to destroying what he called "this monster—Race Prejudice."[37]

In the thesis he had compiled the facts on black novelists as a combination of political and ethical duty, "to spread Truth and Good-will in behalf of millions of oppressed souls." He went on to finish his Ph.D. degree in literature at the University of Iowa in 1946, where Austin Warren, the famed new critic, was his major advisor. (Ford described his relationship with the bantam Warren as congenial, and one that reversed the traditional teacher–student role.)[38] In the fall of 1946, partly because of the immediate seniority he had from having finished his terminal degree, he assumed the chairmanship of the department at Morgan. He wanted to see America properly reformed to incorporate black achievement.

This was not the conservative position in an era when black critics were experts in Elizabethan drama and the British romantic poets. At a conference of Negro teachers in the early 1940s, Ford had faced shock and derision at the idea of offering a course in black literature. To himself, he called these colleagues "dead fossils of a lost generation."[39] Since the early 1930s Ford had been offering year-long courses in African American literature, constructing a syllabus from writers like Phillis Wheatley, Frederick Douglass, James Weldon Johnson, and W.E.B. Du Bois that remains current. His idea about the value of black literature was news to many of his black colleagues, who taught their American literature courses with state-issued materials that regularly ignored any black contributions in literature and history. When the same colleagues knocked the application of fiction and poetry to stem enormous social problems that seemed, at least on the surface, more fully answered by social science, Ford maintained that "the modern novel has done more to focus the attention of the American people upon certain evils in our civilization than any other type of literary production."[40] He understood that *Native Son* cut two ways. It could be both "favorable to the race" and "constructing a Frankenstein which perverts the very devices he uses to win his audience into cudgels of destruction."[41]

Ford wanted blacks to comprise the vanguard in the spread of what he was certain was the viable entity black literature. But he also helped to prime the intellectual practices necessary at the dawn of an interracial society. He made use of the American canon in his scholarship. He placed an essay in *New England Quarterly* in September 1946 called "Henry David Thoreau, Abolitionist" that challenged the assertion by Thoreau biographer Henry Seidel Canby that Thoreau should not be considered a genuine advocate of abolitionism. Intentionally or not, Canby was working to swing the American tradition in literature and history toward the consensus of liberal moderation: radical extremes like abolitionism—and communism—were thought unbecoming for central figures. Arthur Schlesinger Jr. had done the same thing with his work on Andrew Jackson that eliminated both slavery and Indian removal from Jackson's vaunted democracy of the common man.

Ford looked through Thoreau's fourteen volumes of journals and the evidence of his contemporaries to educe a strong pattern of abolitionist practices, including physically assisting runaways and holding rallies to support the actions of John Brown. This was not precisely a new dimension for black critics, but it was one where they had seen virtually no publishing in predominantly white journals and magazines. A couple of years later, Ford investigated Walt Whitman's *Democratic Vistas* to determine that famous poet's sense of democratic rights, the eternal tension between the rights of the individual and those of the mass. In that paper Ford liked noting the fact that Whitman had resigned his job at the *Brooklyn Eagle* on account of his beliefs as a "free-soil democrat."

Indeed, studies of British and American dissenters—abolitionists, free-soilers, satirists like Jonathan Swift and Mark Twain, Irish nationalists like Yeats—were abundant and complementary areas for African American critics to ground a series of critical protocols. Ford had the proper frame of mind. He was one of the first to write criticism of both African- and European-descended American writers. However, his education and exposure onboard the raft of segregation could carry him but so far. When his contemporary Ralph Ellison published a review of John Beecher in *New Republic* in 1946, he showed a concord of interest with Ford but wielded a critical instrument that did not hesitate to draw blood. The problem with the new liberals, and their older forbearers, Ellison thought, was an inability for "sustained thought and organized action"; furthermore, liberals "feel right but lapse into self-interest."[42] Ford was prepared to criticize Hurston for her political failings and pull white liberals under the canopy of combined interest, but he was not prepared to enumerate a white friend's flaws.

These measures resounded well with the public. In 1946, the high point of social realism aggressively targeting the race problem, Ford was invited to address the YWCA Book-of-the-Month Club meeting in formidably segregated Baltimore. He charged the YWCA audience with the stewardship of an American literature that would "revolutionize the thought and action of a whole nation." He pointed to the prominent blacks like Wright, Himes, and Petry, but his bread-and-butter were the books by radically liberal (and Communist) whites: Howard Fast's *Freedom Road*, Henrietta Buckmaster's *Deep River*, Margaret Halsey's *My Best Friends Are Soldiers*, alongside the work of Bucklin Moon, Hodding Carter, and Lillian Smith. He wanted his liberal listeners to remain sutured to the literature of propaganda, and not to be sidelined by the other major modern trends in naturalism or high modernism, which Ford bluntly called a literature of "disorganization and unintelligibility."[43] Ford reasoned that the trend in modern literature spearheaded by Joyce and Faulkner was a calculated response to the tight regimentation of modern industrial bureaucracies.

Ford was unable to sustain his half of the debate in favor of propaganda. During the second half of the 1940s, he tried to codify his own arguments about the important political and social work carried out by the major African American novelists of that decade. He wrote a manuscript called "Fighting With Words," which praised writers central to his creation of a black protest tradition: Richard Wright, Ann Petry, William Attaway, James Weldon Johnson, Jessie Fauset, Arna Bontemps, and Frank Yerby. Ford sent the manuscript out, over four or five years, to the academic and commercial presses. The judgments he made had evolved from his publications in the early 1940s, like "The Negro Novel as a Vehicle of Propaganda" in the *Quarterly Review of Higher Education* and "The Dilemma of the Negro Author" in the *Southwestern Review*. But publication in these all-Negro academic magazines had not evolved enough to face an intellectual climate that had grown suspicious of social realism.

Ford must have had a uniquely anguished moment when Allen Tate rejected his manuscript for Henry Holt in 1947. "I can assure you that it has had several careful readings," Tate wrote, before shunting the manuscript aside with the time-honored brush-off that Holt could not justify its expense.[44] At the time Tate was better known for his tepid defense of segregationist Donald Davidson than for the relationship with black Wiley College poet Melvin Tolson. But Tate's euphemisms must have soothed in contrast to what Ford experienced in the long and ultimately futile journey to publish the book. The work of his mature years was rejected by all of the leading academic presses. University of North Carolina Press wrote him with regret, "I don't know that I can make any suggestions to save this work."[45] The University of Chicago told him the manuscript was "a mere descriptive catalog," "not profound enough," and then finally offered: "Let the author drop all 'literary' considerations and consider the work as a contribution to the social sciences."[46]

Ford went the farthest distance with University of Illinois Press, who expressed interest in the book and sent the manuscript out to readers. For one of about nineteen blacks with a Ph.D. degree in English during his era, the cutting remarks questioned even Ford's basic competency. "Professor Ford is uncertain in his grammar, his spelling, and occasionally in his punctuation. The writing is clear but unimpressive; it should at least be made correct."[47] If, in 1950, the chairperson of Morgan State College's English department was unqualified in the fundamentals of writing, it could not be surprising that his interpretive capacities, let alone his political project, did not rank highly. "The superlatives which he showers on obscure Negro writers do not give the reader a high sense of his critical acumen," the Illinois reviewer thought. Ford tried to revise the manuscript according to the reviewers' suggestions, but still he ran aground. Illinois sent him parting words in December 1950 elaborating upon its decision not to publish. "You have set yourself a difficult task, for you are writing literary criticism about men whose aim is social protest, and at the same time your own commentary is in itself a social protest. Under these circumstances it is pretty hard to avoid critical statements that are unconvincing."[48] To their credit, liberal academic publishers were not averse, as a matter of course, to political stridency from black academics.

But quite possibly, the African Americans whose life experiences might have predisposed them to do what Ford believed was necessary—to write criticism of protest that was itself a protest, to believe that a few more *Native Son* novels were necessary to cross the rubicon of the American racial consciousness—had suffered already a systematic racial discrimination in quality of education that entirely precluded them from making the critique. Then it became a simple model of structural inequality perpetuating itself. Because, of course, the rub was not so much the South Carolina native's hold on grammar as it was Ford's "unconvincing" "critical statement[s]." And the same man who was disinclined toward modernist complexity thought the climate of new criticism obtuse and hypocritical. After twenty years and a bit more academic freedom, Ford would write, "the overwhelming insistence upon *aestheticism* as the major criterion for literary achievement must be repudiated."[49] But Ford was trying to publish in the 1950s, and "social protest" per se was what was believed unconvincing, not the other way around. Antioch, Columbia, and the University of Oklahoma turned him down too, and around 1954, after eight years of trying to publish the book, Ford abandoned the project.

In a fine example of the peculiar toxicity that lay behind innocent liberal suggestions, Antioch Press recommended that he turn to the black colleges for a publisher. "I don't mean to imply a sort of second-rate, Jim Crow publishing," the press wrote to him, not "second-rate," simply all-Negro. Since the general reader would find the book "rather academic and didactic," Ford would do best by appealing to his primary audience, "the Negro college and University student."[50] How better to get to this student than through his or her own college press? By 1950 the segregated black American collegians, their number exploding at the seams with empowered women and veterans, amounted to 209,000.[51] Some quite liberal accounting by the U.S. Census would put the number of African American college graduates at 2.2 percent of the total black American population of more than fifteen million by 1950, an extraordinary increase in the college-educated black population since 1940.[52] But the reality of the caliber of the schools and the graduates they produced meant that there was little demand for a publisher. Howard University Press was founded in 1919, but it did not begin putting out monographs until the 1950s. Carter G. Woodson's Associated Publishers published occasional volumes but slowed considerably in the 1940s and ended with Woodson's death in 1950. African Americans would never develop a viable separate institutional publishing house for first-rank scholarly books, nor could it be said that the arch advocates of "separate but equal" racial segregation wanted to see such an institution in place. Langston Hughes would continue to invoke this problem in 1962, when he pointed to the comparatively favorable situation of black writers in places like Jamaica, Cuba, and Nigeria—or the Third World.[53]

Ford's predicament with his scholarship was the regular pickle for talented black writers and critics living in the segregated society. The years following the end of the Second World War eliminated the legal basis for Jim Crow. President Truman integrated the U.S. Armed Forces in 1948, and lower court cases outlawing racial segregation in housing, education, and employment mounted toward an inevitable crescendo outlawing the legal separation of the races. "Mainstream" America of the large urban metropolis and growing suburban areas appeared ready to accept the black authors who, miraculously enough, had been able to gather the skills necessary to compete on the same level as whites. But what about someone like Ford? Aside from about two years in Des Moines, Iowa, he had lived his entire life in the former slave-holding South and operated within the educational and moral standards set aside there for blacks. When he wrote a short piece describing the impact of racial integration for *New Republic* in 1957, he was fearful and sensing his own irrelevance. "Consider the Negro Teacher" surely described his own tendencies with the comment, "the vast majority of peace-loving and law abiding Negroes avoid the hero's lonely stand."[54] Ford seemed to be talking explicitly about the civil rights crusader, but there was another implicit lonely stand, the isolated turf of the writer who slipped group standards and tastes, the audience and the heritage, the amen corner and the chitterlings. Here was the underside of approaching the new standards of competency and success for the heroic critic, who must now stand apart from those who had nurtured him, and who looked to him for protection.

Ford committed himself to protest novels of race propaganda perhaps for the simple reason that they justified and offered a coherent place of containment for his own anger aimed at a system that had withheld from him precisely that which it demanded he master. He unavoidably called comparison between himself and the young woman he described in his article, a teacher he met at a conference who expressed surprise on learning that there was a state called Maryland. If the reality of racial segregation bandaged him to colleagues who lacked elementary competency, from what source was he supposed to generate adequate profundity for America's college presses? Added to that was Ford's inadequate praising of high modernism in an age critically dominated for Negroes by a young James Baldwin. How might he leap to the position that Baldwin famously claimed in "Everybody's Protest Novel," that humanity was a "burden" not to be battled for, but accepted? Throughout the rest of the 1950s, Ford commented warily on the downfall of segregation and what it meant for underqualified black teachers and the tradition of social realism.

It was hard to misinterpret the logic of the hard-fought NAACP victory at the Supreme Court in 1954. The Court decision was anchored in the logical principle driven home by the lawyer Thurgood Marshall and based partially on evidence provided by social psychologist Kenneth Clark. All-black schools were, fundamentally, inferior. The unanimous decision was remarkable; it won over the former Ku Klux Klan member and associate Supreme Court Justice Hugo Black. Justice Robert Jackson voted in favor of the decision and drafted a memo that celebrated not just the end of the segregated regime, but what it had achieved. "Negro progress under segregation has been spectacular and, tested by the pace of history, his rise is one of the swiftest and most dramatic advances in the annals of man. It is that, indeed, which has enabled him to outgrow the system and to overcome the presumptions on which it is based."[55] In other words, compelling examples of black pride and vigorous resistance had not terminated racial injustice, but rather efficient black submission, assimilation, and acquiescence, a series of practices that of course challenged the notion that there ever had been injustice in the first place. Ford's position that "Negro literature" was a distinctive body of work that had its own discrete rules of rank was quite at odds with the more general drift of American attitudes, that in the two generations between the film *Birth of a Nation* and *Brown v. Board of Education of Topeka*, blacks had achieved the status of at least junior whites.

Nor was it possible to quantify what might crop up under the segregation regime. Segregation had produced, in some small laboratories, such as the departments of English, history, and sociology at Fisk College in Nashville, extraordinary results. Signals of new artistic standards appeared to critics and readers immediately after Brooks's breakthrough with *Annie Allen*. A twenty-eight-year-old veteran named William Demby published with Rinehart a short book called *Beetlecreek* in 1950. Raised in Pittsburgh, Demby had begun his college education at West Virginia State College, where, in spite of a literature class with Margaret Walker, he had determined to become a professional musician. However, when he jammed with fellow GIs from New York during the war, he found that the idiom of musical expression had changed from swing to bop. Demby remained tied to Duke Ellington and his band's great soloist voice on the trumpet, Roy Eldridge.

After the hostilities ended, Demby attended Fisk, where he studied under the young and newly arrived English professor Robert Hayden and wrote a short story called "St. Joey." In 1947 he graduated from college and left the United States for Rome, where he had been stationed during the war. He lived in an art student's apartment on the Via Margutta that gave him the carnival of European life "like out of a Christopher Isherwood novel."[56] He acted in William Saroyan's play *The Time of Our Life*, hung out in an artistic circle that included the painter Carlo Levi, and dated a professional photographer. The move to Italy was "important and liberating,"[57] even though Demby found in Rome among the artists the same "rotten odor of phoniness" that he had known in the United States.[58]

He decided to become a novelist, and he finished his first book *Beetlecreek* overseas. Demby had learned a complex mantra at Fisk in the course of his friendly interactions with Robert Hayden and Arna Bontemps. He was suspicious of anyone who set himself up "as a Negro artist as such," but at the same time, and like Nick Aaron Ford, he believed in "Propaganda of course" but of "honesty and integrity."[59]

Beetlecreek was a precious and vulnerable coming-of-age story, a story of growth stunted not by racism but because of human alienation and fear. The novel was written from the perspective of three characters: Bill Trapp, a white outcast; David Diggs, a frustrated college educated black man in a small rural town in either Pennsylvania or West Virginia; and Johnny Johnson, David's teenage nephew, who yearns for social acceptance. With a sensibility that was shaped by Dostoyevsky and Shirley Jackson and anticipating *Lord of the Flies* author William Golding, Demby wrote a novel of human symbolic ritual. He revealed the aching days in a dying mill town, and three fearful people at different stages along life's way who are trying to achieve fulfillment by pursuing affectionate love from their fellow human beings. Race colored their perspective and, for David, certainly contributed to his sense of impending doom, but the fact of blackness was still only one of many factors. Most important to Demby was revealing the severely truncated mentality of Beetlecreek's citizenry, who persecuted their neighbors for difference and were too jagged to extend warmth and compassion.

Beetlecreek was sad and foreboding, but on its deck of American society a person's race and the power of the environment to cripple or inspire were salient, not determinative, features. Demby had white characters for the American mainstream and modernist psychological interiors for the critics, but he did not allow for any character's tensions to be resolved, so the reviewers were not sure what he had done. The book got a quiet but fair reception in *Nation* and *Saturday Review of Literature*. When Horace Cayton wrote for the *New York Times*, he cut to the quick: "There has been a wave of Negro literature" because "white publishers found out they could make money." Demby's book was different. "This book can stand on its own just as a book. It didn't have to push the point that it was written by a Negro about race prejudice."[60] Demby triumphed over the pitfalls that piqued the critics, the publishers, and the audiences. But he had to leave the United States to do it.

CHAPTER FOURTEEN

Still Looking for Freedom (1949–1954)

The demand to show black American life as composed of the same kind of inner struggle that affected white Americans of the middle class appealed deeply to a cadre of young writers. For some, this did not necessarily mean the abandonment of politics. Vital, hard-working, articulate, professional, and politically committed young people like John Oliver Killens revitalized the ranks of cultural activists, and their group included many ex-veterans using the GI Bill to take college courses. Killens had been politically groomed in the Southern Negro Youth Congress, the National Negro Congress offshoot, and he discovered the work of Richard Wright while taking E. Franklin Frazier's classes at Howard University. Killens had studied law in Washington, D.C., until the war started, when he joined the army and went to war in the Pacific theater. At the end of 1945 he returned to the city and worked for the National Labor Relations Board, then the Congress of Industrial Organizations. By the summer of 1948 the dream of becoming a published novelist sent him to New York, to Columbia University, for a summer course with Dorothy Brewster. Killens returned to Washington long enough to round up his family and then went back to New York, where he enrolled in Helen Hull's writing course at Columbia. He spent the time between 1950 and 1953 taking classes in the General Education Division of New York University, including creative writing with Saul Bellow.

Like many of the young artists and political activists, Killens thought that Richard Wright had captured their intellectual fury along with an essential segment of black American life in *Uncle Tom's Children* and *12 Million Black Voices*. Killens even claimed to have met Wright between 1939 and 1941, but there is little historical evidence to support the assertion.[1] What the probably apocryphal story indicates is the manner that writers of "social conscience" felt driven to define themselves in terms of Wright's achievement. There was an important difference between Killens and members of the Wright school. After *Uncle Tom's Children*, Killens had little use for Wright. He believed that the novelist had become embittered in his subsequent works and had made the error of overly stressing black resignation. If historians and political scientists had missed talking about black psychology, Richard Wright had touched too heavily with his brush, emphasizing only despair. In an early critical exercise at Columbia, Killens decided that the Wright of the 1940s had capitulated. "Nothing Mr. Wright has written subsequently compares with *Uncle Tom's Children*," he explained. "It would appear since this major job was accomplished the author began to cool off. *Native Son*, though a stirring piece of fiction, does not live up to the expectancy created by those five stories of Negro heroism. Certainly *Black Boy* with its defeatism and great despair has no relation to Uncle Tom's 'Fighting' Children."[2] When he reflected on the 1940s, Killens described his mood as one of "militance and revolutionary impertinence."[3] Georgia-born Killens was an excellent example of a writer who believed that Wright was not political enough.

Paul Robeson responded to the ache of the next generation and the chasm between politics and aesthetics by mobilizing a group of Communists, fellow travelers, and black rights supporters around a journal he named *Freedom*, housed in offices on Harlem's great boulevard 125th Street. Robeson had become the public lightning rod for black civil rights and left-wing politics when white rioters stoned the audience at a concert he performed in Peekskill, New York, in 1949. Robeson had spoken the same year at the Communist-organized Paris Peace Conference, declaring black unwillingness to fight in a war against the Soviets. The next year Secretary of State Dean Acheson stripped him of his passport. To edit the paper, Robeson hired Louis Burnham, a labor organizer who had helped to find and operate the Southern Negro Youth Congress. Robeson himself contributed a monthly column, which the *Masses & Mainstream* senior writer Lloyd Brown ghost-wrote. The collaboration suggests the difficult position for the Communist Party. Their national leadership, including leader Eugene Dennis, *Daily Worker* editor John Gates, Harlem City Councilman Benjamin Davis, and the third-ranking CPUSA leader Henry Winston had all received five-year prison sentences for conspiring to overthrow the U.S. government, a violation of the Smith Act. Their 1949 trial took place at the Foley Square Courthouse in New York, and the convictions were upheld by the U.S. Supreme Court in 1951. The American Communist Party was running out of venues as quickly as the artists on the black Left. As a regular broadsheet, *Freedom* provided vital nourishment for the politically conscious creative writers and readers.

The newspaper published occasional reportage by the surviving Communist black intelligentsia: Doxey Wilkerson, Alphaeus Hunton, Eugene Gordon, William L. Patterson, and Lloyd Brown. Also including the maverick leftist John Henrik Clarke, these were highly visible figures connecting the worlds of literature and politics in Harlem and Communist circles. The newspaper gave voice on occasion to a forerunner: Frank Marshall Davis wrote a short piece from his refuge in Hawaii. The most regular contributor was the witty and energetic columnist Alice Childress, the Harlem-bred veteran of the American Negro Theater and playwright, whose play *Trouble in Mind* would win an Obie award in 1956. Childress's column "A Conversation from Life" presented a series of letters from a black domestic named Mildred to her friend Marge. In homespun language, Mildred recounted contemporary issues and politics. Independence

Publishers released the column in book form in 1956 under the title *Like One of the Family: Conversations from a Domestic's Life.*

But the person who took over the cultural field at *Freedom* was the twenty-one-year-old associate editor from Chicago who had completed two years at the University of Wisconsin, Lorraine Hansberry. Attractive, optimistic, and with shoulder-length hair, Hansberry wrote more than twenty articles and reviews for the paper between 1951 and 1955. She enjoyed the mentorship she received from the managing editor, Louis Burnham. A small man with a deep voice, whose conversation ranged easily from the politely academic to the raucous gossip of the barbershop, Burnham emphasized politics in everything, unveiled racism everywhere, and unapologetically romanced the folk. "They are beautiful my child," he would say to Hansberry, looking out of the window and onto the Harlem crowds.[4]

Hansberry's reviews snapped at the sloppy commercial representations of black people. Her first *Freedom* piece, in June 1951, criticized the transformation of two radio programs, *Beulah* and *Amos 'N Andy*, into television shows: "[T]he vicious impression of Negroes the TV and radio moguls strive to create and maintain before the people is no accident." She hit the point hard. "The longer the concept of the half-idiot subhuman can be kept up, the easier to justify economic and every other kind of discrimination, so rampant in this country."[5] This rich vein criticizing black stereotypes was a source of inspiration for Childress as well; the play *Trouble in Mind* scored the black stereotypes held by the most enlightened of the white liberals.

Hansberry was the traditional middle-class collegian drawn to radicalism in arts, politics, and sexuality. In other words, for African America, she was an entirely new quantity. She was, for example, very distinct from Ralph Ellison, another college kid who had been swept up in New York's left-wing artistic swirl fifteen years earlier. Though she disliked people reminding her of it, Hansberry was a debutante, the daughter of a Chicago real estate mogul. Her father, Carl Hansberry, fought segregation up to the Supreme Court—and won. Hansberry was artistically inclined, interested in painting, plays, and sculpture, but with a difference. Unlike her upper-class black peer group, she had not rushed off to Europe; she had studied in Guadalajara, Mexico, during her freshman year summer. But Lorraine Hansberry left the overwhelmingly white University of Wisconsin in 1950 for Greenwich Village to augment what she could not learn in Madison. (Occasional *Partisan Review* critic Horace Gregory described the scene at Wisconsin in the late 1940s: "a huge vacuum filled by the *Chicago Tribune*, the teachings of Yvor Winters and tons and tons of peanut butter and ice cream. If you touch anything it turns to plastic, and if you look again, it's a new Ford or a Buick.")[6] Wisconsin was middle America's version of postwar affluence and cultural homogeneity, and New York enabled a quickening by comparison.

In the Village Hansberry found her voice as an artist, by writing at a Harlem black leftist journal. Working at *Freedom* opened up the left-wing press to Hansberry and she made them initially with her poetry. *Masses & Mainstream* published her lyric "Lynchsong," protesting Mississippi truck driver Willie Mc-Gee's imminent execution, as well as her eloquent and moving "Flag from a Kitchenette Window." At the same time she was writing her political and activist works for the Robeson paper. The exposure in New York to political organizing and mass movements radicalized her, especially the campaign to collect signatures to free McGee from death row for the "crime" of consensual sex with a white woman. She decided then that even though the black middle class had not been examined fully by artists, she would "very arbitrarily, very deliberately" portray black working-class life. Hansberry felt pulsing "sources of life within this milieu."[7]

Hansberry went from cultural issues to politics in her long tenure with the magazine, covering student congresses and black women protestors at the White House, and even traveling to Uruguay to present a lecture in place of the passport-less Paul Robeson. And her bohemian streak had a fascinating component. She had grown up in a household with regular visits from her uncle William Leo Hansberry, the foremost African American authority on blacks in Africa and antiquity. When she thought of her racial ancestry, she was as radical as her point of view regarding social class. She mused in her notebooks that "One thing was certain: she was at one . . . with the sound of the mighty Congo drum . . . Africa claimed her."[8] At *Freedom* she got to know Robeson, Du Bois, and Alphaeus Hunton, the elite from the Council on African Affairs. Her sophisticated interest in the decolonization movement in Egypt, Ghana, and Kenya had multiple sources. She was a writer engaged in the international struggle for black freedom, as her 1951 article "Gold Coast's Rulers Go, Ghana Moves to Freedom" attests. Hansberry would also support the Egyptian and Kikuyu nationalist pursuits. By 1953 Hansberry had cut her hair short and started teaching African American literature at the Jefferson School of Social Science.

Freedom relied on the most prolific black Communist critic, Lloyd L. Brown. Brown spent his busiest professional years editing and reviewing for *Masses & Mainstream* and collaborating with Paul Robeson. (The Robeson partnership produced *Here I Stand*, Robeson's 1958 autobiography.) With the exception of an occasional piece from someone like Carl Ruthven Offord or William Attaway, both of whom published in *Masses & Mainstream* in 1949, Brown was the central black contributor. In Communist circles he could claim a certain distinction as a fiction writer, though his work was far too didactic for the mainstream press. As early as 1946 he had written "Jericho U.S.A." for *New Masses*, followed in 1948 by "All God's Chosen" in *Masses & Mainstream* and "Battle in Canaan" in *Mainstream* in 1948.

His most artistically rich short story was called "Glory Train." In it Brown showed the life and truncated aspiration of a Mississippi railroad fireman, who yearns to be the engineer of a locomotive. He drew a rich portrait of southern black male railroad life—one that Brown had no first-hand experience of—to present the problem of labor, racism, and its inevitable solution: the CPUSA. His protagonist lands in the North after a broken strike and then experiences a wildly improbable epiphanic moment of interracial ethnic unity by way of a handbill picturing Earl Browder and James Ford running for the presidency. In this episode Brown showed as much melodrama as realism, and a fundamentally romantic perception of character that seemed at the core of communist aesthetics. Where he had his flair was as a critic. When he took apart books by his peers, this was nearly always what he opposed—a socially alienated protagonist, sorrowful about his condition. Brown deplored the exercising of this trope, and he revealed well the ideological weakness of the characterization.

In an interesting and perceptive review of Lillian Smith's work in 1949, Brown drew a new frame of reference. Smith had come out fully as a cold warrior as southern reactionaries tried to derail a mild civil rights agenda by smearing it as the work of "nigger-loving communists." But Brown was not merely speaking for the masses when he wrote that in her book *Killers of the Dream*, "Miss Smith is an embattled liberal of the Vital Center type. She deplores lynching, segregation, white supremacy—but she hits hardest at the main enemy: communism."[9] His pun glanced off Arthur Schlesinger's 1949 book of the same title, *The Vital Center*, and Brown perceptively noted how easy the rhetorical shift was becoming for whites to take on the language of racial fairness while glossing over the actual hard work that had been conducted by the Communist Party in defending black rights and black lives since the 1930s.

The swelling liberal consensus in American cultural and political life also threatened to erase some important differences under its big umbrella, and Smith's work, teetering on reactionary attitudes toward the Civil War and blacks, seemed precisely the kind of book capable of wrenching the coalition apart. Less and less satisfied with the shape of things at home, William Gardner Smith duplicated Brown's critique of Lillian Smith in the pages of *New Republic*. The Philadelphia writer found in Smith an innocent in regard to her understanding of the functioning of northern race prejudice, or the role that social class played in racial antagonism.[10]

Lloyd Brown found liberal blacks among the anticommunists as well. When he reviewed J. Saunders Redding's 1951 pamphlet *On Being Negro in America*, he believed that he had found a familiar varnish of anticommunism glossing over Redding's purported journey into his racial identity. After he checked Redding, Brown offered a corrective to the psychoanalytic approach, a liberal favorite, and consistent with Communists' suspicion of the priority of the individual over the group. When Abram Kardiner and Lionel Ovesey's sensational study of black urbanites *The Mark of Oppression* appeared, Brown did not let the credentials of the authors sway him. He viewed the book as dangerously flawed. Brown's article "Psychoanalysis vs. the Negro People" claimed that the study by Columbia University psychologists offered the "New Look in racism": fundamentally, the idea that black inner yearning and striving was to become white.[11] The challenge to the widely accepted theory of assimilation, even amalgamation, was defiant and showed the curious position inside of a strictly disciplined ideological movement; black Communist circles continued to sustain black ethnic fundamentalism. The idea that black Americans had a cultural prerogative other than or outside of assimilation to the advertising agency's glossy ideal of American life would gain ground.

Brown's suggestion in "Psychoanalysis vs. the Negro People" that liberal social scientists were making up a new kind of racism was a bit different from the flaws that piqued Vital Center liberals like Daniel Rosenblatt, who was also alert to blacks internalizing oppression. Writing in *New Republic*, Rosenblatt faulted the "liberal imagination" for spreading the view that "the Negro who adjusts to prejudice and makes the best of his life is the *bad* Negro, the slave, the Uncle Tom, while the Negro who is miserable and suffers, but makes no adequate adjustment, is a better person, more deserving."[12] The heroism of blacks who deftly adopted conspicuous upper-middle-class white American tastes and gave no indication of discomfort at the racial barriers undergirded Anatole Broyard's blasts against Negro "inauthenticity." The idea that the miserable sufferers had an important message or some capacity for leadership along with those who had quietly made the adjustment to segregation inevitably struck a nerve. Naturally enough among blacks, no one wanted to be seen as having made a permanent adjustment to a social order in the process of shifting. But Lloyd Brown's sensibility on the matter of social scientists determining black pathology captured the frustration of many of black writers, even those, like Albert Murray at Tuskegee, who did not share his politics.[13]

By 1951 Brown had completed his major fiction work, the novel *Iron City*. *Freedom* carried a chapter. In the moving book, Brown made a couple of contributions to the literature of black America. He had written the first African American prison drama, part roman à clef and part social documentary novel. It addressed the real-life issue of black men falsely imprisoned on trumped-up charges, and it was modeled after the electrocution in 1941 of a Pennsylvania black man named Willie Jones. But Brown's book would not end with death. At the conclusion, he gave his reader the opportunity for a qualified but realistic hope: the hero Lonnie James is still incarcerated, but on the cusp of a retrial; he sleeps soundly, no longer menaced by the light and night watchman of death row. If Richard Wright had emphasized the world of inevitable doom and execution, Brown envisaged a new land of interracial solidarity and effective communists who could lobby, protest, and fight long enough to turn the tide in the direction of democratic justice. The conclusion to *Iron City* was extraordinary, but so was the governor of Michigan denying the state of Alabama extradition powers in the case of escaped Scottsboro prisoner Haywood Patterson in 1950. Scottsboro, the Martinsville Seven, and the Trenton Six were all cases of ongoing Communist Party legal involvement. For Americans who understood the cases of poor black men casually imprisoned as a direct sequel to chain gangs and slavery, the CPUSA acted courageously.

Brown's book did not soar out far beyond his immediate peers; the book itself was published by Masses & Mainstream Press and, due especially to his limited achievement in the development of individual character, seemed only a propaganda piece. But his fellow critics did notice more prominently his series of assertive essays that year, in March and April in *Masses & Mainstream*, "Which Way for the Negro Writer?" Brown decided that little was gained from two signals that black critics had been sending to black writers. He rejected the 1940 ethos of Sterling Brown and Arthur P. Davis, that "Negro American literature" per se did not exist as a source of distinction, and that black novelists constructing stories without black protagonists was a solid index of racial advance. Most insightfully, Brown opposed the equation of universality with a "raceless" work, or one that avoided elements of black life and history. "What tragic folly for him [the Negro novelist] to turn away from the virtually untapped richness of this subject toward some nebulous and non-existent 'universality'!" Brown hit his final point with emphasis: "the trouble with Negro literature . . . is that *it has not been Negro enough.*"[14]

Blyden Jackson, just over forty, was working for the *Phylon* editorial board; when Alain Locke died in 1954, Jackson would overtake the annual African American literature review. He decided that Brown was wrong, but the debate was important. Jackson faulted Brown for having fundamentally confused propaganda for aesthetics, the contrast between the "artist" and the "person who demands to be read primarily because his cause is just."[15] Importantly, Jackson was willing to take a risk to hear out different political points of view. "And I do not think . . . that his being a representative of the far left plays any appreciable role in my aversion to his flatfooted stand." More or less, here was an important resuturing of convictions by African Americans across lines of politics, education, and social class origin. Brown, the committed Marxist, had advocated a profoundly black-based cultural expression (though he hoped it would avoid the snare of bourgeois nationalism). Jackson, an Aristotelian critic subscribing to the effect produced by the climbing meaning of enjoined literary form and content, which might render an "elixir" of "eternal life," used as his example of "vilely" written work NAACP member Walter White's *Flight*.

Even if two different critics like Lloyd L. Brown in New York, laboring for the embattled Communist Party, and Blyden Jackson, riding out the last two tigerish decades of segregation at Fisk and Southern University, proved to have something like a family commitment to document the existence of black literature, there were other debates that suggested new perspectives that might not be as easily contained. Access still registered as a key problem. Literally having *Masses & Mainstream* in his possession might well have earned Jackson a stretch on the chain gang in Nashville or Baton Rouge; he had to show temerity to keep abreast of the New York leftist critiques. Even the sharpest insights, the most unsentimental examinations by the critics of their own ethnic oeuvre, such as Edward Bland had conducted, were always in danger of falling off the precipice of public view. White peers ignored the black critics, confirming Du Bois's observation from 1903 that rarely did the best class of colored and white get together.

It was not completely surprising that in 1953 when Lionel Trilling edited the collection *Perspectives U.S.A.*, he felt compelled to reprint the two black voices he thought capable of challenging the hegemony of liberal coddling and black racial propaganda. One was James Baldwin, the author of "Everybody's Protest Novel." Trilling knew the other man personally: Richard Gibson. Gibson held Trilling's recommendation to the artist's colony at Yaddo in 1951. The same year, Gibson had published in *Kenyon Review* the opinion piece "A No to Nothing." Trilling thought Gibson "likely to become one of our truly notable men of letters."[16]

A nineteen-year-old undergraduate at Kenyon College in Ohio, Gibson had the inside track to people like sixty-three-year-old John Crowe Ransom, the college professor of Robert Penn Warren and Allen Tate at Vanderbilt and architect of the formalist literary approach. *Kenyon*'s associate editors included Trilling, Warren, and Albert Erskine, and they hosted a summer school of criticism that got under way in 1948. *Kenyon* brought the southern agrarian critics and the New York intellectuals together under one roof. Ransom had founded the review in 1938, shortly after leaving Vanderbilt for Kenyon. His sensibility shifted with the move north, and he became more openly tolerant. Part of the tolerance was expressed by his connection to the heavily Jewish New York group, begun at the 1939 Modern Language Association meeting in New Orleans. By 1941 Ransom wrote that the "righteousness" expressed by firmly hierarchical critics like T. S. Eliot and Allen Tate was "too luxurious for my blood."[17] Mannerly if not from the genteel class, Ransom could show warmth in spite of race if approached deferentially. Near the end of World War II and from a visiting position at Johns Hopkins, he wrote to Arna Bontemps and described "a great pleasure on the train from Washington to Baltimore, following a reading of my verse in the Library of Congress. A number of very animated Negro girls was sitting across the aisle, and finally two of them came over, showed me their notebooks, for they were college students somewhere, and [had] notes about my poems and asked me for my autograph. I liked that very much."[18] The young women may well have been Morgan State College coeds. All the Kenyon critics united in praise of Baldwin, Ellison, and, for a time, Richard Gibson. Ransom judged that "of all the Negro authors I have read," Gibson, on the basis of manuscripts and the *Kenyon* piece, "has the most objective and purely literary spirit."[19]

The ironic scheme of blindness and insight that is American race relations had gotten Gibson to the point of being thought the savior of black writing by leading American critics. As a teenager in Philadelphia, Gibson had read Henry Miller's 1945 homage piece "The Amazing and Invariable Beauford Delany." Gibson wrote a letter that impressed Delany so well that the painter paid a visit to the precocious fourteen-year-old Central High School student when travel took Delany to Philadelphia. Delany took Gibson under his wing, talked to him seriously about art, and had him up to his New York apartment. By 1948 Gibson had met and befriended Delany's protégé James Baldwin.[20] The same year, while working at the *Afro-American* in Philadelphia, Gibson met William Gardner Smith, who worked across the street at the *Pittsburgh Courier* and was flush with success after his novel *Last of the Conquerors*. Gibson went to Kenyon College in the fall of 1949 ambitious, determined, and with a bohemian maturity and sense of nerve. When Robert Lowell visited the campus, Gibson got so drunk in the company of the regularly besotted poet that the sophomore fell into a ditch.

In the spring of 1951 *Kenyon Review* published its first piece by Kenyon's young black recruit to the New Criticism. The article "A No to Nothing" caused a stir, and it aspishly struck out against the publishing industry, American liberals, and every black who had ever picked up a pen. "[T]here is not yet a single work of literature by an American Negro which, when judged without bias, stands out as a masterpiece," Gibson boomed, echoing Richard Wright's "Blueprint for Negro Writing," but for a completely different crowd.[21] Gibson had the ear of the elite American critical aesthetes.

The chief source of his fury was the publishing industry. If the more publicly contented blacks, like *Ebony* magazine editor Era Bell Thompson, claimed that "opportunity for Negro writers is here, but far too few are ready," Gibson was enraged by the publishers' expectations.[22] "The young Negro writer discovers to his bitter amazement that he is nearly trapped by the Problem," he clamored. Neither the "Professional Liberal" nor the "many paranoiac Negroes obsessed with the injustices done them" would allow "a Negro the right to be human, to become a man and walk with his own strength his own way." Gibson believed that anthologies of black writers and poets, such as were published by Sterling Brown, Langston Hughes, and Nick Aaron Ford, exalted the incompetent works of black artists, which had been produced by a "minstrel psychology," a direct overture to what Anatole Broyard had argued in the pages of *Commentary*.[23]

Gibson republished the polemic in *Negro Digest* under the title "Is the Negro Writer Free?" before getting out a short story called "Two Mortuary Sermons" in *Kenyon*. The buildup took place on account of a Whitney Fellowship (courtesy of New Deal black economist Robert Weaver) as well as a fellowship to the turreted, gray-stone Trask Mansion at Yaddo in 1951 when he was nineteen. At Yaddo he befriended Eleanor Clark, who introduced him to her soon-to-be-husband Robert Penn Warren. Gibson might easily have been the first Negro adult whom Warren had had intellectual contact with. Gibson would hold the support of this group through his brief Yaddo stay, where he managed to cause a minor scandal on account of what some of the other guests believed was overt homophobia. But despite his peccadilloes, young Gibson got on quite well with and was liked in return by the best of the white American literary tastemakers. Random House editor Albert Erskine encouraged him to write a protest novel, and Warren told him to remain in the States. Instead, Gibson joined William Demby in Rome.

Even though he did it in one of the standing journals of the New Criticism, Gibson was condemning the tradition of black literature from within. Thirty-year-old Anatole Broyard offered a similar assessment and, by virtue of his morphological ability to pass for a nonblack, prepared his condemnation from without. His article "Keep Cool, Man: The Negro Rejection of Jazz" was his own swan song to black life. Never again would he write on a subject that might cause the editor of *Commentary* to refer to him as an "anatomist of the Negro personality in a white world."[24] For his epilogue, Broyard wanted to talk about shifts in the jazz world away from the hot style of Louis Armstrong to the chilled poise of Miles Davis.

Broyard found entirely objectionable the young jazz artists, backs turned, thumbing their nose at white society from the concert stage. In an era where mixed audiences could enjoy black music, and, perhaps more to the specific point, black men could enjoy the company of white women, Broyard found everyone rejecting the Dionysian ecstasies of the musical ritual. The ungrateful musician "no longer engaged in passionately celebrating his freedom and drowning out his troubles." Instead of achieving a worldly independence, Broyard decided, the musicians were avoiding the possible catharsis of the musical ritual because they were petulant children, which he in turn psychoanalyzed as "a classic attitude of anticipated disappointment." The Negro had become resentful and hurt because of his repeated rejection "in subtle forms by white society." By the end of his essay Broyard had transformed the image of the detached "cool" black performer into a heroin-numbed victim of "self-enslavement."[25] With this assessment of black culture, his decision to refuse to identify as Negro at all made perfect logical sense: he was rejecting slavery. The blacks who accepted and analyzed black culture on white American terms had reached a cul-de-sac.

Broyard's tenderness about his own background had an unusual climax in 1952. In that year Chandler Brossard, in the mid-1940s a close friend, exposed Broyard's racial identity in the novel *Who Walk in Darkness*. Or rather, Brossard tried to reveal Broyard's racial identity, and to use Broyard's ethnic subterfuge as the central conceit for his book. Brossard wrote a roman à clef exploring the Village arts and bohemian scene, with Broyard and Milton Klonsky as the key characters Henry Porter and Max Glazer. The publisher, New Directions, sent Broyard a galley of the book, asking him to sign a release relieving it of grounds for a libel lawsuit. Broyard refused, unless the publishing company removed the language that referred to him as a "Negro," the book's opening sentence. Brossard decided to publish the book and write that Henry Porter was "illegitimate" instead of a "passed Negro." The book made little sense when the door to Porter's dishonorable character hinged on the absence of a marriage certificate. But Brossard's portrait of Broyard as a menacing Lothario who abandons girlfriends once he has gotten them pregnant showed a man of deep psychic malice, completely coincident with the sketch of black personality Broyard himself had written in the essay "The Inauthentic Negro." Deliberately wounding to a man who prided his own savoir faire, Brossard characterized Broyard as the sort of man who wears the school tie to impersonate a graduate of the Ivy League.

Brossard nailed Broyard to the wall as an imposter, which of course was another way of upholding the racial barricades. In the 1950s in New York everyone striving to make something of himself or herself affected airs, and Broyard was famous for supremely casual erudition. He called everyone, men and women alike, "sport." When the recently discharged airman Leroi Jones saw Broyard in the Village in the mid-1950s, he believed that, in comparison with the regulars at the White Horse Tavern and other Village hangouts, Broyard was some kind of a high-fashion model. Broyard followed his jazz piece in 1953 with "Ha! Ha! An Essay," something in *Discovery* that, more than anything else that he had ever done, excluded questions of race and the environment in American society. It was perhaps Broyard's most forced and least memorable work.

Broyard was of course following the exact prescriptions of the entire critical consensus. J. Saunders Redding had reached the cul-de-sac with him. At the beginning of the 1950s, Redding described life as a black man in the United States during the middle of the twentieth century as similar to "having a second ego which is as much the conscious subject of all experience as the natural self. It is not what psychologists call dual personality."[26] The second ego was "complex" and "morbid" and did not lead to enlightenment. Instead, the twin egos forced him to deride that which he was compelled to produce because, in some fashion, Redding's own work closed out the long decade of social realism that had begun with *Uncle Tom's Children.*

In 1950 Redding completed and published *Stranger and Alone,* his novel about black collegians that brought to life the African American middle class, a group that he depicted as nearly a racial caste. But the novel that took him seven years to write was an agonizing act of desperate creation. In 1944 Redding had confided to Richard Wright that finally the "great pressure" with *Stranger* was gradually "easing off." Writing steadily, Redding had tentatively started to believe in his work, but he revealed to Wright the special burden of his writing life and personality: "It's getting to the place where I know where I am; and my evenings and nights aren't filled with the black glooms of discouragement." Redding perfectly captured the dilemma of the black writer as the popularity for realist treatments of the environmental conditions that exacerbated racial injustice gave way to a privileged category of modernist conditions: alienation, sensitivity, and despair.

Stranger and Alone exposed the immense pain of Redding's own life, his own brittle psyche, but the book wound up only linking him to the ragged protesters of the world. As a piece of writing it was ultimately didactic in its the clear depiction of a villain. The novel's protagonist is a desperate man named Shelton Howden—"Shell torn, How then?" the narrator seems to ask. Howden is an orphan who can only suspect that his father was a white man on a visit to a colored brothel. Dull-witted, diffident, and poor, Howden has almost no outstanding qualities, except, perhaps, one: near graduation from fictional New Hope College, he accepts the academic position of racial inferiority. "It never occurred to him that the books he was reading and the lectures he heard might be the scholarship of prejudice, the rationalizations of fallible men whose conclusions were questionable."[27] At first, Howden hopes to become a doctor so that he can become "prosperous, assured" and join the group whose claim to social prestige rests on its material prosperity, "the shiniest cars, the prettiest wives."[28] But after a disastrous encounter with a railroad crew, Howden is crippled, gives up medicine, and turns to education. He works as a college administrator, learning at the feet of President Wimbush at Arcadia College.

A mason cementing the wall between blacks and their justly earned material resources, Wimbush is the illegitimate child of a black woman and a southern planter. He teaches Shelton Howden the showmanship necessary to manage southern blacks away from social and economic equality and to accept their subjugation. Howden falls in love with Wimbush's daughter Gerry, and she and her friends conduct a cheap and hollow Negro high society that imitates the worst of white middle-class life. Wimbush helps Howden completely erase his moral compass. "My God, son, group or race ethics, race morality—it's got nothing to do with us, and it's got nothing to do with reality either."[29] Howden concludes the book as a school supervisor who betrays the black principals organizing to gain equal school apportionments from the state. Redding's Shelton Howden was a pathetic blemish, the novel a study in cowardice. As a protagonist he was nearly completely unsympathetic, a man beyond redemption. On the eve of heroic NAACP success against the structure of racial inequality, it was difficult to believe that people as cowardly, traitorous, and small as Shelton Howden existed.

The darkly pessimistic view questioned the virtue of integration politics. Ralph Ellison reviewed *Stranger and Alone* for the *New York Times Book Review* and declared that the book's only significance was "sociological" and that the writing lacked "high quality."[30] The critic Ulysses Lee more gently disapproved of the novel, and he eased his dispraise with a gesture toward the future: "[T]his might have been the fine and penetrating novel of the tender more painful edges of Negro life that Saunders Redding yet may write."[31] Only those who remained enlisted in the cause of protest writing enjoyed the book heartily. Ann Petry reviewed the novel for *Saturday Review of Literature* and called it "first rate." She also placed Redding in a tradition of black naturalists, if she believed that he had made some important innovations. "Shelton Howden . . . is obviously a victim. But he is not the protesting, outraged Negro who has often been portrayed in novels."[32] Later she wrote to an editor at Harcourt Brace to convey personally her brimming admiration. "I liked S[tranger]&A[lone] so much that I am wholeheartedly recommending it to the membership of Negro Women Incorporated. . . . S&A is a good book and I ended the review this way 'Buy the book, read it and ponder over it.'"[33] Redding received endorsement for his social conscience and sense of responsibility to the race, not for the quality of his execution or the inevitable unfolding of his plot. He had written himself into the same league as his whipping boy Chester Himes.

Stranger did not bring with it the coronation of a magnificent talent in fiction, and yet Redding's literary drive persisted. In 1951 he wrote, compulsively, another memoir. Predictably, instead of escaping the turmoil that held him fast, Redding continued along the path of racial obsession in those years, when he filled a visiting professorship at Brown University, and began justifying himself. He described the core of his problem in a brief note to the editor of the *Saturday Review of Literature*, and, very much unlike Chester Himes's defense of his work during the realists' heyday of 1946, there was regret in his words.

Redding had been included in *Saturday Review*'s 1951 group of notable newcomers to fiction writing. But Redding was ashamed of his fiction, so he wrote about his book that was coming out that year, *On Being Negro in America,* and he revealed something more than shame. "[T]he truth about Negro people seems the most important truth the American democracy needs to learn," he told his readers, in an off-the-shoulder manner. Then he shifted into the mode of a repentant, troubled man. "And so I'm writing one more book about this truth. I want to write it much less than I *need* to write it. (It would probably save my time and labor if I consulted a psychoanalyst.) It's an art of purification, a catharsis." Finally Redding unburdened himself completely: "After it's done, perhaps I can write the books I want to write without feeling that I'm betraying something fundamental in me and American life."[34] As he had said in *On Being Negro in America*, "I want to get on to other things."[35] He wanted to but never would.

Saturday Review's columnist Eloise Perry Hazard wrote up her brief blurb on Redding and eliminated any mention that Redding had written the major novel *Stranger and Alone* within the past year.[36] Having merely delivered a blueprint to his enemies, Redding's catharsis remained unrealized. *On Being Negro in America*, almost a series of positions on questions of racial experience and an accent, at best, to *No Day of Triumph*, came out alongside his narrative history of the black experience, *They Came in Chains*. Redding's flaw was the problem of blacks who had excelled under the segregation regime. If the shell of robust human individuality was torn, how then would black writers and intellectuals fend for themselves in the competition of life? What path would they follow? And how would they understand their past lives, the history they had made, once the barriers came down?

Choosing a new kind of American identity was a confounding problem and one that caused Redding to float along the threshold of American social reality. Redding published three books in two years, an unmitigated distinction for any college professor, and yet his work appeared in part because he was black, an opportunity that, in his own words, was nefarious. Redding wanted nothing better than escape from the race problem. To that end, he decided sometime between 1952 and 1953 to reject his feelings of racial fraternity and to consider the world—phenomenologically. He hacked away some of the tissue of himself, the "emotional baggage," that had been his racial identity. Whatever his books did not do, he believed that he had made an emotional advance. Writing about the period he claimed, "I rid myself of all those requirements and responsibilities that had fallen my lot, and the lot of any American Negro." He stopped referring to other black Americans as "my people" and decided that he had "escaped" and "depersonalize[d]" himself. "I was glad. I was free."[37] He became a kind of expatriate from the country of his own mind.

Or he thought he was free. Nothing signaled the ham-fisted and tongue-tied Negro liberal stance secured to a realist narrative of the race problem that Redding struggled for better than the success of the suave modernism of Ralph Ellison. When Ellison published *Invisible Man* in 1952 he told himself it had taken five years, from the time of his *Horizon* publication, until the final publication. In 1948 he published the same section of the novel again in *48 Magazine of the Year*, minus a blonde's tattooed crotch and a young Negro's projecting erection. In 1952 *Partisan Review* carried the novel's seventeen-page "Prologue" and affirmed Ellison's place with the opinion makers. He joked about using the support of *Partisan Review*, saying to Albert Murray that "I guess I'm now a slightly mammy-made novelist."[38] The novel revealed the extramural senior year of a young black collegian, who graduates into life after being dismissed from college after an embarrassing episode with a white trustee. The young black "invisible man" goes up to New York to seek his fortune, extolling the wisdom of his college and Booker T. Washington. Poverty leads him into the arms of a radical political group called "The Brotherhood," an organization recognizably similar to the Communist Party. After adventures inside the Brotherhood, the Invisible Man questions his purpose, tries to find out who he is, and inadvertently helps to get one of the Harlem Riots going. The weird, asexual, violent, and neurotic character concludes the novel in the place where he started, a cellar in an old building that he got to through a sewer.

The book was not startling in its originality. The principle trope of invisibility and going underground had a long history, and while Ellison admitted some antecedents—Dostoyevsky for one—he pointedly avoided the obvious comparison to Richard Wright's 1944 novella "The Man Who Lived Underground." But what Ellison brought to a commonly shared artistic heritage and set of key concerns was a craftsman's obsession with language, a devoted love of black music and folklore, and a richly ironic sense of humor. In a word, he brought faith in a culture. Gwendolyn Brooks had written in 1945 of the desirability of a bit more from African American life than just "a song in the front yard," or the more conspicuous elements of assimilation. While her work clinically analyzed the sickness inside of black life that was produced by the economic crisis of racism, she did not quite offer a celebration of the native instrument. "Sadie and Maude" was tart and wryly observed, but the poem's power lies in the ironic tragedy of Maude, the "thin brown mouse," more than it is a direct celebration of Sadie, "one of the livingest chits." With characters like Jim Trueblood, Peter Wheastraw, Lucius Brockaway, Mary Rambo, Todd Clifton, Brother Tarp, and Rinehart, Ellison offered an affirmation of indigenous black American culture, and he did it with the idiom of high modernism. The affirmation carried a considerable echo.

Ellison wrote to Albert Murray, his closest friend after Richard Wright left the United States, and said that he was proud to have retained all of the novel's "rough stuff": Rinehart, Ras the Destroyer, and the hero writing in lipstick on the belly of a naked white woman. In a manner, Ellison expected these symbols to be sources of pique if not outright condemnation: urban slick operators who take success on their own terms, violent black nationalists, and a sexual situation across the color line that was deliberately lewd and grotesque. Though only a few of his critics read him properly, the novel was designed as an endorsement of the time-tested regional value of the Old West: physical action. In four places in the novel the hero joins in fisticuffs: first in a battle royal with other black boys, second against an old man in a paint factory, and third in street fight against black nationalists in Harlem. The fourth battle was the most important. In the novel's opening pages the hero descends upon a white man in the streets and nearly kills him, using West Indian tactics. In the move Ellison made his overture to the tradition of the militant 1940s and also sawed at the planks connecting him to his friends Horace Cayton, Wright, and Chester Himes. Ellison resented the articulation of fear as prime component of the black man's inheritance. And he went on to see most of the socially grounded writing exposing the racial condition as an investigation of black fear.

When *Invisible Man* first appeared, readers, all of them, recognized that it was a literary event, and yet they were unprepared to accord lasting significance to the work of a first-time black novelist. Writing for the *Atlantic*, Charles Rolo found himself in the decided rearguard of the literary elite when he said, "My admiration for the book is qualified, which puts me in a dissident minority." Rolo praised the work but steadily pointed to gaffes: "overwriting, stretches of fuzzy thinking, and a tendency to waver, confusingly, between realism and surrealism."[39] In lengthier treatment from the *New Yorker*, the critic Anthony West thought, "Few writers can have made a more commanding first appearance," and he called Ellison's book "exceptionally good."[40] West, however, was even more unilateral in his condemnation than Rolo. He decided that the novel's prologue, the epilogue, and everything that had been written in italics ought to be skipped by the reader. Perhaps the treatment that Ellison received from the magazines that shaped the tastes of the book-buying public explains the first year's sales of about twelve thousand.[41]

The classy conservative academic reviews, homes to the New Criticism, were among Ellison's more vigorous supporters. R.W.B. Lewis, writing for the *Hudson Review*, said that "*Invisible Man* is the most impressive work of fiction in a number of years," and Richard Chase in *Kenyon Review* thought the novel exemplary of "sheer richness of invention."[42] The New York intellectual crowd was represented by creative writers Saul Bellow and Delmore Schwartz, and they were ecstatic over the book. There could not be but a bit of giddiness from Jewish writers, pleased by the challenge that the book represented to the Anglo-American literary aristocracy. Bellow liked the fact that the American literary institutions that had been broadcasting the death of the novel since the end of World War II had not bred Ellison. "It is commonly felt that there is no strength to match the strength of those powers which attack and cripple modern mankind," wrote the up-and-coming novelist. "But what a great thing it is when a brilliant individual victory occurs, like Mr. Ellison's, proving that a truly heroic quality exists among our contemporaries."[43]

Delmore Schwartz flattered the book enough to suggest that he could not really offer it a competent review; only William Faulkner was capable. What Ellison's peers interpreted him as doing was striking a blow against the naysayers of art, who, laying the groundwork for the ideas that became postmodernism, began to argue that art had little ability to improve or even influence the caliber of human understanding in the era of the atomic bomb, genocide, and the totalitarian state. Young American novelists like Bellow recognized in Ellison an optimist, whose faith in the tradition of lyrical eloquence and whose heavy attention to the emotive life of the individual celebrated the resilience of the human being. And in terms of American literary politics, Ellison's talkative, analytical, and self-conscious Invisible Man swung out defiantly against both the emotionally terse and psychologically narrow characters of Hemingway and the hard-boiled naturalists who placed their faith in the determinative powers of the environment.

During the year of publication and the year following when he was the prize-winning author, Ellison predictably bristled at the criticism and thought some of the praise fulsome, and he kept a certain sort of psychological distance from the community of literary celebrity-makers. Certainly the reception he received in the black press and from black writers was enough to keep him humble. To begin with, if *Kenyon* marveled at the sheer creative intensity of the book, his black colleagues thought he was writing straight autobiography. The African American press hedged their support of the prize-winning novel (save Langston Hughes, a lifelong Ellison supporter). J. Saunders Redding reviewed the novel in his regular column at the *Baltimore Afro-American* and put on the table the consistent disappointment voiced by black critics. Powerful though the writer's technique and intelligence might be, Redding believed Ellison's scope was tragically foreshortened and he paddled the first-time novelist. "The book's fault is that a writer of power has put all his power into describing the diurnal life of gnats."[44]

Black newspaper reviewers expressed confusion, not as Aristotelians objecting to the novel's dramatic scope, but rather, looking a bit suspiciously at the novel's characters and their preoccupations: incestuous farmers, bitter and cynical college presidents, and young men blindly aping Booker T. For writers who held regular posts in urban interracial organizations and who were members of the NAACP, the novel hardly reflected their existence. If the "protest" novels of Richard Wright, Ann Petry, and Chester Himes had examined the depravity of black life with a kind of moral fervor, Ellison seemed amused by the plight of black Americans. Writing for the *Chicago Sunday Tribune*, Roi Ottley offered the worn observation that summed up the black middle class's prescriptive approach to the novel-as-public-relations: "I doubt that every Negro's life is only an endless series of defeats and frustrations."[45]

Straightforward animus to Ellison's book came predictably from his old home, New York's black Communists and fellow travelers. Fresh from defending Paul Robeson at a State Department hearing, Lloyd Brown angrily dismissed the novel in *Masses & Mainstream*. "[T]he firstborn of a talented young Negro writer enters the world with no other life than its maggots."[46] And Communist Party member and regular *Daily Worker* contributor Abner Berry, with whom Ellison had debated dialectics and art theory in the late 1930s, rejected the novel as a work of cynicism. Berry claimed that the book was "a maze of corruption, brutality, anti-Communist slander, sex perversion and the sundry inhumanities upon which a dying social system feeds": "good business, but nauseating as art."[47] The black Left thought Ellison was trying to earn bourgeoisie success by way of abstract symbolism, Freudian psychoanalysis, and anticommunism, the coin of the day. In effect, the radicals accused him of being an Uncle Tom and a sellout, draped in the tinsel of existential neurosis. Ellison was slick enough to see the situation for what it was. He permanently changed his base of support.

Another of the negative reviews against Ellison came out in Robeson's journal *Freedom*, where typically the book reviews had fallen to the cultural editor Lorraine Hansberry. Though Hansberry did have a book review in the May 1952 issue of *Freedom*, she gave *Invisible Man* to John O. Killens, whose talent was about to be recognized with the novel *Youngblood* in 1954. Narrowly focused, Killens disparaged the book that July. "It is a modernized 'surrealist' anti-Negro stereotype," he fumed.[48] The unfriendly criticism became a kind of line in the sand between Ellison and those who presented themselves as saviors of black freedom after World War II. Thenceforth Ellison had an impossible time convincing fellow black writers of his political credentials, and he never stood as an impressive figure for the artists of the 1950s who invested heavily in heroic characterizations of black freedom fighters and describing political problems.

However, Killens's remarks were not quite the result of substanceless sectarian politics. In the same issue as Killens's terse, hundred-word Ellison review, *Freedom* carried a lead article "Student Killing Exposes NYU Bias" by Lorraine Hansberry. Hansberry described the death of Enus Christiani, a doctoral student at New York University in economics. The campus police shot Christiani dead after he had repeatedly protested the use of a mammy caricature at a student fundraiser. There were rallies and demonstrations against the university in Christiani's name. Ellison's book obviously anticipated the Christiani murder in the Tod Clifton episode. But instead of the character Clifton righteously protesting the deployment of insulting caricatures by whites, Ellison's sensibility fastened onto the weird complicity between blacks and whites evoked by the minstrel tradition. In fact, nowhere in Ellison's book did a black character directly confront and violently resist unambiguous white racism. The novel

Invisible Man divulged a world without virtue or integrity: it seemed incapable of admitting the value of principled black resistance. To win a politicized black audience in the 1950s, an audience of embattled progressives unafraid of Communist ties, a writer needed to address the martyrdom of Enus Christiani, Mississippi truck-driver Willie McGee, Florida NAACP man Harry Monroe, blood plasma doctor Charles Drew, South Carolina veteran Maceo Snipes, and many a score more.

Not just the embittered Reds made the charge that Ellison concerned himself with the extraneous. Chester Himes admitted to Richard Wright that he and Ellison, whose families had shared Thanksgiving in 1946 in warmth and humor, had bordered on violence in the fall of 1952 at Vandi Haygood's apartment and in the company of Horace Cayton.[49] The ground for the disagreement was Ellison's book. Himes persisted in the accusation that, far from a pure and diligent exercise of talent, Ellison had merely taken advantage of a well-understood literary conceit that would appeal to whites, intimidate blacks, and secure fame, the gist of the John Killens review.[50] By August 1954, the eve of the publication of his novel *The Third Generation*, Himes was convinced that Ellison had met with Luce's *Time* and *Life* editors for vetting, and that *Invisible Man*'s commercial and critical success were "part of a vast propaganda campaign to silence Negro voices raised in protest, and to relegate the Negro to a place of unimportance in the literary world."[51] By 1956, when Ellison visited Wright in Paris in July and saw Himes, his relationship with both men would draw to a close.

A few months before the Supreme Court decided *Brown v. Board of Education* and the legal foundation for racial segregation gave way, Malcolm Cowley observed that the "new fiction represents the extreme point of reaction from 'social realism' as practiced in the 1930s. The new fictionists . . . are determined not to deal with public issues or social environments."[52] Ellison had not evacuated politics from his work, but the complex novel that contemplated the symbolic structure of individual will could easily be read as anticommunist. In a sense, he had successfully buried his leftist past and snuggled up to what Cowley called "the moral dilemmas of individuals, usually in isolated situations where the dilemmas can be studied like specimens in a laboratory."

The praise for the novel *Invisible Man* would sound louder throughout the 1950s, and the critics anticipated Ellison's future work with the special deference awarded to major talents. But his nimble Rinehart-like approach to the shifting cultural politics of the cold war and the Civil Rights Movement cost him mightily in the future. What Ellison did not know was that, in essence, his own career had come to a conclusion in the mid-1950s. He would produce at least two fascinating pieces of critical work after *Invisible Man*—"Change the Joke and Slip the Yoke" in 1958 and "The World and the Jug" in 1963 and 1964— but these were ripostes, not investigations, and they showed him as anxious and touchy. He censored his public career to omit the years between 1937 and 1947—the indignant leftist years—and to maintain this lacuna required an aching acrobatics of rhetoric that looked like something else. Before long Ellison would present himself so seriously and with such pomp that when even friends listened to his lectures they would find him incoherent.[53] The "vigorous" and "aggressive" writer that *Reporter* had sought out in 1949 became pretentious and affected not long after the *Brown* decision. The man thought to have the most abundant talent of all the black creative writers, who had received the kind of artistic respect it had taken more than a generation to achieve, would never publish another novel. Given that, it was difficult to conceive of America as a salutary climate for black writers.

14.1. Chester Himes, 1946   Photograph by Carl Van Vechten, James Weldon Johnson Collection in the Yale Collection of American Literature, Beinecke Rare Book and Manuscript Library, Yale University

14.2. Daisy Brown, Cedric Dover, Sterling Brown, and Owen Dodson, Fisk University, 1948　Cedric Dover Collection, Manuscripts, Archives, and Rare Book Library, Emory University

14.3. Langston Hughes, Horace Cayton, and Arna Bontemps, Fisk University, 1947   Photograph by Carl Van Vechten, James Weldon Johnson Collection in the Yale Collection of American Literature, Beinecke Rare Book and Manuscript Library, Yale University

14.4. *Zero*, spring 1949, cover   Billops-Hatch Collection, Manuscripts, Archives, and Rare Book Library, Emory University

CONTENTS

1

14.5. *Zero*, spring 1949, table of contents   Billops-Hatch Collection, Manuscripts, Archives, and Rare Book Library, Emory University

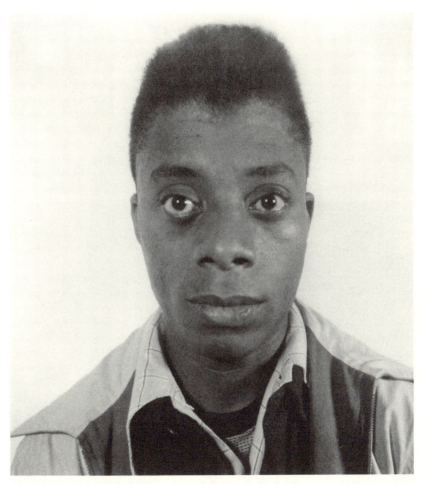

14.6. James Baldwin, 1948   Julius Rosenwald Foundation Papers, special collections, John Hope and Aurelia Elizabeth Franklin Library, Fisk University

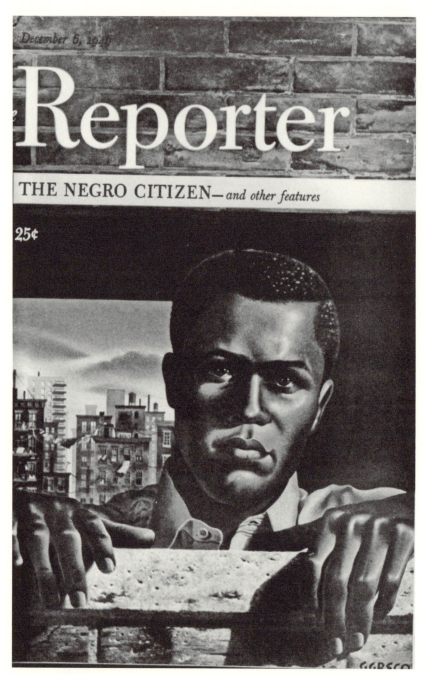

14.7. *Reporter,* "The Negro Citizen," 1949, cover

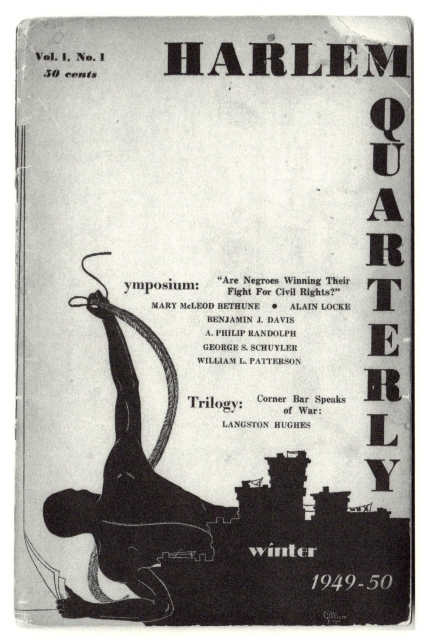

14.8. *Harlem Quarterly* 1.1, 1949–1950, cover   Billops-Hatch Collection, Manuscripts, Archives, and Rare Book Library, Emory University

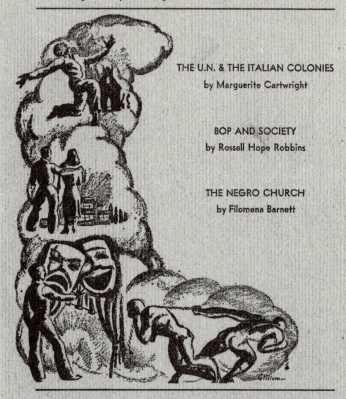

FALL-WINTER, 1950

HARLEM QUARTERLY

"A magazine for enlightenment and entertainment"

THE U.N. & THE ITALIAN COLONIES
by Marguerite Cartwright

BOP AND SOCIETY
by Rossell Hope Robbins

THE NEGRO CHURCH
by Filomena Barnett

Short Stories • Poetry • Articles • Reviews

Vol. I, No. 3 & 4   50 CENTS

14.9. *Harlem Quarterly* 1.3–4, 1950, cover   Billops-Hatch Collection, Manuscripts, Archives, and Rare Book Library, Emory University

HARLEM *QUARTERLY*

"A Magazine for Enlightment and Entertainment"

Fall _ Winter, 1950

Editor-in-Chief

BENJAMIN A. BROWN

Associate Editors

JOHN H. CLARKE
ELEANOR CARLSON
AMERICUS T. LONG

Poetry-Editor

MATTIE L. GOODE

Book Review Editor

ERNEST KAISER

Business Manager

ANATOLE D. PERKINS

Theatre

WALTER CHRISTMAS
CHARLES GRIFFIN

Staff Artists

CLYDE GILLIAM
CLARENCE RICHARDSON

Contributing Editors

LANGSTON HUGHES

SHIRLEY GRAHAM

ALAIN LOCKE

OWEN DODSON

FRANK MARSHALL DAVIS

JEAN BLACKWELL

412

C O N T E N T S

14.10. *Harlem Quarterly* 1.3–4, 1950, table of contents   Billops-Hatch Collection, Manuscripts, Archives, and Rare Book Library, Emory University

14.11. *Masses & Mainstream*, August 1949, cover

NEGRO CULTURE:

Heritage and Weapon

by DOXEY A. WILKERSON

N EGRO culture emerges from and develops as an expression of the struggles of the Negro people for freedom from oppression. It reflects, therefore, the problems and achievements of the developing national liberation movement from whose womb it springs.

Negro culture is also a vital factor in the further development of the Negro's struggle for freedom. Expressing fully the reciprocal relationship between all art and society, it operates as a social force helping to shape the consciousness of Negroes and other Americans, and to move them to social action.

Approached in terms of this frame of reference, Negro culture is seen to have significance, not only in the field of "esthetics," taken in isolation, but also in the wider realm of political struggle. It is from this point of view that the present discussion proceeds.

No attempt is made here to trace the historic development of Negro culture, or to survey the cultural achievements of the Negro people at the present time, or to make technical evaluations of the contributions of Negroes to different fields of culture. Rather, the sole purpose of this discussion is to interpret Negro culture as a social phenomenon which emerges from, and reacts upon, the freedom struggles of the Negro people.

CONCEPT OF NEGRO CULTURE

B ROADLY conceived, the term "culture" is to be equated with the term "civilization." It comprehends the entirety of the superstructure which a society has developed on the basis of its prevailing mode of production, on the economic foundation which under-girds and decisively influences the totality of social being. Thus, a people's gov-

3

14.12. "Negro Culture: Heritage and Weapon" by Doxey A. Wilkerson, *Masses & Mainstream*, August 1949, first page

14.13. Lloyd L. Brown, 1953, jacket photo from *Iron City* Masses & Mainstream
Press. Courtesy of the private collection of Randall K. Burkett

14.14. William Demby, ca. 1950   Photograph by Carl Van Vechten, James Weldon Johnson Collection in the Yale Collection of American Literature, Beinecke Rare Book and Manuscript Library, Yale University

14.15. John O. Killens, 1954 Photograph by Carl Van Vechten, Carl Van Vechten Photographs, Countee Cullen-Harold Jackman Memorial Collection, Robert W. Woodruff Library of the Atlanta University Center

14.16. Lorraine Hansberry, 1959 © Bettmann/Corbis

14.17. Richard Gibson, 1959 Photograph by Carl Van Vechten, Carl Van Vechten Photographs, Countee Cullen-Harold Jackman Memorial Collection, Robert W. Woodruff Library of the Atlanta University Center

CHAPTER FIFTEEN

The Expatriation: The Price of *Brown* and the New Bohemians (1952–1955)

In the middle of the fall in 1952, Chester Himes wrote to Richard Wright in Paris. Himes was in free-fall away from the American literary scene. He claimed in later years that the reception of the novel *Lonely Crusade* deeply wounded him, and the gore was easy to see in his letter to Wright. He refused, in spite of the crescendo in the press moving toward the Supreme Court's refutation of segregated public schools in the middle of 1954, to accept that America was transforming racially.

> The fact is the truth now is as bitter as it has ever been . . . we over here are practically being dared to discuss it. And as you know, they are not only the communists, not only the reactionaries, but the great mainstream of liberals as well who dare us now to tell the truth. . . . As long as you were on the scene and exerted a vital force on the position taken on racial matters by literary criticism and the liberal group, the issues could never entirely be excluded from discussion. You were the only one over whom they could exert no control; and you were the one who had access to the public.[1]

In public forums, in literary journals, and in highbrow intellectual magazines, virtually no one of any rank would share Himes's characterization of the scene.

Himes was becoming unsettled and his observations cast no shadow. His most profound insights were like a resin from the discarded social realist debris of the 1940s. In the novel *Lonely Crusade* Himes's hero Lee Gordon tries to explain to his fellow union organizers the basic problem that prevents blacks from taking full advantage of the benefits of democracy. "They did not want to be just members; they wanted rights and privileges above all other members."[2] This was the basic concept that Himes had brought out in the novel, and it was the one that had irked his readers the most because it completely flew in the face of the idea that blacks were on the threshold of successful assimilation.

But Himes persisted to the point of believing that something extra was necessary, and typically it brought no results. When he wrote to his first publisher Ken McCormick at Doubleday in the spring of 1953, asking for royalty information, editor-in-chief McCormick responded to Himes as if the black writer had displayed deep ingratitude. "We're not accustomed to having our word questioned the way you question it in that letter, Chester."[3] Even though Himes was writing steadily, it had taken him five years to get another book contract. His 1952 novel *Cast the First Stone* was published by a small publisher without much in the way of literary acclaim, Coward-McCann. Himes got a twelve-hundred-dollar advance. None of the big commercial presses such as he had known in the 1940s would touch him, especially not with his primed detonations in the press, at public talks, and in the apartments of friends. Himes the writer seemed to be wandering into something deliberately self-destructive. His novels had become hastily scribbled notes out of his own private history. *Cast the First Stone* seemed to dredge up elements of his personal life that were dangerous. The book recalled his prison experience, including at its center a homosexual affair. The next year Himes worked on another book that was even more deeply personal and not quite thinly fictionalized called *The Third Generation*. He stood naked in front of readers and showed a tortured home life that would make his incarceration at nineteen seem a kind of refuge. Himes seemed alone, a reject, and defeated by his own history.

To deal with his problems Himes drank hard in the early 1950s—and perhaps less than Horace Cayton and Sterling Brown. It was euphemistically called "taking the cure." Himes could get ugly, and a few years later he would lose credibility with some of his New York friends when, at a small party, he tried to beat up his white girlfriend, the former Rosenwald Fellowship officer Vandi Haygood. (He apparently did not suffer the same ostracism when he tried the same thing a bit earlier with his wife Jean and her roommate on Christmas 1952.) Shameless and resourceful, Himes turned the abusive experience into another novel, *The End of a Primitive*. Focusing on the book's assumption of interracial sex, William Targ, the editor at World who had published *Third Generation*, told him that the book "is simply not publishable" and he hoped that Himes wouldn't "confuse it with serious writing."[4] In 1953 Chester Himes left the United States, returned briefly, then took permanent exile, at first in France and then, toward the end of the 1960s, in Franco's Spain. The writers responded to the extremity of the era, and Himes, half-sensualist, half-pimp, did not even recoil the furthest. The *Freedom* cartoonist and painter Oliver Harrington would eventually leave Paris for East Germany.

Himes's glum broadcast to Wright captured the flight and crash of that rare composition, sentient in art and politics and black. Between 1948 and 1955, the seven years immediately following Richard Wright's setting up house a stone's throw from either the Seine or the intellectual cafés of St. Germain de Prés, the epicenter of African American literary affairs shifted. Or it cracked. The new home for black talent was Paris, or at least Europe.

William Demby completed one novel in Rome and had another under way before 1950. He made the most of the international life, marrying an aristocrat and becoming an assistant director for filmmaker Federico Fellini. Nor did he go to a Rome that was at a loss for black talent: the expatriates included actor John Kitzmiller; translator and critic Ben Johnson; Katherine Dunham; Prix de Rome winner John Rhoden; soprano Evelyn Mock; and the globetrotting nightclub owner Ada "Bricktop" Smith.

James Baldwin left the United States in November 1948. He would return after nearly five years when his novel was being published, but he never lived continuously in the United States again. The Philadelphia writer William Gardner Smith, who some people were putting their chips on as the next great writer, left for France in 1951, not long after the publication of the blanched novel *Anger at Innocence*. Once there, Gardner Smith never even pretended to desire returning. Richard Gibson took the trouble to serve out his enlistment in the U.S. Army overseas, beginning in 1951, but starting after he traveled to Italy in the company of Owen Dodson. Gibson settled in Paris in 1953 after his discharge and would return to the United States briefly, then embrace permanent expatriation. All of them, Chester Himes, James Baldwin, William Gardner Smith, William Demby, and Richard Gibson, liked the United States best as tourists.

And even Ralph Ellison, anointed by the reviews from *Sewanee* to *Partisan*, the acknowledged leader among American modernists of whatever race and, from at least 1952 onward, a remarkably stalwart patriot, extended his Prix de Rome fellowship from one year to two and lived in Rome from 1955 through 1957. These male expatriates had as much talent as any comparable group, anywhere, anytime. And they left their native land at precisely the moment that the greatest political and artistic freedom had ever been available to black writers. Confused about his confusion, James Baldwin had written to William Phillips that he followed the Americans to Paris because he did not know where he was or what he wanted.[5] No less jammed up but more direct, Chester Himes said, "I just wanted out from the United States, that was all. I had had it."[6]

There was a great irony to the passages out to Europe. In an eighteen-month span from 1952 to 1953, four key works of African American high modernism appeared: Ellison's *Invisible Man*, Gwendolyn Brooks's *Maud Martha*, Ann Petry's *The Narrows*, and James Baldwin's much anticipated *Go Tell It on the Mountain*. These works, all of them major achievements in narrative form and psychologically complex black characters, would signal the successful acceptance of blacks into American life. Everything collided like an atom burst: the erudite modernists, the vogue of black novelists proving themselves with all-white casts, and the drive to get the hell out of the country.

The singular reaction of black critics against Ralph Ellison's *Invisible Man* showed the bitterness and fury after years of second-class citizenship. It was not even a question of using Ellison to defeat the crude racists with the example of Negro cultivation. After Ellison had received the National Book Award for fiction, black writers were uneasy about his membership as an organic part of the black community, in part undoubtedly because they could not match the recognition accorded Ellison from elite publishers, top-tier white colleges and universities, foundations, media organs and award-granting bodies. His peers were beginning to see Ellison as apart from them. Arna Bontemps's comment to Langston Hughes in October of the same year suggests the abiding cynicism shared by talented and productive black artists who witnessed Ellison being launched by the American culture industry: "Why don't you (as a suggestion) pick out a few of the *ideas* previously used, ideas which seemed to catch the fancy of ofays [whites] who read or reviewed the books, and work up new treatments or new situations in which to air them," Bontemps recommended to Hughes with the wink of his eye. "For example," he continued, in mock seriousness, "the idea of elevating one Negro (like Ralph [Ellison]) while neglecting or closing the eyes to the millions."[7] Bontemps, like Hughes, had always diluted the extreme bitterness of his life with extensive doses of humor.

Ellison had used humor as a palliative too, and it showed in his novel, though not everyone thought he was really funny. In 1954 the Morgan State College literary critic Nick Aaron Ford published an essay in *Phylon* comparing the best-selling well-known male novelists of the time: Wright, Willard Motley, Frank Yerby, and Ellison. Unsurprisingly, Ford wrote about serious problems with the style and approach of *Invisible Man*, specifically the novel's conclusion: "[T]he only avenue open to the Negro who wants to keep his self-respect is complete withdrawal. This seems to be the meaning of the final episode." Ford echoed early criticisms that the novel was uneven, and that the tensions between comedy and tragedy and realism and surrealism were quite strained. Ford thought that Ellison wasn't sure if he "wanted to be serious or comical in his personal attitude."[8]

Langston Hughes was certain about whether or not Ellison was serious. Hughes, who once bragged that he could never finish reading *Invisible Man,* described Ellison's own personality as a fitting counterpart to the kind of alienation that Nick Aaron Ford noticed about the narrator of *Invisible Man.*[9] In Hughes's view, Ellison and Richard Wright "always" perceived "something not quite right in the world around them," "[e]ven on the brightest days . . . something was always wrong."[10]

Perhaps one sign of the world's wrongness to Ellison was the lethargic response of the black critics to his literary style, until they seemed willfully ignorant by doing so. Alain Locke put *Invisible Man* among three peaks of black narrative fiction, alongside Toomer's *Cane* and Wright's *Native Son.* And yet Locke lamented the unnecessary language; the book was "smothered with verbosity and hyperbole."[11] When he first offered his opinion of the book it was possible to sense behind his encomium a desperate hope that Ellison would write another book that made more sense. "For once, too, here is a Negro writer capable of real and sustained irony. *Invisible Man*, evidently years in the making, must not be Ralph Ellison's last novel."

And when blacks did get something from the novel, it was often not what the whites got, at all. The handful of black undergraduates on Harvard's campus, like future U.S. ambassador Walter Carrington, found themselves walking around the yard and muttering under their breath, "Ras the Destroyer!"[12] They were less interested in the jam of existentialism and American exceptionalism that Ellison had proposed as the core philosophy of the book; they enjoyed the symbol for righteous vengeance. The possibility of black assimilation and the triumph of the literary formalism pioneered by T. S. Eliot presented a fascinating paradox. If the method of explaining the literary work of art relied on a belief in tradition, order, hierarchy, original sin, discipline, and the acknowledgment of evil in the world, what would happen to African Americans, people of a related but still different cultural tradition? What happened if one believed that Nat Turner as much as Nathan Hale had made the great sacrifice for the beloved community?

In the third week of October 1952, Margaret Walker held a clearinghouse conference of black writers and critics at Jackson State College in Mississippi. Under the inauspicious but still gutsy title "Seventy-Five Years of the Negro in Literature," the conference attendees gathered for a Sunday afternoon convocation address by Sterling Brown, followed by a full week of papers, panels, and workshops on literature, journalism, and the arts. The conference attendees included Brown, Langston Hughes, Arna Bontemps, Era Bell Thompson, Owen Dodson, Robert Hayden, J. Saunders Redding, Gwendolyn Brooks, Melvin Tolson, and Carl Moses Holman. This group had things to celebrate: Tolson, Brooks, Hughes, and Redding had all just published or were on the verge of publishing major works, and all were at the pinnacle of their creative and intellectual powers. Walker, in the next year, was herself to win a major new fellowship from the Ford Foundation and go to Yale for a year in 1954. The historic crowd did not include Ralph Ellison. Walker confided to Langston Hughes that she had hoped to have the esteemed novelist participate, but, although she had known him since the 1930s, on account of his mainstream success she doubted his interest. "I would very much like to have invited Ralph Ellison to come down also, but our money has run out and we are operating on a much smaller budget than originally expected," she wrote, adding "of course, he may not have accepted."[13]

Excepting Hughes, none of the fast-track black New Yorkers went to Mississippi, and certainly no one expected Richard Wright in from France. Only a few months after the conference in early 1953, Wright published his first novel since *Native Son*, a heavily anticipated book called *The Outsider*. The appearance of Wright's work was still an event, though by 1953 it is certainly difficult to imagine how Americans, black or white, new liberal or old, would have had any use for something he would have said. This was not true outside of the country. In 1953 the great theorist of pan-Africanism, George Padmore, wrote to Gold Coast prime minister Kwame Nkrumah heralding the importance of Wright's new book. For Padmore, the novel was a study of power, the "psychological and philosophical conflict in man's struggle to be free of forces which imprison his personality." Padmore ringingly endorsed the book that tried to answer the question of human freedom and responsibility in a world whose ideologies of power and control were obviously failing. "You must read the book," he advised the newly elected head of what was then yet a British colony.[14]

In his last letter to Ralph Ellison, Wright expressed his belief in the outrageous potential of the book, which would delineate "the Negro's relationship to the Western world."[15] Speaking about the character Cross Damon, Wright called him "by far a more savage guy than Bigger Thomas." Wright was confident of one thing: "I know the Negroes will not like it." Negroes of course meant American blacks, whose civil rights and artistic successes Wright might have felt made them suffer from the same blind innocence that earned white American's abroad such unflattering reputations. Obviously Wright relished his status as the *enfant terrible* among American black writers, and he felt that his hero of existentialism, the murderous intellectual Cross Damon, would vindicate his steady coupling of philosophies of individual responsibility and deadly violence. The book was well received in France. But in America, it only added to the undoing of Wright's public career.

Whatever ultimately can be said of Wright as a craftsman and as a thinker, he never lacked ambition. The novel tried to entertain the question of what might lie beyond Western philosophy and its theories of mental consciousness, if it was possible to get outside of it; by choosing a black protagonist, Wright attempted to begin on the margin of the Western world. The novel, with its love affairs and murders and scenes of flight and escape, rang especially true for Chester Himes, who wrote to Wright that "I'm so goddamned close to that boy I don't want to talk about it."[16] The book pointed to the existential choice as one toehold for human fortitude, though Wright took the next step and had his hero arrive at the conclusion that human existence in isolation is the most acute and disfiguring horror. Arna Bontemps delivered the near epitaph that seemed generally to characterize the reception of the book: "He has had a roll in the hay with the existentialism of Sartre, and apparently he liked it."[17]

To at least one degree, Bontemps completely miscast Wright's effort. *The Outsider* was basically sympathetic to Sartre's foundations, and at one point it even provided a reading list in the philosophy of Heidegger, Kierkegaard, Husserl, and Nietzsche to show the main character's adherence to the policy of alienation. But in the book Wright seemed mainly to have continued to flesh out and detail the narrative of Fred Daniels from "The Man Who Lived Underground," which was written before the rise of Sartre. Furthermore, in this novel he had fulfilled his career up to that point; he had brought the indignant anger of the American bogey of fiction Bigger Thomas into line with the brooding, alienated portrait of himself in *Black Boy*. The deliberately existential hero Cross Damon is in search of fellow "rebels with whom he could feel at home, men who were not outsiders because they had been born black and poor, but because they thought their way through the many veils of illusions."[18]

Of course, given Wright's sense of the violent United States, the protagonist Cross Damon has to murder his way to the cerebral plateau. He kills a totalitarian, manipulative communist and a venal, racist capitalist but, perhaps most important, the killing begins with a black man who represents something like Cross Damon's Sambo alter ego. The murder of "fat black Joe Thomas" makes all the other killings possible. The novel concluded on nearly the same plane as "The Man Who Lived Underground," with the dying hero groping for wisdom to yoke human beings to one another and to themselves. Bleeding to death, Damon tells the hunchbacked district attorney Ely Houston, "Men must meet themselves," and finishes the tale describing the horror that cannot be disconnected from the narrator's feeling of innocence.[19] Just as he had done in *Native Son*, Wright fabricated an interracial conclusion that seemed forced.

Nevertheless, for a self-educated black American whose life had begun on a Mississippi plantation, the book was a bit of a marvel. But the public never warmed to *The Outsider*, as they never warmed to a book from 1951 trying to work through the communist–capitalist–existentialist morass and using elements of detective fiction as well, *Barbary Shore*, Norman Mailer's sophomore novel. The theater of a political narrative beyond right and left was a bit much for the U.S. market during what was then called the Korean Conflict, which left more than fifty thousand Americans and hundreds of thousands of Koreans and Chinese dead. It is also likely that Wright may have been better known at the time as the author of a chapter in *The God That Failed*, Richard Crossman's 1949 collection of anticommunist writings.

The market favorite that year was James Baldwin's novel *Go Tell It on the Mountain*, which appeared a few months after Wright's book, on May 18, 1953. The day before the book became available to the public, the *New York Times* ran a celebratory review. By the time the book was published, Baldwin had romped through Paris for four and a half years, in kind of an intriguing version of postgraduate work that enabled him to run, sometimes, in the same circles as American writers like Saul Bellow, William Styron, George Plimpton, and Norman Mailer. These writers paralleled the stature and work achieved by John Dos Passos, F. Scott Fitzgerald, Ernest Hemingway, Allen Tate, Edmund Wilson, and Malcolm Cowley in the 1920s. After World War II, this group would now include blacks: Richard Wright, because of his steady critiques of American politics, was on the fringe, and Baldwin, his anguished young double, was closer to the center.

Baldwin was a case history in contradiction, who claimed to find amazing resources in his Americaness but was just as easily repelled by it when that was all that was there. He was as conflicted about the quality of his ethnic inheritance, where he was assumed to have expertise, as he was regarding his exile. Bitter about Eisenhower's crushing presidential victory and Eugene McCarthy's Senate inquisitions, he wrote to his agent William Cole that he would rather "be at home getting into trouble" than stranded overseas and explaining to Europeans "quite clearly indefensible American policies."[20] And though he thought that Sartre's support of the Communists as the lesser of two evils would prevent him from offering a blurb for *Go Tell It on the Mountain*, he did think that Albert Camus and Richard Wright might. Always prepared to take advantage of Wright's reputation, Baldwin encouraged his agent to mail out an advance copy of *Go Tell It on the Mountain*. "[W]hy the hell not?," he wrote to Cole, clarifying his position on Wright. "We're perfectly pleasant to each other. I don't think he'll like the novel, but, then, you haven't got to print what he says about it."

The time in Paris in Wright's circles had never curbed Baldwin's tongue. In December 1951, at a Franco-American Fellowship meeting organized by Wright to prod the French government into hiring blacks, Baldwin had publicly accused Wright of exaggerating racial discord between blacks and whites. The outburst made its way onto Wright's extensive FBI file. The first report read, "Wright and his group were the targets of attacks from one James Baldwin, a young Negro writer who was a student in Paris. Baldwin attacked the hatred themes of the Wright writings and the attempt of the Franco-American Fellowship Group to perpetuate 'Uncle Tom Literature Methods.'"[21]

Seven years later, a U.S. Army report made its way to the FBI director on "Possible Subversives among U.S. Personnel in France" and probably better characterized the events of December 1951.[22] Baldwin, who may have reported the conversations of the Franco-American Fellowship, which he was known to attend inebriated, is the "Source" in the memorandum. "Richard WRIGHT asked Source to join a 'protest' group aimed at 'forcing the employment of more of the Americans of African ancestry' in US government jobs in Paris. Source told WRIGHT that it would be better to be certain of facts before 'going off half cocked.' WRIGHT then accused Source of having an 'Uncle Tom attitude.'"[23] The gusto with which the legendary battles between the two men are told tends to eclipse the broad sympathy between their positions, which they both recognized. In late 1951 or 1952 Wright had invited Baldwin to his house for a party and Baldwin had refused, telling William and Mary Smith that Ellen Wright "had a vile tongue."[24] Ellen Wright, who was perhaps a better Communist than

Richard Wright and thus much less disposed to Baldwin than her husband was, did not attend the party.

Baldwin returned to the United States in the year his book was published. Despite the rough edges of life in Paris, the move to France had not been idle for him. Portions of the novel came out in the alert postwar periodicals that everyone was happy to be published by. Before the book's publication, France-based *New Story* printed "The Outing" (alongside an article by William Demby frowning at television), *American Mercury* ran "Exodus," *Commentary* beheld "The Death of the Prophet," and *New World Writing* published perhaps the most crucial section, "Roy's Wound." Some of Baldwin's critical essays had appeared in France, like his bit of anti-Sartrean work "Le Problème Noire en Amérique" in *Rapports France-États Unis*. In the short essay that for any validity with the French audience demanded that he quote Richard Wright, Baldwin conducted an amanuensis performance, speaking for the white American. He decided that the entirely unique situation of American blacks could find its resolution only within the equally remarkable circumstance of American exceptionalism. Baldwin entrusted the "specific American dynamic," which produced "cohesion out of diverse phenomena," as a source for the eventual resolution of the race problem. "[I]mperfect" were the American solutions so far, Baldwin admitted, but "[o]nly totalitarian regimes ask more from human beings."[25]

An anticommunist abroad, Baldwin was hitting both the highbrow and middlebrow in the United States. *Partisan Review* carried "Many Thousands Gone," his explicit rebuttal to Wright's *Native Son*, and *Harper's* carried "Stranger in the Village," his attempt to define black identity outside of Wright's terms. Baldwin's ability to have his work appear in long-standing, widely circulated magazines like *Harper's* and the influential *Partisan Review* forced comparisons with the only other black writers who had done something similar before: Richard Wright and J. Saunders Redding.

Bigger news than his essays and shorter fiction was the novel *Go Tell It on the Mountain*. Baldwin showed mastery with many remarkable features of confident writing. He had sure-handed flashbacks and transitions to present narrative time, and a careful scrutiny of realistic environment and human motive. He attended to ghetto life without any careless pleading or sentimentality. But by far the most exceptional artistic choice was thematic: the book offered chiefly a portrait of a father and a son. Baldwin suggested that his was the first black generation of black sons to have ever known their fathers. The relationship was uneasy. Baldwin pointed to a conflict, intimate, Oedipal, and vicious. His portraits ennobled black women for their suffering the men, but women in his fiction were typically secondary characters. The key conflict of the novel was a primal struggle for dominance between a brutal and ignorant father and a passive, fearful son.

Unsurprisingly, in essence, Baldwin was substituting one conflict for another. His portrait was more than semi-autobiographical, but he was in rebellion from his race as much as he was from his stepfather David Baldwin and his decision for sexuality on his own terms. After the novel had been published, he absolved himself in a letter to Cole, admitting deep feelings that he had concealed in order to win a public career: "I hated and feared white people."[26] But between 1948 and 1952 James Baldwin was not in a position to endorse the view of Horace Cayton and Chester Himes. Although Baldwin's book did carry doses of white brutality in the South and police cruelty in the North, he proposed that instead of an epic confrontation with whites, black men were more deeply invested in a drama of generational internecine war. Death and rejection lay at the core of the black male paternal–filial relationship. He was successful in outrunning the race problem by, essentially, turning Bigger Thomas into a hypocrite preacher and father of five.

With Baldwin, perhaps for the first time the liberal press and the African American intellectuals reached consensus. New Republic reviewed the book and called it "an attempt by a Negro to write a novel about Negroes which is yet not a "Negro novel."[27] Richard Barksdale, who in 1951 had become the second African American to earn a Ph.D. from Harvard's English department, reviewed the novel for Phylon.[28] "It is a story by a Negro, about Negroes, set in a predominately Negro environment; and yet it is not essentially a "Negro" novel. Herein lies Baldwin's signal achievement."[29] It had become imperative to recognize the lay of the land. Better than writing about whites to prove the black writer's objective credentials was to write about blacks but somehow without being "intent on analyzing the social dilemma." Baldwin's friend Richard Gibson had done it in Kenyon Review. His short stories "Two Mortuary Sermons," about African American life in the still-rural Maryland suburbs of Washington, D.C., never betrayed, in either the physical description or the vernacular they used to speak, the characters' racial status. By 1953 this had become the new encomium of distinction: black blacklessness.

Baldwin had done more than Gibson. Go Tell It on the Mountain's permanent contribution to American literature lay in the deeply beautiful portrait of working-class black life, the life of the anonymous common man. The novel operated with a bookend for its main plot: parts 1 and 3 showed the salvation of protagonist John Grimes within the evangelical storefront "The Fire Baptized Church." But the book itself was in the second section, called "The Prayers of the Saints," a profoundly reflective study of John's mother Elizabeth, his stepfather Gabriel, and Gabriel's older sister Florence. Each of their stories, essentially what the individual characters have in mind as they kneel next to John on a Harlem Saturday at their storefront church, is the painful tale of unfulfilled romance. The love story was Baldwin's gift. He delivered up three gritty romances of southern-born black Americans who had moved north in the early twentieth century.

If describing the same period of historical time as Zora Neal Hurston, it seemed impossible in fifteen years to have traveled a further distance in representing the speech of Janie and Tea Cake. Baldwin demurred that he had never even listened to the music of Bessie Smith until he lived in Switzerland in 1951, so he did not attempt to invoke the densely metaphorical black speech and weighty cultural rituals behind speech practices. As great as his gifts of storytelling and narration and psychological depth were, Baldwin retained, throughout his career, a flat ear for black vernacular and Anatole Broyard's suspicion about its wisdom. He did not make the error of commission, but of omission. Baldwin had determined that the difference in speech between southern blacks and whites could really be isolated to three or four gaffes in grammar and syntax— "ain't"; the perfect tense instead of the simple past tense, as in "done" instead of "did"; and "got" instead of "have"—beyond that, the sounds of whites and blacks were just alike.

But it was impossible to quarrel with the breadth and sincerity of ambition of *Go Tell It on the Mountain*. Baldwin wanted to properly humanize the "common nigger," a tag that he put over and again into the mouths of his weary laboring-class characters to invoke differences among poor blacks. He might have wanted Diana and Lionel Trilling to have achieved a deeper kind of estimate of the human profundity of the person who mopped their kitchen and shut their elevator door. But the twenty-five-year-old graduate of the New York intellectuals and Marshall Plan Paris could do this only within a rigidly precise critical framework. The ideal of heroic manhood, a version of which Baldwin had already castigated in American detective fiction, would have to be abolished. John Grimes's stepfather Gabriel, who tries at eight to face white malice with bravery and at twenty-one to redeem the neighborhood's outcast woman, was earmarked as the source of evil.

The novel called rapid attention to its being written by a young gay black American. In the first paragraphs, and, perhaps, in a manner that Baldwin did not exactly intend, he asserted that the novel would revolve around the adolescent hero John's "sexual" problem. John Grimes lives in an environment of depravity, where it was possible to observe couples in condemned buildings making love standing up (which was perhaps to say upside down), and where the sound of his own parent's lovemaking competed with the sound of scurrying rats to mortify him. John's younger brother Roy adjusts to Harlem by determining to become like the rough streets, and to place himself literally into its fleshy chaos. John has not the reediness for such priapic rebellion and makes his adjustment in the form of submission—to the church. Fearful about sex, what it does to his mother "every time her belly began to swell," and knowing that the pregnant swelling "would not end until she was taken away from him," John becomes, in 1950s parlance, an introvert.[30]

On his birthday, John goes to a movie and identifies with the blonde heroine. He soon finds comfort in the charismatic potency of an older teenager named Elisha, a boy struggling to contain his "muscles leaping" and "thighs [that] moved terribly against the cloth of his suit."[31] The novel concludes with John defying his father in order to receive a "holy kiss" from Elisha. This thematic undercurrent of the book (one that ostensibly also lay at the root of the un-sexed narrators in the books by William Demby, Owen Dodson, and Ralph Ellison) was a wasp's nest. It seemed in broad sympathy with the research by psychologists Kardiner and Ovesey in *Mark of Oppression*. The doctors had decided, on the basis of a handful of interviews, that Negro men were impotent and liable to "inversion" as a result of racial oppression. This was a tangent off of Park and Burgess, the solidly liberal duo who had presented "lady of the races" mythology in the early 1920s.[32] The price of black submission to white supremacy might have looked like passivity or mild effeminacy on the surface, but some of the prominent liberal social scientists believed that underneath that was homosexuality.

The distance that the young black writers put between themselves and pro-testing the racial condition is obvious in the rhetoric of another young "mose" who achieved his first fiction publication in 1953, Albert Murray. Murray went over to France on the GI Bill in the spring of 1951 to take French language courses at the University of Paris. He looked up Baldwin and, using his own inimitable black vernacular and deep range of black folklore allusion, sounded out Baldwin's writer's instincts. Baldwin had been raised in the storefront church, yes, but the literal poverty of that tradition had disabled his sensibility toward older cultural resources. Murray put the matter to Ralph Ellison in a letter that year. "I haven't seen Baldwin's book yet, but what I saw of the manu-script in Paris didn't show me much, and I caint figure out why they printed that excerpt in *New World Writing*. As for that style, Baldwin has already admit-ted to me that he really doesn't know anything about the actual grain and texture of Negro expression. But what the hell, man, you been going around signifying for years about castration."[33] Chester Himes was cruder in his characterization of Baldwin's new work. He kindled some warmth with Richard Wright in June 1953, "[H]ave you seen any reviews of 'our boy' Baldwin's book—Go Shit on the Mountain, or whatever the title is."[34]

The private comments of African American male writers expressed a kind of bravado by way of fear and loathing toward homosexuality. What is more curi-ous is that they emerge from a group of men not necessarily in league with one another. A dilettante writer in the early 1950s, Murray ridiculed the work of both Wright and Himes. Ellison, who had talks with Baldwin in the fall of 1952 when Baldwin returned from France, actively disliked Baldwin's work but was too respectful of Baldwin's power, especially as a connected critic, to attack him in public. But Ellison also resisted Chester Himes, and he went on to resist Wright. Himes and Wright were distrustful of Ellison for nearly the same reason that they distrusted Baldwin, though neither man thought Ellison much worse than a curmudgeon who tried to take advantage of current literary rhetoric to advance himself. But for all of them, Baldwin was understood to have abandoned his racial heritage, painted himself white, and turned gay as a result.

The partly phobic attitude of the others toward Baldwin had a great deal to do with sexual anxiety. This racial cannibalism had everything to do with sexuality. During an era when the public and private murder of black men was sometimes accompanied by genital mutilation, black male anxiety about castration dovetailed with homophobia and anxieties about homosexuality. In the novel itself, for example, Baldwin had reproduced the biblical story of Noah and Ham, with tiny Johnny washing his stepfather and hating the man for his serpentlike penis, while he prepares for his father's Noah-like curse. Men like Murray, Himes, Ellison, and Wright, active sentinels of their heterosexual identities, thought of homosexual men as having "castrated" themselves and become women.

In the 1940s Wright had described this condition, especially as it concerned race and sexual identity to Horace Cayton. When the two men sat aboard a Jim Crow train and heard a noticeable change in the tone of a black steward as he addressed his white supervisor, Wright made the observation that the black man's "testicles must have jumped two inches into his stomach." "He does that to emasculate himself, to make himself more feminine, less masculine, more acceptable to a white man," he continued to Cayton, who complained that he preferred not to have a verbal photograph of what was taking place.[35] To these men and at this time, conspicuous homosexuality was the ultimate in the feminization of the male.

Both Baldwin and Albert Murray were writing coming-of-age tales about young men and both came out, a year apart, in the high modernist journal *New World Writing*. Murray's "The Luzanna Cholly Kick" introduced African Americans of the Deep South erecting standards of highly masculine heroic behavior on their own terms. If Baldwin was writing about a Harlem that had no tangible white presence, Murray suggested a different kind of black resistance to white domination. In the short story, the narrator actively seeks to diminish the crisis of black oppression. He makes a glancing remark, which Murray placed in parentheses.

(Naturally Lil' Buddy and I knew about Negroes and white folks, and we knew that there was something generally wrong with white folks, but it didn't seem so very important then. We knew that if you hit a white boy he would turn red and call you nigger that did not sound like the Nigger the Negroes said and he would run and get as many other white boys as he could and come back at you, and we knew that a full-grown white man had to get somebody to back him up too, but we didn't really think about it much, because there were so many other things we were doing then.)[36]

Apparently even such gestures were not enough to convince publishers of the merits of a book trying to be an African American *Adventures of Huckleberry Finn*. Even with the backing of Ralph Ellison, it would take Murray roughly twenty years to publish his paean to the blue-black railroad man Luzanna Cholly, which eventually became the novel *Train Whistle Guitar*.

In vast distinction from Murray, Baldwin's extravagantly praised *Go Tell It on the Mountain* was a contender for the National Book Award in 1954, and Baldwin was told that he lost the award because the foundation refused to honor two black writers in successive years. The award went instead to Saul Bellow's *The Adventures of Augie March*, the first of Bellow's three National Book Awards. Ralph Ellison served on the jury, which probably added to Baldwin's sense that the award had been deliberately steered away from him. Discreetly, Baldwin admitted that he admired Ellison, whom he compared to Faulkner and Robert Penn Warren. He called Ellison "the first Negro novelist I have ever read to utilize in language, and brilliantly, some of the ambiguity and irony of Negro life," but he never went effusive in praise of the man whose career he caught and eclipsed.[37] And the black reviewers liked him more than Ellison, though Baldwin scoffed at the inability of the Negro press to print words like "nigger" and "black bastard." J. Saunders Redding might have missed Baldwin's foraging missions in *Commentary* or *Partisan Review*, but he did not ignore the succulent 1953 novel. He praised Baldwin's book warmly. "No one can quarrel with his literary talent."[38]

An impartial observer might have found a worthy quarrel in the inability of the literary scene to accommodate more than a single example of black literary talent at a time in 1953. Although the high modernist triumphs appeared between 1952 and 1953 in the same kind of jet that had produced the astoundingly popular social realists between 1945 and 1947, the result of the works as a group in public were not that similar. The difficulty apparently was one of digestion: it was simply beyond the ken of reviewers and a public to grant encomium after encomium, to heap up superlatives on distinguished work that seemed to advance black writing to a remarkable new position from a short distance of seven or eight years. It would be difficult to suggest that the new virtuosity was encouraged.

Thus, in Baldwin's successful year Ann Petry earned little for easily her most significant work, her novel debuting on August 17, 1953, *The Narrows*. Probably the sharpest craftsman to review her, Arna Bontemps tried to adjust his compliments to do the most good. Even though *The Narrows* was a "novel about Negroes by a Negro novelist and concerned, in the last analysis, with racial conflict," he explained, "'The Narrows' somehow resists classification as a 'Negro novel,' as contradictory as it may sound."[39] But even this prime ranking was not enough.

A more telling review thought the work not fully capable of climbing the high mast of modernist techniques, the world beyond protest art. Wright Morris, a new chum of Ralph Ellison and Albert Murray and author of *The Works of Love*, took the opportunity to offer a tutorial—to Petry apparently—on literary criticism when he reviewed the book. "Literature is the place to cry havoc," Morris began.

> The Negro in America has known this for some time. To his old cry of havoc something new, recently, has been added. The desire to give it permanence, to stake out a claim in the durable world of art. This ambition transforms the writer's conception of both his suffering and his raw material—he is made aware that his predicament is more than skin deep. Ralph Ellison's "Invisible Man" marked the transition to this higher ground. It set new standards by which the old material must be judged. "The Narrows" reflects these standards in its ambition and its theme of the complexity of evil, but the performance indicates that the goal is not easily attained.[40]

It was becoming obvious that after Ellison's National Book Award, everyone would retreat from the initial criticism of *Invisible Man* and use the work as a new kind of benchmark, and in the process junk the import of several finely made books. But *Invisible Man* had two colossal strengths in 1953. First, it could easily be fitted into a generally anti-Stalinist cold war liberal attitude. Ellison had in fact deleted elements from his manuscript that suggested that black Americans existed in a colonial-style situation. The famous symbolic finale in the sewer, where the protagonist burns the papers that had defined him, was originally designed to include a key text that the Invisible Man could not bring himself to burn: a bible of anticolonial guerilla warfare. Second, while Ellison daringly acknowledged the reality of and psychological tension that resulted from sex between the races, he prudently kept his distance from such descriptions. Undoubtedly here Ralph Ellison had done well to follow his white editorial friends who advised him to chuck the "Othello theme" from his book.

Petry targeted and hit the "durable world of art," but her book was not assimilable in the same way as Ellison's or Baldwin's. The problem of black writers failing to measure up to white standards had been a perennial one. It had not been anticipated that when the artists began to measure up, they would forcefully repudiate the institutions responsible for them. Petry gave over much of the book's theme to exposing the corruption of an industrial war economy and to the African American pursuit of assimilation to white middle-class standards. In every respect *The Narrows* was a better, more intellectually probing, psychologically denser, and artistically richer work than *The Street*. The rickety popular response to the book must have had something to do with the fact that Petry would never again complete a full-length work of adult fiction.

The core narrative of *The Narrows* was a doomed love affair between a young black intellectual and a white heiress. Though the novel combined multiple flashbacks and was better known and beloved for its minor characters, Petry had a fundamentally compact plot. *The Narrows* explored the life of a young man named Link, an orphan raised by Abbie Crunch, the paragon of aging black middle-class propriety, on Dumble Street in a Connecticut river town. Link, the tale's heroic martyr, has graduated from the Ivy League and plans to write a history of U.S. slavery. Abbie has lost her husband and faces declining economic circumstance and old age. Link's heroic course of action changes when he falls in love with a married munitions heiress; eventually he regains his race pride but dies at the hand of the rich adulteress's avenging mother.

Petry presented the case that the achievement of solid middle-class mores threatened blacks with sterility, and obviously this was an early anxiety about integration. Link's final tragedy was premised on a history of tragedy. Abbie's husband Theodore comes home in a stupor one night, and the dutiful middle-class wife fears that a drunken spouse has embarrassed her. Instead the man is suffering from a stroke. A deep tension underlies Abbie's mistake. Abbie Crunch's husband is a self-described descendant of South Carolina "swamp niggers"—maroons—and he passes on stories of levitating African ancestors as well as a more general bitterness about the misery of slavery. The "Major" is the embodiment of the ancestral tradition, and Theodore Crunch intends to transfer these stories to Link, who can connect the era of enslavement to the present generation of African Americans.

But since Abbie Crunch believes that her husband has humiliated her, she neglects medical advice and "Major" dies. During her grief Link falls into the care of the ill-tempered tavern-owner named Bill Hod and his gourmet cook, a schizophrenic called Weak Knees. Though Link eventually returns home and finishes college, he has forged permanent ties to the black lower class. Abbie herself then takes in a roomer, a cropped and mannered professional servant named Malcolm Powther, who in an act of either rebellion or assimilation—it was ambiguous—married Mamie, a Bessie Smith–styled character who oozes with black-bottom sensuality and conducts an open affair with Bill Hod. The Powthers's uninhibited young son J.C. rubs Abbie's nerves raw and complexly represents future black possibility; the novel concludes with Abbie recognizing the treasure in the relationship to the young boy. Petry showed a formidable sense of the structure of the African American community, savvy political concerns, and technically alert literary expression.

J. Saunders Redding picked up on the singular importance of the book in a manner that owed less to literary criticism than it did to the literary politics of race. To Redding's mind, Petry represented the end of social realism and the description of blacks in a category apart. In the "protest" literature of William Attaway, Chester Himes, and Richard Wright, a "creative philosophy" in "realistic idealism" existed that rejected fundamental racial differences. However, Redding thought that these writers had been unable to convince themselves of it emotionally. "The result is that they have writ large the differences and tried, always after the writing, to explain them away," he argued. Petry, the New Englander, had "never written the differences in, nor even implied them."[41] Calling her book strong and valid, Redding applauded the new sensibility that created dramatic tragedy without anything like recourse to sordidness.

Petry's crackling blows against militarism, industrialization, and image-manipulating newspapers, and the heavy irony of her central character—the black historian Link—dying at the hands of the same powers, went unremarked. This was an ominous harbinger: none of the black novelists in the 1950s who tried to slug a thematic home run fared well. Redding saw books like John O. Killen's *Youngblood* and Frank London Brown's *Trumbull Park* as anticlimactic overtures trying to stir activist passions thought to have run their course.

Like clockwork, the magazines and journals that had committed the least to black writers and nothing at all to breaking down eons of stereotypes voiced the greatest impatience with the material. "The mechanics of the tale are familiar to the point of being worn," said *Newsweek*.[42] A blasé attitude toward interracial romance seemed a key feature of the unconscious American reluctance to endorse publicly interracial sex between black men and white women. There had certainly been long-lasting descriptions of sexual relationships between blacks and whites from every major literary period, and Lillian Smith was considered to have brought the thing out in the open and without the stereotypes of the past. But Smith had really done no such thing, nor had Mark Harris in *Let the Trumpet Sound*, nor had any of the half dozen other novelists whose plots exploited the stereotypes and titillated audiences. The work of a serious American writer who was deriding sensationalism but willing to face an explosive (and dangerous) area of American social life was still awaited.

Another black woman's novel got less than it was due in 1953. Gwendolyn Brooks published *Maud Martha* in October 1953, and in all likelihood it was as inauspiciously received then as it would have been in 1947, when she had written the book under its original title "An American Family Brown." In 1947 Brooks's work would have been resisted on account of the turn against social realism. In 1953 the book itself was too slender to compete well with

Baldwin-the-boy-wonder and Ann Petry's major work. Harper, her publisher, decided that she had entered the ranks of Wright and Himes, and in their promotional material they described the book as "the fear that underlies every moment—fear that beyond the safety of the neighborhood world the person born with a dark face will be looked upon as an intruder."[43] A technician of diction, Brooks provided a delightful but highly serious narrative look at Bronzeville. *Maud Martha* was an attempt to add depth to the prosaic existence of a young housewife. Maud Martha Brown did not run from a lynch mob or race riot; she confronted no white scions of dizzying power; but her ordinary life was filled with significance and with a great deal of racially contrived agony.

In terms of the thrust of its chief story line, the book was a kind of detailed narrativization of *The Anniad*. Brooks had taken the issue of blacks adapting to white American standards of beauty and made a mild tour de force. In brief chapter after brief chapter, she showed the successive waves of degradation and humiliation that women faced from unthinking men who hoped in their romantic pursuits to get as close to a white woman as possible without going to jail. The pursuit of whiteness, which both does and does not consume Brooks's heroine, combines seriously with elements of patriarchy and social status striving to divide black relationships, such as mother and daughter, or between sisters.

Similar to her Pulitzer Prize–winning book of poetry *Annie Allen*, in several pointed vignettes Brooks examined the shifting landscape of race in northern, urban America, but without any sensationalism. She took the young couple to the movies where they were the only blacks. Maud Martha visits a milliner suspicious of Negro patronage. One of the climactic moments in the book occurs when the heroine convinces her daughter that Santa Claus does not despise her because of her race.

Brooks showed Maud Martha's first beau, an intellectual who mimics his white peers from the University of Chicago. The haughty young black man is frustrated because he is stranded in the land of Vernon Parrington's 1927 analysis of the "main currents" in American thought—to which he has just been exposed—but which twenty years later is no longer fashionable with his white friends. Here Brooks slyly cut into the debates between social realists and liberal critics. Parrington's "account of the genesis and development in American letters of certain germinal ideas" was deliberately crafted from "the broad path of our political, economic, and social development, rather than the narrower belletristic."[44] But after twenty years, Parrington's *Main Currents in American Thought* was displaced by Lionel Trilling in *The Liberal Imagination*, which faulted Parrington for overly relying on "economic and social determination" and showing inadequate "accuracy and originality."[45]

But perhaps the defining moment of growth in the book occurred at the hairdresser in a chapter called "the self-solace." In the episode, a white peddler casually uses the phrase "work like a nigger" in the presence of Maud Martha and her beautician Sonia Johnson.[46] In a remarkable portrait that collapsed the problems of race, social class, and individual responsibility, the shop owner, a black woman of perfunctory formal education, refuses to condemn the white peddler. Maud Martha convinces herself that she has misheard the young white woman, then is forced to deal with the hard fact that she, herself, is responsible for resolving racial slights. The reader was left to determine where the shared ground lay: between the two women of shared racial ancestry, or the entrepreneurial tie between the coarse beautician and the foul-mouthed peddler. Of course, it was impossible to be sure, which added to the beauty of Brooks's complex ambiguity in rendering the vignette. Listening to a white woman use the word "nigger" and failing to redress her becomes for Maud Martha an important lesson upon which she can forge new standards of adult maturity.

But arguably the era of the poets was in decline, even if they took to prose. Brooks would receive praise from the *New York Times* for her "economy and restraint."[47] The *Chicago Defender* found her book not so much economical as poignant. Her representations of black and white relations were "painfully true."[48] But bringing the project begun so many years earlier to a close was not completely an experience combining relief and satisfaction. Brooks said to Langston Hughes that she was not even an artist any longer. She was only a wretched parent at home, bereft of any time "to call my soul my own."[49] The mother of an elementary-school-age boy and toddling girl told Hughes, "I have not had time to sit down." But Brooks, who planned to write a *Maud Martha* sequel where the husband Paul is killed in a fire, could not hide the anger that, in spite of her bona fide talent, she was not quite making the most of her gifts

Brooks and Hughes were the only African Americans in the early 1950s with contracts at the major publishers. Poets like Melvin B. Tolson soldiered on in search of elusive backers and found subsistence from an unusual source. In 1947 the president of Liberia Joseph Tubman commissioned Tolson to write a long poem to commemorate Liberia's centennial in 1953. Tolson, a 1924 Lincoln University graduate, considered younger Lincoln men like Nnamdi Azikiwe of Nigeria (class of 1930) and Kwame Nkrumah of Ghana (class of 1939) a living part of his tradition. Alongside a coherent belief in his African identity, Tolson remained unrepentantly Marxist. For the centennial, he produced the high modernist African epic *Libretto for the Republic of Liberia*, replete with documentary evidence found in eight pages of footnotes he appended to the text. Black poets may have been erudite, but they were not known for it, Gwendolyn Brooks and Robert Hayden notwithstanding.

Tolson attracted a bit of attention by way of his footnotes to Du Bois and ancient research in African antiquity, his foreign words in Ga, Latin, German, and French, his craving for Songhai and Timbuctu. He had penned a sort of black version of "The Waste Land," but instead of desiccation and atrophy, Tolson pointed to savannah and muscle. Rejecting the line of argument that saw in the founding of Liberia just another act of colonialism, Tolson called Liberia "the quicksilver sparrow / that slips the eagle's claw."[50] Most unlike Eliot's work was the profoundly American exuberance, though basically nodding toward rubber-rich Liberia specifically and Africa in general. The future of Africa could be glimpsed by way of automobile, train, and plane, and it would be glorious. In some manner, it was an intellectually abstract updating of Psalm 68:31, "And Ethiopia shall stretch forth her hands unto God."

But what left bitterness in the caw of the people who had stomach and perception enough to read Tolson was the foreword to the poem written by Allen Tate. In 1945, probably only a few weeks after his notorious editorial in *Sewanee*, "Mr. Davidson and the Race Problem," Tate had written to Charles Johnson at Fisk in pursuit of a black writer suitable for a series jointly undertaken by *Sewanee* and Prentice-Hall. "We would be very much interested in receiving entries in poetry, fiction and the essay from gifted Negro authors, and I hope that you will be able to pass this word on to any interested persons."[51] Johnson sent the message over to Tolson at Wiley, so that he would know about white critics in the process of changing some of their semipublic attitudes, at least.

In Tolson, Tate seemed to have found the real McCoy. "For the first time, it seems to me," the *Sewanee* editor concluded, "a Negro poet has assimilated completely the full poetic language of his time and . . . the language of the Anglo-American poetic tradition." Tate denied that this was the same as saying it had previously been impossible for Negroes to assimilate. Nor did he admire everything about the *Libretto*. He thought the climax "rhetorically effective but not, I think, quite successful as poetry."[52] But what he did do was conflate, once again, white status and objective artistic excellence. "White" and the "Anglo-American poetic tradition" and "*the literary point of view*" were all the same. When J. Saunders Redding saw the collection and Tate's vouchsafing foreword he became apoplectic.[53]

What is more curious, Tolson, who never abandoned his labor organizer's point of view, remained permanently flattered by Tate's attention. He thought that the preface "stripped the underlying esthetic principle of verbiage and bias, in the manner of Socrates, etymologically and semantically."[54] As for the argument that he should stress content and "write down," or simplify his language, for the sake of his membership in an "oppressed minority," Tolson wrote to Tate that "the 'Star Spangled Banner' didn't win the Revolution." Tolson continued to defend himself ably in a letter to Redding's publisher Carl Murphy (well-known for emending columns that appeared in the *Afro* that were not to his liking), and his sense of what the modern tradition might mean for black writers. Tolson considered Tate "the most tough-fibered critic of poetry in the world today," and he had no problem being lumped with Eliot and David Jones for the use of notes, or the critics William Empson and R. P. Blackmur who praised the annotative poets.

For Tolson, contemporary poetry had given way like the other sciences and arts to benign complexity, and, as Heraclitus had said, "Everything is in a state of change and the only thing that doesn't change is the law that everything changes."[55] As for Redding, Tolson believed that his "reaction to contemporary poetry is what mine was twenty years ago." "Away with the simple Negro! This is a book to be chewed and digested." For black scholars who had been in the trenches a long time, like the seventy-six-year-old Victorian-era poet and critic William Stanley Braithwaite, turning Tate from an inveterate apostle of racial inequality was a valuable achievement. "This is a different Allen Tate than I knew twenty-five or thirty years ago who did not accept the Negro artist on the higher level of excellence. It is, apart from anything else, a great achievement to have converted this critical authority to the single standard by which all artists irrespective of race or color should be judged."[56] Braithwaite saw it as the culmination of hoeing a hard row.

Tolson's thorny case presented the American dilemma for the black writer, an artist seeking the broadest intellectual recognition possible yet wishing to remain virtuously connected to the black community and the ideal of overturning racial injustice. Palisades now were setting up where friendship had been. Tolson, who shared the modernist technique of embedded allusion with no one as much as Ralph Ellison, considered himself superior to Ellison, whom he saw doing some political backpedaling. Recently elected mayor of the all-black town of Langston in Oklahoma, teaching at a black college, and enthusiastic poet laureate of Liberia (he visited West Africa for Tubman's third inauguration as president in 1956), Tolson groused in a letter to a friend the summer of Ellison's smash hit, "[i]t's sickening to hear so many ex-Marxists 'singing' to the FBI!" Next Tolson asked, "Have you seen Ralph Ellison's 'The Invisible Eye'? Great!" But the good news had a downside for Tolson, who also thought that Ellison's success was "saddening." "I know Ralph well. He's from Oklahoma. Used to be a Harlem radical."[57]

Ellison did not quite sing to the FBI, but he did take ever more seriously his reputation. When a recent Harvard Ph.D. named Henry Kissinger, editing a journal called *Confluence*, asked Ellison to contribute to a forthcoming edition of the journal devoted to "Tradition in Culture and Politics: The Problem of Minorities," Ellison cleared out some old material from his drawers. What was most telling about the essay "Twentieth Century Fiction and the Black Mask of Humanity," Ellison's principal statement about the idea of the Negro in American literature and culture, were his prefatory remarks. He built up a sense of extraordinary distance from the previous seven years. "When I started rewriting this essay it occurred to me that its value might be somewhat increased if it remained very much as I wrote it during 1946. For in that form it is what a young member of a minority felt about much of our writing. Thus I've left in much of the bias and shortsightedness, for it says as much about me as a member of a minority as it does about literature."[58] Obviously Ellison had overhauled the essay and wanted to stand fully by its contents, but he thought it prudent to repudiate his earlier career. The span of years during the Korean War seemed to signal full-scale retreat from the communitarian ideals of the 1930s and 1940s.

Another successful writer upon whom much hope had been placed seemed intent upon putting some distance between himself and his former work. In 1951 Yaddo opened its doors to the twenty-four-year-old author of two novels William Gardner Smith. His work in the *New Republic* hinted that he was being groomed as the next major black critic on the Left. Smith knew how to bear down and finish a project, but when he sent his new book to Farrar, Straus, editor John Farrar rejected it. The pace of the literary world forced Smith to do some soul searching, a gut-check of his own creative power and political commitments. Yaddo was in upstate New York, but Smith managed to introduce himself to C.L.R. James, who lived in Manhattan during the first half of 1951.

The reigning black Marxist intellectual in the United States, James had just split again with the Socialist Workers Party and had reinvigorated his Hegelian explorations with his coauthored book *State Capitalism and World Revolution*. He and his coauthor Raya Dunayevskaya had spent ten years developing principled points of divergence from Trotsky's Socialist Workers Party and the popular American socialist leader Max Shachtman, especially over the type of government in the Soviet Union (James thought it an example of state capitalism) or the necessity of the Lenin-theorized vanguard revolutionary party (James eventually believed the masses did not require advanced leadership). James and Dunayevskaya called their faction the Johnson-Forest Tendency (James had the pseudonym "Johnson" and Dunayevskaya was "Forest"), and the Chinese American Ph.D. in English Grace Lee Boggs also joined the renegade outfit.

When Smith went to see James, the Trinidadian intellectual was immersed in a study of Herman Melville, in part to prove to the U.S. State Department his abiding and sincere appreciation of U.S. culture and thus avoid being deported. It may have been James who encouraged Smith to seek France as a place to get his writing done. In any event, C.L.R. James was impressed enough by the contact to furnish Smith with Richard Wright's address. Smith wrote to Richard Wright about the possibility of life in France, where he might settle for "a year, two years, or even longer, perhaps."[59] By October 1951 Smith and his young wife Mary had packed their bags and were headed for Le Havre, first port after the transatlantic passage, and only a train ride away from Paris. Smith sent his wife home after six months and lived abroad, mainly in France, until his death in 1974.

Smith had known fame, the lecture circuit, and an invitation to Carl Van Vechten's among the perks of publishing two novels. The novel upon which he had hoped to cement his reputation as a force in American letters was called *South Street*, and in it Smith returned to racial injustice, his first passion. As a teenager, in a bit of political theater, he had shepherded a dozen bandaged protestors through Philadelphia's downtown to dramatize police brutality; *South Street* was intended to reclaim his role as a championship pugilist against racism in the United States.

When the book finally came out in 1954, it proved an interesting failure. Smith's narrative hummed with ambition and scope, yet it was tantalizingly ineffective because of the melodrama, the structural weakness of the plot, and the characterizations that were not fully rounded out. Racist brutality there was good and plenty in the United States, but the public had officially wearied of realism that clunked along with a didactic message. "Novels of Negro life, like the proletarian novels of the Thirties, have come to embody several sets of easily recognizable stereotypes," one critic wrote and then decided that *South Street* "appears to be a portmanteau expression of them all."[60] "The whole thing is earnest, accurate and wooden," said another reviewer.[61] At the *Pittsburgh Courier*, Henry Winslow decided that Smith had "reproduced idiom far better than he has realized his characters."

After two successful novels, Smith had moved, by force of nature it seemed, in the direction of a steely appraisal of the race problem in Philadelphia. The odds against success were high. To his credit, he structured the book around thematic properties heavy with potential: the portrait of a renowned geographic entity, Philadelphia's South Street; the black militant responses to Jim Crow and white hostility; and the dynamic role of African American vernacular culture. The hero of the narrative is Claude Bowers, a well-educated black leader who writes essays in defense of black Americans and has lived in Africa working for the decolonization movement. Claude Bowers closely resembled Paul Robeson, whom a deeply infatuated Smith met once but was unable to intrigue.[62]

Smith's hero Claude Bowers has tired of active duty on the front lines of the struggle for black rights. Bowers has two devoted younger brothers, Philip and Michael, and they have all vowed militancy to avenge their father, lynched by whites in the South for exercising his right to vote. Youngest brother Michael is the impetuous black avenger, and Philip is the classic artist seeking relief from the obligations imposed by racial duty. Together they have begun a radical group called the Negro Action Society. The scant plot revolves around Claude's improbable marriage to an innocent young white violinist and his decision to reject vigorous protest. The novel concludes with the murder of Philip by a white street gang and Claude's decision to renounce his marriage and return to active struggle for black rights.

Smith portrayed working-class South Street with the numbers runner Slim, his girlfriend Lil, a waitress and semiprostitute who has escaped an abusive home, the patrician but corrupt political ward boss Old Man, and the vulgar oracle of the book, The Blues Singer. The Blues Singer was Smith's most interesting character, a lesbian heroin addict, and she carried the black tradition of wisdom, pain, art, and boiling frustration. Her melancholy barking at the world was deliciously magnetic, even to Claude's angelic white wife Kristin. But Smith, who held a reputation as a spellbinding conversationalist, never properly developed scene and setting in his fiction world. In the months following publication of Saul Bellow's *The Adventures of Augie March*, the thin psychological depth of character that Smith had learned from studying Hemingway short-circuited. His potentially rich working-class characters seemed mythic archetypes at best and stick-men at worst. The general theme of the heroin-soaked, gritty blues-performer-as-soothsayer would be taken up and utterly transformed by James Baldwin, who visited with him regularly during Smith's first months in France, in the short story "Sonny's Blues" and in the novel *Another Country*. These are among Baldwin's outstanding portraits of African Americans.

In effect, Smith did not quite know how to put on paper in realistic terms a situation that was absurd. Perhaps the difficulties that Smith himself was having with the book were best represented in the explicit intertextual references he made to the black friends he found in France. Verging on becoming engulfed by hatred of whites, the militant brother Michael Bowers questions the Old Man in a bar.

> "How can you be happy while Negroes are so unhappy?" Michael said suddenly, looking at the Old Man with emotion.
> Again the Old Man chuckled. "Negroes are not unhappy, son. That's a myth created by Richard Wright."[63]

Smith praised Wright since the Old Man represents the path of cynicism, black American complicity with social injustice, and the pursuit of vigorously shallow material success without mores or values.

Closer to the end of the book, Smith gestured to another colleague. The sensitive artist Philip has accepted his own reluctance to serve as a leader in the civil rights struggle. His fiancée tells him,

> "I've just read a book," Raye said. "*If He Hollers, Let Him Go*. By Chester Himes. He's very good."
> Philip nodded.[64]

Himes's protagonist Bob Jones also decides to abandon the path of civil rights leader and upstanding member of the middle class. Praising Wright and Himes showed Smith in the process of defining the ligature of a new tradition. But the intertextual reference to the important black naturalists of the Left Bank got him not even as far as Himes had gotten in 1945. He seems to have proposed that writing down what was not basically conceded would be enough to bring off a victory. For example, he created a black ghetto that produced principled, educated militants. The voluptuous black heroine sold her body to the highest bidder, but she was not a streetwalker. He had given the black struggle for civil rights an international dimension and linked it to decolonization.

The reality is that he had made a political overture similar the one made by the Bajan writer George Lamming in the more lyrically and psychologically intense 1953 bildungsroman *In the Castle of My Skin*. Lamming placed as the thematic crisis of the novel the 1937 Barbados labor riots, and his secondary character Trumper visits the United States and returns to the hero G's home filled with the politics of racial solidarity. Among the other encomiums, Lamming was thought a kind of originator of a pan-Caribbean nationalism in fiction.

But Smith's third novel earned no encomiums for even what he had created. Blyden Jackson, by then perhaps the sharpest of the new black critics, looked at the book and groaned in pain at what had happened. "[T]he most distressing single phenomenon is the continued presence of established writers whose work shows no sign of growth," he told *Phylon* readers in 1955. The culprits were Chester Himes and William Gardner Smith. But Himes's life was a wreck and, according to Jackson, as a writer Himes had always been in love with "putrid matter." "[A]t least in Himes' case the lesion was always there."[65] Smith, on the other hand, had seemed the hope of a generation: young, uncorrupted, disciplined, and talented. "His first novel, *Last of the Conquerors,* was a beautiful book, beautiful in its conception, beautiful in its execution. And now, two novels later, he flounders pitifully through *South Street*, saying nothing clearly, handling nothing with artistic discipline."

Smith got along well in France though. After perfecting his language skills, he managed a job as English language editor at Agence France-Presse. "I had come to a dead end," he told an interviewer. "I felt like I couldn't go down the old road any longer. I mean the road of protest."[66] Whatever he might have meant, for Smith, the rejection of "protest" basically brought an end to his career as a novelist. He published one other novel, *The Stone Face*, in 1963, featuring a semiblind black American, tragically wounded by racism, who falls in love with a European woman, recognizes the prejudice in France against Algerians, and determines to return to the United States to participate fully in the American black freedom struggle.

The theme of both *South Street* and *The Stone Face* depicted the social responsibility of everyone who picked up a pen in the 1950s. Ungainly perhaps, Smith presented educated artists having to make the difficult decision to join the active struggle to win black rights in the face of real challenges to their craft.

It became the chief condition for the black talent that had got on the scene in the 1940s. Not the man with the golden arm Ralph Ellison, not Ann Petry, not Smith, not J. Saunders Redding, not Chester Himes; they had all left the adult novel behind.

There was evidence other than hosannas at the end of 1954 and 1955 that Thomas Jefferson's famous wolf had not perished at the steps of the Supreme Court. New magazines, like Chicago's *The American Negro: "A Magazine of Protest"* portrayed the mounting frustration that grew after each languorous civil rights victory, at the emergence of every new leader, like Birmingham's young Ph.D. Martin King, or the soldierly Medgar Evers of Mississippi, who followed in the bloody footsteps of two other NAACP leaders, both assassinated. Discretion, or taste rather, was having to find new codes. "[T]his magazine has attempted to expose jim crow in all its revolting ugliness, without mincing words or modifying phrases," began the Chicago editor Augustus Savage, who won a seat in the U.S. House of Representatives in 1980. At Roosevelt College after the war, Savage had roomed with another young black Chicago political go-getter named Harold Washington. Anxious and proud, Savage reminded his readers that "there are forces which seek Negro re-enslavement and should spur our readers to greater effort in the fight for equal rights." The editorial itself was entitled "Are Our Efforts in Vain?"[67]

Caught in the middle of the back-and-forth between hope and fury, J. Saunders Redding reviewed the domestic scene and wished more deeply than ever to liberate himself from the obligations of racial duty. He chose to involve himself in the maintenance of national identity. He was by then heading up the English department at Hampton, wanting to put his years at Brown and Columbia to work, but without a genuine signal to his value. Then, in 1952, the State Department invited him to represent the government on a sponsored trip to the recently independent nation of India. Redding, who hoped that American blacks would achieve a meaningful assimilation into American society, agreed to go. When he faced young students armed there with ranking black Communist William Patterson's pamphlet *We Charge Genocide*, the indictment delivered before the United Nations to enlist international help in the cause of black rights, Redding waved them off as badly informed, dogmatic, and excessively paranoid concerning American imperial designs in Asia. The crowds of students harangued him. "Always there was the implication and/or the declaration that American color prejudice is reflected in official American international policy, that our international relations reflect our domestic order."[68]

When he returned to the United States, Redding published his account. In the pages of his travel memoir, Redding put forth his most sincere patriotism tempered by the racial discomfort he could not escape. He admitted his cynicism at being selected to go to India as the representative of a rather coy U.S. liberalism.

Because, invariably in the course of the trip, he celebrated the freedom of a democracy that was not at the core of his own emotional experience. Redding discerned for his readers an India of a contradictory color consciousness, reverse racism ("No White South Africans allowed"), and rabid communism.

The mainstream press looked favorably on his efforts. *Time* magazine, one of the nation's leading weekly news magazines, and unused to news coverage of Negro Americans, did its best to make Redding palatable for its audience. "Saunders Redding, 48, is a good-looking Negro professor of English at Hampton Institute (Va.), one of the nation's best Negro colleges," the article began, adding polish to the Phi Beta Kappa writer of four previous books. "[H]e has told the startling truth about India in a clean, calm book." Of course Redding's achievement had little to do with his hygiene or his tranquility; of a great deal more interest and concern were his politics, his views that could be shaped into a chastisement of India's policy of neutrality toward China and the Soviet Union and then also of India's left-leaning intellectual class. "Redding likens the Reds to wild dogs that run in packs all over India," was *Time*'s quick synopsis of the book.[69] In the year in which the Supreme Court struck down the laws upholding racial segregation, Redding put on the togs of a cold warrior.

Redding's international role as a foil to communism still had considerably less traction domestically. In India his lecture halls were forums for wide-ranging political and aesthetic debate; this simply was not the case at Hampton Institute, even if Hampton had cultivated applicants interested in the debate. The young black talent would still have to find New York, and still they would find it necessary to make do with the rafters and joists that remained of the Communist Party's cultural infrastructure. Out from the ashes of the Harlem Writers Club emerged a regular writers' workshop that finally evolved, around the time of the demise of Robeson's newspaper *Freedom*, into the Harlem Writers Guild. The writers' workshop from the Committee for the Negro in the Arts involved none of the people influential with *Harlem Quarterly*—not Benjamin Brown, Harold Cruse, or Ernest Kaiser. But it could have. Also, the composition of the new group said something about the ease with which African Americans continued to experience shelter, opportunity, and democratic freedom inside of Communist ranks.

In 1951 Rosa Guy solicited help from Philip Bonosky, a published novelist, *Masses & Mainstream* contributing editor, and short story instructor at the Jefferson School. She asked him to guide a fledging writers, workshop.[70] Bonosky, the author of *Brother Bill McKie* and *Burning Valley*, who was leading another workshop that had only white writers, agreed. He knew the unpublished writer Rosa Guy from the 1949 American Society of Composers, Authors, and Publishers conference. For roughly two years he sent out notices, made telephone calls, and welcomed new members to head up the workshop sessions. John Killens inspired the first meeting, held in October 1951 in the same loft on 125th Street that had served as *Freedom's* editorial room. After a couple of amateur poems on nature and sentimental romance, Killens held the group spellbound with chapters from *Youngblood*. After Bonosky departed in 1953, Julian Mayfield would lead the meetings for a time, until an affair with a married woman turned into her divorce and remarriage to Mayfield but basically ruined his effectiveness leading the workshop. Killens then took over the leadership of the group, and almost the entirety of its roster from the 1950s went on to artistic distinction.

Attractive and confident, John Oliver Killens kindled the sparks of the young group. Much of his allure was based on the success of his compelling work about an African American family in the Deep South, *Youngblood*. A native of Macon, Georgia, Killens put about seven years of dutiful labor into the book. In the mid-1940s Killens had met Paul Robeson when he worked in Washington, D.C., as a trade union organizer. After the inspirational meeting, Killens went to New York on behalf of the striking black women in the Cafeteria Workers Union, and Robeson lent his support.[71] Satisfied in having earned recognition from the premier symbol of black politically independent thought, Killens never wavered in his determination to write African American characters who shared at least some of Robeson's outstanding qualities in the arts, athletics, or the arena of the intellect. Few other novels written by African Americans during the cold war more faithfully transmuted into character and scene the principles of left-wing ideology.

Youngblood centered on the lives of the Youngbloods, a family whose mother and father symbolize the union between the petit-bourgeois intelligentsia and the black laboring class. Always a celebrator of family relationships, Killens showcased the undying love and understanding within the Youngblood family, and he specifically sought to strike down the animosity within a family that Wright had put up in *Black Boy*.

In his most famous episode, Killens's heroine Janie Lee is forced to buggy-whip her son Robby to placate a sadistic white sheriff. Much of the rest of the book shows the complex emotional cycle of forgiveness between mother and son and the indication that the son derives an adult maturity from his mother's mandatory violence. Richard Wright had suggested that black families were beaten down in the aftermath of slavery, but Killens, another Deep South native, walked in tandem alongside Theodore Ward and Lloyd Brown. He claimed resilience, fidelity, and love as the most genuine of black traits. Keeping its focus on the South, *Youngblood* proposed to resolve the problem of racial injustice with batches of black pride, leftist organizers, and interracial unity.

Killens had a number of supporters after Dial Press brought his book out in June 1954, among them his former instructor Saul Bellow and the critic Maxwell

Geismar. Geismar thought Killens more faithful to the complexity of African American life than some of his well-regarded peers, like Ralph Ellison, whom Geismar had dismissed after Ellison gave an "art-for-art's sake" speech at a Brooklyn library in 1954.[72] In the year after its publication, *Youngblood* sold about three thousand copies, a modest showing, but which did not deflate Killens.[73] To date, no one had really written a novel that acknowledged the destructive force of southern white prejudice while turning the black characters into heroes.

One of his fans in Philadelphia brought home the distinction that made him unique. "I was terrifically impressed with what you said about *Youngblood's* being a novel of affirmation; of wholesome, hearty Negro people with faith in progress and their future," the admirer wrote.[74] By contrast, the workshop in Philadelphia also included a writer who possessed "great admiration for Richard Wright" and who was excitedly embarking upon a short story "about a degenerate Negro on a NY subway." "Needless to say, Philadelphia and I both concur in our admiration for your writing." Killens derived considerable prestige from his decision to make his characters morally chaste, like Ann Petry's heroine from *The Street*. Once again, the Communist Party's 1950s literary aesthetics conformed exceptionally well with middlebrow America.

Killens took to the lecture circuit and took seriously the job of building up the other writers of the workshop. The younger writers fulfilled their extraordinary promise and included the likes of Brooklyn College graduate Paule Marshall, ex-showgirl Maya Angelou, teen poet Audre Lorde, playwright Loyle Hairston, *Freedom* columnist and actress Alice Childress, budding novelist Sarah Wright, football-player-turned-actor, playwright, and theater company founder Douglas Turner Ward, John Henrik Clarke, actor and playwright Clayton Riley, Rosa Guy, novelist Louise Meriwether, playwright, screenwriter, and actor Lonnie Elder III, and Julian Mayfield.

The best-known Harlem writer did not have a permanent address in the United States between 1953 and 1955, though he was in America getting out a new novel, staging his first play, and pulling together a collection of essays. James Baldwin had gone abroad to find himself, but in the early 1950s he was still emotionally dealing with deep feelings of shame and guilt connected to his blackness, his family, and his having escaped them. In 1953 Baldwin published in *Harper's* the essay "Stranger in the Village," perhaps his most thorough advancing of the idea that degradation, shame, and historical absence lay at the base of the slave inheritance. Baldwin translated the academic notions about ethnic assimilation into a sabbatical he had taken in a small Swiss village. He decided that the Swiss peasants, even the "most illiterate among them[,] is related, in a way that I am not, to Dante, Shakespeare, Michelangelo, Aeschylus, Da Vinci, Rembrandt, and Racine. . . . Go back a few centuries and they are in their full glory—but I am in Africa, watching the conquerors arrive."[75]

To a degree, this was something like a philosophy of black powerlessness, but one that Baldwin had not necessarily connected to the experience in America. Six years later the historian Stanley Elkins published a provocative book called *Slavery: A Problem in American Institutional and Intellectual Life*. Elkins suggested that contemporary inequality, as well as the black caricatures that Broyard had reported in the pages of *Commentary* and *Partisan Review*, were the result of the condition of slavery itself, which in turn had eerily resembled Nazi concentration camps. To survive the brutal regime, blacks had appropriated the behavior style of the clownlike "Sambo," which was not merely a mask of duplicity, but a kind of permanent psychological degeneration. Baldwin's line of reasoning did not go so far as Sambo, but it did still suggest that slavery for African Americans was an embarrassing topic and that Africa held nothing to help shore up an African American's identity.

His decision to use this language and to render the descriptions of blacks and Africans as wards of the West was fraught with trepidation. When he was in his late forties, Baldwin candidly assessed himself at the precise moment of the publication of "Stranger in the Village" and *Go Tell It on the Mountain*. He described this moment as the onset of his disillusionment with American liberalism. "I began to be profoundly uncomfortable. It was a strange kind of discomfort, a terrified apprehension that I had lost my bearings. I did not altogether understand what I was hearing. I did not trust what I heard myself saying. . . . I felt an increasing chill, as though the rest of my life would have to be lived in silence."[76] During the 1950s he described the twenty-four months spent in the United States between *Go Tell It on the Mountain* and the 1955 collected essays *Notes of a Native Son* in another way: he told a close friend he was having a "breakdown," a nervous collapse.[77]

But deception and collapse played well to his audience. The publication of *Notes of a Native Son* in 1955 consolidated James Baldwin's reputation. The book itself was the brainchild of Sol Stein, the most literary among Baldwin's high school friends. After mustering out from the military and finishing a Ph.D. degree at Columbia, Stein had become executive editor of the American Committee for Cultural Freedom, Sydney Hook's anticommunist cultural program. Organized in 1950 by Melvin Lasky, a GI who had worked in intelligence during the war and written for *New Leader* and *Partisan Review*, the Committee for Cultural Freedom basically operated to spank the Soviet Union. The committee itself included many prominent New York writers and critics, and Baldwin's name sat beside Max Yergan and George Schuyler. (Schuyler resented the presence of so many socialists who were anti-Stalin but not sufficiently anticommunist, and he liked the committee's work so well that he thought it needed to be expanded to the faculties at colleges and high schools.)[78] Sol Stein selected the contents of *Notes of a Native Son*, mostly what Baldwin had done between

1949 and 1954, but not his French essay. The book operated with the cold war as a perceptible canvas: America was flawed, but not permanently, and in modernist complexity lay the hope of the future. The race problem was chiefly one of individual perception.

J. Saunders Redding picked up on this sensibility immediately and began to be suspicious of Baldwin. Nearly everyone was anxious to see Wright's stature eclipsed, even in the course of promoting even higher literary standards. It is unclear precisely which work of Baldwin's that Redding, now serving on the editorial board of *American Scholar*, read as it came out in journals, reviews, and the major monthlies. But Redding saw white-hot betrayal when he looked at *Notes of a Native Son*, specifically "Stranger in the Village." He blamed Baldwin for capitulating to the venery of bohemian life, capricious intellectual fashion, and purposeless aesthetics. He felt uncomfortable with Baldwin's modern attitudes, his imposition of individual self-made values, and his apparently casual disdain toward the idea of a tradition of African American literature that Redding had worked so hard to write into existence and then to cultivate. While Redding left alone Baldwin's famous dismissals of the social realist literary tradition. . . "Can Baldwin believe that the American Negro is unqualified (not merely disqualified!) in the very nature of him and in experience to find his identity in America?" the critic seethed.[79]

As for Baldwin's largest audience, the response was diametrically opposite. Sol Stein had said of that essay specifically in the book's prefatory note, "when we consider the concluding chapter of this book, 'Stranger in the Village,' and try to think of a greater essay ever written by a member of Mr. Baldwin's race, we cannot name it."[80] Stein's comment was included in the bound galleys but then removed from the hardcover printing. After about twelve months *Notes of a Native Son* reappeared in paperback, a book in Stein's "Contemporary Affairs Series" that included André Malraux, Sidney Hook, George Orwell, and Arthur Koestler. These were the most prominent literary anticommunists of the twentieth century.

Langston Hughes seems to have had instincts that matched J. Saunders Redding's when he reviewed *Notes* for the *New York Times Book Review*, a signal that the pace of the civil rights movement was demanding blacks of stature for the national press, which was now able to forgive Hughes his leftist past. Hughes gave and took away, demanding that readers remain ambivalent about Baldwin, in essence pricking the helium-filled balloon that was James Baldwin's career. "Few American writers handle words more effectively in the essay form than James Baldwin," Hughes began with apparent praise and mildness. Then, knowing Baldwin's ambition as a novelist, Hughes cut him down. "To my way of thinking, he is much better at provoking thought in essay than he is in arousing emotion in fiction. I much prefer 'Notes of a Native Son' to his novel, 'Go Tell It on the Mountain,' where the surface excellence and poetry of his writing did not seem to me to suit the earthiness of his subject-matter."[81] Baldwin was not in the United States when the review came out. But although neither Hughes nor Redding had any reputation in Baldwin's world of Paris, Greenwich Village, or *Partisan Review*, their conception of Negro identity and their confidence concerning black life mattered to him. James Baldwin's need for the approval— the love—of black men of stature like Richard Wright went deep, as deep as his need for the elusive approval of David Baldwin, the man whose blood he did not share but whose last name he was making famous.

CHAPTER SIXTEEN

Liberal Friends No More: The Rubble
of White Patronage (1956–1958)

In 1956 James Baldwin published his third book and his second novel, *Giovanni's Room*. For a novel that carried at its core a homosexual affair, it was charitably received, even though Baldwin had been warned that it might ruin his career and the book was rejected by Knopf, which had a right of refusal for his second piece of fiction. Granville Hicks, who had survived his Communist associations, wrote approvingly, "even as one is dismayed by Mr. Baldwin's materials, one rejoices in the skill with which he renders them."[1] The book spent itself on the American colony in Paris, and it featured not a single black character. However, despite the curiosity of a book without black characters, *Giovanni's Room* offered a clear-sighted focus on the subject at hand, which perhaps had not quite been attempted by black writers before: the thoroughgoing perfidy of liberal whites.

The character Giovanni, a swarthy Italian, conveys the sympathetic heart of the book. If Baldwin had made Giovanni Algerian, he would have given the book a more enduring political significance, an absence that undoubtedly contributed to its neglect. A non-European Giovanni would also have secured Baldwin the crown in a conversation about primal American male identity that had in its depths an unacknowledged, uncomfortable, and submerged erotic desire between a white male subject and greatly objectified nonwhite male Other. Leslie Fiedler had turned up the volume of the conversation in 1948 by pointing out the pairs that dominated nineteenth-century American fiction: James Fenimore Cooper's Natty Bumpo and Chingachgook, Herman Melville's Ishmael and Queequeg, and Mark Twain's Huckleberry Finn and Nigger Jim. But Baldwin missed the opportunity, though he too revisited the conundrum with the characters Vivaldo and Rufus in *Another Country*.

Instead, his real achievement was to confront the waffling and antiseptic white American Adamic hero. Baldwin claimed that he was rewriting the Henry James novel *The American*, and he provided a nimbly drawn portrait of a tragic American hero, caught between a kind of zestful and hedonistic youth and the obligations of adult maturity. In the process, the narrator David destroys lives. David is supposed to be essentially American. "For I am—or I was," the narrator tells the reader, "one of those people who pride themselves on their willpower, on their ability to make a decision and carry it through."[2] Providing evidence of the independence that would lead him in new directions, Baldwin used David to unravel the ideological underpinning of the formalist critical method and sensibility—which ennobled literary ambiguity. Speaking of his mighty will, David finally decides that "[t]his virtue, like most virtues, is ambiguity itself. People who believe that they are strong-willed and the masters of their destiny can only continue to believe this by becoming specialists in self-deception. Their decisions are not really decisions at all . . . but elaborate systems of evasion, of illusion, designed to make themselves appear to be what they and the world are not."[3]

Though on its face the novel seemed a plea for tolerance toward gays, which, in terms of the plot, might have prevented Giovanni's execution, the book really was a plea to end the myth of American innocence. In 1955 the young critic R.W.B. Lewis had published a book called *American Adam* that located in American literature between 1820 and 1860 a stock archetype—the mythic male Adam in the American Garden of Eden. "[A] figure of heroic innocence and vast potentiality, poised at the start of a new history," observed Lewis.[4] Baldwin wanted to puncture the sensibility that craved purity and wished so completely to mask all its actions in a psychological supper of willful innocence and counterfeit masculine posture. Instead of returns to Edenic myth, American men needed to risk madness by recalling, in pain, the loss of innocence. "Nobody can stay in the garden of Eden," the character Jacques tells the narrator toward the finale. Baldwin concentrated on the problem of a perpetually shallow American liberal attitude, a belief that liked to stick its toe in the edge of the pond but disliked the thought of baptism in the river.

Baldwin had never been to Africa, but he was leaving one country for another. In the months following the daring novel he took a hard look at his African peers, began his disentanglement with the American liberal intelligentsia, and stood toe-to-toe with the Nobel laureate William Faulkner. In his work and in his personal life, Faulkner had been a rather outspoken proponent of racial fairness. His classic 1936 novel *Absalom, Absalom!*, for instance, offered an audacious concluding sentence. "[I]n a few thousand years, I who regard you will also have sprung from the loins of African kings," says Shreve, after hearing Quentin Compson's saga of a Mississippi family tortured by fictions of racial purity.[5] It was not an NAACP membership, but it was impossible to see such words coming from a simpleminded bigot. Faulkner had written brief notes to fellow Mississippian Richard Wright, and, in a 1955 trip to Japan, he told an audience about Ralph Ellison, whom he had met: "Ellison has talent and so far he has managed to stay away from being first a Negro, he is still first a writer."[6] These were considered words of genuine warmth and bonhomie, and Ellison was proud enough of them to print them on a dust jacket of his essay collection *Shadow and Act* in 1964.

But that well of goodwill evaporated on March 5, 1956, when *Life* magazine published Faulkner's ill-considered "A Letter to the North." The letter opposed the tempo of integration and did not reveal any deep resources of wisdom or courage in the man who had won the 1949 Nobel Prize for Literature. In the letter and in interviews over the next couple of months, Faulkner would show himself a white man first and a writer second. The byline ran, "William Faulkner, the South's most foremost writer, warns on integration—'Stop Now for a Moment.'" Ostensibly, Faulkner feared for the safety of Authurine Lucy, a young black woman attempting to sit for classes at the University of Alabama. But in reality he was showing an inept understanding of the region he had lived in all his life and the feeble quality of his own convictions. "Now I must go on record as opposing the forces outside the South which would use legal or police compulsion to eradicate the evil overnight."[7] Part of the problem was that though his novels gripped the handle of shared black and white existence in the South, Faulkner had never before gone on record for anything.

Faulkner recommended "gradual" change to the NAACP (the majority of whose 400,000 members lived in the South) with full knowledge of Emmett Till's lynching in 1955 and the murder a few months later of black filling station attendant Clinton Melton, shot dead for adding too much gas to a white man's car, only a few miles from where Till's mutilated body was discovered. This was only Mississippi's terrorism aimed at penning black Americans socially. It was not exactly the same as the political terrorism that led to the shooting of Reverend George Washington Lee in 1955, the first black registered to vote in Humphreys County since Reconstruction. To add insult to injury, a short time after the *Life* letter, a reportedly inebriated Faulkner told a journalist that he would remain loyal to Mississippi, even if "going out into the streets and shooting Negroes" became necessary.[8] Of course, this was already taking place. These statements did not invoke the specter of race war as much as they did the willingness of armed white southern mobs to continue slavery by another name.

While the Faulkner stew simmered, Robert Penn Warren was gently trying to break ranks with his old confederates by way of the 1956 chapbook *Segregation: The Inner Conflict in the South*. The book had started out as a series of *Life* magazine articles, and Warren tore so gently that he did not effect any break. His most important novel *All the King's Men* had contained typically insulting depictions of indolent and unredeemable "nigger[s]," "boy[s]," and "comely wench[es]" when he did not erase African-descended people from the Louisiana landscape entirely. His 1955 *Band of Angels*, a novel about a woman raised white and then sold into slavery, appeared an angelic reconsideration of his opinions. But Warren, who, in the company of his new wife Eleanor Clark, had without ceremony begun to befriend Negroes (and also Jews) like Richard Gibson and, in Rome in 1956, Ralph Ellison, did not have the psychological sensitivity, the political interest, nor the investigative spirit to do much with the topic. Nor did his presence in the field inspire the writers who had been traditionally engaged. In 1956 Warren recommended Ralph Ellison to Irving Kristol at *Encounter*, and Ellison agreed to write an essay on the civil rights struggle. But, already wrestling with the angels and demons of his new acceptance into the upper echelons of white society, Ellison never completed the work.

Perhaps because he taught at Yale and no longer lived in the South, Warren did not want to burn any southern bridges. *Segregation* offered the point of view of the proverbial southern man-on-the-street, without the "distortion" that Warren believed came from the northern press. From another angle, the book was a one-sided, white supremacist version of events. Warren balanced the murder of Till with the claim that a white woman was raped by a black gang in Tennessee. He averred that the citizens of Glendora, Mississippi, where a friend of Till's killers had shot Clinton Melton, might have acquitted their suspect but did everything they could to help the Melton family. Warren did not mention that despite the goodwill of Glendora, a week before the trial of the man accused of shooting her husband, Melton's wife had been run off of the road and into a bayou where she drowned. Or that Medgar Evers later found that the "goodwill" of the Lions Club and white citizens to take care of the widow and send Melton's children to college amounted to twenty-six dollars. Warren ended his travels and talks through Tennessee, Mississippi, Alabama, and Louisiana by suggesting that after developing the virtues of patience and humility, to end segregation blacks would have to produce magnanimity, or forgiveness. "I am glad the white people have no problem as hard as that," was Warren's attempt at graceful understatement.[9] He interviewed himself at the end of the book and decided that he was for gradualism and the education of white and black prior to actual desegregation. He was faithful, if more vague, to what he had said in 1932.

Since James Baldwin was a confirmed expatriate, it is curious that he stepped into this national breech, and in clearly the medium of national cultural intellectual leadership, *Partisan Review*. Baldwin had returned to the United States from France twice: in 1952 to get *Go Tell It on the Mountain* ready for Knopf, and in 1954 for a longer visit, when he launched a play at Howard University with Owen Dodson, worked at the McDowell Writers Colony with Sol Stein on a number of projects, including *Notes of a Native Son*, and was arrested in New York for disorderly conduct and spent a night howling in the city jail. But by 1956 it had become almost the exclusive job of the thirty-two-year-old former Harlemite to represent to the American intellectual class the deep feelings of black intellectuals as a group and to fire out against acts of racial chauvinism.

Even though few published black writers knew less about the South than Baldwin, he did not chafe this time against the presumption that his pigment lent him experience. He was compassionate and respectful, but completely at odds with Faulkner's version of events. In his essay Faulkner had asked for time. Baldwin responded with tidy eloquence. "[T]he time Faulkner asks for does not exist," Baldwin submitted, warming up to preach. "There is never time in the future which will work out our salvation. The challenge is in the moment, the time is always now."[10]

Even if he had little southern exposure, Baldwin had not misrepresented the case or the tenor of the other black writers. As a group, they were impressed and inspired by Faulkner's body of work, his dense psychological portraits of the gnarled webs of genealogy and heritage. African American writers in the 1950s tended to agree that Faulkner aptly rendered the American social scene. Perhaps it was not so much that he had been considered liberal—tolerant, excited by diversity—as unflinchingly honest. But both qualities were now proved thin and anemic.

Albert Murray felt deeply betrayed by one of his literary heroes. "Saw that Faulkner piece in *Life*," he began in an uncharacteristic epistolary tirade to Ralph Ellison.

> Sad, pitiful and stupid thing for a writer like that to do. That underdog shit makes me puke. How can a son of a bitch sit up and fuckup morality like that? . . . Man, a motherfucker ain't got no business even sticking with the whole godamned USA against *Freedom*. Son of a bitch prefers a handful of anachronistic crackers to everything that really gives him reason not only for being but for writing. I'm watching his ass but close forevermore. Imagine a fastass traveling all around the world selling humanity for the State Dept and then going back home pulling that kind of crap at the first sign of real progress. . . . Sounds like all of the other "safe liberals."[11]

Even for a private letter, and even for Murray, an expert in barracks-talk, it was an unusual amount of profanity. And it seemed that the profane, the black vernacular and proper use of it, held a key in the dispute. In a flash, Murray had cornered the point that the universal values debate often rested on a core of the particular. Black writers too had some core obligations to fulfill.

But Murray published, or perhaps could publish, nothing to express himself fully. He did not inspire his friend Ellison to shoulder a musket in the fight. John Oliver Killens begged *Reporter* to publish his rebuttal; Faulkner had been an idol to him as well. He had to content himself with drafting an unpublished reply, surely what several other black writers were doing. Baldwin and everybody else had noted Faulkner's undying pride in his ancestry. "I have not seen a single statement of Faulkner's concerning desegregation which does not inform us that his family has lived in the same part of Mississippi for generations, that his great-grandfather owned slaves, and that his ancestors fought and died in the Civil War," Baldwin reminded his reader.[12] John Killens acknowledged the remark with a rejoinder. He had a different kind of toast to bring from down home. "My great grandmother was a child of slavery and hated it," he replied.[13]

The voice of the Harlem Writers Guild, Killens wanted to drive down the pegs of big tent liberalism. Faulkner's point of view over time had been generally liberal and intelligent, and *Go Down, Moses* (1942) and *Intruder in the Dust* (1948) had been explicit, even if *Requiem for a Nun* (1951) was a bit of a setback. Like Baldwin, Killens was more than solicitous, his tone polite. "Don't align yourself with them," he pleaded. "Them" referred to Mississippi's reactionary White Citizens Council. "We deemed you much bigger than Mississippi. So many Americans, especially of the liberal persuasion, have looked to you for intellectual leadership, and particularly on this burning question."[14] But Faulkner provided them with nothing.

In fact, after Faulkner avowed his willingness to shoot Negroes in the comment to Russell Howe for the London *Sunday Times*, Killens added a postscript to his essay. Faulkner had "deceived" the liberals and suffered from the pathology of the plantation owner. In *Commonweal*, the young southern writer Walker Percy published a view and pointed to the deep problem in the South, where ruling-class southerners seemed to be abandoning the fight for tolerance and fairness, at least in part because of the decline in manners, "the Negro's demanding his rights instead of being thankful for the squire's generosity."[15] The contrêtemps stirred Baldwin from his French hibernation. For the first time, in 1958, writing essays for *Harper's* and *Partisan Review*, he would travel to the American South, move to the rear of an American bus, and introduce himself to a young, Boston-educated minister, famous for having led a boycott against a bus company in Montgomery, Alabama.

William Faulkner had not annoyed only black writers with his attempts to slow the barely doddering pace of racial integration. By early 1957, during the weeks surrounding the victory of boycotters in Montgomery (where Martin Luther King, Jr., had been convicted and fined for operating an illegal boycott and the charges had been dropped against whites suspected of bombing private homes and black churches) and when King's portrait appeared on the cover of *Time* magazine, Norman Mailer's friend Stuart Lyle, editor of *Independent*, wagered that if Mailer expressed his true opinions on reluctant southern integration, a major paper would carry the pyrotechnics. Mailer forged ahead with gusto and volatility, writing:

> Can't we have some honesty about what's going on now in the South? Everybody who knows the South knows the white man fears the sexual potency of the Negro. And in turn the Negro has been storing his hatred and yet growing stronger, carrying with him the painful wound that he was usually powerless to keep from being cuckolded.

For the white, symbolically and materially, has possessed Negro womanhood for two centuries. Which is what all the literary critics mean when they talk about the blood guilt of the South.

The comedy is that the white loathes the idea of the Negro attaining equality in the classroom because the white feels that the Negro already enjoys sensual superiority.[16]

Mailer was deliberately stating with embarrassing candor what everyone knew. Southern whites of official responsibility had admitted a version of it. Norman Brittin, an Alabama school administrator, had noted the white fear of sexual promiscuity in the pages of *Antioch Review* shortly after the 1954 Supreme Court decision in *Brown v. Board of Education*. "By and large, Alabama Negroes are still primitives," he tried to persuade his audience that year.[17] To Brittin, black Americans had "taken over the vices of civilization but not its virtues. Their emotionality, which is so hard for them to bridle, leads them to excess. Their power of restraint, on which civilization rests, being so fragile, does not keep them within the pattern of white morality. One is likely constantly to be shocked by Negroes." This basic claim was shared widely by southerners and also stood at the center of the analyses of many of the black naturalists: regardless of blame, the alley shack–dwelling African Americans had not achieved the fullness of Western civilization. Black historian Rayford Logan had also written of the white unconscious threatened by the desegregation movement. "For desegregation arouses fear of intermarriage or of sexual relations without benefit of clergy. In whatever form discussion of the problem may be disguised, fundamentally this fear dominates the thinking of most opponents of desegregation."[18] There was little wonder then when in 1957 two black eight-year-old boys were sentenced to reform school terms in North Carolina for kissing a white girl on the cheek.

It was natural that the creative artist would make bread with all this yeast. In the wake of Freud, Nietzsche, and Marx, "shocking" the audience had been one of the prime desires of the serious artist, and both Faulkner and Mailer could claim laurels for American modernist literary exploration. Faulkner had responded to his black critics with an article in *Ebony*. He responded to Mailer by direct mail.

I have heard this idea expressed several times during the last twenty years, though not before by a man.

The others were ladies, northern or middle-western ladies, usually around forty or forty-five years of age. I don't know what a psychiatrist would make of this.[19]

Mailer was a war veteran and a celebrated novelist, but he perhaps willfully missed the irony of Faulkner's tart note. In the 1932 novel *Light in August*

Faulkner had created the character Joanna Burden; the twenty-five-year-old tale fleshed out Faulkner's response and had been built itself from what Mailer touted as a fresh insight. After the initial exchange, Mailer responded again, calling Faulkner "timid" and grounding his theory of black sexual potency and white fear in what to him were irrefutably authentic sources that he insisted were beyond Faulkner's habitat: a black car-washer in Queens, a mulatto pimp, and the drug-pushing madam of a Charleston bordello. When the diverse exchange was published, it received appropriate cries of horror from W.E.B. Du Bois (known to some for his own "sensual superiority"), Eleanor Roosevelt, and others. The group was horrified that Mailer had dredged up this mythology at all. But it did become a news event.

Nor was this enough for Mailer, fishing around for a subject for his next novel. He had evolved away from the committed social realist of the acclaimed World War II novel *The Naked and the Dead* (1948), to the Henry Wallace Progressive and Trotskyite of *Barbary Shore* (1951), to the phallic narcissist of *The Deer Park* (1955). Mailer was now becoming a key player in the American sexual revolution. Herman Wouk had stirred the jug in 1955 by producing the scheming and witty Hunter College student aiming for Broadway in *Marjorie Morningstar*, a youngster who feels shame and loss after sex and winds up married and living in suburban Mamaroneck. But a handful of years later in "The Time of Her Time," Mailer would turn that world upside down with his hard-boiled, psychoanalyzed, nineteen-year-old New York University undergraduate, who convulses into orgasm after a combination of anal sex and having her lover whisper to her, "You dirty little Jew."[20]

In spite of his fondness for sensational topics, as a writer Mailer was hardworking, streaky, and independent. He had taken on both professional Communist and anticommunist writers at the Waldorf Astoria Conference in 1949. He could sense that his oeuvre was light in the area of race relations and civil rights, and with the Faulkner exchange he reached his destination for the latter half of the 1950s: hipsterism. Mailer decided to develop an essay that theorized more broadly the latest American rebellion. Although that train had already pulled out of the station eight years earlier with Anatole Broyard, the great hipster hero Charlie Parker had just died of consumption in 1956. Mailer would confront Faulkner and the liberal crowd with new work, an essay entitled "The White Negro." The essay did as he had hoped—it transformed his career.

"The White Negro" came out in Irving Howe's young socialist cultural journal *Dissent*. The magazine-without-an-office had started in 1954, in response to the increasingly politically centrist and Joseph McCarthy–scared *Partisan Review*. Mailer's incendiary article helped *Dissent* sell a record-breaking fourteen thousand copies.[21] Though Howe thought the magazine uneven from one issue to the next, he stood up tall to carry out his liberal commitments. He opposed

McCarthy and gave journal space to C. Wright Mills, the forceful analyst of social structure who radically critiqued 1950s American democracy as having shifted power to the elites of the military, government, and corporations. Unlike *Partisan Review* and *Commentary*, Irving Howe did not limit *Dissent's* pages to one or two homegrown blacks. L. D. Reddick, at work on a biography of Martin Luther King, Jr., published "The Anxious South" in the same issue as Mailer, proof to Reddick's friends that he had not died by going back to the South, first to Atlanta University and then to Alabama State. By the summer of 1961 *Dissent* would publish "Harlem, My Harlem," the riveting social realist work of the young black writer Claude Brown. Howe became a devoted admirer of Richard Wright, visited him in France, and published some of Wright's work, leading to Howe's famous 1963 essay exalting Wright's achievement, "Black Boys and Native Sons."

Mailer's "The White Negro" was a manifesto, purporting to describe the "second revolution" of the twentieth century, considering the Bolshevik the first. This revolution was the movement of human beings away from the field of "action and more rational equitable distribution, but backward toward being and the secrets of human energy." And if T. S. Eliot had found some of it with the ancient Aryans, Norman Mailer spied it in Sapphire and Stagolee. He called the hipster a "frontiersman in the Wild West of American night life," a key American icon, the "menage-a-trois" between bohemian, juvenile delinquent, and Negro.[22] Mailer wanted to tie together the spiritual energy of the African American jazzman and the legendary defiance of the well-known black street-corner hustler and the burgeoning "Beat" artistic movement of Allen Ginsberg and Jack Kerouac.

The formula was indebted to what was in the news: juvenile delinquency, hydrogen bomb holocaust, and the death of a heroin-shooting jazz giant like Parker. But the infusion of the Negro into the atomic era avant-garde was quite normal, considering that poets LeRoi Jones, Ted Joans, and Bob Kaufman also made early contributions to the countercultural, spontaneous movement that emphatically embraced the diverse breadth of American experience, even if the black poets had not been at Columbia with Ginsberg and Kerouac. Mailer himself was more interested in "cool" and violence than the Beats, who tended toward Buddhism. But he correctly identified the jazz soundtrack, the bohemian interracial attitudes, and the black argot that could bring Beats and hipsters into the same sphere.

While the essay rang out with unchecked hyperbole, underneath it bravely celebrated urban American life and the unpredictable cultural jam of the streets, the opposite of what was being taught in the new university "American Studies" courses. The American urban jam got its sweetness from the "cultural dowry" of the Negro. Picking up on the central theme of writers like Chester

Himes and Ralph Ellison without acknowledging any black writer, Mailer decided that blacks retained a valuable psychological attitude because "[t]he Negro has the simplest of alternatives: live a life of constant humility or ever threatening danger."[23] The hip blacks lived life on the razor's edge. The danger of black life was equally tragic and life-giving, a nonconforming key to turn the engine of productive spontaneity. In floaty language Mailer endowed it all with a theological purpose. "Hip" was the potential salvation of American society and the solution to the crisis of existence in a world of atomic warfare and radical disillusionment that Irving Howe had begun calling "post-modern."[24]

The essay's natural peak was its interest in the powerful erotic life of hipsters, or Negroes. These people were capable of making "an ethical differentiation between the good and the bad in every human activity," and the principal human activity that aroused Mailer was sex.[25] Mailer decided that by dunking himself in Negro attitudes toward life and Negro cultural behavior, he might gain a health-sustaining, psychologically potent orgasm, in keeping with the orgone energy theory of the reigning, credentialed sex-guru Wilhelm Reich. It was garishly sophomoric, to a point. But there was a kernel of sustenance in Mailer's impudent formula. An attraction to rhythmic unbridled sexual intercourse and the fear of Negro slave rebellion were really—as much as American exceptionalism and the American Adam—at the core of the collective U.S. cultural unconscious.

The work was graphic but not really original. Before Broyard, Ralph Ellison had written in a 1946 *New Republic* essay that the "'Negro Problem' is actually a guilt problem charged with pain. . . . [I]t is practically impossible for the white American to think of sex, economics, his children or womenfolk, or of sweeping socio-political changes, without summoning into consciousness fear-flecked images of black men."[26] Mailer had above all else inflated the "fear-flecked" image. Anatole Broyard had stirred the same principal elements but would have jeopardized his chances at acceptance if he had written the jive-talking, gage-smoking, street-corner sharpie as ecstatically as Mailer did. The writer whose complete body of work in the 1940s and 1950s has no memorable black character had, for the sake of black civil rights, become the pot-smoking John Brown for the 1950s.

"The White Negro" swung with bravura and recalled Thomas Sancton when it claimed, "if the Negro can win his equality, he will possess a potential superiority, a superiority so feared that the fear itself has become the underground drama of domestic politics."[27] But on almost all accounts, black writers saw Mailer as having a barely crude perception, perhaps cruder than Faulkner's, an amusing irony. The hearty rejection showed the wide gulf between the two races, a willfully determined gulf of language and history that blacks believed needed a vast bridge with pylons and tension cables, and liberal whites thought could be leaped across with a resolute bound. The famous portraits of black men that followed in roughly the next dozen years—William Styron's protagonist in *The Confessions of Nat Turner* (1968), Saul Bellow's black pickpocket in *Mr. Sammler's Planet* (1970), John Updike's Skeeter in *Rabbit Redux* (1971), and Bernard Malamud's Willie Spearmint in *The Tenants* (1971)—testified to this profound and enduring chasm.

The quintessential illustration of the tendency that Mailer had noted and the failure of even the most bohemian of the liberals was Jack Kerouac's novel *The Subterraneans*, published by Grove in February 1958. Kerouac liked to speak of his novel writing as spontaneous, and on the dedication page of his own successful poem *Howl* Allen Ginsberg had famously called it "spontaneous bop prosody."[28] But Kerouac's follow-up to the underground smash *On the Road* was more formally an extremely disciplined bop solo, and one that carried with it as much of an attempt at social significance as Baldwin had sought in *Giovanni's Room*. The book explored the tragic romance between Kerouac and a black girlfriend in North Beach, San Francisco, during the second half of the 1950s, and all the prominent members of the movement—Ginsberg, William Burroughs, Neal Cassady—made their appearances in the roman à clef.

Kerouac was testing the limits of Beat here. If a white man, a prototype for the heroic American, could disavow the pursuit of upward mobility, if he could not only disavow homophobia but, in some fashion, even embrace his own homoerotic tendencies, if he could explore his puritan-based sexual insecurities, could he triumph finally by romantically accepting a black mate? Was the white American male hero ready to put away his quest for purity and innocence? It was as if the American Adam were told to accept Jezebel for his wife.

The Subterraneans said that it was still impossible. The simple plot detailed the summertime love affair between beautiful, rough-hewn poet-hero Leo Percepied and the equally desirable, chic, and sexually active Mardou Fox. Leo loses Mardou after a two-month-long ambiguity about the relationship results in Mardou's accepting a younger lover.

The uninhibited and unmoored duo Leo and Mardou should have pointed the way to a more stable platform of American possibilities within an ethnically diverse society. But the disabilities are too much, and in North Beach among the Beats, there are not lynchers and brutes, but psychology and American conditioning to exact the heavy toll. Leo wants to take "Hip" as an antidote, but he can't "make it" there fast enough. If sexual intimacy is the place where Hipness is forged, Leo is castrated in a sense by his Western inheritance, and this has nothing to do with a portrait of Mardou as a primitive. Like Mailer, Leo has succumbed to Reichianism and is hoping for the exceptional orgasmic experience with Mardou. But to claim the categories of Reich is to pursue a sexual taxonomy that relies on key terms like "clarity . . . scientific, Germanic, beautiful, true."[29] At one point Leo examines Mardou's vulva and clitoris under a lightbulb because "I saw some kind of black thing I've never seen before, hanging, like it scared me."[30] The fright, the threat of contamination, the undercurrent of mythological or hermaphroditic difference, contributes to Leo's suspicion that Mardou is a thief, stealing his white purity.

Kerouac captured the idea of theft with extraordinarily powerful symbolism. Leo habitually accuses Mardou of having stolen white male homosexual pornography from his friend. The black woman threatens to steal the provenance of exclusively white male sexual activity that precludes her by its very genre. And there is a greater danger than Mardou's threat to white men's homosocial erotic lives. Even when Leo overcomes the horror of "pernicious and pizen juices" when he and Mardou have intercourse, Leo admits to being overwhelmed by the sheer muscular force of her vagina, the "greatstrength of womb." "I now wonder and suspect if our little chick didn't really intend to bust us in half," the narrator reveals.[31] Leo's lingering anxieties, and his regular belief that Mardou is a feral land bequeathed to white men, prevent him from getting Hip.

Kerouac had several virtues, and sterling among them was honesty. His angling toward "Hip," the conceptual cocktail of heroin, jazz, black trim, and black joint, was unsteady and dangerous, even if it seemed to hold out freedom. "Beat," the term that Baldwin said originated with the black Harlem gamins denouncing their newly unemployed "beat-to-the-socks" fathers, was a far distance from Hip.[32] Kerouac also showed the distance in aesthetics. Leo Percepied likes white jazz artists like Gerry Mulligan, creator of the "cool" sound of "West Coast" jazz, and Stan Kenton, who brought out "progressive jazz" with a string orchestra and rarely featured black regular musicians. Norman Mailer tried to show himself beyond the Beats when he labeled Thelonius Monk the Moses of "hip" and Dave Brubeck, the first jazz musician on the cover of *Time*, a talented "square."[33] At nearly the same time, Ralph Ellison wrote about four figures and turned the rudder of the jazz discussion in the other direction, back to its source: the queen of gospel Mahalia Jackson; Ellison's Oklahoma City buddies the singer Jimmy Rushing and the guitarist Charlie Christian, who had died in the 1942; and Charlie Parker, whom Ellison thought vastly overrated by precisely the forces represented by Mailer and Kerouac. There were multiple schools then: white cool imitators, black northern jazz experimental innovators, and black southern and western jazz artists who conspicuously drew from the native tradition.

Kerouac strode out against the novel of manners and the conformity of the 1950s, but he was not seeking out the sources of jazz. Leo Percepied's journey from Beat to Hip showed the stony path to the promised land. Beyond the physical difference of race, he fears a permanent tie to his black girlfriend because it "would preclude completely the possibility of living in the South, like in that Faulknerian pillar homestead in the Old Granddad moonlight I'd so long envisioned for myself."[34] Leo becomes capable of admitting that Mardou has significance in his life, but he clings to his "dumb little phantasy, a shack in the middle of the Mississippi woods, Mardou with me, damn the lynchers."[35] Ultimately Leo's attempt to fashion an Eden by way of his interracial relationship to Mardou is half-hearted on his part and completely ignores Mardou, who tells him in the final pages of the novel, "don't call me Eve."[36]

Only obliquely could Kerouac focus attention on the subaltern among the subterranean. If the heroic beat Leo Percepied is foiled in his journey because he clings to rational discourse, hip Mardou is being driven insane by the Beats. Percepied doubts the relationship on account of two, intertwined reasons: "because she was a negro" and "because I knew she'd been seriously insane."[37] Mardou's mental instability, her regular psychoanalytic counseling, is inseparable from her dilemma of being a black, sexually attractive female in the company of white men. The Beats want Mardou for her body, and Leo especially angles toward becoming Hip through sex and association with a black woman. But at every level he actively seeks to limit the intensity of the connection.

As early as *On the Road*, Kerouac had written of "wanting to be vital, alive like a Negro," and he included the same passage in *The Subterraneans*. Leo claims fondness for this old dream, the storied bedrock of Kerouac's interracial sensibility. Naturally this feeling of gargantuan envy was Kerouac's deepest kinship with Mailer. But though Mardou "was always talking about" "her Negro fear of American society," in the entirety of Leo's confessional novel about the romance, he records none of it.[38] Leo pursues Negro carnal ebullience but eliminates the anxiety, the peril, and the political responsibility that accompany black identity.

Necessarily then, very few of the black writers thought any of the Beats or white Negroes especially Hip. Generous and indulgent with his friends, and a little in love with Mailer, James Baldwin claimed disbelief at the "White Negro." He had met Mailer in 1956 at the Paris home of Mailer's guru, the Trotskyite philosopher Jean Malaquais. Though Mailer had graduated from Harvard and Baldwin had not had any college, living in Paris and running with the American writer's crowd, especially for an American black, was a great prize. When it came to discussing black culture, Baldwin thought that Mailer's tool was so dull that "helplessly maligns" the black "periphery" was the nicest thing he could say about "The White Negro."[39] Secure in his belief that "the Negro jazz musicians, among whom we sometimes found ourselves, who really liked Norman, did not for an instant consider him even remotely 'hip' and Norman did not know this," Baldwin extended compassion to Mailer.

The Beats themselves were opposed to Mailer's pulling their movement along beside the hipster's ideal of coldness and violence. "I thought the essay was very square, and Kerouac thought that Norman was being an intellectual fool," recalled Allen Ginsberg.[40] "Norman's notion of the hipster as being cool and psychopathic and cutting his way through society with jujitsu was a kind of macho folly we giggled at," he continued, and probably James Baldwin felt similarly. Jean Malaquais published a typical opinion in *Dissent*: "It was a seasonal thing, a romantic extrapolation of what came to be known as the guilt complex among American intellectuals." A bit closer to the intellectual center of American life, William Phillips said he did not feel the guilt and that he would not have published the essay in *Partisan Review* because it was "intellectually non-acceptable," though, preparing the way for Saul Bellow, he did think it had a place in fiction.[41]

Still, Mailer's provocative work presented a challenge. Phillips's young Brooklyn-born and Cambridge-educated protégé Norman Podhoretz tried to show how unacceptable Jack Kerouac and Mailer were intellectually in the article "No Nothing Bohemians." Podhoretz, who had dismissed Saul Bellow's acclaimed *Augie March*, thought Mailer in league with the Beats; as for Mailer's exploration of blackness, that signaled a tawdry fondness for sex orgy. But Podhoretz hit the mark when he looked at the Beat celebration of blacks. He said that both Kerouac's and Mailer's celebration of "primitive spontaneity" left out of the account the blacks they actually knew. Podhoretz asserted that "even if it were true that American Negroes, by virtue of their position in our culture, have been able to retain a degree of primitive spontaneity, the last place you would expect to find evidence of this is among Bohemian Negroes."[42] He went on to raise the key point that the Communists had struggled with in their umbrella organizations. "Bohemianism, after all, is for the negro a means of entry into the world of whites, and no negro Bohemian is going to cooperate in the attempt to identify him with Harlem or Dixieland." Podhoretz had accurately observed bohemia—an amorphous zone that seemed large enough to capture Beat and Hip—as an entry point for blacks. However, underneath his just observation was a sneer: black bohemians were inauthentic fakes who really only desired assimilation—or escape—however they could.

And yet, Podhoretz wound up making more space for new voices than Norman Mailer. A twenty-four-year-old black poet who lived in a Village walk-up apartment and worked at a record store defended his right to enter wherever he liked. LeRoi Jones, who hailed from New Jersey and had founded a journal, said that the Negro bohemian was an artist who needed other artists. The concerned young writer rejected Podhoretz's and Mailer's assumption that "Harlem" signified anything. Jones's girlfriend Hettie Cohen, a Jewish Mary Washington College graduate, worked as the circulation manager at *Partisan Review*. The journal published Jones's rebuttal of Podhoretz and launched Jones into a league that included Richard Wright, Sterling Brown, Anatole Broyard, James Baldwin, and Ralph Ellison.

Jones began his considerable career with strong words. "The Negro bohe-mian's flight from Harlem is not a flight from the world of color but . . . [a flight from] the provinciality, philistinism, and moral hypocrisy of American life." Jones thought of Harlem in terms of 409 Edgecombe and Convent Place; it was "the veritable capital city of the Black Bourgeoisie."[43] Mailer's hipsters were not glamorous, but cut-rate hustlers and knife-scarred con-men to be shunned.

Jones embodied the new spirit bubbling from the young black vanguard, the art-curious parvenus and upstarts taken less by the heritage of earnest, Communist-backed black writers' collectives than by the sexy, interracial free-for-all available in Greenwich Village. He had nearly completed his college training at Howard University, but he did not take his degree. His mother had graduated from Tuskegee and his father worked for the U.S. Post Office: Jones was easily the African American version of the middle class. But at Howard he had been reprimanded for eating watermelon too close to the city street, which, at least from the point of view of the dean of men, might have confirmed white stereotypes. Jones rebelled by learning the dialectic and Fichte from Margaret Juste Butcher, the heir to Alain Locke's cultural criticism at Howard, and taking Dante from the brilliant University of Chicago-trained philosopher and theolo-gian Nathan Scott. Jones poured his aptitude into his course with Sterling Brown, visiting Brown's home and believing him when Brown pointed to his voluminous phonograph recordings of Ma Rainey and Bessie Smith and told the young college student, "That's your history." Brown's best gift was his non-chalance, his cool. "He wasn't trying to prove that he knew something," Jones recalled.[44]

Howard's demanding propriety pushed Jones into the U.S. Air Force in 1955. His high school friend and rival Allen Polite had moved to a Greenwich Village apartment on Bedford Street, started wearing a beard, and begun to live with a white girlfriend. These were the accoutrements to the new, hip life, a domestic version of what the expatriates pursued in Paris and Rome. On his furloughs from a military base in Puerto Rico, Jones visited Polite, took out a subscription to *Partisan Review*, and started sending out poems to the magazines. Quickly he became disenchanted by mainstream American writing, especially when it came in the mechanically polished poems appearing in the *New Yorker*. Embar-rassed, Jones confided to himself that "there was something in me so *out*, so unconnected with . . . what that magazine was."[45] The disillusionment became an awakening. He also managed to get discharged from the military on account of his subversive literature. The full absurdity of the American political scene was revealed to Jones when air force officials used his copies of *Partisan Review* as the prime evidence against him.

Jones arrived in the Village in 1956, found a job at The Record Changer music shop, and became a jazz aficionado. That year when he glanced in the windows of the bookshops on Eighth Avenue, he noticed the photograph of a young, colored, gentle-faced man with a sparse mustache and wearing a cumbersome sweater on the front cover of a new book. It was James Baldwin's *Notes of a Native Son*. Familiar figures like Langston Hughes were reading poetry to the accompaniment of Charles Mingus at the new Village club the Five Spot. And just as easily, Jones flowed into the circles of abstract painters and Black Mountain Poets clustering at Cedar Tavern on University Place. He started a family and married Cohen. Several of his close friends and artistic comrades, like Allen Ginsberg and Frank O'Hara, were homosexual. He had street fights with the bass player Mingus and ushered into playing venues the most unorthodox of the jazz musicians, the Albert Aylers, Thelonius Monks, and Ornette Colemans of the world. He shot horse with the painter Bob Thompson.

At the time of the reply to Podhoretz in *Partisan Review*, Jones and Cohen were editing a magazine called *Yugen: A New Consciousness in the Arts*. "Yugen" was a Japanese word that meant "elegance, beauty, grace, transcendence of these things, and also nothing at all."[46] The couple produced the journal until 1962, and in 1958 and 1959 they published poetry by William Carlos Williams and the anchors of the Beat poetry movement: Allen Ginsberg, Diane di Prima, Jack Kerouac, Frank O'Hara, Robert Creeley, Gregory Corso, Gilbert Sorrentino, Peter Orlovsky, and William S. Burroughs. Jones was more interested in claiming the East Village talent than in promoting himself; he published his own poetry occasionally as he mastered the new idiom, the open defiance to the disciplined, emotionally restrained, and encyclopedically erudite Eliotic tradition in poetry.

Jones brought to bohemia the point of view of black American frustration and cultural finesse and united them with the perspective of the late 1950s intellectual rebels. His brew enabled him to make an original contribution to an artistic tendency that prized spontaneity and alternatives to traditional politics. One of his earliest published poems, "Lines to Garcia Lorca," began with an epigraph from a Negro spiritual "Climin up the mountain, Chilrun" and then addressed the murdered poet of the Spanish Civil War. "Slice of Life" was a slyly comic piece revealing an angel descended upon segregation's epicenter in South Carolina. The second number in 1958 contained Jones's "Suppose Sorrow Was a Time Machine," a dismayed homage to Jones's grandparents, the Booker T. Washington generation. The poem showed the channeled rage that the younger blacks felt, but which came out in tormented philosophical angst.

> Tom, are you going to let him cry like that? Are you going to let the me that was, before the stoneage metapmorphosis, suffer? Have you no feeling for the child? A sympathy for the post-prebirth enlightenment, the pre-promethean banality of childhood? The boy is sensitive, Tom, say something before you move on to grounds more fertile for random vibrations.[47]

The young editor was ribald, and always near the edge. Alongside Jones's New Jersey friend Allen Polite and Howard classmate Ben (A. B.) Spellman, Mason Jordan Mason was one of the other blacks published in the magazine, and he wrote "The Curse of Ham." The poem concluded with a gesture to Mailer's "White Negro" as much as it alluded to a kind of anatomical curiosity that also provided fuel to the bohemian movement. Answering the question about black docility by way of explaining God painting the black male body except for the mouth and genitals, the poet explained, "And that is why his mouth / and his peter is / never nobodies slave yet."[48] Black folklore and tale-telling, rural and urban, was replete with libidinal celebrations. But to continue this working-class effort in literature, mainstream or avant-garde, was risky for a serious artist.

The barriers of race, social class, and sexual orientation fell at the Jones-led dance parties where Ornette Coleman played saxophone solos unencumbered by reference to any melody and Allen Ginsberg met Langston Hughes.[49] Jones was successful enough that, by dint of his own artistic talent and personality, in conjunction with the circumstances of the time, he was able to project to his peers the importance of black contributions to American culture. Poet Robert Creeley would write that "Negro consciousness . . . has become *the* dominant reality in the States today."[50] Norman Mailer believed precisely the same thing. Experimental poet Frank O'Hara and several of the other young writers appearing in *Yugen* thought the attitude, sensibility, and culture—explicitly the music—of Negro America was the source of a unique fertility that their young movement might successfully harness as a basis for experimental artistic creation.[51] Jones was obviously out front as a physical symbol for a large group of artists and because of his own work. His poetry was humorous, obscene, conscious of his African heritage, but without sloganeering or crude slander directed at the apparatus of American commercial might and middle-class cultural mores. Jones seemed an authentic new breed: disregarding middle-class success, too cynical for communism, eclectically educated, celebrating his ethnicity, and openly associating with whites. He had a great deal in common with Richard Wright from the mid-1930s.

Some of the white writers admitted the pleasures of historic African American sites of life while pointing out the conformity to mainstream tastes that was also found there. Seymour Krim had made it as a reviewer in the mainstream literary world, a "prison," until he discovered the Beats who revived him. He fell in love with the "protest writing, fresh writing, fantastic crazy nutty grim honest liberating fertilizing writing, words and thoughts that come untouched by Madison Avenue's manicured robotic hand."[52] Jones had shared precisely the same sentiments regarding the tightly controlled *New Yorker* poetry.

In his personal affairs, Krim was nearly a double for the character James Baldwin would name Vivaldo in the 1961 novel *Another Country*. A habitué of

Harlem for what it had to offer of hop and hip trim, Krim had written an article on white hipsters for the *Village Voice*, a newspaper partially founded and funded by Norman Mailer in 1955. In "Anti-Jazz: A Question of Self Identity," he tried to assert two painful facts. First, jazz was created by a despondent and degraded group of African Americans who lingered near the bottom of the American social order, and it therefore could not be safely romanticized—or imitated. "Jazz is the music of the colored people," the essay began without controversy before landing a fist. "It came out of squalor, ignorance, the most ignoble and pathetic kind of conditions, which ultimately produced its beauty and its excitement."[53] The second point was naturally related to the first: the whites who listened to jazz—which meant both Beat and Hip whites—were romanticizing black squalor and were shameless voyeurs acting out fantasies that they would reject in the world of whites. The whites were doing everything but painting their faces black in their efforts "to behave and be like a Negro." "It seems to me that this permanent problem is at the bottom of every white man who plays jazz."

Krim closed the work by refusing to flatter anybody and, after a fashion, aligning his sense of ethnic politics to Norman Podhoretz's. "Most ordinary Negroes, whose emotions are naturally put into jazz, know only too well the ecstasy of their music comes out of a rough and often abysmal life: they would gladly have sacrificed their music to a white skin and a less brutal standard of living."[54] Bucklin Moon had had his black college president make the same assertion about the origin of the blues in *Without Magnolias*, but he had not gone as far as saying that blacks wanted to be white. Krim refused dignity in the music and pride in the musicians. In the process, he picked up new enemies in the Village from among the fledgling breed of "tense, self-conscious, easily-offended Negroes" who could not afford the fare to Paris and had decided to take New York where it seemed vulnerable.[55] The young *Village Voice* fielded so many letters, most of them scowling at what they believed was the evidence of pathetic racism, that Krim wrote an essay eighteen months later clarifying his experiences in Harlem, called "Ask for a White Cadillac." The essay was a Kerouacian tour de force that showed Krim hunting black hustling women above 116th Street.

If the *Village Voice* published essays by white hipsters and dealt with squalor, sex, and jazz, the *Saturday Review*, renamed from the *Saturday Review of Literature* in 1952 and on the downside of its quarter-century dominance of American literary tastes, was its antipode. By 1958 no one appeared more republican in his tastes than Ralph Ellison. He thought, in line with Norman Podhoretz, that "The White Negro" was "[t]he same old primitivism crap in a new package."[56] Ellison devoted his work during the second half of the 1950s, when he was a celebrated writer with access to publication outlets, to trying to make the point that Krim was wrong about the proving ground of jazz music and that

Mailer was wrong about the mystery of the black ghetto. His essays on Charlie Christian, Minton's Play House, Jimmy Rushing, Mahalia Jackson, and Charlie Parker turned out to be nearly concluding gestures for his career as a published writer. He wanted to rewrite jazz history, its origin myths, and, really, to defend the antisqualor point of view regarding the creation of black culture. By 1958 Ellison had a sense of confidence that made him, at forty-five, patrician and a bit haughty. When Charlie Christian's work was rereleased, Ellison read the liner notes and addressed the *Saturday Review*'s audience, "it would be well that here I offer a correction. . . . Al Avakian and Bob Prince are mistaken when they assume that Christian was innocent of contact with musical forms more sophisticated than the blues."[57]

Naturally the American mainstream regarded Ellison as hesitantly as James Baldwin's black jazz musicians did Norman Mailer. Ellison, like any other black writer, would bleed into whatever image popular culture placed before them—jazz-blowing hipster, Bigger Thomas, or Uncle Remus—whether or not he had begun to take a banker's approach to his work. Describing what it implied was his frenzied approach to writing, *Time* magazine called him a "jazzed-up, Joyced-up intellectual."[58] Ellison recognized and explained the contradiction, between his work to cultivate the underlying shared American cultural history and the mask that he continued to wear in the performance of his everyday life. He accomplished the unusual feat in an essay that stylishly managed to say that white liberals—Faulkner, Mailer, and Ellison's friend and one-time mentor Stanley Edgar Hyman—had in a sense worn out their welcome. The essay "Change the Joke and Slip the Yoke" appeared in 1958 in *Partisan Review*, making Ellison and James Baldwin the most influential African American essayists. Looking now to publish in *Saturday Review* and *Partisan Review* after 1955, when the journal had squandered its moral authority by failing to vocally resist McCarthy and was considered to be marking time, Ellison was now, officially, no longer radical; Baldwin never had been.[59]

Ellison claimed that in the essay "The Trickster in American Fiction," the bookish and sincere Stanley Hyman had mistakenly presumed that the "darky entertainer" was at the core of black American culture. To make the point, Hyman had pointed out minstrel caricatures. Ellison countered Hyman's cultural proof, which had seemed only basic prima facie evidence, by claiming that the well-known figures filling in the century between Tambo and Bones and Step-n-Fetchit did "not find [their] popularity among Negroes but among whites" and that all of these figures originated "not from the Negro but from the Anglo-Saxon branch of American folklore."[60] Instead, Ellison pointed to minstrelsy as a national theater and declared that "America is the land of masking jokers," and he included icons like Benjamin Franklin and Abraham Lincoln. He said this with a combination of authority, resolve, and distance that, from the pen of a Negro writer, would not have been thought possible ten years earlier. On the basis of the piece, LeRoi Jones sent Ellison a letter of approval and declared his joyful excitement for Ellison's essay on Charlie Christian, "the finest piece of Jazz writing I have seen in quite a while."[61] Jones suggested that the two of them share a craftsmen's rendezvous.

The overture from Jones was remarkable. Ellison's decision to send work to *Saturday Review* served as an obvious sign of his acceptance by and his contentedness with what the critics—especially Jones—railed against, the complacent and socially conservative American "middlebrow." The meeting never occurred. When Ellison himself had been twenty-four, he had been, within days of arriving in New York, warmly befriended by Langston Hughes, Alain Locke, and Richmond Barthé. By 1958, though, he had become the kind of artist incapable of such generosity—at least toward fellow blacks. Ellison and Jones would clash, with a vigor that increased every year, throughout the 1960s.

James Baldwin registered his point of view on the topic commensurate with Mailer, in the summer of 1957, with what may have been his greatest fiction achievement, the short story "Sonny's Blues." He had written to his friend Owen Dodson in the second half of 1956 and described the genesis of the important story. Near the middle of 1955 Baldwin had begun a story dealing with a Negro jazz musician "as tragic hero." "The great technical difficulty," he allowed, "is that jazz musicians are practically by definition inarticulate."[62] "Sonny's Blues" appeared in 1957 in *Partisan Review* and sought to detail the life of a young hip musician named Sonny, and it deliberately emphasized what Kerouac and Mailer could not conceive: the peril of hip, its steady border with the abyss.

After his battle with Faulkner, Baldwin fiercely told the black hipster's story in a language that would make callow any casual appropriation of Harlem's jungles of narcotic addiction for the sake of fashion. Sonny, the story's tragic hero, is a jazz musician who has turned to heroin as a form of solace not necessarily to escape but to engage at all the problem of choosing a path for existence. Sonny's brilliance and angelic humanity are constantly contrasted with his older brother's tendency for pettiness and false piety. Baldwin had pursued a genuine fictionalization, in a sense, of Hip and Square, and no whites were involved.

Moreover, Baldwin never lost sight of the blues as a central component of Sonny's hip life and behavior. Mailer had not accounted for the aching despair of the blues. His entire theoretical apparatus, his philosophical approach and Nietzschean ethical relativism, was, in fact, designed to preclude or eliminate the blues. Black identity in his view did not involve thoughtful tragedy; it served to multiply ecstasy exponentially. The gulf was between adrenalin- and endorphin-based action, on one side, and the high-pitched and low-moaned laughter and resignation of mind frosting heroin, on the other.

Ultimately, this then was the central difference among the artists regarding how black integration into American life would take shape. Mailer's "The White Negro" made a suggestion that whites could be "Negro," or more accurately "Hip," without having to take on the historical burden of Negro blues. This was the happy magic of integration for white artists and the simultaneous reluctance of black novelists to imagine a fiction world where this integration was successfully taking place. Outrageous white liberal writers like Mailer seemed to propose that Negro identity might be donned like a suit of clothes without paying the price for the coat. Straight-laced critics like Lionel Trilling only wanted blacks to shoulder their individual responsibility—with or without a social transformation of American reality. Baldwin's black figure Sonny buckles under the burden of being the Native Son—providing culture and shouldering his individual burden from the bottom—and he has to make his own identity out from the rubble of addiction. Baldwin deliberately chose the addict, precisely the figure most often cast out by the snide rhetorical posture of the righteous, by the Milton Klonskys of the world reproducing the hopped-up Harlem snake-eyed man.

However, the situation remained complex, forever entangled. There was a glittering presupposition in Mailer's hipster response to Faulkner's protection of segregation. Mailer had said in kooky Reichian-Kierkegaardian-Erich Frommian-Max Weberian jargon that the black lower class had cut into the American social bedrock a form of life, complete with desirable routes to possibility and admirable resistance in the face of slavery, segregation, lynching, miseducation, scorn, and dishonor. He was pointing to the crude-oil vitality of ill-bred American culture, of which "the Negro" was the undeniable silt foundation. Mailer had unsettled whites and several of the black elites because he suggested that a rather churlish class of blacks had created a tantalizing style—a history, a commodity—by accepting their lives. He was also unsettling to others of black elites, a different kind from the first, because he called for the white majority to skillfully soak up the resources there. Belonging to both camps of these black elites, the young writer Lorraine Hansberry called Mailer a "New Paternalist[s]" who had "mistaken the *oppression* of the Negro *for* 'the Negro.'"[63]

432

16.1. Jackson State College Writers' Conference, 1952 Standing, *left to right*, Arna Bontemps, Melvin Tolson, unidentified, Owen Dodson, Robert Hayden; seated, *left to right*, Sterling Brown, unidentified (probably Ruth Dease), Margaret Walker, and Langston Hughes. Library of Congress

SUNDAY, OCTOBER 19

4:00 P.M. — Dansby Hall — Auditorium

VESPER SERVICES

President Jacob L. Reddix, Presiding

Prelude—Spiritual Medley ....Arranged by Young and Davis

Call to Worship
Processional Hymn..."How Firm a Foundation"

        How firm a foundation, ye saints of the Lord
        Is laid for your faith in his excellent Word!
        What more can he say than to you he hath said,
        To you who for refuge to Jesus have fled?
        To you who for refuge to Jesus have fled?

        Fear not, I am with thee, O be not dismayed,
        For I am thy God, I will still give thee aid;
        I'll strengthen thee, help thee, and cause thee to stand,
        Upheld by my righteous, omnipotent hand,
        Upheld by my righteous, omnipotent hand.

        When thro' the deep waters I call thee to go,
        The rivers of sorrow shall not overflow!
        For I will be with thee, thy troubles to bless,
        And sanctify to thee thy deepest distress,
        And sanctify to thee thy deepest distress.

                                      Amen.

Invocation—Rev. D. M. Ray, Pastor Central Methodist Church, Jackson,
    Mississippi

The Occasion...Jesse Stegall

Special Music—"Thanks Be to God"...................................Handel
        The Jackson College Vesper Choir

Introduction of Speaker.....................President Jacob L. Reddix

Address: "Seventy-five Years of Literature by Negroes in America"
        Dr. Sterling A. Brown, Professor of English, Howard University,
        Washington, D. C.

Spiritual—"When I Was Sinking Down"........................Arr. Johnson

Recessional—"Now the Day Is Over"

Benediction

Seven-fold Amen

Postlude—"Theme Oppressione"..............................Young, arr. by Davis

MONDAY, OCTOBER 20

9:00 A.M. — Dansby Hall — Lecture Room

Student Workshop in Journalism—"The Negro in the News and the History
    of the Negro Neswpaper."
    Leader: Mr. Rollin P. Greene
    Consultants: William Peterson
                Era Bell Thompson
                Claude Barnett
                Percy Greene
                Purser Hewitt

    Student Participants...................Sam Hannibal, Magnoria Meekins

16.2. Program, "Seventy-Five Years of the Negro in American Literature Conference," Jackson State College, Mississippi, 1952   Arna Bontemps Papers, Special Collections Research Center, Syracuse University Library

434

WEDNESDAY, OCTOBER 22

10:00 A.M. — Dansby Hall — Auditorium

Dean Lionel B. Frazier, Presiding

Prelude

Scripture and Prayer...Speech Choir

Hymn: "Battle Hymn of the Republic."

Mine eyes have seen the glory of the coming of the Lord;
He is trampling out the vintage where the grapes of
   wrath are stored;
He has loosed the fateful lightning of his terrible
   swift sword;
His truth is marching on.

I have seen him in the watchfires of a hundred
   circling camps,
They have builded him an altar in the evening dews
   and damps;
I can read His righteous sentence by the dim and
   flaring lamps
His day is marching on.

Refrain

Glory! glory! Hallelujah!
Glory! glory! Hallelujah!
Glory! glory! Hallelujah!

(1) His truth is marching on.

(2) His day is marching on.

Introduction of Speaker...Mr. Rollin P. Greene

Address: "The Negro Novelist and the
   Southern Scene"...Dr. J. Saunders Redding

Vocal Solo—"Oh, What a Beautiful City"...............................Arr. Johnson
                              Cora Bell Wade

Announcement of Winners of Literary
   Contest..Mrs. Margaret W. Alexander

Presentation of Awards and Prizes.......................President Jacob L. Reddix

Introduction of Guests

Announcements

Postlude

4:00 P.M. — Dansby Hall — Lecture Room and Lobby

BOOK FAIR AND AUTOGRAPH PARTY

7:00 P.M. — Dansby Hall — Auditorium

Organ Prelude

Music—"Lift Every Voice and Sing"

Symposium: "The Contemporary Novel: Themes and Writers."
   Arna Bontemps, Presiding

Postlude

16.3. Program, "Seventy-Five Years of the Negro in American Literature Conference," Jackson State College, Mississippi, 1952   Arna Bontemps Papers, Special Collections Research Center, Syracuse University Library

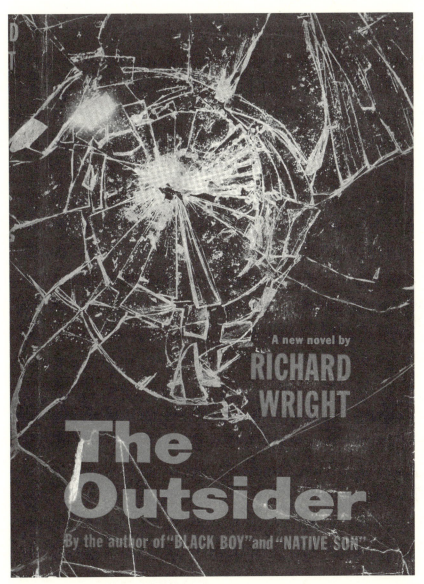

16.4. *The Outsider* by Richard Wright, 1953, cover   Copyright 1953 by Richard Wright; renewed © 1981 by Ellen Wright. Reprinted by permission of HarperCollins Publishers

16.5. Speaker's platform, opening session, Congress of African Writers and Artists, September 19, 1956   *Seated*, left to right, Richard Wright, unidentified, Alioune Diop (standing), unidentified, Jean Price-Mars, Paul Hazoumé, Aimé Césaire, unidentified

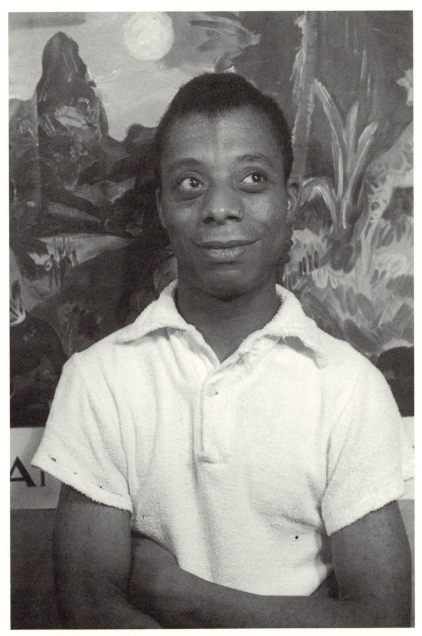

16.6. James Baldwin, 1955 Photograph by Carl Van Vechten, James Weldon Johnson Collection in the Yale Collection of American Literature, Beinecke Rare Book and Manuscript Library, Yale University

16.7. William Gardner Smith, 1948   Photograph by Carl Van Vechten, Carl Van Vechten Photographs, Countee Cullen-Harold Jackman Memorial Collection, Robert W. Woodruff Library of the Atlanta University Center

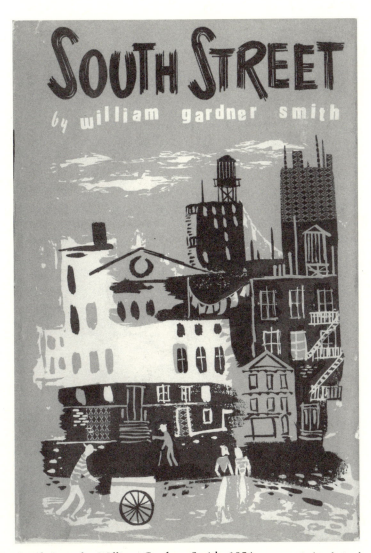

16.8. *South Street* by William Gardner Smith, 1954, cover   Jacket design by Carl
Malouf from *South Street* by William Gardner Smith. Jacket design copyright © 1954 by Carl Malouf. Reprinted by permission of Farrar, Straus and Giroux

16.9. LeRoi Jones (Amiri Baraka), 1962   Photograph by Carl Van Vechten, Carl Van Vechten Photographs, Countee Cullen-Harold Jackman Memorial Collection, Robert W. Woodruff Library of the Atlanta University Center

16.10. Julian Mayfield, 1959   Photograph by Carl Van Vechten, Carl Van Vechten Photographs, Countee Cullen-Harold Jackman Memorial Collection, Robert W. Woodruff Library of the Atlanta University Center

16.11. AMSAC Negro Writers' Conference, Hudson Hotel, New York, 1959   Standing, *left to right*, John Davis, Langston Hughes, J. Saunders Redding; seated, *left to right*, Arna Bontemps, Lorraine Hansberry. *The American Negro Writer and His Roots: Selected Papers from the First Conference of Negro Writers*, March 1959. New York: American Society of African Culture, ©1960

16.12. Ralph Ellison at the National Book Awards, 1958   Photograph by Alfred
Eisenstaedt, Time & Life Pictures© Getty Images

CHAPTER SEVENTEEN

The End of the Negro Writer (1955–1960)

The distinguished sociology professor E. Franklin Frazier went to France in 1949 and then returned in 1952 and 1953, to Paris, as the chief of the Division of Applied Sciences for the United Nations Educational Scientific and Cultural Organization (UNESCO) in France. Perhaps he considered the time abroad a well-earned reward. Frazier had gained remarkable distinction on account of his formidable researches and strongly articulated views, but he also deserved recognition because of his personal courage. Born in Baltimore in 1894, Frazier had known steadily mounting racial segregation for most of his life. But racial oppression had never slowed his pursuit of professional and intellectual goals. He taught at Tuskegee, at tiny St. Paul's in Lawrenceville, Virginia, and at Morehouse, where in 1927 he was forced to flee after publishing a psycho-sociological analysis of the white mob who had lynched an African American man. When teaching at Fisk, he defied the ban on blacks at Vanderbilt and ate in the cafeteria.[1] Frazier finished his doctorate at the University of Chicago and then published commanding books in the sociological field, like *The Negro Family in the United States*. By 1941 he had become the chairman of the department of sociology at Howard University, a rank that he would hold for twenty years. Even his white peers recognized him, and he became president of the American Sociological Association in 1948.

Frazier stayed abreast of developments in other fields, and he may have shared with Ralph Ellison the wealthy New York patron, the heiress, Communist Party sympathizer, and American Labor Party supporter Ida Guggenheimer. Like some others of Howard's faculty, Frazier had some standing on the far Left. He claimed, when his cohort at Howard was brought before Joseph McCarthy's Senate committee, to have ridiculed his questioners. It was an event that "scared the hell" out of Arthur P. Davis.[2] During his 1953 sojourn to France he wrote to Guggenheimer, reporting that he had read Ellison's *Invisible Man*, which he liked, even though on its face the novel was dogmatically anticommunist, which Frazier did not like. At the time, Frazier was working on a curious book that he would publish in Paris in 1955 and called *Bourgeoisie Noir*. For a book about black Americans published in a foreign language, Frazier had unusual success, winning the MacIver Award from the American Sociological Society. The English edition of the book was published in 1957 and then began to receive reviews from the American press. The English version, *Black Bourgeoisie*, became an instant classic, quoted especially by the literary radicals of the second half of the 1950s who had taken full flight from the goal of American middle-class standing. An African American rejection of the mainstream, that distant pursuit for much of the twentieth century, was afoot; sixty-three-year-old Frazier was the majordomo.

The succinct *Black Bourgeoisie* neither was the result of new research nor did it deliver a startlingly precise definition of what the black middle class was. The salient points to Frazier's reviewers, like Chester Himes's brother Joseph, a sociologist in North Carolina, was the facile discussion of social science, aboard a raft of anecdote and cultural study, which coalesced into a kind of prophetic vision. But more notably, Frazier threw down the gauntlet in his brief account. He said that the achievement of black middle-class standing amounted to nothing. "[W]hen Negroes attain middle-class status, their lives generally lose both content and significance."[3] He implied that racial integration, even the basic desegregation of American institutions, was worthless.

The book suggested that on account of preconditions that went back to slavery, black achievers tended to plateau into an illusory world of black "society." Frazier wrote with frustration and evident contempt at the lackadaisical puritan resolve for which the black middle class, and blacks as a whole, were known. Black Americans who had succeeded under segregation stood "without cultural roots in either the Negro world with which it refuses to identify, or the white world which refuses to permit the black bourgeoisie to share its life." They had an "inferiority complex" and ran to "a world of make-believe in which it attempts to escape the disdain of whites and fulfill its wish for status in American life."[4] For his footnotes Frazier relied completely on black press accounts and his Howard colleagues for the disparaging remarks that led him to dismiss the middle class. Everyone knew that he was basically writing autobiography. One of his reviewers joined him to J. Saunders Redding. Both men were accused of having fallen "for publicity and fortune" and sold "their own people down the river."[5] Frazier was in Europe and Redding had made the New York publishers, but it was not quite possible to say that they had earned ransoms by issuing their mordant views.

Frazier's book was also a satire, the implicit humor sometimes sulfurous, qualities that helped the book endure for future readers. His set portraits of black doctors and educators calling the Negro a "child race" before whites seemed painful and ridiculous, as had the portraits of black educators in Redding's *No Day of Triumph* and *Stranger and Alone* and Ralph Ellison's *Invisible Man*. Certainly from the perspective of black artists the ridicule made sense: with such small numbers, the only way to survive was to reach the middle class and distress it into vomiting up a group of new writers with a radically different kind of social conscience. What had been left unarticulated was whether or not this sort of devastating trend would continue as racial barriers eased. Would the teeny upper class of blacks merely exchange the debutante cotillion and Sigma Pi Phi Boulé for the comparably banal rituals of white American society? Frazier hoped they would not. He had used a skywriter to claim this imitation the height of idiocy, the Greek societies spending two and a half million dollars in conspicuous consumption over a Christmas holiday, the professional black couple who served fifty-six people a nine-course meal. Of the American nation's nineteen million Negroes, he expected better from the 20 percent of them who lived in households with incomes above two thousand dollars a year.

Without question he had found a style and method that reached black citizens. He received a plaintive, pencil-written note from Virginia thanking him. "Here was a book put in words I had been thinking for 40 years," the letter began. "I found out from your book a person dont need to Be Book Scoo[led] to think. I dont Know the Wright words to thank you for what your book did for me. I only wish more of our people could think like you."[6] A Harlem photographer named Lloyd Yearwood compared the book to Gwendolyn Brooks's *Maud Martha*. The middle-class blacks of New York "can rattle off the different brands of liquor, different styles of clothing, books written by White Authors," Yearwood wrote in despair to Frazier. "I can't find one to discuss the work of Gwendolyn Brooks or literature of Africa. They have only heard of Mary Bethune or George Washington Carver. Very few have taken the trouble to search and to find out for themselves the true achievements of those truly great American Negroes. And for goodness sake don't mention gospel music to them."[7] For his part, the Harvard University political science Ph.D. candidate Martin Kilson believed that Frazier had written a new black gospel. "I have taken on a sort of personal crusade to have it read by every college educated Negro I come in contact with," he wrote.[8]

Frazier had, like so many others, found another measure of freedom overseas. France had the mixed blessing of being an old society when it came face-to-face with its colonial past after the end of the Second World War. Perhaps for that reason it could appear nonchalant when the African writers of *Présence Africaine*, a journal Richard Wright had had a hand in founding, decided to conduct an intellectual conference in 1956, the year after the Indonesian Bandung Conference of Non-Aligned Nations. In fact, Alioune Diop, the Senegalese herald of the conference, called it a "Second Bandung." Still, this important clearinghouse for what was called "Black Africa" at the time was curious. France still had an active colonial empire, portions of which had recently become "departments," which could then send elected representatives to the French National Assembly. Architect of the *assimilé* model, France seemed most reluctant to jettison the colonial system in toto, especially after its loss of the prize Vietnam in 1954.

France's most troublesome African property was directly on the other side of the Mediterranean Sea, in Algeria, where about half a million white Christian French citizens lived. An especially vicious and complicated war broke out there, which the Algerians were successful in bringing to the streets of the metropolis, where five thousand people were killed at cafes. Perhaps the claims of West African and Caribbean blacks seemed rather tame by comparison. In September 1956 the major black figures in the francophone intellectual world appeared for three days at the Sorbonne in the Salle Descartes.

James Baldwin covered the conference for the British journal *Encounter*, edited by Stephen Spender and the American Irving Kristol. His article appeared in January 1957. *Encounter*, like the Congress for Cultural Freedom, was an active organ of the U.S. State Department and received its funds through the Fairfield Foundation, under the guidance of agent Michael Josselson of the Central Intelligence Agency.[9] Kristol would become a leader of the neoconservative movement in the United States in the later 1960s, and he shared a pedigree with so many of Baldwin's close associates: Jewish, City College graduate, former Trotskyite, and one-time *Commentary* editor. Baldwin, who kept writing for *Encounter* into the 1960s, may have been chagrined a couple of years later when British theater critic Ken Tynan told him in no uncertain terms that he was, in effect, working for a U.S. government bureau, but his journalistic essay did not give itself over to selling Coca Cola and Cadillacs or sermonizing against Communist wrongdoing.[10]

In the article "Princes and Powers," Baldwin dispassionately reviewed the pan-African writers conference. The best that could be said from the point of view of his backers was that he was eerily distant from the proceedings. He called the meeting the "Conference of Negro-African Writers and Artists," a title that would be understood as redundant, odd, or delusional, or all three, in a few short years. And he described the American Negro participants with that magically racist word "colored," which by 1956 was still in widespread use but thought by black intellectuals an embarrassing term that made shadowy reference to the forced concubinage of an illegitimate, dishonored race. "Colored" was also one of the key intermediate racial designations used by the invigorated white racist regime in South Africa.

Baldwin could see the referendum coming out from the colonies in what he thought were the exceptionally charismatic and cunning voices of Leopold Senghor from Senegal and the Communist Aimé Césaire of Martinique. (Césaire would resign from the Communist Party in a couple of months after the Soviet Union invaded Hungary in November 1956.) Senghor startled Baldwin's senses most because he described a black extrasensory perception, what he called *Sentir c'est apercevoir*, that made feeling and perceiving the same thing.[11] In the 1960s this would be called "soul," and Paul Robeson, among other blacks, was known for similar, informal suggestions.[12] Senghor was followed by equally prestigious, equally adamant men. The Senegalese chemist Cheikh Anta Diop ignored the time limit and launched into a full-scale condemnation of European historians and archeologists. Diop claimed that the entirety of ancient Egyptian civilization belonged properly to the black African past. In other words, the use of a term like "black Africa" made no sense. The American term borrowed from Spanish, "Negro," was even more ridiculous.

Baldwin had a context to appreciate the ideas of the West Africans Senghhor and Diop and it was not a privileged one. He had gained familiarity with black cultural nationalism in storefront churches and on angry Harlem street corners. He had seen it at the Coptic Church on 125th Street, from members of the Moorish Science temple, and the remnants of the Garvey legions. He had read the flamboyant and alarming signs at Elder Lewis Michaux's National Memorial Bookstore on Seventh Avenue, the "House of Common Sense and Proper Propaganda," and may not have felt exactly welcomed by the West Indian intellectual elegance and light-colored skin of proprietor Richard B. Moore at his Frederick Douglass Book Center. And he had at least sensed it roaring at the center of his stepfather's version of Christianity, which would one day bring black men into glory and destroy the white enemy.

But this notion of shared racial traits and the idea of cultural superiority were at odds with his literary training and his influences and his common sense. He despised his stepfather for reasons other than religion or politics, and he connected the man's hatred of whites to basic, simian ignorance. Harlem's problack fighters, like its streets, were something to escape, not to wax nostalgically about. Despite his sensibility, Baldwin did not completely shout down the idea of a shared welcome-table in the African past, the "way of life" Baldwin "could only very dimly and perhaps somewhat wistfully imagine."[13] Senghor went on to suggest even that Richard Wright's *Black Boy* had an African spirit lurking in its past—divergent from its more obvious links to the western narrative tradition. This put Baldwin in what must have been a regrettable position for him. He had to wave the flag, claim Wright, and repeat Harper's advertisement for the book by saying, "*Black Boy* is one of the major American autobiographies."[14]

For Baldwin to have to echo Senghor's words and praise *Black Boy*, in some fashion, must have reduced him again to Wright, who was, by very far, the dominant American-born Negro at the conference, and arguably the dominant writer-intellectual figure there period. In reality, Baldwin wrote privately at the time that he considered Richard Wright pathetic: "as an enemy, frankly, he's much less embarrassing."[15] The general attitude against Wright's position, the indifference to Wright's international stature, and the reluctance to identify strongly with Africa obviously endeared Baldwin to America's powerful cultural cold warriors moving about in Europe. But that attitude did not necessarily win him esteem from other black writers. George Lamming, who thought a good deal of Baldwin's writing abilities, lumped Baldwin together with the Trinidadian V. S. Naipaul on account of his unfailing personal identification with European culture. "[I]n Baldwin's case," wrote Lamming, "it seems that the intelligence suffers a kind of arthritis. There is a swift and total paralysis of native pride."[16]

Of course, Richard Wright cherished a political commitment to black people across the globe that never seemed to express itself as a joyful pride in being black. In 1954, two years before the Paris black writers' conference, Wright had visited Kwame Nkrumah in Ghana and written the book *Black Power: A Record of Reaction in a Land of Pathos* to describe his experience. He was the first prominent black American creative writer to visit West Africa and write a narrative about his experiences there, and the book itself was not kind; its general tenor was pro-Western government enough for a chunk of it to appear in *Encounter*. Nevertheless, Wright accepted a leadership role on the international scene on behalf of Africa and people who traced their origin to that continent, tirelessly putting his prestige and talent as a writer to work. Following up *Black Power,* Wright published *The Color Curtain* (1956), a narrative assessment of Indonesia and the Bandung Conference between Asian and African nations.

Wright's support for the developing world and his earnest desire to end colonialism did not stem from a commitment to Négritude. He remained a fairly conservative, Marx-grounded intellectual, believing in the importance of material conditions, stages of progress, and individual responsibility. His experiences in Africa and acquaintance with African writing led him to believe in the difficulty of eradicating the formidable psychology of dependence in colonized and formerly enslaved peoples. He stuck to the establishment and maintenance of the secular nation-state. More stiffly, in such speeches as "Tradition and Industrialization: The Tragic Plight of African Elites," Wright's contribution to the Paris conference, he offered a bitter prescription for the transformation of societies mired in what Wright characterized as "superstition." If the West had needed the seventeenth-century English, eighteenth-century French, and nineteenth-century American civil wars to eradicate superstition, religious mysticism, feudalism, slavery, and economic backwardness, Wright challenged his audience to brace themselves for similarly difficult phases of historical evolution in Africa and Asia. Wright was insistent: "[T]hese newly created national states, must be given *carte* blanche to modernize their lands without overlordship of the west, and we must understand the methods that they will feel compelled to use. . . . [they] will necessarily use quasi-dictatorial methods to hasten the process of social evolution and to establish order in their lands. . . . Why pretend to be shocked at this?"[17] Pessimistic regarding the condition of the African intellectuals, especially their mental independence, Wright encouraged the production of a generation free from ties to the past. He was capable of endorsing dictators to push old errors out of the way.

When he took the podium at at the conference and presented his abrupt ideas, Richard Wright also said that colonialism had freed Africans from superstitious religions and uncritical philosophy. He advocated the "new" black man who, benefiting from the European enlightenment, could escape the "rot" of a primitive tradition. Surely this view pleased the U.S. State Department, and Baldwin showed some of his own independence by taking the opportunity to call the address "a tactless way of phrasing a debatable idea."[18] But four years after "Many Thousands Gone," and three years after Wright had defiantly put an ocean of distance between his own social realist works by way of the novel *The Outsider*, the two writers could easily see their strong common ground. After he finished talking, Wright introduced Baldwin to the American delegates. Surely there was some joking about the senior and junior black writers of great stature. Ralph Ellison had gathered with Wright, Chester Himes, and James Baldwin at Wright's house in early July 1956. Ellison had also been invited to cover the conference but had declined in favor of a Congress of Cultural Freedom jaunt to Mexico, where he would be on the dole of the now hard-charging Central Intelligence Agency.

Baldwin did not write about the final morning address "Racism and Culture" given on Thursday, September 20, by the dashing Martinican psychiatrist Frantz Fanon, who had now begun to work with National Liberation Front (FLN) in Algeria. Fanon, a member of the Martinican delegation, delivered an address that was uncompromising and, under the circumstances of the conference, perhaps a bit incomprehensible. Fanon presented himself in classic clinical fashion, diagnosing the sclerosis of the West. He disposed of the imperialism project of Western enlightenment science and history and summed up his points by way of a series of stunning one-liners. He described the degradation of the "chattel-man" produced by the colonial powers, and he credited Richard Wright's "early novels" for their "very detailed description" of the psychological complexes engendered in the oppressed. The psychiatrist abruptly dismissed the great claim of American and Western liberalism, that racism was the work of individuals: "The habit should be abandoned of regarding racism as a disposition of the mind, a psychological flaw."[19] Fanon demanded utter simplicity on two points, "Either a society is racist or it is not. There are no degrees of racism," which corresponded directly to his other, "But, let us repeat, every colonial group is racist."[20] With those principles, the end point was clear. Fanon suggested that natives would use traditional cultures as an avenue to liberation, and that once the native cultural renaissance had begun in earnest, at the moment the native begins "to fight against all forms of exploitation,"[21] the savvy resistance from colonialism would take the form of liberal tolerance. "[T]he occupying power, at this point, will multiply its appeals to assimilation, and subsequently to integration and community."[22] In the final stage, after "the eternally inferiorised spring suddenly to life and emerge in battle,"[23] Fanon predicted a "reciprocal relativism of differing cultures" as the final universalism.[24]

Fanon's practical work in the field of psychoanalysis was leading him to the conclusion beyond what C.L.R. James had written in 1938 about the relation between base and superstructure where race became involved. James had decided then that material facts were paramount in a Marxist analysis, but to examine global economy without taking into account the exercise of racism was a crushing error. But based on his psychiatric treatment of soldiers involved in the torture and massacre of Algerians, Fanon believed that both portions—the "base" material and economic conditions that structured inequality and the "superstructure" effect of prejudice on the basis of cultural and ethnic belonging—were generated simultaneously. Fanon was arriving at the modern definition of racism—the conjoined system of effects that includes gross material disparity, violence, and cognitive bias.

He refined his conference address and later published a fuller account in a book that set the world on fire, the classic *Wretched of the Earth*. "In the colonies," Fanon wrote, "the economic substructure is also a superstructure. The cause is the consequence; you are rich because you are white, you are white because you are rich."[25] After that hurdle, Fanon's next analytical certainty was the use of violent means, and the participation of the native intellectual class in the implementation of violent means, as the only possible route to the overthrow of the colonial system.

If the question of violent struggle against European colonial power had not come up in the discussions of the conference, certainly by later 1956, North African war would have made the topic unavoidable. In a few weeks France would invade Egypt in a joint operation with Britain and Israel and seize, for a time, the Suez Canal. But Baldwin did note the popular reception given Fanon's teacher, Aimé Césaire. Baldwin described the schoolteacher Césaire, one of the architects of French "departmental" policy that enabled some political representation and formal citizenship for former colonies, as a man with an intelligence that was "penetrating" but also "demagogic." Césaire theorized the manner in which culture might overcome colonialism, and what followed were sharp exchanges between him and the American delegates.

The American blacks were in an awkward position because neither of the black leftist international heroes W.E.B. Du Bois nor Paul Robeson was in possession of a passport. At the conference a telegram from Du Bois was read in which he protested the U.S. State Department's refusal to allow him to travel and cheered socialism in Africa. "I trust the black writers of the world will . . . set themselves to lead Africa towards the light and not backward toward a new colonialism where hand in hand with Britain, France, and the United States, black capital enslaves black labor."[26] Baldwin thought the missive "extremely ill-considered," and partially for the compromising effect it had on the black Americans present: Howard University romance department chairman Mercer Cook, Lincoln University president Horace Mann Bond, political scientist and New York City College professor John Davis, University of Pennsylvania philosophy professor William Fontaine, and *Crisis* magazine editor James Ivy. Thurgood Marshall and Duke Ellington attended some of the sessions as well, and rounding out an all-male delegation that included some of the lightest colored in skin and straightest texture of hair in all of African America. As it turned out, of course, the delegates' travel had been funded by U.S. government bureaus. Less well known, the conference bore fruit in 1957 in an organization called the American Society for African Culture and in 1958 in a book edited by Davis, *Africa Seen by American Negroes.*

Baldwin's view of the Africans was limited by other, psychologically messy factors. He wrote to Sol Stein, who was encouraging Baldwin to produce a tour de force on blacks in America, and admitted to a confrontation with his own antiblack prejudice. "'Letter to My Younger Brother' has been suffering from my ignorance concerning Africans; an ignorance which I've decided to utilize, for I will never really understand any more of Africa than the insights afforded me by some of the Africans I meet. More than that, though, it's suffered from a certain unsuspected condescension I've got in me towards Africans."[27]

When he described the Africans, the descriptive tool he seemed most comfortable with was "very dark", though some were "chocolate" or "caramel." But this was preferable to the manner in which he described three Negro Americans, whom he wrote about more than anyone else: his stepfather David Baldwin, Richard Wright, and himself. Baldwin reserved the term "pickaninny" for himself and Wright; he once referred to his stepfather as a "monkey."[28] He was completely unique in the employ of deeply painful language for himself and the others with whom he experienced elements of a paternal relationship. Wandering into the land of self-hate and self-rejection was perhaps too high a price for anyone to have to pay for the sake of clarity or the appearance of utter objectivity.

But Baldwin's white friends could sense his increasing charity toward the black radicals, partly on account of the wars against Kenya by England and against Algeria by France, and the hardening of black defiance in the United States. Predictably, Baldwin's friend Stein, who had just left his position as executive director of the American Committee for Cultural Freedom, disputed "Princes and Powers" as soft on communism. He accused Baldwin of making excuses for an irresponsible Du Bois. "You look at it much too much in terms of black and white," Stein griped. The Committee for Cultural Freedom had traditionally attacked the Soviet policy of regularly withholding passports from its citizens. Now the same committee rationalized the necessity of the U.S. State Department withholding passports from American citizens. Baldwin wrote Stein a long letter that seems to have been the end of their lengthy correspondence. Stein of course wound up having more to do than anybody else with making Baldwin's American reputation, as the editor and original spirit behind the collection *Notes of a Native Son*.

The American blacks at the conference could not decide if they would throw in their lot with their ancient past, regardless of ESP or black Egypt. In a situation common among the American blacks of his time, Baldwin had lived in an apartment with a woman who had spent a good portion of her life in bondage; his very presence at the conference, his ability to read a single word, abounded with promethean significance. The remarkable stride forward common to U.S. blacks made the claims of Diop and the demands of Césaire seem a bit dramatic, a bit overzealous and blind. Baldwin thought that he had found something of a hypocrite in Césaire, whose "speech left out of account one of the great effects of the colonial experience: its creation, precisely, of men like himself."[29]

But the observation about Césaire's curious position would in the months ahead lose its sharp edge, and, had he any expertise in political theory, Baldwin might have anticipated it. The magnificent Paris boulevards and cafes, the casual wisdom among the French who considered themselves too sophisticated for the crude racism that was quite palpable in America during the 1950s, did not exhibit the same quality of refuge for Baldwin in 1956 as it had in 1949. In the early days, Baldwin had palled with Algerian and Tunisian street boys and moneyed Egyptians. But in 1956 the Algerian War of the countryside moved to the city of Algiers itself and the European quarter. The situation in France for American blacks rapidly became more tense, and their exercise of relative personal freedom more difficult, more like home. Baldwin's friend Richard Gibson, who had finished his U.S. Army service in Germany and was now living in Paris, had noted the increased scrutiny from the police, who now regularly asked him for his papers. With light skin, full lips, and tightly curled hair, he was regularly mistaken for a native Algerian. The contrite response from the police at the sight of his American passport—the return of their human friendliness—more completely revealed the arbitrary impersonal violence of the modern Western nation-state to the young intellectual.

As a writer for the French news agency, William Gardner Smith kept up on the developments in Algeria, which had begun to shake loose some of the idealism he had had about France. In what Nick Aaron Ford thought was his best work, Smith's 1963 novel *The Stone Face* characterized the period and the international tensions in a dialogue between an Arab and black American named Simeon.

> "The Negroes in America should revolt like we did."
> Simeon said, "We don't have any Algeria to free."
> "You have a country. Africa."
> It was hard to explain. Africa was far away, in time as well as miles, and most American Negroes, while enthusiastic about the independence movement in Africa, would feel and be treated like complete foreigners there. The American Negro had, because of a specific experience, become something specific—neither African nor typically American. Things were changing, things were evolving, and perhaps some day—
> He finally said, "A lot of Negroes will go to Africa. But not all. You can't make it a revolutionary program."
> "And you?"
> "I don't know where I'm going."[30]

Smith's character's confusion of "country" for continent was sloppy, but it seems more disarming in the contemporary period than it was in the era when no individual West African nation was more than five years old. The major European powers had all taken colonies in 1884 and had really been none too concerned with talking about what had been there before. The reality of the international situation of armed movements for decolonization became apparent, then pressing upon the black writers living in Europe by the time the French called in paratroopers and gave them full civil authority in the Algerian capital city of Algiers in 1957. The alienated ennui of Smith's narrator exposed the Left Bank grunge-style café life as frivolous. What had seemed a principled stand against American babbittry and earnest pledges for artwork uninfected by what Richard Gibson had called in 1951 the "minstrel psychology" of "the Problem" did not hold up to the urgency of Algeria or even Montgomery, Alabama.

Expatriate life in France was nearing losing its shine on account of politics, but few American whites were redrawing the old boundaries back home. In his 1959 omnibus of remarkable over self-confidence, a collection of his *Village Voice* columns called *Advertisements for Myself*, Norman Mailer basically broke the color barrier by way of a strained and lengthy acknowledgment of Ralph Ellison, whom he described as a fierce and worthy competitor, and James Baldwin, whose delicate style, such as he had evinced in the rebuttal to Faulkner, struck Mailer as effeminate. If Mailer appeared to respect Ellison more as a man than Baldwin, he still believed that Ellison's major premise was backward. Mailer found it impossible to ignore these writers because "the Negro is the least invisible of all people in America." And for Mailer blacks were not just highly visible, they had aesthetic grace. He claimed that by the time that they were twenty, most blacks, among whom he definitely would have considered Ellison and Baldwin, had created "a face which is a work of art."[31]

The work of art that was the black writers' artistic face began to appear with a new kind of difference by the end of the war in Korea. By the mid-1950s, bearded black men reading French poetry and black women wearing all-black clothes had become characteristic of the Greenwich Village scene. Young black poets, men and women, lived openly, if precariously, with white lovers in the Village. Mailer envied and also resented these young people who had challenged Seymour Krim because they could navigate Harlem from the inside, come downtown, and still have direct access to the jazz musicians at Café Society and the Village clubs, the Five Spot (Mailer's maestro Thelonius Monk returned to the scene in 1957) and the Village Vanguard. It was precisely this access that preserved James Baldwin's sense of, if not superiority, at least fit competitiveness. Some of the young blacks in the Village were serious artists and politically sophisticated. While they did not have as high a profile as the expatriates, there were black writers anxious to describe the bubbling vitality of the black lower class, and they did not find out about its value through Mailer.

Julian Mayfield was probably the most energetic and successful member of what by the mid-1950s had become the Harlem Writers Guild, the group known by its leader John Oliver Killens. Mayfield had grown up in Washington, D.C., and, like William Gardner Smith, joined the U.S. Army as an eighteen-year-old in 1946. Mayfield shot up to Harlem after a restless year at Lincoln College in Pennsylvania. He signed on to the Communist Party in 1949 and joined the small entourage of athletes who defended Paul Robeson from physical assault. Mayfield, the young Bajan actor and U.S. Army washout Sidney Poitier, dramatist Leon Bibb, and New Yorker Harry Belafonte escorted Robeson through the streets, staring down the right-wing vigilantes.

A foot soldier for communism, Mayfield walked sentry at all the public causes at the end of the 1940s and the beginning of the 1950s: Willie McGhee, the Martinsville Seven, Rosa Ingram, and the Ethel and Julius Rosenberg case—he even visited the freshly electrocuted couple lying in state at their Brooklyn home. Mayfield and other young members of the Committee for the Negro in the Arts workshop—which became the Harlem Writers Guild—like Audre Lorde spent their free time traveling to Washington, D.C., to carry placards of protest at the White House. But the 1950s of the standing House Committee on Un-American Activities, the McCarthy Senate Investigations Subcommittee, the federal Loyalty Oath, and the Smith Act was a far cry from the heroic 1930s and the successes with the Scottsboro Boys and Angelo Herndon. The young actor and his buddies were always on the losing side. "[A]fter a few years of fighting for such causes and losing them all, one must begin to question if the cause is worth fighting for," Mayfield thought, then adding, "or if the method is the most effective one."[32]

It made better sense to diversify the terrain of radical struggle; the arts, certainly theater continued to hold the bright promise of reaching a broad audience and bringing out the issues. Alongside fellow workshop members like the playwright and columnist Rosa Guy, Mayfield turned to acting and producing for the Committee for the Negro in the Arts. He appeared in the 1949 Harlem play *A Medal for Willie* and wrote some of his own plays, like *417*, an off-Broadway production about winning the outlawed "policy" game. He and Sidney Poitier vied with one another for roles and, in an odd twist of fate, Poitier shucked professional theater in favor of Hollywood for the 1949 film *No Way Out*. In his place he left Mayfield with the Broadway role of Absalom Kumalo in *Lost in the Stars*, the adaptation of Alan Paton's novel *Cry the Beloved Country*. The play ran in 1949 and 1950.

Mayfield followed up his Broadway success with civil rights. In 1951 he led a CNA subcommittee in getting statistics on the number of blacks employed in theater, television, and radio,[33] and in November he performed alongside Katherine Dunham at the Equal Rights for Negroes in the Arts, Sciences and Professions Conference.[34] The next year he produced Ossie Davis's play *Alice in Wonder*, a tale of a singer who faces blacklisting, and obviously a dramatic allegory of Paul Robeson's public agony. To win a victory, the play needed widespread support from blacks in Harlem and whites downtown in the Village, and the Communist press to bring them together. The resistance to the idea would crystallize Mayfield's suspicion of whites on the Left.

The experience producing *Alice in Wonder* itself showed the terrain uneasily shared by Soviet supporters, anticommunist liberals, and civil rights radicals. Though the play needed Communist press and organizational support to generate a buzz among the young left-wing theatergoers, its writers had not made the typical overtures to the Communist crowd. For one thing, Ossie Davis had committed heresy by failing to show an example of black and white unity, a hallmark of Communist-inspired dramas. For another, the play's protagonist bore an obvious resemblance to Paul Robeson, a major gaffe to some of the Communist policy makers. They believed that invoking Robeson's case potentially detracted from their strategies to win back the singer's passport. However, the young black artists considered an essential figure like Robeson and an analysis of the racial scene areas of proprietary right. Mayfield, who certainly may have distinguished between the black-run and white-run elements of the Communist Party, began to consider that in his sphere, the white version of the Communist Party had little more going for it than talk. He needed no mandate authorizing his personal experience of blackness in America. These conversations, along with the emphasis on Africa and decolonization, were the lifeblood of the CNA writers' workshops.

One young friend, better placed than Mayfield and Davis, shielded the young thespians. Lorraine Hansberry helped broker inexpensive advertisement rates and publicity from *Freedom*, and she defended Mayfield and coproducer Maxwell Granville to *Freedom*'s editor Louis Burnham, who had some influence with the *Daily Worker, Masses & Mainstream*, and *Political Affairs*, publications whose support was deemed crucial for the play's success. Ultimately the effort flopped and the play lost money, but Mayfield had weathered successfully and shown leadership skill, and he stepped into the chairmanship of the CNA writers' workshop.

In 1953 he arranged for Hansberry, whom he considered "brilliant," to write a script for yet another fundraiser aimed at helping Robeson win back his passport.[35] It was her first time taking a project to the stage. The same year Mayfield directed another Ossie Davis play, *Big Deal*. By 1954 the CNA writers' workshop had been completely swallowed by the Harlem Writers Guild, and the CNA itself was defunct. John Henrik Clarke dated the collapse of CNA in a letter he wrote in March 1954. "As far as I can see only the workshop is functioning and it has already changed its name to Harlem Writer's Workshop or something like that."[36] Mayfield worked on several projects in the CNA literature workshop and started developing a novel from his play.

The search for a natural audience for black drama that neither emphasized white relationships nor grounded itself in comedy, song, and dance was unending. The Communists were also showing themselves as less agile after the conviction of their leadership ranks following the 1949 Foley Square trials. It had become unclear, for example, precisely how well they would adhere to the concept "Negro self-determination," which had been fully revived after the Nazi defeat, now that racial "integration," or at least the demise of the legal doctrine of racial segregation, appeared imminent. Mayfield had taken his youthful inspiration from their bold tactics and shocking beliefs, the party's confidence that the rest of the country was backward in its racism. But he started to notice that the perky Communists who appeared in Harlem always consisted of a gang of black men and white women, a "visual image [that] was certain to lose half of your potential audience," meaning black women.[37] Personal rivalries and jealousies further diminished the efforts.

Mayfield detested one young Communist in particular, Harold Cruse, but he shared an important view with Cruse on the effect of the Communist Party in Harlem in the 1950s. "[P]aternalism existed which black Communists, especially the younger ones, came more and more to resent."[38] A central feature of the paternalism was the inflation of the mildly competent into the spectacular. This was never clearer for Mayfield than when he took Davis's play away from the theater on 126th Street to the Yugoslav Playhouse downtown. During the intermission, V. J. Jerome, then cultural director for the Communist Party, assured him that, at every level artistically and politically, first-time playwright Ossie Davis surpassed Arthur Miller as a dramatist.

To keep his sanity and develop his craft, Mayfield befriended older members of the Harlem intelligentsia who were also determined to win their way as writers. The veteran writer John Henrik Clarke, thirteen years older than Mayfield, recognized the serious drive of the talented younger man and served as his literary secretary when Mayfield married, formally resigned from the CNA, and left the writers' workshop to live in Puerto Rico in 1954. Mayfield moved the same year that four Puerto Rican nationalists loosed a fusillade of gunfire from the visitors' gallery at the U.S. House of Representatives, wounding five members of Congress. Mayfield worked in Puerto Rico with his wife, the physician Anna Livia Cordero, who was taking over a hospital in Naranjito. In Puerto Rico Mayfield set up an English-language radio broadcast and began the difficult work of transforming his play into a novel.

His friend John Henrik Clarke was still interested in fiction writing, but increasingly he was becoming known as a historian with a Garveyite vision, and he shared his interests in classical era black civilization with Mayfield. Clarke was turning into a bibliophile and keeper of a new brace of African American sacred texts written to disprove the notion of black primitivism in antiquity. This collection of interests inspired his career as a teacher and fueled the history course that he taught at the New School in the later 1950s. Clarke contributed to a direction of black vindicationist historical writing that included Oklahoma City writer Drusilla Dunjee Houston's 1926 book *The Wonderful Ethiopians of the Ancient Cushite Empire* (she was probably the first writer, black or white, that Ralph Ellison ever knew); classics professor George James's 1954 *Stolen Legacy*, which claimed that all of Greek philosophy was purloined; and, after a decade, translations of Cheikh Anta Diop's work *The African Origins of Civilization*, which Diop had attempted to render in its entirety at the 1956 Paris conference. Chancellor Williams, who had written fiction and poetry but finished a Ph.D. at American University in the 1950s, would turn his career in the same direction and have his biggest hit, *The Destruction of Black Civilizations*, in the 1970s.

Mayfield also rendered the unapologetic historical consciousness in his own work. Readers were undoubtedly a bit startled to read in his 1962 novel of civil rights politics *The Grand Parade*: "[T]he first great rulers of the earth, so far as the scholars could determine, were neither white, nor yellow, but black men who controlled empires from the valley of the Ganges, the banks of the Euphrates, and the Nile Rivers."[39] Or that the "obviously African" Sphinx represented the race of the "pharaohs who ordered it, the artists and engineers who designed it, and the slaves who built it." The information in and of itself was toxic to the "colored" water fountain sign, the back-of-the-bus tradition. The epistemological revision was also reforming some of the assumptions behind the longed-for value of interracial collaboration. During an era when young black leftists in New York—be they in Harlem or the Village—were bombarded by whites, Mayfield would later record that an entire generation of black artists was having a change of attitude. "By the middle 1950's, many of us felt simply the need to talk to each other alone."[40]

Mayfield was making a transition that caused his belief in an urgent civil rights agenda and artistic excellence to collide. As he worked on two novellas about Harlem life, *The Hit* and *The Long Night*, he observed to Clarke his distaste for the State Department's version of black intellectual life. He had become aware of James Baldwin and Richard Gibson through Lionel Trilling's issue of the journal *Perspectives USA* and characterized Baldwin and Gibson as playful but unimportant. Writing about Baldwin's "Everybody's Protest Novel," he voiced displeasure at the hint of new criticism. "Didn't like those two articles myself. Digging up *Uncle Tom's Cabin* to probe a present day situation strikes me as something like going to Brooklyn from Manhattan by way of the Bronx." He considered the articles provocative, and he pondered the international appearance of black American critics in the context of the workshop in Harlem. He did not miss it. He thought that perhaps the workshop, with its egos and jealousies, had only operated in a minor key. "I doubt if workshops, even good ones, are as valuable as we must suppose the salons of the last century were."[41]

Increasingly the work of the previous century was becoming important. For the first time, Mayfield had started reading Henry James seriously, and he had to overcome considerable prejudice to do it. Mayfield had held a view typical in Communist circles: Henry James's work dealt with one sphere of human life—the wealthy upper-middle class—and was thus irrelevant, if not frivolous. "I don't believe that his people nor his situations have any real meaning for our times (nor had any for his)," Mayfield initially estimated.[42] "[F]or our generation James' work lacks passion . . . because James was never really passionately involved with mankind, only with the weaving of his beautiful psychological tapestries."

John Henrik Clarke was prone to agree with this line of reasoning. In July 1955 he reviewed George Lamming's second novel, *The Emigrants*, for Robeson's paper *Freedom* and thought it good, but still marred by "a style that leans too heavily sometimes on James Joyce" and "the occasional affected mannerism."[43] However, as Mayfield began to take seriously the task of creating his own novels, he found himself wandering back through the garden of Henry James and revising himself. "[N]ow that I have been reading him for several weeks, I find him easy reading, and fascinating! I have really begun to get involved in his situations and take attitudes toward some of his people."[44] Mayfield did not know James Baldwin, but what he was learning would cause him to appreciate Baldwin's style.

In 1957 Vanguard Press, James Farrell's publisher, well known for social realist fiction and for chance-taking with unknown authors, brought out Mayfield's first novel, paying him a five hundred dollar advance. Mayfield did not go head over heels into a psychological characterization or interior monologues in his novels of Harlem. He emphasized black families facing down giants to stay together. *The Hit*'s hero was James Lee Cooley, a young Korean veteran and cab driver who is slowly learning that there is more to the world than the exercise of his own will. His disgruntled father, Hubert, a building superintendent, has won the local policy game after years of throwing his money away. Instead of a favorable opportunity, Hubert's winning number or "hit" mentally disables him. He already spends his days shaking his fist in anger, and hitting the lottery only augments his escapist fantasies. "If I had been born white this would have been the kind of life I would have led."[45] Hubert imagines himself living in San Francisco with Sister Clarice, a woman he impulsively seeks to marry. Hubert is an absurdly futile figure, and even when he is let down by the numbers banker, he still clings to his packed suitcase, with which he had hoped to flee Harlem, his family, and everything familiar.

James Lee Cooley has a struggle identical to his father's, but with the possibility for growth. He is "all mixed up" and doesn't "know whether I'm coming or going,"[46] and he entertains feelings that his "life was slipping away from him."[47] A Harlem-bred seducer, but not an initiate to Norman Mailer's and Jack Kerouac's sexual revolution, James Lee comes into full understanding as his girlfriend Essie Dee gains the courage to leave him. At that exact moment James Lee wants to hit his girlfriend, and both characters recognize the degradation behind his violent impulse: his playground masculinity has dehumanized them both. So instead of an exhortation for sexual "kicks," Mayfield had his hero break through the Hollywood cloud of machismo. "Where did I get these silly ideas I've been carrying around with me," asks James Lee of himself, before deciding that Essie has eyes like his own mother.[48] "How many times have I wanted really to talk to Essie," he wonders. Though the relationship itself is irreparable, the achievement of a new consciousness for James Lee continues. The narrative culminates with his girlfriend Essie leaving James in an act of self-defining confidence. "For the first time since she had known him he was listening to everything she was saying . . . as she looked at him she could not keep her anger down." Here was a new development, black male novelists noting the satisfied arrival of black women, no longer taming the anger down, but turning the energy behind the anger into the fuel for a new movement.

Even younger than Mayfield and a stylist in the mold of early Ann Petry and William Gardner Smith, the twenty-six-year-old St. Louis writer Herbert Simmons captured the 1957 Houghton Mifflin Literary Prize and published a novel called *Corner Boy*. Simmons had begun his gritty novel of black urban life as a precocious undergraduate at Washington University in his hometown. With its hip narrative tone that seemed to call attention to the race of the narrator, the book made people uncomfortable. Somehow, in a plot describing three post–high school romances, Simmons graphically revealed the institutionalization of narcotics and gang violence in urban America. He anticipated the decline of America's cities and the faltering industrial economy after a booming black migration that would take more than half of African Americans to metropolitan areas of the United States by 1950, and more than three-quarters by 1980.[49]

Corner Boy's protagonist, Jake Adams, is a nineteen-year-old drug dealer working for a crime syndicate. Jake's best friend Scar is a junkie. Still, Jake and Scar are deeply moral—loyal, honest, dignified—though in a way barely recognizable to the Christian prayer-in-public-school morality of the 1950s. If he invoked a more complicated, adaptive moral standard for the 1950s, Simmons returned to the 1930s with some of his naturalist environmental descriptions. He peppered the narrative with chunks of postwar squalor that embarrassed Americans at the peak of a century-long drive for material well-being. "The baby cries, the kids chasing each other through the gangways. In the hallways the fellows and the girls. The shrill burglar alarms at Judiheimer's pawn shop where the gaping hole in the window protested of trespassing."[50] He also seemed to have the same investment as Redding, Wright, Ellison, and now LeRoi Jones in clarifying the betrayal by the black middle class, especially the educators. "The bald head of the principal ... seemed to accentuate his personality. He had bowed and scraped for years. .... His life was a direct opposite of the inspired message he delivered to the students."[51]

Young Simmons registered the grit of the American city, but he also showed the inner workings of a culture. In one of his finer scenes he reproduced a jazz "cutting contest." Simmons rebuilt a ritual by portraying two jazz saxophonists conducting a private discussion, a conversation that was opaque to "squares." The musicians play The Dozens, the hallowed verbal game of ritualistic insult, and they signify against each other in a native tongue known only to the hep cats. "People looked at each other, swept along by the rhythm of the music, but not understanding the meaning. People cajoled the guys in the know about what was happening. The guys in the know said, Be cool, so they could hear what was going on. The squares went along with the guys in the know caught in the fervor of the music."[52] Simmons's solidly midwestern voice contributed, from that great distance, to the contentions roiling in the East. He dismissed Norman Mailer's ontological basis for hipsters and made it into an argument about knowledge and experience, keeping the blues nearby. He also seemed uniquely confident that African Americans had produced a private language, perhaps profane, but the evidence of a culture nonetheless.

When Gilbert Millstein reviewed the book in the *New York Times* he was probably right when he said that "[t]he transmutation that lifts a novel above the merely naturalistic does not take place."[53] However, the crux of the argument published in the *Times* was that Simmons's story had been done before by Chester Himes, who had never written about drugs, and whose characters were typically middle class. The critique of redundancy was also what Julian Mayfield had received from Henry Volkening, literary agent to major African American novelists and liberal whites. Naturally, the black press carried the other flag. The *Pittsburgh Courier*'s Harold Keith thought that Simmons's protagonist was a weak imitation of a "hep cat."[54]

The press's natural bias against youth ignored the accuracy of the younger generation's measure of postwar America. Behind it all—hipsters, social protest realism, black nationalist politics, caginess about mainstream assimilation—lay Africa. How hip or how cool was it to be African, for an American black to praise dark skin and curled hair? It was a question that everyone began to grapple with, in terms of culture. In 1957, the same year as the successful desegregation of the public bus system in Montgomery, Alabama, after a two-year-long boycott, J. Saunders Redding was invited to join the American Society of African Culture. Alioune Diop headed the International Society of African Culture, and, in the United States, John Davis became the Executive Secretary of the American counterpart.

The American Society of African Culture (AMSAC) had grown out of the success of the Paris Conference from the year before, and it was as if the Council on African Affairs had been reconstituted but without the black Americans who had had the most long-standing and public interest in Africa: Paul Robeson and W.E.B. Du Bois. Because, of course, at its genesis, AMSAC was product of American liberal political strategies during the cold war, which was to say that AMSAC was depoliticized in public and anticommunist in private. Instead of darts at U.S. foreign policy or emphasis on socialist politics in the emerging African nations, AMSAC specialized in the cultural exchange between African descendants in America and on the African continent. At its June 1957 founding the conveners determined that the organization would "provide an understanding of the validity of African and Negro cultural contributions in order to provide a basis of mutual respect between Americans and Africans, and indeed between Africans and other citizens of the world."[55]

When AMSAC published a bulletin following its first annual conference in June 1958, the second plank of the organization's platform bore all the tell-tale markers of the committed American struggle to defeat communism. "[T]his is a society concerned with intellectual studies and artistic attainment," the organizing secretary had written. "It is not a political organization. The cultural justification of such an organization must be the ideal of the free man—the independent man—who owes no allegiance to any power that would, or could restrict the free expression or exchange of ideas, or trammel the free expression of the individual artistic genius." By 1960 AMSAC would hold its annual conference, publish the journals *Africa Forum* and *Africa Report*, and operate with an annual budget of $260,000.[56]

The group's driving force was John A. Davis, who had graduated summa cum laude from Williams College and held a doctoral degree from Columbia. Davis had taught at Lincoln for nearly twenty years and certainly felt comfortable with Africans like Ghana's prime minister Kwame Nkrumah and Nigeria's president Nnamdi Azikiwe. After Lincoln, Davis moved to Ohio State in 1951 before settling into a job in the political science department at New York University in 1953. Initially Davis ran AMSAC out of the same East 40th Street offices as the Council on Race and Caste in World Affairs (CORAC), his organization that received its money outright from the Central Intelligence Agency. AMSAC merged in 1958 with CORAC, which had an early budget of almost $94,000.[57] Located just a block east of the New York Public Library, the organization took its additional funding by the early 1960s through CIA front groups like the Norman Foundation and the J. Frederick Brown Foundation.[58]

It is unclear precisely which members of the leadership knew of the government role, but the source of the funding seemed obvious to the more alert and politically seasoned of the black writers. (Implausibly, John Davis denied knowledge of the ultimate origin for the organization's funding when the sources became public in 1967.[59]) During cocktails at AMSAC's first Negro Writers' Conference, Lloyd Brown said to Langston Hughes that the conference was funded by "somebody who can print all of the dough he needs."[60] Of course, as in the case with the Congress for Cultural Freedom, the idea of a one-to-one correspondence between financier and policy is impossible to prove. Perhaps the agency's support was designed chiefly to suggest to African nations in the queue for liberation behind Ghana that the United States did not cling tenaciously to its history of slavery and racial discrimination.

But AMSAC's leadership, which was limited to African Americans, removed any voluble leftist. Certainly on occasion the first president Horace Mann Bond, deposed from the presidency of Lincoln in 1957 and landing on his feet as the dean of education at Atlanta University, could be called vociferously anticommunist.[61] When J. Saunders Redding went to Africa on AMSAC business in 1962, he tried to get a fellowship for a South African refugee, Joe Lowe, and in his correspondence he assured his colleagues of the ideological purity of the man he supported. "A point I should like to emphasize is that, whereas Joe Lowe rejected an invitation to go East, some of his fellow refugees (not only from S. Africa, but from Angola, Mozambique, etc.) have not."[62] If the organization publicly avoided politics, its inner circle was typically anticommunist.

Davis tried to bring onboard the best regarded of black scholars who were making the move into white universities, like himself and Redding. All the original delegates to the 1956 Paris conference remained. Characteristically, Redding was uncomfortable with the rhetorical focus, and he proposed to insert the word "Negro" into the title to indicate the organization's domestic status. He did not so much strike a nerve as try to revive a moribund sensibility. "You have raised the question of the name of the Society," Davis wrote to him.

> Briefly, as the American affiliate to the International Society of African Culture, we are more or less obliged to use that name. More important, however, is the fact that the Society (both international and national) does concern itself specifically with African culture. That is Africa as a geographic, political and cultural entity. From this you can see that "Negro" would hardly be more adequate. Furthermore, as you may know, Africans rarely identify themselves as "Negroes"—a term which for them (and perhaps for many of us) has certain sociological and biological connotations which they find unhappy. . . . We raised the same question that you propose with regard to the name of the international society. The Paris committee reacted strongly.[63]

If Redding felt that he needed to go out of his way to remind the international group of a particular U.S. domestic sensibility, the continental Africans operating in Europe did not always exactly admire American blacks. AMSAC's Mercer Cook, the envoy to the French-based Society of African Culture and member of its executive council, met with formidable resistance from his Senegalese colleagues Alioune Diop and Cheikh Anta Diop at the beginning of 1960. On the verge of publishing his research on black Egypt, Cheikh Anta Diop told the executive council that Cook did not "believe in Africa" enough to bear the responsibility of serving as art editor for *Présence Africaine*, unless he had supervision from a council member from Africa or the West Indies.[64] In a heated exchange, Diop extended the idea of disloyalty to Africa to American blacks generally, a minority group that Diop believed were seeking integration in a white country, not building a national destiny of their own.

Nor did all American blacks blithely carry out the emperor's bidding. When John Davis asked E. Franklin Frazier to host the 1960 AMSAC conference at Howard, Frazier refused on account of the group's rightward political profile. "We are concerned primarily with teaching and research in regard to Africa and do not feel we should engage in activities which are promotional or concern ourselves with some program or policy with reference to Africa," he diplomatically wrote to Davis in October 1959.[65]

The men and women of J. Saunders Redding's generation were giving way. The most systematic opponent to everything that had been meant by the term Negro, but especially its suggestion of racial assimilation, was a man on the edge of his fortieth birthday, the journeyman critic Harold Cruse. By the mid-1950s he was no longer a Communist Party member or attending Committee for the Negro in the Arts meetings. Cruse left the *Daily Worker* and claimed now that his years of being a "philosophical Marxist"—his euphemism for Communist Party membership—had come to an end in 1952. He also liked to say he had left "the *church*."[66]

His reasons for leaving the Communist Party were numerous, but they boiled down to basic feelings of racial discrimination. Not one to go quietly, he sounded off in letters to party officials: "All this talk about 'Negro-White' unity is something you whites harp about but only practice when, how, and where you see fit."[67] Internally he was a bit more somber. Through hard work and sacrifice he had "become sophisticated in the ways of a high level revolutionary manners and customs" and risen to "the highest intellectual mastery of Marxism that was within his capacity."[68] His reward was gall: the "personal desolation of disillusionment, not with the Marxist philosophical system of thought, but with the little men who considered Marxism their personal property but who swore by Lenin they were bestowing it on the working class and the Negro People."

As for the Committee for the Negro in Arts, Cruse called it "a sad flop," an example of "the dishonest, ignorant, arrogant and opportunistic tomfoolery of the leftwing movement in its approach to the Negro in cultural fields."[69] Specifically, Cruse would never forgive what he perceived as a series of slights in 1952 and 1953 on the part of Walter Christmas and Ruth Jett, who once asked him to leave the room and guard the door during a reading of William Branch's working draft of *A Medal for Willie*. When it came time for his own play, "Delta Rose," to be read, Christmas called it "unacceptable," and Jett and Stella Holt, the white manager of the Greenwich Mews theater company, kept the script for a couple of months and then told him he wasn't ready for prime time.[70] Convinced that they—to wit, middle-class, college-educated American blacks, dedicated black and white communists, lighter-complexioned American blacks, West Indian blacks, friendly left-wing liberal whites—considered him a "lesser breed," Cruse dedicated himself to their demise.

By 1954 he was getting by as a waiter on 14th Street near his apartment, writing a musical comedy called "Headline Hetty," as well as serious political fare like the play "Furlough to Cradle," and hoping to breathe life into a new club that he christened the "Afro-American Cultural Society."[71] Cruse seems to have hoped to have had the more sober-minded, intellectually grounded, and inconspicuous black Harlem Marxists and ex-Harlem Writers Club members John Henrik Clarke and Ernest Kaiser join him in the venture. Cruse planned a monthly magazine called "SCENE" to disseminate the organization's views, and he was explicit regarding the importance of African American culture. "[O]ur approach to the Negro question has been all wrong," he told his friends.[72]

"[I]n terms of Negro unity, the cultural side is more important than the political in view of the fact that politics is run by "them" not "us" in addition to "them" having all the economic power." Cruse would promote cultural nationalism, the hallmark of his 1967 magnum opus, *The Crisis of the Negro Intellectual.*

But neither his plays, his work as a television studio technician, nor his writers' club amounted to much. He was relegated to sending angry letters to the *New York Post* about the sorry state of cultural affairs and badgering his former CNA comrade Harry Belafonte about what Cruse thought an "insufferable" and specifically West Indian presumptuousness about North American black life. That scuffle came to a head around the Nat King Cole affair. Cole, quiet on civil rights and content to play before whites-only audiences, was assaulted onstage by an organized group of white men in Alabama in April 1956. Before the end of the month he paid up in full an NAACP lifetime membership. A New York native himself, Belafonte had suggested that Cole was a Johnny-come-lately to the struggle, and only when in dire personal straits, a tendency typical of American blacks who, when compared to those of Caribbean origin, lacked personal courage and group loyalty. Cruse replied that he remembered Belafonte from the Harlem CNA and "[p]ersonally I found you and most of the others up there a bunch of snobs."[73] Over and again, in life and death, Cruse would be written off as a crank, but the criticism that he was among the first to bring was deep and retains its sting: the left-wing movement in the United States, and the Communist Party in particular, drew many of its most prominent black leaders from the middle class—really what was the upper class—and thus at least tacitly endorsed the phenomenon of racial caste in American society. In other words, in contradiction to a foundational ideological principle to empower the working class, the CPUSA and the leftist structure more broadly tended to sustain in their own organizations long-standing disparities in American life.

Cruse found a refuge in a novel of politics and ideas. By 1955 or 1956 he was devoting himself full time to writing up his experiences in a remarkably accurate and historically important roman à clef called "The Education of a Rebel." He had a draft of the project by 1957, and publishers like Viking were encouraging but asked for rewrites.[74] A stroke of luck took him away from the imaginative field and back in the direction of his old reviews for the *Daily Worker.* If the sensibility was the same, the venue was different and suggested a new possibility. Cruse published a big, bouncy essay in the December 1957/January 1958 number of *Présence Africaine,* carrying on his favorite crusade: it sought to put the black middle class in its place.

"An Afro-American's Cultural Views" continued E. Franklin Frazier's critique by calling into question what was being thought of as the next step after the dismantling of the segregation barrier: racial integration. Cruse urged for the baby not to be thrown out with the bathwater, and his water had Mau Mau soap. "These are the days of 'racial integration' among our leaders, professionals and intellectuals, and anything that smacks of 'racial culture' or 'nationalism' is strictly taboo," he lamented.[75] National cultural expression for Cruse was an antidote to the "debilitating sickness" of "Caucasian idolatry in the arts, abandonment of true identity, and immature childlike mimicry of white aesthetics."[76] "[I]t is we Afro-Americans who are out of step with the rest of the colonial world," Cruse promised his reader.[77] "They are seeking their identity while we are endeavoring to lose ours in exchange for a brand of freedom in a never-never-land of assimilated racial differences."[78]

Cruse always reserved his sharpest enmity for blacks of privilege. He ridiculed anyone cheering the falling racial barriers as a carrier of "assimilation tendencies." The "bourgeois leaders of this movement" had as their "main objective" the achievement of a "status and a social position approximating as closely as possible that pre-eminence enjoyed by the great Anglo-American middle class."[79] "Progress for Afro-Americans," Cruse argued, "demands the strongest kind of racial unity and cooperative endeavor." But he thought the high ground of racial unity impossible to reach, "in the face of the extreme racial and cultural diffidence toward our heritage." This was a strong 'and plebeian black pride, as Langston Hughes had written of in the 1926 in "The Negro Artist and the Racial Mountain," and Richard Wright had inflected through Marxism in 1937 in "Blueprint for Negro Writing." But it had less to do with an identification with American Negro heritage, the sort of feeling that was quite hearty in the case of J. Saunders Redding and Ralph Ellison, less hearty in the case of James Baldwin, and erased in the case of Anatole Broyard. Cruse was writing of a blackness that crossed national barriers, and he was talking about protecting it from rapacious middlemen.

Although Cruse was no longer in the Communist Party, because of his critique of integrationism as a new kind of Jim Crow-of-the-mind he was remarkably in step with Harry Haywood, the black Communist pioneer of the "nation within a nation" theory. Seeing William Foster as a continuation of Earl Browder, Haywood thought the Communists had fully turned to the American establishment during the cold war era, and he feuded with much of the old school leadership. Haywood confronted not only the titular leadership, but also blacks like Ben Davis and Doxey Wilkerson, who were fully sympathetic toward the NAACP's legalistic approach to resolving the civil rights crisis.[80] In Wilkerson's 1952 *Political Affairs* essay "Race, Nation and the Concept 'Negro'," he had sought to minimize discussions of race and to end the use of the term "Negro." Opposing Wilkerson and Davis, Cruse extended Haywood's line of reasoning to his colleague John Killens in a January 1959 screed of ten pages, where he probed nearly every element of the Communist association with black writers in New York, hoping to debut the attack at the upcoming Negro Writers' Conference organized by Killens under AMSAC auspices.

On behalf of the contented elements within AMSAC, J. Saunders Redding challenged Cruse to a debate, which Cruse excused as "ill-timed and ill-prepared and, thus, inconclusive."[81] Of course, given Redding's prickliness about his own identity, it might not be surprising that the debate did not take place in *Présence Africaine*. The polemic began when the two men squared off on a panel at the second annual AMSAC conference in June 1959. The event consisted of ten panels over four days that brought together continental Africans with American Africans and featured a keynote address by Kenya's second minister after Tom Mboya, the prominent Kenyan nationalist Gikonyo Kiano. Kiano, a leader of the black delegation petitioning in London in the months before the release of Jomo Kenyatta and the British lifting of the "state of emergency," perhaps sparked the imagination of Lorraine Hansberry, who started work on a new play in 1959, eventually called *Les Blancs*, about revolution in Africa.[82]

The Waldorf Astoria gathering was a long work-weekend for Redding, who chaired a panel on Friday on American Negro Literature with William Fontaine, Sterling Brown, and Richard Gibson, taking the place of James Baldwin. Then, Saturday afternoon, the conference featured the mano a mano debate between Redding and Cruse at the Panel on Negro Literature—African. The entire conference was memorable for the appearance by a young senator from Massachusetts who chaired the African Affairs Subcommittee on the Senate's Committee on Foreign Relations, John Fitzgerald Kennedy. Kennedy made two points. First, he assured the guests during his remarks that "racial segregation and violence, which badly distorts our image abroad while weakening us here at home, constitute only a small part of the American scene."[83] Then he tried to get out far ahead on the battlefield of hearts and minds: "never let us assist Africa mainly because we are afraid of Russian assistance to Africa. Let us never convince the people of that continent that we are interested in them only as pawns in the cold war." The conference's cultural finale butted up the famed Nigerian percussionist Babatunde Olatunji with the lyric soprano Camilla Williams, the first black hired by a major opera company.

Six months after Redding and Cruse's public showdown, *New Leader* served as the venue for Redding's written reply to Cruse. In the *New Leader* article "Negro Writing in America," Redding claimed that Cruse was "not only wrong but wrong-headed."[84] Home to Baldwin's early anticommunist work, in the early 1960s *New Leader* would publish Ralph Ellison's famous disavowal of political art and the politicized artist, "The World and the Jug." Cruse took Redding's opposition as an example of AMSAC's organizational unwillingness to "implement the Paris body's cultural program among American Negroes."[85] Echoing Baldwin's French essay of 1951 that rejected the colonial analogy between U.S.

and West African blacks, Redding abhorred the growing tendency among the younger urban blacks to equate the situations between blacks at home and abroad, especially in African countries gaining independence. Redding claimed that it was foolish and sentimental to regard a similarity between black Americans and Africans, whose political independence came out of racial nationalism. "The American Negro people are not a *people*," replied an irritated Redding, "[t]he distinction between American Negro literature and American literature is only the distinction between bough and branch."[86]

Redding must have thought it careless to stress heavily distant kinships at the beginning of the collapse of sixty years worth of legally enforced American apartheid. But Cruse preferred not to be reduced to something as expendable as a tree branch. He sounded a battle cry that would only increase its volume. "[I]ntegrationists such as Redding present a greater liability in terms of an intellectual renaissance in black thought than Marxist integrationists. . . . The Reddings stand still, afraid of the risks incident to pushing forward into the virgin territory of black and white relations in literature and art."[87] Cruse came to see Redding as an old "traditionalist," "never able to break the custom barriers to any kind of originality."[88] Redding had always remarked that he had taken to integration unwillingly and with suspicion, but it was becoming impossible to straddle the camps between integrationists and the growing tribe of impatient militants who determinedly entwined culture and politics. Cruse made a simple but accurate point about black intellectual life in 1958: "We are in severe cultural crisis!"[89]

And on a more personal level Cruse was completely right; Redding was standing still. He never published his redemptive second novel. Redding had traveled to India by way of the State Department and then later made a less happy trip to West and Central Africa by way of AMSAC in 1962. Cruse's travels, by comparison, would turn him into the high priest of the radicals. He journeyed to Fidel Castro's revolutionary Cuba, and in 1962 he constructed the explosive article "Revolutionary Nationalism and the Afro-American," which would shape the thinking of Nation of Islam minister Malcolm X, ex-marine and Wilmington, North Carolina, NAACP president Robert F. Williams, and part-time college student Max Stanford, a cofounder of the Revolutionary Action Movement. The writings, public speeches, and political activities that grew from the three broad tendencies and organizations connected to these men—ideologically resolute black separatism, southern-based armed black militancy, and northern-based black urban militancy—forged the essential framework of thought and the historical events behind the LeRoi Jones–led Black Arts Movement of the second half of the 1960s and 1970s.[90]

CHAPTER EIGHTEEN

The Reformation of Black New Liberals (1958–1960)

In 1954 *Time* magazine had published an article about Frank Yerby called the "Golden Corn," which regaled Yerby's success as a commercial phenomenon, his becoming a millionaire, and his life of ease in the South of France. In an article four years later called "Amid the Alien Corn," *Time* contrasted the happy commercial success of Yerby to the disgruntled whining about U.S. racial discrimination by the black writers who continued to live abroad. *Time* picked an auspicious occasion to run the piece, not long after scandal and physical assault had rent the intimate, if prickly and often penniless, group of black writers who gathered at Café de Tournon and Café de Flore in Paris's Latin Quarter. Richard Gibson, who returned to the United States to attempt a job as a television newscaster in 1958, was at the center of dispute, along with his fellow Philadelphian William Gardner Smith.

The year before, apparently at the behest of Smith, whom he had known since high school, Gibson wrote a letter to *Life* magazine under the cartoonist Ollie Harrington's name loudly protesting the French war in Algeria. Remarkably the letter was printed, and the identity of the writer was never authenticated. Originally the scheme between Smith and Gibson had been to draw attention to the Algerian war without formally violating their French visas, which obliged foreign visitors to remain publicly neutral on topics of French politics.

After suggesting the ruse of writing in each other's names to afford nominal legal protection, Smith then reported Gibson to the French police. Added to this was the fact that Gibson and Harrington had earlier had a fistfight over the use of an apartment. Once Gibson admitted the forgery, he had no problems in France, other than being fired from Agence France-Presse, where Smith also worked. For his part in the scandal, William Gardner Smith continued on in high-level capacities in the French news service, then moved to Ghana in 1964 and never spoke to Gibson again. The American Negro artists' hope for finding a sanctuary had reached its limit.

After the deportations of black Communist Claudia Jones and socialist C.L.R. James, the collapse of Robeson's *Freedom* in 1953, the end of the Committee for the Negro in the Arts in 1954, and the closing of *Masses & Mainstream* in 1956, the American Communist Party had basically ended its 1950s role as a major vehicle for activism and black art. However, the placement of the 1957 *Time* article and *Life* magazine letter showed the future targets of concern for U.S. government investigation: black dissidents and anti-imperialists. The glossy magazines sought to expose the next batch of radicals who no longer necessarily carried bona fide Communist credentials. *Time* treated the very phenomenon of Negroes abroad as curious, although the essay portrayed Gibson as a conscientious civil rights crusader. All the black writers were rendered as in flight from punishing white racism. One unit lived in Rome and consisted of Ralph Ellison, William Demby, and Ben Johnson. Gibson gratuitously observed that the men lived in southern Europe "because of social and political causes which everyone knows. The bright young white boys, after the end of their Fulbright scholarships, are able to return with reasonably light hearts to the dens of Madison Avenue or to the provincial Ph.D. factories. It is still impossible for an American Negro to return to the land of his birth in the same spirit."[1]

The phenomenon of expatriation made good political fodder and did not originate with *Time*. The black press—*Our World*, *Ebony*, and the *Afro*—carried regular articles about Negro artists abroad. When they had the chance, black artists themselves, especially the more left leaning of them, confronted the issue. In late spring of 1957 Langston Hughes addressed the National Assembly of Authors and Dramatists at the Alvin Theater in New York and told the crowd, "We have in America today about a dozen top flight, frequently published and really good Negro writers. Do you not think it strange that [of a] dozen, at least half of them live abroad, far away from their people, their problems, and the sources of their material?"[2] Hughes mentioned by name Richard Wright, Chester Himes, James Baldwin, William Demby, Ralph Ellison, Frank Yerby, and Willard Motley. He said the men had fled because of "the stones thrown at Arthurine Lucy at the University of Alabama . . . the shadow of Montgomery and the bombs under Rev. King's house." He added that "[o]ne of the writers I've mentioned, when last I saw him before he went abroad, said to me, 'I don't want my children to grow up in the shadow of Jim Crow.'"

Hughes had been responsible enough not to quote Richard Wright by name and cause him problems. When *Time* had run its article, it devoted most of its description to Chester Himes, but it was Richard Wright, the "dean of Negro writers abroad," who was credited with the most inflammatory remarks. "The Negro problem in America has not changed in 300 years," Wright was quoted as having said.[3] Mysteriously enough, Wright had not spoken to any *Time* reporter.[4] His well-known views were suspected to have been supplied by the photographer Gisèle Freund. And when Wright complained by way of his lawyer, *Time* refused a retraction. The entire episode seemed to sustain some of Richard Wright's more improbable fears; it was as if favorably portrayed Gibson really did work for a U.S. intelligence agency.

In the United States Ralph Ellison had joined America's most misunderstood men, and he was misunderstood principally by persons who knew him. Ellison smarted at having to justify living abroad, and he disliked being forced into a gaggle on account of race and Italy. His personal ambition at stake, he expended his energy to clarify the public record. Surprisingly, this would become his dominant role as a public critic between roughly 1958 and 1965. Unwilling to publish his novel, and unprepared to write criticism of his contemporaries, he famously, sometimes with humor and sometimes with vinegar, clarified his own point of view. The obligation, which included the two-part essay "The World and the Jug" of 1963 and 1964, began with "Amid the Alien Corn."

Unlike Richard Wright, who had not been misquoted but whose remarks had been entirely fabricated, Ellison rebutted the very mention of his name. It took three months for his correction to appear. Ellison's dogged response in *Time*'s February 1958 issue made clear that he had not voluntarily exiled himself in Rome from late 1955 until late 1957 to escape the race problem, which he wanted everyone to know he was capable of facing head-on. Instead of imposing upon himself "self-exile," Ellison (who disliked Gibson) felt it important to robe himself in the garment of American triumph:

> I returned to the U.S. a year and three months ago—not from voluntary exile, "for
> social and political causes," as Richard Gibson's rhetoric would have it, but from a
> stay at the American Academy in Rome, which was my privilege as winner of the
> 1955 Fellowship in Literature granted by the American Academy of Arts and Let-
> ters. Admittedly, two years may seem a long time in this swiftly changing country
> even for purposes of broadening one's personal culture—which is the aim of
> fellowship—but exile is, fortunately (and even for Negro Americans) largely a state
> of mind.[5]

But Ellison's state of mind combined the element of withdrawal with the pursuit of inclusion. He had not been famous enough in the radical war years to be smeared by the Red witch-hunting. During his stay at the American Academy he had jousted mentally with American writers and critics like R. P. Blackmur, Archibald MacLeish, and Van Wyck Brooks and engaged especially "pleasurable" intellectual "roaming" with Robert Penn Warren. "[B]ars to our friendship that might have been imposed by Southern manners and history went down the drain and left the well-known Fugitive poet and the fledgling writer and grandson of Freedmen marvelously free to enjoy themselves as human beings," he wrote grandiloquently to Nathan Scott in the 1980s.[6] But when he wrote to his vernacular equal Albert Murray in April 1957, he felt the need to justify the friendship with Warren. "Warren is a man who's lived and thought his way free of a lot of irrational illusions."[7] The justifying of American racism was to have been the more irrational of Warren's illusions.

If Ellison had become able to cozy with whites, there were always whites cozy with blacks. Following Vernon Loggins's 1931 Columbia Ph.D. dissertation, *The Negro Author: His Development in America to 1900*, a second book-length study of black literature by an Ivy League white American came out in 1958. Robert Bone, a Yale Ph.D., had written a legitimate and comprehensive study of the black literary tradition, and he showed the power of having a legitimate and comprehensive library at his fingertips.[8] Bone quite usefully provided a bibliography that showed the criticism that had been produced by black writers but had not been collected or anthologized. The work was academically thorough and technically conducted to a high standard.

At the outset of the volume Bone had thanked Sterling Brown and "my colored friends" for teaching him what could not be found in books. It seemed, initially, like he was after the deep sources of the cultural tradition that manifested itself in the African American novel. But throughout the work, Bone exclusively derived his hanging-judge's conclusions from other books, and he resorted to hierarchies of excellence that branded him a product of Yale, the home of the formalist method New Critics. With a tradition of knowledge drawn only from the library and a method of explication from Cleanth Brooks and Robert Penn Warren, it became difficult to see the impact of his "colored friends." Which is not to say that Bone's assertions about black literature were out of step with what black critics had had to say. But the white scholar's tone of condescension toward the tradition, which culminated in an appendix that ranked books written by African Americans in order of significance and determined the brunt of the tradition filled with what he defined as "Mediocre novels: run of the mill," and "Poor novels: also-rans," undercut the largesse of his magnanimity.[9] The import that Bone seemed to place on his reader's knowing his assertion of willingness to engage in interracial friendship seemed little better than a new kind of noblesse oblige. Blyden Jackson, who himself enjoyed the task of evaluating black literature according to lofty standards of art, would credit Bone only with capturing a "shadow" of the "magnitude" of black literature.[10]

By the end of the 1950s, the writers who had come on the scene at the beginning of the decade wanted less to do with white liberals. Chief among the impatients, surprisingly, was Richard Gibson, back in the United States and relinquishing his membership in the tribe of New Critics. In a review of Robert Bone's book in the *Nation*, Gibson could praise the tradition of black literature. "The overall literary achievement of American Negroes since the publication of William Wells Brown's *Clotel* is impressive, especially when viewed against the Negro's status in the United States." In his most startling assessment, Gibson claimed that "Today the Negro artist is torn between the two poles of assimilationism and black nationalism."[11] This was the first time in the history of the

Nation that the term "black nationalism," usually confined to African liberation struggles in the 1950s, had been used to describe American blacks.

Good-looking, stylish, and successful in amour, Gibson seemed an unlikely match to Harold Cruse, but Gibson's *Nation* review and Cruse's *Présence Africaine* article provide solid evidence of intellectual commitment to something that looked an awful lot like an artistic peak jutting out from a mountain of black nationalism by 1958. Bone would only have been able to anticipate that Gibson was an easy ally in the imputation of the standards of high art to black fiction—a tradition he thought an unattractive weal of protest against segregation. But Gibson's streak of independent thought seemed in search of redemption. Referring to his and James Baldwin's anti–social realist essays from *Perspectives USA*, Gibson explained himself. "Baldwin and I were, and are, mainly interested in combating the once-widespread notion that Negroes' writing ought to be dedicated entirely to attacking 'the Problem' and hence propagandistic."

No longer concerned to please Lionel Trilling and John Crowe Ransom and, apparently face-to-face with his own black nationalism, Gibson took umbrage at Bone's work. He viewed *The Negro Novel in America* as a nothing more than a white man stooping to conquer. "[H]is freehanded distributions of merits and demerits to Negro writers is a wild distortion of literary criticism," Gibson wrote. When Bone responded with a letter to the editor at *Nation* calling Gibson's review "fanciful," Gibson reviewed the book again. Now he said that both Carl Milton Hughes's *The Negro Novelist* and Hugh Gloster's *Negro Voices in American Fiction* had done more important work. In his final point, Gibson asserted his militant race politics by both accusing an avowedly liberal white of something very close to racism and also rejecting the prescription of a narrow ambit for the black creative writer. Gibson may have indicated the contradictions of a young black nationalist movement's intelligentsia when he scoffed that Bone wanted blacks to "devote their creative efforts to an 'autonomous Negro art.' A lovely ghetto, I am sure."[12] The young nationalists seemed to want both control over the black literary tradition and total freedom for artistic expression, and both desires were matched by an intense determination for black-directed political change.

Gibson had additional important work to do around the time that he was reviewing Bone. A few months earlier, with the English publisher Anthony Blond, he had brought out his own narrative fiction. The novel itself and its publication in England were unusual. Gibson seems to have been influenced by no other black writer as much as Baldwin, and the influence showed in his only novel of sin, evil, the Fall, and redemption, *A Mirror for Magistrates*. The book was ignored in the United States. Set at a rural Pennsylvania Christian school for boys, the novel was more like a stage play, with seven fully drawn characters: Bubba, the wounded black World War II veteran employed to keep the gate;

Bessie, a young reformed woman from off the street corner; Ferdy, a well-to-do adolescent student with strong homosexual tendencies; Fireman, the handyman who tends the school boiler; Wilmer, the gardener; Fernsworth, the school proctor and a religious extremist; and Edgeworth, the headmaster. The novel was Bubba's story of descent and ascent, away from the poverty of his home in Chambersburg to the mildly Edenic setting of the school, only to be cast out again. Gibson did not make any condemnation per se of white Americans or segregation. But he did make several revealing symbolic choices about the "nature" of white society.

Bubba, a poor man who is barely eking out a living, gets his job as a reward for the personal bravery and loyalty he has shown during the American invasion of Italy. He saves the well-to-do major, a pederast, during a German shelling. At the academy, Bubba falls in love with Bessie, only to have the romantic world torpedoed by Ferdy, who has fallen in love with Bubba and despises Bessie, and is persuaded by the religious fanatic Fernsworth to make false charges of rape against Bubba. The novel concludes with the dramatic showdown of all the principals. "Well you have put me in your hell," Bubba tells his two accusers. "You want me to be frightened of something neither you nor I have seen." Then, in defiance, the unlettered black man tells them, "I'm not going to be your scapegoat."[13]

A more consciously aware Bubba courageously resolves to determine the truth, in the face of the deepening and protofascist religious fervor of the white administrators. In the middle of a snowstorm, he and Bessie, who has been exposed as a former prostitute, dope-addict, and thief, leave the institute together. Gibson suggested that white America protected itself by means of an unconscious racism that was roused to extremes by the slow but steady enlightenment of the debased and scorned black American. He also seemed to view homosexuality as a social riddle that he determined to answer, and he discussed it in conjunction with white elites. But more generally, he hinted that at the base of white American society was a core of corrupt values. Gibson had written a mildly Manichean drama of protest that contrasted sharply with his early short stories.

Gibson was not the only writer maturing into being convinced that the reigning pressures for the creative wing of the black intelligentsia no longer revolved around making reasonable adjustments to white society. The "crisis" of black nationalism ranked importantly with the group assembled at the Negro Writer and His Roots Conference, held at the Henry Hudson Hotel in New York on the last day of February in 1959. Feeling strong now about his ethnic connections, Gibson participated on the panel "The Problem of Social Responsibility and the Role of Protest in Writing of Negro Authors." Perhaps he could have done no less because the American Society of African Culture's First Conference of Negro Writers was a roll call. The larger Paris-based Société Africaine

Conference (SAC) promoted the gathering in order to "assess" the "progress" of American blacks and "their relationship to their roots."[14]

On account of the cold war political attitudes of AMSAC's leadership, it was quite savvy for them to have farmed out the planning and execution of a conference to John Oliver Killens, the sterling example of the successful, sophisticated, politically progressive black writer of unimpeachable race loyalty. Under Killens's guidance, the deep range of black writers came out, from Harlem Renaissance pioneers like Langston Hughes and Arna Bontemps, to Chicago's *Ebony* editor and just published novelist Frank London Brown, author of the 1959 integration-terror conspiracy-thriller *Trumbull Park*. It was an event for one solid reason in particular: the conference brought into conversation professional artists, professional activists, and professional scholars, the great majority of them black. However, when the proceedings were published in *The American Negro Writer and His Roots*, it could clearly be seen that the old guard was giving way and that the future generational conflict would find its definition in the language with which Gibson had reviewed Robert Bone: assimilationism versus black nationalism. Immediately losses were suffered. This was the end of the commanding influence of *Phylon*, and, at least for a time, the newly founded *CLA* journal, published by the College Language Association. The black academics would face a kind of questioning from the students that was inconceivable as the 1950s began. But it was, in a sense, only to be expected; the ground of their authority had completely shifted.

J. Saunders Redding began the conference by putting himself a bit beyond the concerns of the other writers. He called himself the boy who "through native disability" could not play the game but enjoyed watching others play with his ball.[15] Redding stressed that the writers responded to an "American situation," but he did not bluster against the American Negro's African identity. Redding's colleague from Howard, Arthur P. Davis, forewarned of the oncoming integration. Langston Hughes pointed out the money-making white "black" writers who "have certainly been financially more successful than any of us real negroes have ever been."[16] Hughes pointed uncontroversially to George Gershwin, DuBose Heyward, William Faulkner, Marc Connelly, and Paul Green, particularly those writers' fondness for the "whore" archetype when creating their black female characters. Hughes was amiably, humorously, dyspeptic. "As for marketing, however, blackness seen through black eyes may be too black for wide white consumption. . . . Or else try becoming a good *bad* writer or a black *white* writer, in which case you might, with luck, do as well as white *black* writers do."

The keenly observant Horace Cayton, who had resumed his column with the *Pittsburgh Courier* in 1957, popped back on the cultural scene to attend the conference. Considering writing an autobiography, Cayton sat in the audience and thought the writers obsessed with easy money, found in "commercial, slick and not too slick magazine and TV writing." Cayton noticed something else that "disturbed" him: the prominent reaction in the crowd that he defined as a "sentimental interest in Africa." But he did not mean exactly that Negroes had become romantic racialist; rather, that there were no Africans in attendance and that the meetings sustained little "analysis of what relationship the American Negro should have toward this upheaval" of "European imperialist civilization."[17]

The papers tended to question, radically, the psychological, cultural, and developmental value that lay at the bottom of the ideal of fully embracing— "integrating"—into a society that had been content to persecute Americans of African descent. The successful playwright Loften Mitchell showed a spirited disavowal in his paper "The Negro Writer and His Materials," noting the way that the style of social protest had been disfavored.

> Integration may be on the march in America, but the fear that the Negro's roots will be obliterated by a white society seems groundless. The rising tide of African nationalism and the uprooting of colonialism have brought reality crashing against the lies of history. The restless stirring in our own southland is from people turning *towards* their roots, not seeking to lose this newly found identity. New challenges and new horizons stir the American Negro writer towards continued creativity. While it is true that American Negroes are arguing for integration—or more correctly, desegregation—and they have been too long influenced by a white majority, the majority of the present-day, shrinking world happens to be colored.[18]

The most vocal of the determined young contenders were the most accomplished: the successful novelist Julian Mayfield, back from the Caribbean, and Lorraine Hansberry, who had weathered the downfall of Robeson's paper and had moved herself from critical left-wing journalism into the field of theater. For Mayfield, the key argument by 1959 really revolved around the very desirability of an American identity. "[I]f scholars convince him that he is indeed an American," he told the gathering, the black writer needed to question "if this condition must be the extent of his vision."[19] The myth that Americanism comprised "the best the world could offer," Mayfield suggested, "has shown signs of being discredited." A critical evaluation was in order, and repudiation might well be the end result. "[B]ut if, as the writer has reason to suspect, integration means completely identifying the Negro with the American image—that great-power face that the world knows and the Negro knows better—then the writer must not be judged too harshly for balking at the prospect."

In a fully ironic turnabout to the steady condemnation of black writing for its provincialism, Mayfield offered, instead of patriotism, universalism. "The Negro writer may conclude that his best salvation lies in escaping the narrow national orbit—artistic, cultural and political—and soaring into the space of more universal experience."[20] "Universal experience" did not necessarily include Europe or the Western tradition. Mayfield scorned the technical excellence of the earlier generations of American writers on account of their thematic weakness, their giant "lack of concern" about "the great questions facing the peoples of the world."

The February 1959 Hudson conference was well attended and princely funded, but, as Cayton had noted, it had no African writers. Both Robeson and Du Bois had their passports returned in 1958, and it may have been easier for American radicals to go abroad than to have the foreign radicals stirring up the United States. The State Department had sent Dizzy Gillespie and the Harlem Globetrotters to tour Europe and Asia, and there were funds for black writers with a flattering eye toward U.S. government policy.[21] The American Society of African Culture flew a contingent of fourteen to Rome in April for the international conference on The Unity and Responsibility of Negro African Culture. New AMSAC president Horace Mann Bond headed an academic group that featured remarkable American Negroes like William Fontaine, a philosophy professor at the University of Pennsylvania, and Adelaide Cromwell Hill, a Boston University sociologist. They were living proof that America had addressed elements of the color barrier—at least in the urban North. Most of the others were educators, and the acknowledged leader was Saunders Redding, who gave an address called "Sanctions of the American Negroes Literary Art." Samuel Allen, an instructor at Texas Southern's School of Law, was the main radical capable of imagining genuinely productive links between American blacks and their continental African cousins.[22]

The international Society of African Culture might have hoped for a bit more from the traditional black American intelligentsia, who were inching in the direction of shared interest with blacks in Africa and the Caribbean but typically averse to the charge of political (or sometime cultural) radicalism. People like Mayfield very much tended toward a position of militant black internationalism, deliberately looking outside the borders of the continental United States. The pole between black nationalism and assimilationism was apparent to Horace Cayton at the next conference in March. Cayton made precisely the same assessment that Cheikh Anta Diop had made in his contretemps with Mercer Cook.

There is no doubt that there is a feeling of kinship between all people of color. But this feeling is limited. I may sympathize with the West African Mau Mau [sic], but their problem is different from mine. The Africans have a continent to win; ours is to be able to buy a Cadillac. The end of their struggle is to rule their independent states. Our cause is to become amalgamated and blend into the general population, to lose our identification as a group.

This thing of integration is causing some concern among many Negro intellectuals. Born and bred in a culture that set them apart, they have become accustomed to their separateness. They find the racial identity, which has cursed them
hard to give up [sic]. I have known several persons in New York who have lived in
the "Village." They lived there in spite of the antagonism of landlords and sometimes hostile neighbors. But now that the City of New York has passed a law that
allows Negroes to live any place, they have gone home to Harlem. But there is a
movement of younger people out of the black ghetto. Both Movements are going
on at the same time.[23]

Cayton was nearing sixty and no longer straining to lead the charge, but the
appraisal revealed the great divide of the coming age, and the role that even the
conservative-appearing critics and writers would play in it. Writers reared in
segregation had of necessity defined themselves in terms of black pride, and
several would not leave it too easily, even though their education in the first half
of the twentieth century had presented them with scientific proof of amalgamation. On the other hand, the dramatic exercise of the new legal guarantees of
opportunity occurred at almost precisely the same time as the question of full
identification with continental Africa was presented. Old black American pride,
the conspicuous exercise of constitutional rights, and identification with Africa
were the principal spheres of concern of the politicized artist in the 1960s.

Some writers were sour both about identification with Africa and about the
expression of militancy. Ralph Ellison had evolved as a writer at black institutions like the 135th Street branch of the New York Public Library and the National Negro Congress, but he no longer had any intention of participating in
gatherings like an AMSAC conference. Because of Ellison's deep concern with
myth and archetype, and his adulation of T. S. Eliot, a white southerner who had
gone "home" to England, his was a conspicuous absence that revealed a lingering problem. The most elite of black writers, sanctioned by white literary authority, might always remain at bay. Richard Wright was the least surprising invited
figure unavailable, since he lived in France and begged out of the conference.
Wright was working on the novel Island of Hallucination, as he had claimed, but
was also reluctant to support AMSAC, which he considered too tame.[24]

But Ellison, who lived a couple of miles from the conference, was even further away than Paris. Ellison had spent half of 1955 and all of 1956 and 1957 in
Rome, working on a novel that his backers were building up as extraordinary.
Some versions of the book had a white narrator; major portions of the book
featured a Joe Christmas–like character who is frequently in the company of
blacks but looks white. Ellison's personal life seemed to mirror the racial ambiguity of his characters. For at least several months while he lived in Rome, Ellison conducted an open sexual affair with a young, married white woman,

whom he hoped to marry.[25] If a well-known and admired writer having an affair, even an interracial affair, is not unusual, Ellison's thoughts about a permanent tie are a bit more revealing. He had become a contributing editor at Saul Bellow's journal *Noble Savage*, and he had not exactly welcomed in any black writers to the literary clique with Bellow. His relations with the younger breed were already strained. When teaching at Rutgers University, he had shut his door to escape Henry Dumas, a talented if high-spirited young black writer who would go on to write extraordinary short stories before being killed by a policeman.[26] By 1959 Ellison was actually living in Tivoli, near the Catskill Mountains, house-sitting at Saul Bellow's ramshackle estate, an act alone that might have struck some of his black contemporaries as rather excessively pursuing white fraternity. Ellison sometimes tried to run in circles where he was not welcomed and, at least by Gore Vidal, had his attention called to this fact.[27] Nonetheless, the end of the 1950s contained bouts of Ellison's increasing personal interracial delight, and public reluctance to condemn racism.

Neither did James Baldwin, an AMSAC member since 1958, attend the February 1959 Killens-organized conference, although the organizers desperately wanted him there. They wanted Baldwin to take his lumps, mainly for what looked like commercial success and distance from other blacks. The black writers in touch with the Harlem Writers Guild and who had slogged through the 1950s guessed Baldwin a "dilettante phony."[28] Undoubtedly the militant vigor and protest of so many of the speeches would have struck Baldwin as a kind of rehash of the 1956 Paris Conference. He would have found it necessary at the Hudson Hotel to have conferred with Langston Hughes, whose collected poems he would pillory in the opening sentence of a March 1959 *New York Times Book Review* article: "Every time I read Langston Hughes I am amazed all over again by his genuine gifts—and depressed that he has done so little with them."[29] Baldwin was apparently irked by the frequent reference to Hughes as the "poet laureate" of Negro America, but he did admit at the end of the piece that the main problem was that Hughes had found "the war between his social and artistic responsibilities irreconcilable."

AMSAC attendee Lloyd Brown rushed to Hughes's defense in the pages of the *Times* and against "a small group of alienated Negro writers." But Brown no longer rode the thoroughbred horse of social class in preference to the bobtail nag of race. "Langston Hughes does not agree that white is right, and as a writer he does not bow to the dictum that only white is art . . . in his writings he is a Negro, voicing with rare genius the very heart of Negro America."[30] The Communist Party would formally sever its connection to the "Black Belt Thesis" of Negro Self-Determination in 1959, but it left throughout the United States and especially in the persons of Louise Thompson Patterson, Marvel Cooke, James and Esther Jackson, John Henrik Clarke, Harold Cruse and Lloyd Brown in

New York, Audley "Queen Mother" Moore in Philadelphia (relocated from New York), Harry Haywood in Detroit, and Ishmael Flory in Chicago well-trained and ideologically unwavering black activists who took pleasure in introducing to the generation of the 1960s the range of debates that had been mulled over by Claude McKay, George Padmore, Haywood, Claudia Jones, C.L.R. James, Otto Huiswood, Cyril Briggs, Grace Campbell, and Richard B. Moore for better than forty years. In a sense, the radical cry of "black nationalism" was not a gesture of racial solidarity, but the observation of a tradition.

The rally in favor of the loveable Hughes and the clever stands of the young anti-mainstream black artists presented a new front that made solo maneuvering more difficult for Baldwin. Julian Mayfield organized a party at his house in East Elmhurst, Queens, and invited Baldwin over to meet with contemporary black writers, among them John Henrik Clarke and Sterling Brown. Most of the people who considered themselves in the trenches of black literary debate since the 1940s did not know Baldwin, who lived abroad for almost the entirety of the 1950s. Alice Childress was one of a few persons within Killens's Harlem Writers Guild circle who could claim intimacy with Baldwin's work in March 1959. Mayfield had too much integrity to plot a roast, but the party went flat and Baldwin sat "in stiff, eager silence, wanting to like and be liked."[31] There was little amity between the guarded man who had grown up on 131st Street and his sociable, pro-Robeson, southern migrant peers from the Harlem Writers Guild. After the others left, Baldwin talked passionately with Mayfield until the next morning.

Baldwin was scheduled to appear on the June program of the AMSAC's second annual conference, but after the programs had been printed, Richard Gibson had to sub for him. Of course, in those confines, Baldwin must have engaged J. Saunders Redding, an unpleasant task after Redding had accused him of dereliction in street corner jargon. At the conference the changed man Richard Gibson changed again. Apparently feeling a sense of duty to the duo's ideals, Gibson began his Friday afternoon paper by echoing his 1951 blast "A No to Nothing": "American Negro literature is not a very impressive body of work from any standpoint, whether aesthetic or social."[32] He then went on to declare that Ellison's *Invisible Man* "marks the end of a specifically *Negro* 'Literature.'" But where he pointed out something a bit curious and where he might have anticipated Baldwin by a couple of months, was in his concluding remark. He had decided that black writers had no real shared interest, that "[p]rotest fiction, with its under-current of emotion and sentimentality, has always failed to reveal [the] complexity," but also that high modernist "pure" art was "an excuse for subjectivism, solipsism and self-pity." Finally, at the end, Gibson showed the influence of the black nationalist zeitgeist, wearing a button-down shirt and tweed blazer in 1959. "In an age of push-button destruction, the intellectual, because he still has some freedom of thought, bears a tremendous responsibility.

But freedom always implies responsibility. And the responsibilities of Negro intellectuals are global."

The speech had begun with the kick of a New Critic and concluded crying "Geronimo!" alongside, if need be perhaps, the Algerian Liberation Front. Gibson, the most traditionally groomed writer of his time, showed evidence of almost precisely the same coming-of-age that had happened to Mayfield, who had been the more orthodox leftist and black political activist. American racism had kicked out the expatriate writers to Europe. Now African independence was bringing them home, fundamentally changed.

As he verged on becoming the most sought-after writer and black intellectual, the direct descendant of Richard Wright, James Baldwin was now having to take his cues from blacks who were interested in relations with the world beyond North America and Europe. He faced an assessment from a group of younger, graduate school–trained, privileged critics like Charles Nichols. Nichols admired Baldwin's work generally but thought Baldwin completely enthralled by an "unrelieved" sense of Calvinist "determinism, doom and feeling of depravity"—the same gloom that Baldwin himself had recognized in Richard Wright and Harriet Beecher Stowe in 1949.[33] And now, from blacks with specified scholastic tools, came a sharp bite. Nichols wondered aloud if it was that "[h]is acceptance of the damnation of the black man finds a quick response in white readers, and one might venture to say that his rapid rise as a writer owes something to this." But the connection between Baldwin's popular success and his portrait of black character had not been a topic of discussion before. Implicitly, Nichols's review of *Giovanni's Room* seemed to question the significance of the "response in white readers," an about-face from what had been considered a prime achievement for black writers. Fostering a sympathetic identification with the white reader in fact had been considered the basic definition of a black writer's universality. The estimate of the book hit close to home, undeniably in part because it appeared in *Commentary*.

The corrections and recalibrations as more and more blacks claimed an intellectual independence had the impact of making Baldwin a bit suspicious of his erstwhile patrons. He made a red carpet appearance as the rare black at a June 1959 Conference on Mass Culture jointly sponsored by the Tamiment Institute and *Daedelus*, the journal of the American Academy of Arts and Sciences. Held at a Pennsylvania resort in the Pocono Mountains, the conference was an official gathering of the "new liberal" intelligentsia and attended by Hannah Arendt, William Phillips, Sydney Hook, Daniel Bell, Randall Jarrell, Nathan Glazer, and Arthur Schlesinger Jr.

Baldwin had been in their midst for a long time, but now he would decide not to be one of them. In brief initial remarks Baldwin called Americans "empty," "tame," and "ugly."[34] It had been in the same crowd, filled even with American

Jews, that a French woman had once looked him in the eye at a party and said that America had fought on the wrong side during the Second World War.[35] In the open discussion that followed his talk, Baldwin said that he was happy to live in the present and not the past when, like his Maryland ancestors, he would have been enslaved. He told his friends that he welcomed, "the end of a whole era . . . the whole European era."[36]

The response to his disobedience came indirectly. Poet Randall Jarrell dominated the artists' roundtable by exalting poetic language and rallying the crowd to the defense of highbrow art. In a kind of ritual exchange with the lone black who had written himself out of poverty, Jarrell accused Baldwin of being ignorant of T. S. Eliot. Baldwin then appropriately dramatized his concluding remarks and did not just belittle Europe. "Life in this country is appalling," he said. Though editor William Phillips never stopped delighting in what Baldwin could do for *Partisan Review*, he recalled the speech as "sentimental and demagogic."[37] The rift would widen, and quickly.

Baldwin's foray to North Carolina in 1958 and his trip to Georgia the same year as the conference, his own personal investigations into the drama of civil rights, had changed him. The articles "The Hard Kind of Courage" for *Harper's* and "A Letter from the South" for *Partisan Review* revealed a confidence in ordinary blacks that he had not felt before. His association with white liberals had begun to make him feel guilty, and he was becoming snappish with them and needed more liquor to keep smiling. Baldwin sneered at his editor Phillips that blacks never told whites the truth. The relationship between sponsor and client was unraveling. Baldwin published a portion of his novel *Another Country* in Phillips's *Partisan Review* in the spring of 1960 and then never published with the liberal intellectual magazines again.[38] *Another Country*, like *Giovanni's Room*, was a formidable anatomy of the hypocrisy of American liberalism. And in this book, set largely in America, Baldwin explicitly made the novel's martyr the black hero Rufus Scott, who in his hour of need is neglected by his white friend Vivaldo.

The 1961 novel was his best-selling work up to that time, but Baldwin's technique and his perception were being challenged increasingly now, even though he had befriended Martin Luther King, Jr., and written approvingly about the resistance movement in the South. When he published in *Esquire* the article "Fifth Avenue Uptown" in 1960, condemning the high-rise apartments designed to alleviate ghetto overcrowding, he clearly needed a new constituency. In the essay he famously called the swank Riverton Housing Apartment Complex "naturally a slum" and teeming with fornicators in the halls, urine in the elevator, and heroin on the playground. *Esquire* visually reinforced his bias with pages of grim photos of rubble. But the *Amsterdam News* took it upon itself to refute him and detail Harlem's bourgeois triumph. "We are fed up-right up to here," began the editorial page in June 1960, "by the army of 'writers' both negro and white, who sell themselves to downtown publications as 'experts' on Harlem, and, who then proceed to sell these publications reams and reams of libel about the struggling but respected Negro and Puerto Rican population above 110th Street, commonly known as Harlem."[39] The paper denounced Baldwin personally. "[W]e only know him as a man who once wrote a book filled with trash about the sex life of homosexuals in Rome."

Riverton residents wrote in describing the freshly waxed hallways and clipped grass out front, and the newspaper ran a directory of the prominent, professionally titled Negroes who lived there. Baldwin now failed to juggle the same intellectual spheres he had castigated William Faulkner for dropping. He had begun his career by scrupulously refusing to represent his race. He had become the righteous liberal crusading for tolerance, then catching it from those he claimed to represent. By the end of the 1950s, to hold the post of representative authority for black America, a writer would have to appeal to the streets, seem capable of commercial success, be independent of orthodox communism, and espouse a radicalism that would make whites as uncomfortable as middle-class blacks.

It was not that long before Baldwin did take to the rostrum with conference organizer John Oliver Killens, in June 1961 at the Martinique Hotel.[40] The Conference on Nationalism, Colonialism and the United States was sponsored by the Liberation Committee for Africa. The same month Malcolm X was calling Phoenix, Arizona, to the home of the founder of the Nation of Islam, Elijah Muhammad. Both men, but particularly Muhammad, were gushing over Baldwin's "wonderful" activities, especially a speech he had given on the morning of June 26.[41] Elijah Muhammad invited James Baldwin to dinner on July 16, 1961, and Baldwin used the experience to write the essay "Down at the Cross," which became the backbone of his most important book, *The Fire Next Time* (1963). Like Richard Gibson, who would take a planeload of black radicals to Cuba and then take himself to Algeria, Baldwin had lost patience with white liberals and the politics of moderation.

CHAPTER NINETEEN

Prometheus Unbound (1958–1960)

Lorraine Hansberry had the excellent personal fortune of being introduced to the American public at almost precisely the same moment as the Nation of Islam national spokesman Malcolm X. The television broadcaster Mike Wallace interviewed Hansberry for his news program on May 8, 1959, the result of her winning the New York Drama Critics Circle Award. Wallace was then hard at work on the exposé of the Nation of Islam called *The Hate That Hate Produced*, a five-part series televised in July. The famous broadcast would be the first time that most Americans, black or white, had ever heard of organized black nationalism, proponents of black segregation and statism, and black supremacy. Nor had people typically been exposed to the articulate, charismatic, and visibly convinced ex-convict Malcolm X. These topics were of considerable interest to Wallace when he interviewed Hansberry, apparently so much so that he ignored questions from two other areas.

The first area he neglected was Hansberry's long association with Paul Robeson, *Freedom* newspaper, the Committee for the Negro in the Arts, and the Communist Party. The other point in the news, never brought up by Wallace, was the startling fact that an NAACP president in Monroe, North Carolina, named Robert F. Williams had also said in May 1959, "We must be willing to kill . . . if it's necessary to stop lynching with lynching, then we must be willing to resort to that method."[1] The May 7, 1959, *New York Times* headline ran "N.A.A.C.P. Leader Urges Violence." In some respects, Williams, a committed integrationist who wanted to organize African American self-defense efforts, a strategy that he called "armed self-reliance," seemed a more threatening black leader than Malcolm X, a black separatist and devotee to a cultlike religion. It was better not to invoke a man like Williams at all.

At the close of Wallace's interview with Hansberry, the CBS reporter steered the conversation to Hansberry's feelings about the rhetorically radical Nation of Islam minister. Hansberry claimed never to have heard of the Nation of Islam, which might have been true, though the gospel according to Malcolm X was old news to the crowd at the Harlem bookstores and street-corner rallies that Hansberry knew as a prominent feature of black New York life. She conceded to Wallace that she was completely opposed to anti-Semitism, which the pressing reporter wrung from her by emphasizing that he had recorded speakers who were explicitly anti-Zionist.

Then Wallace overplayed his hand. "Even black racism, you do understand?" he feigned. Hansberry closed out the final seconds of the interview with a response that knocked his air out.

> Let's keep in mind that we are talking about oppressed peoples who are saying that they must assert themselves in the world. . . . I've fought against color prejudice all my life. I'm not interested in having white babies murdered anymore than I can countenance the murder of Kikuyu babies in Kenya. . . . Let's not equalize the oppressed with the oppressor and when people stand up and say, "We don't want anymore of this," they are now talking about a new kind of racism. My position is that we have a great deal to be angry about. Serious about. You know it's 1959 and they are still lynching Negroes in America. I feel, as our African friends do, that we need to point toward the total liberation of the African peoples all over the world.[2]

American Negro writers, fully integrated into American society, who had moved beyond even middle-class status, were now capable of designating themselves one of the "African peoples" in need of liberation. This was a new understanding of blackness in the imagination. And, in not quite five years, it became shared and quite forcibly articulated by Malcolm X, who changed his name and founded a new forum called the Organization of Afro-American Unity to promote his views. The two black activists who shared the same birthday died within weeks of each other in early 1965, and X, then calling himself Malik Shabazz, attended Hansberry's funeral. The joining of blacks from privilege and from prison was unique and recalled the unions from the era of enslavement.

Lorraine Hansberry had not had her New York premier when the John Killens–hosted AMSAC Negro Writers' Conference got under way in February 1959. But her impending success, palpable by that time, would certainly be linked to other sources than the caprice of New York critics, or Hansberry's much talked about upper-middle-class background. To begin with, Hansberry had her head on straight about her African heritage, which she did not see as a source of shame and ignobility. She was not humiliated to be a descendant of Africans or slaves. And she held the workers of the world in esteem and paid a debt to them by working hard herself at writing. She was a unifier. Like the sophomore Fisk student activist Diane Nash, Lorraine Hansberry believed firmly in women's rights, that is, women's basic and fundamental capacity for excellence in historically male-dominated fields. And certainly the people who knew the intimate details of her life by 1959 would note the broad diversity of her experience as her admission requirement to free thinking.

In 1953 Hansberry had married a white New York University graduate student in literature named Robert Nemiroff and kept her own name. The courtship with Nemiroff was spent on picket lines and writing protest pamphlets and circulars. Hansberry expressed an iconoclastic suspicion toward her own romance, which she never completely reconciled herself to. On the verge of marriage in December 1952, she wrote Nemiroff from Chicago after tearing up a longer letter. "I have finally admitted to myself that I *do* love you; it said I have a terrific, no, exciting idea for a play."[3] The day before a modest wedding ceremony, the couple were protesting the execution of Ethel and Julius Rosenberg. They lived at 337 Bleecker Street in Greenwich Village, amid the poets, painters, and jazz musicians.

The Village in the 1950s was no interracial Eden; there were also Italian gangs, anxious Jewish merchants, and other white ethnics struggling for a foothold in Manhattan. According to LeRoi Jones's wife Hettie Cohen, "[t]here weren't half-dozen steady interracial couples in the Village" in the late 1950s.[4] Catcalls and worse were a matter of course walking below 14th Street between Broadway and the Hudson River. Bohemia might have been opportunity, but it was not sanctuary. Even in 1961 James Baldwin, who had his Village apartment at 81 Horatio Street, would open the novel *Another Country* by describing the regular looks of raw hatred from whites at the sight of an interracial couple in Washington Square. And as early as July 1956, FBI agents followed Hansberry and reported her whereabouts to the New York and Washington, D.C., offices.[5]

Hansberry had begun to consider herself a dramatist in the context of the demise of *Freedom* in 1955, her marriage to a literature student and songwriter, and her occasional course on African American literature at the Jefferson School. One evening around 1956 she returned from the theater determined to write an engaging and accurate portrait of black American life. By 1956 Nemiroff was earning a steady annuity by way of part ownership of the lyrics to the hit song "Cindy, Oh Cindy," and Hansberry was able to stage readings and small productions of her dramatic works. When she looked for actors to translate her language and ideas into action, she turned to the tightly knit group from her days with the Committee for the Negro in the Arts, the actors Sidney Poitier, Lonnie Elder III, Ruby Dee, and Ossie Davis. In January 1959 her first complete play, *A Raisin in the Sun*, opened in New Haven, then summoned rave reviews in Philadelphia. The play got to New York, to Broadway's Barrymore Theater, in the middle of March.

Killens and Hansberry had known of each other at least since Killens's 1952 *Invisible Man* review in *Freedom*. He arranged for Hansberry to deliver a keynote address during the final night of the Negro Writers' Conference. Hansberry read the paper "The Negro Writer and His Roots: Toward a New Romanticism" to a large crowd. Her paper was perhaps the most incendiary address at the conference. She hoped to ignite a total revolution in sensibility, and she explicitly repudiated the pursuit of middle-class status. Comparing the ebullient vitality of Sean O'Casey with the despondent cynicism of Tennessee Williams, Hansberry pronounced America in the "death agonies of a dying and panic-stricken social order." Nor did she do this from the rather chic point of view of the "vague" and "non-inspirational" Beat writers, whom she believed completely lost in the fog of illusion and the mistaken belief that they had no choice in shaping the world. Hansberry embraced the ideal of social change and the artist's responsibility. Nor did her intensity detract an iota from her racial pride and black radicalism. She discredited the twin signs of upward mobility for blacks: the showy materialist trinkets and "the absence of recognizable Negro idiom or inflection." "It is still the dark ages," she told her audience, reminding them of their responsibility, and then she led them to their feet. "[I]t is time to shout again."[6]

On the eve of her international celebrity, Hansberry was shouting out the value of folk vitality, by way of dense, if romanticized, portraits of black working-class life. The sometimes shiny characters broached the never-ending conflict with book publishers and theater producers. At the conference Hansberry talked to highly regarded playwrights Alice Childress, William Branch, and Langston Hughes and bemoaned the perennial problem of having to prove that black work did not necessarily limit itself "to the Negro problem or question."[7] Richard Gibson had stated this point the loudest in "A No to Nothing" during his phase among the New Critics. Still, with an agenda to reach an audience and heroicize the character, Hansberry basically rubbed against high modernists, whose intellectual brush with the world seemed to have left them convinced mainly of the permanence of despair. She encouraged her peers to take their cues from the audience and move art away from the realm of the exclusive journals and the hierarchy-prone formalist professors.

Hansberry had good reason to challenge her peers with confidence. *A Raisin in the Sun* introduced the possibility of a sentimentally moving, politically relevant drama with an all-black cast on the big stage. In a sense, it was the sequel to Wright's *Native Son* for a different era.[8] Thematically, America was returned to the city of Chicago for its nativity scene, and a Chicago social realist writer living in New York was once again the pacesetter. "There's no contradiction between protest and art and good art," Hansberry could say, triumphantly and publicly, calling the play a protest, "actively so." In private correspondence with ranking Communist William Patterson, she wrote, "My play was an effort to say that principal decisions are not abstract style but are the very fabric of existence."[9] Also remarkable, the play was directed by a black American who had earned his way as an actor with the Greenwich Mews Company, Lloyd Richards, the first time that had ever happened on Broadway. Black playwright Louis Peterson's 1953 Broadway hit *Take a Giant Step* had deftly delivered a Negro family in a mixed-race neighborhood, and the drama took its shape by way of interracial friendships. But Hansberry's play spent its time exclusively on the lives of a working-class black family dreaming of upward mobility while living in a tumble-down Chicago apartment. And if the play dwelled on the lives of black hewers and drawers, it could not have been more distinct from film director Otto Preminger's 1959 revivification of Cat Fish Row, *Porgy and Bess*, and starring Dorothy Dandridge, Sammy Davis, Jr., Pearl Bailey, and Sidney Poitier.

Hansberry's central characters all pray for new lives after an insurance policy matures and promises a lump sum of ten thousand dollars. A chauffeur in his middle thirties, the lead character Walter Lee Younger hopes to open a liquor store and become a prosperous member of the petit bourgeois. His mother Lena, a lifelong domestic worker, wants to use her husband's insurance policy to purchase an affordable home outside of the black ghetto. Ruth Younger, Walter's pregnant wife, is hoping to be able to afford to have the baby. Beneatha Younger, fifteen years younger than her brother, is a college student who plans to go to medical school. She entertains two well-endowed black suitors during the play: the pompous heir to a real-estate fortune and an exchange student from West Africa's Gold Coast who awaits his country's national independence.

Hansberry's claim that the play was basically a bildungsroman for Walter Lee was also undercut by a strenuous feminist politics.[10] In 1957 she had sent a long letter of support to the nation's first widely circulated lesbian magazine, *The Ladder*. Undoubtedly she was a vocal advocate for women's rights. She wrote, "I feel that women, without wishing to foster any strict *separatist* notions, homo or hetero, indeed have a need for their own publications and organizations. . . . Women, like other oppressed groups of one kind or another, have particularly had to pay a price for the intellectual impoverishment that the second class status imposed on us for centuries created and sustained."[11] Hansberry regarded lesbian causes highly, and she at least insisted on women's decision-making and political power, if she did not explicitly celebrate women erotically. Her play itself is a series of explicit criticisms of Walter's masculine heroism, borne out in the relations he has with his mother, wife, and sister. *A Raisin in the Sun* was a clear declaration of the liberation of black women from the iron shackle of patriarchy, a form of life fundamentally discounted in the play's formal structure by the fact that the patriarch "Big" Walter Younger is, at the beginning of the dramatic action, already dead. This left the role of natural authority to the character Lena Younger, called "Mama" throughout the play by everyone except her daughter-in-law.

Hansberry revealed a concord of sensibility with Harold Cruse, Richard Gibson, and Julian Mayfield when she described Lena Younger as having the "noble bearing of the women of the Hereros of southwest Africa." This was a learned intellectual description, remote, and a bit odd. She had not just called the woman black, or even African, she had named her to a tribe, which might have been understood in some quarters as similar to calling her a cannibal. Even for those unshaped by the poisonous stereotypes, the description was obscure. It meant tangibly nothing to directors, actors, and audiences in a country that did not regularly teach courses on sub-Saharan Africa in its colleges any more than it allowed Kwame Nkrumah's finance minister a seat for breakfast at its Delaware eateries.[12] But for posterity it represented the vanguard in problack thought; it was also a description of a woman actively battling colonial rule.

The playwright's determination to connect Lena Younger to Africa pronounced the mother's centrality and stature, and no other character, certainly not her son Walter, was offered such an important description. Despite Hansberry's creation of an ostensible situation to show the valor of her male lead, Walter Lee was as frivolous and flawed as his dream of upward mobility—a pursuit that a privileged but socially conscious Hansberry demolished throughout her career in the 1950s and 1960s. Additionally, Walter is given moral flaws: he deceives his family and he lacks the wisdom to perceive his own deception by his business partners. The undergirding of the plot, where Walter cheats his sister, then is cheated, first by Bobo, and then Bobo and Walter are both cheated by Willie, is the fulfillment of the audience's desire for misfortune to befall Walter on account of his overgrown pride. Walter Lee's comeuppance provides a preliminary dramatic catharsis in the play; the mildly foppish black man returns to his place.

Walter Lee's ultimate heroic test is to resist a bribe from the Clyburne Park homeowner association, a necessary act that allows the family to move into Lena Younger's new home. Obviously this was the dream of the middle class: homeownership and education enough to grasp white-collar jobs. But Hansberry did not end the play with lines that might have sealed Walter Lee's own self-created transformation. She concludes with Lena Younger's observation to her daughter-in-law that Walter "finally come into his manhood today." It seems apparent that Walter will have as much "manhood" or adult wisdom as he has mother and wife who provide for and guide him. In the sentiment of the concluding lines, Hansberry's audience could touch the familiar strength of the mother, pushing the family toward the purchase of a home and bedrock twentieth-century American middle-class values. The black female domestic was the African American that they knew. And arguably it was this that the white American audience noted, as they packed the thousand-seat Barrymore, night after night, for more than a year. They saw a black family that operated on a matriarchal foundation striving to escape the malevolence of the black inner city. They saw their maids and nannies and cooks obtaining a room of their own.

Perhaps the strongest assertion of women's rights made in the play occurred in the frustrating of aptly named Beneatha, the character poised to contribute the resources of college to the black working class: scientific rationalism, atheism, African history and the struggle to end the colonial regimes, and the obliteration of European standards of beauty. Beneatha hurls Nietzsche at her mother at the peak of an argument, asserting, "God is dead." For such defiance, Lena Younger slaps her daughter in the mouth and then forces her to admit that, "in my mother's house there is still a God."[13] Hansberry seemed to have safely skirted the problem of communism.

In terms of black nationalism, Hansberry got away with more depth. Beneatha's relationship with her African suitor Joseph Asagi offered arguably the most elaborate view of African American ancestry in letters, perhaps with the exception of Melvin B. Tolson's *Libretto*. Hansberry said that she gave Asagi the most important line in the play. Asagi dismisses the popular argument, central to the 1958 play *The Blacks* written by Jean Genet, that freedom from the colonial powers is inconsequential because native Africans will obviously reproduce a corruption similar to the Europeans'. But Asagai tells Beneatha, "[d]on't you see that there will be young men and women—not British soldiers then, but my own black countrymen—to step out of the shadows some evening and slit my then useless throat?"[14] Asagi refuses compromise with the first principle of complete decolonization, then he suggests his own willingness to embrace social-class suicide to make the revolution permanent. Hansberry had fortified Asagi with an "ideological preparation." After the play opened, she told the Chicago writer Studs Terkel that "history always solves its own questions, but you have to get to first things first. . . . [B]efore you start talking about what's wrong with independence, get it!"[15]

In what was to have been the play's most dramatic moment, and showing the evolution in thought made possible by a college education and a relationship with an African actively involved in ridding his country of the European powers, Beneatha cuts the permanent lye relaxer out of her hair and wears a short Afro. This act of aesthetic resistance occurs after a conversation with Asagi, who chides her about "mutilating" her hair. However, according to Robert Nemiroff, the producers of the play decided that the short hairstyle did not suit the actress Diana Sands and the New York audience lost that powerful symbolic rejection of assimilation.

The Afro hairstyle had broken into high fashion at New York art shows in the 1950s.[16] Afro-wearing Miriam Makeba of South Africa and the singer Odetta were becoming famous at the time, and there were examples of black women writers like Sara Wright wearing short hair. Still, in 1959 there was no single greater aesthetic gesture of repudiating the heritage of Europe and whiteness than this. (When Sara Wright integrated a Lower East Side apartment building, at the sight of her the woman underneath her apartment would shout through the window, "Nigger whore! Nigger whore!")[17] Nor was it entirely clear if the characters would have more than a dialectical relationship between assimilation and materialism and international black consciousness and ascribing value to their southern heritage. The play concludes with Walter the chauffeur still entertaining fantasies of becoming an executive. Beneatha's tuition money has been squandered, and Walter still counsels her to marry George Murchinson, the model of the rapacious bourgeoisie.

Alongside politically relevant films like Harry Belafonte's notable *Islands in the Sun* of 1957 and Sidney Poitier's more popular *The Defiant Ones* of 1958, Hansberry's successful play seemed a sweet vindication for the veterans from *Freedom* and the Committee for the Negro in the Arts. After she won the New York Drama Critics Circle Award in April 1959 for best play, Hansberry moved into an orbit of influence shared with very few other black American artists. For a time, Hansberry garnered unique privileges. Interviewers and photographers from *Harper's Bazaar* and the *Times* were invited to the Bleecker Street apartment. She even managed to write an article for the *New York Times* about herself in the third person. "Her literary god is Sean O'Casey," Hansberry wrote, "the Irish playwright, who, she says, 'establishes the nobility of man by showing him in all his marvelous complexity.'"[18] She seemed here, not like a woman who had broken with middle-class gradualism and the integrationist movement, but like a comfortable New Critic and aesthete. But this was not the case, as her regular references to the Communist O'Casey suggested.

Initially Hansberry submitted to positioning herself as an ingénue, which might account for the reason why her Robeson affiliations never emerged in the popular press. At the start of her celebrity run in March 1959, she allowed the *Times* reporter Nan Robertson to misquote her as having said, "most of our playwrights are retarded. They show the Negro as all good and the white man as bad. That isn't the truth."[19] It may well have been precisely what she said, since the remark was completely consistent with her traditional fight against the snobbish black middle class. But the rapid appearance of the stock answer considered "smart" from the mouth of an African American revealed the regular pattern used to manage dissent. The newspapers and the critics would emphasize Hansberry's commitment to artistic standards and disconnect her from more radical politics of social change, a pursuit joined to the inept craftsman. She would be presented to the public as the antidote, the black writer who possessed a refinement and marketability that the provincial black artists lacked.

When the hard-boiled Mike Wallace interrogated her in May 1959 and asked if her remarks in the *Times* were not proof of the low aspiration of all Negro writers, Hansberry said that the *Times* had mangled her words. "I was interviewed by a very capable young woman who, however, certainly misunderstood this," she told Wallace, puffing on her cigarette. "What I feel happens to be exactly the opposite," she clarified. "We haven't had the benefit of enough Negro writers on Broadway to know what they would say about anything." At twenty-nine Hansberry seemed completely sure of herself, capable of having popular success without sacrificing her integrity.

And after not even a full year in the public eye, Hansberry showed herself as uncompromising and moving into a position of outright defiance. As an advocate of black liberation in Africa and determined to make the connection between decolonization and domestic American racial policies, and as a popular writer, Hansberry was completely in a class by herself. And for a short window she reared formidably in the circles of influence. Half a year after her award, the *Times* gave her space for a 1,200-word profile of an eighteen-year-old boy from the Harlem streets called "Stanley Gleason and the Lights That Need Not Die." The piece depicted the life of an ordinary boy—neither sinner nor saint. Hansberry called him "a problem to his society by his very existence." The essay showed the successive wave of alienation and rejection that an ordinary, "non-headline mak[ing]" black young person who pushes carts in the garment district might experience.[20]

Gleason's alienation begins after a typical course in the public schools with its trips to the Museum of Natural History featuring trees of human evolution that show the African native as the intermediary between apes and Europeans who are lodged at the main "trunk" of civilization. The Stanley Gleasons of the world evolve cultural means to deal with this kind of rejection. "It was after the museum that Stanley developed his way of walking. . . . His bouncy figure seems to be an act of defiance; a symbol of almost omnipotent awareness that he has played a telling trick on somebody by sticking it out. It is as if he is saying, "*Man, I am here!*"[21] This of course was the philosophical extension of the famous placard that protesting followers of Martin Luther King, Jr., would carry shortly, "I am a man."

Next, a policeman hits Stanley in the mouth one night for failing to move on. After that, he is told that opportunity is there for him if he shows "imagination" and "industriousness." Hansberry begged for "guidance and opportunity rather than correction." She was in step with the times. Black students at a small southern college would kick off a regionwide sit-in movement the next month, February 1960. A mass civil rights movement in the South would very soon be joined by a black political and economic empowerment movement in the North, identified very much with Malcolm X.

Chicago continued its roar as a literary center when the young activist and writer Frank London Brown published the large social realist novel *Trumbull Park* in 1959. The four-hundred-page novel attacked the tendency to sentimentalize the enactment of racial integration in American neighborhoods at the end of the 1950s. Trumbull Park was the name of a housing project in Chicago that had become the site of an organized terrorist bombing campaign when African Americans families had moved in. The sounds of violence and race friction dominated the action of the book. Brown began his tale with the senseless death of a two-year-old at a rundown apartment house on Chicago's South

Side; the little girl falls through a rotting porch railing. Helen and Louis "Buggy" Martin are obviously greatly in need of a new apartment, but their move to federally funded housing in Trumbull Park is anything but serene. Vigilantes' bricks, curses, and dynamite fall on them like rain. They are as troubled by the white policemen who harass them and turn a blind eye toward their persecutors. Buggy, a defense industries worker, eventually learns about the nature of his own courage and begins to develop an organization of his black neighbors that starts to uncover the inner workings of the "mob."

Like Killens and Mayfield, Brown had written a serious work of fiction that went beyond the cardboard cutout of a masculine hero. Buggy Martin is in steady dialog with his wife Helen, and he recognizes the unique—and sometime superior—qualities of courage that his wife possesses. At the same time, and although Brown and his wife had actually lived in the Trumbull Street housing projects, Brown resisted the artistic trap of making his protagonist an intellectual whose views might easily stand for the author's. He successfully brought together political relevance and artistic value. Nor did Brown seem to be writing with a superego of whiteness standing over him; he wrote directly out of the John Killens school of social realism, with the occasional intrusion of high modernist narrative technique. A keen fan of *Youngblood* and a friend of Killens's, Brown emphasized the exploitation of the working class by a cabal of corporate and political misanthropes.

Brown revived the importance of narrative-length accounts of the urban crisis. But the best example from a writer just as young as Hansberry and Mayfield and taking advantage of the new aesthetic and political confidence was the phenomenally polished and astute fiction of exodus novelist Paule Burke Marshall. Marshall was born in Brooklyn, the daughter of a Bajan couple who had immigrated to the United States during the era of the First World War, just prior to the eugenics-based Racial Exclusion Act of 1924, which eliminated black immigration from the Caribbean. Her father Samuel Burke migrated illegally from Cuba and eventually joined one of the black evangelist Father Divine's "kingdoms." Marshall grew up as a reader in the Macon Street branch of the Brooklyn library, attended Brooklyn College, and earned Phi Beta Kappa membership during the era of Charles Glicksberg's critical enterprise in African American literature. She finished her undergraduate degree in 1953, before the arrival of John Hope Franklin, who took over the history department in 1956. In her second book, the short story collection *Soul Clap, Hands Sing*, she wrote a chapter called "Brooklyn" that revealed the relationship between a fastidious Old World professor and a young black woman from Virginia, attempting to earn a master's degree. The European professor vainly attempts to seduce the young woman, and the short story ends with her assertion of psychological maturity and defiance. Those would have been qualities that Marshall herself would have needed to complete her undergraduate degree.

After college, Marshall landed a job with *Our World*, the New York black glossy magazine styled after Chicago's *Ebony*, married, and worked on a coming-of-age novel. The staff of *Our World* had to concentrate on getting out saccharine copy, fast, and she remembered the anxiety-filled days as a journalist on a paper "about to fold at any moment."[22] Marshall often talked about the great novel waiting to be written, and all she needed was the discipline to write, even though she had not heard of any black writer except Langston Hughes until the 1950s. The timing however, of the young woman who took as her model Thomas Mann's *Buddenbrooks* could not have been more perfect. She met John Oliver Killens, who lived in Brooklyn, and began attending the Harlem Writers Guild meetings. Somehow she met Hiram Haydn and was offered a book contrct by Random House. When she got her editorial suggestions back from Haydn, she sojourned to her parents' homeland Barbados to complete the work.

On August 11, 1959, Random House published Marshall's *Brown Girl, Brownstones*. It was a filling bildungsroman that traced the development of young Selina Boyce inside of the confines of a Caribbean American family living in the Brownsville and Flatbush areas of Brooklyn. The portrait was magnificent. Selina, her extraordinary mother Silla, and her whimsical father Deighton were drawn so compellingly as to immediately become among the most remarkably vivid characters created by a black writer in American fiction. But the strong central characters did not detract from equally marvelous secondary characters, like the roomer Sugie Skeete, or the neighborhood hairdresser Ms. Thompson, the "sore-foot" woman. Marshall worked both sides of the Second World War for her time period, introspectively scrutinizing black Brooklyn family life and the transformation made possible by the war: City College for Selina, and the war industries for her mother and father. *Brown Girl* did not anchor the happiness of its characters to the achievement of assimilation; rather, in a centrifugal dynamic out from the United States and back to the Caribbean, it adhered Selina futuristically to nations of black people.

Naturally enough, the novel was a Joycean exploration of the peril that befalls the artist in a cruel family struggle of movement from the working class to the petit bourgeois; certainly this too, along with a concentration on courtship rituals, had been the concern of Gwendolyn Brooks. But Marshall's resources in the Caribbean enabled her to advance to a point of being comfortable with her skin and her heritage. The book was not the apology for a dark girl, such as Brooks had written. It happily explored the beauty and tempest of a bright black girl, including her sexuality. Marshall evoked such vivid imagery, depicted convincingly and unpretentiously Caribbean dialect, and captured the cycles of birth, death, and rebirth throughout with powerful symbols. Her work indicated a remarkable maturity for the black novel, and it was the sharpest description of black family life that existed.

The great center of Marshall's epic tale of a family's adjustment to the United States, one that requires the family, from the matriarch Silla Boyce's point of view, to "buy house," "take yuh mouth and make a gun," and "learn to run these machines to live," was the heroine's youthful repudiation of the upward mobility narrative as well as the goal of personal greed and willfulness. Hansberry had seemed to offer an affordable suburban home as at least the possibility of black success and determination, but Paule Marshall implied little reward at the epicenter of prideful American middle-class status. Selina's mother gets a house at the conclusion, but bodies are piled high in her wake, including her own husband's. When the coveted houses are being torn down to make way for public housing projects, Selina symbolically leaves a part of her heritage there and then seems most interested in taking the rest to the Caribbean, to a Bajan ancestral legacy that she has never visited.

The anti-assimilationist political stance necessary for that kind of self-definition was obvious, and it was also obvious that only modernist struggles with identity could make it possible. To emphasize this point, Marshall enabled Selina to reach the most genuine sense of herself through a relationship with two artists, Clive, a war-scarred and neurotic painter, and Rachel Fine, a Jewish classmate at college in Manhattan. If Selina's mother Silla had fled Barbados's small town Bimshire and its one-crop system modeled on slavery, the generation coming of age after World War II did not retain sullen anger toward the newly independent former colonies. Their anger would be directed domestically, and the old colonies, not the American West, would become resources of possibility.

But Marshall had easily outstripped the capacity of her audience, and her great strength was to continue to write. Perhaps the tepid reception to her achievement was easily explained by the fact that she was a black woman who had featured a young black woman protagonist and only minor white characters. And also, without much by way of an African American family on their literary canvas, critics were unprepared to accord recognition to the Anglophone Caribbean. Perhaps, too, she was already uncomfortably close to African, non-American roots. Southern University's John Lash said that she was "delicately close to a translation of Negroes into people," but that her selection of experiences "is not always as judicious as it might be."[23] Nick Aaron Ford, brimming over with pride about the "first class" "chocolate-colored Brooklyn-born writer" decided in 1962 that he loved Marshall's collection of short stories *Soul Clap, Hands Sing*, but that *Brown Girl* "contained no promise as great as this."[24] Ford had misjudged; *Brown Girl* was the most significant narrative of the decade written after 1953.

If the 1940s and early 1950s had not proven the unequivocal arrival of the African American woman novelist and poet, the end of the decade showed black women writers moving into increasing confidence and certainty. In 1960 Gwendolyn Brooks created her epitome, and probably the most beloved and best-recognized work of her career, *The Bean Eaters*. Brooks showed her own inclinations regarding the debates about blacks entering the mainstream with the book, which resisted the obscure language and dense structure of *Annie Allen*. At some point in the 1950s and in the midst of her ongoing life on Chicago's South Side, Brooks accepted the realization that racism and segregation could not be defeated like an advancing Nazi column. This was a discouraging coming-to-terms, and it carried with it a sense of waste and lost time, including a recognition of a basic dishonesty among liberals for encouraging opacity in high art and distance from the audience. The 1950s had been tough for Brooks. After she won the Pulitzer, even her supporters at *Poetry* had remained picky about her submissions.[25] But if she contorted her work to keep her Chicago friends, she no longer felt the need to prove herself a poet on the terms set out by the tastemakers at reviews like *Kenyon*, *Sewanee*, or *Hudson*.

The Bean Eaters was her resolution. It brought together the folk-spun lyricism of *A Street in Bronzeville* with the demanding modernist thematic responsibility of *Annie Allen*. Clearly Brooks wanted to recapture a portion of her audience, and in doing so, she would pay the same price that Langston Hughes paid perpetually, to be called "trite" and "sentimental," as she was in the *New York Times*.[26] Again she returned to her great themes, the slow drying and emaciation of black life, and the fight for full citizenship. Brooks brought explicitly political poems into her purview for the first time, and two of them recorded the horrifying 1955 murder of Chicago boy Emmett Till, "The Last Quatrain of the Ballad of Emmett Till" and the lengthy "A Bronzeville Mother Loiters in Mississippi, Meanwhile a Mississippi Mother Burns Bacon."

The better-known "A Bronzeville Mother" would not receive applause from the critics, but in effective allegory it sought to capture the restrained fury of black citizens eyeing the funeral of a disfigured and decomposed black boy. Brooks chose to approach the long poem from the point of view of Carolyn Bryant, whose husband Roy admitted to *Look* magazine that he had indeed killed the fourteen-year-old Bronzeville youth. Brooks placed her imagination in conversation with the chivalric myth she believed Carolyn Bryant clutched, the grown woman threatened by the teenage Till, the poem's "Dark villain." At the morning breakfast table, the myth and Roy Bryant's ready violence bubble uneasily underneath the surface of a masquerade of purportedly normal American family life.

Other poems kept at current events. She broached the integration of Central High School in Arkansas with "The Chicago *Defender* Sends a Man to Little Rock," concluding the poem in a manner that showed precisely the nature of heroic martyrdom that she now attributed black Americans: "The loveliest lynchee was our Lord."[27] Critics responded to the line as if they had been personally insulted. But Brooks went much further into the saintly ideal of black martyrs and western white villainy. She complimented Lorraine Hansberry's *A Raisin in the Sun* with "The Ballad of Rudolph Reed," a poem featuring a black man who moves his family from a slum with falling plaster and fat roaches to a house of suburban splendor, where every room "will be full of room." The problem is the neighbors. Brooks's poem concluded with Rudolph Reed sinking a butcher knife into one of his white assailants and dying in the middle of his briefly racially integrated street.

The Bean Eaters closed a door for the foremost black modernist poet of the 1940s and 1950s. It was her last book of new work with the white press in the United States. Harvey Shapiro offered the typical criticism of really any black artist's work by saying that Brooks's poems worked best when they were not political. But neither Brooks nor the others were listening to the critical pronouncements in the same way anymore. Her fellow Chicagoan Frank London Brown picked up on the shift and wrote a bop review of *Bean Eaters*, comparing Brooks to Miles Davis and Thelonius Monk. "Gwendolyn Brooks is from the set," Brown began in the dense idiom of the black streets. "She grew up on the stroll. She has seen and known the cool ones, and the down ones, and the ones with dark glasses 'round 'bout midnight."[28] Brooks herself was beginning to show a new kind of confidence that would lead in 1967 to her own transformation in favor of militant black aesthetics. "Of course, to be anything in this world as it is 'socially' constructed is 'political,' " she believed. "Whites, too, and all other distinctions operate politically as to offense, defense, and response—even when they don't know it."[29]

As for the Valhalla of middle-class life and what racial assimilation signified, Brooks was as unrepentant at the end of the decade as she had been with her sharply satiric portrait of David McKemster in *Maud Martha*. Her protagonist in "A Man of the Middle Class" says

> I have loved directions.
> I have loved orders and an iron stride, I,
> Whose hands are papers now,
> Fit only for tossing in this outrageous air.[30]

Brooks showed her impatience not just with the status of civil rights, but also the numbing materialism and devaluation of human values that hit black Americans, old and young, especially hard. In a signature poem like "The Bean Eaters," she showed the huge gaps in the celebrated prosperity of the Eisenhower era, like an old couple eating beans amidst deterioration, feeding off memories of more brilliant times. But perhaps the most famous single poem from the book captured a postwar crisis in urban America that would prove so powerful it would dismantle the gains of civil rights.

Like *Cornerboy* author Herbert Simmons, she caught sight of the development of an ever-growing cadre of black urban young people with few prospects and mounting disillusionment. During a period when black employment was at its historic postslavery high, Brooks tuned in the street-corner denizens. The succinct poem "We Real Cool: The Pool Players, Seven at the Golden Shovel" addresses the driving, syncopated, clicking of a generation of young people out for "kicks" and moving from the house, onto the city streets, and to the cemetery without so much as a civil rights organization or a church in between.

> We real cool. We
> Left school. We
>
> Lurk late. We
> Strike straight. We
>
> Thin gin. We
> Sing sin. We
>
> Jazz June. We
> Die soon.

Brooks had created an anthem of sorts for the 1960s, a foretaste of a swelling attitude of alienation and disaffection by black youth toward a society that really had no place for them.

In February 1960 a group of students from North Carolina Agricultural and Technical University expressed their disgust with the slow pace of racial change by sitting-in—occupying the seats and refusing to leave—at a lunch counter in downtown Greensboro. Within a few short weeks the defiant gesture was duplicated throughout the South, involving tens of thousands of black and white collegians. Martin Luther King, Jr.'s, Southern Christian Leadership Conference and the northern-based Congress of Racial Equality (CORE) were quick to help with the organizing. The "sit-in" resistance of the mainly black southern collegians then mushroomed into a larger movement. CORE, which had conducted tests of the federal laws protecting interracial interstate travel since the 1940s, began staging larger challenges to Jim Crow customs onboard buses called "Freedom Rides." In another year, college students began registering black voters in the Deep South in an even more dramatic gesture to harness political power. Fairly static for decades, the concrete relations of America's racial groups took on a new and dramatic tempo for rapid change. Even jazz music itself, which had been typical of entertainment's disinterest with politics, had begun to make explicit its own radical tempo.

Unsurprisingly, the great percussionists led the way in taking inspiration from Africa and the freedom struggle. Art Blakey, a leader of the "hard bop" sound, a soul-rich, beat-driven jazz music designed to return the African American audience to jazz, began in 1953 with songs like "Message from Kenya" and by the end of the decade was producing albums like *Africaine* (1959), *The Freedom Rider* (1961), and *The African Beat* (1962). Blakey's premier sidemen, like Jackie Mclean and Lee Morgan, followed suit, with McLean making the song "Appointment in Ghana" (1960) and Morgan naming another "Mr. Kenyatta" (1964).

Perhaps bebop's greatest drummer, Max Roach, was the most politically and culturally conscious of all the jazz musicians. He was also becoming the angriest. Roach, his wife Abbey Lincoln, Oscar Brown, Jr., and formidable saxophonist Coleman Hawkins put out their *WE INSIST! Max Roach's Freedom Now Suite* a couple of months after the students had begun to crash the southern barricades. The record was overtly political and filled with songs like "Driva' Man," a document of slavery's brutal work conditions, and "All Africa," where Abbey Lincoln sang out the names of African ethnic groups and Nigerian percussionist Olatunji, who had entertained at the AMSAC conference, played the rhythms. Bass player Charles Mingus had been censored by Columbia records for his 1959 "Fables of Fauvus," a song protesting Arkansas governor Orval Faubus's using the national guard to prevent black students from integrating the Little Rock, Arkansas, high school. A year later and on another record label, Mingus released the uncut version of the song, "Original Fables of Fauvus."

The writers of course prided themselves on being more intellectual than jazz musicians, and they began to insist on higher levels of engagement. And Richard Gibson may have been the most outrageous case of biting the hand that had fed him after he returned to the United States and started working for CBS. Like his estranged friend William Gardner Smith, Gibson was reconsidering the value of more direct resistance to Western imperialism and neo-imperialist policies. He began to involve himself in politics in his native hemisphere, specifically the Caribbean island of Cuba.

In April 1960 Gibson joined the Fair Play for Cuba Committee (FPCC) and worked as a United Nations correspondent for Fidel Castro's newspaper *Revolucion*.[31] Designed to promote an impartial portrait of the Castro-led Cuban Revolution to the American press, the FPCC was founded by filmmaker Robert Taber, who had made a documentary of the Cuban Revolution in 1957 called *Rebels of the Sierra Maestra*, and Alan Sanger, a New Jersey contractor and Democratic Party politico.[32] The FPCC had started out as a public relations effort designed to lure investment to revolutionary Cuba, and it had included Jackie Robinson among its members. By the time Gibson got involved in 1959, the organization was perhaps understood as a cross between a Communist-front and a revolutionary nationalist advocacy group.

Because of his newly radical politics, Gibson found himself "eased out" of his news job, and he responded by enrolling at Columbia's journalism school. He met Malcolm X, and at the United Nations he began bringing together Algerians, Arabs, African Americans, Cubans, and liberal whites. The committee organized fact-finding missions and public relations initiatives, and it proposed taking writers to Cuba. Gibson planned to convene a group for a trip to Cuba in the summer of 1960. He approached the Harlem Writers Guild, his friend James Baldwin, and Langston Hughes.

He was able to convince prominent black organizers and intellectuals like John Henrik Clarke, Harold Cruse, Sara Wright, and the embattled NAACP militant Robert F. Williams to visit Cuba. After learning that Langston Hughes was unable to attend, Gibson personally invited LeRoi Jones to join the group. He said to Jones, "I thought that since you were a poet you might like to know what's *really* going on down there."[33] Jones had rejected an overture from the CPUSA to edit a literary magazine in 1959; he was still feeling his way politically. "It had never entered my mind that I might really like to find out for once what was actually happening some place else in the world," thought Jones. The young Beat editor and poet did not exactly approve of the people he was traveling with. "One embarrassingly dull (white) communist, his professional Negro (*i.e.*, unstraightened hair . . .) wife . . . [t]wo middle-class young negro ladies from Philadelphia . . . [o]ne 1920s 'New negro' type African scholar (one of those terrible examples of what the 'Harlem Renaissance' was at its worst). One 1930s type Negro 'essayist' who turned out to be marvelously un-lied to."[34] In spite of his travel companions, the trip to Cuba had a "clarifying role" for Jones's political development.[35] More or less, he adopted precisely the point of view that Hansberry had unfolded in her Negro Writers' Conference speech: the Beats were abdicating responsibility for a more democratic, racially egalitarian future.

Julian Mayfield too reached a turning point in 1960 when he joined the entourage of Robert Williams's supporters in Cuba in the middle of the year. He interviewed the leader of integrationist militants from Monroe, North Carolina, and grew to think of him as an Abraham Lincoln figure. When Williams told him that he was pursuing freedom, and that he would make it to that place, Mayfield felt as if he was in the presence of a man taking his chance to become a citizen of the world. When the bunch was still in Cuba as Castro's guests for the celebration of the revolution, Williams got word that the Klan had threatened his family in North Carolina and that local authorities had downplayed the obvious danger. The lynching of Mack Parker in Mississippi and the rape of Betty Jean Owens in Florida in 1959 emphasized the obvious reality of the threat. Armed with a pistol, Williams told the U.S. ambassador that if anything happened to his family in North Carolina, he would begin killing American citizens in Cuba, beginning with the ambassador. "Militant self-reliance" had become a kind of creed that enabled Williams to live out his beliefs and gave to him the aura of nineteenth-century figures like Lincoln and Frederick Douglass. But Jones and Mayfield were especially impressed, and shortly after the visit they began to provide clandestine military assistance to Williams. Jones assisted in storing weapons destined for North Carolina at the Phoenix Book Shop on Cornelia Street in New York, where the poet Diane di Prima worked.[36]

Harold Cruse gained inspiration from the Cuba trip. The events of the Cuban overthrow of the colonial regime sharpened Cruse's perceptions too, stimulating the production of the article "Revolutionary Nationalism and the Afro-American" in about eighteen months. The essay would lead him to his hefty reconsideration of twentieth-century black intellectual history, *The Crisis of the Negro Intellectual*. After the end of his Cuba trip, Harold Cruse would be fully done with the tutelage he had experienced at anyone's hands. "From the beginning, the American Negro has existed as a colonial being," he would write. "His enslavement coincided with the colonial expansion of European powers and was nothing more or less than a condition of domestic colonialism."[37] This was even further than Cruse had been in the contretemps with Redding over the idea of black cultural nationalism. Cruse had moved into the train of thought of C.L.R. James, who had taken the socialist theory to an ultraradical plane in 1948 when he had suggested in "The Revolutionary Answer to the Negro Problem" that blacks constituted their own revolutionary vanguard, without white help or coaching.

But with independent Cuba—a heavily black, Marxist-based society in the Western Hemisphere—there was tangible evidence that someone other than European urban workers might be embraced by the historical spirit of dialectical materialism and transform a society. Instead of assimilating to the white mainstream, blacks would reap greater theoretical and historical fruit by joining themselves to the colonial world, a tropical zone of black and brown and yellow people now remaking itself. "The failure of Marxists to understand the bond between the Negro and the colonial peoples of the world has led to their failure to develop theories that would be of value to Negroes in the United States," Cruse proposed.[38] The declaration for black Marxism from Cruse sounded his newfound independence and his international direction. (Cruse in fact later became close colleagues with Cheikh Anta Diop, who would have a university in his native Dakar in his name.) His carrying over into the 1960s the fundamental Marxist tools he had plied as a young playwright and theater critic after the war magnified the direct link back to the mid-1930s and that powerful incubator for radical black creative writers: the Communist Party and their writers' institutions.

No one would have been more surprised than Richard Wright at the political conversion of Richard Gibson or the steady heroics of a tried-and-true Chicago socialite like Lorraine Hansberry. In the weeks leading up to his unusual death in November 1960, Richard Wright reflected broadly on a career that had taken him to several continents and afforded him an international reputation: he was still the best-known writer of African descent publishing in the Western world. In the final months of his life, Wright had become increasingly conscious of the circumstances that enabled him to develop as a writer and intellectual in the United States. He believed firmly that he had "escaped being conditioned," and he claimed that, "luckily," the state government of Mississippi did not provide school for Negroes beyond the eighth grade. Wright thought the neglect of black schools in Mississippi an unintended "gift," because he had not received an education that forced on him values that did not correspond to the narrow life-choices available to American Negroes. His triumph was to have dodged the mental limits of the "pet nigger," a condition that he believed he would have succumbed to in the United States, particularly at an African American college. "I would have been too conditioned to prudence to have ever written a single book," he said to an audience.[39] Wright upheld the tradition of autodidacticism, of self-made freedom.

Wright was outspoken. He relished as his most important contribution his hardheaded opposition to the Western powers and his correspondingly unflattering estimates of fellow blacks who seemed attracted to them. He believed that because of his uncompromising attitudes he was a specific target of American governmental agents. Many of his suspicions began with the resistance he met when he tried unsuccessfully to produce a film of the novel *Native Son* in France in 1948. His feeling of persecution matured with swirling rumors of FBI and CIA operatives infiltrating the Parisian café circuit frequented by black American writers. The open spats with James Baldwin in the early 1950s in cafés and inside of the short-lived Franco-American Fellowship itself left him feeling paranoid and unsheltered. Every criticism of his work by Baldwin or Richard Gibson had seemed to disguise a more menacing threat.

At times Wright tried to play both ends against the middle. For example, Wright himself had apparently reported to a member of the U.S. State Department when he visited the Bandung Conference in Indonesia in 1954 that Eugene Gordon had been an early member of the Communist Party.[40] He took his turn in *Encounter*. He also believed that the journal *Présence Africaine* was being infiltrated and disrupted by the French government, and Americans like Kay Boyle reported to Wright himself the rumors that swirled in the American colony in Paris that Wright was an informant and had been spotted leaving the U.S. Embassy. After Richard Gibson had been arrested and released by French police for forging Oliver Harrington's name in 1957, Wright sat Gibson down and asked him dozens of questions, writing down the answers in longhand. After the interview with Gibson, he had a new enemy, William Gardner Smith.

Wright had mainly used his fiction as an anchor in a frighteningly chaotic world. He returned to the novel in 1958 with *The Long Dream*. In his last published work of narrative fiction, he sought to provide a template for the timeless practice of racial subjugation in the United States. The intellectual challenges of existentialist philosophy no longer stirred him deeply; he wanted to resist the image of black patriarchal abandonment and black male weakness. This key image of the defeated black male adult circulated broadly and reached its deafening crescendo in 1965 with New York Senator Daniel Moynihan's report "The Negro Family: The Case for National Action." In *The Long Dream*, Wright seemed to wish to refute, point by terrible point, James Baldwin's interpretation of black fathers, sons, and male life generally in *Go Tell It on the Mountain*.

Wright's hero Fishbelly is the son of Tyree Tucker, a prosperous undertaker whose source of wealth seems to have little connection to the white world. In theory, this was the ideal situation for some kind of resolution with the environment of racial subjugation. Wright then showed the contradictions that made the resolution impossible: a white gambler briefly abducts tiny Fishbelly into an alley crap game, fondling him for luck; Fishbelly and his gang of older friends cruelly ostracize a boy for his effeminate behavior, a ritual that they all recognize as a parallel of whites do to them; Fishbelly's father Tyree has to prepare the body of a teen castrated and lynched for sex relations with a white prostitute; and an appalled Fishbelly witnesses his father weepingly beg the chief of police. Ultimately Fishbelly grows to despise his father, who stands at the center of the town's corrupt power structure. Then, after Tyree Tucker is murdered by the police chief, Fishbelly recognizes the fundamental wisdom and humanity in unlettered but cunning black men like his father. The novel ends with Fishbelly on the plane for Paris.

In the father-and-son relationship, Wright presented a series of primordial interactions that transparently emphasized bonds of love and the manner of their attenuation under the condition of racism. But the regimented case study of black men submitting to racial subjugation in the South that might have made the work a classic to audiences digesting it in translation seemed comparatively crude to Americans. U.S. reviewers were prepared for more fundamentally psychologically insular works, and especially works that gestured to the world after segregation had ended. People wondered why Wright had not emphasized optimism and heroism following the U.S. Supreme Court's decisions to overturn racial segregation, King's growing international fame, and federal intervention to open high schools to blacks in Arkansas. Cold war calculations pitted the publishers, reviewers, and public against Wright's hugely negative portrait of the United States. Ghana gained independence in 1957, and in 1958 the U.S. State Department was encouraging African and Asian countries away from the Soviet Union, to the point of reinforcing federal civil rights laws so that the diplomats would not be humiliated visiting Jim Crow Washington, D.C., and Maryland.[41] As Baldwin had said to Sol Stein in 1956, Wright continued to embarrass.

All *The Long Dream*'s major reviews were mixed. Some said Wright had powerfully revealed the truth, others said he had written with competence, but no review claimed that he had done both. Granville Hicks said that "Wright is telling the truth about the situation of the American Negro and the truth cannot fail to shock us," but then Hicks decided that Wright had fumbled in terms of technique.[42] Educated blacks, who had praised him mightily in the past, levied a sharp rebuke. The professional "Negro" Saunders Redding said, "Wright has been away too long," and even Nick Aaron Ford found the book "a colossal disappointment" and encouraged Wright to "return to his native land."[43] But return to Mississippi was obviously not what Wright desired, and his dim vision of the magnolia state would be brightly vindicated by 1963. But for the 1950s, Wright had lost his American audience.

The book's failed potential exacerbated Wright's gargantuan sense of doom, an anxiety that made its way into his letters to his friend, the translator Margrit de Sabloniére: "The American State Department and the Pentagon are hard on my neck, for my work, though anti-Communist, falls like a black shadow over what they are trying to do in Asia and Africa. They are trying to drive me back to the USA, but I'd give up my American citizenship rather than do that, for they would shut me up and physically destroy me."[44] Wright could never obtain compromise with what he clearly understood as his personal enemy.

After *The Long Dream* he wrote a manuscript treating African American expatriate life in Paris and the infiltration of the black group by government agencies. Wright was preparing to publish the manuscript *Island of Hallucination* when he died. The book was a roman à clef that suggested that James Baldwin, William Gardner Smith, and Richard Gibson were spies and CIA operatives. To a degree, in his 1967 book *The Man Who Cried I Am*, John A. Williams would complement this view, although Williams had not seen any portions of Wright's manuscript.

Wright must have found the events of 1960 odd, as Richard Gibson emerged as a revolutionary figure. In a short time Gibson would be followed, a bit less forcefully, by James Baldwin beating the drum and bearing witness to the cacophony, bitterness, and failed liberal promises of the 1950s. Wright's three manuscripts between 1958 and 1960—*The Long Dream*, *A Father's Law*, and *Island of Hallucination*—reflect fascinatingly if obliquely on his relationship with James Baldwin, who superseded Wright as the world's most famous black writer and the most important literary figure involved in the civil rights movement. That street ran both ways. Baldwin had told Wright in 1953 in a famous dispute and in the presence of Chester Himes that he considered Wright a father figure.[45]

On November 8, 1960, in the auditorium of the American Church in Paris, Richard Wright prepared to read a long paper on the Negro writer to an audience mainly of American students. He had over thirty pages of typed notes that were really a kind of cultural and intellectual history that lay behind the manuscript *Island of Hallucination*. The paper itself was an exposure of James Baldwin and Ralph Ellison as examples of artists who unsuccessfully struggled to keep their integrity. Wright began reading the paper, which described the cultural confusion and impossible situation of the black writer. But according to a news report, after a sip of water, several minutes into the address, he stopped reading, took off his glasses, and put away his notes. The *Chicago Defender* reported that he then launched into his real preoccupation, the tension between the United States and the Soviet Union over the Congo. He praised the elected Congolese leader Patrice Lumumba as "an able man" and the "legal head of a legal government."[46] Wright called Tshombe, head of the rebellious Katanga province, a puppet, and then he denounced the puppeteers, agent provocateurs, and government agents that he had known in the United States and as he had written about in *Island of Hallucination*. "How much longer can the West afford the luxury of preaching at home and practicing abroad?," a fundamental contradiction in ethics, he asked his audience.

Wright would be dead even before Lumumba. In less than three weeks Richard Wright's heart failed at a Paris hospital he had never before visited, where he had rushed to be treated for liver poisoning, a condition caused by the medicine that his doctor had prescribed for him. His final works shouted to a close the era that he had begun.

Coda

The combination of radical politics, militant defiance, and black writers' groups, the hallmark of the 1960s, all cohered in February 1961 when black Americans learned of the assassination of the Congolese Prime Minister Patrice Lumumba. Belgian and U.N. troops had militarily supported the rebellion of the resource-rich Katanga province, then, with advisers and U.S. intelligence reports, orchestrated the coup against Lumumba's government that led to his murder. The Soviet Union publicly accused the U.N. Secretary Dag Hammarskjold of conspiring to assassinate Lumumba, and U.S. Ambassador Adlai Stevenson addressed the Security Council to prop Hammarskjold back up. During the session on February 15, 1961, fifty African Americans distinguished by black armbands and veils packed the visitors' gallery of the Security Council to hear Stevenson's speech. The group included Max Roach, Abbey Lincoln, LeRoi Jones, and Harlem Writers Guild members Maya Angelou and Rosa Guy.[47] When the activists stood in silence to protest Stevenson's remarks, security officers approached them, and tussling and loud outbursts ensued. Outside of the U.N. building, more demonstrations and fistfights between police and Lumumba supporters took place.

The unprecedented public denunciation of Hammarskjold and the ensuing melee made the international news. The demonstration was the culmination of the fiery speeches of Mayfield and Hansberry at the Negro Writers' Conference, Richard Gibson's coordination of the Cuba visit so that the black intellectuals might see an outbreaking revolution up close, and then a famous September 1960 visit to Harlem by Fidel Castro and his meeting with Malcolm X. The embarrassed U.N. undersecretary Ralph Bunche formally apologized to his U.N. colleagues for the demonstrations, which he claimed were "in no way representative of the American Negro."[48] A month later, in March 1961, Lorraine Hansberry, who had not been at the United Nations, did her part by apologizing for Ralph Bunche in the pages of the *New York Times* to the widow of Patrice Lumumba.[49]

Hansberry's speedy and flip rebuttal of the highest-ranking black American international diplomat proved that she had outgrown her usefulness for much of the liberal press. In an article she wrote that April for the black publication *The Urbanite*, Hansberry socratically rejected her Western education—including "[t]hat racist" Camus—and supported Algeria for Algerians.[50] And she was filled with praise for the taut essay by James Baldwin, "A Negro Assays the Negro Mood," which the *Times* had published on March 12. Baldwin had planned to attend the U.N. demonstration and in his report called "the Negro's status in this country not only a cruel injustice but a grave national liability."[51] He pointed to the sit-in movement as an "act of faith" that took as its creed the "essential decency" of white people. But Baldwin knew that the assumptions held by the black collegians were in the process of change and he said so.

Furthermore, the U.N. protest had not been made by the colleges, but had involved groups like LeRoi Jones and Calvin Hicks's On Guard, by then old-guard black radical and Communist Benjamin Davis, ex-gang members who had turned Muslim, the Harlem Writers Guild, Abbey Lincoln's Cultural Association for Women of African Heritage, James Lawson's United African Nationalist Movement, Dan Watts's Liberation Committee for Africa, the African Nationalist Pioneer Movement, and African American Muslim groups. Although the Nation of Islam formally denied involvement in the protest, national spokesman Malcolm X assured the press that he refused to condemn other black nationalists groups.[52] Informally, Malcolm X was the mentor and confidant of many of the activist leaders, and colleagues of his like Louis X (Farrakhan) believed him to be the key organizer.[53] In any event, the Nation of Islam, or "Black Muslims" as they were frequently called, became indelibly, if erroneously, connected to radical militancy and protorevolutionary activism.

In the public mind Malcolm X and other Muslims appeared as the opposite of civil rights–concerned, domestic, nonviolent, integrationist activism. Baldwin rightly understood that the righteous indignation behind the civil rights movement of students and ministers in the South would evolve quite differently in the northern black ghetto.

In his earlier years Baldwin had served as a foil for what the radicalism of social realism seemed to threaten, but he was no longer keeping the lid on things. He told his liberal friends that it was "quite impossible to argue with a Muslim [a member of the Nation of Islam, called "Muslim" in the essay] concerning the actual state of Negroes in this country—the truth, after all, is the truth."[54] Baldwin, the product of the Congress for Cultural Freedom, then quoted Hansberry scorning the politics of racial integration during a January roundtable discussion with Langston Hughes, editor Emile Capouya, and literary critic Alfred Kazin. Hansberry had told Kazin, who had been faithfully tendering the moderate liberal position, that she was "not at all sure that I want to be integrated into a burning house." Writing plays about Toussaint L'Ouverture and the principled Mau Mau violence in Kenya, the playwright took the opportunity to remind Kazin that the twentieth century's famed portraits of black American life— Faulkner's Dilsey from *Sound and the Fury* was the case in point—were satisfactory only because whites had never "sat in a Negro home . . . [and] heard the nuances of hatred, of total contempt" from their black servants. Then she confronted Kazin personally. "[F]or you this is a fulfilling image, because you haven't either."[55] Few whites had an interest in sitting in the kitchen and listening to denunciations by blacks of the serving class as a necessary requirement for the health of the country. But the new order of the day was obvious to James Baldwin. "[T]he American Negro can no longer, nor will he ever again, be controlled by white America's image of him. This fact has everything to do with the rise of Africa in world affairs."[56]

Leading the way in outrunning the white American image of blacks, and the federal government itself, was Robert F. Williams. Williams outfoxed a government dragnet in early 1961 and fled the United States for safety in Cuba. Shortly after his arrival there, the Kennedy administration sent trained militia to Cuba to topple the socialist regime, almost in the manner of Napoleon's General Leclerc going to Haiti to reinstitute slavery. But after the operation was under way Kennedy lost his nerve and refused air and naval support to the stalled anti-Castro militants. The Bay of Pigs disaster went on to join other key moments in the defeat of Western imperialism, like the 1954 French defeat in Vietnam at Dien Bien Phu. Julian Mayfield, implicated in supplying weapons to Robert Williams and enabling his escape from the United States and whose essays had increasingly characterized the militant rejection of assimilation, fled in September 1961 for Ghana. He served as one of Nkrumah's advisors until the

Ghanaian government was overthrown during Nkrumah's visit to North Vietnam in 1966. William Gardner Smith joined Mayfield in Ghana from France, and Maya Angelou joined them from the United States. W.E.B. Du Bois and his wife Shirley Graham Du Bois arrived in 1961 and became citizens in 1963. And then in early 1962 Richard Gibson, facing federal indictment, pushed off for Algiers to become a spokesperson for the FLN, partially filling the void left by Frantz Fanon, who died in December 1961.

Black American writers engaged in a second wave of expatriation, but no longer to find acceptance in a Western country that would allow them the personal liberty to define themselves individually. As Baldwin had noted, this had everything to do with the "rise of Africa in world affairs." Like Joseph Cinque 130 years before them, the vanguard now determined to set its sails in reverse.

NOTES

MANUSCRIPT COLLECTIONS ABBREVIATIONS

AB   Arna Bontemps Papers, Special Collections Research Center, Syracuse University Library

AL   Alain Locke Papers, Moorland-Spingarn Research Center, Howard University

ALB   Alice Browning Papers, Vivian Harsh Collection, Carter G. Woodson Branch, Chicago Public Library

ALP   Ann Petry Papers, Howard Gottlieb Archival Research Center, Boston University

AMSAC   American Society of African Culture Papers, Moorland-Spingarn Research Center, Howard University

APD   Arthur P. Davis Papers, Moorland-Spingarn Research Center, Howard University

BM   Bucklin Moon Papers, Manuscripts and Archives, Rollins College

CH   Chester Himes Papers, Amistad Research Center, Tulane University

DW   Dorothy West Papers, Schlesinger Library, Harvard University

EFF   E. Franklin Frazier Papers, Moorland-Spingarn Research Center, Howard University

FHC   Frank and Helen Chisholm Papers, Manuscripts, Archives and Rare Book Library, Emory University

HAB   Selected Records of Harper & Brothers, Department of Rare Books and Special Collections, Firestone Library, Princeton University

HAC   Harold Cruse Papers, Tamiment Library, Elmer Holmes Bobst Library, New York University

HC   Horace Cayton Papers, Vivian Harsh Collection, Carter G. Woodson Branch, Chicago Public Library

HJ   Harold Jackman Papers, Trevor Arnett Library, Atlanta University

JB   James Baldwin Mss., Lilly Library, Indiana University

JHC   John Henrik Clarke Papers, Manuscripts, Archives and Rare Books Division, Schomburg Center for Research in Black Culture, New York Public Library, Astor, Lenox and Tilden Foundations

JM   Julian Mayfield Papers, Manuscripts, Archives and Rare Books Division, Schomburg Center for Research in Black Culture, New York Public Library, Astor, Lenox and Tilden Foundations

JOK   John Oliver Killen Papers, Manuscripts, Archives, and Rare Book Library, Emory University

JSR   J. Saunders Redding Papers, John Hay Library, Brown University

JUL   Julius Rosenwald Papers, John Hope and Aurelia E. Franklin Library, Fisk University

KMD   Ken McCormick/Doubleday Papers, Manuscripts Division, Library of Congress

LH   Langston Hughes Papers, Beinecke Library, Yale University

MA   Max Ascoli Papers, Harold Gottlieb Archives and Research Center, Boston University

MBT   Melvin B. Tolson Papers, Manuscripts Division, Library of Congress
MC   Malcolm Cowley Papers, Midwest Writers Collection, Newberry Library
MEC   Library of Matt and Evelyn Crawford, Manuscripts, Archives and Rare Book Library, Emory University
MF   Michel Fabre Papers, Manuscript Archives and Rare Book Library, Emory University
NAF   Nick Aaron Ford Papers, South Caroliniana Library, University of South Carolina
PM   *Poetry Magazine* Papers, Regenstein Library, University of Chicago
PR   *Partisan Review* Papers, Howard Gottlieb Archival Research Center, Boston University
RE   Ralph Ellison Papers, Manuscript Division, Library of Congress
RW   Richard Wright Papers, Beinecke Library, Yale University
SAB   Sterling A. Brown Papers, Moorland-Spingarn Research Center, Howard University
WM   Willard Motley Papers, Vivian Harsh Collection, Carter G. Woodson Branch, Chicago Public Library
YA   Yaddo Papers Collection, Manuscripts and Archives Division, New York Public Library

INTRODUCTION: IRREDEEMABLE PROMISE

1. J. Saunders Redding, letter to Henry Allen Moe, 1 January 1959, JSR, box 3.

2. Saunders Redding, *On Being Negro in America* (1951; New York: Bantam, 1964), 14. From [Scrapbooks, vol. 2, JSR, p. 12,] William Shirer, "An Eloquent and Passionately Written Book," *New York Herald Tribune Book Review*, 11 November 1951, n.p.

3. Ralph Ellison, letter to Richard Wright, 22 April 1940, RW, box 97, folder 1314.

4. Horace Kallen, "Democracy versus the Melting Pot," *Nation*, 25 February 1915, 220.

5. Gary Gerstle, "The Protean Character of American Liberalism," *American Historical Review* (October 1994): 1052.

6. John Dewey, *Liberalism and Social Action* (New York: Putnam, 1935), 27.

7. Dewey, *Liberalism and Social Action*, 48.

8. Irving Howe, "The New York Intellectuals," in *Selected Writings, 1900–1950* (San Diego: Harcourt Brace Jovanovich, 1990), 251.

9. Michael Kimmage, *The Conservative Turn: Lionel Trilling, Whittaker Chambers, and the Lessons of Anti-Communism* (Cambridge: Harvard University Press, 2009), 4–6.

10. Lionel Trilling, *The Liberal Imagination* (New York: Scribner's, 1976), xv.

11. See Darryl Scott, *Contempt and Pity: Social Policy and the Damaged Black Psyche: 1880–1996* (Chapel Hill: University of North Carolina Press, 1997).

12. Ralph Ellison, "A Rejoinder," *New Leader*, 3 February 1964, 15, in *Shadow and Act* (New York: Vintage, 1995), 122.

13. Arthur P. Davis, "Integration and Race Literature," *Phylon* (Spring 1956): 145.

14. The political scientist Adolph Reed suggests that the New Deal era's economic and cultural shifts outmoded "ethnic particularity" and with it the teeth of race prejudice. He argues that the civil rights movement was ideologically corporatist in its designs and aims, a condition that indicates essentially that racial prejudice had become inefficient within the framework of monopoly capitalism. Adolph Reed, "Ethnic Particularity

Reconsidered," *Is It Nation Time?*, ed. Eddie Glaude (Chicago: University of Chicago Press, 2003).

15. J. Saunders Redding, *Stranger and Alone* (1950; Boston: Northeastern University Press, 1989), 71.

16. Bob Bone, "The Changing Status of the Negro," *Dissent* (Spring 1955): 130.

17. Redding, *On Being a Negro in America*, 35.

CHAPTER 1: THREE SWINGING SISTERS

1. Malcolm Cowley, *Exiles Return: A Narrative of Ideas* (New York: Norton, 1934), 11.

2. J. Donald Adams, "The Lost Generation's Sad Story," *New York Times Book Review*, 27 May 1934, 2.

3. Cowley, *Exiles Return*, 300–301.

4. J. Saunders Redding, *To Make a Poet Black* (1939; Ithaca: Cornell, University Press, 1988), 120.

5. Harold Rosenberg, "The Situation in American Writing: Seven Questions," *Partisan Review* (Summer 1939): 48.

6. Wallace Thurman, "Nephews of Uncle Remus," *Independent*, 24 September 1927, 298; quoted in Charles Scruggs, "All Dressed Up but No Place to Go: The Black Writer and His Audience during the Harlem Renaissance," *American Literature* 48 (1977): 560.

7. Alain Locke, "1928: A Retrospective Review," *Opportunity* (January 1929): 8.

8. Alain Locke, "This Year of Grace," *Opportunity* (February 1931): 48.

9. Langston Hughes, *The Big Sea* (1940; New York: Hill and Wang, 1963), 334.

10. Michael Denning, *The Cultural Front* (New York: Verso, 1998), 4. Denning recognizes the era between 1934 and 1948 as the historic bloc "Popular Front," "a radical historical bloc uniting industrial unionists, Communists, independent socialists, community activists, and émigré anti-fascists around laborist social democracy, anti-fascism, and anti-lynching." In Harlem, for example, the movement combined key organizations like A. Phillip Randolph's Brotherhood of Sleeping Car Porters Union, Adam Clayton Powell Jr.'s Abyssinia Baptist Church and *People's Voice* newspaper, Communist lawyer and politician Benjamin Davis Jr., and the National Negro Congress (15).

11. Sterling Brown, "Ralph Bunche—Statesman," *Reporter*, 6 December 1949, 4.

12. St. Clair Drake and Horace Cayton, *Black Metropolis: A Study of Life in a Northern City* (New York: Harcourt, Brace, 1945), 8.

13. Edwin R. Embree, *Brown America: The Story of a Tenth of the Nation* (New York: Viking, 1943), 107–8.

14. Harry Washington Greene, *Holders of Doctorates among American Negroes* (Boston: Meador, 1943), 26.

15. Winston James, *Holding Aloft the Banner of Ethiopia: Caribbean Radicalism in the Twentieth Century* (New York: Verso, 1998), 175.

16. Glenda Gilmore, *Defying Dixie: The Radical Roots of Civil Rights, 1919–1950* (New York: Norton, 2008), 51; and Mark Solomon, *The Cry Was Unity: Communists and African Americans, 1917–1936* (Jackson: University of Mississippi Press, 1998), 26–27.

17. Harold Cruse, *Crisis of the Negro Intellectual* (New York: Morrow, 1967), 127–30; James, *Holding Aloft the Banner of Ethiopia*, 274–81. James offers an important revision of how Cruse understood W. A. Domingo's famous report "Socialism Imperilled, or the Negro—A Potential Menace to American Radicalism."

18. Waldo Frank, *Memoirs of Waldo Frank* (Amherst: University of Massachusetts Press, 1973), 187–88.

19. Harvey Klehr, *The Heyday of American Communism* (New York: Basic Books, 1984), 347.

20. Gilmore, *Defying Dixie*, 61–65.

21. Solomon, *The Cry Was Unity*, 77.

22. Edmund Wilson, *Red, Black, Blond and Olive: Studies in Four Civilizations: Zuni, Haitia, Soviet Russia, Israel* (New York: Oxford, 1956), 271.

23. Herbert Alper, *Goodbye Union Square* (Chicago: Quadrangle, 1970), 147.

24. Woodford McClellan, "Africans and Black Americans in the Comintern Schools, 1925–1934," *International Journal of African Historical Studies* 26 (1977): 371–72.

25. Eric Homberger, "Proletarian Literature and the John Reed Clubs," *American Studies* 13 (1979): 221.

26. Philip Rahv, review of *Scottsboro Limited* by Langston Hughes, *Rebel Poet* (August 1932): 7.

27. Richard Wright, *Black Boy (American Hunger)*, restored by Library of America 1991 (New York: HarperCollins, 1993), 381.

28. Bettina Drew, *Nelson Algren: A Life on the Wild Side* (Austin: University of Texas Press, 1989), 83.

29. Richard Wright, "I Tried to Be a Communist," *Atlantic* (August 1944): 69.

30. Arnold Rampersad, *The Life of Langston Hughes*, Vol. 1: *1902–1941, I, Too, Sing America* (New York: Oxford University Press, 1986), 217.

31. Langston Hughes, inscription to Matt and Evelyn Crawford, 15 May 1934, *The Ways of White Folks*, MEC.

32. Rampersad, *The Life of Langston Hughes*, 323.

33. Verner D. Mitchell and Cynthia Davis, "Dorothy West and Her Circle," introduction to *Where the Wild Grape Grows: Selected Writings, 1930–1950* by Dorothy West, ed. Mitchell and Davis (Amherst: University of Massachusetts Press, 2005), 21.

34. George S. Messersmith, U.S. Consul General, Berlin Consulate memorandum, 30 August 1932, U.S. State Department Decimal Files, RG 59, 861.5017, 1930–1939; Solomon, *Cry Was Unity*, 174–77.

35. Mitchell and Davis, "Dorothy West," 24.

36. James Weldon Johnson, letter to Dorothy West, 7 February 1934, quoted in Abby A. Johnson and Ronald M. Johnson, *Propaganda and Aesthetics: The Literary Politics of African-American Magazines in the Twentieth Century* (Amherst: University of Massachusetts Press, 1991), 113.

37. James Weldon Johnson, "Race Prejudice and the Negro Artist," *Harper's Magazine* (November 1928): 776.

38. James Weldon Johnson, "Negro Authors and White Publishers," *Crisis* 36 (July 1929): 229.

39. Countee Cullen, letter to Dorothy West, 25 October 1933, DW, box 85-M139, folder 6.

40. Frank Yerby, letter to Dorothy West, 1 June 1934, DW, box 85-M139, folder 18.

41. Wallace Thurman, letter to Dorothy West, 12 September 1934, DW, box 85-M139, folder 2.

42. Zora Neale Hurston, "Characteristics of Negro Folk Expression," in *Negro: An Anthology*, ed. Nancy Cunard (London: Wishart, 1934), 39.

43. Zora Neale Hurston, *Their Eyes Were Watching God* (1937; Urbana: University of Illinois Press, 1978), 285.

44. Zora Neale Hurston, *Dust Tracks on the Road* (Philadelphia: J. B. Lippincott, 1942), 217; Charles A. Madison, *Book Publishing in America* (New York: McGraw Hill, 1966), 219.

45. "Zora Neale Hurston," in *Twentieth Century Authors,* ed. Stanley Kunitz and Howard Haycraft (New York: H. W. Wilson, 1942), 694–95.

46. Zora Neale Hurston, letter to Thomas E. Jones, 12 October 1934, in *Zora Neale Hurston: A Life in Letters,* collected and ed. Carla Kaplan (New York: Doubleday, 2002), 315.

47. Sterling Brown, quoted in *Zora Neale Hurston: A Literary Biography* by Robert Hemenway (Urbana: University of Illinois Press, 1980), 219.

48. Harold Preece, "Negro Folk Cult," *Crisis* 43 (December 1936): 374, 364.

49. Joanne Gabbin, *Sterling A. Brown: Building a Black Aesthetic Tradition* (Westport, CT: Greenwood, 1985), 15–35. The biographical information on Brown comes from Gabbin.

50. Sterling A. Brown, "Southern Road," in *Collected Poems of Sterling A. Brown,* ed. Michael Harper (Evanston, IL: Triquarterly, 1996), 52–53.

51. Sterling Brown, Arthur P. Davis, and Ulysses Lee, introduction to *Negro Caravan,* ed. Brown, Davis, and Lee (New York: Dryden Press, 1941), 5.

52. Walter Lippman, *Public Opinion* (1922; New York: Free Press, 1965), 59.

53. Sterling Brown, "Negro Character as Seen by White Authors," *Journal of Negro Education* (January 1933): 179, 198.

54. Genevieve Ekaete, "Sterling Brown: A Living Legend," *New Directions: The Howard University Magazine* 1 (Winter 1974): 9; in Gabbin, *Sterling A. Brown,* 199.

55. Marita Bonner, "Tin Can," in *Frye Street and Environs* (Boston: Beacon, 1987), 139, 137.

56. Sterling Brown, "Imitation of Life: Once a Pancake," *Opportunity* (March 1935): 88.

57. Fannie Hurst, "Miss Fannie Hurst," *Opportunity* (April 1935): 121.

58. Sterling Brown, "Mr. Sterling Brown," *Opportunity* (April 1935): 122.

59. Sterling Brown, "Southern Cross Sections," *Opportunity* (December 1935): 380.

CHAPTER 2: THE BLACK AVANT-GARDE BETWEEN LEFT AND RIGHT

1. Arthur Casciato, "Citizen Writers: A History of the League of American Writers, 1935–1942," Ph.D. diss., University of Virginia, 1986, 25.

2. Ibid., 26–27.

3. Michael Denning, *The Cultural Front* (New York: Verso, 1998), 203.

4. Harvey Klehr, *Heyday of American Communism: The Depression Decade* (New York: Basic Books, 1984), 331, 339.

5. "Police End Harlem Riot; Mayor Starts Inquiry; Dodge Sees a Red Plot," *New York Times,* 21 March 1935, 1; "Boy, Cause of Riot, Put on Probation," *New York Times,* 28 March 1935, 44; "Blamed for Riot, Harlem Girl Fined," *New York Times,* 24 March 1935, 19.

6. "Police Condemned by Harlem Inquiry," *New York Times,* 10 August 1935, 10.

7. "Harlem Riots Laid to Neglect by City," *New York Times,* 13 April 1935, 3.

8. "Communist Hail Soviet Peace Aid," *New York Times,* 27 January 1936, 4.

9. Gerald Horne, *Black Liberation/Red Scare: Ben Davis and the Communist Party* (Newark: University of Delaware Press, 1994), 111.

10. Claude McKay, *Harlem: Negro Metropolis* (New York: Harcourt, 1940), 248–49.

11. Earl Browder, "Communism and Literature," in *American Writers Congress*, ed. Henry Hart (New York: International Publishers, 1935), 69.

12. Langston Hughes, "To Negro Writers," in ibid., 140, 139.

13. Langston Hughes, "The Negro Artist and the Racial Mountain," *Nation*, 23 June 1926, 692–94.

14. Alan Wald, *Exiles from a Future Time: The Forging of the Mid-Twentieth-Century Literary Left* (Chapel Hill: University of North Carolina Press, 2002), 82.

15. Eugene Gordon, "Social and Political Problems of the Negro Writer," in *American Writers Congress*, ed. Hart, 141, 144.

16. "New Contributors," *Partisan Review: A Bi-Monthly of Revolutionary Literature* (July–August 1935), inside cover.

17. McKinney, *Mordecai*, 87.

18. Eugene Clay, "The Negro in Recent American Literature," in *American Writers Congress*, ed. Hart, 147, 152.

19. Lydia Filatova, "Langston Hughes: American Writer," *International Literature* 1 (1933): 107, quoted in Anthony Dawahare, "Langston Hughes's Radical Poetry and the "End of Race," *MELUS* (Autumn 1998): 21–41.

20. James T. Farrell, *Notes on Literary Criticism* (New York: Vanguard, 1936), 29, 32.

21. Michel Fabre, *The Unfinished Quest of Richard Wright* (1971; Jackson: University of Mississippi Press, 1998), 123, 121.

22. "The Coming Writers Congress," *Partisan Review* (January–February 1935): 96.

23. Robert Van Gelder, review of *The New Caravan* edited by Alfred Kreymbourg, Lewis Mumford, and Paul Rosenfeld, *New York Times*, 2 November 1936, 19.

24. Sterling Brown, "The Literary Scene: Two Negro Poets," *Opportunity* (March 1936): 216, 220.

25. Sterling Brown, "Transfer," *Partisan Review* (October 1936): 21.

26. Wald, *New York Intellectuals*, 141–47.

27. "Editorial Statement," *Partisan Review* (December 1937): 3.

28. Wald, *New York Intellectuals*, 143.

29. Philip Rahv, letter to Richard Wright, n.d. [ca. 1939], RW, box 103, folder 1528.

30. T. J. Arnold, interview, November 2004.

31. Mark Naison, *Communists in Harlem during the Depression* (1983; New York: Grove, 1984), 170.

32. See Mary Poole, *The Segregated Origins of Social Security: African Americans and the Welfare State* (Chapel Hill: University of North Carolina Press, 2006).

33. Jere Mangione, *The Dream and the Deal* (Boston: Little, Brown, 1972), 29.

34. Ibid., 9.

35. Bernard DeVoto, "Unemployed Writers," *Saturday Review of Literature*, 31 October 1936, 8.

36. Mangione, *Dream*, 98–99.

37. Ibid., 194.

38. Gabbin, *Sterling A. Brown*, 70; Monty Penkower, *The Federal Writers' Project* (Urbana: University of Illinois Press, 1977) 67. For her statistic, Gabbin cites the work of Allen Francis Kifer, "The Negro under the New Deal, 1933–1941," Ph.D. diss., University of Wisconsin, 1961, 237.

39. Anzia Yezierska, *Red Ribbon on a White Horse* (London: Virago, 1987), 188–89.

40. Mangione, *Dream*, 9.

41. Gabbin, *Sterling A. Brown*, 68.

42. Sterling A. Brown, "The Negro in Washington," in *Washington: City and Capital* (Washington, DC: U.S. Government Printing Office, 1936), 90, quoted in ibid., 81.

43. Mangione, *Dream*, 259.

44. Norman Yetman, "Ex-Slave Interviews and the Historiography of Slavery," *American Quarterly* (Summer 1984): 181–210; see also Earl Lewis, "To Turn as on a Pivot: Writing African Americans into a History of Overlapping Diasporas," *American Historical Review* 100 (June 1995): 765–87, esp. 772 and the discussion of "near total autonomist" historians John Blassingame, George Rawick, Herbert Guttman, Lawrence Levine, and Sterling Stuckey; and John W. Blassingame, "Using the Testimony of Ex-Slaves: Approaches and Problems," *Journal of Southern History* (November 1975): 473–92.

45. Editorial Comment, *Direction: Special Issue American Stuff* (February 1938): 2.

46. Editorial Comment, *Direction* (May 1938): 32.

47. George A. Rollins, letter to Sterling Brown, 2 and 8 March and 23 April 1937, reel 23, in *New Deal Agencies and Black America*, ed. John Kirby (Frederick, MD: University Publications of America, 1983).

48. John B. Streater, Jr., "The National Negro Congress, 1936–1947," Ph.D. diss., University of Cincinnati, 1981, 3–4; Robert H. Brisbane, *The Black Vanguard* (1970; Valley Forge, PA: Judson, 1975), 150; Klehr, *The Heyday of American Communism*, 345.

49. Louis E. Martin, "The National Negro Congress," *Challenge* (June 1936): 30, 32.

50. A. N. Fields, "Red Scare at Race Congress Proves to Be a Colossal Joke," *Chicago Defender*, 22 February 1936, 2.

51. John P. Davis, letter to Richard Wright, 29 January 1936, RW, box 102, folder 1490.

52. Fields, "Red Scare."

53. Klehr, *Heyday*, 348.

54. Ibid., 346.

55. Walker, "Richard Wright," *How I Wrote Jubilee and Other Essays on Life and Literature* (New York: Feminist Press, 1990), 34.

56. Margaret Walker, *Richard Wright: Daemonic Genius* (1988; New York: Amistad, 1991), 71.

57. Alan Wald, *Exiles from a Future Time* (Chapel Hill: University of North Carolina Press, 2002,) 158.

58. Walker, "Richard Wright," 35; Robert Bone, "Richard Wright and the Chicago Renaissance," *Callaloo* (Summer 1986): 462; Walker, *Daemonic Genius*, 71–72.

59. Rena Fraden, *Blueprints for a Black Federal Theatre 1935–1939* (1994; New York: Cambridge University Press, 1996), 128.

60. Frank Marshall Davis, *Livin' the Blues* (Madison: University of Wisconsin Press, 1992), 245.

61. Fern Gayden, interview with Horace Cayton, notes, HC, box 12, folder "Gayden, Fern."

62. Monroe N. Work, *Negro Year Book and Annual Encyclopedia of the Negro* (Tuskegee: Monroe N. Work, 1935, 1936, 1937).

63. Marian Minus, letter to Dorothy West, n.d. [ca. 6 Oct. 1936], DW, box 2, folder "Letters."

64. Walker, "Richard Wright," 37, 47–48.

65. Margaret Walker, letter to Richard Wright, 7 June 1939, RW, box 107, folder 1667.

66. Davis, *Livin'*, 241.

67. Wright, *Black Boy*, 285–86.

68. Richard Wright, "Black Confessions," RW, box 9, folder 202.

69. Gayden, interview with Cayton.

70. Margaret Walker, letter to Richard Wright, n.d., RW.

71. Fraden, *Blueprints*, 122.

72. Mangione, *Dream*, 155.

73. Lionel Abel, *The Intellectual Follies* (New York: Norton, 1984), 60.

74. Ellen Tarry, *The Third Door* (1955; Westport, CT: Negro Universities Press, 1971), 140–41.

75. Mangione, *Dream*, 175.

76. Penkower, *Federal Writers' Project*, 190–91.

77. Yezierska, *Red Ribbon*, 170.

78. "WPA Writers Firm I 'Stay-In' Strike," *New York Times*, 4 December 1936, 4.

79. Alfred Kazin, *Starting Out in the Thirties* (1965; Ithaca: Cornell University Press, 1989), 139.

80. Kathleen Hauke, *Ted Poston: Pioneer American Journalist* (Athens: University of Georgia Press, 1998), 73.

81. Harry Roskolenko, *When I Was Last on Cherry Street* (New York: Stein and Day, 1965), 153.

82. Mangione, *Dream*, 309.

CHAPTER 3: A NEW KIND OF *CHALLENGE*

1. Wayne Cooper, *Claude McKay: Rebel Sojourner in the Harlem Renaissance* (Baton Rouge: Louisiana State University Press, 1987), 218.

2. Ibid., 327.

3. Frank, *Memoirs of Waldo Frank*, 188.

4. Cooper, *Claude McKay*, 307, 311.

5. Claude McKay, *A Long Way from Home* (1937; New York: Harcourt, 1970), 345.

6. Marian Minus, "Present Trends of Negro Literature," *Challenge* (Spring 1937): 10.

7. Dorothy West, "Dear Reader," *Challenge* (Spring 1937): 41.

8. Richard Wright, "Negro Writers Launch Literary Quarterly," *Daily Worker*, 8 June 1937, 7.

9. Thomas Wolfe, Jr., "The League of American Writers: Communist Organizational Activity among American Writers, 1929–1942," Ph.D. diss., Yale University, 1956, 159.

10. Earl Browder, untitled, in *The Writer in a Changing World*, ed. Henry Hart (New York: American Writers Congress, 1937), 52–53.

11. Ellen Tarry, *The Third Door: The Autobiography of an American Negro Woman* (New York: David McKay, 1955), 132.

12. Mary McCarthy, *Intellectual Memoirs* (New York: Harcourt Brace Jovanovich, 1992), 72.

13. Franklin Folsom, *Days of Anger, Days of Hope* (Niwot: University of Colorado Press, 1994), 96.

14. Claude McKay, letter to Dorothy West, 10 June 1937, DW, carton 1, folder 10.

15. Saxe Commins, letter to Richard Wright, 21 July 1937, RW, box 105, folder 1570.

16. Richard Wright, letter to Alain Locke, 8 July 1937, AL, box 164–96, folder 3.

17. Ibid.

18. Dorothy West, letter to Alain Locke, 14 September 1937, AL, box 164–74, folder "New Challenge."

19. Alain Locke, "Spiritual Truancy," *New Challenge* 1 (1937): 84.

20. Ibid.; see Lawrence Jackson, "The Aftermath: The Harlem Renaissance Twenty Years Later," in *Cambridge Companion to the Harlem Renaissance,* ed. George Hutchinson, (New York: Cambridge University Press, 2007), 239–53.

21. Richard Wright, "Blueprint for Negro Writing," draft typescript, RW, box 5, folder 76.

22. Richard Wright, "Blueprint for Negro Writing," *New Challenge* 1 (1937): 53.

23. Ibid., 58.

24. Hurston, *Their Eyes Were Watching God*, 254, 255.

25. Marian Minus, "Their Eyes Were Watching God," *New Challenge* (Spring 1937): 87.

26. Robert Hemenway, *Zora Neale Hurston: A Literary Biography* (Urbana: University of Illinois Press, 1977), 96–97.

27. Gabbin, *Sterling A. Brown*, 51.

28. Sterling Brown, "Luck Is a Fortune," *Nation*, 16 October 1937, 210.

29. Ibid.

30. Richard Wright, "Between Laughter and Tears," *New Masses*, 5 October 1937, 23+.

31. W. A. Hunton, "The Adventures of the Brown Girl in Search of Her Life," *Journal of Negro Education* (January 1938): 72.

32. Nick Aaron Ford, *The Contemporary Negro Novel* (Boston: Meador, 1936), 96.

33. Ibid., 93, 102.

34. Elizabeth Hart, "Within the All Negro World," review of *Ollie Miss* by George Wylie Henderson, *New York Herald Tribune*, 24 February 1935, 4.

35. James Hubert, "They Happen to Be Black," review of *Ollie Miss* by George Wylie Henderson, *Survey Graphic* (June 1935): 308.

36. For Margaret Walker, see Alan Wald, *Exiles from a Future Time* (Chapel Hill: University of North Carolina Press, 2002,) 158. For Ralph Ellison, see Barbara Foley, "Ralph Ellison as Proletarian Journalist," *Science and Society* (Winter 1998–1999): 537–56; Foley, "Reading Redness: Politics and Audience in Ralph Ellison's Early Short Fiction," *Journal of Narrative Theory* 29 (Fall 1999) 323–39; Foley, "From Communism to Brotherhood: The Drafts of *Invisible Man*," in *Left of the Color Line: Race, Radicalism, and Twentieth-Century Literature of the United States*, ed. Bill V. Mullen and James Smethurst (Chapel Hill: University of North Carolina Press, 2003), 163–82; and Arnold Rampersad, *Ralph Ellison: A Biography* (New York: Knopf, 2007), 93.

37. Marian Minus, "Retrospect and Analysis: After the Genteel Tradition," DW, box 3, folder 58.

38. Robert Hayden, "Diana," DW, box 3, folder 58.

CHAPTER 4: THE TRIUMPH OF CHICAGO REALISM

1. "15,000 Attend Exposition of Negro Advance," *Chicago Tribune*, 19 July 1940, 25.

2. St. Claire Drake and Horace Cayton, *Black Metropolis: A Study of Negro Life in a Northern City* (New York: Harcourt, Brace, 1945), 399, 217.

3. James B. McKee, *Sociology and the Race Problem: A Failure of Perspective* (Urbana: University of Illinois Press, 1993), 109–10.

4. See Jerry G. Watts, "On Reconsidering Park, Johnson, Du Bois, Frazier and Reid: Reply to Benjamin Bowser's 'The Contributions of Blacks to Sociological Knowledge,'" *Phylon* (Fall 1983): 282–85.

5. Langston Hughes, letter to Arna Bontemps, n.d. [Friday], in *Arna Bontemps–Langston Hughes, Letters 1925–1967*, selected and ed. Charles H. Nichols (1980; New York: Paragon, 1990), 110.

6. Paul Healy, "Former Nomad Heads Largest Negro Center," *Chicago Tribune*, 5 April 1942, S6; Richard S. Hobbs, *Cayton Legacy: An African American Family* (Pullman: Washington State University Press, 2002), 117.

7. Grace Lee, letter to Horace Cayton, 22 November 1963, HC, box 1, folder "Boggs, Grace Lee."

8. Edwin Embree, *Investment in People: The Story of the Julius Rosenwald Fund* (New York: Harper, 1949), 15.

9. Embree, *Investment in People*, 176.

10. Edwin Embree, "Timid Billions," *Harpers Magazine* (March 1949): 32.

11. Ibid., 31.

12. Embree, *Investment in People*, 155.

13. Jayne R. Beilke, "The Changing Emphasis of the Rosenwald Fellowship Program 1928–1948," *Journal of Negro Education* 66 (1997): 9. Beilke is quoting a "Meeting of the Rosenwald Fund" report from May 1934.

14. Embree, *Investment in People*, 152.

15. "The Changing Emphasis of the Rosenwald Fellowship," 12. Beilke is citing a "Memorandum from Charles S. Johnson," 10 February 1948.

16. Margaret Walker, *How I Wrote Jubilee and Other Essays*, ed. Maryemma Graham (New York: Feminist Press, 1990), 16.

17. Gwendolyn Brooks, *Report from Part One* (Detroit: Broadside Press, 1972), 68.

18. Anne Knupfer, *The Chicago Black Renaissance and Women's Activism* (Urbana: University Illinois Press, 2006), 61. Knupfer quotes an unnamed librarian from a Chicago *Bee* article of 18 February 1945: 9.

19. Margaret Burroughs, interview, July 2008.

20. Frank Marshall Davis, "Chicago's Congo," *I Am the American Negro* (1937), in *Black Moods: Collected Poems of Frank Marshall Davis*, ed. John Edgar Tidwell (Urbana: University of Illinois Press, 2002), 5.

21. Frank Marshall Davis, "Ebony over Granite: VIII. Roosevelt Smith," *Black Man's Verse* (1935), in *Black Moods*, 52.

22. Frank Marshall Davis, "Forewarning," *I Am the American Negro*, in *Black Moods*, 57.

23. Margaret Walker, "Preface," *This Is My Century: New and Collected Poems* (Athens: University of Georgia Press, 1989), xii.

24. Walker, *How I Wrote Jubilee*, 35.

25. "Poet Attends Reception Honoring 200 Writers," *Chicago Defender*, 5 December 1942, 4.

26. Charles H. Nichols, prologue, in *Arna Bontemps—Langston Hughes, Letters 1925–1967*, 5; Kirkland Jones, *Renaissance Man from Louisiana: A Biography of Arna Wendell Bontemps* (Westport, CT: Greenwood, 1992), 87–89.

27. Jere Mangione, *Dream and the Deal: The Federal Writers' Project, 1935–1943* (Syracuse: Syracuse University Press, 1996), 126.

28. Lucy Tompkins, " 'In Dubious Battle' and Other Recent Works of Fiction: Slave's Rebellion," *New York Time Book Review*, 2 February 1936, 7.

29. Julie Goldsmith Gilbert, *Ferber: A Biography* (New York: Doubleday, 1978), 295.

30. Ibid., 295.

31. Waters Turpin, *These Low Grounds* (New York: Harper, 1937), 313.

32. Augusta Tucker "A Distinguished Novel of Negroes in Maryland," *New York Times*, 26 September 1937, 98.

33. Ralph Ellison, "Creative and Cultural Lag," *New Challenge* 2 (1937): 90.

34. Alfred Kazin, "Odyssey of the Twenties: An Affectionate and Moving Chronicle of Middle-Class Negro Life," review of *O Canaan!* by Waters Turpin, *New York Herald Tribune*, 23 July 1939, 4.

35. Ulysses Lee, "Novels of Chicago," *Opportunity* (October 1939): 312.

36. "Brick Slayer Is Likened to a Jungle Beast: Ferocity Is Reflected in Nixon's Features," *Chicago Tribune*, 5 June 1938, 6.

37. Richard Wright, letter to Eleanor Roosevelt, n.d. [1938], RW, box 105, folder 1582.

38. Eleanor Roosevelt, letter to Eugene Saxton, 4 March 1938, RW, box 105, folder 1582.

39. Sterling Brown, "From the Inside," *Nation,* 16 April 1938, 448.

40. Gabbin, *Sterling A. Brown*, 81.

41. Sterling Brown, letter to Richard Wright, 22 May 1939, RW, box 95 folder 1238.

42. Sterling A. Brown, "Bitter Fruit of the Tree," *Nation*, 26 August 1939, 223.

43. Brown to Wright, 23 January 1939, RW.

44. Sterling Brown, "The American Race Problem as Reflected in American Literature," *Journal of Negro Higher Education* (July 1939): 289.

45. J. Saunders Redding, *No Day of Triumph* (New York: Harper, 1942), 39.

46. Horace Cayton, "*Black Boy*: Negroes Hatred of Whites and Fear of His Hate in Wright's Autobiography," *Pittsburgh Courier*, 13 January 1945, 7; Horace Cayton, "The Psychological Approach to Race Relations," *Reed College Bulletin* 25 (November 1946): 6, 9, 10, 15, 26.

47. Anthony Platt, "The Rebellious Teaching Career of E. Franklin Frazier," *Journal of Blacks in Higher Education* (Autumn 1996): 88.

48. J. Saunders Redding, *To Make a Poet Black* (1939; Cornell University Press, 1988), 10.

49. Ibid., 120.

50. Richard Wright, *Native Son* (New York: Harpers, 1940), 62.

51. Ibid., 292.

52. Ibid., 40, 46.

53. Ibid., 331–32.

54. Richard Kluger, *Simple Justice* (New York: Vintage, 1977), 166.

55. Richard Wright, letter to Paul Reynolds, 13 February 1940, RW, box 103, folder 1531.

56. Richard Wright, "How Bigger Was Born," *Native Son*, restored ed. (1940; New York: Harper Perennial, 1994), 583.

57. Hazel Rowley, *Richard Wright: The Life and Times* (New York: Holt, 2001), 202.

58. Bucklin Moon, *High Cost of Prejudice* (New York: Julian Messner, 1947), 38.

59. Joan Shelly Rubin, "Early History of the Book of the Month Club," *Journal of American History* (March 1985): 783, 797.

60. John Farrar, "Ten Years of Book Clubs," *English Journal* (May 1936): 351–52.

61. Dorothy Canfield Fisher, introduction to *Native Son* by Richard Wright (New York: Harper's, 1940), x.

62. "Public Stampedes," *Publisher's Weekly*, 9 March 1940, n.p.; "Native Son Sells Rapidly," *Publisher's Weekly*, 16 March 1940, 1161; "Best Sellers of the Week," *Publisher's Weekly*, 18 May 1940, 1918; "Best Sellers of the Week," *Publisher's Weekly*, 15 June 1940, 2281.

63. "Best Sellers of 1940," *Publisher's Weekly*, 18 January 1941, 226–28.

64. Rowley, *Richard Wright*, 229.

65. Paul Reynolds, *The Middleman* (New York: Morrow, 1972), 133–34.

66. James W. Ivy, *Crisis* (April 1940): 122.

67. Sterling A. Brown, *Opportunity* (June 1940): 185–86.

68. *Chicago Defender*, 16 March 1940, 22.

69. Arna Bontemps, letter to Langston Hughes, 26 January 1941, in Rowley, *Richard Wright*, 228.

70. Lillian Johnson, "'Native Son Is a Personal Triumph but of No Value to a Nation," *Baltimore Afro-American*, 13 April 1940, 13.

71. Ben Davis, Jr., *Sunday Worker*, 14 April 1940, sec. 2, pp. 4, 6.

72. Chester Himes, "'Native Son': Pros and Cons," *New Masses*, 21 May 1940, 23–24.

73. Sterling A. Brown, "Insight, Courage, Craftsmanship," review of *Native Son* by Richard Wright, *Opportunity* (June 1940): 185.

74. Ralph Ellison, letter to Richard Wright, 22 April 1940, RW, box 97, folder 1314.

75. Alain Locke, "Of Native Sons, Real and Otherwise," *Opportunity* (January 1941): 8.

76. Horace Cayton, "English Liberals: Writer's Account of S. Carolina Lynching Proves Distasteful," *Pittsburgh Courier*, 28 June 1947, 7.

77. For example, the *New Yorker's* description of opera singer Marian Anderson in "Talk of the Town: Dark Contralto," *New Yorker*, 18 January 1936, 9–10. In this short profile, the magazine wrote, "She made her first concert appearance . . . with another pickaninny"; "Her father sold ice and coal, and her mother took in washing; the family lived in a single rented room. They all used to sing spirituals on rainy Sundays to keep cheerful"; "There's no trace of a southern Negro accent in her voice" (9). See also A. J. Liebling, "Sparring Partner," *New Yorker*, 24 June 1939, 25–28; Henry Roth, "Broker," *New Yorker*, 18 November 1939, 60–64; Margaret Case Harriman, "Nirvana Is Near Savannah," *New Yorker*, 3 February 1940: 32, 34, 36, 38–39. However, by November 1940 the tenor of the fiction was a bit different. A short story by Edward Newhouse, "Ten Years on a Desert Island," *New Yorker*, 23 November 1940, 20–22, featured black defiance and aggressiveness in the face of white provocation. Horace Cayton noted the problem of the *New Yorker* in the magazine's mishandling of a lynching story, "Opera in Greenville."

78. Theodore G. Bilbo, "An African Home for Our Negroes," *Living Age* (June 1940): 328, 330.

79. David L. Cohn, "Sharecropping in the Delta," *Atlantic Monthly* (May 1937): 583. Cohn wrote several pieces for the magazine on the South and international affairs, and he steadily offered his patronizing view of blacks in essays like "Black Troubadour," in the *Atlantic* from July 1938.

80. David L. Cohn, "The Negro Novel: Richard Wright," *Atlantic Monthly* (May 1940): 659.

81. Richard Wright, "I Bite the Hand That Feeds Me," *Atlantic Monthly* (June 1940): 828.

CHAPTER 5: BIGGER THOMAS AMONG THE LIBERALS

1. "Common Council for American Unity," *Common Ground* (Autumn 1940): front cover.

2. J. Saunders Redding, "A Second Look: There Is a magazine Called Common Ground," *Baltimore Afro-American*, 6 April 1946, 4.

3. Archibald MacLeish, "New Land: New World," *Common Ground* (Summer 1941): 3.

4. Phillip McGuire, "Desegregation of the Armed Forces: Black Leadership, Protest and World War II," *Journal of Negro History* (Spring 1983): 154; "Defeatist Press Scored by MacLeish," *New York Times*, 18 April 1942, 13.

5. "Apology," *Phylon* (1st Quarter 1940): 4.

6. Abby Arthur Johnson and Ronald Mayberry Johnson, *Propaganda and Aesthetics: The Literary Politics of African American Magazines in the Twentieth Century* (Amherst: University of Massachusetts Press, 1991), 145.

7. Elmer Carter, letter to John Henrik Clarke, 5 September 1941, JHC, box 7, folder "general correspondence 1940–1944."

8. "From Where I Sit," advertisement for *If He Hollers Let Him Go* by Chester Himes, *Publisher's Weekly*, 10 January 1945, 29.

9. "Foreward," *Negro Youth* (April 1941): n.p.

10. Ernest Kaiser, letter to the author, April 1999. Negro Publication Society board member Ernest Kaiser claims that the group published a number in 1944 called "The South Moves West."

11. Ralph Ellison, "Recent Negro Fiction," *New Masses*, 5 August 1941, 24, 26.

12. "Statement of Policy," *Negro Quarterly* (Spring 1942): 4.

13. Sterling Brown, "The Negro Author and His Publisher," *Negro Quarterly* (Spring 1942): 14.

14. Stanley Young, "Tough and Tender," *New York Times Book Review*, 25 June 1939: sec. 6, p. 7.

15. V. F. Calverton, letter to Melvin B. Tolson, 17 October 1939, MBT, box 1, folder "C."

16. Hugh Gloster, "Zora Neale Hurston, Novelist and Folklorist," *Phylon* (2nd Quarter 1943): 158

17. Arna Bontemps, review of *Dust Tracks on the Road*, *New York Tribune Book Review*, 22 November 1942, 3.

18. "Zora Hurston Denies Saying the Race Better Off in the South," *Atlanta Daily World*, 3 March 1943, 3.

19. Langston Hughes, *The Big Sea* (1940; New York: Thunder's Mouth, 1986), 228.

20. William Wells Brown, slave-born author of *Clotel: Or the President's Daughter*, published in 1858 and considered in the 1940s the first novel by an African American.

21. J. Saunders Redding, letter to Richard Wright, 18 August 1942, RW, box 105, folder 1572.

22. J. Saunders Redding, "The Alien Land of Richard Wright," in *Soon, One Morning*, ed. Herbert Hill (New York: Knopf, 1968), 53.

23. Richard Wright, introduction to *No Day of Triumph* by J. Saunders Redding (New York: Harper's, 1943), n.p.

24. J. Saunders Redding, *No Day of Triumph* (New York: Harpers, 1942), 119–20.

25. Ibid., 138.

26. Ibid., 170.

27. Ibid. 300.

28. Ibid., 260, 295.

29. See W. T. Couch "Publisher's Introduction," in *What the Negro Wants*, ed. Rayford Logan (University of North Carolina Press, 1944), x–xxi; Kenneth Janken, *Rayford Logan: The Dilemma of the African American Intellectual* (Amherst: University of Massachusetts Press, 1993), 154–55.

30. Redding, *No Day of Triumph*, dust jacket interior flap.

31. Wallace Stegner, "How Serious Is Our Race Problem," *Atlantic* (December 1942): 130.

32. Malcolm Cowley, "Journey in the Slave States," *New Republic*, 12 October 1942, 470.

33. William Shands Meacham, "Paradoxes in Our Society," *New York Times Book Review*, 25 October 1942, 8.

34. Edward Aswell, letter to J. Saunders Redding, 16 April 1942, JSR, box 9, folder 31.

35. N.T., review of *No Day of Triumph* by J. Saunders Redding, *Phylon* (1st Quarter 1943): 88, 89.

36. John Lovell, "The Things So Strange and So Marvelous," *Journal of Negro Education* 12 (Spring 1943): 220.

37. W. M. Brewer, "No Day of Triumph," *Journal of Negro History* (January 1943): 109.

38. J. Saunders Redding, *On Being Negro in America* (1951; New York: Bantam, 1964), 62, 90.

39. Horace Cayton, letter to Richard Wright, 15 December 1943, RW, box 95, folder 1254.

40. Cayton to Wright, 22 January 1945.

41. Horace R. Cayton, "Negro Morale," *Opportunity* (December 1941): 375.

42. Ralph Ellison, draft letter to Horace Cayton, n.d. [ca. May 1942], RE, box 21, folder "Negro Quarterly"; Lawrence Jackson, *Ralph Ellison: Emergence of Genius* (New York: Wiley, 2002), 268.

43. Ellison, draft letter to Cayton.

44. Horace R. Cayton, "Fighting for White Folks," *Nation* (September 1942): 268.

45. Richard S. Hobbs, *Cayton Legacy: An African American Family* (Pullman: Washington State University Press, 2002), 123–24. Cayton became aware of the investigation in 1941.

46. Chester B. Himes, "Now Is the Time! Here Is the Place!," *Opportunity* (September 1942): 271.

47. See Harvard Sitkoff, "Racial Militancy and Interracial Violence," *American Journal of History* (January 1971): 661–81.

48. Chester B. Himes, "Negro Martyrs Are Needed," *Crisis* (May 1944): 159.

49. Chester Himes, Federal Bureau of Investigation file #105-2502; SAC New York, letter to J. Edgar Hoover, 12 June 1944.

50. J. Saunders Redding, "A Negro Speaks for His People," *Atlantic Monthly* (March 1943): 63, 62.

51. Ibid., 62.

52. Edward Larocquetinker, "New Editions, Fine and Otherwise," *New York Times Book Review*, 13 April 1941, 24; "Antioch Takes Up Post-War Problems," 22 June 1941, D4.

53. Luis Alberto Sanchez y Sanchez, "The North-American Negro," *Antioch Review* (Fall 1942): 365.

54. J. Saunders Redding, "The Black Man's Burden," *Antioch Review* (Winter 1943): 587.

55. Ibid., 594.

56. Pearl T. Robinson, "Blacks in the Republican Party," *Political Science Quarterly* (Summer 1982): 211 (table 1).

57. Chester Himes, *Lonely Crusade* (1947; New York: Thunder's Mouth Press, 1986), 144.

58. James Boyd, "Strategy for Negroes," *Nation,* 26 June 1943, 886.

59. Horace Cayton, "The Negro's Challenge," *Nation,* 3 July 1943, 10.

60. Cayton, "The Negro's Challenge," 11.

61. Charles V. Hamilton, *Adam Clayton Powell Jr.: The Political Biography of an American Dilemma* (New York: Atheneum, 1991), 105.

62. Constance Webb, *Not Without Love: Memoirs* (Hanover, NH: University Press of New England, 2003), 148-49.

63. Alan Wald, *Trinity of Passion* (Chapel Hill: University of North Carolina Press, 2007), 111.

64. Wald, *Trinity of Passion,* 111-18 passim.

65. Ann Petry, letter to Ewart Guinier, 10 June 1942, ALP, box 7, folder 20.

66. Eileen Lange, letter to George Bye, 1 December 1943, DW, carton 1, folder 20 "Correspondence with Agents and Publishers 1943-1946."

67. Elizabeth Boutelle, letter to George Bye, 3 April 1944, DW.

68. Hugh MacNair Kahler, letter to George Bye, 11 October 1944, DW.

69. Eleanor Daniels, letter to Ann Petry, 28 February 1944, ALP, box 14, folder 11.

70. Carl Ruthaven Offord, *The White Face* (New York: Robert McBride, 1943), 312.

71. Claudia Jones, "Maiden Book of New Author Deals with Negro Problems," *Daily Worker* 13 June 1943, 7, quoted in Wald, *Trinity of Passion*, 138.

72. Henry Lee Moon, "The Promised Land," *New Republic*, 31 May 1943, 741.

73. Rose Feld, "Flight to Harlem," *New York Times Book Review*, 23 May 1943, 12.

74. Diana Trilling, "Fiction in Review," *Nation*, 5 June 1943, 816.

75. Edwin Embree, letter to Horace Cayton, 29 April 1943, JUL, box 178, folder 7.

76. Jervis Anderson, *A. Philip Randolph: A Biographical Portrait* (New York: Harcourt, 1973); Merle Reed, "The FBI, MOWM, and CORE: 1941-1947," *Journal of Black Studies* (June 1991): 465-69; Hilmar Jensen, "The Rise of an African American Left: John P. Davis and the National Negro Congress," Ph.D. diss. Cornell University 1997), 508-18; "Editorial Comment," *Negro Quarterly* (Winter–Spring 1943): 298-99. The editorial board of *Negro Quarterly* was made up of Angelo Herndon, Communist and ex-political prisoner, Ralph Ellison, *New Masses* journalist and League of American Writers officer, and Ernest Kaiser, Schomburg librarian.

77. Cayton to Wright, 30 October 1944.

CHAPTER 6: FRIENDS IN NEED OF NEGROES

1. John Hope Franklin, interview, October 2004.

2. Harry Washington Greene, *Holders of Doctorates among American Negroes* (Boston: Meador, 1943), 225.

3. L. D. Swingler, "Thrown From Train: August 1942," *Atlanta Daily World*, 27 August 1942, in *Reporting Civil Rights: Part One American Journalism* (New York: Library of America, 1997), 21.

4. Lillian Smith, letter to William Haygood, 10 February 1943, in *How Am I to Be Heard: Letters of Lillian Smith*, ed. Margaret Rose Gladney (Chapel Hill: University of North Carolina Press, 1993), 67–70.

5. Bucklin Moon, letter to Edwin Embree, 24 November 1944, JUL, box 436, folder "Moon."

6. "Bucklin Moon, 'Lighter Brother'," *Chicago Defender*, 29 September 1945, 11.

7. Valerie Boyd, *Wrapped in Rainbows* (New York: Scribner, 2003), 241–43.

8. Bucklin Moon, "Boats for Hire," *Harper's Magazine* (September 1938): 344–51.

9. The early work of Lawrence D. Reddick was especially devoted to debunking popular stereotypes of sentimental blacks, and he worked with the National Negro Congress and the Hollywood Mobilization Committee to write a code for representations of blacks in film. See "The Year's Worst Novel," *Opportunity* (December 1941): 376–77; "Get Tough with Racial Slander," *New Masses*, 20 October 1942: 25–26; "Educational Programs for the Improvement of Race Relations: Motion Pictures Radio, The Press, and Libraries (in Educational Programs for the Improvement of Race Relations)," *Journal of Negro Education* (Summer 1944): 367–89.

10. Bucklin Moon, *Darker Brother* (New York: Doubleday, 1943), 245.

11. Rackham Holt, "Latest Fiction," *New York Times Book Review*, 19 September 1943, 5.

12. Thomas Sancton, "Novels and Negroes," *New Republic*, 4 October 1943, 464.

13. Elizabeth Lee Wheaton, *Mr. George's Joint* (New York: Dutton, 1941), 54, 66.

14. C. M. "Books and Authors," *New York Times Book Review*, 9 January 1944, 10; "Doubleday, Doran Plans Carver Award," *Publisher's Weekly*, 18 December 1943, 2239.

15. Bucklin Moon, "Book Boom," *Negro Digest* (April 1946): 79–80.

16. Bucklin Moon, "Memoir," BM, box 1, folder 18.

17. Will Lissner, "Soule Is Dropped by New Republic," *New York Times*, 20 December 1946, 21.

18. James T. Farell, "Seven Questions," *Partisan Review* (Summer 1939): 31, 32.

19. Malcolm Cowley, *The Dream of the Golden Mountains* (1964; New York: Penguin, 1980), 289.

20. George Orwell, "'Liberal' Fifth Column," *Partisan Review* (Summer 1946): 279–93.

21. Thomas Sancton, letter to Edwin Embree, 11 April 1943, JUL, box 445, folder 9.

22. Tess Crager, letter to Lebaron Barker, 31 May 1953, KMD, box 153, folder "Tess Crager Correspondence."

23. Fannie Cook, "Somebody," *New York Times Book Review*, 20 October 1947, 10.

24. Stephen Jay Gould, *The Mismeasure of Man* (New York: Norton, 1981), 175, 191–92, 219–20.

25. Sydney Bailey, "America's Race Problem," *Contemporary Review* 168 (1945): 43–48; see also "The Negro: His Future in America," *New Republic*, 18 October 1943, 537. Editors reproduce a table from Otto Klineburg's "Race Differences," featuring intelligence test data from black and white World War I army recruits.

26. Virginius Dabney, "Nearer and Nearer the Precipice," *Atlantic Monthly* (January 1943): 94–100; James Boyd, "Strategy for Negroes," *Nation*, 26 June 1943, 884–887.

27. Thomas Sancton, "The Waller Case," *New Republic*, 13 July 1942, 46.

28. Thomas Sancton, "To the Curator of the Nieman Foundation," January 1947, JUL, box 445, folder 9.

29. Robert Penn Warren, "The Briar Patch," in *I'll Take My Stand*, by Twelve Southerners (New York: Harper, 1930), 260, 264.

30. Egerton, *Speak Now Against the Day*, 66; Forrest G. Robinson, "A Combat with the Past: Robert Penn Warren on Race and Slavery," *American Literature* (September 1995): 511–30.

31. Robert Penn Warren, "Cowley's Faulkner," *New Republic*, 26 August 1946, 235.

32. Richard Pells, *The Liberal Mind in a Conservative Age: American Intellectuals in the 1940s and 1950s* (New York: Harper, 1985), 65.

33. Donald Davidson, "Preface to Decision," *Sewanee* (Summer 1945): 409. .

34. Ibid., 394, 409.

35. Anthony Julius, *T. S. Eliot, Anti-Semitism, and Literary Form* (New York: Thames and Hudson, 2003).

36. Allen Tate, "Mr. Davidson and the Race Problem," *Sewanee Review* (Fall 1945): 660.

37. Hodding Carter, *The Winds of Fear* (New York: Farrar, Rinehart, 1943), 77.

38. Thomas Sancton, "Southern Liberal," *New Republic*, 9 September 1946, 292.

39. [Unsigned editorial], "The Negro: His Future in America, A Special Section," *New Republic*, 18 October 1943, 535, 536.

40. Thomas Sancton, "The South Needs Help," *Common Ground* (Winter 1943): 12.

41. Thomas Sancton, "Race Clash," *Harper's* (January 1944): 136.

42. Thomas Sancton, "The Silver Horn," *Harper's* (February 1944): 266.

43. Thomas Sancton, "The Race Question," *Negro Quarterly* (Fall 1942): 199, 200.

44. Ann Petry, letter to Helen Chisholm, n.d. [ca. summer 1943], FHC, box 7, folder 5.

CHAPTER 7: "BEATING THAT BOY"

1. Edwin Seaver, *So Far So Good* (Westport, CT: Lawrence Hill, 1986), 146.

2. Edwin Seaver, preface to *Cross-Section* (New York: L. B. Fischer, 1944), viii.

3. Edwin Seaver, letter to Richard Wright, 8 September 1943, and memorandum to Max Scherman, RW, box 106, folder 1604.

4. Lillian Smith, letter to Sterling Brown, 29 April 1943, SAB, box 9, folder "S."

5. Lillian Smith, "Democracy Was Not a Candidate," *Common Ground* (Winter 1943): 7–10; Smith, "Growing into Freedom," *Common Ground* (Autumn 1943): 47–52; Smith, "Southern Defensive-II," *Common Ground* (Spring 1944): 43–45.

6. Anne C. Loveland, *Lillian Smith: A Southerner Confronting the South* (Baton Rouge: Louisiana State University Press, 1986), 76.

7. "Best Sellers of the Week," *Publisher's Weekly*, 26 February 1944, 972; 25 March 1944, 1301.

8. Curtis Hitchcock, "Boston and 'Strange Fruit'," *Publisher's Weekly*, 8 April 1944, 1447–48.

9. "Candidates for the Best Seller List," *Publisher's Weekly*, 1 April 1944, 1375; "Best Sellers of the Week," *Publisher's Weekly*, 8 April 1944, 1468

10. "Best Sellers of the Week," *Publisher's Weekly*, 15 April 1944, 1537; 22 April 1944, 1615; 29 April 1944, 1708.

11. "Publishers Weekly-Ad Club Award Goes to Reynal and Hitchcock," *Publishers Weekly*, 10 March 1945, 1113.

12. "Best Sellers of the Week," *Publisher's Weekly,* 1 July 1944, 42; 12 August 1944, 513; "The Best Sellers of 1944," *Publisher's Weekly,* 20 January 1945, 223.

13. Lillian Smith, *Strange Fruit* (1944; New York: Harcourt, 1972), 142.

14. Ibid., 6.

15. Ibid., 113.

16. Ibid., 103.

17. R.E.C., "Hard Facts and Harder Truths," *Phylon* 11 (3rd Quarter 1950): 81.

18. Smith to Sterling Brown, 15 June 1945.

19. Kenneth Janken, *Rayford Logan: The Dilemma of the African American Intellectual* (Amherst: University Massachusetts Press, 1993), 154–55.

20. W. T. Couch, "Publisher's Introduction," in *What the Negro Wants,* ed. Rayford Logan (Chapel Hill: University of North Carolina Press, 1944), x–xi, xxi.

21. Eugene Holmes, "What the Negro Wants," *Journal of Negro History* (January 1945): 91.

22. Bill Mullen, *Popular Fronts: Chicago and African-American Cultural Politics, 1935–1946* (Champaign: University of Illinois Press, 1999), 198.

23. Kenneth Clark, "The Zoot Effect in Personality: A Race Riot Participant," *Journal of Abnormal Psychology* (April 1945): 141–48.

24. Gunnar Myrdal, *An American Dilemma* (New York: Harper, 1944), 24.

25. Eugene Exman, *The House of Harper: One Hundred and Fifty Years of Publishing* (New York: Harper, 1967), 233.

26. Myrdal, *American Dilemma,* 751–52.

27. Ibid., 56.

28. Ralph Ellison, "An American Dilemma," in *Shadow and Act* (New York: Random House, 1964), 316.

29. Horace Cayton, letter to Richard Wright, 22 October 1944, RW, box 95, folder 1254.

30. Horace Cayton, *Long Old Road* (1964; Seattle: University of Washington Press, 1970), 257–67.

31. Ibid., 310.

32. Richard Wright, introduction to *Black Metropolis,* by St. Clair Drake and Horace Cayton (New York: Harcourt, Brace, 1945), xxvii.

33. Richard Wright, letter to Ralph Ellison, 25 July 1945, RE, box 27, folder "Richard Wright."

34. Horace Cayton, interview, 1964.

35. J. Saunders Redding, "The Alien Land of Richard Wright," in *Black Voices: New Writing by American Negroes,* ed. Herbert Hill (London: Elek Books, 1963), 55.

36. St. Clair Drake and Horace Cayton, *Black Metropolis* (New York: Harcourt, Brace, 1945), 757.

37. Ibid., 284.

38. Ibid., 564.

39. William Tindall, "The Sociological Best Seller," *College English* (November 1947): 55; Robert Gorham Davis, "State of American Writing," *Partisan Review* (August 1948): 869; Lionel Trilling, "Preface," in *Liberal Imagination,* 10; Trilling "Reality in America," in *Liberal Imagination,* 31.

40. Drake and Cayton, *Black Metropolis,* 766.

41. Elaine Ogden McNeil and Horace R. Cayton, "Research on the Urban Negro," *American Journal of Sociology* (September 1941): 183.

42. Charles I. Glicksberg, "Negro Americans and the African Dream," *Phylon* (4th Quarter 1947): 324.

43. Charles I. Glicksberg, "The Negro Cult of the Primitive," *Antioch Review* (March 1944): 48–49.

44. See Jonathan Scott Holloway, *Confronting the Veil: Abram Harris Jr., E. Franklin Frazier, and Ralph Bunche, 1919–1941* (Chapel Hill: University of North Carolina Press, 2002), 127–34.

45. Alan Wald, *The New York Intellectuals* (Chapel Hill: University of North Carolina Press, 1987), 36.

46. Lionel Trilling, "The Mind of Robert Warshow," *Commentary* (June 1961): 502–3.

47. Lionel Trilling, "Elements That Are Wanted," *Partisan Review* (September–October 1940): 368–69.

48. Howard Odum, *Race and Rumors of Race* (Chapel Hill: University of North Carolina Press, 1943), 73–80, 86–89.

49. Lionel Trilling, "The Other Margaret," *Partisan Review* (Fall 1945): 498.

50. Margaret Rodriguiz, "I Had a Colored Maid," *Negro Story* (May–June 1944): 5–8.

51. James T. Farrell, *Literature and Morality* (New York: Vanguard, 1946), 13.

52. Irving Howe, "James T. Farrell: The Critic Calcified," *Partisan Review* (September–October 1947): 545–51.

53. Trilling, "Preface," in *Liberal Imagination*, 10.

54. Trilling, "Reality in America," in *Liberal Imagination*, 31.

CHAPTER 8: AFROLIBERALS AND THE END OF WORLD WAR II

1. Roi Ottley, "Harlem Is Confident But Cautious," *New York Times*, 1 June 1947, SM20.

2. Mary McCarthy, "The Man in the Brooks Brothers Shirt," in *The Company She Keeps* (New York: Simon and Schuster, 1942), 83, 130.

3. Paul Blanchard, "Negro Delinquency in New York," *Journal of Educational Sociology* (October 1942): 120.

4. Richard Wright, letter to Paul Reynolds, 7 March 1939, box 103, folder 1531, RW.

5. Horace Cayton, "A Memoir: The Curtain," *Negro Digest* (December 1968): 15.

6. Constance Webb, *Not Without Love: Memoirs* (Hanover, NH: University Press of New England, 2003), 188–92.

7. Dorothy Canfield Fisher, letter to Richard Wright, 1 July 1944, HAB, box 33, folder 19.

8. Dorothy Canfield Fisher, letter to Edward Aswell, 12 July 1944, HAB, box 33; Fisher, *Keeping Fires Night and Day: Selected Letters of Dorothy Canfield Fisher*, ed. Mark J. Madigan (Columbia: University of Missouri Press, 1993), 235.

9. Richard Wright, *Black Boy* (New York: Harper, 1945), 227.

10. J. Saunders Redding, "The Negro Author: His Publisher, His Public, His Purse," *Publishers' Weekly*, 24 March 1945, 1288; "Candidates for the Best Seller List," *Publishers' Weekly*, 24 March 1945, 1307; "National Best Sellers—March," *Publishers' Weekly*, 7 April 1945, 1471.

11. "Best Sellers of the Week," *Publishers' Weekly*, 28 April 1945, 1768.

12. "Best Sellers of the Week," *Publishers' Weekly*, 30 June 1945, 2527.

13. "The Best Sellers of 1945," *Publishers' Weekly*, 19 January 1946, 298.

14. http://www3.isrl.uiuc.edu/~unsworth/courses/bestsellers/best70.cgi; graph is based on Bowker reports.

15. Ralph Ellison, "Richard Wright's Blues," *Antioch Review* (Summer 1945), in *Shadow and Act*, by Ralph Ellison (New York: Random House, 1964), 79.

16. Richard Wright, *Black Boy* (1945; New York: HarperPerennial, 1993), 172–73.

17. Ibid., 33.

18. Ibid.

19. Leon Edel, *Henry James: The Conquest of London: 1870–1881* (New York: Avon, 1978), 388.

20. Wright, *Black Boy*, 33.

21. Richard Wright, "Black Confessions" [handwritten draft], RW, box 9, folder 202.

22. Ibid., folder 203.

23. Ibid., folder 211.

24. Gwendolyn Brooks, letter to Elizabeth Lawrence, 25 March 1945, HAB, box 5.

25. Daryl Scott, *Contempt and Pity: Social Policy and the Image of the Damaged Black Psyche* (Chapel Hill: University of North Carolina Press, 1997), 98–103.

26. "Topics of the Times," *New York Times*, 13 May 1945, E8.

27. Jere Mangione, letter to Horace Cayton, 28 December 1968, HC, box 2, folder "Jere Mangione."

28. Samuel Sillen, "Richard Wright in Retreat," *New Masses,* 29 August 1944, 25.

29. "Negro Author Criticizes Reds as Intolerant," *New York Herald Tribune*, 28 July 1944, 11, reprinted in *Conversations with Richard Wright*, ed. Kenneth Kinnamon and Michel Fabre (Jackson: University of Mississippi Press, 1993), 51.

30. Ellison, "Richard Wright's Blues," 77.

31. Horace Cayton, "Writing Schools: Mr. Cayton May Be Saying Reality Inhibits Only a Dark and Furtive Zone," *Pittsburgh Courier,* 15 June 1946, 7.

32. Ralph Ellison, addendum draft of letter to Richard Wright, 5 August 1945, RW, box 97, folder 1314; see Lawrence Jackson, *Ralph Ellison: Emergence of Genius* (New York: Wiley, 2002), 314–17.

33. Rampersad, *Ralph Ellison*, 172–73.

34. Brooks, *Report from Part One*, 69.

35. Ibid.

36. Mullen, *Popular Fronts*, 115, 124.

37. "Our Contributors," *Negro Story* (March–April 1945): 57.

38. Alice Browning, "Autobiographical Sketch," ALB, box 1, folder 16.

39. Alice Browning, interview with Horace Cayton, tape recording, HC.

40. Edward Bland, "Social Forces Shaping the Negro Novel," *Negro Quarterly* (Fall 1942): 241, 246, 247.

41. Edward Bland, "Racial Bias and Negro Poetry," *Poetry* (March 1944): 332, 333.

42. Brooks, *Report from Part One*, photo insert, 108.

43. Richard Wright, letter to Edward Aswell, 18 September 1944, HAB, box 33.

44. B.L., review of *A Street in Bronzeville* by Gwendolyn Brooks, *Phylon* (3rd Quarter 1945): 297.

45. John Parker, "A New Singer from the Middle West," *Journal of Negro Education* (Spring 1946): 201.

46. Elizabeth Lawrence, letter to Gwendolyn Brooks, 22 September 1944, microfilm [1976], HAB.

47. Brooks to Lawrence, 28 September 1944.

48. Brooks to Lawrence, 25 October 1944.

49. Brooks to Lawrence, 25 February 1945.

50. Lawrence to Brooks, 20 March 1945.

51. Robert Hayden, *Collected Prose*, ed. Frank Glaysher (Ann Arbor: University of Michigan Press, 1984), 162.

52. Robert Hayden, "Middle Passage," *Phylon* (3rd Quarter 1945), 251.

53. Ibid.

54. Bucklin Moon, *A Street in Bronzeville* (New York: Harpers, 1945), dust jacket.

55. Ralph Ellison, "Beating That Boy," *New Republic*, 22 October 1945, 535-36, in *Shadow and Act*, 99.

56. Ibid.

57. Thomas Sancton, "Unfinished Business," *New Republic*, 3 December 1945, 770.

58. Doxey Wilkerson, "The Negro Press," *Journal of Negro Education* (Autumn 1947): 514.

59. J. Saunders Redding, "A Second Look," *Baltimore Afro-American*, 17 March 1945, 4.

60. Ibid.,10 November 1945, 4.

61. Ibid., 21 April 1945, 4.

62. Ibid.

63. Ibid., 13 April 1946, 4.

64. Ibid., 20 April 1946, 4.

65. Ibid., 29 September 1945, 4.

66. Ibid., 15 September 1945, 4.

67. Ibid., 18 March 1944, 4.

68. Eric F. Goldman, *The Crucial Decade and After: America, 1945-1960* (New York: Vintage, 1961), 52-57.

69. J. Saunders Redding, review of *Trees Along the Highway* by Gloria Pritchard, *Baltimore Afro-American*, 24 April 1954, 2.

70. J. Saunders Redding, "It Is Strange," *Baltimore Afro-American*, 6 February 1950, 6; Redding, "Plea for Book Buying Readers," *Baltimore Afro-American*, 18 January 1958, 2.

71. For a discussion of the industry in the 1890s, and 1920s, see Gene Jarrett, *Deans and Truants* (Philadelphia: University of Pennsylvania Press, 2006); George Hutchinson, *The Harlem Renaissance in Black and White* (Cambridge: Belknap Press of Harvard University, 1995); and John Young, *Black Writers, White Publishers: Marketplace Politics in Twentieth Century African American Literature* (Jackson: University of Mississippi Press, 2006).

72. Sterling A. Brown, "The Negro Author and His Publisher," *Quarterly Review of Higher Education among Negroes* (July 1941): 144.

73. J. Saunders Redding, "A Second Look: Prejudiced Publishers?," *Baltimore Afro-American*, 14 October 1944, 4

74. Hiram Haydn, *Words and Faces* (New York: Harcourt, Brace, Jovanovich, 1974), 51.

75. See Lawrence Jackson, "Saying Things on Paper That Should Never Be Written: Publishing Chester Himes at Doubleday," *African American Review*, forthcoming.

76. J. Saunders Redding, review of *U.S. Stories* edited by Martha Foley and Abraham Rothberg, *Baltimore Afro-American*, 13 August 1949, 6.

77. Redding, "The Negro Author," 1288.

CHAPTER 9: BLACK FUTILITARIANISTS AND THE WELCOME TABLE

1. Chester Himes, "All God's Chilluns Got Pride," *Crisis* (June 1944): 189.

2. Chester Himes, *If He Hollers Let Him Go* (1945; New York: Thunder's Mouth Press, 1986), 121.

3. Edward Margolies and Michel Fabre, *The Several Lives of Chester Himes* (Jackson: University of Mississippi Press, 1997), 34.

4. Himes, *If He Hollers*, 87–88.

5. Isaac Rosenfeld, "With Best Intentions," *New Republic*, 31 December 1945, 909.

6. Patsy Graves, "The Minority Is Hollering," *Opportunity* (April–June 1946): 99.

7. R.E.C., "Race in the Rough," *Phylon* (2nd Quarter 1946): 210–11.

8. J. Saunders Redding, "A Second Look," *Baltimore Afro-American*, 1 June 1946, 4.

9. Horace R. Cayton, "Writing Schools: Mr. Cayton May Be Saying Reality Inhibits [*sic*] Only a Dark and Furtive Zone," *Pittsburgh Courier*, 15 June 1946, 7.

10. Horace R. Cayton, " 'If He Hollers': Los Angeles Writer Has Produced Powerful Novel of American Life," *Pittsburgh Courier*, 3 November 1945, 7.

11. Horace R. Cayton, "Newest 'Hit' Author, Ralph Ellison, Lives Literary World New Form, Writing Style," *Pittsburgh Courier*, 10 May 1952, 9.

12. Horace R. Cayton, "State of Fear: Constant Fear Largely Due to Oppression of Race in Southland," *Pittsburgh Courier*, 13 April 1946, 7.

13. Horace Cayton, "*Black Boy*: Negroes Hatred of Whites and Fear of His Hate in Wright's Autobiography," *Pittsburgh Courier*, 13 January 1945, 7.

14. Horace R. Cayton, "The Psychological Approach to Race Relations," *Reed College Bulletin* (November 1946): 16.

15. Cayton, *Long Old Road*, 299.

16. Chester B. Himes, " 'If He Hollers Let Him Go'," *Saturday Review of Literature* 16 February 1946: 13.

17. Chester Himes, letter to Richard Wright, n.d., RW, box 99, folder 1393.

18. Mabel Robinson, letter to Ann Petry, 16 August 1945, ALP, box 7, folder 20.

19. "Tips from Publishers: Houghton Mifflin," *Publisher's Weekly*, 23 February 1946, 1261–62.

20. Charles Poore, "A Baleful Street in Harlem Tragedy Inevitable at End," *New York Times*, 7 February 1946, 31; Alfred Butterfield, "The Dark Heartbeat of Harlem," *New York Times Book Review*, 10 February 1946, 117.

21. Gertrude Rodenchiser, letter to Ann Petry, 7 December 1945, ALP, box 14, folder 11.

22. Malcolm X and Alex Haley, *The Autobiography of Malcolm X* (1965; New York: Ballantine, 1993), 105.

23. Ann Petry, *The Street* (1946; Boston: Houghton Mifflin, 1988), 147.

24. Ibid., 99.

25. Ibid., 147.

26. Ibid., 308.

27. Ibid., 324.

28. Ibid., 387–88.

29. Ibid., 154.

30. Ibid., 206.

31. Ibid., 315.

32. Lucy Ann Clemmons, "Grime, Garbage, and Ugliness," *Phylon* (1st Quarter 1946): 99.

33. Alfred Butterfield, "The Dark Heartbeat of Harlem," *New York Times*, 10 February 1946, 117.

34. Arthur P. Davis, "Hard Boiled Fiction," *Journal of Negro Education* (Autumn 1946): 648, 649.

35. Diana Trilling, "Class and Color," *Nation*, 9 March 1946, 291.

36. Yerby had written and published steadily up to the release of *Foxes Harrow*: "The Thunder of God," *New Anvil* (April–May 1939): n.p.; "Health Card," *Harper's* (May 1944): 448–53; "White Magnolias," *Phylon* (Fall 1944): 319–26; "Roads Going Down," *Common Ground* (Summer 1945): 67–72; "My Brother Went to College," *Tomorrow* (January 1946): 9–12; "The Homecoming," *Common Ground* (Spring 1946): 41–47; "How and Why I Write the Costume Novel," *Harper's* (October 1959): 145–50.

37. Frank Yerby, letter to Muriel Fuller, 22 July 1943, in Gene Jarrett *Deans and Truants: Race and Realism in African American Literature* (Philadelphia: University of Pennsylvania Press, 2006), 150.

38. Yerby to Fuller, 25 November 1943, in ibid., 152.

39. "Frank Yerby," *Afro-American Writers, 1940–1955. Dictionary of Literary Biography*, vol. 76, ed. Trudier Harris and Thadious M. Davis (Detroit: Gale Research, 1988), 227.

40. Ken McCormick, letter to Frederick Warburg, 11 May 1949, KMD, box 78 folder "Bucklin Moon 1948–1950."

41. William Tindall, "The Sociological Best Seller," *College English* (November 1947): 55.

42. Robert Gorham Davis, "State of American Writing," *Partisan Review* (August 1948): 869.

43. "National Best Sellers-March," *Publishers' Weekly*, 6 April 1946, 1979.

44. "The Best Sellers of 1946," *Publishers' Weekly*, 25 January 1946, 415.

45. U.S. Census Bureau, "Nativity and Parentage of the Population: 1890–1930, 1960, and 1970," table 12, available at www.census.gov/population/www/documentation/twps0029/tab12.html. In 1930 the percentage of Americans of "foreign stock" was 32.8 percent.

46. Frank Yerby, *Foxes of Harrow* (New York: Dial, 1946), 375.

47. Ibid., 259.

48. Ibid., 406.

49. J. Saunders Redding, review of *The Policy King* by L.A.H. Caldwell, *Baltimore Afro-American*, 15 June 1946, 4.

50. Curtis Lucas, *Third Ward Newark* (Chicago: Ziff Davis, 1946), 59.

51. Ibid., 69.

52. J. Saunders Redding, review of *Third Ward Newark* by Curtis Lucas, *Baltimore Afro-American*, 4 January 1947, 4.

53. Elizabeth Ames, letter to Malcolm Cowley, 23 May 1942, MC, box 2, folder 86.

54. Ames to Malcolm Cowley, 23 May 1942 and 5 September 1947, MC.

55. Granville Hicks, letter to Elizabeth Ames, 29 February 1948, YA, box 278, folder 17.

56. J. Saunders Redding, letter to Arna Bontemps, 3 October 1948, AB, box 23, folder "J. Sanders Redding."

57. Elizabeth Hardwick, *The Ghostly Lover* (1945; New York: Ecco, 1982), 27.

58. Harvey Breit, John Cheever, Eleanor Clark, Alfred Kazin, Kappo Phelan, letter [to former Yaddo guests], 21 March 1949, AB, box 29, folder "Yaddo."

59. Helen B. Parker, "Evasive Polemic," *New York Times*, 13 July 1947, 168.

60. "Best Sellers of the Week," *Publisher's Weekly*, 5 July 1947, 67; 26 July 1947, 337.

61. J. Saunders Redding, "Book Review: *Kingsblood Royal*," *Baltimore Afro-American*, 28 June 1947, 4.

62. Sinclair Lewis, *Kingsblood Royal* (New York: Random House, 1947), 339.

63. Horace Cayton, *Long Old Road* (1964; Seattle: University of Washington Press, 1974), 300.

64. Mark Schorer, *Sinclair Lewis: An American Life* (New York: McGraw Hill, 1961), 762. Cayton wrote of the visit in his autobiography *Long Old Road* as if it took place on July 4, 1947, but his letter to Elizabeth Ames on July 7 indicates specifically that Cayton spent July 12–14 with Sinclair Lewis. Horace Cayton, letter to Elizabeth Ames, 7 July 1947, YA, box 234, folder "Horace Cayton."

65. Fanny Butcher, "The Literary Spotlight," *Chicago Tribune*, 6 August 1944, E14.

66. Herman Kogan, "His Fiction Realistic? He Even Went to Jail to Obtain Background," [no publication information] WM, box 1, clipping file.

67. Petry, *Street*, 435.

68. Willard Motley, *Knock on Any Door* (New York: Appleton Century, 1947), 9.

69. Ibid., 42–43.

70. Ibid., 149.

71. Ibid., 423.

72. Ibid., 289.

73. Ibid., 419.

74. Ibid., 452.

75. "Candidates for the Best Seller List," *Publisher's Weekly*, 5 July 1947, 67.

76. Horace R. Cayton, "Literary Expansion: Another Best-Seller by a Negro Is Not of the Negro or His Environs," *Pittsburgh Courier*, 24 May 1947, 7.

77. Horace R. Cayton, "A Terrifying Cross Section of Chicago," *Chicago Daily Tribune*, 4 May 1947, B3.

78. Alain Locke, "A Critical Retrospect of the Literature of the Negro for 1947," *Phylon* (1st Quarter 1948): 7.

79. Thomas Jerrett, "Sociology and Imagery in the Great American Novel," *English Journal* (November 1939): 518.

80. Orville Prescott, "Books of the Times," *New York Times*, 5 May 1947, 21.

81. Charles Lee, "Disciple of Dresier," *New York Times Book Review*, 4 May 1947, 3.

CHAPTER 10: THE PERIL OF SOMETHING NEW

1. W. G. Rogers, "Another Renaissance Noted in Negro Arts," *Washington Post*, 26 January 1947, S10.

2. Harry Overstreet, "Images and the Negro," *Saturday Review of Literature*, 27 August 1946, 5–6; and "The Negro Writer as Spokesperson," *Saturday Review of Literature*, 2 September 1946, 26–27.

3. Alfred Kazin, "Midtown and the Village," *Harper's Magazine* (January 1971): 83.

4. Thomas Sancton, "Southern Train," *Common Ground* (Winter 1949): 61–67; Sancton, "They Belonged," *Common Ground* (Summer 1949): 75–78.

5. Lawrence Jackson, *Ralph Ellison: Emergence of Genius* (New York: John Wiley, 2002), 340–50.

6. Fern Marja Eckman, *The Furious Passage of James Baldwin* (New York: Martin Evans, 1966), 108.

7. "James Baldwin," 1930 U.S. Census, New York City, sheet No. 10A (18).

8. James Baldwin, interview with Studs Terkel, 29 September 1962.

9. James Baldwin, "The Price of the Ticket," in *The Price of the Ticket: Collected Non Fiction 1948–1985* (New York: St. Martin's, 1985), xiii.

10. Ibid.

11. Al Silverman, *The Time of Their Lives* (New York: St. Martin's, 2008), 180–81.

12. Bucklin Moon, letter of reference, James Arthur Baldwin, Julius Rosenwald Application: 1948, JUL, box 391, folder 2 "Baldwin."

13. For details of Young's trouble in the army and a more optimistic view of the aftermath, see Douglass Henry Daniels, *Lester Leaps In: The Life and Times of Lester "Pres" Young* (Boston: Beacon Press, 2002). John Hope Franklin, *Mirror to America* (New York: Farrar, Straus and Giroux, 2007) 17, 128–30. Franklin's brother, a high school principal, was degraded during his military service and committed suicide after his discharge.

14. Eckman, *The Furious Passage of James Baldwin*, 94, 103.

15. Constance Webb, *Not Without Love: Memoirs* (Hanover, NH: University of New England Press, 2003), 122–23.

16. Baldwin, "The Price of the Ticket," xi.

17. James Baldwin, 27 December 1945 and undated, letter to Richard Wright, RW, box 94, folder 1201.

18. Baldwin, "The Price of the Ticket," ix.

19. McKay published the following: "Negro Author Sees Disaster If the Communist Party Gains Control of Negro Workers," *New Leader*, 10 September 1938, 5; "Everybody's Doing It: Anti-Semitic Propaganda Fails to Attract Negroes; Harlemites Face Problems of All Other Slum Dwellers," *New Leader*, 20 May 1939, 5–6; "Where the News Ends," *New Leader*, 10 June 1939, 8; "Claude McKay Replies to Poston on Solution of Negro Problems," *New Leader*, 7 December 1940, 5; "Negroes are Anti-Nazi, but Fight Anglo-U.S. Discrimination; Soap Boxers in Harlem Typify Negro Resentments," *New Leader* 25 October 1941, 4.

20. Diana Trilling, review of *Passage from Home* by Isaac Rosenfeld, *Nation*, 18 May 1946, 606.

21. Isaac Rosenfeld, *Passage from Home* (Cleveland: World Publishing, 1946), 117, 118.

22. Isaac Rosenfeld, letter of reference for James Arthur Baldwin, JUL, box 391, folder James Baldwin.

23. Mary McCarthy, "A Memory of James Baldwin," *New York Review of Books*, 27 April 1989, 48; "Baldwin," in *James Baldwin: The Legacy*, ed. Quincy Troupe (New York: Touchstone, 1989), 48.

24. James Baldwin, "When War Hits Brownsville," review of *The Amboy Dukes* by Irving Shulman, *New Leader*, 17 May 1947, 12.

25. James Baldwin, "Smaller Than Life," review of *There Was Once a Slave* by Shirley Graham, *Nation*, 19 July 1947, 78.

26. Chester Himes, letter to Carl Van Vechten, n.d. "Wednesday" [11 September 1947], Box 8, folder 7, Amistad Research Center, Tulane University. Himes's letter to Van Vechten is far less conspiratorial than his 1972 autobiography, *The Quality of Hurt.*

27. Earl Conrad, "Author 'Discovers' Negro," *Chicago Defender*, 13 April 1946, 13.

28. Chester Himes, *The Quality of Hurt* (1972; New York: Paragon, 1990), 103.

29. Ralph Ellison, letter to Richard Wright, 1 February 1948, RW, box 97, folder 1314.

30. Phillip Butcher, review of *Lonely Crusade* by Chester Himes, *Opportunity* (Winter 1948): 23.

31. John Farrelly, "Fiction Parade," review of *Lonely Crusade* by Chester Himes, *New Republic*, 6 October 1947, 30.

32. J. Saunders Redding, review of *Lonely Crusade* by Chester Himes, *Baltimore Afro-American*, 13 September 1947, 4.

33. Horace R. Cayton, " Scared of White Folk?: Sure, Most of Us Are, Points Out Author of Challenging Book," *Pittsburgh Courier*, 11 October 1947, 7.

34. James Baldwin, "The Art of Fiction LXXVIII: James Baldwin," interview with Jordan Elgrably and George Plimpton, in *Conversations with James Baldwin*, ed. Fred L. Standley and Louis H. Pratt (Jackson: University of Mississippi Press, 1989), 237.

35. James Baldwin, "History as Nightmare," review of *Lonely Crusade* by Chester Himes, *New Leader*, 25 October 1947, 11.

36. Lloyd L. Brown, "White Flag," review of *Lonely Crusade* by Chester Himes," *New Masses*, 9 September 1947, 18.

37. James Baldwin, "History as Nightmare," 11.

38. Milton Klonsky, "The Writing on the Wall," *Commentary* (February 1948): 190.

39. Anatole Broyard, *When Kafka Was the Rage* (New York: Vintage, 1997), 69.

40. William Phillips, *A Partisan View* (New Brunswick, NJ: Transaction, 2004), 113.

41. Lionel Trilling, review of *Black Boy* by Richard Wright, *Nation*, 7 April 1945, 390.

42. Ibid.

43. Horace R. Cayton, "Cayton: White People Should Read Moon's Book Because They Can't Laugh It Off," *Pittsburgh Courier*, 23 April 1949, 14.

44. Richard Dier, "One Block of Paris Has More Freedom than Whole U.S.," *Afro Magazine*, 22 February 1947, M7.

45. J. Saunders Redding, "What I Think of Richard Wright: Redding Calls Him a New Type of Writer Whose Creations Rise Above Race," *Baltimore Afro-American*, 1 March 1947, M2.

46. Frank Yerby, "How and Why I Write the Costume Novel," *Harper's Magazine* (October 1959): 145.

47. "The Individual in Our Writing World," JUL, box 421, folder 1 "Chester Himes."

48. Chester Himes, "Author's Protest," *Commentary* (May 1948): 474.

49. Chester Himes, "Dilemma of the Negro Novelist in the U.S.," in *Beyond the Angry Black*, ed. John A. Williams (New York: Cooper Square, 1969), 57.

50. Ibid., 53.

51. Chester Himes, letter to John A. Williams, October 20, 1962, in *Dear John, Dear Chester:Letters Between Chester Himes and John A. Williams*, by John A. Williams (Detroit: Wayne State University Press, 2008), 26.

52. Arna Bontemps, letter to Langston Hughes, 17 October 1948, in *Arna Bontemps—Langston Hughes, Letters 1925–1967*, 239.

CHAPTER 11: THE NEGRO NEW LIBERAL CRITIC AND THE BIG LITTLE MAGAZINE

1. Hugh Gloster, *Negro Voices in American Fiction* (Chapel Hill: University of North Carolina Press, 1948), 202.

2. Ibid., 158.

3. Hugh Gloster, "The Van Vechten Vogue," *Phylon* (4th Quarter 1945): 310, 314.

4. Carl Van Vechten, letter to Langston Hughes, 8 October 1942, in *Remember Me to Harlem*, ed. Emily Bernard (New York: Random House, 2001), 211.

5. J. Saunders Redding, review of *We Have Tomorrow* by Arna Bontemps, *Baltimore Afro-American*, 10 August 1946, 4.

6. Blyden Jackson, "Largo for Adonis," *Journal of Negro Education* (Spring 1948): 173.

7. John S. Lash, "What Is Negro Literature?," *College English* (October 1947): 42.

8. Waters Turpin, "Evaluating the Work of the Contemporary Negro Novelist," *Negro History Bulletin* (December 1947): 64.

9. Norman Podhoretz, *Making It* (1967; New York: Harper, 1980), 100.

10. Phillips, *A Partisan View*, 162.

11. Edward Shapiro, "World War II and Modern Jewish Identity," *Modern Judaism* (February 1990): 78.

12. Nathan Glazer and Daniel Patrick Moynihan, *Beyond the Melting Pot: The Negroes, Puerto Ricans, Jews, Italians, and Irish of New York City* (Cambridge: MIT and Harvard University Press, 1963), 53.

13. Shapiro, "World War II and Modern Jewish Identity," 72.

14. Eckman, *The Furious Passage of James Baldwin*, 108.

15. Lionel Trilling, "The Mind of Robert Warshow," *Commentary* (June 1961): 501–6.

16. James Baldwin, "Harlem Ghetto," in *Notes of a Native Son* (1955; Boston: Beacon, 1984), 68.

17. Ibid., 64.

18. Eckman, *The Furious Passage of James Baldwin*, 109.

19. Baldwin, "Harlem Ghetto," 58.

20. Arna Bontemps, letter to Langston Hughes, 17 February 1948, in *Arna Bontemps—Langston Hughes, Letters 1925–1967*, 229.

21. Alain Locke, letter to Eliot Cohen, 28 October 1948, AL, box 164, folder 21 "Eliot Cohen."

22. Ralph Ellison, "Harlem Is Nowhere," in *Shadow and Act*, 296.

23. Phillips, *A Partisan View*, 116.

24. Julian McKee, letter to Ann Petry, 9 May 1950, ALP, box 13, folder 6.

25. Ann Petry, "Harlem," *Holiday* (April 1949): 110, 168.

26. Eckman, *The Furious Passage of James Baldwin*, 103; James Baldwin, "The Price of the Ticket," xiii.

27. James Baldwin, letter to William Phillips, April 1949, PR, box 1, folder 2.

28. Richard Wright, "The Position of the Negro Artist and Intellectual in the United States," 27 (33), RW, box 3, folder 41.

29. James Baldwin, "Previous Condition," *Commentary* (October 1948): 337.

30. Ibid., 342.

31. Edmund Wilson, "No! No! No! My Soul Ain't Yours Mas'r," *New Yorker*, 27 November 1948, 134.

32. Delmore Schwarz, "The Writings of Edmund Wilson," *Accent* (Spring 1942): 179.

33. Stanley Edgar Hyman, *The Armed Vision* (New York: Knopf, 1948), 20, 35, 21.

34. Ibid., 35.

35. Ibid., 21

36. William Barrett, *The Truants: Adventures among the Intellectuals* (Garden City, NY: Anchor, 1982), 63.

37. Ibid. , 68.

38. Robert N. Linscott, Reader's Report "Crying Holy," 23 July 1948, PR, box 1, folder 11; Linscott, letter to Philip Rahv, 15 October 1948, PR, box 1, folder 11.

39. Linscott to Rahv, 15 October 1948.

40. Phillips, *A Partisan View*, 138, 145; Philip Rahv, letter to Marcus Cunliffe, 26 June 1958, PR, box 12, folder 6.

41. Rahv to Arthur Schlesinger Jr., 4 September 1947, PR, box 1, folder 17.

42. Baldwin to Phillips, May 1949.

43. Federal Bureau of Investigation, Report Date 11 December 1963, File "James Arthur Baldwin," Part 1, 187.

44. James Campbell, *Exiled in Paris: Richard Wright, James Baldwin, Samuel Beckett, and Others on the Left Bank* (New York: Scribner's 1995), 28; Baldwin to Phillips, April 1949.

45. Dabney Lewis, *Edmund Wilson: A Life in Literature* (New York: Farrar, Straus and Giroux, 2005); Philip Rahv, "Disillusionment and Partial Answers," *Partisan Review* (May 1948): 519–25. Lewis interviewed McCarthy for his Wilson biography and she described her pattern of targeting Wilson during the years around the breakup of her marriage in 1946.

46. Julian Mayfield, letter to John Henrik Clarke, 19 June 1955, JHC, box 5, folder 5.

47. James Baldwin, "Everybody's Protest Novel," in *Notes of a Native Son*, 9.

48. Ibid., 11.

49. Ibid., 14.

50. Sidney Hook, "Report on the International Day Against Dictatorship and War," *Partisan Review* (July 1949): 732.

51. David Dempsey, "American Dilemma, Army Model," *New York Times Book Review*, 5 September 1948, 6.

52. Blyden Jackson, "An Essay in Criticism," *Phylon* (4th Quarter 1950): 341.

53. Alain Locke, "Dawn Patrol," *Phylon* (1st Quarter 1949): 9.

54. Seymour Krim, "Boston Black Belt," *New York Time Book Review*, 16 May 1948, 5.

55. Broyard, *When Kafka Was the Rage* (New York: Vintage, 1997), 41.

56. Ibid., 107.

57. Ibid., 46.

58. Ibid., 72.

59. Ibid., 110.

60. Barrett, *Truants*, 72.

61. Anatole Broyard, "Portrait of the Hipster," *Partisan Review* (June 1948): 726.

62. Ibid., 727.

63. Broyard, *When Kafka Was the Rage*, 70.

64. Henry Louis Gates, Jr., "The Passing of Anatole Broyard," in *Thirteen Ways of Looking at a Black Man* (New York: Random House, 1997), 187.

65. Several authors talked about either their experiences in the 1950s or even earlier and the attitudes toward blacks, including Seymour Krim, "Ask for a White Cadillac," in *Beyond the Angry Black*, ed. John A. Williams (1962; New York: Cooper Union, 1966), 102–17; and Norman Podhoretz, "My Negro Problem and Ours," *Commentary* (February 1963): 93–101.

66. Milton Klonsky, "Greenwich Village: Decline and Fall, Bohemia's Age of Lead," *Commentary* (November 1948): 462.

67. Anatole Broyard, "Portrait of the Inauthentic Negro," *Commentary* (July 1950): 57.

68. Ibid., 56.

69. James Baldwin, "The Death of the Prophet," *Commentary* (March 1950): 257.

70. Broyard, "Portrait of the Inauthentic Negro," 63.

71. Ibid.

CHAPTER 12: THE COMMUNIST DREAM OF AFRICAN AMERICAN MODERNISM

1. Cyril Connolly, "Introduction," *Horizon* (October 1947): 3, 8–9.

2. Saul Bellow, "Man Underground," *Commentary* (June 1952): 608.

3. Ralph Ellison, "The Invisible Man," *Horizon* (October 1947): 104.

4. Ellison, "The Invisible Man," 104–5.

5. Hurston, *Their Eyes Were Watching God*, 89.

6. Alyce McComb, "From Where I Stand," *Reporter*, 30 August 1949, 27.

7. Kenneth B. Clark, "Another Stand," *Reporter*, 27 September 1949, 40.

8. John Hope Franklin, *From Slavery to Freedom: A History of American Negroes* (New York: Knopf, 1947), 3.

9. James Baldwin, "Too Late, Too Late," *Commentary* (January 1949): 98.

10. Blyden Jackson, "Full Circle," *Phylon* (1st Quarter 1948): 30, 34, 31.

11. Kenneth M. Stampp, preface to *The Peculiar Institution: Slavery in the Ante-bellum South* (New York: Knopf, 1956), vii.

12. John A. Williams, *The Man Who Cried I Am* (1969; New York: Thunder's Mouth, 1985), 105.

13. Claudia Jones, "On the Right to Self-Determination for the Negro People in the Black Belt," *Political Affairs* (January 1946); 73.

14. Ibid., 70–71.

15. Harold Cruse, "The Education of a Rebel," p. 10, HAC, box 3, folder "The Education of a Rebel"; Cruse, interviewed by Van Gosse, "An Interview with Harold Cruse," *Radical History Review* (Spring 1998): 107. In the interview with Van Gosse, Cruse claims that Bennett was married to Huiswood; the biographical entries on Bennett do not support his view and suggest that she left Harlem around the end of World War II.

16. Sandra Govan, "After the Renaissance: Gwendolyn Bennett and the WPA Years," *MAWA Review* (December 1988): 30–31.

17. Lloyd L. Brown, "Words and White Chauvinism," *Masses & Mainstream* (February 1950): 17.

18. Lloyd L. Brown, "The Legacy of Willie Jones," *Masses & Mainstream* (February 1952): 44–51.

19. Lloyd L. Brown, "My People, My Party," *Masses & Mainstream* (February 1949): 6; Robin Kelley, email to author, August 2006.

20. Ibid., 6.

21. Ted Ward, "Five Negro Novelists," *Mainstream* (Winter 1947): 106.

22. Samuel Sillen, letter to Melvin B. Tolson, 21 November 1946, MBT, box 1, folder "S."

23. Saunders Redding, "Saga of a City Jungle Boy," review of *Taffy* by Phillip B. Kaye, *New York Herald Tribune*, 19 November 1950, 18

24. "Art Notes," *New York Times*, 5 February 1944: 11.

25. "Leftist School Will Close Soon," *New York Times*, 28 November 1946, 6.

26. L. D. Reddick, "No Kafka in the South," *Phylon* (4th Quarter 1950): 380–88; Broyard, *When Kafka Was the Rage*.

27. Skip Gates and Ted Joans, "Ted Joans: Tri-Contintental Poet," *Transition* 48 (1975): 8.

28. Doxey Wilkerson, "Freedom—Through Victory in War and Peace," in *What the Negro Wants,* ed. Rayford Logan (Chapel Hill: University of North Carolina Press, 1944), 196.

29. Doxey Wilkerson, "The Fight Against Segregated Schools," *Political Affairs* (July 1954): 42–43.

30. "Group Discusses Fight on Race Bias," *New York Times*, 17 March 1947, 16.

31. John Baxter Streater, Jr., "The National Negro Congress: 1936–1947," Ph.D. diss., University of Cincinnati, 1981, 342–53. Streater cites the loss of influence in the Automobile Workers Union and the National Maritime Union as final blows to the efficacy of the organization.

32. Glenda Gilmore, *Defying Dixie* (New York: Norton, 2008), 436–37.

33. Marvel Cooke, interview no. 5 with Kathleen Currie, 1 November 1989, Women in Journalism, Oral History Project, Washington Press Club Foundation.

34. Doxey A. Wilkerson, "What's Happening to 'Peoples Voice'?," *Daily Worker*, 18 December 1947, 10; "Harlem Paper Held Aiding Negroes' Foes; Plays 'Uncle Tom' Role, Red Critic Says," *New York Times*, 19 December 1947, 52.

35. George Streator, "Rift in Negro Unit Is Laid to Leftists," *New York Times*, 6 April 1948, 46.

36. David Henry Anthony III, *Max Yergan: Race Man, Internationalist, Cold Warrior* (New York: New York University Press, 2006), 236–65.

37. Lewis Nichols, "Visitor from Harlem," *New York Times*, 10 September 1944, x1.

38. Aram Goudsouzian, *Sidney Poitier: Man, Actor, Icon* (Chapel Hill: University of North Carolina Press, 2004), 55.

39. Erroll Hill and James Hatch, *A History of African American Theater* (New York: Cambridge University Press, 2003), 359; Philip Bonosky, "Odyssey of a Writers' Workshop in the 1950s," http://www.phillipbonosky.com/html/harlemworkshop.html; Phillip Bonosky, interview, July 2008.

40. Doxey Wilkerson, "Negro Culture Heritage and Weapon," *Masses & Mainstream* (August 1949): 22.

41. Ibid., 5.

42. Ibid., 21.

43. Harold Cruse, *Crisis of the Negro Intellectual* (1967; New York: Quill, 1984), 217–18.

44. Cruse and Van Gosse, "Locating the Black Intellectual," 106.

45. Untitled handwritten notes, HAC, box 3, folder "Memoirs of a Self-Taught Journalist."

46. Harold Cruse, "Letter on the American Negro Theater Production of 'Freight,'" *Daily Worker*, 9 March 1949, 13.

47. Harold Cruse, "Purblind Slant on Africa," *Daily Worker*, 29 November 1950, reprinted in Harold Cruse, *Rebellion or Revolution* (New York: Morrow, 1968), 32.

48. Harold Cruse, "Negro Soldier Sequences Censored in "Call Me Mister," *Daily Worker*, 2 February 1951, reprinted in *Rebellion or Revolution*, 32–35; Cruse, "Salute to Josephine Baker," *Daily Worker*, 14 March 1951, reprinted in *Rebellion or Revolution* 36–40.

49. Harold Cruse, introduction to *Rebellion or Revolution,* 19.

50. Harold Cruse, " 'Green Pastures' Twenty years Ago and Today," *Daily Worker,* 30 March and 2 April 1951, reprinted in *Rebellion or Revolution,* 41–47.

51. Harry Washington Greene, *Holders of the Doctorate among Negroes: An Educational and Social Study of Negroes Who Have Earned Doctoral Degrees in Course* (Boston: Meador, 1946).

52. Lloyd Brown, "Aptheker and Myrdal's Dilemma," in *African American History and Radical Historiography: Essays in Honor of Herbert Aptheker,* ed. Herbert Shapiro (Minneapolis: MEP Publications, 1998), 112.

53. John Henrik Clarke, *John Henrik Clarke: The Early Years,* comp. Barbara E. Adams (Newport News, VA: United Brothers and Sisters, 1992), 24–31.

54. Ernest Kaiser, "Racial Dialectics: The Aptheker–Myrdal Controversy," *Phylon* (4th Quarter 1948): 298

55. Ibid., 299.

56. Benjamin Brown, letter to Langston Hughes, 3 August 1949, LH, box 74, folder 1432.

57. Langston Hughes, letter to Benjamin Brown, 17 August 1949, LH, box 74, folder 1432.

58. Arnold Rampersad, *The Life of Langston Hughes,* Vol. 2: *1941–1967, I Dream a World* (New York: Oxford, 1988), 90–91.

59. Ernest Kaiser, "*Harlem Quarterly* Scope," *Harlem Quarterly* (Winter 1949–1950): 19.

60. Editors, "Prospectus," *Harlem Quarterly* (Fall–Winter 1950): 1.

61. Ralph Ellison, letter to Richard Wright, [undated "Your wire reached me about noon,"] RW, box 97, folder 1314.

62. Ernest Kaiser, letter to author, July 1999.

63. "Some Notes on Policy," 3 March 1948, MA, box 49, folder 11.

64. Phillip Horton, letter to Max Ascoli, 7 July 1949, MA, box 85, folder 1.

65. John Nickel, "Disabling African American Men: Liberalism and the Message Films," *Cinema Journal* (Autumn 2004): 25.

66. Max Ascoli, letter to Phillip Horton, 30 August1949, MA, box 85, folder 1.

67. P.H., "Editorial: The Negro's International Vote," *Reporter,* 6 December 1949, 2.

68. Ralph Ellison, letter to Albert Murray, 2 January 1950, in *Trading Twelves* (New York: Modern American Library, 2001), 8.

69. Ellison to Murray, 4 February 1952, in *Trading Twelves,* 27.

70. Cruse, *Crisis,* 217–20.

71. James Baldwin, "The Negro in Paris," *Reporter,* 6 June 1950, 34, 36.

72. Bucklin Moon, "Literature of Protest," *Reporter,* 6 December 1949, 36–37.

73. Bucklin Moon, memorandum "All Salesmen," KMD, box 78, folder "Bucklin Moon 1948–1950."

74. William Weaver, "Southern Negroes' World," review of *Without Magnolias* by Bucklin Moon, *New York Times Book Review,* 10 April 1949, 4.

75. Bucklin Moon, *Without Magnolias* (New York: Avon, Pocket Books, 1950), 371.

76. Horace R. Cayton, "Cayton: White People Should Read Moon's Book Because They Can't Laugh It Off," *Pittsburgh Courier,* 23 April 1949, 14.

77. Charles Glicksberg, "The Alienation of Negro Literature," *Phylon* (1st Quarter 1950): 50.

78. Marvin Elkoff, "Black and White Unite," *Commentary* (April 1953): 378.

79. "Editor Loses Job, Charges a Smear," *New York Times*, 18 April 1953: 9; Bucklin Boon, "Memoir," BM, box 1.

CHAPTER 13: THE INSINUATING POETICS OF THE MAINSTREAM

1. Gwendolyn Brooks, "Poets Who Are Negroes," *Phylon* (4th Quarter 1950): 298.

2. Elizabeth Lawrence, letter to Gwendolyn Brooks, 15 February 1946, microfilm, HAB.

3. Brooks to Elizabeth Lawrence, 25 February 1946.

4. Marguerite, letter to Elizabeth Lawrence, 1 July 1947.

5. Russell Lynes, "I'm afraid not. Nice but not enough," n.d., microfilm, HAB.

6. Elizabeth Lawrence, letter to Gwendolyn Brooks, 26 September 1947.

7. Gwendolyn Brooks, *Maud Martha*, in *Blacks* (Chicago: Third World Press, 1994), 229–30.

8. Arna Bontemps, "A 'White Negro' 'Passes'," review of *Alien Land* by Willard Savoy, *New York Herald Tribune*, 17 April 1949, 6.

9. Ann Petry, "Outcast," review of *Alien Land* by Willard Savoy, *Saturday Review*, 30 April 1949, 16.

10. Lawrence to Brooks, 5 December 1945.

11. Gwendolyn Brooks, "Ballad of Pearl May Lee," *A Street in Bronzeville*, in *Blacks*, 60.

12. Gwendolyn Brooks, letter to Langston Hughes, 25 October 1948, LH, box 24, folder 479.

13. Brooks, "Ballad of Pearl May Lee," 61.

14. Brooks to Hughes, 25 October 1948.

15. Brooks, "Ballad of Pearl May Lee," 63.

16. J. Saunders Redding, "American Negro Literature," *American Scholar* (Spring 1949): 137, 148.

17. Gwendolyn Brooks, "Intermission, 3," *Annie Allen*, in *Blacks*, 137; "The Anniad," 100.

18. Phyllis McGinley, "Poetry for Prose Readers," *New York Times*, 22 January 1950, 177.

19. Paul Engle, "Miss Brooks Shows a Talent of Rare Quality," *Chicago Tribune*, 11 September 1949, K7.

20. William Jay Smith, "Performers and Poets," *Sewanee* 58 (1950): 533, 534.

21. F. Cudworth Flint, "Seven among the Poets," *Virginia Quarterly Review* (Winter 1950): 155.

22. Margaret Walker, "New Poets," *Phylon* (4th Quarter 1950): 352, 354.

23. J. Saunders Redding, review of *Annie Allen* by Gwendolyn Brooks, *Afro American Magazine*, 27 August 1949, 3.

24. Blyden Jackson, "Full Circle," *Phylon* (1st Quarter 1948): 34.

25. Redding, review of *Annie Allen*, 3.

26. Julian Mayfield, "Autobiography: Chapter Two," JM, box 2, folder 9.

27. Alain Locke, "Self Criticism: The Third Dimension in Culture," *Phylon* (4th Quarter 1950): 392.

28. William Gardner Smith, "The Negro Writer Looks at His World," *Phylon* (4th Quarter 1950): 298.

29. Blyden Jackson, "An Essay in Criticism," *Phylon* (4th Quarter 1950): 338.

30. Hugh M. Gloster, "Race and the Negro Writer," *Phylon* (4th Quarter 1950): 371.

31. Thomas D. Jarrett, "Toward Unfettered Creativity: A Note on the Negro Novelist's Coming of Age," *Phylon* (4th Quarter 1950): 313.

32. Ulysses Lee, "Criticism at Mid-Century," *Phylon* (4th Quarter 1950): 337, 329.

33. Locke, "Self Criticism," 393.

34. Walker, "New Poets," 353.

35. Ibid., 350.

36. Ford, "I Teach Negro Literature," *College English* (March 1941): 534.

37. Nick Aaron Ford, unaddressed form letter ["Because I feel that you are a Christian"], n.d., NAF.

38. Nick Aaron Ford, *"Seeking a Newer World": Memoirs of a Black American Teacher* (Great Neck, NY: Todd & Honeywell, 1983), 195–97.

39. Ford, "I Teach Negro Literature," 531.

40. Ibid.

41. Nick Aaron Ford, "The Negro Novel as a Vehicle of Propaganda," *Quarterly Review of Higher Education* (July 1941): 138.

42. Ralph Ellison, "The Booker T," *New Republic*, 18 February 1946, 262.

43. Nick Aaron Ford, "Books Can Revolutionize the Thought and Action of a Nation," *Vital Speeches of the Day*, 15 January 1947, 216, 220.

44. Allen Tate, letter to Nick Aaron Ford, 24 March 1947, NAF.

45. Thomas Wilson, letter to Nick Aaron Ford, 19 March 1946, NAF.

46. Marian Scott letter to Nick Aaron Ford, 30 January 1946, NAF.

47. University of Illinois Reader's Report, 24 July 1950, NAF.

48. Donald Jackson, letter to Nick Aaron Ford, 6 December 1950, NAF.

49. Nick Aaron Ford, "Black Literature and the Problem of Evaluation," *College English* (February 1971): 538.

50. Freeman Champney, letter to Nick Aaron Ford, 12 December 1951, NAF.

51. *Current Population Reports: Population Characteristics*, Educational Attainment in the United States: March 1975, 6, table D.

52. U.S. Bureau of the Census, "A Half Century of Learning: Historical Statistics of Educational Attainment in the United States, 1940–2000," table 4, available at http://www.census.gov/population/www/socdemo/education/phct41.html; U.S. Bureau of the Census, "Historical Census Statistics on Population Totals by Race, 1790–1990, and by Hispanic Origin, 1970 to 1990, for the United States, Regions, Divisions, and States," by Campbell Gibson and Kay Jung, table 1, available at http://www.census.gov/population/www/documentation/twps005 /twps0056.htm.

53. Langston Hughes, James Baldwin, Lorraine Hansberry, Alfred Kazin, Emile Capouya, roundtable discussion, May 1962, audiocassette.

54. Nick Aaron Ford, "Consider the Negro Teacher, *New Republic*, 15 April 1957, 15.

55. Bernard Schwartz, "Justice Rehnquist, Justice Jackson, and the 'Brown' Case," *Supreme Court Review* (1988): 262.

56. William Demby, letter to Arna Bontemps 4 November 1947, AB, box 6, folder "William Demby."

57. Demby to Bontemps, 18 December 1948.

58. Demby to Bontemps, 5 December n.d. [1947].

59. Ibid.

60. Horace R. Cayton, "Defeated Lives," review of *Beetlecreek* by William Demby, *New York Times Book Review*, 26 February 1950, 4.

CHAPTER 14: STILL LOOKING FOR FREEDOM

1. John Oliver Killens, "The Impact of Richard Wright Upon Afro-American Literature," JOK, box 33, folder "The Impact of Richard Wright Upon Afro-American Literature."

2. John Oliver Killens, "Wright's Rebels: A Book Review of Uncle Tom's Children," 24 March 1949, General Studies 16, JOK, box 32, folder 6.

3. John Oliver Killens, "The Impact of Richard Wright upon Afro-American Literature," JOK, box 33, folder 18.

4. Lorraine Hansberry, *To Be Young, Gifted and Black,* adapted by Robert Nemiroff (New York: Signet, 1970), 100.

5. Lorraine Hansberry, "Negroes Cast in Same Old Roles in TV Shows," *Freedom* (June 1951): 7.

6. Horace Gregory, letter to William Barrett, 22 July 1947, PR, box 1, folder 7.

7. James Baldwin, Emile Capouya, Lorraine Hansberry, Langston Hughes, and Alfred Kazin, "The Negro in American Culture," 10 January 1961, audiocassette.

8. Hansberry, *To Be Young, Gifted and Black,* 75.

9. Lloyd L. Brown, "More Dilemma," *Masses & Mainstream* (January 1950): 90.

10. William Gardener Smith, "Status of the Negro," *New Republic,* 17 April 1950, 27–28.

11. Lloyd L. Brown, "Psychoanalysis vs. the Negro People," *Masses & Mainstream* (October 1951): 24.

12. Daniel Rosenblatt, "The Negro Personality," *New Republic,* 4 February 1952, 20–21.

13. Albert Murray, letter to Ralph Ellison, n.d. [early 1952], in *Trading Twelves,* 26.

14. Lloyd L. Brown, "Which Way the Negro Writer: Part Two," *Masses & Mainstream* (April 1951): 53, 54.

15. Blyden Jackson, "Faith without Works in Negro Literature," *Phylon* (4th Quarter 1951): 386, 380.

16. Lionel Trilling, letter to Elizabeth Ames, 22 December 1950, YA, box 248, folder 11.

17. Grant Webster, *Republic of Letters* (Baltimore: Johns Hopkins University Press, 1979), 104.

18. John Crowe Ransom, letter to Arna Bontemps, 19 April 1945, AB, box 23, folder "John Crowe Ransom."

19. John Crowe Ransom, letter to Elizabeth Ames, 2 January 1951, YA, box 248, folder 11.

20. Richard Gibson, taped interview, December 2006.

21. Richard Gibson, "A No to Nothing," *Kenyon Review* (Spring 1951): 255.

22. Era Bell Thompson, "Negro Publications and the Writer," *Phylon* (4th Quarter 1950): 306.

23. Gibson, "A No to Nothing," 252, 253, 255.

24. Editor's note, "Keep Cool Man: The Negro Rejection of Jazz," *Commentary* (April 1951): 359.

25. Anatole Broyard, "Keep Cool Man: The Negro Rejection of Jazz," *Commentary* (April 1951): 360.

26. Redding, *On Being Negro in America,* 3.

27. Redding, *Stranger and Alone,* 48.

28. Ibid., 50.

29. Ibid., 157.

30. Ralph Ellison, "Stranger and Alone," *New York Times Magazine Book Review,* 19 February 1950, 4.

31. Ulysses Lee, "Hatred and Betrayal," *Phylon* 11 (Spring 1950): 181.

32. Ann Petry, "Race Betrayal," *Saturday Review of Literature,* 25 February 1950, 18.

33. Ann Petry, letter to Denver Lindley, 17 January 1950, JSR, box 10, scrapbook volume 2.

34. J. Saunders Redding, letter to Ms. Hazard, 28 January 1951, JSR, box 9, folder 112.

35. Redding, *On Being Negro in America,* 14.

36. Eloise Perry Hazard, "Notes on Novices," *Saturday Review of Literature,* 17 February 1951, 9–12.

37. J. Saunders Redding, *An American in India* (Indianapolis: Bobbs-Merrill, 1954),10–11.

38. Ralph Ellison, letter to Albert Murray, 8 January 1952, in *Trading Twelves,* 25.

39. Charles Rolo, "Candide in Harlem: Ralph Ellison's *Invisible Man,*" *Atlantic* (July 1952): 83.

40. Anthony West, "Black Man's Burden," *New Yorker,* 31 May 1952, 94.

41. Jackson, *Ralph Ellison,* 440.

42. Richard W. B. Lewis, "Eccentric's Pilgrimage," *Hudson Review* 6 (1953): 148; Richard Chase, "A Novel Is a Novel," *Kenyon Review* 14 (1952): 681.

43. Saul Bellow, "Man Underground," *Commentary* (June 1952): 608; Delmore Schwartz, "Fiction Chronicle: The Wrongs of Innocence and Experience," *Partisan Review* (May–June 1952): 354–59.

44. J. Saunders Redding, "Invisible Man," *Baltimore Afro-American,* 10 May 1952, 10.

45. Roi Ottley, "Blazing Novel Relates a Negro's Frustrations," *Chicago Sunday Tribune,* 11 May 1952, 4.

46. Lloyd Brown, "The Deep Pit," *Masses & Mainstream* (June 1952): 62; John Oliver Killens, review of *Invisible Man* by Ralph Ellison, *Freedom* (June 1952): 7.

47. Abner Berry, "Ralph Ellison's Novel *Invisible Man* Shows Snobbery, Contempt for Negro People," *The Worker,* 1 June 1952, 7.

48. John Killens, review of *Invisible Man* by Ralph Ellison, *Freedom* (July 1952): 7.

49. Ralph Ellison, letter to Richard Wright, 21 January 1953, RW, box 97, folder 1314.

50. Richard Wright, "The Position of the Negro Artist and Intellectual in American Society," 25, RW, box 3, folder 41.

51. Chester Himes, letter to William Targ, 13 August 1954, CH, box 9, folder "Targ."

52. Malcolm Cowley, "American Novels since the War," *New Republic,* 28 December 1953, 16.

53. Rampersad, *Ralph Ellison,* 383.

CHAPTER 15: THE EXPATRIATION

1. Chester Himes, letter to Richard Wright, 19 October 1952, RW, box 99, folder 1393.

2. Himes, *Lonely Crusade,* 138.

3. Ken McCormick, letter to Chester Himes, 1 April 1953, KMD, box 1, folder "Chester Himes 1953," Manuscripts and Archives, Library of Congress.

4. William Targ, letter to Chester Himes, 1 July 1954, CH, box 3, folder 6.

5. James Baldwin, letter to William Philips, April 1949, PR, box 1 folder 2.

6. Himes, *The Quality of Hurt*, 141.

7. Arna Bontemps, letter to Langston Hughes, 8 October 1953, in *Arna Bontemps—Langston Hughes, Letters 1925-1967*, 315.

8. Nick Aaron Ford, "Four Popular Negro Novelists," *Phylon* (1st Quarter 1954): 35, 36.

9. Rampersad, *The Life of Langston Hughes*, Vol. 2, 201.

10. Langston Hughes, *I Wonder as I Wander* (1956; New York: Thunder's Mouth, 1989), 120.

11. Alain Locke, "From *Native Son* to *Invisible Man*: A Review of Literature of the Negro for 1952," *Phylon* (1st Quarter 1953), 34.

12. Walter Carrington, interview, January 1999.

13. Margaret Walker, letter to Langston Hughes, 22 July 1952, LH, box 107, folder 1667.

14. George Padmore, letter to Kwame Nkrumah, 14 April 1953, MF, box 13, folder 20.

15. Richard Wright, letter to Ralph Ellison, 21 October 1952, RW, box 97, folder 1314; Hazel Rowley, *Richard Wright: The Life and Times* (New York: Henry Holt, 2001), 407.

16. Himes, letter to Wright, n.d. [1953].

17. Arna Bontemps, review of *The Outsider* by Richard Wright, *Saturday Review*, 28 March 1953, 15-16.

18. Richard Wright, *The Outsider* (New York: Harpers, 1953), 25.

19. Ibid., 404.

20. James Baldwin, letter to William Cole, n.d. [ca. November 1952], JB.

21. Federal Bureau of Investigation, "Richard Wright," 17 July 1953, Richard Wright File, part 2.

22. Federal Bureau of Investigation, Legat, Paris, letter to FBI Director, 11 February 1960, Richard Wright File, part 2.

23. Natalie Robins, *Alien Ink: The FBI's War on Freedom of Expression* (New York: Morrow, 1992), 345.

24. Mary Sewell Smith, interview, December 2006.

25. James Baldwin, "Le Problème Noire en Amérique," *Rapports France-États Unis* (September 1951): 38 ("ce dynamisme spécifiquement américain qui donne leur unite à tant de phénomènes divers"), 47 ("imparfaits. On ne saurait le leur reprocher. Seuls, les régimes totalitares demandent davantage des humains et c'est en quoi consiste leur mensonge").

26. Baldwin to Cole, n.d. [ca. November 1952], 6.

27. John Henry Raleigh, "Messages and Sagas," *New Republic* (22 June 1953): 21.

28. Dolan Hubbard, "An Interview with Richard K. Barksdale," *Black American Literature Forum* (Winter 1985): 139. In 1949 Dave Dickson was the first African American Ph.D. in English at Harvard. The philological requirements of Old and Middle English and German and medieval Latin changed after the Second World War.

29. Richard Barksdale, "Temple of the Fire Baptized," review of *Go Tell It on the Mountain* by James Baldwin, *Phylon* (3rd Quarter 1953): 326.

30. James Baldwin, *Go Tell It on the Mountain* (1953; New York: Dell, 1985), 11-12, 16.

31. Ibid., 16.

32. Robert Park and Ernest W. Burgess, *Introduction to the Science of Sociology*, 3rd rev. ed. (1921; Chicago: University of Chicago Press, 1969), 139.

33. Albert Murray, letter to Ralph Ellison, [Spring 1953,] in *Trading Twelves*, 48.

34. Himes to Wright, 1 June 1953.

35. Horace Cayton, "The Curtain," *Negro Digest* (December 1968): 14.

36. Albert Murray, "The Luzanna Cholly Kick," in *New World Writing* (New York: Mentor, 1953), 235.

37. James Baldwin, "Autobiographical Notes," in *Notes of a Native Son*, 8.

38. J. Saunders Redding, review of *Go Tell It on the Mountain* by James Baldwin, *Baltimore Afro-American*, 16 May 1953, 2.

39. Arna Bontemps, "The Line," review of *The Narrows* by Ann Petry, *Saturday Review of Literature*, 22 August 1953, 11.

40. Wright Morris, "The Complexity of Evil," review of *The Narrows* by Ann Petry, *New York Times Book Review*, 16 August 1953, 4.

41. J. Saunders Redding, review of *The Narrows* by Ann Petry, 12 September 1953, 2.

42. "Out of a Fog," *Newsweek*, 17 August 1953, 95

43. "First Novel by Pulitzer Prize Winner Is Published," *Amsterdam News*, 17 October 1953, 12.

44. Vernon Parrington, *Main Currents in American Thought: The Colonial Mind 1620–1800*, vol. 1 (1927; Norman: University of Oklahoma Press, 1989), xvii.

45. Lionel Trilling, "Reality in America," in *Liberal Imagination* (1950; New York: Doubleday, 1953), 15.

46. Gwendolyn Brooks, *Maud Martha* (New York: Harper & Brothers, 1953), 139.

47. Hubert Creekmore, "Daydreams in Flight," *New York Times Book Review*, 4 October 1953, 4.

48. Gertrude Martin, "Book Reviews," review of *Maud Martha* by Gwendolyn Brooks, *Chicago Defender*, 17 October 1953, 7.

49. Gwendolyn Brooks, letter to Langston Hughes, 11 December 1951.

50. Melvin B. Tolson, *Libretto for the Republic of Liberia* (New York: Twayne, 1953).

51. Charles S. Johnson, letter to Melvin B. Tolson, 9 September 1945, MBT, box 2, folder "Routine Business 1941–1949."

52. Allen Tate, preface to *Libretto for the Republic of Liberia* by Melvin B. Tolson (1953; London: Collier, 1970), 10–11.

53. J. Saunders Redding, review of *Libretto of Liberia* by Melvin B. Tolson, *Baltimore Afro-American*, 23 January 1954, 2.

54. Melvin B. Tolson, letter to Allen Tate, 4 March 1950, MBT, box 1, folder "T."

55. Melvin B. Tolson, letter to Carl Murphy, 26 January 1954, MBT, box 1, folder "M."

56. William S. Braithwaite, letter to Melvin B. Tolson, 24 January 1954, MBT, box 1, folder "B."

57. "I shall get to New York this summer," Anonymous, n.d. [1952], MBT, box 1, folder "T."

58. Ralph Ellison, "Twentieth Century Fiction and the Black Mask of Humanity," *Confluence* 2 (December 1953): 3–21, in *Shadow and Act*, 24.

59. William Gardner Smith, letter to Richard Wright, 14 June 1951, RW, box 106, folder 1614.

60. Gilbert Milstein, "The Problem as Before," review of *South Street* by William Gardner Smith, *New York Times Book Review*, 31 October 1954, 34.

61. Henry F. Winslow, "Philadelphia's South Street," *Pittsburgh Courier*, 19 March 1955, A12.

62. Mary Smith, interview.

63. William Gardner Smith, *South Street* (New York: Farrar, Strauss, 1954), 17.

64. Ibid., 295.

65. Blyden Jackson, "The Blithe Newcomers, Resume of Negro Literature in 1954: Part I," *Phylon* (1st Quarter 1955), 9.

66. LeRoy S. Hodges, Jr., *Portrait of an Expatriate: William Gardner Smith, Writer* (Westport, CT: Greenwood, 1985), 49.

67. "Are Our Efforts in Vain," *The American Negro: A Magazine of Protest* (April 1956) 4.

68. Saunders Redding, "A Report from India," *American Scholar* (Autumn 1953): 444.

69. "The Wild Dogs Are Close," *Time*, 20 September 1954, 116, 120.

70. Philip Bonosky, telephone interview, July 2008.

71. John Killens, untitled notes on memo pad "About 25 yrs ago," 1971, JOK, box 18, folder "Ad Hoc Committee to Memorialize Paul Robeson."

72. Maxwell Geismar, letter to John Oliver Killens, n.d., JOK, box 3, folder "Incoming Correspondence."

73. "Youngblood Royalty Statements, May 20, 1954–June 30, 1961," box 23, folder 12, JOK.

74. Rose, letter to John Oliver Killens, 14 February 1955, JOK, box 3, folder "Incoming Correspondence."

75. James Baldwin, "Stranger in the Village," in *Notes of a Native Son*, 165.

76. James Baldwin, "Take Me to the Water," in *No Name in the Street* (New York: Dell, 1972), 32.

77. James Baldwin, letter to Sol Stein, 9 January 1956, in *James Baldwin and Sol Stein: Native Sons*, ed. Sol Stein (New York: One World Books, 2004), 69.

78. George S. Schuyler, *Black and Conservative: The Autobiography of George S. Schuyler* (New Rochelle, NY: Arlington House, 1966), 329.

79. J. Saunders Redding, review of *Notes of a Native Son* by James Baldwin, *Baltimore Afro-American*, 17 March 1956, 2.

80. Sol Stein, "Editor's Prefatory Note," in *James Baldwin and Sol Stein*, 71.

81. Langston Hughes, "From Harlem to Paris," review of *Notes of a Native Son* by James Baldwin, *New York Times Book Review*, 26 February 1956: 14.

CHAPTER 16: LIBERAL FRIENDS NO MORE

1. Granville Hicks, "Tormented Triangle," review of *Giovanni's Room* by James Baldwin, *New York Times Book Review*, 14 October 1956, 3.

2. James Baldwin, *Giovanni's Room* (1956; New York: Dell, 1988), 30.

3. Ibid., 35.

4. R.W.B. Lewis, *American Adam* (Chicago: University of Chicago Press, 1955), 1.

5. William Faulkner, *Absalom, Absalom!* (1936; New York: Random House, 1964), 378.

6. William Faulkner, from *Faulkner at Nagano*, dust jacket notes, in *Shadow and Act*, by Ralph Ellison.

7. William Faulkner, "A Letter to the North," *Life*, 5 March 1956, 51.

8. Joseph Blotner, *Faulkner: A Biography,* single vol. edition (New York Vintage, 1991), 618.

9. Robert Penn Warren, *Segregation: The Inner Conflict in the South* (New York: Vintage, 1956), 107.

10. James Baldwin, "Faulkner and Desegregation," in *Nobody Knows My Name* (1961; New York: Vintage, 1993), 126.

11. Albert Murray, letter to Ralph Ellison, 19 April 1956, in *Trading Twelves*, 125.

12. Baldwin, "Faulkner and Desegregation," 123.

13. John Oliver Killens, "A Letter to William Faulkner and His Middle Grounders," JOK, box 33, folder 17.

14. Ibid.

15. Walker Percy, "Stoicism in the South," *Commonweal*, 6 July 1956: 344.

16. Norman Mailer, *Advertisements for Myself* (1959; New York: Putnam, 1969), 307.

17. Norman A. Brittin, "Non-Segregation, or Quality, in Schools of the Deep South," *Antioch Review* (December 1954): 387–96.

18. Rayford Logan, "The Realities and Ethics of Desegregation," *Antioch Review* (December 1954): 399–404.

19. Mailer, *Advertisements for Myself*, 308.

20. Mailer, "The Time of Her Time," in ibid., 464.

21. Irving Howe, *A Margin of Hope: An Intellectual Autobiography* (New York: Harcourt, Brace, Jovanovich: 1982), 240.

22. Mailer, *Advertisements for Myself*, 313.

23. Ibid., 314.

24. Irving Howe, "Mass Society and Post-Modern Fiction," *Partisan Review* (Summer 1959): 420–36.

25. Mailer, *Advertisements for Myself*, 321–22.

26. Ralph Ellison, "Beating That Boy," in *Shadow and Act*, 100.

27. Mailer, *Advertisements for Myself*, 329.

28. Allen Ginsberg, *Howl, and Other Poems* (San Francisco: City Lights, 1959).

29. Jack Kerouac, *The Subterraneans* (1958; New York: Grove, 1994), 45, 46.

30. Ibid., 46.

31. Ibid., 76.

32. James Baldwin, "If Black English Isn't a Language, then Tell Me What Is?," in *The Price of the Ticket: Collected Non Fiction 1948-1985* (New York: St. Martin's, 1985), 650.

33. Mailer, "The Hip and the Square," in *Advertisements for Myself*, 389.

34. Kerouac, *Subterraneans*, 45.

35. Ibid., 60.

36. Ibid., 109.

37. Ibid., 43.

38. Ibid., 69.

39. James Baldwin, "The Black Boy Looks at the White Boy," in *Nobody Knows My Name*, 218.

40. Peter Manso, ed., *Mailer: His Life and Times* (New York: Simon and Schuster, 1985), 254–55.

41. Ibid., 256.

42. Norman Podhoretz, "Know-Nothing Bohemians," *Partisan Review* (Spring 1958): 311–12.

43. LeRoi Jones, "The Beat Generation," *Partisan Review* (Summer 1958): 473.

44. Amiri Baraka [formerly LeRoi Jones] interview, December 2006.

45. Amiri Baraka, *The Autobiography of Leroi Jones* (New York: Freundlich, 1984), 118.

46. LeRoi Jones and Hettie Cohen, eds., *Yugen: A New Consciousness in Arts and Letters*, 1 (1958): 1.

47. LeRoi Jones, "Suppose Sorrow Was a Time Machine," *Yugen* 2 (1958): 11.

48. Mason Jordan Mason, "The Curse of Ham," *Yugen* 3 (1958): 16.

49. John Genari, "Baraka's Bohemian Blues," *African American Review* (Summer–Autumn 2003), 254.

50. Robert Creeley, *The Collected Essays of Robert Creeley* (Berkeley: University of California Press, 1989), 531–32.

51. See Michael Magee, "Tribes of New York: Frank O'Hara, Amiri Baraka, and the Poetics of the Five Spot," *Contemporary Literature* (Winter 2001): 694–726.

52. Joseph Wenke, "Seymour Krim," in *Dictionary of Literary Biography*, vol. 16: *The Beats: Literary Bohemians in Postwar America,* ed. Ann Charters (Columbia, SC: Bruccoli Clark, 1983), 316–20.

53. Seymour Krim, "Anti-Jazz: A Question of Self Identity," *Village Voice,* 30 October 1957, 4.

54. Ibid., 16.

55. Seymour Krim, "Ask for a White Cadillac," in *Beyond the Angry Black,* ed. John A. Williams (New York: Cooper Square, 1969), 103.

56. Ellison to Murray, 28 September 1958, in *Trading Twelves,* 198.

57. Ralph Ellison, "The Charlie Christian Story," *Saturday Review,* 17 May 1958, in *Shadow and Act,* 235.

58. "Skin Game," review of *A Place Without Twilight* by Peter S. Feibelman, *Time,* 3 March 1958.

59. Grant Webster, *Republic of Letters* (Baltimore: Johns Hopkins University Press, 1979), 222.

60. Ralph Ellison, "Change the Joke and Slip the Yoke," *Partisan Review* (Spring 1958), in *Shadow and Act,* 47.

61. Leroi Jones, letter to Ralph Ellison, n.d. [1958], in Rampersad, *Ralph Ellison: A Biography,* 380.

62. James Baldwin, letter to Owen Dodson, n.d. [after July 1956], HJ.

63. Hansberry, *To Be Young, Gifted and Black,* 211.

CHAPTER 17: THE END OF THE NEGRO WRITER

1. Anthony Platt, *E. Franklin Frazier Reconsidered* (New Brunswick, NJ: Rutgers University Press, 1991), 102.

2. Arthur P. Davis, "Notes for Autobiography," 133, APD, box 2, folder "Notes for autobiography."

3. E. Franklin Frazier, *The Black Bourgeoisie* (1955 [French edition];1957 [first English edition]; New York: Collier, 1962), 195.

4. Ibid., 27, 28.

5. Wilson Record, review of *Black Bourgeoisie* by E. Franklin Frazier, *Social Forces* (July 1957): 45.

6. Caleb Henderson, letter to E. Franklin Frazier, 25 January 1958, EFF, box 131–26, folder "correspondence g–l."

7. Lloyd Yearwood, letter to E. Franklin Frazier, 29 March 1959, EFF, box 131–26, folder "correspondence q–z."

8. Martin Kilson, letter to E. Franklin Frazier n.d. [ca. 20 July 1959], EFF, box 131–26, folder "correspondence q–z."

9. Frances Stonor Saunders, *The Cultural Cold War: The CIA and the World of Arts and Letters* (New York: New Press, 1999), 165–79.

10. Richard Gibson, email to author, August 2007.

11. James Baldwin, "Princes and Powers," in *Nobody Knows My Name*, 23.

12. Ralph Ellison, letter to Richard Wright, 5 August 1945, RW, box 97, folder 1314.

13. James Baldwin, "Princes and Powers," in *Nobody Knows My Name*, 24–25.

14. Ibid., 31

15. James Baldwin, letter to William Cole, n.d. [ca. August 1953], JB.

16. George Lamming, *The Pleasures of Exile* (1960; London: Pluto, 2005), 34.

17. Richard Wright, "Tradition and Industrialization," in *White Man, Listen!* (1957; New York: 1995), 66.

18. Baldwin, "Princes and Powers," 46.

19. Frantz Fanon, "Racism and Culture," *Presence Africain: Cultural Journal of the Negro World* (June–November 1956), 125, 127, 129, 128, 130, 131.

20. Ibid., 127.

21. Ibid., 129.

22. Ibid., 128.

23. Ibid., 130.

24. Ibid., 131.

25. Frantz Fanon, *The Wretched of the Earth*, trans. Constance Farrington (1961; New York: Grove Wiedenfield, 1967), 40.

26. Aprés le Congres, *Présence Africaine*, 11 December 1956: 383; David Macey, *Frantz Fanon: A Biography* (New York: Picador, 2000), 281.

27. James Baldwin, letter to Sol Stein, 9 November 1956, in *James Baldwin and Sol Stein*, 82.

28. James Baldwin, "The Discovery of What It Means to be an American," *New York Times Book Review*, 25 January 1959, in *Nobody Knows My Name*; James Baldwin, "The Survival of Richard Wright," *Reporter*, 16 March 1961, reprinted as "Alas, Poor Richard," in *Nobody Knows My Name*; James Baldwin, "Notes of a Native Son" in *Notes of a Native Son*, 102.

29. Baldwin, "Princes and Powers," 37.

30. William Gardner Smith, *The Stone Face* (New York: Farrar, Straus and Giroux, 1963), 93.

31. Mailer, *Advertisements for Myself*, 434.

32. Julian Mayfield, "Autobiography," 109, JM, box 15, folder 9.

33. "Group to Discuss Employment," *New York Times*, 24 July 1951, 21.

34. "Negroes Plan Special Show," *New York Times*, 6 November 1951, 34.

35. Mayfield, "Autobiography," 101.

36. John Henrik Clarke, letter to Alice, 24 March 1954, JHC, in Rebeccah Welch, "Black Art and Activism in Postwar New York, 1950–1965," Ph.D. diss., New York University, 2002, 138. According to a 1955 letter from journalist and Marvel Cooke to John Killens, the Committee for the Negro in the Arts was "put out of existence by the same forces threatening us." Marvel Cooke, letter to John Killens, 27 May 1955, JOK, box 3, folder "Incoming Correspondence."

37. Mayfield, "Autobiography," 120.

38. Ibid., 121.

39. Julian Mayfield, *The Grand Parade* (New York: Vanguard, 1961), 240–41.

40. Welch, "Black Art and Activism," 156.

41. Julian Mayfield, letter to John Henrik Clarke, 6 July 1955, JHC, box 6, folder 5.

42. Mayfield to Clarke, 23 January 1955.

43. John Henrik Clarke, "Lamming's Second Novel," review of *The Emigrants* by George Lamming, *Freedom* (July–August 1955): 8.

44. Mayfield to Clarke, 23 January 1955.

45. Julian Mayfield, *The Hit* (New York: Vanguard, 1957), 154.

46. Ibid., 22.

47. Ibid., 102.

48. Ibid., 146.

49. John Hope Franklin and Alfred A. Moss Jr., *From Slavery to Freedom* (New York: McGraw-Hill, 1988), 420.

50. Herbert Simmons, *Corner Boy* (1957; New York: Norton, 1996), 91, 81.

51. Ibid., 93.

52. Gilbert Millstein, "Pre-Tested Mixture," *New York Times Book Review*, 5 January 1958, 24.

53. "The Weeks Books: Top Novel and Jazz World," *Pittsburgh Courier*, 9 November 1957, B2.

54. "A Statement on the American Society of African Culture and Its Purposes and Activities" n.d. [ca. June 1957], AMSAC, box 4, folder "Memorandum on AMSAC."

55. "AMSAC Report Proposed Budget 1960–1961," ibid.

56. "Revised CORAC Budget," 1958," AMSAC, box 8, folder "John A. Davis,"

57. John M. Crewdson, "C.I.A. Link to Cherne Unit Is Denied," *New York Times*, 21 February 1976, 11; see also John M. Crewdson, "Worldwide Propaganda Network Built By the C.I.A.," *New York Times*, 26 December 1977, A1, 37.

58. Neil Sheehan, "5 New Groups Tied to C.I.A. Conduits," *New York Times*, 17 February 1967, 16; Brenda Gayle Plummer, *Rising Wind: Black Americans and U.S. Foreign Affairs, 1935–1960* (Chapel Hill: University of North Carolina Press, 1996), 254.

59. Mary Helen Washington, "Desegregating the 1950s: The Case of Frank London Brown," *Japanese Journal of American Studies* 10 (1999): 28.

60. Wayne J. Urban, *Black Scholar: Horace Mann Bond, 1904–1972* (Athens: University of Georgia Press, 1992), 159–64.

61. J. Saunders Redding, letter to James K. Baker [AMSAC], 27 September 1962, box 8, folder "Saunders Redding Lagos, Nigeria," AMSAC.

62. John A. Davis and James T. Harris to J. Saunders Redding, 31 October 1957, JSR, box 4, folder 61.

63. Mercer Cook, letter to John A. Davis, 23 January 1960, box 8, folder "John A. Davis," AMSAC.

64. E. Franklin Frazier, letter to John Davis, 16 October 1959, EFF, box 131-8, folder "Davis, John B."

65. E. Franklin Frazier, letter to John Davis, 16 October 1959, EFF, box 131-8, folder "Davis, John B."

66. Harold Cruse, "Biography: AMSAC June 1959," AMSAC, box 9, folder "2nd Conference." In the 1998 interview "Locating the Black Intellectual: An Interview with Harold Cruse," by Van Gosse, *Radical History Review* 71 (Spring 1998): 96–120, Cruse put the date at 1953. In a 1958 letter to "Jimmie," he put the date at 1951. Harold Cruse to Jimmie, 18 May 1958, HAC, box 2, folder "Correspondence 1952–1959."

67. Harold Cruse, letter to "Dear Sir," 11 October 1954, and Harold Cruse, letter to anonymous n.d., HAC, box 7, folder "Correspondence," in Welch, "Black Art and Activism," 137.

68. Cruse, "The Education of a Rebel," 280.

69. Welch, "Black Art and Activism," 140.

70. Harold Cruse, "A list of Particulars on Committee for the Negro in the Arts," 23 October 1952; Harold Cruse, letter to Stella Holt, 26 June 1953, HAC, box 2, folder "Correspondence 1952–1959."

71. Van Gosse, "More Than Just a Politician," in *Harold Cruse's The Crisis of the Negro Intellectual Reconsidered* (New York: Routledge, 2004), 22; Peniel Joseph, "Harold Cruse, Black Nationalism and the Black Power Movement," in *Harold Cruse's The Crisis of the Negro Intellectual Reconsidered*, 245.

72. Harold Cruse, letter to John, 20 August 1956, HAC, box 2, folder "Correspondence 1952–1956."

73. Harold Cruse, letter to Harry Belafonte, *New York Post*, 11 November 1956, HAC, box 2, folder "Correspondence 1952–1959."

74. Harold Cruse, letter to Hubert, 3 April 1957, HAC, box 2, folder "Correspondence 1952–1959."

75. Harold Cruse, "An Afro-American's Cultural Views," in *Rebellion or Revolution* (New York: Morrow, 1968), 49.

76. Ibid., 56.

77. Ibid., 61.

78. Ibid., 63.

79. Ibid., , 66.

80. Harry Haywood, *Black Bolshevik* (Chicago: Liberator Press, 1978), 577–604. Haywood refers explicitly to Doxey Wilkerson's essay "Race, Nation and the Concept 'Negro'," *Political Affairs* (August 1952): 15.

81. Harold Cruse, introduction to *Rebellion or Revolution* (New York: Morrow, 1968), 22.

82. "Dr. Kiano Will Speak at AMSAC Banquet Here," *Amsterdam News*, 9 May 1959, 5; "Second Conference on Culture June 26," *Amsterdam News*, 6 June 1959, 5.

83. John F. Kennedy, untitled remarks, AMSAC, box 9, folder "2nd Conference Correspondence."

84. J. Saunders Redding, "Negro Writing in America," *New Leader* (May 1960): 8.

85. Cruse, introduction to *Rebellion or Revolution*, 22.

86. Redding, "Negro Writing in America," 8, 9.

87. Cruse, introduction to *Rebellion or Revolution*, 23, 24.

88. Ibid., 24.

89. Cruse, "An Afro-American's Cultural Views," 55.

90. Muhammad Ahmad [Maxwell Stanford, Jr.], *We Will Return in the Whirlwind* (Chicago: Charles Kerr, 2007), 97; Imamu Amiri Baraka, *The Autobiography: Leroi Jones/Amiri Baraka* (New York: Freundlich, 1984), 200–204, 213. See also Komozi Woodard, *A Nation within a Nation: Amiri Baraka (LeRoi Jones) and Black Power Politics* (Chapell Hill: University of North Carolina Press, 1999).

CHAPTER 18: THE REFORMATION OF BLACK NEW LIBERALS

1. "Amid the Alien Corn," *Time*, 17 November 1957, 28; Leroy S. Hodges, *Portrait of an Expatriate: William Gardner Smith, Writer* (Westport, CT: Greenwood, 1985), 54–58; Richard Gibson, "Richard Wright's 'Island of Hallucination' and the 'Gibson Affair'," *Modern Fiction Studies* (Winter 2005): 896–920; Richard Gibson, taped interview, December 2006.

2. Langston Hughes, "The Writers Position in America," 7 May 1957, APD, box 3, folder "Subject files."

3. "Amid the Alien Corn," 28.

4. Rowley, *Richard Wright*, 496.

5. Ralph Ellison, "At Home," letter to the editor, *Time*, 9 February 1958, 2.

6. Ralph Ellison, letter to Nathan Scott, 17 July 1989, in *Robert Penn Warren*, by Joseph Blotner (New York: Random House, 1997), 536.

7. Ralph Ellison, letter to Albert Murray, April 1957, in *Trading Twelves*, 158.

8. Dorothy Porter, "The African Collection at Howard University," *African Studies Bulletin* (January 1959): 17-18. Howard University's Moorland-Spingarn Research Center, grounded in three thousand books and manuscript donated in 1914 by bibliophile Jesse Edward Moorland and the 1946 purchase of the library of NAACP president Arthur B. Spingarn, carried wonderful and rare books written by and about blacks. However, this was not the same as having a library set up with an endowment and staff to stay abreast of publications by twentieth-century black writers who had published in the mainstream, the artistic vanguard, or the left-wing press.

9. Robert Bone, *The Negro Novel in America* (New Haven: Yale University Press, 1958), 227. Bone removed the five-page ranking from later reprintings of the book.

10. Blyden Jackson, "Shadow of the Magnitude," review of *The Negro Novel in America* by Robert Bone, *Phylon* (2nd Quarter 1959): 198.

11. Richard Gibson, "The Color of Experience," *Nation*, 7 February 1959, 123.

12. Richard Gibson, "The Negro Novelist," *Nation*, 28 February 1959, 189

13. Richard Gibson, *A Mirror for Magistrates* (London: Anthony Blond, 1958), 167.

14. John L. Davis, preface to *The American Negro Writer and His Roots* (New York: Carnegie Press, 1960), iii.

15. J. Saunders Redding, "The Negro Writer and His Relationship to His Roots," in ibid., 1.

16. Langston Hughes, "Writers: Black and White," in ibid., 42.

17. Horace Cayton, "World at Large," *Pittsburgh Courier*, 14 March 1959, A6.

18. Loften Mitchell, "The Negro Writer and His Materials," in *The American Negro Writer and His Roots*, 60.

19. Julian Mayfield, "Into the Mainstream and Oblivion," in ibid., 30.

20. Ibid., 32.

21. Penny Von Eschen, *Race against Empire: Black Americans and Anti-Colonialism, 1937-1957* (Ithaca: Cornell University Press, 1997), 177-78.

22. "14 American Artists Attend Rome Congress," *Chicago Defender*, 4 April 1959, 20.

23. Horace Cayton, "World at Large," *Pittsburgh Courier*, 21 March 1959, A6.

24. Michel Fabre, *The Unfinished Quest of Richard Wright*, 2nd ed. (1973; Urbana: University of Illinois Press, 1993), 489-91.

25. Rampersad, *Ralph Ellison*, 336-46.

26. Jeffrey Leake, *From Sweethome to Harlem: The Lives of Henry Dumas* (Athens: University of Georgia Press, forthcoming).

27. Rampersad, *Ralph Ellison*, 370.

28. Julian Mayfield, "And Then Came Baldwin," *Freedomways* (Spring 1963): 150.

29. James Baldwin, "Sermons and the Blues," *New York Times Book Review*, 29 March 1959, 6.

30. Lloyd Brown, "The Negro Writer," *New York Times Book Review*, 24 May 1959, 42.

31. Mayfield, "And Then Came Baldwin," 151.

32. Richard Gibson, "The Proper Function and Role of American Negro Literature," 1, 6, AMSAC, box 10, [no folder, loose].

33. Charles H. Nichols, "The New Calvinism," review of *Giovanni's Room* by James Baldwin, *Commentary* (January 1957): 96.

34. James Baldwin, "Mass Culture and the Creative Artist: Some Personal Notes," in *Culture for the Millions?: Mass Media in Modern Society*, ed. Norman Jacobs (1959; Boston: Beacon, 1964), 123.

35. James Baldwin, "'Take Me to the Water,'" in *No Name in the Street* (New York: Dell, 1972), 32.

36. Baldwin, "Mass Culture and the Creative Artist," 187.

37. Phillips, *A Partisan View*, 218.

38. His last article in *Commentary* was "On Catfish Row: Porgy and Bess at the Movies" in 1959. He appeared internationally in the CIA-funded journals *Preuves* in February 1961 and *Encounter* in April 1961 with articles on the death of Richard Wright: "Richard Wright, tel que je l'ai connu" and "Richard Wright."

39. "Plain Libel," *Amsterdam News*, 18 June 1960, 10; Robert Freeman, Sr., "Riverton Defense," *Amsterdam News*, 2 July 1960, 10.

40. Federal Bureau of Investigation, "Nationalism, Colonialism and the United States," FBI Field Report, James Baldwin FBI File, Section 1961–1964, 28.

41. Federal Bureau of Investigation, U.S. Government Memorandum, SAC Chicago to SAC Boston, 7 July 1961, Memo of telephone conversation between Elijah Muhammad and Malcolm X Little, 26 June 1961, 2, James Baldwin FBI File, Section 1961–1964, 15.

CHAPTER 19: PROMETHEUS UNBOUND

1. Timothy Tyson, *Radio Free Dixie* (Chapel Hill: University of North Carolina Press, 1999), 149.

2. Lorraine Hansberry, interview with Mike Wallace, 8 May 1959, *Lorraine Hansberry Speaks Out: Art and the Black Revolution*, LP, Caedmon, 1974.

3. Hansberry, *To Be Young, Gifted and Black*, 105.

4. Hettie Jones, *How I Became Hettie Jones* (New York: Dutton, 1990), 36.

5. Federal Bureau of Investigation, Lorraine Hansberry file, 25 July 1956.

6. Lorraine Hansberry, "The Negro Writer and His Roots: Toward a New Romanticism," in *Speech and Power*, vol. 2, ed. Gerald Early (Hopewell, NJ: Ecco, 1993), 131, 141, 135.

7. Hansberry, interview with Wallace, 8 May 1959.

8. Keith Gilyard has elaborated upon this point in his textbook, *African American Literature* (New York: Pearson Longman, 2004).

9. Lorraine Hansberry to William Patterson, 27 March 1959, in Rebeccah Welch, "Black Art and Activism in Postwar New York, 1950–1965," Ph.D. diss., New York University, 2002, 132.

10. Lorraine Hansberry, James Baldwin, Langston Hughes, Emile Capouya, and Alfred Kazin, "The Negro Writer in America," 10 January 1961, audiocassette. During the interview she reinforced the centrality of Walter Lee when Langston Hughes suggested that the actress Claudia McNeil had made a remarkable performance.

11. L.H.N., letter to the editor, *The Ladder* (May 1957): 26.

12. Brenda Gayle Plummer, *Rising Wind* (Chapel Hill: University of North Carolina Press, 1996), 270; "Restaurant Bars African Leader," *New York Times*, 9 October 1957, 20.

13. Lorraine Hansberry, *A Raisin in the Sun* (1959; New York: Vintage, 1988), 51.

14. Ibid., 136.

15. Lorraine Hansberry, interview with Studs Terkel, 12 May 1959, in *Lorraine Hansberry Speaks Out*.

16. Robin Kelley, "Nap Time: Historicizing the Afro," *Fashion Theory* 1 (1997): 341.

17. Sara Wright, "The Lower East Side: A Rebirth of World Vision," *African American Review* (Winter 1993): 593.

18. Lorraine Hansberry, "Her Dream Came True," *New York Times*, 9 April 1959, 37.

19. Nan Robertson, "Dramatist Against the Odds," *New York Times*, 8 March 1959, 3.

20. Lorraine Hansberry, "Stanley Gleason And the Lights That Need Not Die," *New York Times*, 16 January 1960, AD11.

21. Ibid.

22. Joyce Pettis and Paule Marshall, "A *MELUS* Interview: Paule Marshall," *MELUS* (Winter 1991–1992): 119.

23. John S. Lash, "Expostulation and Reply: A Critical Summary of Literature by and about Negroes in 1959," *Phylon* (2nd Quarter 1960): 112, 120.

24. Nick Aaron Ford, "Search for Identity: A Critical Survey of Belles-Lettres by and about Negroes Published in 1961," *Phylon* (2nd Quarter 1962): 136.

25. Anonymous, letter to Gwendolyn Brooks, 20 August 1952, PM, box 52, folder 9.

26. Harvey Shapiro, "A Quartet of Younger Singers," *New York Times Book Review*, 23 October 1960, 32.

27. Gwendolyn Brooks, *The Bean Eaters* (New York: Harper, 1960), 34.

28. Frank London Brown, review of *Maud Martha* by Gwendolyn Brooks, *Chicago Defender*, 21 June 1960, 13.

29. D. H. Melhem, *Gwendolyn Brooks: Poetry and the Heroic Voice* (Lexington: University of Kentucky Press, 1988), 101.

30. Brooks, *Bean Eaters*, 42.

31. Richard Gibson, "Richard Wright's 'Island of Hallucination' and the 'Gibson Affair,'" *Modern Fiction Studies* (Winter 2005): 914; Wayne Phillips, "Castro Is Seeking Negroes' Support," *New York Times*, 21 September 1960, 17. Fair Play for Cuba also involved one of American history's most infamous and enigmatic figures, Lee Harvey Oswald.

32. Van Gosse, *Where the Boys Are* (New York: Verso, 1993), 138–40.

33. LeRoi Jones, "Cuba Libre," *Home: Social Essays* (New York: Morrow 1966), 12.

34. Ibid., 13.

35. Amiri Baraka [formerly LeRoi Jones] interview, December 2006.

36. Diane di Prima, *Recollections of My Life as a Woman* (New York: Viking, 2001), 215–16.

37. Harold Cruse, "Revolutionary Nationalism and the Afro-American," in *Rebellion or Revolution* (New York: Morrow, 1968), 76.

38. Ibid., 74–75.

39. Richard Wright, "The Position of Negro Artist and Intellectual in American Society" [1960], 9, RW; Rowley, *Richard Wright*, 521.

40. Richard Wright, U.S. State Department File, 20 April 1955, telegram #1921 from Djakarta; Rowley, *Richard Wright*, 480.

41. Mary Dudziak, "Desegregation as a Cold War Imperative," *Stanford Law Review* 41 (November 1988): 61–120.

42. Granville Hicks, "The Power of Richard Wright," *Saturday Review*, 18 October 1958, 13, 65, in *Richard Wright: The Critical Reception*, ed. John M. Reilly (New York: Burt Franklin, 1978) 325.

43. J. Saunders Redding, "The Way It Was," *New York Times Book Review*, 26 October 1958, 4, 38; Nick Aaron Ford, "A Long Way from Home," *Phylon* (4th Quarter 1958): 435–36, in *Richard Wright: The Critical Reception*, 329, 335, 336.

44. Richard Wright, letter to Margit de Sablonière, 22 March 1960, MF, box 15, folder 6.

45. Chester Himes, *The Quality of Hurt* (New York: Doubleday, 1972), 200–201; James Campbell, *Talking at the Gates* (New York: Viking, 1991), 65–69.

46. Edward Reeves, "Richard Wright Hits U.S. Racial Hypocrisy," *Chicago Defender*, 28 November 1960, 13.

47. Plummer, *Rising Wind*, 302–3; "Riot in Gallery Halts U.N. Debate," *New York Times*, 16 February 1961, 1, 10.

48. "Bunche Deplores Riot by Negroes in Council," *New York Times*, 18 February 1961, 3.

49. Lorraine Hansberry, "Congolese Patriot," *New York Times*, 26 March 1961, SM4.

50. Lorraine Hansberry, "Containing Wholesome Intentions and Some Sass," *Urbanite* (April 1961): 11.

51. James Baldwin, "A Negro Assays the Negro Mood," *New York Times Magazine*, 12 March 1961, reprinted as "East River Downtown," in *Nobody Knows My Name*, 74.

52. Peniel Joseph, *Waiting 'Til the Midnight Hour* (New York: Holt, 2007), 42.

53. Louis Farrakhan, "Address at Malcolm X College," Chicago 1990, recording.

54. Baldwin, "A Negro Assays the Negro Mood," 76.

55. Hansberry, Baldwin, Hughes, Capouya, and Kazin, "The Negro Writer in America."

56. Baldwin, "A Negro Assays the Negro Mood," 79.

INDEX